QUANTITATIVE APPROACHES TO BUSINESS DECISION MAKING

RICHARD M. BURTON
Duke University

JOHN S. CHANDLER
University of Illinois, Urbana

H. PETER HOLZER
University of Illinois, Urbana

HARPER & ROW, PUBLISHERS, New York
Cambridge, Philadelphia, San Francisco,
London, Mexico City, São Paulo, Singapore, Sydney

Material from the Certificate in Management Accounting Examinations, Copyright © 1977, 1978, 1979, 1980, and 1981 by the National Association of Accountants, is reprinted with permission.

Material from Uniform CPA Examination Questions and Unofficial Answers, Copyright © 1971, 1973, 1974, 1975, 1976, 1977, and 1978 by the American Institute of Certified Public Accountants, Inc., is reprinted with permission.

Sponsoring Editor: Jayne Maerker
Project Editor: Eleanor Castellano
Cover Design: 20/20 Services, Inc., Mark Berghash
Text Art: Fineline Illustrations, Inc.
Production: Willie Lane
Compositor: The Clarinda Company
Printer and Binder: R. R. Donnelley & Sons Company

Quantitative Approaches to Business Decision Making

Copyright © 1986 **Richard M. Burton, John S. Chandler, and H. Peter Holzer**

All rights reserved. Printed in the United States of America. No part of this book may be used or reproduced in any manner whatsoever without written permission, except in the case of brief quotations embodied in critical articles and reviews. For information address Harper & Row, Publishers, Inc., 10 East 53d Street, New York, NY 10022.

Library of Congress Cataloging in Publication Data

Burton, Richard M.
   Quantitative approaches to business decision making.

   Includes bibliographies and index.
   1. Management science.   I. Chandler, John S.
II. Holzer, H. Peter.   III. Title.
HD30.25.B872   1986   658.4′03   85-915
ISBN 0-06-041086-8

85 86 87 88 9 8 7 6 5 4 3 2 1

Contents

Preface xiii
Acknowledgments xvii

1 INTRODUCTION TO QUANTITATIVE METHODS 1

1.1 Perspective on Quantitative Methods 2
History and Development of Quantitative Methods 2
Objectives of Quantitative Methods 3

1.2 Analysis with Models 4
Simulation Models and Heuristic Models 5
More About Mathematical Models 6

1.3 Summary 8
Glossary 9
Problems 9

2 SURVEY OF PROBABILITY CONCEPTS 11

2.1 Basic Foundation of Probability 12
Introduction 12
Definition of Probability 13
Events 13
Objective and Subjective Probabilities 14
Probability Notation and Rules 15
Addition of Mutually Exclusive Events 15
Independent Events 17
Dependent Events 18
Conditional, Marginal, and Joint Probabilities 20

2.2 Analysis of Probabilistic Situations 20
Probability Tree Diagrams and Joint Probability Tables 20
The Revision of Probabilities and Bayes' Theorem 23

2.3 Business Decisions Under Uncertainty 26
Conditional Profits and Opportunity Losses 26
Expected Profits 28
Expected Profits with Perfect Information 31
Expected Profits with Imperfect Information 33

2.4 Summary 39
Glossary 39
Problems 40
References 55

3 PROBABILITY DISTRIBUTIONS AND DECISION THEORY 57

3.1 Introduction to Probability Distributions 58
Introduction 58
Random Variables and Probability Distributions 58
Expected Value 59
The Variance 60
Discrete and Continuous Distributions 61

3.2 Specific Probability Distributions and Their Use 63
The Binomial Distribution 63
The Normal Distribution 67

3.3 Decision Theory 72
Different Decision Criteria 73
Utility and Decisions 77
Measuring Utility 79

3.4 Summary 85
Glossary 85
Problems 86
References 96

4 LINEAR PROGRAMMING—A GRAPHICAL APPROACH 97

4.1 Perspective 98

4.2 A Problem To Be Solved 98

4.3 Setting up the Graphical Approach 100
The Constraints: Feasibility 103
The Objective Function: Optimality 105

4.4 The Graphical Solution 107

Contents / v

4.5 **Variations** 110

4.6 **Marginal Values at the Optimal Solution** 114
Marginal Value of Another Unit of Machining 115
Marginal Value of Another Unit of Assembling 116

4.7 **The Dual Formulation** 117
The Dual Problem 117
Solution to the Dual 118

4.8 **A Comprehensive Problem** 121

4.9 **Summary** 125
Glossary 125
Problems 126
References 145

5 LINEAR PROGRAMMING—THE SIMPLEX METHOD 147

5.1 **Introduction** 148

5.2 **The Simplex Method** 149
Standard Form 149
The Initial Tableau—Step 0 150
Can We Do Better?—Is It Profitable to Produce Different Products?—Step 1 153
Choosing Which Product to Produce—Step 2 154
How Much Can We Produce?—Step 3 155
How Much of Other Products to Produce—Step 4 156
What Are the New Technological Rates of Substitution?—Step 5 157
Can We Do Better?—Step 6 159

5.3 **The Second Iteration** 159

5.4 **The Third Iteration** 161

5.5 **The Optimal Solution—Primal and Dual** 163

5.6 **Variations** 164
Unbounded Solutions 165
Degenerate Solutions 166
Multiple Optimal Solutions 168

5.7 **Extensions** 169
Artificial Variables 169
Surplus Variables 169
Minimization 171

5.8 **Sensitivity Analysis and the Limits of the Solution** 171
Changes in Profit Coefficients 172
Changes in the Availability of Resources 174

5.9 Summary 177
Glossary 177
Problems 178
References 188

6 THE TRANSPORTATION MODEL 189

6.1 Introduction 190
A Transportation Problem 190
A Graphical Basis 192

6.2 A Simplex Approach 193
The Initial Tableau—The Northwest Corner Rule 194
The Initial Tableau—Vogel's Approximation Method 195
Can We Do Better?—The Simplex Criterion (Stepping-stone Method) 199

6.3 Dummy Distributors and Factories 206

6.4 A Special Situation: Degeneracy 207

6.5 Applications 209

6.6 The General Linear Programming Formulation of the Transportation Model 210

6.7 Summary 211
Glossary 211
Problems 212
References 215

7 INVENTORY MODELS WITH DETERMINISTIC DEMAND 217

7.1 Introduction 218

7.2 Cycle Inventories—Economic Order Quantity (EOQ) Model 221

7.3 Data, Errors, and Sensitivity 226

7.4 Economic Production Lot Size Model 229
An Example 231

7.5 Quantity Discounts and the EOQ Model 232

7.6 Inventory Models with Stockouts and Backorders 234

7.7 Summary 238
Glossary 238
Problems 239
References 246
Appendix. Derivation of Optimal Order Size Q and Optimal Shortage V 247

8 INVENTORY MODELS WITH PROBABILISTIC DEMAND 249

- 8.1 Introduction 250
- 8.2 When to Order: An Example 250
- 8.3 Reorder Point and Safety Stock 251
- 8.4 Optimal Levels of Safety Stock 254
  Assuming Independence Between Safety Stock and Order Quantity 254
  Assuming Dependence of ROP and EOQ 258
- 8.5 Note on Normally Distributed Demand During Lead Time 263
- 8.6 Safety Stock When Stockout Costs Are Unknown 265
- 8.7 Constant Order Cycle Systems and Periodic Review Systems 267
- 8.8 Some General Remarks 268
- 8.9 ABC Inventory Systems 269
- 8.10 Summary 271
  Glossary 271
  Problems 272
  References 280
  Appendix. Derivation of Optimal Q and ROP Under Uncertainty (shortages backordered) 280

9 PROJECT SCHEDULING AND CONTROL USING CPM AND PERT 283

- 9.1 Introduction 284
- 9.2 The Project Structure 285
  An Example: Test Marketing of New Products 285
- 9.3 The Project Network 286
- 9.4 A Dummy Task 289
- 9.5 PERT 290
- 9.6 PERT/Cost 293
- 9.7 CPM with Limited Resources 297
  Limited Resources Approach 297
- 9.8 A Comprehensive Example for CPM with Limited Resources 299
- 9.9 Summary 302
  Glossary 303
  Problems 303
  References 314

10 FORECASTING AND COST ESTIMATION 315

10.1 Introduction 316

10.2 Extrapolations of Historical Observations (Time Series) 316
The Simple Average 318
The Moving Average 318
The Weighted Average 319
Exponential Smoothing 320
Estimation of Linear Trends 324

10.3 Prediction Models 326
Regression Analysis 327
Coefficient of Determination 331
Testing the Significance of the Regression Coefficient 334
Confidence Intervals for the Regression Coefficient b 335
Confidence Intervals for the Expected Value of y' 336

10.4 Multiple Regression 337

10.5 Learning Curves and Cost Estimation 339

10.6 Summary 343
Glossary 344
Problems 345
References 358
Appendix. Development of the Normal Equations from Least Squares 359

11 INTRODUCTION TO SIMULATION 361

11.1 Introduction 362

11.2 An Accounting Model: A Deterministic Simulation 363
Concepts and Issues in Simulation 364
Validation of the Model 365
Expanding the Basic Model 366

11.3 Monte Carlo Simulation 370
Using a Random Number Table 371
Sampling and Inference 374
Confidence Intervals 374
Hypothesis Testing 375
The Sample Size: How Many Trials to Perform 375

11.4 Simulation of Analytic Models 377
An Inventory Application 377
Variations on the Inventory Model 378
A Queuing Application 380

13.7 **Summary** 439
  Glossary 439
  Problems 440
  References 445

14 QUEUING THEORY 447

14.1 **Introduction** 448

14.2 **Waiting-line Systems** 449
  The Population 450
  The Waiting Line 451
  The Service Facility 451
  Served Units 452
  Steady-state Versus Transient-stage Operating Characteristics 453
  Definitions and Notations of Operating Characteristics 453

14.3 **The Single-channel Model** 454

14.4 **Multiple-channel Waiting Lines** 460

14.5 **Other Queuing Models** 463

14.6 **Summary** 463
  Glossary 464
  Problems 464
  References 469
  Appendix. The Poisson Process and Distributions; the Exponential Distribution 469

15 MARKOV PROCESSES 473

15.1 **Introduction** 474

15.2 **Two Examples** 474
  A Brand-switching Model 474
  A Health-planning Model 477

15.3 **Markov Process Concepts and Terms** 478
  Calculating Steady-state Probabilities 479
  An Intuitive Meaning for Steady-state Probabilities 480

15.4 **Decision Making and Markov Processes** 482
  Brand Switching: An Advertising Decision 482
  Health Planning: A Public-sector Decision 483

15.5 **Summary** 485
  Glossary 485
  Problems 485
  References 490

11.5 **Summary** 383
Glossary 384
Problems 385
References 392

12 SIMULATION: CORPORATE MODELING AND IMPLEMENTATION 395

12.1 **Introduction** 396

12.2 **Steps in Corporate Simulation Modeling** 397
Creating the Data Base 397
Constructing the Corporate Model 397
Using the Model for Managerial Reports 399

12.3 **An Example of a Corporate Model** 399

12.4 **Expanding the Corporate Model: Cash Flow** 400

12.5 **What Are "What If?" Questions?** 401

12.6 **The "What If?" Response Matrix** 403

12.7 **Corporate Modeling on Spreadsheets** 404

12.8 **The Combination of Simulation and Optimization Techniques** 405
Optimization as an Idea Generator for Simulation 405
Optimization as a Submodel in the Larger Simulation Model 406

12.9 **Reviewing the Simulation Technique** 406

12.10 **Summary** 409
Glossary 409
Problems 409
References 418

13 DYNAMIC PROGRAMMING 421

13.1 Introduction 422

13.2 Stages and State Variables 422

13.3 The Shortest-route Problem 423

13.4 An Investment Problem 426

13.5 A Purchasing Problem 432

13.6 A Production Planning Problem 433
Stage I 435
Stage II 435

16 ORGANIZATIONAL IMPLICATIONS FOR THE IMPLEMENTATION OF QUANTITATIVE METHODS 493

16.1 Introduction 494
16.2 Extent of Practical Applications 494
16.3 Problems in Applying Quantitative Methods 497
Interaction Between Model Builder and Managers 497
16.4 Difficulty of Demonstrating a Satisfactory Cost/Benefit Relation 497
16.5 Difficulty in Obtaining Information Needed as Inputs for Quantitative Models 498
16.6 The Bottom Line 499
16.7 Summary 500
References 501

APPENDIX A: A REVIEW OF DIFFERENTIAL CALCULUS 503

APPENDIX B: A REVIEW OF MATRIX ALGEBRA 509

APPENDIX C: TABLES 515

Table 1 Random Numbers 516
Table 2 The Standardized Normal Distribution Function, $F_N(Z)$ 517
Table 3 Student's t-Distribution 518
Table 4 Cumulative Binomial Distribution $P(R \geq r\ n,p)$ 519
Table 5 Unit Normal Linear Loss Integral 536

Course Outlines 538

Index 539

Preface

The increasing use of quantitative methods by business makes it mandatory for today's business students to have a basic understanding of these modern tools of management and decision making. Such basic comprehension enables them to identify situations in which quantitative methods might usefully be applied, as well as to understand the information inputs required in using decision models. With the increasing availability of microcomputers and analytic software, managers have the opportunity to apply quantitative models to their decision situations. Thus, today's business student needs to be prepared for this decision-making environment.

Quantitative Approaches to Business Decision Making is designed to provide the student with an introduction to quantitative methods and the business problems to which they apply in a straightforward and understandable manner. Many of the students may not have extensive mathematical training, so the text presumes only an understanding of college algebra. An introductory statistics course is taken concurrently. Most of the material in this book was designed for and has been class-tested in an undergraduate course in quantitative methods.

The many business problems and examples in this book make the application of the quantitative methods more relevant for the student. Many of the problems and examples in this text are adapted from professional examinations, including those for the Certified Public Accountant (CPA), Certified Management Accountant (CMA), Certified Internal Auditor (CIA), and, in Canada, the Registered Industrial Accountant (RIA). A Solutions Manual is available with the text.

PEDAGOGICAL AIDS

Many different pedagogical techniques are presented here to aid both the instructor and the student. The main ones are:

1. Chapter outlines. Each chapter begins with a short topical outline to help the reader put the forthcoming topics into perspective.

2. Figures and tables. There is liberal use of visual presentation of data and techniques to facilitate learning.
3. Chapter summaries. Each chapter concludes with a brief synopsis of the main points of the chapter.
4. Content review questions. Each chapter has numerous short answer questions relating to the content of the current chapter.
5. Professional examination questions. Each chapter contains several more difficult problems that have been adapted from recent professional examinations, making this book an ideal vehicle for students preparing for the quantitative methods section of CPA, CMA, CIA, and RIA examinations.
6. Short case applications. More involved problems are presented throughout the text to provide the student with opportunities to apply their new knowledge in real-world settings.
7. Glossaries. Each chapter contains a glossary of the new concepts and terms that were introduced in that chapter.
8. Spreadsheet applications. Chapters 11 and 12 on simulation contain several problems that have been designed for solution on an electronic spreadsheet. Templates for these problems are included in the instructors manual.

CHAPTER SYNOPSES

The book begins with an introduction to quantitative methods and reviews important probability concepts in Chapters 1 and 2. The question and problem material of this section stresses business-related applications. Chapter 3 presents significant probability distributions and an introduction to decision theory.

Linear programming is first discussed in Chapter 4 with basic concepts being developed through graphical analysis. A unique feature is the early incorporation of shadow prices, sensitivity analysis, and the dual formulation of problems. The next two chapters cover the simplex method and the transportation model.

Chapters 7 and 8 describe inventory models, developing the economic order quantity model and the notions of stockouts, safety stock, and reorder points. Chapter 9 discusses project planning and control, using Program Evaluation and Review Technique (PERT) and the Critical Path Method (CPM). Chapter 10 deals with forecasting and cost estimation, employing various averaging techniques, regression analysis, and learning curves.

Simulation techniques are examined in Chapter 11 through a simple pro forma financial accounting model with a step-by-step increase in sophistication. With the presentation of the familiar income statement and balance sheet model, the notions of state and transition variables are introduced, definitional and behavioral relationships are developed, and probability distributions are incorporated. Applications to inventory management and waiting-line problems conclude this introductory chapter. The following chapter, "Corporate Modeling and Implementation," deals with some planning models that are widely used today.

Chapter 13 introduces dynamic programming concepts by presenting a number of illustrative examples. Chapter 14 discusses queuing theory, giving two simple applications with particular emphasis on the underlying assumptions. Chapter 15 covers Markov processes, using brand-switching and health-care examples as vehicles to present transition and steady-state probabilities and their application to decision making. A review of quantitative method applications in business, which appears in Chapter 16, isolates some of the major problems involved. It synthesizes the topics of previous chapters.

We gratefully acknowledge permission given by the Institute of Management Accounting of the National Association of Accountants, the Society of Management Accountants of Canada, and the American Institute of Certified Public Accountants for the use of their problems throughout the book. These problems are designated parenthetically as *(SMA)* or *(CMA)* when they occur in the text.

Richard M. Burton
John S. Chandler
H. Peter Holzer

Acknowledgments

We wish to thank many of our colleagues who have critically reviewed parts of the manuscript. We would like to give special acknowledgment for the assistance given by the reviewers listed below. Professor Song Kim deserves special credit for class testing some of the material. Several students have contributed greatly to the generation of problems and to the editing of textual content. They include Liz Bauer, Amy Kopko, Jody Johnson, and Chuck Westphal. For their invaluable assistance in preparing the manuscript we owe a great deal to Mrs. Kathleen Melton, Mrs. Norma Hubbard, and Mrs. Mary Lou Dunker.

Professor Gordon B. Harwood
Georgia State University
Atlanta, Georgia

Professor John C. Camillus
University of Pittsburgh
Pittsburgh, Pennsylvania

Professor Ted M. Smith
Temple University
Philadelphia, Pennsylvania

Professor Stanley Brooking
University of Southern Mississippi
Hattiesburg, Mississippi

Professor David Ashley
University of Missouri
Kansas City, Missouri

Professor Wayland P. Smith
Western Michigan University
Kalamazoo, Michigan

Mr. Douglas Vaughn
Sarasota, Florida

Professor William Ziemba
University of British Columbia
Vancouver, B.C., Canada

Professor Terry Dielman
Texas Christian University
Fort Worth, Texas

Professor Ed P. Winkofsky
Virginia Polytechnic Institute &
    State University
Blacksburg, Virginia

Professor John A. Lawrence
California State University
Fullerton, California

Professor Song K. Kim
University of Illinois at Urbana-Champaign
Urbana, Illinois

Professor William A. Verdini
Arizona State University
Tempe, Arizona

Professor Edward Stafford
University of South Carolina
Columbia, South Carolina

Professor Donald R. Williams
North Texas State University
Denton, Texas

Dr. Frank G. Landram
West Texas State University
Canyon, Texas

CHAPTER 1
Introduction to Quantitative Methods

1.1 Perspective on Quantitative Methods
History and Development of Quantitative Methods
Objectives of Quantitative Methods

1.2 Analysis with Models
Simulation Models and Heuristic Models
More About Mathematical Models

1.3 Summary

Glossary

Problems

Key Concepts

Analog model	Mathematical model
Constraints	Model
Decision variables	Objective function
Deterministic model	Parameters
Heuristic models	Simulation models
Iconic model	Stochastic model
	Validity of models

1.1 Perspective on Quantitative Methods

HISTORY AND DEVELOPMENT OF QUANTITATIVE METHODS

The application of quantitative methods to realistic decision problems on a large scale can be traced back to World War II, when British scientists used mathematical and other scientific approaches to solve military problems. These efforts proved very successful and led to the formation of similar teams of scientists in the U.S. armed forces. After the war some of the same scientists tried to apply many of the techniques to problems in business and industry. Their success, which was greatly facilitated by the growing availability of computers, motivated many scientists to develop new methods and techniques and to apply them to an ever-increasing number of business problems. The evolution of this rapidly growing body of knowledge led to a discipline variably referred to as operations research, management science, or simply quantitative methods for decision making.

Today these efforts continue. Quantitative methods are widely applied in industry and government. New applications are being developed in such areas as production, marketing, accounting, finance, personnel, health care, and energy policy.

The movement of management toward more quantitative analysis is clear. The most popular periodicals and textbooks of the 1950s in production, marketing, finance, and managerial accounting covered very few, if any, of the techniques discussed in this book. Today, the leading texts and journals in all these fields contain discussions on and applications of at least some of the techniques, in particular, decision theory, linear programming, and simulation. Quantitative techniques are a basic part of the language and approach of modern management.

The study and practice of management will likely continue to become even more quantitative. As management education continues to stress quantitative analysis, the gap between the manager and the quantitative specialist will decrease. This barrier to implementation will gradually disappear as more managers will have studied quantitative methods throughout their management education. Regardless of the reader's specific interest in management, a basic understanding of quantitative methods and their application to management problems is essential for today's management student and tomorrow's manager.

OBJECTIVES OF QUANTITATIVE METHODS

The purpose of quantitative methods is to assist managers in making decisions. Decisions involve choosing courses of action to attain goals. Especially with crucial decisions, managers want to identify the most effective course of action. It is in the evaluation of alternative courses of action that the use of quantitative methods can help managers to make better decisions. The problems that have been successfully analyzed and solved through the use of quantitative methods include inventory and production scheduling, distribution channel analyses, plant location, forecasting, and resource allocation.

The decision-making process of management can be viewed as including the following steps:

1. Recognize and define the problem.
2. Develop a set of possible alternative courses of action and state criteria for their evaluation.
3. Evaluate the alternative courses of action.
4. Select the best possible alternative.

To illustrate, consider a company that wants to market a new product nationally (see Figure 1–1). The problem, (1), is to determine what

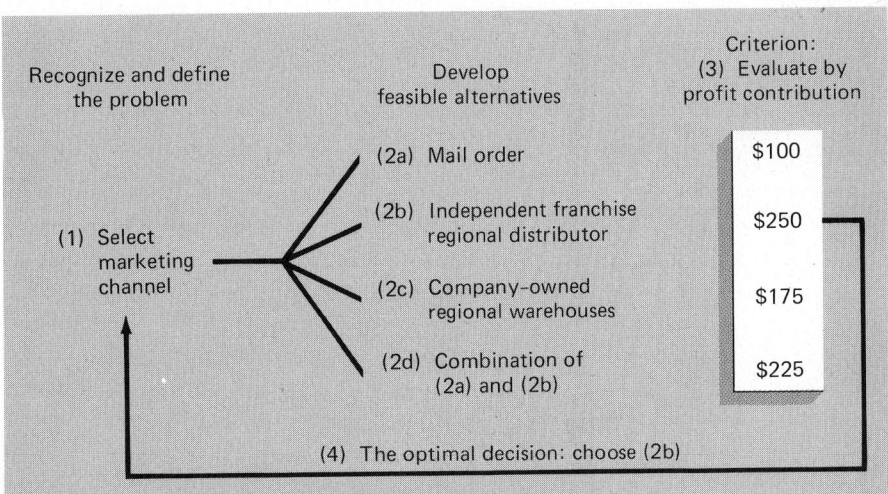

Figure 1–1. The decision-making process.

marketing channel for the product is optimal. The set of alternatives under consideration include mail-order marketing (2a), selling through independent franchised regional distributors (2b), selling through company-owned regional warehouses (2c), or a defined combination (2d) of (2a) and (2b). The criterion for evaluation used by the company is contribution to company profit. Each of the four possible marketing alternatives is now evaluated in terms of its contribution to company profit (3). Using the profitability criterion, the most profitable marketing channel is then selected (4).

Obviously, the quantitative criterion of profitability will not be used as an exclusive evaluator. Many qualitative aspects, including social, political, and environmental considerations that cannot be quantified, will play an important role in the final decision. The quantitative evaluation of the alternative courses of action, however, is a very important, and often the most important part in the overall evaluation of alternatives. The basic objective in employing quantitative methods, therefore, is to help managers make better decisions.

1.2 Analysis with Models

How does one go about evaluating the profitability of different marketing channels? Most generally we employ an analysis that compares revenues and costs of each channel as follows:

$$PC_i = R_i - C_i$$

where, for each marketing channel, PC_i is the profit contribution, R_i is the revenue, and C_i is the cost. In calculating this profit contribution we have used a model, in particular, an accounting model.

A *model* can be defined as a representation of a real situation or system. There are several kinds of models. An *iconic* or *prototype model* is usually a scaled-down replica of the real object. A small wooden airplane is an iconic model used to represent a real airplane in wind tunnel tests. *Analog models* do not bear any resemblance to the real object or system, but they measure important characteristics of the real-world system. Examples are automobile speedometers, thermometers, and clocks. They also include two-dimensional visual presentations, such as charts, maps, and diagrams.

Mathematical models represent the real system or situation through a system of symbols and mathematical functions. In this book we are concerned primarily with such models. Mathematical models are abstract, having no outward resemblance to the real system, and are simplified representations of the real system. These models try to reflect a real situation by selecting only the most important variables, because the real situation or system is often so complex that it is impossible to analyze all its variables and their interrelationships at one time. The accounting model we used in the analysis of marketing channels in the preceding section is an example of a mathematical model. It is a simple equation that, by the use of accounting numbers, tests the profitability of highly complex marketing systems.

The usefulness of solutions or measures obtained from models depends on their validity in representing the real situation. We use a model to help us make decisions in a real setting. The advantage of analyzing the above marketing alternatives by means of a model is that models can be tested and evaluated before taking any real action. Thus, very costly mistakes can be avoided. The *validity* of an analysis by model depends on how closely the cost-revenue projections of the model represent the real revenues and costs incurred when the product is actually marketed.

SIMULATION MODELS AND HEURISTIC MODELS

Mathematical models should be distinguished from simulation models. Mathematical models are usually algorithms that enable us to arrive at optimal solutions. *Simulation models,* on the other hand, are symbolic, mathematical representations that imitate the behavior of real systems, usually with the help of a computer. Once the model is constructed, it is usually run on a trial-and-error basis. Thus, we can learn how the system behaves under a given set of assumptions. Simulation models have the advantage of being more flexible and less theoretically constrained. Therefore, the behavior of many ill-structured systems that defy mathematical modeling can be analyzed with the aid of a simulation model. On the other hand, simulation models do not produce "optimal" solutions.

Heuristic[1] *models* generally involve the application of intuitive rules, or guidelines, based on experience, to a complex situation for which an optimal solution cannot be developed because it is either impossible or too expensive to do. Usually it involves finding an initial feasible solution and a subsequent search for better solutions until a "satisfactory" solution is discovered.

Any model, of course, must be tested for its *validity.* We must determine how reliable the model is in representing reality. In the marketing problem we should question and test the validity of all the parameters, such as price, cost, capacity constraints, and all other assumptions. (For example, is it valid to assume that we can combine actions 2a and 2b?) The methods for determining validity vary with the type of model. Mathematical models, for example, have a battery of

---

[1] The term is derived from the Greek word for discovery.

sophisticated systematic techniques to analyze model validity called *sensitivity analysis*. Simulation and heuristic models can be validated through statistical analysis or trial and error.

MORE ABOUT MATHEMATICAL MODELS

When analyzing important problems in a business setting, we usually find that managers have an objective or goal in mind. In the analysis of the marketing channels, their goal was to find the most profitable solution. In the context of mathematical modeling, we say that their objective was to find the solution (i.e., the marketing channel) that would maximize the profit contribution from the new product. For other problems the objective may be to find the solution that would minimize cost.

Assume, for example, that a company located in Chicago must ship some manufacturing equipment to its subsidiary in São Paulo in Brazil. Various combinations of routes and means of transportation must be considered. In order to avoid costly delays, however, top management decrees that the equipment must arrive before October 1, 198—. Obviously, we are dealing with a cost-minimization problem, but we are not free just to look for the cheapest route available. We must restrict our evaluation of alternatives to those that also guarantee arrival of the equipment by October 1. Such a restriction of the available alternatives is called a *constraint*. We shall illustrate the concepts of objective function and constraint in the context of mathematical modeling with the following example.

Assume that an importer on a business trip in Taiwan discovers a new, very appealing Christmas toy. Upon his return to the United States, he surveys the potential market for the toy and finds that he can sell an almost unlimited quantity of the toys for about $10 per unit during the pre-Christmas season. The cost of the imported toy to the importer is approximately $6.50 per unit when delivered to his Chicago warehouse. Additional distribution costs are estimated at $0.50 per unit. From the estimated arrival time of the shipment to Christmas, only 10 weeks will be available to sell the toys. The toys have to be repacked in the warehouse, but because of other demands, no more than 5000 items can be packed and shipped per week. The importer wants to know how many units of the toys he should purchase.

The objective for this simple problem is to maximize the profit of the importer. The *objective function* is expressed as

$$\text{Maximize} \quad CM = X[10 - (6.5 + 0.5)] = 3X$$

where CM is the contribution or profit margin, X is the number of units that should be bought and sold, and [10 − (6.5 + 0.5)] represents the dollar amount of the contribution to profit or the contribution margin per unit. The warehouse packing constraint can be expressed as $X \leq 5000$ (units per week) · 10 (weeks), which means that the total quantity he can sell must not exceed 50,000 units. A second constraint, $X \geq 0$, means simply that the units sold must be zero or larger, excluding solutions with negative numbers.

The solution to this problem is obvious. The importer should purchase and sell 50,000 units; the total contribution to profit will be $150,000. The solution here is simple and does not require formulation as a mathematical model. Later in the book we shall discuss similar problems involving several products and constraints, where obtaining an optimal solution would be difficult without the use of mathematical models.

In constructing mathematical models, we distinguish between *decision variables* and *parameters*. Decision variables are those that can be influenced or controlled by the decision maker and are also referred to as controllable variables. In our simple model, X is a decision variable. The importer can decide how many toys to import and sell. *Parameters* are the factors in the model that are assumed as given. In our example, the unit selling price, the unit buying cost, the limited packaging capacity, and the additional packaging costs are the parameters of the model. At least in the short run, we usually assume that parameters cannot be influenced by the decision maker. They are, therefore, also referred to as noncontrollable model inputs.

When we are certain about the values of the parameters of a model, we are dealing with a *deterministic model*. The simple model about the imported toy is a deterministic model because we assumed that all the values of its parameters are known with certainty. If any parameter is not known with certainty and can assume different values, we are dealing with a *stochastic* or probabilistic model. For example, in the importer model we assumed that the sales price for the toy was a definite $10. If we were uncertain about the sales price, such that we had reason to believe that the price could be $9, $10, or $11, we would have to construct a stochastic model that takes these possible variations into account.

In the first section we listed four steps in the decision-making process as follows: (1) Recognize and define the problem; (2) develop a set of possible alternative courses of action and state criteria for evaluation; (3) evaluate the alternatives; and (4) select the best possible alternative. When we want to develop a mathematical model to aid management in the decision-making process, we shall slightly modify these steps and state them as follows:

1. Define the problem.
2. Identify the decision variables.
3. Define the objective.
4. Identify the parameters.
5. Develop the model; that is, state the objective as a function of decision variables and parameters.
6. Find the solution that optimizes the objective.

These steps are illustrated in Figure 1–2.

In the real world setting we recognize and define a problem. From this setting we must now abstract those factors that are the most important and relevant to the problem. Using these factors, we formulate the problem in quantitative terms; that is, we develop the model. We then manipulate the mathematical model until we find a solution. The decision suggested by the model may then be implemented.

1.3 Summary

This book is an introduction to the quantitative methods used by managers in the decision-making process. After briefly discussing the evolution of quantitative methods as a useful tool in decision making, we identified a sequence of logical steps involved in problem solving. The concept of models as abstract representations of reality was introduced and a simple example was used to show how a mathematical model can be formulated. In presenting the steps involved in developing and using models for problem solving, the need for testing the validity of

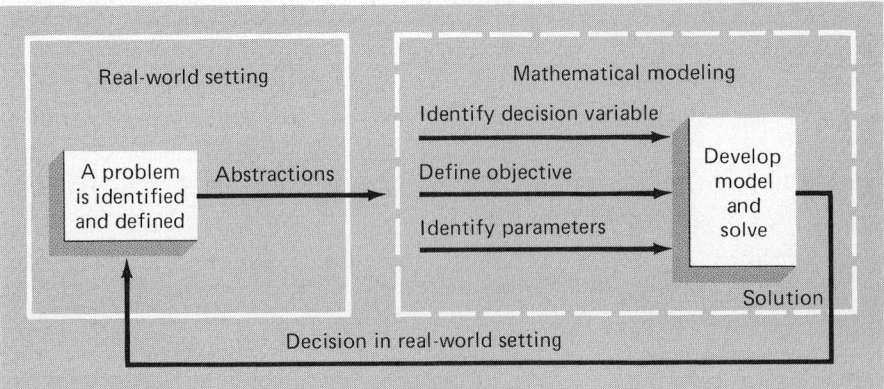

Figure 1–2. Decision making with mathematical modeling.

the model before accepting solutions for decision-making purposes was emphasized.

Glossary

Analog model. An abstract representation of a real system.
Constraints. Restrictions imposed on a problem that limit the set of possible solutions.
Decision variables. Variables for which the value can be influenced by the decision maker; also called controllable variables.
Deterministic model. A mathematical model for which all parameters are known with certainty.
Heuristic model. A model that tries to improve a feasible solution through a systematic search for other solutions following some intuitive rules.
Iconic model. A replica or physically similar representation of a real system.
Mathematical model. A representation of a real system through a system of symbols and mathematical functions.
Model. A representation of a real situation or system.
Objective function. A mathematical function expressing the goals or objectives of a system.
Parameters. Factors in a model that are not influenced by the decision maker; also called noncontrollable model input.
Simulation model. A symbolic, mathematical representation of a real system that is developed for the purpose of analyzing the behavior of the real system.
Stochastic model. A mathematical model that has at least one parameter that can assume different values.
Validity of models. The reliability of a model in representing reality.

Problems

1. For each of the following situations, identify a problem, define a criterion or goal for solution, and generate at least three alternative courses of action.
    a. You have a doctor's appointment at 10:00 A.M. You get in your car at 9:30 A.M. and it does not start.
    b. You have a 20-page term paper due at the end of the semester in economics. It is now the sixth week of the semester and you have not yet started.
    c. You run a small dress-making shop. Your profits have been good and business is booming. Your six sewing machines are 15 years old and are constantly in need of repair. New machines cost $10,000 apiece.
2. The following are items shown on ABC Company's balance sheet (the dollar amounts have been omitted because they are not relevant to the problem).

```
                            ABC
                Balance sheet as of Dec. 31, 1981

    Cash                    XX      Accounts Payable      XX
    Accounts Receivable     XX      Mortgage Payable      XX
    Inventories             XX      Owners' Equity        XX
    Fixed Assets            XX                            ___
                           XXX                            XXX
```

REQUIRED

Select any three of the items listed on the balance sheet. For each item, identify and define a realistic problem situation, define a criterion or goal for a solution, and develop at least three alternative courses of action. For example, assume that the problem area is collection of accounts receivable. A goal could be to maximize cash inflow and the alternatives could be (1) allow for discounts, (2) reduce interest charges, and (3) aggressively pursue legal action.

3. The ABC Company's income statement shows the following items:

```
            Sales                       XXXX
            Cost of Goods Sold          XXXX
            Gross Margin                 XXX
            Selling Expenses              XX
            Administrative Expenses       XX
            Net Income                    XX
```

REQUIRED

Select any three of the items listed on the income statement. For each item, identify and define a realistic problem situation, define a criterion or goal for a solution, and develop at least three alternative courses of action.

4. A local bank is opening a new branch close to the campus of a large Midwestern university. Management has to decide how many tellers' windows to install to serve clients during business hours.

REQUIRED

Define the problem and propose criteria for possible solutions. Describe in your own words what factors would determine the "best" solution.

CHAPTER 2
Survey of Probability Concepts

2.1 Basic Foundation of Probability
Introduction
Definition of Probability
Events
Objective and Subjective Probabilities
Probability Notation and Rules
Addition of Mutually Exclusive Events
Independent Events
Dependent Events
Conditional, Marginal, and Joint Probabilities

2.2 Analysis of Probabilistic Situations
Probability Tree Diagrams and Joint Probability Tables
The Revision of Probabilities and Bayes' Theorem

2.3 Business Decisions Under Uncertainty
Conditional Profits and Opportunity Losses
Expected Profits
Expected Profits with Perfect Information
Expected Profits with Imperfect Information

2.4 Summary

Glossary

Problems

References

Key Concepts

Bayes' theorem
Conditional probability
Dependent events
Expected monetary profits
Expected value of perfect/imperfect information
Imperfect information
Independent events
Joint probability

Marginal probability
Mutually exclusive events
Objective probability
Opportunity loss
Perfect information
Probability
Sample space
Subjective probability

Key Applications
Decision making under uncertainty, including marketing, production, and investment planning

2.1 Basic Foundation of Probability

INTRODUCTION

Uncertainty about the future is an ever-present fact of life. When the weather forecast tells us that there is a 90 percent chance of rain, we shall most likely cancel our plans for a picnic. Card players continuously decide what cards to play, even though they do not know their opponent's hand. Everybody, sooner or later, makes important decisions even though the consequences of these decisions cannot be predicted with certainty.

As a practical example, a college student, usually in the sophomore year, has to decide on a major field to study. This decision is, in most cases, based on expectations of satisfying intellectual curiosity and planning for a professional career. Regardless of the student's talents and determination, there will always remain a degree of uncertainty as to whether these expectations will come true. Many unexpected events may happen; unforeseen financial or health problems, and unexpected changes in the job market are only two examples. Certainly, careful planning and evaluation of possible contingencies may reduce the student's uncertainty about the future, but it can never completely eliminate it. Despite this uncertainty, the young sophomore must decide on a major field of study.

The uncertainties of the business environment are even more pronounced than those of the academic environment. The manager of a sporting goods store, for example, has to decide how many tennis rackets, balls, shoes, and related equipment to purchase and store even though he can never be absolutely sure how many he will sell. He may understock and lose sales and customers, or he may overstock and have to sell slow-moving items at greatly reduced margins or at a loss. A manufacturing company may decide to construct a new plant based on the expectation that the new products produced can be marketed profitably, even though there is a chance that the investment may fail.

Before making their decision, the manager of the sporting goods store and the executives of the manufacturing company have either implicitly or explicitly assessed the chances of incurring losses. They have come to the conclusion, however, that the chances of a successful, profitable outcome are higher than the chances of a loss. Practically all business decisions must be made in the face of varying degrees of uncertainty. When the problem is not very important, it is often sufficient to make an intuitive, less quantitative, decision. There are also instances where the outcome is relatively certain and, therefore, a thorough analysis of very improbable alternative possibilities can be ignored. There are many problem situations, however, where a careful analysis of the uncertain outcomes is very useful. In this chapter we introduce some of the basic concepts of probability that help assess and measure the uncertainty of alternative outcomes.

DEFINITION OF PROBABILITY

In general terms, we define a *probability* as a numerical value that measures the relative likelihood that a certain outcome will occur. Probabilities are measured as fractions ($\frac{1}{4}$, $\frac{1}{8}$, $\frac{1}{2}$, etc.) or decimals (0.25, 0.5, 0.6) between zero and one, inclusive. A probability of 1 means that something will always occur; a probability of zero means that something will never occur.

EVENTS

An outcome is called an *event*. With regard to tomorrow's weather, for example, rain would be an event. Before assigning a probability to an event, we must identify all possible events (outcomes) of an uncertain situation. An exhaustive listing of *all* possible events is called a *sample space*. When only one of the events listed can occur at a given time, the events are said to be *mutually exclusive*.

Naturally occurring examples of events and sample spaces are commonplace. The sample space for a single toss of a coin contains two events, head and tail, only one of which can occur. Another example of an event is the drawing of *one* card from a shuffled deck of 52 cards, where the 52 cards represent the sample space. As a final mathematical example, consider the tossing of a die. Here the sample space is made up of the number of dots on each of the six sides. Thus, we can say that the sample space equals the set of events (1, 2, 3, 4, 5, 6). The six possible events are mutually exclusive: only one event can occur at one time because the die can land only on one side. If two or more events can occur at the same time, they are not mutually exclusive.

From a business perspective, consider the classic make-or-buy decision of management accounting. A manager would like to sell a new product but currently does not have the capability to do so. The manager must decide whether to manufacture the product in-house (possibly involving new machinery, an increased labor force, and greater material costs) or to purchase the completed product from an outside manufacturer. Depending on the subsequent analysis, the manager may also have the option of producing a portion of the product in-house and purchasing the remainder. Of course, the manager can always forego the extension of his business and not manufacture or purchase any new product.

In this setting the events in the sample space are those decisions available to the manager. Specifically, the sample space S contains four possible events: make all, buy all, make portion/buy remainder, make none/buy none. These events are exhaustive in that there are no other alternatives available to the manager. These events in S are also mutually exclusive in that the manager cannot make and buy all at the same time, cannot make or buy all and none at the same time, and cannot make or buy all and a portion at the same time.

OBJECTIVE AND SUBJECTIVE PROBABILITIES

Conceptually, we can distinguish between two classes of probability. *Objective* or classical *probability* is based on the outcomes of frequently repeated experiments; that is, it is based on, and may be verified by, reliable objective evidence. *Subjective probability*, on the other hand, is based mainly on the judgment, belief, intuition, and experience of the person making the probability estimate.

Objective probabilities may be determined in two ways. If all the possible events for a subset A are known and the events in sample space S are exhaustive, mutually exclusive, and equally likely, then the probability that an event in A occurs is

$$P(A) = \frac{\text{number of events in the subset } A}{\text{total number of events in the sample space } S} \quad (2\text{–}1)$$

For example, in tossing a fair coin once, there are two possible outcomes (or subsets): a head or a tail. Head and tail represent the total number of possible events for our experiment for the denominator of Eq. (2–1). The probability of a head represents a selected event from the sample space, and, therefore, is the numerator of Eq. (2–1). Thus, the probability of a head is $\frac{1}{2}$.

A second definition of objective probabilities is needed if the events in the sample space are not equally likely. Probability can then be established empirically through numerous observations of events under identical conditions. Thus, the probability of A is

$$P(A) = \frac{f(A)}{N}$$

where $f(A)$ is the number (frequency) of observations that fall into subset A and N is the total number of observations. For example, toss

10,000 coins and observe the number of heads that occur. The probability of a head on any given toss is then the number of heads observed divided by 10,000. We are basing our probability on an observed frequency distribution. Thus, objective probabilities can be supported through repeated experimentation.

Objective probabilities are frequently not available in a business environment. Empirical or historical information is either not available or not relevant. The kind of rigorous, logical analysis that underlies the assignment of probabilities in well-defined games of chance is impossible in the complex real world confronting the business decision maker. For example, what is the probability of successful introduction of a new product? Thus, probabilities must be assigned to possible outcomes by business people and managers on the basis of experience, sound judgment, and intuition. These are therefore called subjective probabilities. Only rarely will different persons or groups assign exactly the same subjective probabilities when facing identical sets of possible outcomes. The principal advantage of using subjective probabilities is that their elicitation and use in the decision process imposes on the decision maker the need for a careful analysis of possible outcomes and their consequences.

PROBABILITY NOTATION AND RULES

Probability is represented as a numerical value between zero and one that measures the relative likelihood of the occurrence of an event. If $P(A)$ is the probability of occurrence for event A, we have

$$0 \leq P(A) \leq 1 \qquad (2\text{--}2)$$

where $P(A)$ is the probability of occurrence of the event (also called the marginal or unconditional probability of A). $1 - P(A)$ is the probability of nonoccurrence (or complement) of the event.

In most applications of probability theory we must combine the probabilities of related events. In the following we discuss the fundamental combinations of probabilities.

ADDITION OF MUTUALLY EXCLUSIVE EVENTS

The probability that one *or* another of two *mutually exclusive events* A and B occur is the sum of their respective probabilities:

$$P(A \text{ or } B) = P(A) + P(B) \qquad (2\text{-}3)$$

For example, if we want to know the probability of getting either a 2 or a 4 when throwing a die, we have

$P(2) = \frac{1}{6}$
$P(4) = \frac{1}{6}$

Therefore

$$P(2 \text{ or } 4) = \tfrac{1}{6} + \tfrac{1}{6} = \tfrac{1}{3}$$

As a further example, assume that on the basis of a geological survey, the chances of finding oil or gas when drilling a hole have been estimated as follows:

Event	Probability
A = dry hole	0.2
B = gas only	0.4
C = oil only	0.25
D = gas and oil	0.15

Because these are the only possible outcomes, the outcomes are exhaustive. Also, we are dealing with mutually exclusive events, as only one event of the defined events can occur. In Figure 2–1 such a sample space is illustrated. The probability of finding either gas or oil, or both, is

$$P(B \text{ or } C \text{ or } D) = 0.4 + 0.25 + 0.15 = 0.8$$

and the probability of having a dry hole or finding only gas is

$$P(A \text{ or } B) = 0.2 + 0.4 = 0.6.$$

When two events are not mutually exclusive, they may occur at the same time. For example, the event of a student taking an English course and the event of a student taking an accountancy course may occur at the same time. If we were seeking the probability of a student being in either class, we would have to account for students in both classes. We must therefore subtract the probability of their occurring

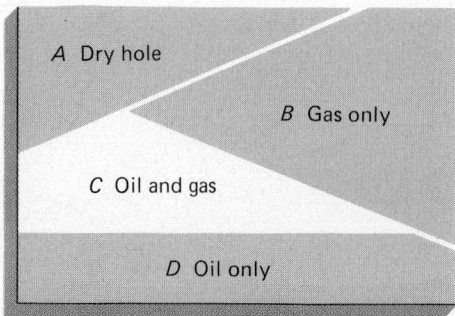

Figure 2–1. Sample space of geological survey.

at the same time in order to avoid double counting. Thus, the probability is determined as follows:

$$P(A \text{ or } B) = P(A) + P(B) - P(A \text{ and } B) \qquad (2-4)$$

where $P(A \text{ and } B)$ stands for the probability of the two events happening simultaneously. [Note that for mutually exclusive events, $P(A \text{ and } B) = 0$ and the above formula is identical to Eq. (2–3)].

Suppose that we have a deck of 52 cards and we want to know the probability of drawing either an ace (A) or a heart (H). We have

$$P(H \text{ or } A) = P(H) + P(A) - P(H \text{ and } A)$$
$$= \tfrac{13}{52} + \tfrac{4}{52} - \tfrac{1}{52} = \tfrac{16}{52}$$

We must subtract $\tfrac{1}{52}$ because one card is both an ace and a heart. To verify this probability, note that the subset (H or A) is the set of all hearts (13) plus the three remaining aces of spades, clubs, and diamonds, for a total of 16.

INDEPENDENT EVENTS

We distinguish between statistically *independent* and *dependent events*. Two events are said to be independent when the occurrence of one event does not affect the probability of occurrence or nonoccurrence of the second event. Statistical dependence or independence does not imply the presence or absence of any causal relationship. When the terms of dependence or independence are used, they refer only to statistical dependence or independence. If A and B are independent events, then the probability that both will occur, called the *joint probability*, is given by the product of their *marginal probabilities*:

$$P(A \text{ and } B) = P(A) \times P(B) \qquad (2-5)$$

When we toss a fair coin twice, we are dealing with two independent events because the outcome of the first event, either head (H_1) or tail (T_1), in no way affects the outcome of the second event, either head (H_2) or tail (T_2). The probability of obtaining two heads is thus

$$P(H_1 \text{ and } H_2) = P(H_1) \times P(H_2)$$
$$= \tfrac{1}{2} \times \tfrac{1}{2} = \tfrac{1}{4}$$

The probability of three heads in a row, therefore, is

$$P(H_1 \text{ and } H_2 \text{ and } H_3) = \tfrac{1}{2} \times \tfrac{1}{2} \times \tfrac{1}{2} = \tfrac{1}{8}$$

Another example is the throwing of two dice at the same time. The probability of obtaining a 6 on both dice is given by

$$P(6 \text{ and } 6) = P(6 \text{ die}_1) \times P(6 \text{ die}_2)$$
$$= \tfrac{1}{6} \times \tfrac{1}{6} = \tfrac{1}{36}$$

A business example is drilling two holes in separate locations. The probability of drilling two dry holes is

$$P(\text{dry hole and dry hole}) = P(\text{dry hole}) \times P(\text{dry hole})$$
$$= 0.2 \times 0.2 = 0.04$$

DEPENDENT EVENTS

Two events are said to be *dependent* when the occurrence of one event *does* affect the probability of occurrence of the second event. For example, assume that we have a box into which we put 10 pieces of paper with the family names of 10 students. Three of the students are white and female, one student is black and female, two are white and male, whereas the remaining four are black and male. The probability of randomly drawing any name from the box is 0.1. Table 2–1 summarizes these facts.

TABLE 2–1. Probability of Events

Student No.	Probability of Event (Drawing a Name)	
1	0.1	
2	0.1	White and female
3	0.1	
4	0.1	White and male
5	0.1	
6	0.1	Black and female
7	0.1	
8	0.1	Black and male
9	0.1	
10	0.1	

Suppose that somebody draws a name from the box and tells us that it is the name of a black student. What is the probability that it is the name of a male student? This probability is called a *conditional probability*. Symbolically, we can write this as $P(M|B)$ and read it as the probability of having drawn the name of a male student (M) given that the student is black (B). Referring to Table 2–1, we see that the probability of drawing the name of a black student is 0.5; that is, $P(B) = 0.5$, because five of the 10 students are black. Knowing that we are dealing only with the group of five black students and that four of them are male, we should readily see that there are four in five chances of getting the name of a male black student from the group of all black students. In symbols we can write $P(M|B) = \frac{4}{5} = 0.8$.

Using the same reasoning, we can answer the question of what is the probability of having drawn the name of a female, given that it is the name of a white student. We see from the table that drawing the

2.1 / Basic Foundation of Probability

name of a white student is $P(W) = 0.5$. Because three of the whites are female, we have

$$P(F|W) = \frac{3}{5}$$

Note that the 3 in the numerator means three out of 10 and is identical with the joint probability of randomly selecting a girl who is both female and white; that is, $P(F \text{ and } W) = 0.3$. To obtain the probability of $\frac{3}{5}$, we have simply divided $P(F \text{ and } W)$ by $P(W)$, hence we can state that

$$P(F|W) = \frac{P(F \text{ and } W)}{P(W)} = \frac{0.3}{0.5} = 0.6$$

The general formula for conditional probability under statistical dependence is expressed as

$$P(A|B) = \frac{P(A \text{ and } B)}{P(B)} \quad \text{where} \quad P(B) \neq 0 \tag{2-6}$$

By referring to Figure 2–2 and using the general formula, we can now determine additional conditional probabilities.

$$P(F|B) = \frac{P(F \text{ and } B)}{P(B)} = \frac{0.1}{0.5} = 0.2$$

$$P(M|W) = \frac{P(M \text{ and } W)}{P(W)} = \frac{0.2}{0.5} = 0.4$$

Finally, we can calculate $P(W|M)$ and $P(B|F)$:

$$P(W|M) = \frac{P(W \text{ and } M)}{P(M)} = \frac{0.2}{0.6} = \frac{2}{6} = 0.33$$

and

$$P(B|F) = \frac{P(B \text{ and } F)}{P(F)} = \frac{0.1}{0.4} = 0.25$$

$P(F \text{ and } W) = 0.3$

$P(M \text{ and } W) = 0.2$

$P(W) = 0.5$ Whites

Female

Male

$P(B) = 0.5$ Blacks

Female

Male

$P(F \text{ and } B) = 0.1$

$P(M \text{ and } B) = 0.4$

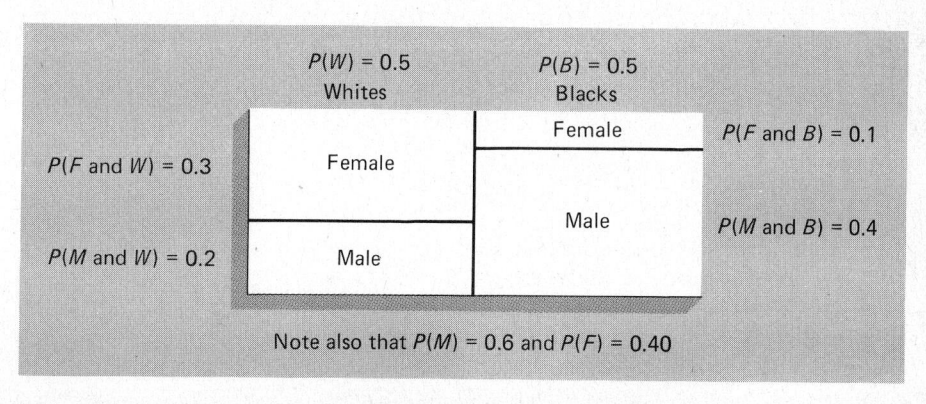

Note also that $P(M) = 0.6$ and $P(F) = 0.40$

Figure 2–2. Sample space for drawing names.

CONDITIONAL, MARGINAL, AND JOINT PROBABILITIES

Equation (2–6), $P(A|B) = P(A \text{ and } B)/P(B)$, *where* $P(B) \neq 0$, can be written as $P(A \text{ and } B) = P(A|B) P(B)$. This tells us that the joint probability of A and B is equal to the conditional probability of A given B times the marginal probability of B.

Let us now examine the above equations under the assumption of independence. From Eq. (2–5) we know that $P(A \text{ and } B) = P(A) \times P(B)$; substituting this expression in Eq. (2–6), we get $P(A|B) = P(A) \times P(B)/P(B) = P(A)$. This, of course, is based on the definition of statistical independence given earlier.

Our discussion of probabilities under the assumptions of statistical independence and dependence can now be summarized in Table 2–2.

TABLE 2–2. Probability Notation

Type of Probability	Symbol	Independence	Dependence
Marginal (unconditional)	$P(A)$	$P(A)$	$P(A)$
Joint	$P(A \text{ and } B)$	$P(A) \times P(B)$	$P(A|B) P(B)$
Conditional	$P(A|B)$	$P(A)$	$P(A \text{ and } B)/P(B)$

2.2 Analysis of Probabilistic Situations

PROBABILITY TREE DIAGRAMS AND JOINT PROBABILITY TABLES

In this section we use an example to show the use of tree diagrams and joint probability tables in analyzing probabilities. We develop unconditional or marginal probabilities, conditional probabilities such as $P(A|B)$ and $P(B|A)$, and joint probabilities such as $P(A \text{ and } B)$. We have used $P(A \text{ and } B)$ to denote the joint probability of A and B. Other common notations for joint probabilities are $P(A \cap B)$, $P(AB)$, and $P(A, B)$. To simplify notation, we shall use $P(A, B)$ from now on to denote joint probabilities.

TABLE 2–3. Given Probabilities

Sales high in first year	$= P(SH_1) = 0.8$
Sales low in first year	$= P(SL_1) = 0.2$
Sales high in second year, given that sales were high in first year	$= P(SH_2|SH_1) = 0.9$
Sales low in second year, given that sales were high in first year	$= P(SL_2|SH_1) = 0.1$
Sales high in second year, given that sales were low in first year	$= P(SH_2|SL_1) = 0.3$
Sales low in second year, given that sales were low in first year	$= P(SL_2|SL_1) = 0.7$

2.2 / Analysis of Probabilistic Situations

Suppose that we are given the probabilities in Table 2–3 concerning the sales of a newly introduced product during the next 2 years. $P(SH_1)$ and $P(SL_1)$ are assumed to be mutually exclusive events. Based on the probabilities given in Table 2–3, we can calculate the joint probabilities as shown in Table 2–4. The first-year probabilities are referred to as unconditional probabilities. The possible sales outcomes for the 2 years can also be shown in the tree diagram of Figure 2–3.

TABLE 2–4. Calculated Joint Probabilities

High sales in both years:

$$P(SH_1, SH_2) = P(SH_1) \times P(SH_2|SH_1) = (0.8)(0.9) = 0.72$$

High sales in first year, low sales in second year:

$$P(SH_1, SL_2) = P(SH_1) \times P(SL_2|SH_1) = (0.8)(0.1) = 0.08$$

Low sales in both years:

$$P(SL_1, SL_2) = P(SL_1) \times P(SL_2|SL_1) = (0.2)(0.7) = 0.14$$

Low sales in first year, high sales in second year:

$$P(SL_1, SH_2) = P(SL_1) \times P(SH_2|SL_1) = (0.2)(0.3) = 0.06$$

There are a number of important relations to note:

$$P(SH_1) + P(SL_1) = 0.8 + 0.2 = 1$$

and that sales in the first year are either high or low;

$$P(SH_2|SH_1) + P(SL_2|SH_1) = 0.9 + 0.1 = 1$$

which means that if sales are high in the first year, sales will either be

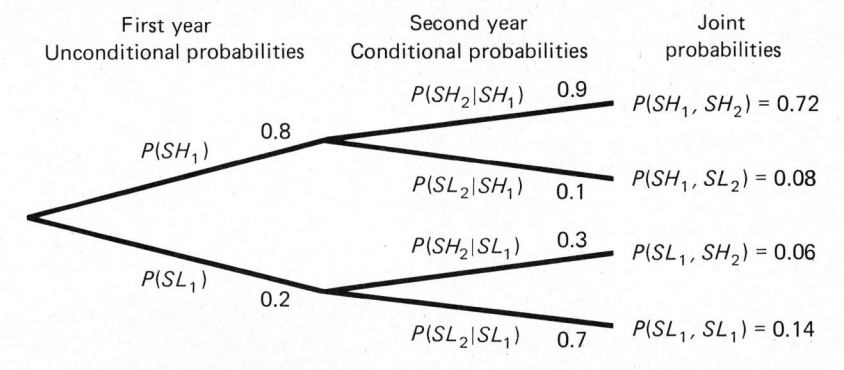

Figure 2–3. Tree diagram of new product sales for the first 2 years.

high or low in the second year. Note also that $P(SH_2|SL_1) + P(SL_2|SL_1) = 1$. Finally, we have

$$P(SH_1, SH_2) + P(SH_1, SL_2) + P(SL_1, SH_2) + P(SL_1, SL_2)$$
$$= 0.72 + 0.08 + 0.06 + 0.14 = 1$$

The same information can be summarized in a joint probability table (Table 2–5).

TABLE 2–5. Joint Probability Table

FIRST YEAR SALES \ SECOND YEAR SALES	HIGH	LOW	MARGINAL PROBABILITIES OF FIRST-YEAR SALES
High	0.72	0.08	$P(SH_1) = 0.80$
Low	0.06	0.14	$P(SL_1) = 0.2$
Marginal Probabilities of Second Year Sales	$P(SH_2) = 0.78$	$P(SL_2) = 0.22$	1.00

The joint probability table summarizes the information of the tree diagram in slightly different form. We can now read joint probability of low sales for both years; it is 0.14. The joint probability of high sales for both years is 0.72. The column on the right gives us the marginal or unconditional probabilities for the possible events of the first year and the bottom row shows the marginal or unconditional probabilities for the second year. (*Note:* The term marginal probabilities is derived from the fact that these probabilities are in the margin of the probability table.) The relation between joint probabilities and marginal probabilities is

$$P(SH_1) = P(SH_1, SH_2) + P(SH_1, SL_2) = 0.72 + 0.08 = 0.8$$

and

$$P(SH_2) = P(SH_2, SH_1) + P(SH_2, SL_1) = 0.72 + 0.06 = 0.78$$

We can find the probability of having high sales in the second year, given that we had high sales in the first year, as

$$P(SH_2|SH_1) = \frac{P(SH_2, SH_1)}{P(SH_1)} = \frac{0.72}{0.80} = 0.9$$

which is the conditional probability originally given.

2.2 / Analysis of Probabilistic Situations

We can also determine the probability of having had high sales in the first year, given that we had low sales in the second:

$$P(SH_1|SL_2) = \frac{P(SH_1, SL_2)}{P(SL_2)} = \frac{0.08}{0.22} = 0.36$$

And for low sales in the first year given that we have low sales in the second year, we get

$$P(SL_1|SL_2) = \frac{P(SL_1, SL_2)}{P(SL_2)} = \frac{0.14}{0.22} = 0.64$$

This reverse reasoning is useful when we want to change an initial (prior) distribution on the basis of new evidence, for example, through sampling, to obtain a new (a posteriori) distribution.

THE REVISION OF PROBABILITIES AND BAYES' THEOREM

It should be obvious that initial probability estimates may have to be revised when additional relevant information becomes available. Such additional information may be obtained through experiments, samples, simple inquiries, or observations. For example, on the basis of the first month's sales of a new product, we may want to revise the probabilities that annual sales will be high. This additional information changes our original ideas (probability estimates) about high sales. The procedure we shall use for revising probabilities is based on *Bayes' theorem*. We begin with an illustrative example of its application and proceed to a more general development.

Suppose that we have a box containing 10 similar coins. We assume that seven of the 10 are fair, that is, the probability of a head equals that of a tail, and the remaining three are unfair, that is, the probability of a head differs from that of a tail. Thus, our initial guess or a priori assumption is that there is a 0.7 probability of picking a fair coin and a 0.3 probability of drawing an unfair coin. Assume also that we know for the unfair coins the probabilities for heads and tails are 0.9 and 0.1, respectively. For fair coins, of course, the probabilities for heads and tails are 0.5 and 0.5, respectively. We can now, without making any experimental tosses, calculate the probabilities of tossing a tail after randomly selecting a coin.

Let $P(F)$ be the probability that a randomly selected coin is fair and let $P(U)$ be the probability that the coin is unfair, and let $P(T)$ and $P(H)$ be the probabilities of heads and tails. Then

$$P(F) = 0.7$$
$$P(U) = 0.3$$
$$P(T|F) = 0.5$$
$$P(T|U) = 0.1$$

The probability of obtaining a tail is

$$P(T) = P(F, T) + P(U, T)$$
$$= P(T|F) \times P(F) + P(T|U) \times P(U)$$
$$= 0.5(0.7) + 0.1(0.3) = 0.38$$

The first part of the equation states that the marginal probability $P(T)$ is the sum of the appropriate joint probabilities, $P(F, T)$ and $P(U, T)$. These joint probabilities are then restated in terms of the conditional probabilities and marginal probabilities.

Assume now that we randomly select a coin and toss it only once and observe a tail. With this additional information and using the probability concepts discussed earlier, we can reassess our prior probabilities as to whether the coin is or is not fair. We find the probabilities of a fair or unfair coin, given that we obtained a tail on an experimental toss. These are

$$P(F|T) = \frac{P(F, T)}{P(T)} = \frac{0.35}{0.38} = 0.92$$

$$P(U|T) = \frac{P(U, T)}{P(T)} = \frac{0.03}{0.38} = 0.08$$

The prior probabilities indicate that if the coin is not fair, there is only one chance in 10 of obtaining a tail on a toss of the coin. Obtaining a tail from the experiment makes us revise our prior probabilities concerning the fairness of the coin according to Table 2–6. These proba-

TABLE 2–6. Probability Revisions

	Prior to Tossing the Coin	After Tossing the Coin
$P(F)$	0.7	0.92
$P(U)$	0.3	0.08

bilities may be calculated directly from Bayes' theorem, which states that the revised probability of A given that B has occurred is

$$P(A|B) = \frac{P(B|A) \times P(A)}{P(B|A) \times P(A) + P(B|\overline{A}) \times P(\overline{A})} = \frac{P(A, B)}{P(B)} \quad (2\text{--}7)$$

where $\overline{A}$ is the complement of A, or *not A*. It means the probability of B, given that A has not occurred. Thus, the revised probability that the coin is fair as

2.2 / Analysis of Probabilistic Situations

$$P(F|T) = \frac{P(F) \times P(T|F)}{P(F) \times P(T|F) + P(U) \times P(T|U)}$$

$$= \frac{(0.7) \times (0.5)}{(0.7) \times (0.5) + (0.3) \times (0.1)}$$

$$= \frac{0.35}{0.38} = 0.92$$

$P(F)$ is the prior probability that the coin is fair. $P(F|T)$ is the revised probability that the coin is fair. Similarly, the revised probability that the coin is unfair is

$$P(U|T) = \frac{P(U) \times P(T|U)}{P(U) \times P(T|U) + P(F) \times P(T|F)}$$

$$= \frac{0.3 \times 0.1}{0.3 \times 0.1 + 0.7 \times 0.5}$$

$$= \frac{0.03}{0.38} = 0.08$$

The proof of Bayes' theorem involves simply the repeated application of the definition of joint, conditional, and marginal probability relations. The above example concerning the fairness of the coin is essentially a constructive proof of Bayes' theorem. By the definition of conditional probability,

$$P(F|T) = \frac{P(F, T)}{P(T)}$$

By the definitions of joint and marginal probabilities,

$$P(F, T) = P(F) \times P(T|F)$$

and

$$P(T) = P(F) \times P(T|F) + P(U) \times P(T|U)$$

Substituting these two expressions into the first expression, we have Bayes' theorem:

$$P(F|T) = \frac{P(F) \times P(T|F)}{P(F) \times P(T|F) + P(U) \times P(T|U)}$$

Bayes' theorem is a powerful statistical tool for revising prior probability estimates based on limited evidence. New experimental evidence, provided in our example by the toss of a randomly selected coin, used in conjunction with the probability rules developed, enables us to revise our initial probability estimate, that is, to make a more accurate assessment of an uncertain situation.

2.3 Business Decisions Under Uncertainty

CONDITIONAL PROFITS AND OPPORTUNITY LOSSES

In the following sections we discuss the application of probability concepts to business decisions under uncertainty. We develop the concepts of *conditional* and *expected monetary profit* or payoffs and estimates for the cost of uncertainty.

In many business decisions under uncertainty, it may be assumed that the decision maker wants to maximize expected monetary profits. Even if maximization of profits is not *the* decision criterion, we may safely assume that it will have an important influence on the decision. In the following section we describe a generalization of expected monetary profit and other criteria. From the following example, we develop the important concepts of *conditional profits* and *opportunity loss*, which are needed to calculate expected monetary profits.

Assume that every morning a retailer stocks a perishable commodity, which deteriorates on the shelf so that stock which remains unsold at the end of the day must be salvaged at a fraction of its full value. The commodity is bought by the retailer for $2.50 per unit and is offered for sale at $3.50 per unit during the day, yielding a $1.00 profit per unit sold. Leftover stock has a salvage value of $0.50 per unit, and it is assumed that the retailer can sell all leftovers. Based on experience and an intimate knowledge of the market, the retailer has assigned probabilities to each possible level of demand as shown in Table 2–7 for the "next day's demand." He now consults you to determine how many units he should stock. (This is a version of the classic newsboy problem, in which the newsboy must decide how many papers to take to his street corner, not knowing how many he will sell.)

TABLE 2–7. Probabilities of Next Day's Demand

Next Day's Demand z	Probability* for Demand $P(z)$
0	0.05
1	0.10
2	0.30
3	0.25
4	0.20
5	0.10

*These probabilities constitute a probability distribution. A more detailed discussion of probability distribution follows in Chapter 2.

2.3 / Business Decisions Under Uncertainty

We can now prepare a table showing in the first column the number of units that may be demanded (events) and in the corresponding rows the range of reasonable actions by the retailer (Table 2–8). For each possible demand and the corresponding action, we enter the profit or loss that would result from a given action. Because these profits or losses depend on the occurrence of an event *and* a given action, they are called *conditional* profits or losses.

To verify some of the entries in this table, assume that the demand was three and the retailer stocked four units. He will sell three units and realize a profit of $3, but because he will not be able to sell the fourth unit, he must sell it at salvage value and lose $2. Thus, overall he would realize a profit of only $1. Now assume that demand was two and the retailer stocked four units. He will realize a $2 profit on the two units sold but lose $4 on the unsold two units, resulting in a net loss of $2. It is left to the reader to verify the other entries in Table 2–8.

Table 2–8 shows that for a given level of demand, the profit is highest when only the quantity demanded is stocked. This, however, requires demand for five units, and a decision to stock five units. If the demand were four units, then it would be best to stock four units, yielding a profit of $4. Stocking three units would result in a lower profit ($3). On the other hand, a stock of five units would yield a loss on the fifth unit, which decreases the total profit to $2. Thus, the best action in terms of conditional profit for each level of demand is to stock exactly the amount demanded.

TABLE 2–8. Conditional Profit Table

EVENTS: Demand	Stock: 0	1	2	3	4	5	Best Action
0	0	−2.0	−4.0	−6.0	−8.0	−10.0	0
1	0	1.0	−1	−3.0	−5.0	−7.0	1
2	0	1.0	2.0	0	−2.0	−4.0	2
3	0	1.0	2.0	3.0	1.0	−1.0	3
4	0	1.0	2.0	3.0	4.0	2.0	4
5	0	1.0	2.0	3.0	4.0	5.0	5

There are two kinds of losses possible-one from understocking, and the other from overstocking. These losses are referred to as opportunity losses, and we want to consider them more formally. An *opportunity loss* is defined as the difference between the profit of the best or optimal act for any given event and the profit (or loss) realized through the act selected. An alternative definition is the amount of profit foregone or of loss suffered by not taking the best action for a given event.

We can now construct an analysis of the opportunity losses as in Table 2–9. The diagonal values are all zero, denoting no opportunity loss; the best action is to stock exactly the quantity demanded. If the demand is four units and we stock three, we lose the profit on the fourth unit: $3.50 − $2.50 or $1.00. If we stock five units, we lose $2.00 on the fifth unit, buying it at $2.50 and salvaging at $0.50. The remainder of Table 2–9 can be completed by the same reasoning.

TABLE 2–9. Conditional Opportunity Loss Table

DEMAND (Event)	Stock: 0	1	2	3	4	5
0	0	2	4	6	8	10
1	1	0	2	4	6	8
2	2	1	0	2	4	6
3	3	2	1	0	2	4
4	4	3	2	1	0	2
5	5	4	3	2	1	0

*Calculations of opportunity losses:

Event	Optimal Action	Profit of the Optimal Action	0	1	2	3	4	5
0	0	0	0	[0 − (−2)] = 2	[0−(−4)] = 4	[0 − (−6)] = 6	[0 − (−8)] = 8	[0 − (−10)] = 10
1	1	1	1 − 0	(1 − 1) = 0	1 − (−1) = 2	[1 − (−3)] = 4	[1 − (−5)] = 6	[1 − (−7)] = 8
2	2	2	2 − 0	(2 − 1) = 1	2 − 2 = 0	(2 − 0) = 2	[2 − (−2)] = 4	[2 − (−4)] = 6
3	3	3	3 − 0	(3 − 1) = 2	3 − 2 = 1	3 − 3 = 0	(3 − 1) = 2	[3 − (−1)] = 4
4	4	4	4 − 0	(4 − 1) = 3	4 − 2 = 2	4 − 3 = 1	4 − 4 = 0	(4 − 2) = 2
5	5	5	5 − 0	(5 − 1) = 4	5 − 2 = 3	5 − 3 = 2	5 − 4 = 1	5 − 5 = 0

EXPECTED PROFITS

The conditional profits and opportunity losses calculated above are useful information. To make an optimal choice, however, we must know what event happened. To determine the best action under uncertainty, we calculate the *expected monetary profits* for each possible act. This is done by weighting the conditional values of each act from Table 2–8 by the corresponding probability and adding the products. This approach is also called the expected monetary value (EMV) approach. Table 2–10 illustrates this procedure.

The amounts in the expected-value column are calculated by multiplying the probabilities times the conditional value. For example, for

TABLE 2-10. Expected Profits for Different Acts

Demand (Event)	P (Demand)	STOCK 0 Conditional Value	STOCK 0 Expected Value	STOCK 1 Conditional Value	STOCK 1 Expected Value	STOCK 2 Conditional Value	STOCK 2 Expected Value	STOCK 3 Conditional Value	STOCK 3 Expected Value	STOCK 4 Conditional Value	STOCK 4 Expected Value	STOCK 5 Conditional Value	STOCK 5 Expected Value
0	0.05	$0	$0	$−2	$−0.10	$−4	$−0.20	$−6.00	$−0.30	$−8	$−0.40	$−10	$−0.50
1	0.10	0	0	1	0.10	−1	−0.10	−3.00	−0.30	−5	−0.50	−7	−0.70
2	0.30	0	0	1	0.30	2	0.60	0	0	−2	−0.60	−4	−1.20
3	0.25	0	0	1	0.25	2	0.50	3	0.75	1	0.25	−1	−0.25
4	0.20	0	0	1	0.20	2	0.40	3	0.60	4	0.80	2	0.40
5	0.10	0	0	1	0.10	2	0.20	3	0.30	4	0.40	5	0.50
Expected profits			$0		$0.85		$1.40		$1.05		$−0.05		$−1.75

TABLE 2-11. Expected Opportunity Losses

Demand (Event)	P (Demand)	STOCK 0 Conditional Value	STOCK 0 Expected Value	STOCK 1 Conditional Value	STOCK 1 Expected Value	STOCK 2 Conditional Value	STOCK 2 Expected Value	STOCK 3 Conditional Value	STOCK 3 Expected Value	STOCK 4 Conditional Value	STOCK 4 Expected Value	STOCK 5 Conditional Value	STOCK 5 Expected Value
0	0.05	$0	$0	$2	$0.10	$4	$0.20	$6	$0.30	$8	$0.40	$10	$0.50
1	0.10	1	0.10	0	0	2	0.20	4	0.40	6	0.60	8	0.80
2	0.30	2	0.60	1	0.30	0	0	2	0.60	4	1.20	6	1.80
3	0.25	3	0.75	2	0.50	1	0.25	0	0	2	0.40	4	1.00
4	0.20	4	0.80	3	0.60	2	0.40	1	0.20	0	0	2	0.40
5	0.10	5	0.50	4	0.40	3	0.30	2	0.20	1	0.10	0	0
			$2.75		$1.90		$1.35		$1.70		$2.70		$4.50

30

stocking one unit and a demand of zero, we get 0.05 × $−2.00 = $−0.10. After calculating the expected values (or profits) for each possible act, the highest expected profit results if the retailer stocks two units of the perishable commodity every morning on the basis of expected profits. In a similar manner, we calculate the expected opportunity losses. The best act will be the one with the least expected opportunity loss as given in Table 2–11.

Initially, it may come as a surprise that opportunity losses indicate that the best act is to stock two units. That is, the maximization of expected profits implies the same decision as the minimization of the expected losses. This is a general result for all decision problems under uncertainty. The basic idea is intuitively appealing: The decision that yields the higher expected profits is the same as the one that minimizes the expected opportunity losses. They are, in fact, equivalent ways to consider the same problem. Using the concept of conditional profits, we have developed the idea of *expected profit* and found that, in our example, the action that yields the highest expected profit would seem to be the most desirable one. We used the notion of conditional opportunity losses to calculate *expected opportunity losses,* and found that the smaller expected opportunity loss indicates the same optimal act as the highest expected profit.

EXPECTED PROFITS WITH PERFECT INFORMATION

We might assume that our retailer arrived at the probability distribution for demand after close observations of the market over a long period of time. He could, in addition, engage the services of a marketing specialist who, through additional studies, might improve the knowledge of his market. In this context it would be useful to ask: "What is the value of the best information this specialist can offer?" In other words, if the specialist provided the retailer with *perfect information* about tomorrow's market, what would be the expected profit?

We can calculate the *expected profit with perfect information* and compare it with our present optimum expected profit to give us an idea of the worth of the additional information. In doing so, we calculate the expected profit under the assumption that we know tomorrow's demand and take the best action. To find the expected payoff with perfect information, we simply take the highest conditional profit for each event from Table 2–8 and weight it by the probability as shown in Table 2–12.

Recall that in Table 2–10 we calculated the maximum expected profit under uncertainty and found it to be $1.40. Subtracting this $1.40 from the expected profit with perfect information of $2.75 yields a difference of $1.35, which is called the *expected value of perfect information (EVPI)*. It is a general result that this expected value of perfect

TABLE 2–12. Expected Profit with Perfect Information

Demand (Event)	P (Demand)	Best Act	Maximum Conditional Profit	Expected Profit Under Certainty
0	0.05	Stock 0	0	0
1	0.10	Stock 1	1.0	0.10
2	0.30	Stock 2	2.0	0.60
3	0.25	Stock 3	3.0	0.75
4	0.20	Stock 4	4.0	0.80
5	0.10	Stock 5	5.0	0.50
				$2.75

information is equal to the minimum expected opportunity loss in Table 2–11. This relationship is more intuitive if you note that you never incur an opportunity loss with perfect information. The $1.35 is the maximum amount the retailer should be willing to pay for perfect information. In real life, perfect information will only rarely be available. But the expected value of perfect information puts an upper bound on the value of imperfect information. And the expected value of perfect information is easier to calculate than the value of imperfect information.

To summarize, for Table 2–10 we calculated the highest expected profit of $1.40. It indicated that the retailer should stock two units if he wants to maximize his long-run profits. For Table 2–11 we calculated the minimum expected opportunity loss of $1.35. It also indicated that two units should be stocked. Finally, for Table 2–12 we determine the *expected profit with perfect information* of $2.75. Thus the following basic relations for the value of information under uncertainty are established:

Expected profit with perfect information	$2.75
Minus expected maximum profit (under uncertainty)	1.40
Equals the *expected value of perfect information* (EVPI) which is also equal to the minimum expected opportunity loss.	$1.35

In Table 2–13 we show that the expected opportunity loss of any act plus the expected profit of the same act sum to the expected profit with perfect information. Only the expected opportunity loss of the optimal act, however, is equal to the expected value of perfect information ($1.35). These results are general and establish the basic relations for the value of information under uncertainty.

2.3 / Business Decisions Under Uncertainty

TABLE 2-13. Expected Profit with Perfect Information for All Acts

Stock	OPTIMAL ACT					
	0	1	2	3	4	5
Expected opportunity loss	$2.75	$1.90	$1.35	$1.70	$2.70	$4.50
Plus expected profit (under uncertainty)	0	0.85	1.40	1.05	0.05	−1.75
Expected profit with perfect information	$2.75	$2.75	$2.75	$2.75	$2.75	$2.75

EXPECTED PROFITS WITH IMPERFECT INFORMATION

Imperfect information is the situation where you know more about the future than without additional information, but less than with perfect information. Examples of imperfect information are weather forecasts, test market results, financial climate predictions, and much of the information obtained in audits. Obviously, the value of imperfect information is less than that of perfect information. Knowing the value of such imperfect information would be a good indicator as to the amount that should be spent in order to obtain it. To make these calculations, we use Bayes' theorem for the revision of probabilities.

To illustrate, suppose that an investor can choose among three alternatives, where the first alternative is to put his money in the bank, the second is to speculate in soybeans, and the third is to sell short in the stock market. These alternatives are called a_1, a_2, and a_3, respectively. These acts can have varying degrees of success, depending on what happens in the economy. The economy can move into a mild recession, remain as is, or experience a rapid takeoff (or growth). These three events are labeled e_1, e_2, and e_3, respectively, with probabilities of 0.25, 0.5, and 0.25, in Table 2-14. To analyze the investor's

TABLE 2-14. Conditional Profit

Events		ACTS		
		a_1	a_2	a_3
Mild recession	$e_1 = 0.25$	100	50	400
No change	$e_2 = 0.5$	100	200	0
Rapid takeoff	$e_3 = 0.25$	100	150	75

problem, column a_2 indicates what happens to the investor who decides to speculate in soybeans; that is, if there is no change in the economy, his profit is $200. The expected profits of the acts have been calculated in part A of Table 2-15.

The best choice is a_2, that is, speculating in soybeans. The expected profit with perfect information of $237.50 has been determined in part B of Table 2–15. Thus, the expected value of perfect information (EVPI) is 87.5, (237.50 − 150). This is identical with the expected opportunity loss for a_2, which is 87.50 as shown in part C of Table 2–15. These results establish the bound on the value of perfect information. The value of imperfect information is between zero and 87.50.

Our investor can also hire a forecasting service called Bust and Boom (B&B). If he does, he wants to know the value of their forecast. To simplify the problem, let us assume that B&B never forecasts that things will remain as they are. The forecasting service gives only one of two predictions: A recession (R) is coming, or a rapid expansion (G) is coming.

TABLE 2–15. Analysis of Investor's Decision

PART A: EXPECTED PROFIT OF ACTS

$E(a_1) = (0.25) \times (100) + (0.5) \times (100) + (0.25) \times (100) = 100$
$E(a_2) = (0.25) \times (50)\ \ + (0.5) \times (200) + (0.25) \times (150) = 150$
$E(a_3) = (0.25) \times (400) + (0.5) \times (0)\ \ \ \ + (0.25) \times (75)\ \ = 118.75$

PART B. EXPECTED PROFIT WITH PERFECT INFORMATION

Event	Probability	Best Act	Maximum Conditional Profit	Expected Profit Under Uncertainty
Mild recession	0.25	a_3	400	100
No change	0.50	a_2	200	100
Rapid takeoff	0.25	a_2	150	37.50
				237.50

$EVPI$ = (expected profit with perfect information)
       = (maximum expected profit under uncertainty)
       = (237.50) − (150.00) = 87.50

PART C. EXPECTED OPPORTUNITY LOSSES: LOSS TABLE

Event	Probability	a_1*		a_2*		a_3*	
Mild recession	0.25	300	75	350	87.50	0	0
No change	0.50	100	50	0	0	200	100
Rapid takeoff	0.25	50	12.50	0	0	75	18.75
			137.50		87.50		118.75

*In each of these columns, the left-hand side represents conditional values, whereas the right-hand side represents expected values.

2.3 / Business Decisions Under Uncertainty

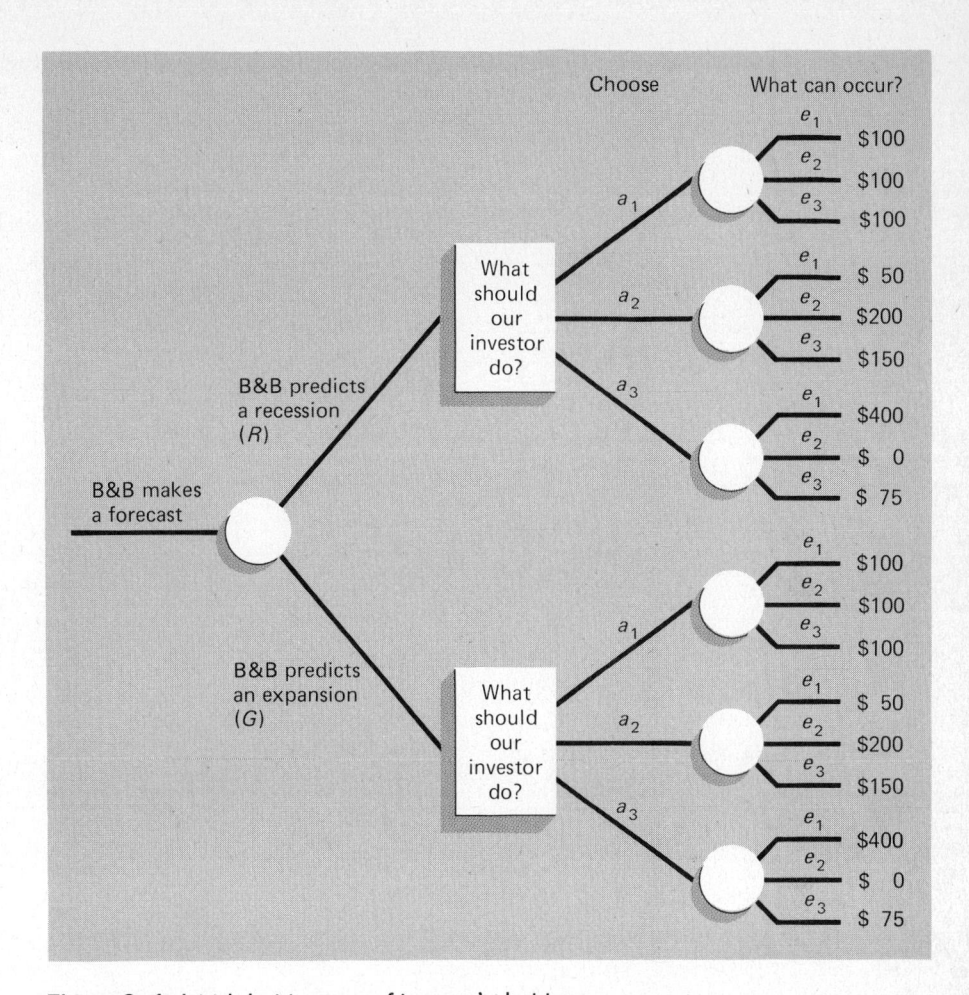

Figure 2–4. Initial decision tree of investor's decisions.

We can now lay out a decision tree that will permit us to summarize how to use the information and calculate its value (Figure 2–4). Starting from the left, B&B makes a forecast. It will either predict a recession (R), or an expansion (G). If it predicts a recession, our investor must choose among a_1, a_2, or a_3. If he chooses a_2, then one of events e_1, e_2, or e_3 will occur with the conditional profits given at the right. But we do not know the probability of the events e_1, e_2, e_3, given that B&B forecasts a recession (R); that is, we need $P(e_1|R)$, $P(e_2|R)$, $P(e_3|R)$. Similarly, we could follow through the lower half of the chart and note that we need $P(e_1|G)$, $P(e_2|G)$, and $P(e_3|G)$.

Now, B&B is not new at forecasting. It has been in business for some time and has an established track record. When a recession did occur, it forecasted a recession seven times out of 10, and an expansion three times. When there was no change, it predicted a recession one-half of the time and an expansion the other half. When an expansion occurred, it predicted a recession four times out of ten, and an expansion six times out of ten. This information can be stated in the following conditional probability terms:

$P(R|e_1) = 0.7 \quad P(R|e_2) = 0.5 \quad P(R|e_3) = 0.4$
$P(G|e_1) = 0.3 \quad P(G|e_2) = 0.5 \quad P(G|e_3) = 0.6$

Also, we know that our best forecast without any additional information is

$P(e_1) = 0.25, \quad P(e_2) = 0.5 \quad \text{and} \quad P(e_3) = 0.25.$

as given in Table 2–13. These required conditional probabilities can be directly calculated using Bayes' theorem.

It is more illustrative, however, to use only the basic concepts of probability, and, essentially, reconstruct the result. As an example, we develop the value for $P(e_1|R)$. By definition of joint probability in terms of conditional probabilities:

$P(e_1, R) = P(e_1|R) P(R) = P(R|e_1) P(e_1)$

Rewriting, we get

$$P(e_1|R) = \frac{P(R|e_1) P(e_1)}{P(R)}$$

$$= \frac{(0.7) \cdot (0.25)}{P(R)}$$

Now, we need to know the probability that Bust and Boom will forecast a recession, $P(R)$. Since the sample space for R is exhaustive and mutually exclusive,

$P(R) = P(R, e_1) + P(R, e_2) + P(R, e_3)$

Using the definition for conditional probabilities:

$P(R) = P(R|e_1) P(e_1) + P(R|e_2) P(e_2) + P(R|e_3) P(e_3)$
$\quad = (0.7) \times (0.25) + (0.5) \times (0.5) + (0.4) \times (0.25)$
$\quad = 0.525$

then

$$P(e_1|R) = \frac{(0.7) \times (0.25)}{(0.525)} = 0.333$$

2.3 / Business Decisions Under Uncertainty

Similarly,

$$P(e_2|R) = \frac{P(R|e_2)\,P(e_2)}{P(R)}$$

$$= \left(\frac{(0.5)\times(0.5)}{0.525}\right)$$

$$= 0.475$$

and

$$P(e_3|R) = \frac{P(R|e_3)\times P(e_3)}{P(R)}$$

$$= \frac{(0.4)\times(0.25)}{0.525} = 0.190$$

Problem 20 asks you to verify that

$P(e_1|G) = 0.158 \qquad P(e_2|G) = 0.526 \qquad P(e_3|G) = 0.316 \qquad P(G) = 0.475$

We now return to Figure 2–4 and fill in the missing probabilities, yielding Figure 2–5. The numbers in the circles above a_1, a_2, a_3 are the expected values—for example, the expected value of a_3 when R is predicted is:

$$(0.333 \times 400) + (0.476 \times 0) + (0.190 \times 75) = 147.6$$

This is the highest expected value when a recession is predicted. Thus, we can say that the best act, when a recession is predicted, is to choose a_3. Similarly, the best act when expansion is predicted is a_2, with an expected return of 160.5 (see Figure 2–6). The expected return from the forecast is the probability that a recession is predicted times the best return plus the probability that a takeoff is predicted times its best return, or

$$(0.525 \times 147.6) + (0.475 \times 160.5) = 153.625$$

This is the expected profit with this imperfect information. The expected value of imperfect information (EVII) is

$$EVII = 153.94 - 150 = 3.94$$

that is, the expected return with the information minus the expected return without the information. This is not very high and is considerably less than the 87.50 value of perfect information. This is not surprising when one notes that B&B never predicts that the economy will remain as it is, and this occurs half of the time.

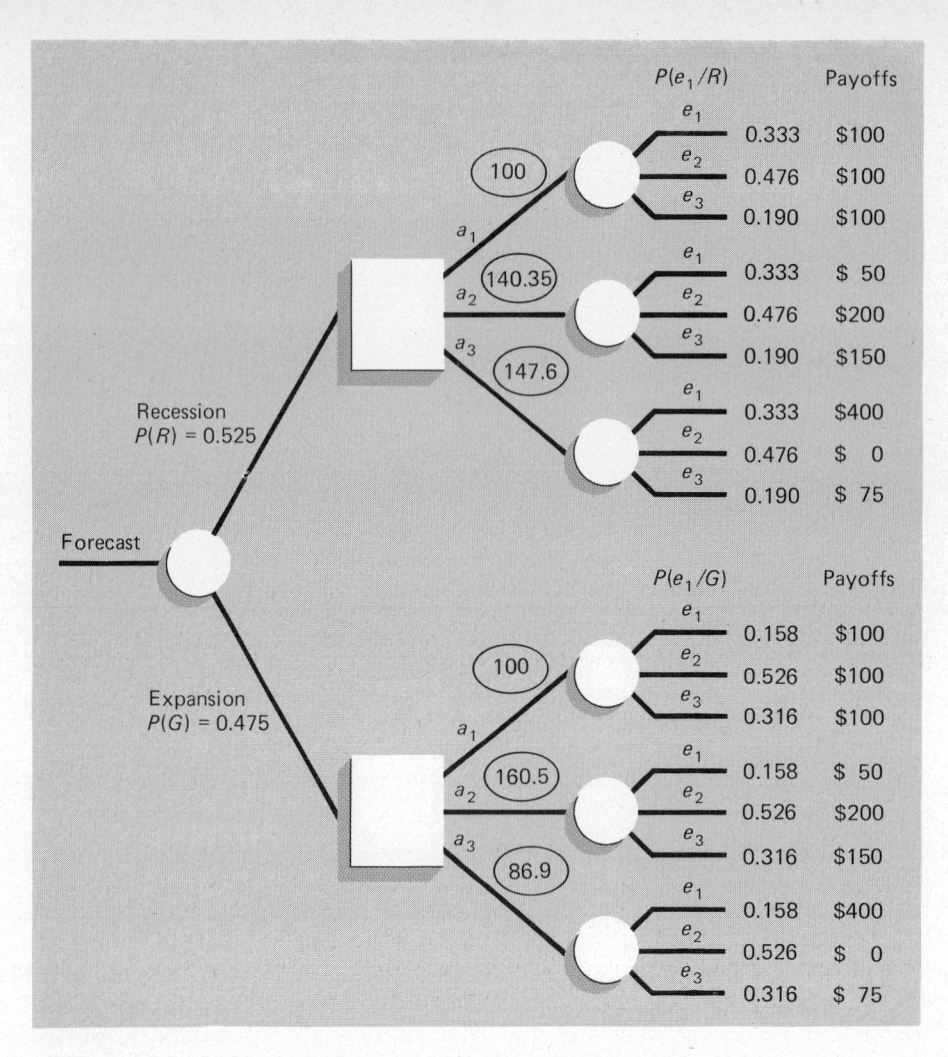

Figure 2–5. Intermediate decision tree of investor's decisions.

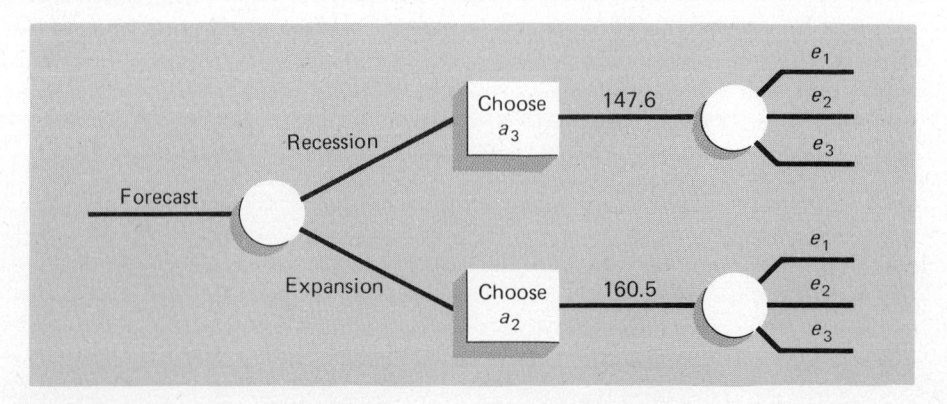

Figure 2–6. Optimal decision tree.

2.4 Summary

We have considered the problem of decision making in the face of uncertain outcomes. We began with a review of basic probability notions and proceeded to the value of better information. Bayes' theorem is the basic theorem that permits us to revise our notions about the future based on sample information.

Glossary

Bayes' theorem. A probability statement that revises the probability of given events based on new information. For example, the probability that the price of a stock goes up can be revised by information from a broker. The formal probability statement of Bayes' theorem is

$$P(A|B) = \frac{P(B|A) \times P(A)}{P(B|A) \times P(A) + P(B|\overline{A}) \times P(\overline{A})}$$

Conditional probability. The probability of an event, given that a different event has occurred.

Dependent events. The occurrence of one event affects the probability of occurrence of another event.

Expected monetary profits. The mean (average) value for a given alternative.

Expected value of imperfect information (EVII). The expected additional profit from having additional imperfect information. Also called the expected value of incremental information.

Expected value of perfect information (EVPI). The expected additional profit from having perfect information. It is also the minimal expected opportunity loss. Note that perfect information eliminates opportunity losses.

Imperfect information. Additional knowledge that a given event will occur, although some uncertainty remains. For example, you have information that there is a 0.9 probability of rain tomorrow. This is not perfect information, but it is better information than the yearly average, which says that there is a 0.2 probability of rain on any given day.

Independent events. The occurrence of one event does not affect the occurrence of another event. For example, when tossing two coins, the event of a head or tail on one coin says nothing about what will occur upon tossing the second coin. The outcomes are independent.

Joint probability. The probability of two or more events occurring simultaneously. For example, $P(A, B)$ is the probability that events A and B will both occur.

Marginal probability. The probability of an event occurring, independent of the occurrence of another event.

Mutually exclusive events. The occurrence of one event excludes the occurrence of another event. For example, the events, head and tail, are mutually exclusive for the toss of one coin.

Objective probability. A probability measure based on physical measures or empirically observable measures that can be based on experimentation. For example, the probability of a head upon the toss of a coin and the probability of a redhead in a population of 100,000 Americans are objective probabilities.

Opportunity loss. A loss of profits due to making an incorrect decision when a better decision was possible. For example, the opportunity to sell an item and make a profit when you are out of stock is an opportunity loss.

Perfect information. The knowledge that a given event will occur. For example, if you have information that it will rain tomorrow, this is perfect information. It does not imply that you can control the weather, only predict it.

Probability. The likelihood that an event A will occur: $0 \leq P(A) \leq 1$.

Sample space. An exhaustive listing of all possible events.

Subjective probability. A probability measure based on judgment and intuition, and not based on physical measures or verifiable through repeated experimentation. For example, the probability of success of a new product is a subjective probability.

Problems

1. During a rainy fall you face the problem of going out with or without an umbrella. While you are outside it may or may not rain. In this situation, there are four possible results, or payoffs. Make up a payoff table that indicates alternatives, events, and results.
2. Consider the toss of one die.
   a. What is the probability of a 4?
   b. What is the probability of a 3 or a 4?
   c. What is the probability of a 3 and a 4?
3. Consider the simultaneous toss of a red die and a white die.
   a. What is the probability of a 4 on the red die and a 3 on the white die?
   b. What is the probability of a 4 on one die (either color) and a 3 on the other one?
   c. What is the probability that the sum of dots showing on both dice equals 7?
4. *(SMA)* "Fast-Toonup," a franchise operation with a "satisfaction-guaranteed" motto, employs four licensed mechanics. The mechanics are trained to work on any type of car.

   Two of the mechanics, Andre and Bill, who are both quite experienced, evenly split 65 percent of the new work. They have very few unsatisfied customers (0.7 percent and 1.5 percent, respectively) who return to have faulty work redone. The balance of the new work is distributed to the other two mechanics, Jacques and Nigel, on a 20 percent and 15 percent basis, respectively. Not as experienced as Andre and Bill, they work slower and more of their customers return to have repair errors corrected (3.5 percent each for Jacques and Nigel).

REQUIRED
If a customer returns requesting that faulty work be corrected, calculate the following probabilities:
   a. Andre did the original work.
   b. Andre *or* Bill did the original work.
   c. Nigel did the original work. (Answers should be to four decimal places.)

5. (SMA) Sonny's Restaurant is noted for the exceptional food served. The menu is small, consisting of two items—pizza and spaghetti—only. Due to Sonny's Secret Spaghetti Sauce, 75 percent of the customers order spaghetti. Two types of beverages are served, coffee and soft drinks. Coffee is ordered by 80 percent of the customers and soft drinks by the remainder. The probability that a customer will leave a good tip is 0.8 if he has spaghetti and coffee, 0.4 if he has spaghetti and soft drinks, 0.6 if he has pizza and coffee, and 0.2 if he has pizza and soft drinks.

REQUIRED
   a. What are the probabilities that a customer will order:
      (1) Spaghetti and coffee
      (2) Spaghetti and soft drinks
      (3) Pizza and coffee
      (4) Pizza and soft drinks
   b. What is the probability that the waiter will get a good tip from a particular customer? (No knowledge of this customer's order.)
   c. If the waiter receives a good tip, what is the probability that the customer ordered:
      (1) Spaghetti and coffee
      (2) Spaghetti and soft drinks
      (3) Pizza and coffee
      (4) Pizza and soft drinks

6. (SMA) A coin is tossed five times. The coin is known to be biased, with a 0.6 probability of landing heads and a 0.4 probability of landing tails. The results of this experiment can then be any one of the following simple events:

Event	Probability
$A = 0$ heads	$P(A) = 0.010$
$B = 1$ head	$P(B) = 0.077$
$C = 2$ heads	$P(C) = 0.230$
$D = 3$ heads	$P(D) = 0.346$
$E = 4$ heads	$P(E) = 0.259$
$F = 5$ heads	$P(F) = \underline{0.078}$
	1.000

REQUIRED
   a. Determine $P(E \text{ or } F)$.
   b. Determine $P(B,C)$.

c. Determine $P(\overline{A} \text{ or } \overline{B})$.
d. Determine $P(\overline{D},\overline{C})$.

Given event G: at least 3 heads show up.

e. Determine $P(G)$.
f. Determine $P(D|G)$.
g. Determine $P(G|E)$.
h. Determine $P(G,D)$.
i. Are events A and G independent? Explain.
j. Are events D and G mutually exclusive? Explain.
k. Are events G and B complementary? Explain.

7. *(SMA)* A random sample is drawn from a large population of students, 30 percent of which are women. The sample result can then be any one of the following simple events (for a sample of size 5):

Event	Probability
A: 0 women	$P(A) = 0.168$
B: 1 woman	$P(B) = 0.360$
C: 2 women	$P(C) = 0.309$
D: 3 women	$P(D) = 0.132$
E: 4 women	$P(E) = 0.029$
F: 5 women	$P(F) = 0.002$

REQUIRED

a. Determine $P(A \text{ or } B)$.
b. Determine $P(C,D)$.
c. Given that event G is as follows: G: There are more women than men in the sample. Determine $P(G)$.
d. Given that event H is as follows: H: There are at most four women in the sample. Determine $P(H)$.
e. Determine $P(G,H)$.
f. Determine $P(G \text{ or } H)$.
g. Determine $P(\overline{A} \text{ or } \overline{B})$.
h. Determine $P(F|G)$.
i. Determine $P(H|C)$.
j. Are events A and G independent?
k. Are events E and H mutually exclusive?
l. Are events G and C complementary?

8. *(SMA)* Three bookkeepers (A, B, and C) are employed in your accounting department to handle accounts receivable. A, who is more experienced than either B or C, handles 40 percent of the invoices; the balance is divided evenly between B and C. Errors are found in 2 percent of the invoices handled by A, 5 percent by B, and 7 percent by C.

REQUIRED

a. What is the probability that any particular invoice is handled by B?
b. What is the probability that any particular invoice will be in error?

c. Given that an error is found in an invoice, what is the probability that the invoice was handled by:
   (1) A
   (2) B
   (3) C
9. Duke Oil has recently purchased the right to drill for oil off the North Carolina coast for $0.5 million. In similar land formations throughout the world, the probability of striking "super pet," a high-grade petroleum, is 0.3. The probability of a medium hole is 0.6, and the probability of a dry hole is 0.1. Duke can either drill or not. If they hit "super pet," they will realize $5 million profit; for a medium hole, a profit of $3 million; and for a dry hole, a loss of $8 million.

REQUIRED:
   a. What should Duke do in order to maximize expected profits?
   b. Mr. Horace Huntington IV has been quoted as saying: "I'd give my right arm to know how much oil is out there." What is the value of Mr. Huntington's arm?
10. *(SMA)* An eastern Canada manufacturer of snowmobiles is contemplating the purchase of motors from a Swedish manufacturer. The motors are currently produced internally and, from experience, it is known that approximately 96 percent of all internally produced motors are nondefective. The Swedish product, although available at a unit cost of $2 less than the cost to produce the motor internally, has an uncertain quality.

Based on the best available information, the following probability distribution describes the quality (fraction defective) of motors supplied by this Swedish manufacturer:

Fraction Defective	Probability
0.01	0.35
0.05	0.45
0.10	0.15
0.15	0.05

The average cost (to the snowmobile manufacturer) to replace or repair a unit with a defective motor is estimated to be $175.

REQUIRED

Assuming that the manufacturer will require 60,000 motors during the coming year, should he purchase them from the Swedish supplier or manufacture them internally?

Please be clear in your quantitative analysis, and indicate the savings ($) between the two plans.

11. Consider the following payoff table:

EVENTS

	e_1	e_2	e_3
a_1	1	1	1
a_2	-2	10	6
a_3	20	-3	7
PROBABILITY	$\frac{1}{3}$	$\frac{1}{3}$	$\frac{1}{3}$

ACTS

Select the best action using the expected monetary value criterion.

12. Electro Generator Company (EGC) makes large steam turbine electrical generators. Unlike their competitors, who manufacture to order, EGC manufactures before the order. To the best of its knowledge, EGC believes that it can sell one generator with a probability of 0.3; two generators with a probability of 0.5; and three generators with a probability of 0.2. EGC can choose to manufacture either one, two, or three generators during the next year, but once it begins, it cannot vary the manufacturing quantity. The total cost for generators is

Quantity	1	2	3	
Total Cost	$2.0	$4.0	$5.0	millions

Generators sell in the market for $3 million, and unsold generators have a value of $0.5 million as scrap.

REQUIRED
  a. Calculate the payoff table for EGC.
  b. Calculate the loss table, and calculate the expected payoff.
  c. Delphi, a consulting firm, has a "track record" for predicting generator sales. Their current fee is $1 million. Should EGC
     (1) Employ Delphi
     (2) Not employ Delphi
     (3) Not enough information to say.
     Pick the correct response and indicate why it is correct.

13. Mr. Bayes, an auditor for Gros Huite, frequently visits the Flimsy Gadget Company. On this visit he plans to sample a single transaction from the cash account. It is well known that cash accounts are badly managed throughout the industry. The best industry standards suggest that there is a 0.3 probability of irregularities in any particular company's account. For Flimsy Gadget, Mr. Bayes has determined from past visits that there is a 0.2 probability that a correct transaction is found when there have been irregularities.

REQUIRED
  a. Assume that Mr. Bayes takes one transaction at random and observes it is correct. What is his revised probability that the account is in order?

b. Flimsy Gadget is rethinking its decision to engage Mr. Bayes to audit the cash account. For each visit, Mr. Bayes charges $100 (whether he goes home early or not). Flimsy Gadget believes the cost to them is $400 when they have irregularities and zero when they do not. Should Flimsy Gadget retain Mr. Bayes or not? Assume that Mr. Bayes fixes the account if he stays on.

14. A spare parts distributor serves his clients in a region through two parts depots. Demand for a regularly demanded part at each depot has varied quite consistently between 10 and 13 units, and the probability distribution below is considered to be a good indication of future demand variability for both depots.

Demand	Probability
10	0.1
11	0.5
12	0.3
13	0.1

Suppose that each depot follows a policy of stocking 12 units at the beginning of each week and that the demand for the part in both locations is independent.

REQUIRED
   a. What is the probability that there will be a stockout in one or the other locations?
   b. What is the probability that there will be a stockout in both locations?
   c. Suppose that a marketing study found that total demand for both regions would not be affected if they were served from a single, larger, centrally located depot.
      (1) Determine the demand distribution for the single location.
      (2) Assume that the new depot carries 24 units at the beginning of each week. Calculate the probability of being out of stock by 1 unit and by 2 units. Compare your answers with the ones obtained in parts a and b.

15. An American (A) and a German (G) car manufacturer are simultaneously trying to develop a revolutionary engine that will reduce gas consumption by as much as 80 percent. 1988 is the target date for having the design ready for mass production. The probability that A will succeed in meeting the target is $\frac{3}{4}$, provided that G succeeds. G will succeed with a probability of $\frac{4}{5}$, provided that A succeeds. Whether A succeeds or not, G will meet the target with a probability of $\frac{2}{3}$.

REQUIRED
   a. What is the probability that A will succeed regardless of the outcome of G?

b. What is the probability that both companies will meet the 1988 target date?
   c. What is the probability that at least one will succeed?
   d. What is the probability that G will succeed and A will not?
16. *(SMA)* One of British Columbia's larger department store chains is considering the following marketing proposal:

   A 40-channel CB radio will be offered to its credit card holders over a 6-month period. The sets will be advertised on literature sent with each monthly statement and will be sold for $175 each, including an automotive antenna. Setup costs for this promotion will be $225,000 and the average variable cost per delivered radio will be $100. There will be no constraint on supply. The department store chain has 125,000 credit card holders provincially.

   The chain's market research department has assessed the following probabilities for the percentage of credit card holders who would participate in the offer:

Percentage (%) Participation	Probability
1	0.15
2	0.45
3	0.25
4	0.10
5	0.05

REQUIRED
   a. Construct the expected profits table.
   b. Construct the opportunity loss table.
   c. Determine the optimal action under conditions of uncertainty.
   d. Calculate the expected value of perfect information. Briefly explain what this value represents.
17. *(SMA)* An astute milkman desires to determine how many 4-liter packs of milk to stock in his truck on a daily basis. Historical data generated on his fixed route have shown the following demand pattern:

Quantity Demanded (4-liter packs)	Number of Days on Which Given Level of Demand Occurred
100	8
101	12
102	30
103	100
104	40
105	10
	200

To facilitate calculations, assume that stock levels are restricted to the range 100–105. Also, milk left unsold at the end of the day must be discarded due to the lack of refrigeration equipment in the delivery truck. Milk costs the milkman $1.75 per 4-liter pack, which he sells for $2.50 per pack.

REQUIRED

Calculate all answers to the nearest cent.
- a. (1) Construct an expected profits table.
  - (2) How many 4-liter packs should the milkman stock in order to maximize expected profits? *Show all calculations.*
  - (3) How much would the milkman be willing to pay to know the exact quantity demanded?
- b. (1) Construct an opportunity loss table.
  - (2) How many 4-liter packs should the milkman stock in order to minimize expected opportunity loss? *Show all calculations.*

18. (SMA) Regional Development Limited owns a large tract of land on which it is considering erecting multi-unit residential housing. Regional has been waiting, however, for an announcement by Gigantic Manufacturing regarding its plans for locating a factor in the area.

    Regional has contracted with a local million construction firm to erect 24-unit apartment buildings at a cost of $1 million each. The contract provides that Regional will pay the full $1 million price once construction is started. Building codes will allow construction of a maximum of two such buildings on Regional's tract of land.

    If Gigantic should decide to locate in the area, Regional feels that demand for housing would ensure full occupancy and that each apartment building could be sold for $1 million. If Gigantic does not decide to locate in the area, any apartment buildings constructed could be sold for only $800,000 each. If Regional decides not to construct any buildings, the tract of land will be sold for $100,000.

    Regional's president believes that a decision can be delayed no longer and asks you for an analysis of the problem and a recommended course of action. You estimate that there is a 30 percent chance of Gigantic locating its plant in this area.

REQUIRED

- a. Construct a payoff table.
- b. How many buildings should be constructed to maximize expected payoff?
- c. How much should Regional be willing to pay for perfect information regarding Gigantic's decision?
- d. A consultant claims to be able to predict whether Gigantic will locate in the area. You believe this consultant will be correct 9 times out of 10. How much should Regional pay the consultant for his prediction?

19. (SMA) Depending upon its adjustment, a machine produces either 5, 10, or 20 percent defectives with probability 0.6, 0.3, and 0.1, respectively. The machine can be checked each day, at a cost of $800, to guarantee that it

will produce 5 percent defectives for the day. If the machine is not checked and produces 10 percent defectives, the extra cost created is $500; for 20 percent defectives, the extra cost created is $2500.

REQUIRED
  a. Construct a payoff table.
  b. If the objective is to minimize cost, should the machine be checked daily?
  c. Determine the EVPI.
  d. A sample of 10 items produced by the machine contains 1 defective. What is the value of the information contained in this sample?

20. For the investor in Figure 2–5, verify that

$$P(e_1|G) = 0.158 \quad P(e_2|G) = 0.526 \quad P(e_3|G) = 0.316 \quad P(G) = 0.475$$

21. The manager of a company is faced with a decision as to whether to allocate some expenditures for marketing research in region R for a new product P. Market research in that region costs $5,000, and a 20 percent probability exists that R will be receptive to product P. If the company decides that it will open a new market in that region, it will have to incur expenses which have a present worth of $20,000. The result may be success in establishing a market or in failure to do so. The present worth of the company's income in the case of success is $100,000, and in that of failure is $10,000. The probabilities of success are as follows:

  (1) If market research is conducted and a receptive market is indicated, the probability is 95 percent.
  (2) If market research is conducted and a nonreceptive market is indicated, the probability is 10 percent.
  (3) If no market research is conducted, the probability is 27 percent.

REQUIRED
  a. Draw a decision tree for this problem and compute the expected monetary values for the acts "conducting a market research," and "not conducting a market research."
  b. Should the manager conduct a market research?

22. A company engaged in prospecting for oil is contemplating a search in a certain area. The company has two options, either to conduct an initial study that would cost $10,000 or not to conduct it. It has been the experience of the company in similar areas that initial studies indicated with a 5 percent probability that an oil field was likely to exist in the area, and with a 95 percent probability that such a field was not likely to exist. If the company decides to take up drilling, the cost will be $200,000. If oil is hit, the present worth of return will be $2 million, whereas if no oil is found, no return will be earned. The probabilities of hitting oil are as follows:

  (1) If an initial study is conducted and the likelihood of the existence of a field is indicated, the probability is 90 percent.
  (2) If an initial study is conducted and the likelihood of the existence of a field is found to be remote, the probability is 2 percent.

REQUIRED
- a. Find the posterior probability of hitting oil after conducting the initial study.
- b. What is the value of the information provided by the initial study?
- c. Should the company conduct the initial study?
- d. What are the assumptions implied in the formulation of the problem? Discuss their validity according to your own judgment.

23. A grocery store manager wants to estimate the optimal daily amount of strawberries that he should carry in his store. Past sales show that the daily demand in cases of strawberries are

Event: Demand	Event: Probability
25 cases	0.1
50 cases	0.2
70 cases	0.4
100 cases	0.3

Assuming a sale price and a cost of $1.00 and $0.50 per case, respectively, and that the daily overstock can be sold at $0.20 per case to an out-of-town (outside the local market) jam factory, answer the following:

REQUIRED
- a. Prepare a table of conditional profits for the different possible acts.
- b. Prepare a table of conditional opportunity losses for the different possible acts.
- c. Prepare a table of expected monetary values.
- d. Prepare a table of opportunity losses.
- e. Calculate an expected monetary value for each act and rank the different acts.
- f. Compute the expected profit and the expected loss with perfect information.
- g. Compute the expected value of perfect information.

24. *(CMA)* Strotz Brewery produces and sells nationally a popular premium beer and has enjoyed good profits for many years. However, in recent years its sales volume has not grown with the general market. This lack of growth is due to the increasing popularity of light beer and the fact that Strotz has not entered the light beer market.

Strotz is now developing its own light beer and is considering potential marketing strategies. Introducing the new light beer nationally would require a large commitment of resources for a full nationwide promotion and distribution campaign. In addition, there is some risk in a nationwide introduction because Strotz is a late entry into the light beer market. Strotz's advertising agency has helped assess the market risk and has convinced the Strotz management that there are only two reasonable alternative strategies to pursue.

Strategy 1—Perform a test advertising and sales campaign in a limited number of states for a 6-mo period. Strotz would decide whether to introduce the light beer nationally on the basis of the results of the test campaign.

Strategy 2—Conduct a nationwide promotion campaign and make the new light beer available in all 50 states immediately without conducting any test campaign. The nationwide promotion and distribution campaign would be allowed to run for a full 2 yr before a decision would be made to continue the light beer nationally.

Strotz management believes that if Strategy 2 is selected there is only a 50 percent chance of it being successful. The introduction of light beer nationally will be considered a success if $40 million of revenue is generated while $30 million of variable costs are being incurred during the 2-yr period the nationwide promotion and distribution campaign is in effect. If the 2-yr nationwide campaign is unsuccessful, revenues are expected to be $16 million and variable costs will be $12 million. Total fixed costs for the 2-yr period will amount to $6 million regardless of the result.

The advertising agency consultants recognize that if Strategy 1 is selected there is a chance that the test will indicate Strotz should conduct a nationwide promotion and distribution campaign when, in fact, a nationwide campaign would be unsuccessful. Also, the consultants recognize that there is a chance that the test results will indicate Strotz should not conduct a nationwide promotion and distribution campaign when, in fact, a nationwide campaign would be successful.

REQUIRED
  a. Represent Strotz Brewery's decision problem through the use of a tree diagram. The tree diagram should identify all decision alternatives and possible outcomes.
  b. Calculate the expected monetary value (EMV) of Strategy 2 for Strotz Brewery.
  c. Assume Strategy 1, the test campaign, could predict perfectly whether or not a nationwide campaign would be successful. Using EMV as the decision criterion, calculate the maximum dollar amount Strotz Brewery should be willing to pay for the perfect information.
  d. The expected monetary value (EMV) criterion used by Strotz Brewery is often criticized as being inadequate for real decision problems. Identify and discuss at least three criticisms of the EMV criterion.
25. A production engineer is faced with the decision to purchase a new machine to be used in manufacturing a new product. It is not known in advance how long the need for the product will continue in the market, but it is generally believed that it will not last more than 8 yr. Four types of machines are available, M_1, M_2, M_3, and M_4, with expected lives of 2, 4, 6, and 8 yr, respectively. Cost and return data have been estimated for each of the four machines, assuming four different market conditions, S_1, S_2, S_3, and S_4, corresponding to 2, 4, 6, and 8 yr of product survival in the market. The following matrix shows the present worth of the net return before

Problems

taxes per $100 of invested capital, after deducting all expenses, including the cost of capital.

	S_1	S_2	S_3	S_4
M_1	100	90	80	70
M_2	60	120	110	90
M_3	30	90	150	140
M_4	-10	45	100	200

REQUIRED

a. If the production engineer has no knowledge of the probabilities of market conditions and assumes that each state of nature is equally likely, how should he make his decision?

b. Suppose that the following estimates of the probabilities were given to him:

States	S_1	S_2	S_3	S_4
Probabilities	10%	30%	40%	20%

Which machine should he choose?

26. In planning next year's budget, a company has two options for the allocation of $10,000:

   a. To invest in new product research, which may end up in one of two outcomes:
      (1) No significant product improvement, resulting in no change in company earnings. The probability of this occurrence is 70 percent.
      (2) A breakthrough in product design (30 percent probability). The company may then:
         (i) Substitute the new product for similar old ones, with the expectation of:
            Eighty percent probability of $100,000 additional return
            Twenty percent probability of $20,000 of additional return
         (ii) Produce a new product side by side with old ones, with the expectation of:
            Ninety percent probability of $80,000 for additional revenue
            Ten percent probability of $40,000 for additional revenue
         The two possible outcomes under each course of action depend on whether the new product will be acceptable to the market or not.
   b. To invest in advertising. The possible outcomes are
      (1) Overcoming competitor's advertising and innovation, with an additional revenue of $60,000 at a probability of 40 percent
      (2) No improvement on the present earnings, at a probability of 60 percent

   Should the company invest in research or advertising? *Note:* Returns are expressed as their present worth over all years for which additional earnings are attributable to the investment.

27. (*CMA*) The Jessica Co. has been searching for more formal ways to analyze its alternative courses of action. The expected-value decision model is among those being considered. In order to test the effectiveness of the expected-value model, a 1-yr trial in a small department has been authorized. This department buys and resells a perishable product. A large purchase at the beginning of each month provides a lower cost than more frequent purchases and also assures that Jessica Co. can buy all of the item it wants. Unfortunately, if too much is purchased, the product unsold at the end of the month is worthless and must be discarded.

If an adequate quantity is purchased, additional quantities probably cannot be purchased. If any should be available, they would probably be of poor quality and overpriced. Jessica chooses to lose the potential sales rather than furnish poor-quality product. The standard purchase arrangement is $50,000 plus $0.50 for each unit purchased for orders of 100,000 units or more. Jessica is paid $1.25 per unit by its customers.

The needs of Jessica's customers limit the possible sales volumes to only four quantities per month—100,000, 120,000, 140,000, or 180,000 units. However, the total quantity needed for a given month cannot be determined prior to the date Jessica must make its purchases. The sales managers are willing to place a probability estimate on each of the four possible sales volumes each month. They note that the probabilities for the four sales volumes change from month to month because of the seasonal nature of the customers' business. Their probability estimates for December 1978 sales units are 10 percent for 100,000, 30 percent for 120,000, 40 percent for 140,000, and 20 percent for 180,000.

The following schedule shows the quantity purchased each month based on the expected-value decision model. The actual units sold and product discarded or sales lost are also shown.

	QUANTITY (IN UNITS)			Sales Units Lost
	Purchased	Sold	Discarded	
January	100,000	100,000		20,000
February	120,000	100,000	20,000	
March	180,000	140,000	40,000	
April	100,000	100,000		80,000
May	100,000	100,000		
June	140,000	140,000		
July	140,000	100,000	40,000	
August	140,000	120,000	20,000	
September	120,000	100,000	20,000	
October	120,000	120,000		20,000
November	180,000	140,000	40,000	

Problems

REQUIRED

a. What quantity should be ordered for December 1978 if the expected-value decision model is used?

b. Suppose that Jessica Co. could ascertain its customers' needs prior to placing its purchase order rather than relying on the expected-value decision model. How much would it pay to obtain this information for December?

c. The model did not result in purchases equal to potential sales except during 2 months. Is the model unsuitable in this case, or is this a characteristic of the model? Explain your answer.

28. (CMA) Jackston, Inc., manufactures and distributes a line of Christmas toys. The company has neglected to keep its doll house line current. As a result, sales have decreased to approximately 10,000 units per year from a previous high of 50,000 units. The doll house has recently been redesigned and is considered by company officials to be comparable to its competitors' models. The company plans to redesign the doll house each year in order to compete effectively. Joan Blocke, the sales manager, is not sure how many units can be sold next year, but she is willing to place probabilities on her estimates. Blocke's estimates of the number of units that can be sold during the next year and the related probabilities are as follows:

Estimated Sales in Units	Probability
20,000	0.10
30,000	0.40
40,000	0.30
50,000	0.20

The units would be sold for $20 each.

The inability to estimate the sales more precisely is a problem for Jackston, Inc. The number of units of this product is small enough to schedule the entire year's sales in one production run. If the demand is greater than the number of units manufactured, sales will be lost. If demand is less than supply, the extra units cannot be carried over to the next season and would be given away to various charitable organizations. The production and distribution cost estimates are listed below.

	UNITS MANUFACTURED			
	20,000	30,000	40,000	50,000
Variable costs	$180,000	$270,000	$360,000	$450,000
Fixed costs	140,000	140,000	160,000	160,000
Total costs	$320,000	$410,000	$520,000	$610,000

The company intends to analyze the data to facilitate making a decision as to the proper size of the production run.

a. Prepare a payoff table for the different sizes of production runs required to meet the four sales estimates prepared by Joan Blocke for Jackston, Inc. If Jackston, Inc., relied solely on the expected-monetary-value approach to make decisions, what size production run would be selected?

b. Identify the basic steps in any decision process. Explain each step by reference to the situation presented in the problem and your answer for part a.

29. (*CMA*) The Unimat Company manufacturers a unique thermostat, which yields dramatic cost savings from effective climatic control of large buildings. The efficiency of the thermostat is dependent on the quality of a specialized thermocoupler. These thermocouplers are purchased from Cosmic Company for $15 each.

    Since early 1976, an average of 10 percent of the thermocouplers purchased from Cosmic have not met Unimat's quality requirements. The number of unusable thermocouplers has ranged from 5 to 25 percent of the total number purchased, and has resulted in failures to meet production schedules. In addition, Unimat has incurred additional costs to replace the defective units, because the rejection rate of the units is within the range agreed upon in the contract.

    Unimat is considering a proposal to manufacture the thermocouplers. The company has the facilities and equipment to produce the components. The engineering department has designed a manufacturing system that will produce the thermocouplers with a defect rate of 4 percent of the number of units produced. The schedule below presents the engineers' estimates of the probabilities that different levels of variable manufacturing cost per thermocoupler will be incurred under this system. The variable manufacturing cost per unit includes a cost adjustment for the defective units at a 4 percent rate. Additional annual fixed costs incurred by Unimat if it manufactures the thermocoupler will amount to $32,500.

Estimate Variable Manufacturing Cost Good Thermocoupler Unit	Probability of Occurrence
$10.00	0.10
12.00	0.30
14.00	0.40
16.00	0.20
	1.00

Unimat Company will need 18,000 thermocouplers to meet its annual demand requirements.

Prepare an expected-value analysis to determine whether Unimat Company should manufacture the thermocouplers.

References

Dyckman, T. R., Smidt, S., and McAdams, A. K. *Management Decision Making Under Uncertainty.* New York: Macmillan, 1969.

Feller, W. *An Introduction to Probability Theory and Its Applications,* 3d. ed., vol. 1. New York: Wiley, 1968.

Kemeny, John G., Minkil, H., Snell, J. L., and Thompson, G. *Finite Mathematical Structures.* Englewood Cliffs, N.J.: Prentice-Hall, 1959.

Lapin, Lawrence L. *Quantitative Methods for Business Decisions.* New York: Harcourt Brace Jovanovich, 1976.

Raiffa, Howard. *Decision Analysis.* Reading, Mass.: Addison-Wesley, 1968.

Spurr, W. A., and Bonini, C. P. *Statistical Analysis for Business Decisions.* Homewood, Ill.: Irwin, 1967.

Winkler, Robert L. *An Introduction to Bayesian Inference and Decision.* New York: Holt, Rinehart and Winston, 1972.

Winkler, Robert L., and Hays, W. L. *Statistics: Probability, Inference, and Decision,* 2d ed. New York: Holt, Rinehart and Winston, 1975.

CHAPTER 3
Probability Distributions and Decision Theory

3.1 Introduction to Probability Distributions
Introduction
Random Variables and Probability Distributions
Expected Value
The Variance
Discrete and Continuous Distributions

3.2 Specific Probability Distributions and Their Use
The Binomial Distribution
The Normal Distribution

3.3 Decision Theory
Different Decision Criteria
Utility and Decisions
Measuring Utility

3.4 Summary

Glossary

Problems

Key Concepts

Binomial distribution	Normal deviate
Continuous probability function	Normal distribution
Cumulative distribution	Probability distribution
Decision theory	Random variable
Discrete probability function	Risk averse
Equal likelihood criterion	Risk neutral
Expected value	Risk seeking
Maximax criterion	Standard deviation
Maximin criterion	Utility
Maximum expected value criterion	Utility function
Maximum likelihood criterion	Variance
Minimax regret criterion	

Key Applications

Financial decision making	Sampling
Quality control	Statistical analysis
Risk analysis	

3.1 Introduction to Probability Distributions

INTRODUCTION

In the first part of this chapter, we continue our discussion of probability concepts by introducing the notions of random variables and probability distributions. The variance and standard deviation are introduced as measures of the variability or dispersion of the values that may be assumed by a random variable. We then present two of the most widely used probability distributions, the binomial and the normal distribution. Examples are presented to show how these distributions can be used in calculating probabilities of outcomes.

In the second part of the chapter the reader is introduced to some basic concepts of decision theory. Different decision criteria useful in choosing among possible courses of action are discussed and illustrated. The utility function is explained as a measure of an individual's attitude toward risk, such as risk aversion, risk neutrality, and risk seeking. The decision implications of each risk attitude are illustrated.

RANDOM VARIABLES AND PROBABILITY DISTRIBUTIONS

In the example in Chapter 2 of the retailer who faces an uncertain demand for the next day, we saw that conditional profits or losses could assume different numerical values depending on the actual demand and the stocking decision. Because these numerical values vary, we shall consider the demand as variable. When the value that a variable can assume is subject to chance (probability), we speak of a *random variable*. The probabilities assigned to each of the possible values of that variable in our example, the probabilities for sales of 0, 1, 2, 3, 4, and 5, constitute a *probability distribution*.

The possible number of heads we obtain when tossing a fair coin twice also defines a random variable. Each random variable value corresponds to a particular event in the underlying sample space (in this case *HH*, *HT*, *TH*, *TT*). The possible values this variable may assume are 0, 1, and 2, and the probabilities for these are $\frac{1}{4}$, $\frac{1}{2}$, and $\frac{1}{4}$. Note that

3.1 / Introduction to Probability Distributions

the probabilities of $\frac{1}{4}$, $\frac{1}{2}$, and $\frac{1}{4}$ constitute the probability distribution for the experiment. A probability distribution summarizes the relationship between a random variable's possible values and their probabilities. Table 3–1 shows these relationships for tossing a coin. Note again that these probabilities sum to 1.00, that the random variable values correspond to events, and that the events are collectively exhaustive and mutually exclusive.

TABLE 3–1. Probability Distribution Function

Events	Possible Values of X*	Probability of Each Value	
TT	0	0.25	
TH } HT }	1	0.50	Probability distribution
HH	2	0.25	
		1.00	

*X is defined as the possible number of heads in two tosses of a fair coin, i.e., the random variable.

When random variables can assume only a limited number of values—such as the one illustrated in Table 3–1, we speak of a *discrete random variable*. A *continuous random variable*, on the other hand, may assume any value on a continuous scale for a given range. Examples are travel times of trucks between two cities, weights of persons, and scores on IQ tests.

EXPECTED VALUE

In the preceding chapter we developed the concept of *expected value* of a discrete random variable. We now formally define it as the sum of the values of the random variable weighted by the probability that the random variable will assume that value. In Table 3–2 we again show

TABLE 3–2. Expected Value

Demand (D), in units	$P(D)$	$D \times P(D)$
10	0.20	2
11	0.20	2.2
12	0.30	3.6
13	0.20	2.6
14	0.10	1.4
	1.00	
Expected or mean demand		11.8

the calculation of the expected value or the mean of a discretely distributed random variable. The mathematical definition of the mean of the probability distribution is

$$E(D) = \sum_{i=1}^{n} D_i \, P(D_i)$$

where $E(D)$ is the expected or mean demand and $\sum_{i=1}^{n}$ simply denotes that we have to sum the products of each random variable value D_i multiplied by its associated probability $P(D_i)$. The expected value corresponds to what is generally referred to as an average. As pointed out in the preceding chapter, expected value is a frequently used criterion in ranking the outcomes of different decisions.

THE VARIANCE

The expected value, or mean, measures only what value we expect on the average or in the long run. Statistically this is referred to as a measure of central tendency. Very often a decision maker wants or needs to know something about the degree to which the values of a random variable will deviate from the mean or vary among themselves. In quantitative analysis the most frequently used measure for this variability or dispersion is the *variance*. The variance is defined as the sum of the squared deviations of values of the random variable from the mean weighted by the probability of the random variable. Very often we also use the square root of the variance as a measure of variability, which is called *standard deviation*. In simple mathematical notation we write:

$$\text{VAR}(D) = \sum_{i=1}^{n} [D_i - E(D)]^2 \, P(D_i)$$

Table 3–3 shows how to calculate the variance and the standard deviation for a discrete probability distribution. VAR(D) is 1.56, and the *standard deviation* (often denoted as σ) is

$$\sigma = \sqrt{1.56} = 1.249$$

In evaluating different alternatives or choices among outcomes that are random variables, the variance or the standard deviation provides useful additional information to the decision maker because each can be used as a meaningful measure of risk. The concept of variance is also very useful in evaluating information obtained from sampling.

3.1 / Introduction to Probability Distributions

TABLE 3–3. Variance and Standard Deviation

Demand (D)	P(D)	Squared Deviation from the Mean $[D_i - E(D)]^2$	$[D_i - E(D)]^2 P(D_i)$
10	0.20	$(10. - 11.8)^2 = 3.24$	0.648
11	0.20	$(11. - 11.8)^2 = 0.64$	0.128
12	0.30	$(12. - 11.8)^2 = 0.04$	0.012
13	0.20	$(13. - 11.8)^2 = 1.44$	0.288
14	0.10	$(14. - 11.8)^2 = 4.84$	0.484
	1.00		
	$\text{VAR}(D) = \sum_{i=1}^{n} (D_i - 11.8)^2 P(D_i) =$		1.56

DISCRETE AND CONTINUOUS DISTRIBUTIONS

Earlier we distinguished between discrete and continuous random variables. A probability distribution that assigns probabilities to the *discrete* values that can be assumed by a random variable is referred to as a *discrete probability function* or a *probability mass* function. When the random variable may assume *any* value within a *defined range*, we are dealing with a *continuous probability distribution* or a *probability density function*.

TABLE 3–4. Table for a Discrete Probability Function

Next Day's Demand (D)	P(d)
0	0.05
1	0.10
2	0.30
3	0.25
4	0.20
5	0.10

Table 3–4 and Figure 3–1 show the table and the graph of the discrete levels of demand we assumed for our retailer's problem in the preceding chapter. On the horizontal axis of the graph we mark all possible values that the random variable may assume. The height of the vertical lines measures the probability of occurrence.

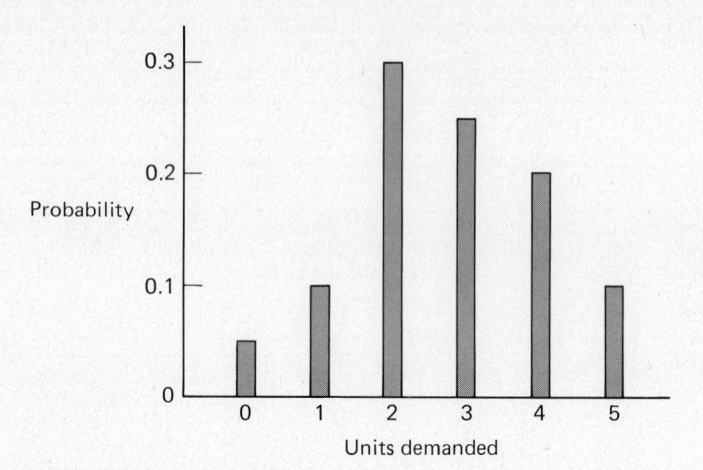

Figure 3–1. Graph for a discrete probability function.

These probabilities could also be presented as cumulative distributions. *Cumulative distributions* show the probabilities as "less than or equal" any given values for D, that is, $[P(D \leq 4)]$. They could also be shown as the probability of D being equal to or "more than" a certain value D, that is, $[P(D \geq 4)]$. In Table 3–5 and Figure 3–2 we show our retailer's cumulative less-than-or-equal distribution and the corresponding graph for the same distribution.

TABLE 3–5. Table of the Cumulative Distribution

D	$P(D = d)$	$P(D \leq d)$
0	0.05	0.05
1	0.10	0.15
2	0.30	0.45
3	0.25	0.70
4	0.20	0.90
5	0.10	1.00
	1.00	

For a continuous distribution, probability is measured by the area under the curve over a defined interval on the horizontal axis of the graph. See Figure 3–3. The curve itself (the probability density function) measures only the height of the graph for any value of the random variable. Figure 3–3 shows the curve for the normal probability distribution, which will be discussed in more detail in Section 3.2. The area under the curve must be equal to 1 because it represents the probability for all possible values of the random variable.

3.2 / Specific Probability Distributions and Their Use

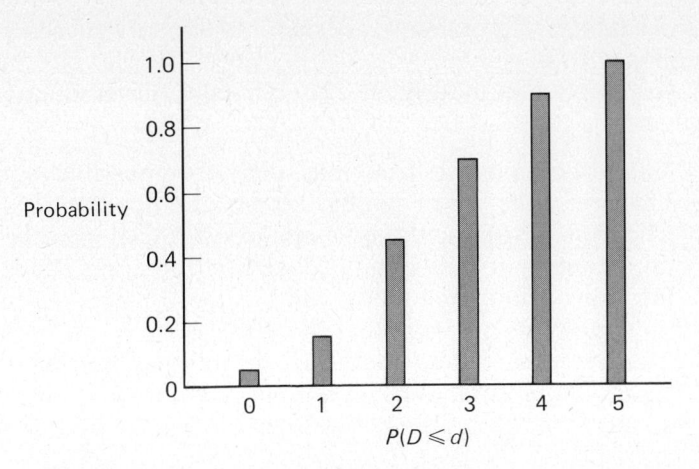

Figure 3–2. Graph of the cumulative distribution.

3.2 Specific Probability Distributions and Their Use

THE BINOMIAL DISTRIBUTION

The *binomial distribution* is a very useful and widely used probability distribution. It is based on the Bernoulli process, which is characterized by repeated trials, where each trial has *only two possible outcomes*, usually referred to as *success* or *failure*. Here are some examples of questions we can answer by employing the binomial distribution. What is the probability of getting five heads in 12 tosses of a coin? What is the chance that five out of 20 persons will respond to a mail questionnaire? What is the probability that five or more products out of a lot of 100 will be defective? In each case we are interested in

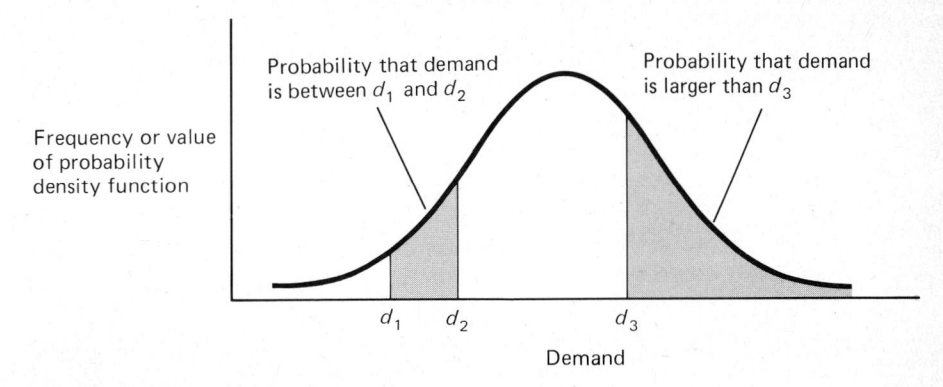

Figure 3–3. Normal probability function.

the probability of obtaining a certain number of "successes" in a given number of trials.

Assumptions underlying the binomial distribution are the following:

1. The process (each trial) has only two possible outcomes (e.g., heads or tails; yes or no; black or white; good or defective; etc.).
2. The *probability* for the outcome of each trial *must be constant*. As an example, consider the probability of getting heads by tossing a fair coin. That probability will remain a stable 0.5, regardless of how many times we repeat the process.
3. The outcome of any trial must be independent of any preceding trial; for our coin-tossing example, this means simply that the outcome of one toss does not affect the outcome of other tosses.

When the outcomes of trials are the result of a Bernoulli process, the number of successes is a random variable with a binomial distribution. Before we work an example, we must define some symbols used when working with the binomial distribution. We shall use R to indicate the number of successes (our random variable); p as the constant probability of success that characterizes the process; $1 - p$, obviously, as the probability of failure; and, finally, n as the number of trials. The binomial probability is

$$P(R = r | n, p) = \frac{n!}{r!(n-r)!} p^r (1-p)^{n-r}$$

We read the expression to the left of the equality sign as the probability of obtaining a number of r successes in n trials and with the constant probability of success p. The term $n!$ is read as "n factorial," meaning $n! = n(n-1)(n-2) \ldots 1$. For example, if $n = 4$, then $4! = 4 \times 3 \times 2 \times 1 = 24$, or if $n = 5$, then $5! = 120$. $0!$ is defined as equal to 1. We demonstrate this formula by applying it to three tosses of a fair coin.

Let us first list all possible outcomes of our coin-tossing experiment and show the applicable probabilities. (Table 3–6). Then we shall use the binomial probability formula to calculate a few probabilities:

1. The probability of *three tails* in *three* tosses. We write this as $P(R = 3 | n = 3, p = 0.5)$; the tails are the successes (R), n is the number of trials, and p is the constant probability of the underlying process. Entering these values in the formula, we obtain

$$P(R = 3 | n = 3, p = 0.5) = \frac{3!}{3!0!} (0.5)^3 (0.5)^0 = 0.125$$

3.2 / Specific Probability Distributions and Their Use

TABLE 3–6. Binomial Distribution

Possible Outcomes	R Value	Probability of Each Outcome
HHH	0	0.125
HHT	1	0.125
HTT	2	0.125
TTT	3	0.125
THT	2	0.125
THH	1	0.125
TTH	2	0.125
HTH	1	0.125
		1.000

Of course, we could have obtained this answer by inspection or by using the probability rule for the joint probability of independent events, that is $P(T) \times P(T) \times P(T) = \frac{1}{2} \times \frac{1}{2} \times \frac{1}{2} = \frac{1}{8} = 0.125$.

2. The probability of getting *two or more* tails. We write $P(R \geq 2 | n = 3, p = 0.5)$; because we already know the probability for three tails and that there cannot be more than three tails, we need to calculate only the probability for two tails and add that for three tails.

$$P(R = 2 | n = 3, p = 0.5) = \frac{3!}{2!1!} \times 0.5^2 \times 0.5^1 = 0.375$$

plus

$$P(R = 3 | n = 3, p = 0.5) = \underline{0.125}$$
$$ 0.500$$

Inspection of Table 3–6 verifies our answer.

We can also obtain this answer from the binomial distribution in Table 4 in Appendix C. In Table 3–7 we have reproduced the section of the table that applies to the problem at hand. The applicable probabilities are found in the lower right-hand corner under $P = 50$ (meaning $p = 0.50$). The probabilities are cumulative, "more than" probabilities, which, using our notation, are represented by $P(R \geq r | r, p)$. Thus, the probability of two or more tails ($r = 2$) can be read directly as 0.5000.

3. One notices from Table 3–6 that there is no entry for $r = 0$, that is, the probability of zero tails. To find the value we must look at the complement of $P(R - c)$; that is, $P(R = 0) = [1 - P(R \geq 1)]$. $P(R \geq 1)$ is 0.8750 in our table. Therefore, $P(R = 0) = 1 - 0.8750 = 0.1250$.

TABLE 3–7. Excerpt from Cumulative Binomial Distribution

$n = 3$

P	01	02	03	04	05	06	07	08	09	10
1	0297	0588	0873	1153	1426	1694	1956	2213	2464	2710
2	0003	0012	0026	0047	0073	0104	0140	0182	0228	0280
3				0001	0001	0002	0003	0005	0007	0010

P	11	12	13	14	15	16	17	18	19	20
1	2950	3185	3415	3639	3859	4073	4282	4486	4686	4880
2	0336	0397	0463	0533	0608	0686	0769	0855	0946	1040
3	0013	0017	0022	0027	0034	0041	0049	0058	0069	0080

P	21	22	23	24	25	26	27	28	29	30
1	5070	5254	5435	5610	5781	5948	6110	6268	6421	6570
2	1138	1239	1344	1452	1563	1676	1793	1913	2035	2160
3	0093	0106	0122	0138	0156	0176	0197	0220	0244	0270

P	31	32	33	34	35	36	37	38	39	40
1	6715	6856	6992	7125	7254	7379	7500	7617	7730	7840
2	2287	2417	2548	2682	2818	2955	3094	3235	3377	3520
3	0298	0328	0359	0393	0429	0467	0507	0549	0593	0640

P	41	42	43	44	45	46	47	48	49	50
1	7946	8049	8148	8244	8336	8425	8511	8594	8673	8750
2	3665	3810	3957	4104	4253	4401	4551	4700	4850	5000
3	0689	0741	0795	0052	0911	0973	1038	1106	1176	1850

4. Finally, we want to obtain the probability of getting *fewer than two tails*. We write

$$P(R < 2 | n = 3, p = 0.5)$$

This is the probability of obtaining zero and one tail. We could, of course, calculate each of these probabilities using the binomial formula and add them. However, because $P(R \geq 2) + P(R < 2) = 1$,

$$P(R < 2) = 1 - P(R \geq 2)$$

and because $P(R \geq 2) = 0.5$, we have

$$P(R < 2) = 1 - 0.5 = 0.5$$

This can also be readily verified from Table 3–6.

As another example, assume that an electrical manufacturer produces a huge quantity of a certain component for digital watches.

These circuits are used in watches made by another division of the company and are also supplied to several other manufacturers. Five percent of all the circuits eventually turn out to be slightly defective and are exchanged when returned by customers. This percentage of defectives is considered satisfactory, as it was anticipated when the process was designed. We assume that all assumptions underlying the binomial distribution are satisfied. We now take a random sample of 20 of these circuits. The following probabilities concerning that sample can help the management of the electrical firm evaluate the quality of their product. (The reader should refer to Table 4 in the Appendix.)

1. For zero defectives, $P(R = 0|n = 20, p = 0.05) = P(R \geq 0) - P(R \geq 1) = 1.000 - 0.6415 = 0.3585$.
2. For one or more defectives, $P(R \geq 1|n = 20, p = 0.05) = 0.6415$. This is read directly from Table 4 in Appendix C.
3. For fewer than two defectives, $P(R < 2|n = 20, p = 0.05)$. This is $1 - p(R \geq 2)$; $P(R \geq 2)$ is obtained directly from Appendix Table 4 as 0.2642, and $1 - 0.2642 = 0.7358$.
4. For exactly three defectives, $P(R = 3|n = 20, p = 0.05)$, $P(R \geq 3) - P(R \geq 4) = 0.0755 - 0.0159 = 0.0596$.

THE NORMAL DISTRIBUTION

The *normal distribution* is one of the most important continuous probability functions. It describes very accurately many actually observed frequency distributions in the real world. Examples are the height and weight of people, human intelligence as measured by IQ tests, and observed variations in the time required for certain tasks in industry. In addition to the fact that many variables in real life are normally distributed, the normal distribution is also a reasonable approximation for many other distributions (including binomial distributions).

Figure 3-4 shows that the normal distribution is a continuous, smooth and symmetric bell-shaped curve. The area under the curve is equal to 1, as it must be for all probability density functions. It represents, for any given interval on the horizontal axis, the probability that the random variable, in our case x, assumes *any* value in that interval.

The normal distribution is determined completely by its mean, denoted by μ (mu) and its standard deviation σ (sigma). Its tails are asymptotic, which means that they keep coming closer and closer to the horizontal axis without ever touching it.[1]

---

[1]Mathematically, the height of this function is given by

$$f(x) = \frac{1}{\sqrt{2\pi}\sigma} \times e^{-(x-\mu)^2/2\sigma^2}.$$

where $\pi = 3.1416$ and e is the base of the natural logarithm (2.7183).

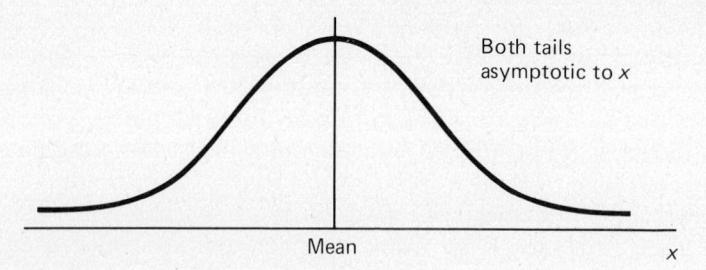

Figure 3-4. The normal density function.

The mean μ is always located in the center where the curve reaches its maximum height. The shape of a particular normal distribution is determined by its standard deviation. Figure 3–5 presents two different normal distributions with the same mean but different standard deviations. Note that the greater standard deviation labeled σ_2, produces a much flatter and wider bell-shaped curve.

We shall now discuss some important characteristics of the normal distribution with respect to the area under the curve. Figure 3–6 shows a normal distribution with a mean of zero and a standard deviation of 1. (This is referred to as the standard normal curve.) It is a characteristic of the normal distribution that the area under the curve within plus or minus one standard deviation (σ) of the mean represents 68.26 percent of the total area under the curve, within $\pm 2\sigma$ the area under the curve represents 95.44 percent of the total area, and within $\pm 3\sigma$ represents 99.73 percent of the total area under the curve. To find the probabilities for different values of a normally distributed random variable, we must determine the *area* of the applicable portions under the normal curve. These areas represent the probabilities of occurrence for a particular *range* of values.

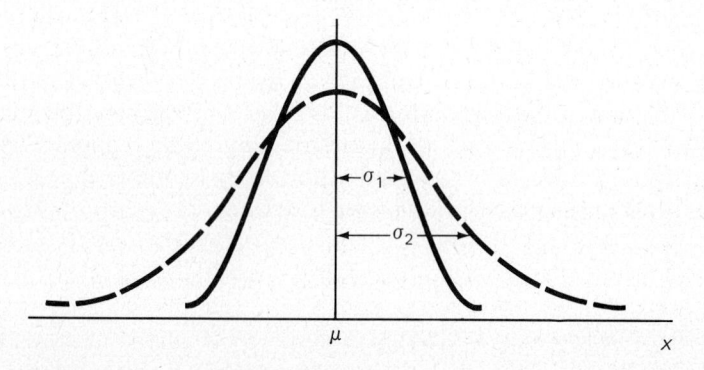

Figure 3-5. Two normal distributions.

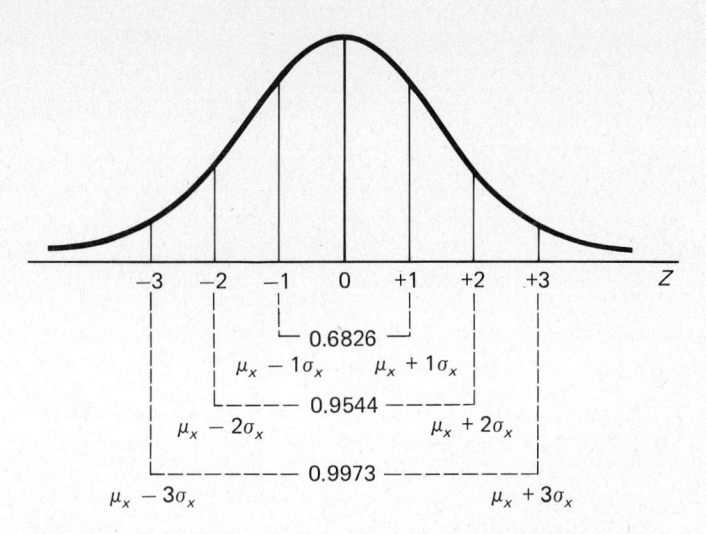

3.2 / Specific Probability Distributions and Their Use

Figure 3–6. Characteristics of the normal distribution.

To find areas under the normal curve, we use Table 2 in the Appendix. We shall illustrate the procedure by using the following example. An automatic machine in a manufacturing process produces thousands of small bolts per hour. The diameter of these bolts is very crucial for their subsequent use. From experience we know that if the machine is working properly, the diameters of the bolts produced are normally distributed with a mean μ of 20 millimeters (mm) and a standard deviation σ of 0.5 mm.

Even without consulting the table in the Appendix, we can make some statements with regard to the diameter of a randomly selected bolt. For example, the probability of randomly selecting a bolt with a diameter *greater than* 20 mm is 0.5. Obviously, then, the probability of selecting one with a diameter of less than 20 mm is also 0.5. But what is the probability of selecting a bolt with a diameter of more than 20.5 mm? Let us refer to Figure 3–7. We see that 20.5 mm is 0.5 mm or exactly one standard deviation larger than the mean. Earlier we learned that the area within one standard deviation on either side of the mean is 68.26 percent of the total area under the curve. But we are now interested in the shaded area to the right of 20.5. Knowing that the area under the curve to the left of 20.0 is 0.5 and the area between 20 and 20.5 is one-half of 0.6826 or 0.3413, we know that the probability of randomly selecting a bolt of less than 20.5 mm is 0.5 + 0.3413 or 0.8413. Hence, the probability of picking one with a diameter of more than 20.5 mm is 1 − 0.8413 or 0.1587.

Table 2 in the Appendix has been calculated for the standard normal curve giving the area from $-\infty$, that is, the beginning of the left

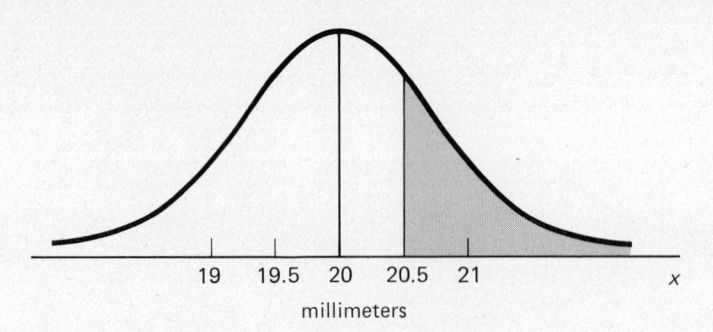

Figure 3–7. The normal distribution for a bolt.

tail, to any value above the mean measured in standard deviations. This distance from the mean measured in standard deviations is considered as a variable and denoted as Z for any value x of our random variable. The value of Z is sometimes referred to as *standard normal deviate*. We calculate Z as follows:

$$Z = \frac{x - \mu}{\sigma}$$

Note that Z simply measures the distance from the mean μ in terms of standard deviations (σ). Calculating for our example, we get

$$Z = \frac{20.5 - 20}{0.5} = 1$$

We now refer to Table 2 in the Appendix. The first column of Table 2 gives us the values for Z, so we look up Z = 1.0 and find the value 0.8413. This constitutes the entire area under the curve to the left of the mean plus the area to the right up to one standard deviation from the mean. Because we want to know the probability of picking a bolt with diameter greater than 20.5 mm, we must subtract from 1, that is, 1 − 0.8413 = 0.1587, to obtain the probability.

What is the probability of randomly selecting a bolt with a diameter of less than 20.78 mm? We obtain

$$Z = \frac{20.78 - 20}{0.5} = 1.56$$

We now look up in the table the value for Z = 1.56 and find 0.9406. This represents the entire area under the curve up to 1.56 standard deviations to the right of the mean. Hence, the probability of randomly selecting a bolt with a diameter of less than 20.78 is 0.9406.

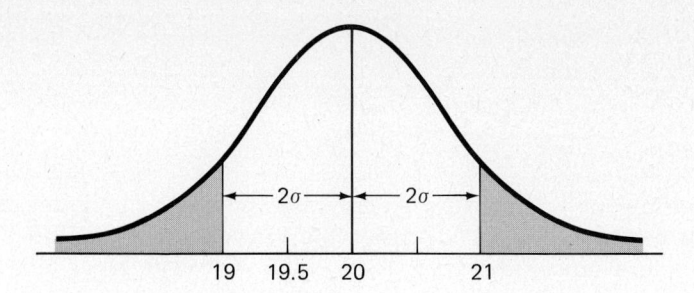

3.2 / Specific Probability Distributions and Their Use

Figure 3–8. The bolt example: $x \leq 19$.

Now let us find the probability of selecting a bolt with a diameter of less than 19 mm. We get

$$Z = \frac{19 - 20}{0.5} = -2$$

Table 4 gives us only the cumulative area from $-\infty$ to Z. We need the area beyond -2 standard deviations in the left tail of the curve (see Figure 3–8). Because the curve is symmetric, the area beyond two standard deviations on the right is identical to the corresponding area on the left. Looking up 2Z in the table, we find 0.9772; the area beyond that is $1 - 0.9772 = 0.02285$. Thus, the probability of obtaining a bolt with a diameter of less than 19 mm is also 0.02285.

As a final example, let us find the probability of randomly selecting a bolt with a diameter between 19.6 and 20.6 mm. Figure 3–9 shows that this probability is represented by the shaded area between the values of 19.6 and 20.6. This problem is more complicated because we have to find areas both to the right and to the left of the mean, whereas our table gives us only cumulative areas to the right of the mean. To

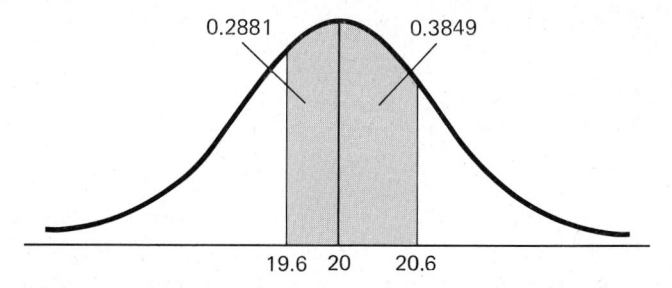

Figure 3–9. The bolt example: $19.6 \leq x \leq 20.6$.

find the relevant total area, let us first calculate the shaded area to the right of the mean:

$$Z = \frac{20.6 - 20}{0.5} = 1.2$$

Looking up 1.2, we find 0.8849; this, however, includes the entire left half or 0.5 of the area under the curve, which we do not need and therefore must subtract: $0.8849 - 0.5 = 0.3849$. Here 0.3849 represents the area to the right of the mean. To find the area to the left of the mean, we first calculate Z:

$$Z = \frac{19.6 - 20}{0.5} = -0.8$$

We therefore need the area under the curve to the left of mean up to a distance of -0.8 standard deviation. Defined areas to the left of the mean are identical to equidistant areas to the right, and we can use our table to find the equivalent area to the right. Looking up the Z value for 0.8, we find 0.7881; again, we must subtract 0.5 to get 0.2881. The total shaded area therefore is $0.2881 + 0.3849 = 0.6730$. Hence, the probability of randomly selecting a bolt with a diameter between 19.6 and 20.6 mm is 0.673.

3.3 Decision Theory

Decision theory is concerned with establishing systematic procedures for making decisions under uncertainty. A knowledge of decision theory should help the decision maker to analyze a problem in a complicated and uncertain setting, to develop alternatives, and to identify possible outcomes. The decision maker then selects the alternative that best meets his or her objectives and psychological desires. In the preceding chapter we used the *expected value criterion* for measuring a decision maker's choice preference. In so doing we assumed that decision makers will choose the act that results in the highest payoff in terms of expected value. There are, however, other *criteria* that may be used to select desirable acts under conditions of uncertainty.

In this chapter we survey some important theoretical decision concepts, including a brief discussion of utility. In a broad sense, all the chapters of this book deal with decision theory, albeit each one with some special aspect. For reasons that we shall explain, the expected value criterion discussed in Chapter 2 is preferred by most decision makers.

DIFFERENT DECISION CRITERIA

Using an example, we shall introduce and explain the following decision criteria. (Note that some of these criteria assume that there is a known probability function for possible outcomes, whereas others deal with unknown probability distributions.)

1. *The maximax criterion.* The decision maker chooses the act that offers the maximum possible return or payoff.
2. *The equal likelihood criterion* (also called the criterion of insufficient reason). The decision maker has no information regarding the probabilities of possible outcomes. He or she therefore considers every event as equally likely, assigns equal probabilities to all events, and then chooses the act with the highest expected payoff.
3. *The maximin criterion.* The decision maker wants to maximize the minimum possible payoff or minimize the possible losses. The decision maker selects the best of the worst possible outcomes.
4. *The minimax regret criterion.* Under this criterion the decision maker attempts to minimize the regret that may be experienced after the fact.
5. *The maximum likelihood criterion.* Here the decision maker selects the outcome or event that is most likely to occur, that is, the outcome with the highest probability, and chooses the act that will produce the highest payoff.
6. *The maximum expected value criterion.* This is the criterion we used in Chapter 2, where the decision maker chooses the act that yields the highest expected profit.

To illustrate the application of these decision criteria, we construct an example similar to the one we used to analyze the retailer's stocking decision in Chapter 2. Assume that a retailer is committed to purchasing either five, six, or seven units of a certain product. Each unit sells for $10, each unit costs $7, and unsold units are worthless. The demand distribution for these five to seven units and the conditional profits are given in Tables 3–8 and 3–9.

TABLE 3–8. Demand Distribution

Demand (d) (in units)	$p(d)$
5	0.10
6	0.60
7	0.30
	1.00

TABLE 3–9. Conditional Profits

IF DEMAND IS		POSSIBLE ACTIONS (a_j)	
	a_1	a_2	a_3
Buy	5	6	7
5	15	8	1
6	15	18	11
7	15	18	21

In the following discussion we assume that the decision maker has a linear utility function with respect to profits and losses. For the moment, this simply means that the decision maker considers a profit of $2000 to be twice as desirable as a profit of $1000 and a loss of $400 to be four times as undesirable as a loss of $100. Obviously this assumption may not be true for wide ranges of profits and losses.

Maximax. A decision maker who uses maximax as a decision criterion chooses the action that leads to maximum profit. In so doing the decision maker ignores the possibility of incurring losses and the probabilities assigned to the possible outcomes. Such a person might obtain the high payoffs, but would obviously be a loser in the long run. In our example we would buy seven units, because this is the only act that would make the maximum profit of $21 possible.

Equal Likelihood. Under the equal likelihood criterion it is assumed that the decision maker has little or no knowledge about the probabilities of the possible outcomes. In such a case it could be argued that we should assign equal probabilities to the possible states of nature. In our example we would have to assume that the given probability assumption is not available and that we would assign a probability of $\frac{1}{3}$ to the possible demand situations. It is left to the reader to verify that under these assumptions buying five units would yield the highest expected payoff ($15).

Maximin. Maximin is essentially the criterion for the rather pessimistic decision maker. The goal is to make sure that one earns at least X dollars or loses at most Y dollars. The decision maker first selects for each act the lowest possible payoff and then chooses for action the highest of these payoffs. In our example we have 15, 8, and 1 as the lowest payoff. Because 15 is the highest, we would buy five units.

Minimax Regret Criterion. As mentioned in the definition, the decision maker tries to minimize the regret that may be experienced. Regret is measured by the difference in payoff of an action and the best possible action assuming that we had known the actual state of nature. To do this we construct a regret matrix for our example as shown in Table 3–10. In the payoff column we first reproduce the conditional profits of Table 3–9. To obtain the amounts in the regret column we subtract the payoff of each line from the largest payoff. The largest payoff of the line represents the best possible action; its regret value is zero. For example, if we buy five and the demand is five, we realize a profit of $15; buying five was the best possible act, hence we have no regrets and enter zero in the regret column. If we buy five and the actual demand is six, we realize a profit of $15, but had we bought six we could have made $18, hence our regret is $3. Buying five when the actual demand turns out to be seven, we experience a regret of $6 ($21 − $15). Buying seven units when the demand is seven yields a payoff of $21, which is the result of the best possible action, hence, a zero regret. Buying seven when demand is six gives a payoff of $11, or $7 less than the $18 we could have obtained by buying only six. On the bottom line we show the maximum regret of each column and identify the minimum of these maximum regrets.

TABLE 3–10. Payoff of Acts and Regrets

Demand	ACT a_1, BUY 5 Payoff	Regret	ACT a_2, BUY 6 Payoff	Regret	ACT a_3, BUY 7 Payoff	Regret
5	15	0	8	7	1	14
6	15	3	18	0	11	7
7	15	6	18	3	21	0
Maximum regret		6		7		14

Minimum of maximum regret

Maximum Likelihood. In this case the decision maker looks for the most likely event, that is, the one with the highest probability, and then chooses the action with the highest payoff. In our example the most probable event is a demand for six units, and the act yielding the highest profit is to buy six units. Although this criterion may seem reasonable in many situations, it has the disadvantage of ignoring available information; that is, the other possible events and their consequences are not considered.

Maximum Expected Value. As pointed out in Chapter 2 under the maximum expected value criterion, we compute the expected value of each act by multiplying each conditional payoff (profit or loss) by its associated probability and totaling the resulting expected values. We then choose the act with the maximum expected value. Although this procedure was fully demonstrated in Chapter 2, we apply it again to the example of this chapter in Table 3–11 in order to point out some additional aspects of the maximum expected value criterion. Table 3–11 shows that the highest expected value is obtained when we buy six units of product. What distinguishes the expected value criterion from all the others mentioned so far is the fact that it alone incorporates *all the information* that is available.

TABLE 3–11. Expected Value

a_1 Buy 5	a_2 Buy 6	a_3 Buy 7
15 × 0.10 = 1.50	8 × 0.10 = 0.80	(1) × 0.10 = 0.1
15 × 0.60 = 9.00	18 × 0.60 = 10.80	8 × 0.60 = 4.8
15 × 0.30 = 4.50	18 × 0.30 = 5.40	221 × 0.30 = 6.3
15.00	17.00	11.2

Table 3–12 compares the attributes of the decision criteria. The maximax criterion ignores probabilities and other possible outcomes. The equal likelihood criterion ignores the fact that different outcomes most likely have different probabilities. The maximin criterion and minimax regret criteria ignore probabilities. The last four criteria mentioned, therefore, do not incorporate the knowledge available concerning the different chances for the possible outcomes. And, finally, the maximum likelihood criterion considers only one probability and ignores all the others.

TABLE 3–12. Comparison of Decision Criteria

	Takes into Account All Probabilities	Takes into Account One Probability	Ignores All Probabilities
Takes into account all outcomes	Maximum expected value	Maximum likelihood	Equal likelihood Maximin Minimax
Takes into account one outcome only			Maximax

A further advantage of the maximum expected value criterion is that it enables us, as we demonstrated in Chapter 2, to extend it and to incorporate sampling and experimental information. One of its major disadvantages is that it does not consider the fact that different alternatives, though having identical expected values, may involve vastly different magnitudes of risk. A simple example will illustrate this point.

Suppose that a young mechanic endowed with lots of business initiative wants to open a gas station with repair facilities at a location that he thinks is excellent. He considers two alternatives: A_1, a large station with six pumps and six stalls for repair and maintenance work; and A_2, a small station with only two pumps and two stalls. After analyzing the possible cash flows with an MBA friend, they come up with the decision structure shown in Table 3–13. According to our expected value criterion, both alternatives are equally attractive, although it would seem likely that some young mechanics may prefer A_2 because it avoids the risk of a $200,000 loss. This problem can be solved by using values for our payoffs that include a consideration of risk and therefore reflect more realistically their value to a decision maker. The theory of *utility*, discussed in the next section, offers us such payoff scales.

TABLE 3–13. Decision Structure for Gas Station Problem

Event	Probability	A_1 LARGE STATION Conditional Profit*	Expected Profit	A_2 SMALL STATION Conditional Profit	Expected Profit
E_1: Gasoline prices continue to increase	0.5	$(200,000)	$(100,000)	$ 50,000	$ 25,000
E_2: Gasoline prices stabilize	0.5	400,000	200,000	150,000	75,000
Expected profits			$ 100,000		$100,000

*Present value of future profits

UTILITY AND DECISIONS

In the example of our mechanic, we showed that alternatives with identical expected profits may involve greatly differing risks. Because people have *different attitudes to risk*, two persons faced with an identical set of alternatives may each prefer a different one. In the gas station example in the preceding section, it is quite possible that some people would prefer alternative A_1 to the less risky A_2, especially when they can afford a large loss. To further illustrate this point, take the case of a homeowner who is considering a fire insurance policy on her

$100,000 house. Table 3–14 shows the relevant conditional and expected values. The probability for home fires has been calculated by the insurance company on the basis of past experience, and a premium of $300 would seem quite reasonable for most areas in the United States. Let us disregard the possibility of partial damage in this example and consider only the chances of total destruction of the home. Clearly, the expected value criterion would tell the homeowner not to insure her home. Yet how many homeowners would willingly assume the risk of the total loss of what is for most of them their biggest lifetime investment? Obviously we are dealing here with a situation where the expected value criterion does not apply. This is because homeowners are willing to pay more than expected value because they value the peace of mind and feeling of security resulting from a good policy with a reputable insurance company more than any disadvantage in expected value.

TABLE 3–14. Conditional and Expected Values for Fire Insurance of Home

		A_1 BUY INSURANCE		A_2 DO NOT BUY INSURANCE	
Event	Probability	Conditional Value	Expected Value	Conditional Value	Expected Value
Fire	0.0015	(300)	(0.45)	(100,000)	(150)
No fire	0.9985	(300)	(299.55)	0	0
			(300.00)		(150)

Utility theory tries to explain the phenomenon that people do often very obviously depart from the expected value criterion and apply different payoff measures. Utility theory can be viewed as an attempt to measure *a person's* attitude toward risk. In uncertain situations persons are assumed to maximize expected utility and not expected dollar payoffs. Returning to our example of the homeowner, we can say that she derives greater utility from having insurance. In the possible losses expressed in dollars, we find that most people fear increased losses far more than is indicated by their proportionate increase. A young man with a total fortune of $10,000 may view the loss of say $500 with relative calm, but he would be more than twice as upset when the loss is $1000. Generally, we can say that when losses reach a level where they hurt and worry a person, the amount of anguish and worry (negative utility) increases much faster than the proportiate increase in losses. The same can be said for monetary gains. An additional profit of

$20,000 will produce a greater sense of well-being (utility) for a person currently earning $10,000 than for a millionaire.

MEASURING UTILITY

Utility theory suggests that each person has a measurable preference for different choices involving risk. This attitude toward risk is called *utility*. The measurement unit used for measuring utilities is called a *utile*. In the following we shall try to illustrate how measures of risk preferences can be used to construct a person's utility function. To do this we assume that utilities can be measured on a cardinal or interval scale. That means that if, of two risky alternatives, one is twice as preferable as the other, the more preferable alternative will be assigned twice as many utiles.

TABLE 3–15. Initial Expected Utiles

		A_1 BUY INSURANCE		A_2 DO NOT BUY INSURANCE	
Event	Probability	Utiles	Expected Utility	Utiles	Expected Utility
Fire	0.0075	−2	−0.0003	−10,000	−15
No fire	0.9985	−2	−1.9997	0	0
			−2.00		−15

Let us first return to the fire insurance example. Assume that we have already estimated the homeowner's utility function. On the basis of this hypothetical function, we assign −2 utiles to the cost of the insurance and −10,000 utiles to the total loss of the home. In Table 3–15 we use this information to calculate the expected utilities for the two acts. Note that the arithmetic of calculating the expected utility is similar to that used in calculating expected monetary values. Instead of conditional monetary values we use utiles and express the expected value as an expected utility.

On the basis of the expected value criterion in Table 3–14, we found that it would be preferable *not* to insure the home. Using a measure of utility in Table 3–15 that reflects the homeowner's risk preference, we find that in terms of expected utility, it is clearly preferable to insure the home.

Having a person's utility function available would permit us to relate the number of utiles (or utility) to corresponding monetary values. By means of a simple example we shall show how a person's utility function can be developed.

TABLE 3–16. Conditional Profits

	Probability	a_1	a_2	a_3
			ACTS	
Event 1	0.2	$60	$75	$30
Event 2	0.5	30	15	30
Event 3	0.3	20	−10	30
Expected values		$33	$25.5	$30

Assume that a manager has to choose among three alternatives, each with three possible outcomes, as shown in Table 3–16. On the basis of expected profits, action a_1 is selected as the best. If we want to evaluate this decision problem in terms of utilities, we need for each conditional value its equivalent in terms of utiles.

To do this, we proceed as follows: First we arbitrarily assign a value of zero utiles to the lowest profit (−$10) and 100 utiles to the highest profit ($75). Second, to obtain the next utility measure, we must ask the decision maker, the manager, to choose between:

A. An investment on which he is guaranteed to make a profit of $60. (the second highest profit in the conditional profit table), or
B. Playing in a lottery where he could lose $10 or make $75.

A is referred to as a certainty equivalent. Obviously our manager is not able to decide between A and B unless he knows the probabilities of the lottery.

We begin by arbitrarily assigning a probability, say, 0.8, to winning in B. If, with this probability, the manager prefers B, we shall lower it step by step until the manager is *indifferent* between the alternatives. If he prefers A with the initial probability, the probability has to be increased until the point of *indifference* is reached. This indifference between the utility of a certainty and the expected utility of an uncertain game of chance can be stated as the following indifference equation:

$$U(\$60) = P[U(\$75)] + (1 - P)[U(-\$10)]$$

where $U(i)$ is utiles of outcome i and the utiles on the right-hand side are 100 and zero, respectively. Verbally we read this equation as the utiles of a certain $60 equalling the expected utility of a lottery involving a possible gain of $75 or a loss of $10. The amount on the left side of the equation, in this case $60, is the certainty equivalent. Note that the probabilities on the right side of our equation are obtained by repeated questioning of the manager.

3.3 / Decision Theory

Suppose that the manager preferred B when we gave him the probability of 0.75. After several trials, we find that he is indifferent between A and B when given the probability of 0.95. We now solve the above equation

$$U(\$60) = 0.95(100) + 0.05(0) = 95 \text{ utiles}$$

We now proceed to the conditional profit or certainty equivalent of $30 and repeat the same questions, except that A is now stated as a certain profit of $30. B is still the same lottery involving a chance of winning $75 and losing $10. Suppose that we reach the point of indifference with a probability of 0.80; then we obtain

$$U(\$30) = 0.80(100) + 0.20(0) = 80 \text{ utiles}$$

We repeat the procedure for the other conditional profits in the table; suppose that we obtain utiles as follows:

$U(\$20) = 70$ utiles
$U(\$15) = 60$ utiles

These values can now be plotted on the graph of Figure 3–10. By connecting the points plotted, we obtain the manager's utility function. From the graph we can read the equivalent in utiles for all the dollar profits included. For example, a $40 profit corresponds to 85 utiles. This means that our manager is indifferent between a certain profit of $40 and our lottery involving an 85 percent chance of winning $75 and a 20 percent probability of losing $10. We could actually use this point (40, 85) or the function to test the validity of the function by submitting

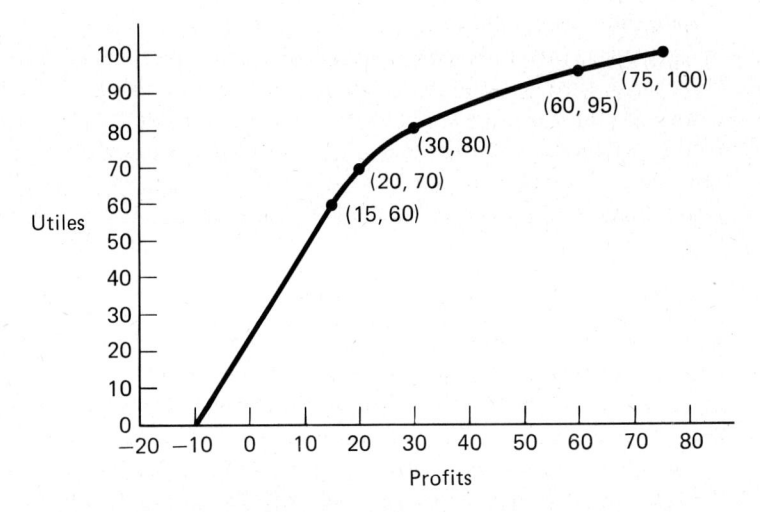

Figure 3–10. Utility function of profits.

the implied question to our manager. In Table 3–17 we show the conditional profit table with the associated utiles and calculate the expected utility for the three acts. Acts a_3 and a_1 have the highest expected utility and would be equally preferable in accordance with our hypothetical manager's utility function.

TABLE 3–17. Conditional Profits and Utiles

	Probability	a_1 $	a_1 Utiles	a_2 $	a_2 Utiles	a_3 $	a_3 Utiles
Event 1	.2	60	95	75	100	30	80
Event 2	.5	30	80	15	60	30	80
Event 3	.3	20	70	−10	0	30	80
Expected values in dollars		33		25.5		30	
Expected values in utiles			80		50		80

Under the expected value criterion only, act a_1 would have been optimal.

In Table 3–18 we outline again the steps we went through when estimating the manager's utility function. A few comments are in order. The scale selected for measuring utility (we used zero to 100) could be changed to any other cardinal scale, just as temperature can be measured on the Celsius or the Fahrenheit scale. The concepts of utility theory are undoubtedly useful in analyzing decision problems. Yet there are serious practical measurement difficulties in obtaining utility functions. It should be obvious that obtaining consistent answers to the lottery questions is no easy task. In addition, we do not know how stable the function is. Major changes in the personal, political, and economic environment can significantly influence a person's attitude to risk. The fact that many important business decisions are made by groups rather than individuals complicates the problem. Obtaining the utility function of a group is obviously more complicated than obtaining one for a single person.

Although utility functions are very individualistic, some general statements can be made. More money is preferable to less, and therefore the function for monetary gains will usually have a positive slope. The slope can be regarded as an indicator of the marginal utility of money (gains). If that slope is constant (i.e., the function is a straight line), each additional dollar has exactly the same utility over the entire

3.3 / Decision Theory

TABLE 3-18. Steps in Estimating Utility Functions

I. Rank outcomes from most desirable to least desirable and assign utiles to extreme outcomes

Max conditional profit	75	100 utiles
	60	x
	30	x
	20	x
	15	x
Max loss	−10	0 utiles

Utiles for these outcomes must be found (for the intermediate values)

II. Formulate decision maker's hypothetical choice between

A: guaranteed profit of a certain amount (the certainty equivalent)

B: playing a hypothetical lottery involving the most desirable and the least desirable outcomes

For each intermediate outcome, ask the decision maker for the probability of winning that will make him or her indifferent between A and B.

III. Determine utiles for each certainty equivalent by solving

$$U(\text{certainty equivalent}) = P(U)(\text{most desirable outcome}) + (1 - P)(U)(\text{least desirable outcome})$$

---

range of the function (see the function labeled *a* in Figure 3-11). Persons with a linear utility function are also referred to as *risk neutral*.

If the slope increases at a decreasing rate (function *b* in Figure 3-11), it indicates an attitude that is described as *risk averse*. Most middle-class people seem to fall into this category. They take out insurance for which the expected value is less than the perceived expected utility. A risk-averse person typically makes conservative investments and dislikes actions that involve high risks. The marginal utility of money decreases as more and more becomes available.

If the slope increases at an increasing rate, it indicates a *risk-seeking* attitude (function *c* in Figure 3-11). A *risk seeker* is attracted by high rewards; the risk seeker will often accept gambles with negative expected values as long as there is even a small chance for a high payoff. The marginal utility of money is increasing; additional money enhances the risk seeker's sense of well-being at an increasing rate.

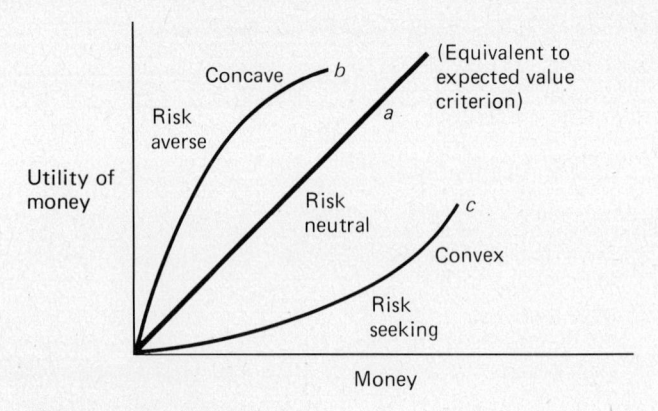

Figure 3–11. Utility functions.

Obviously, people cannot be simply categorized as falling into these three categories. Most persons will display all three attitudes to risk at varying degrees, depending on, among other factors, their age, station in life, and individual wealth. The function in Figure 3–12 may be indicative of a hypothetical professional person's changing attitudes to risk at different stages of her career. During her student years, our future professional is understandably risk averse. Risking her limited wealth might endanger her education and ruin her career. As she enters professional life and begins to enjoy a successful career, her risk aversion changes to risk neutrality. As her career unfolds and her increasing wealth assures her security and a high standard of living, she becomes a risk seeker willing to take chances on risky investments that promise a chance of high rewards. As she approaches retirement, she

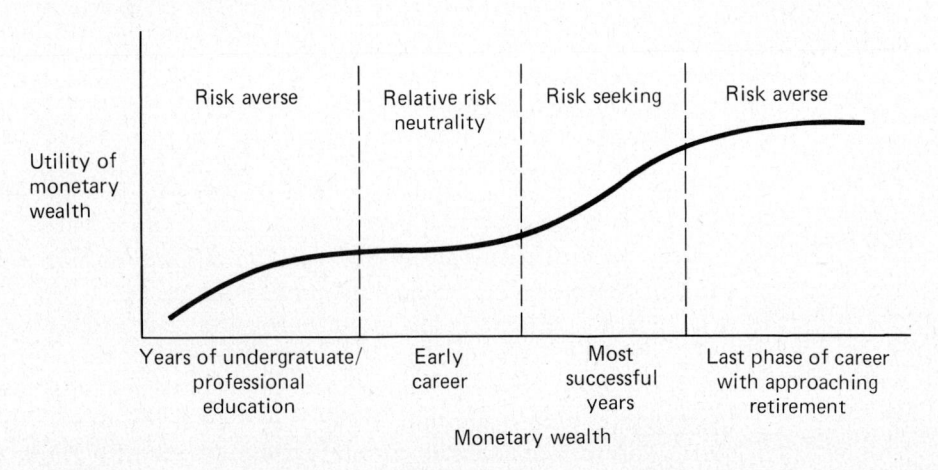

Figure 3–12. Utility as a function of professional age.

again changes back to risk aversion, preferring conservative ventures with relatively certain payoffs.

Needless to say, such a function is hypothetical. Although it is possible to establish a person's attitude to risk when he or she is faced with well-defined options, it would be extremely difficult to develop a function such as the one in Figure 3–12 that would be valid over the long run. Too many factors can and do cause changes of individual attitudes over time.

3.4 Summary

In this chapter we have expanded our discussion of probability concepts to include the notion of a random variable. Two widely used distributions, the binomial and the normal distribution, were presented and investigated. Both are frequently applied in the analysis of business problems. The binomial distribution gives the probability of "successes" in a given number of attempts. The normal distribution is a continuous distribution. The problem section illustrates a number of applications.

Our earlier discussion of decision theory was expanded to include different criteria for selecting an alternative course of action: maximax, equal likelihood, maximin, minimax regret, maximum likelihood, and a new rationale for expected value. Another approach to considering risk is utility theory. A method for determining a decision maker's utility function was presented and applied to the evaluation of courses of action. The notions of risk aversion, risk seeking, and risk neutrality were defined, illustrated, and discussed.

Glossary

Binomial distribution. Distribution based on a process characterized by repeated trials, where each trial has only two possible outcomes (success or failure). The probabilities for the outcomes are constant over time, and the outcomes of any trial are independent of all preceding or following trials. It is a discrete probability function.

Continuous probability function. A probability function that allows the random variable to assume any value within a given range. It is also called a probability density function.

Cumulative distribution. A distribution that states the probability of a random variable for a value "less than or equal to" the given value.

Decision theory. The analysis of decisions under uncertainty.

Discrete probability function. A probability function that allows the random variable to assume only a finite number of values. It is also called a mass probability function.

Equal likelihood criterion. The assumption that the decision maker has no knowledge of the probabilities of possible outcomes and therefore considers all events as equally likely. It is also called the criterion of insufficient reason.

Expected value. The sum of the probability values times the random variable values, summed over all values.

Maximax criterion. A criterion for optimists under which a decision maker consistently chooses the act with the highest possible payoff.

Maximin criterion. A criterion for pessimists. The decision maker chooses the highest from the lowest possible payoffs of each act.

Maximum expected value criterion. A criterion by which the decision maker chooses the alternative that maximizes the expected value.

Maximum likelihood criterion. A criterion by which the decision maker considers only the most probable event and selects the act with the highest payoff.

Minimax regret criterion. A criterion by which the decision maker tries to minimize the regret that might be experienced.

Normal deviate (Z). Measures distance from the mean of a normal distribution in standard deviations: $Z = (x - \mu)/\sigma$.

Normal distribution. A symmetrical, bell-shaped distribution of a continuous random variable with asymptotic tails. It is a continuous probability function.

Probability distribution. A list of the possible outcomes and their associated probabilities. It summarizes the relationship between a random variable's possible values and their probabilities.

Random variable. A variable that assumes values subject to chance.

Risk averse. A decision maker who values additional money less. He or she would have a risk-averse utility function.

Risk neutral. An individual who values additional money at a constant rate. He or she would have a risk-neutral utility function, which is the expected value criterion.

Risk seeking. A decision maker who values additional money more. He or she would have a risk-seeking utility function.

Standard deviation. The square root of the variance.

Utility. The relative satisfaction that would be experienced by individuals if certain outcomes and payoff occurred.

Utility function. Assigns numerical measures of satisfaction to possible uncertain events.

Variance. A measure of dispersion around the mean.

Problems

1. A fair coin is tossed seven times. Without using Table 2 in the Appendix, determine the probabilities for the following outcomes:
   a. Exactly two heads
   b. Exactly four tails

Problems

    c. No heads
    d. Exactly three tails
2. A fair coin is tossed three times. Determine the probability distribution for the number of tails and calculate the expected number of tails.
3. A fair coin is tossed 20 times. Using Table 4 in the Appendix, determine the following probabilities for the number of heads:
    a. More than or equal to 8
    b. Less than 15
    c. More than 20
    d. Equal to 12
    e. More than or equal to 10
    f. Between 9 and 15 inclusively
4. A fair die is rolled four times. Without using Table 4 in the Appendix, determine the probabilities of the following outcomes:
    a. Exactly two 6s
    b. One 3 or one 4
    c. No 2s
    Using Appendix Table 4 ($P = 0.17$) determine the following probabilities:
    d. Four 6s in a row
    e. No 4s
    f. Each roll yields a 1, 2, or 3
5. Find the probabilities shown below for a normally distributed random variable X:

    a. $\mu = 0; \sigma = 1$
$$P(x \geq 0.75)$$
$$P(x \leq 0.75)$$
$$P(x \geq -0.75)$$
$$P(x < 1.00)$$
$$P(-0.8 \leq x \leq +0.8)$$
$$P(-0.8 \leq x \leq -0.4)$$

    b. $\mu = 5; \sigma = 2$
$$P(x > 7)$$
$$P(x \leq 7)$$
$$P(x \geq -7)$$
$$P(x < 3)$$
$$P(3 \leq x \leq 7)$$
$$P(6 \leq x \leq 7)$$

    c. $\mu = 5; \sigma = 1$
$$P(x > 7)$$
$$P(x \leq 7)$$
$$P(x \geq -7)$$
$$P(x < 3)$$
$$P(3 \leq x \leq 7)$$
$$P(6 \leq x \leq 7)$$

d. $\mu = 3.5$; $\sigma = 2$
   $P(x > 4)$
   $P(x \geq 4)$
   $P(x \leq 2.5)$
   $P(2 \leq x \leq 3)$
   $P(4 \leq x \leq 5)$
   $P(3 \leq x \leq 6)$

6. a. Given that X is a normally distributed random variable with a mean of zero and a standard deviation of 1. If $P(Z > z) = 0.02068$, what is the values of x?
   b. The random variable X again is normal, the mean is 8, and the standard deviation 3. If $P(Z > z) = 0.1587$, what is the value of x?
   c. Assume the same facts as in part b. If $P(Z \leq z) = 0.7224$, what is the value of x?
   d. Assume that X is normally distributed and has a mean of 12 and a standard deviation of 2. If $P(Z > z) = 0.02331$, what is the value of x?

7. *(SMA)* Y is a random variable with probability distribution

Y	P(Y)
−1	0.5
0	0.2
a	0.3

and $E(Y) = 1.0$

REQUIRED
   a. Determine the numerical value of a.
   b. A second random variable x is defined by $X = 2Y + 4$. Determine $E(X)$.
   c. Determine the variance of Y.

8. A machine has been set up to produce an axle for a small electric motor. The axle should have a diameter of 2 mm, but the electric motors will accept axles with diameters in the range of 1.99–2.01 mm without affecting their quality. To control the diameter of the axles, periodic random samples are taken, and, when necessary, the machine is stopped for adjustments. Assume that the distribution of these sample means is normal, has a standard deviation of 0.005 mm, and that the machine is stopped whenever the sample means are smaller than 1.99 mm or larger than 2.01 mm.
   a. What is the probability that the machine is stopped for adjustments (because a sample mean is less than 1.99 or more than 2.01), although the machine is actually operating within the prescribed limits and no adjustment is necessary?
   b. Suppose that the machine is actually turning out axles with a mean diameter of 1.98 mm. What is the probability that a random sample will *not* signal this shift, and the machine continues to operate, even though there is a need for an adjustment?

Problems

c. Suppose that something has caused the machine to turn out axles with a diameter of 1.99. What is the probability that a random sample will indicate that the machine needs adjustment?

9. (SMA) The Occult Company Ltd. manufactures various types of dolls. The daily demand for Wombats dolls is normally distributed with a mean of 500 units and a standard deviation of 80 units.

REQUIRED
(Answer the following questions to four decimal places.)
   a. On any particular day, what is the probability that Wombats demand exceeds 620 units?
   b. On any particular day, what is the probability that Wombats demand is between 400 and 600 units?
   c. What is the probability that Wombats demand exceeds 560 units on each of two successive days?
   d. What is the probability that Wombats demand exceeds 560 units on exactly one of two successive days?
   e. What quantity of Wombats should be on hand at the start of a day to ensure only a 3 percent chance of being out of stock before the end of the day?
   f. What is the probability that weekly demand exceeds 4200 units?

10. (SMA) The life of type A transistors is normally distributed with a mean of 6000 hours and a variance of 360,000 hours.

REQUIRED
   a. What percentage of type A transistors have a life shorter than 7000 hours?
   b. What percentage of type A transistors have a life between 5400 and 7200 hours?
   c. Two type A transistors are used as components in a model X radio. What is the probability that both transistors fail before 5600 hours of life?
   d. What is the probability that exactly one of the two type A transistors in a model X radio fails before 5600 hours of life?
   e. The life of type B transistors is also normally distributed. Ten percent of type B transistors fail before 6000 hours of life, and 10 percent fail after 7300 hours. What is the mean life of type B transistors?

11. (SMA) A study has shown that 75 percent of a bank's checking account customers do not object to paying extra for personalized checks.

REQUIRED
Find the probability that of nine randomly selected checking account customers, at most seven will not object to paying extra for their personalized checks. (Answer should be to four places of decimals.)

12. (SMA) A random sample of 25 people were asked to state a preference for Brand A or Brand B. There is actually no difference in the two brands.

REQUIRED
- a. What is the probability that 15 or more people will state a preference for Brand A?
- b. What is the probability that 15 or more people will state a preference for one of the brands?
- c. What is the expected number of preferences for Brand A?
- d. What is the variance of preferences for Brand A?
- e. What is the actual binomial probability that between 5 and 20 people (inclusive) state a preference for Brand A?

13. *(SMA)* The life of a certain type of light bulb is normally distributed with a mean of 1000 hours and a standard deviation of 100 hours.

REQUIRED
- a. What is the probability that one of these bulbs fails prior to being used 850 hours?
- b. What percentage of these bulbs will have a life between 900 and 1200 hours?
- c. What is the median life of these bulbs?
- d. A particular lighting fixture utilizes two of these bulbs. What is the probability that both bulbs fail prior to being used for 900 hours?
- e. What is the probability that exactly one of the two bulbs in the light fixture described in (d) fails before 960 hours of use?
- f. A second type of light bulb has the same mean life of 1000 hours, and 88.1 percent of these bulbs fail before 1236 hours of life. If the lives of these bulbs are also normally distributed, what is the standard deviation for this type of bulb?

14. *(SMA)* Fishfinders Limited manufactures depth-sounders that are very sensitive and are also used as fish-locating devices. Eastcoast Marine Supplies buys these depth-sounders for installation in commercial fishing vessels. Fishfinders Limited claims that their production process, when in control, produces an average defective rate of 2 percent. Eastcoast Marine specifies that shipments received must contain no more than 3 percent defectives. Eastcoast Marine places an order for 200 depth-sounders at a time when it is known that the manufacturing process is in control.

REQUIRED
Calculate the probability that Eastcoast Marine Supplies' specifications will be met. (Answer to four places of decimals.)

15. *(SMA)* Data collected from service records of a particular compact car used for food delivery showed that 80 percent of the cars required a major engine overhaul at 60,000 or more kilometers. The data were normally distributed with a variance of 20,250,000 km^2.

REQUIRED
Calculate the average (mean) number of kilometers that you would expect this type of car to travel before requiring a major engine overhaul.

Problems

16. *(SMA)* Experience has provided evidence that 4 percent of the computer software packages supplied by a particular computer manufacturer require extensive (and expensive) modification by the customer before application.

REQUIRED
(Answer required to four places of decimals.) What is the probability that *at least* two of nine software packages, supplied by the computer manufacturer, will require extensive modification by the customer before application?

17. *(SMA)* A supplier of "Sun-screen," a silvered plastic film designed to keep houses warmer in winter and cooler in summer when applied to windows, is debating whether or not to expand its market by setting up a sales outlet in a large northern Alberta city. The area contains an estimated 125,000 single family homes.

   In the past "Sun-screen," a rather expensive product, has appealed mainly to home owners in the $80,000 and higher price range. With increasing costs of energy, the sales manager wishes to ascertain the sales potential of this market and gathers the following data from the city's tax department:

   Average market price of the 125,000 single family homes in the area is $70,000, with a standard deviation of $6000.

REQUIRED
   a. Assuming that the market prices are normally distributed, estimate the number of single family homes that are in the $80,000 and higher price range.
   b. If "Sun-screen" were to be produced in a thinner gauge plastic (but less durable), it could be sold at a 20 percent discount, and probably would also appeal to owners of homes in the $65,000 to $80,000 price bracket. If this were true, by what *percentage* would the market be *increased*?
   c. What is the potential market for homes of $90,000 and over?

18. *(CMA)* Racell Corporation is a food manufacturer that produces several different kinds of cereals. Krinkles, one of Racell's cereals, is packaged and sold in a 500 g(gram) box. The filling equipment used to fill the boxes cannot be set precisely enough to guarantee that each box will contain exactly 500 g. The volume by weight of cereal put in the boxes is normally distributed with a standard deviation of 12 g. The filling equipment can be adjusted to vary the mean fill, but the standard deviation is constant. Management has specified that the filling equipment be set so that no more than 3 boxes out of 100 have less than 500 g. If a box does have less than 500 g, the box is emptied and the contents are reentered into the filling process.

   The manufacturer of the filling equipment being used by Racell has informed the company that an attachment is available that can improve the performance of the filling operation. The manufacturer estimates that the standard deviation of the filling operation for Krinkles can be reduced to 8 g. The attachment would have to be replaced after 150,000 boxes were filled and would cost $1500.

Racell sells 900,000 boxes of Krinkles annually. Krinkles are sold on the retail market for $1.35 a box; the wholesale price is $1.10 a box. The standard variable production cost is $0.75 to produce 500 g.

REQUIRED

Racell Corporation's filling equipment can be set to achieve a specified mean with a standard deviation of 12 g. Explain what is meant by the terms:

1. Mean
2. Standard

Calculate the mean fill setting required for Racell Corporation's filling equipment in order to meet the specifications set by management, assuming the new attachment is not added.

Should Racell Corporation acquire the attachment that would reduce the standard deviation of the filling process from 12 to 8 g? Support your decision with appropriate calculations.

19. You own an $80,000 home in an attractive suburb of a large midwestern city. A national fire insurance company offers you full coverage against fire loss for a premium of $350 per annum. After discussing the proposal with some friends, you learn that the probability of a major damage to your home from fire is 0.0025.

REQUIRED
    a. Set up a payoff table.
    b. List the decision criteria discussed in this chapter that would be consistent with your decision to take out a fire insurance policy for $350.

20. A local insurance firm offers you full coverage against fire loss for a premium of $300 per annum. Because they are local, they have lower overhead costs and can also inspect the house annually, which lowers the probability of damage to 0.0020.

REQUIRED

a. Set up a payoff table.
b. Compare the local offer with the national offer in Problem 19. Which one should you choose, and why?

21. A large manufacturer of automotive products is planning to build a new plant for the manufacture and assembly of electrical products (generators, electric motors, etc.) to be used in cars and trucks. Three different plant sizes have been proposed. Each plant size represents a capacity ideally suited, and, therefore, most profitable for a corresponding level of demand. The payoff table on page 93 shows the possible payoffs for each plant size, the three demand levels, and their corresponding probabilities.

Determine the best decision with regard to plant size using the following criteria
    a. Maximin
    b. Minimax regret
    c. Maximax
    d. Equal likelihood
    e. Expected value
Discuss results.

Problems

	Plant Size $P(D_i)$	P_1	P_2	P_3
Low demand, D_1	0.5	25	−10	−20
Medium demand, D_2	0.25	−4	32	12
High demand, D_3	0.25	0	6	40

22. *(CMA)* Decision theory provides possible techniques for assisting managers of organizations in making decisions when all the facts are not known with certainty. For each decision situation managers have several alternative solutions, each of which has different consequences for the organization. Managers need decision criteria to help them select the alternative that will best achieve the company's objectives as established by top management.

   Many decision criteria that managers could adopt have been identified and defined. Five of the possible decision criteria are:

   1. Minimax regret criterion
   2. Maximax criterion
   3. Laplace criterion (criterion of insufficient reason; equally likely)
   4. Maximum likelihood criterion
   5. Bayes decision rule

   REQUIRED
   Select any three of the five decision criteria identified and for each of the three selected decision criteria:
   a. Define the criterion.
   b. Describe the type of circumstance in which the criterion could be applied.
   c. Explain the difficulties of applying the criterion in a business decision.

23. You have inherited $10,000 from a distant relative and are thinking of investing most of it. A friend recommends the stock of two companies: Venture Engineering and Reliable Water Co. During the last year the price of the two shares fluctuated as shown below:

| VENTURE ENGINEERING || RELIABLE WATER ||
Price	Percent of Time Price Was Quoted	Price	Percent of Time Price Was Quoted
$ 50	0.05	$190	0.10
100	0.07	200	0.25
150	0.10	210	0.50
250	0.05	215	0.15
300	0.10		
350	0.15		
400	0.12		
450	0.10		
550	0.12		
575	0.14		

From your broker you learn that the price fluctuations of the two stocks are expected to continue in the next 2 yr in the same manner, over the same range of prices. Both stock currently sell for $200 and pay dividends of $200 annually. Assume that the given frequency distribution for the past 2 yr can be used as probability distributions of price fluctuations for the next 2 yr.
a. Calculate the expected price for each share.
b. Should you select the one with the highest expected price? Discuss. (Graphing the price versus the percentage of time may provide some insight.)

24. Assume a decision problem where the possible monetary outcomes range from $-1000 to +$10,000. You have been asked to interview the responsible executive for the purpose of estimating his utility function. You do this by arbitrarily assigning 100 utiles to the possible maximum profit of $10,000 and 0 utiles to the possible loss of $1000. You then select certainty equivalents of $1500, $2500, $4700, and $7500 and ask the executive to state his indifference by equating the certainty equivalent (CE) with a lottery offering a chance of winning $1000 or losing $1000 by submitting to him the following equation:

$$U(CE) = P(100) + (1 - P)(0)$$

where U stands for the number of utiles for the certainty equivalent and P is the probability of winning. The 100 and the zero on the right side are the utiles you assigned to the profit of $10,000 and the loss of $1000, respectively. You begin with $7500 and ask him what probability of winning $10,000 would make him indifferent. After repeated questioning, you find the probability to be 0.85, thus yielding 85 utiles. Using much patience, you repeat the questioning for the certainty equivalent amounts, finally arriving at the following results:

Certainty Equivalent	Utiles
$1500	50
2500	60
4700	75
7500	90

REQUIRED
a. Draw the executive's estimated utility function.
b. Is he a risk seeker or a risk avoider?
c. Approximately how many utiles correspond to a certainty equivalent of a profit of $2500?
d. What is the approximate certainty equivalent of 20 utiles?

25. The decision maker in Problem 24 has refined his current problem to the point where there are four possible alternative acts. The profits and probabilities of three of the possible outcomes are shown in the following table.

Problems

	Probability	CONDITIONAL PROFITS			
		Act$_1$	Act$_2$	Act$_3$	Act$_4$
Event 1	0.4	2000	6000	−500	4000
Event 2	0.1	5000	600	500	4000
Event 3	0.5	1000	2000	9000	2000

REQUIRED
  a. Based on expected values, what should the decision maker do?
  b. Based on the utility data you collected in Problem 24, what should the decision maker do?
  c. Comment on any differences between parts a and b.

26. An analysis manager's utility function reveals that her utility index for a loss of $1000 is zero, and the index for a profit of $3000 is 100. We find her to be indifferent between a certain profit of $1000 and the following gamble: A 0.4 probability of losing $1000 and a 0.6 chance of winning $3000. What is her utility index for a profit of $1000? Is she a risk seeker?

27. Consider the following choice problem concerning the selection of an alternative marketing method for one of your products:

   (1) Stick with the present marketing arrangements, which assure you an almost certain profit contribution of $100,000.
   (2) Change over to a new method of marketing, for which the possible outcomes vary between $−500,000 and $+1,000,000.

You are asked to interview the marketing manager, the accountant, and the personnel manager for the purpose of obtaining their utility functions. You arbitrarily assign zero utiles to the possible maximum loss of −500,000 and 100 utiles to the possible maximum profit of $1,000,000. You then proceed to question each individual in the manner outlined in the chapter. Following are some partial results of your interview.

	$	Utiles	$	Utiles	$	Utiles	$	Utiles
Accountant	−300	48	0	72	400	90	800	97
Personnel manager	−300	13	0	35	400	60	800	87
Marketing manager	−300	0	0	5	400	18	800	55

REQUIRED
Graph the utility function of the three persons involved. What can you say about their attitude to risk?

28. Suppose that you are offered a choice of (a_1) a guaranteed payment of $1000 or ($a_2$) a gamble that involves flipping a fair coin. If heads come up on the first toss, you receive $2; if tails come up on the first toss and heads on the second, you receive $2^2 or $4; if two tails in a row are followed by a

head, you receive $8. In general terms, you receive 2^n for every toss of a fair coin, where n is the number of times a fair coin is flipped until a head comes up.

REQUIRED
a. What is your choice? Give reasons.
b. Develop a general expression for the expected monetary value of the gamble.

References

See references at the end of Chapter 2.

CHAPTER 4
Linear Programming—A Graphical Approach

4.1 Perspective

4.2 A Problem to Be Solved

4.3 Setting up the Graphical Approach
The Constraints: Feasibility
The Objective Function: Optimality

4.4 The Graphical Solution

4.5 Variations

4.6 Marginal Values at the Optimal Solution
Marginal Value of Another Hour of Machining
Marginal Value of Another Unit of Assembly

4.7 The Dual Formulation
The Dual Problem
Solution to the Dual

4.8 A Comprehensive Problem

4.9 Summary

Glossary

Problems

References

Key Concepts
Constraint
Dual linear program
Extreme point
Feasible area
Feasible solution
Linear program
Marginal value
Nonnegativity constraint
Objective function
Optimal solution
Primal linear program
Shadow price

Key Applications
Managerial accounting
Production planning
Resource allocation problems

4.1 Perspective

Business decisions are made in an environment of scarce resources. There is only a limited supply of coal and raw ore to make steel. The consumer can bear only a certain level of price increase before the consumer does not buy anymore. A bank will lend a company only what is creditworthy, not all that may be asked for. It is the job of management to recognize these limitations in the real business world and still make the best decisions possible. Managers use experience, intuition, the advice of others, forecasting, and other approaches. One approach designed specifically to attack the problem of using scarce resources effectively to reach a goal is *linear programming*.

A significant problem for the business decision maker is deciding how to allocate effectively the available levels of scarce resources to the possible uses. The problem is worsened by the fact that, usually, the potential consumers of these scarce resources are competing for these resources. In other words, the users are not mutually exclusive. If an auto manufacturer decides to make small cars, the company will not be able to make as many large cars as it did before; thus, a tradeoff must be made between small and large cars. These decisions are usually maximization or minimization decisions—maximization of profits or contribution and minimization of costs. Depending on the level of acceptable goal achievement (e.g., how much profit is enough), the required levels of the scarce resources can change dynamically. As the number of scarce resources and limitations increases, one can easily see that the business decision maker may become buried by the number of possible combinations of alternatives and solutions. It is to these types of complex, yet common, business decisions that linear programming is directed.

4.2 A Problem to Be Solved

In order to illustrate the linear programming approach, let us examine a simple, yet typical, business situation involving scarce resources. A

4.2 / A Problem to Be Solved

small manufacturing shop produces two products, high-quality unicycles and bicycles. Let X_1 be the quantity of unicycles to be produced, and let X_2 be the quantity of bicycles. It can sell these two products in a perfectly competitive market; that is, the shop can sell any number of cycles at the given prices. It also buys raw materials from perfectly competitive markets, and thus each unit of either product sold has a constant profit margin; that is, the profit per unit is equal to the selling price per unit minus the variable cost per unit. The profit per unit for X_1 is $200 and for X_2, $300. In the shop there are three departments (machining, assembling, and painting). The manufacture of cycles requires processing in each of the departments.

The three production departments do not have infinite capacity to make X_1's and X_2's. In the machining department there are only 30,000 hr of machine time available per month to make either cycle. Each unicycle (X_1) requires 10 hr of machine time, and each bicycle (X_2) requires 20 hr of machine time. The assembly department also has 30,000 hr of available time per month. A unicycle (X_1), because of its special balancing problems, requires 15 hr of assembly, whereas a bicycle (X_2) can be assembled in only 5 hr. And finally, the painting department is much smaller and has only 6250 hr of painting hours available per month. These can be used to paint a unicycle (X_1) in 1.25 hr or to paint a bicycle (X_2) in 5 hr.

Let us first formulate this decision problem as a mathematical model. The *objective function* is a statement of what we want to accomplish, a goal. In this case we want to determine the quantities of unicycles and bicycles to produce in order to maximize profits, or, more specifically, to maximize the contribution to profits and overhead. Algebraically, we can state this as

Maximize: $P = 200X_1 + 300X_2$

where

P = the total contribution to profits and overhead
X_1 = the number of unicycles produced and sold
X_2 = the number of bicycles produced and sold
200, 300 = the coefficients (in this case the unit contributions to profit and overhead) for X_1 and X_2, respectively

Clearly this is not a complete formulation of any realistic problem. The maximization of this objective function would be quite simple. The shop should simply produce an infinite amount of X_1, or X_2, or both, and realize an infinite profit. Unfortunately, such maximization is impossible because it disregards the fact that limited inputs prevent us from producing infinite amounts of products. These limiting factors, referred to as constraints, may be related to production capacity or inherent market factors.

In our example, we have three production departments, each of which has a finite production capacity. Examining the machining department first, one can describe its capacity limits as the following *constraint:* The total time used in machining unicycles (X_1) plus the total time used in machining bicycles (X_2) must be equal to or less than the total machine time available for the month. The total machining time for a given product is the machine time per unit (10 for X_1 and 20 for X_2) times the number of units produced. Algebraically, this can be stated as:

$$10X_1 + 20X_2 \leq 30{,}000$$

The parameters of the assembly department (30,000 hr available, 15 hr per X_1, and 5 hr per X_2) can be formulated in a like manner:

$$15X_1 + 5X_2 \leq 30{,}000$$

And, finally, the painting department constraint can be expressed as

$$1.25X_1 + 5X_2 \leq 6250$$

These constraints are sometimes called *structural constraints* in that they define the structure or relationships underlying the mathematical model. Because negative (less than zero) production quantities have no economic meaning, we also want the production quantities in our model to be nonnegative. Thus, *nonnegativity constraints* are added to our model in the following form:

$$X_1 \geq 0 \qquad X_2 \geq 0$$

This finishes the formulation of the problem mathematically. The resultant formulation is called a *linear programming model.* The complete model is summarized as follows:

$$
\begin{aligned}
\text{Max:} \quad & P = 200X_1 + 300X_2 \\
\text{Subject to:} \quad & 10X_1 + 20X_2 \leq 30{,}000 \\
& 15X_1 + 5X_2 \leq 30{,}000 \\
& 1.25X_1 + 5X_2 \leq 5{,}250 \\
& X_1 \geq 0 \qquad X_2 \geq 0
\end{aligned}
$$

4.3 Setting up the Graphical Approach

The preceding mathematical model may appear to be a formidable approach to a solution. Without benefit of a systematic approach or procedure (such as the method to be described in the next chapter), one would probably use a trial-and-error approach: Select values of X_1 and X_2 and determine if they satisfy all the constraints. Another alternative for business decisions with only two variables, such as the current ex-

4.3 / Setting up the Graphical Approach

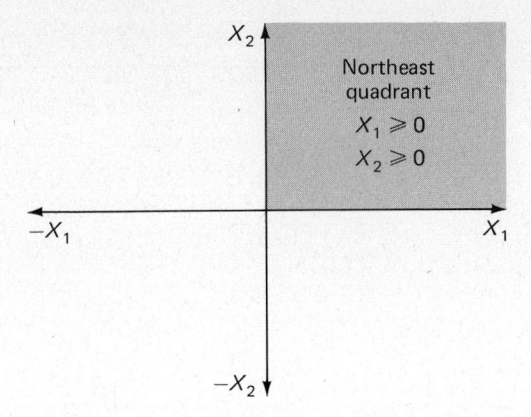

Figure 4–1. Nonnegativity constraint.

ample, is a graphical approach. Obviously, such an approach is limited to only two variables and is of little aid in the more complex, and more typical, business decisions. Valuable insight can be gained, however, into the relationships of the constraints to each other and to the objective function by examining the graphical approach and solution. It also lays the foundation for the systematic linear programming algorithm to develop in Chapter 5. The same processes that will be performed graphically here will be performed mathematically later. Thus, this approach is a logical first step toward understanding the linear programming methodology.

A prefatory remark with respect to the graphical approach concerns the nonnegative constraints. With both X_1 and X_2 greater than or equal to zero, the area of the cartesian plane of concern is the northeast quadrant (see Figure 4–1). All of our structural constraints and our objective function may, theoretically, extend over the entire cartesian plane, but for linear programming problems they are relevant only in this quadrant.

Assume for the moment that we had initially used a trial-and-error method to solve our problem. The results of this approach are presented in Table 4–1 and plotted in Figure 4–2. To evaluate each point as to its validity, we substitute the X_1 and X_2 values into each constraint until one of them is violated or all three are satisfied. For example, by substituting point A into the machining constraint, we find that it is violated,

$$10(0) + 20(4,000) = 80,000 \not\leq 30,000$$

and by substituting point F into the assembly constraint, we find another violation,

$$15(2,000) + 5(2,000) = 40,000 \not\leq 30,000$$

TABLE 4–1. Trial-and-Error Results

Point	X_1	X_2	Constraints Violated	P
A	0	4000	Machining, painting	Not relevant
B	500	500	None	250,000
C	500	1000	None	400,000
D	1000	1000	None	500,000
E	2000	0	None	400,000
F	2000	2000	All three	Not relevant
G	2500	500	Machining, assembling	Not relevant

Although point A violates two constraints, it still satisfies the assembly constraint:

$$15(0) + 5(4,000) = 20,000 \leq 30,000$$

The remaining points (B, C, D, and E) are all possible candidates for solution; that is, they are *feasible* alternatives. From this set we

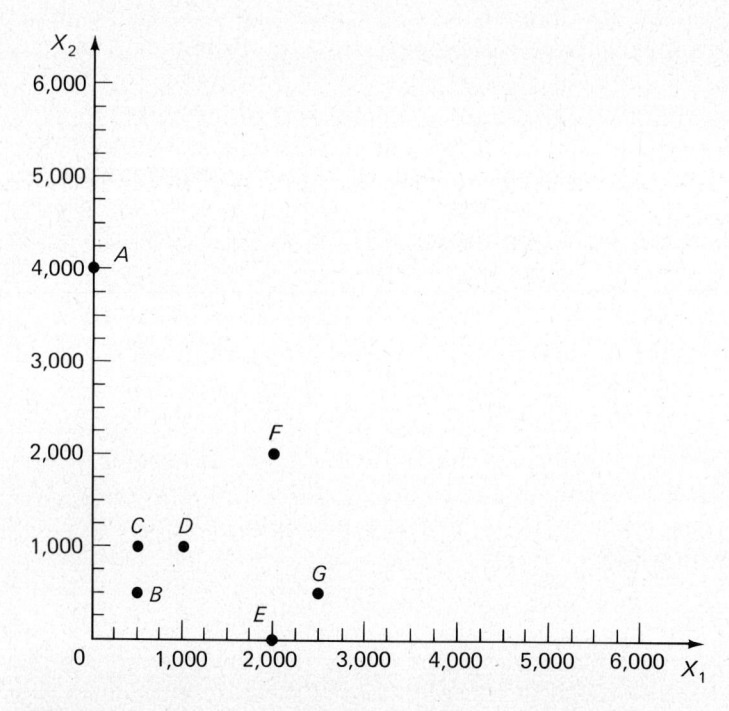

Figure 4–2. Plot of trial-and-error approach.

would obviously choose point D: make 1000 unicycles and 1000 bicycles, for a total profit contribution of $500,000. But are we sure that this is the best that we can do? Is it an optimal solution? If we had stopped at point B as soon as we had a feasible alternative, we would have had a 50 percent lower profit than we now know is possible. But what evidence do we have that point D is not also 50 percent of some other solution point? Linear programming answers these questions of feasibility and optimality. The following discussion of the graphical approach demonstrates how these conditions are determined and achieved.

THE CONSTRAINTS: FEASIBILITY

From the above discussion of the trial-and-error approach, the relationship of a potential solution point to the structural constraint was a key factor. Therefore, let us begin by graphing these constraints. Consider the machining constraint, $10X_1 + 20X_2 \leq 30,000$. This constraint produces two half-planes in the northeast quadrant: the area where $10X_1 + 20X_2 \leq 30,000$, and the area where $10X_1 + 20X_2 > 30,000$. Those in the first area are the feasible points relative to this constraint. To graph this inequality we first graph the boundary line, $10X_1 + 20X_2 = 30,000$. To determine a line, all we need is two points. By setting $X_1 = 0$ and solving for $X_2(1500)$ and then setting $X_2 = 0$ and solving for $X_1(3000)$, we obtain the points $P_1(0, 1500)$ and $P_2(3000, 0)$. Plotting these points and connecting them yields the boundary line $P_1 - P_2$ (see Figure 4–3). Because the inequality is "less than or equal to," the area below and on the boundary line represents the area where values of X_1 and X_2 satisfy the constraint, that is, the *feasible region* for the machining constraint.

We can now easily see how points A, F, and G fail to satisfy the machining constraint. Also, points B, C, and E are easily seen to be feasible points. Point D, although on the boundary line $P_1 - P_2$, is also feasible, because the constraint was "less than or equal to." In the case of point D, all the machine hours are used up, that is, there is no idle time. From this constraint alone, however, we cannot determine which of the four remaining points, if any, is the most profitable solution.

In a similar fashion, the assembly constraint can be graphed as shown in Figure 4–4. Solving for the X_1 and X_2 intercept points in the boundary line equation $15X_1 + 5X_2 = 30,000$ yields $P_1 = (0, 6000)$ and $P_2 = (2000, 0)$. Relative to this constraint, all points except F and G are feasible. Finally, the painting constraint can be graphed as shown in Figure 4–5. The boundary line intercepts are $P_1 = (0, 1250)$ and $P_2 = (5000, 0)$. As noted in the trial-and-error analysis, points A and F are infeasible. Also note that point D is again on the boundary of this constraint, yet it is still feasible.

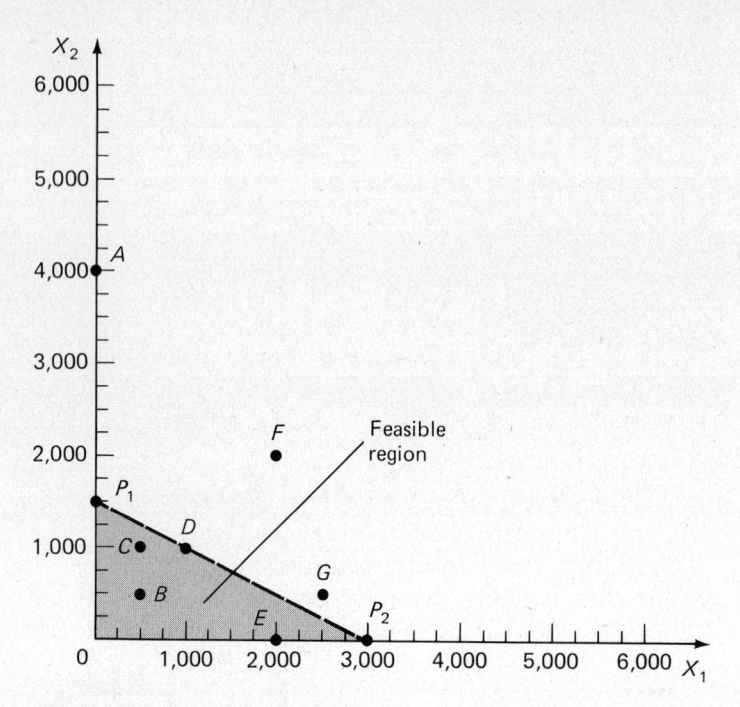

Figure 4-3. Machining constraint.

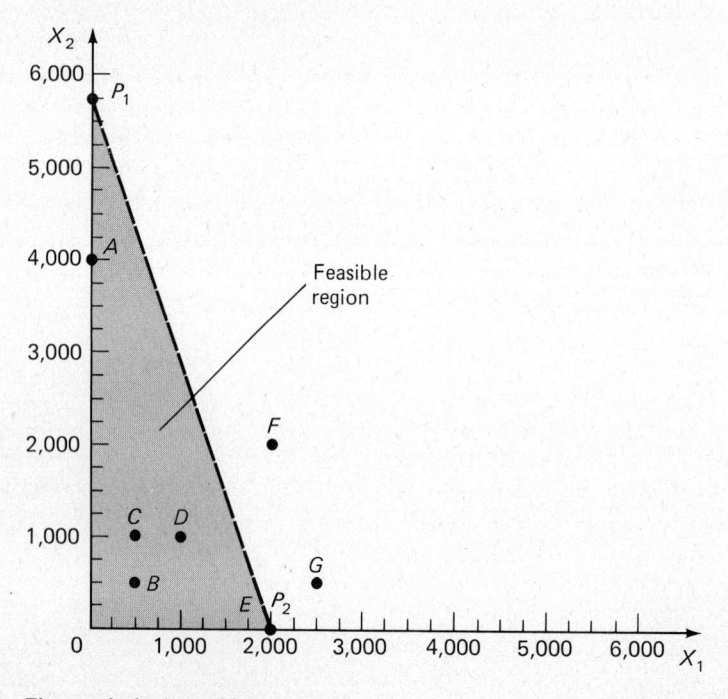

Figure 4-4. Assembly constraint.

4.3 / Setting up the Graphical Approach

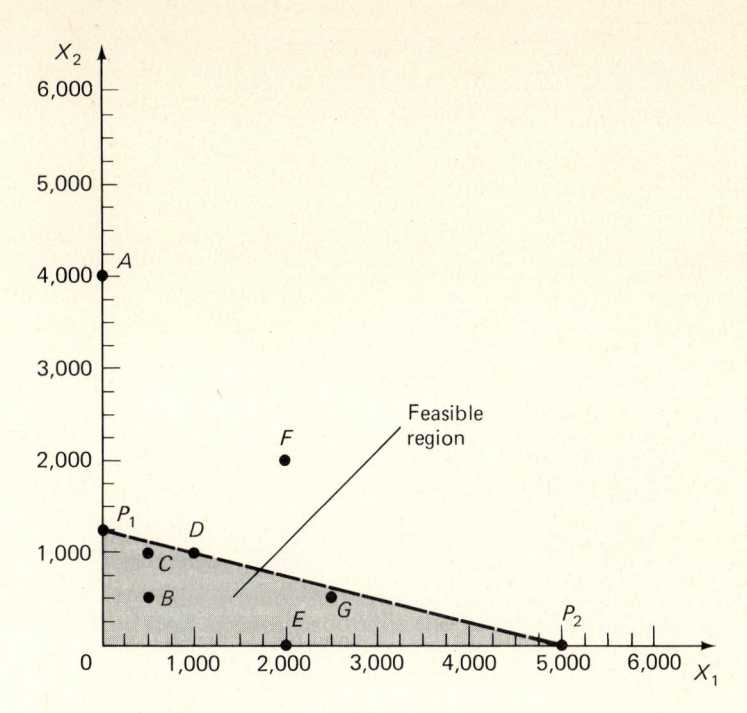

Figure 4–5. Painting constraint.

For a point to be a potential candidate for solution to this decision problem, it must satisfy all three feasible regions just graphed. Thus, the feasible region for the complete linear model is the intersection of the three feasible regions from Figures 4–3, 4–4, and 4–5. This combined region is shown in Figure 4–6. Here we can see that points B, C, D, and E satisfy all three points. We thus have developed a method for determining the feasibility of alternatives by intersecting the feasible regions of all the constraints.

THE OBJECTIVE FUNCTION: OPTIMALITY

Our remaining problem is to determine the optimality of the feasible alternatives. Optimality is relative to our goal on our objective function, which in the case of our example is the maximization of $P = 200X_1 + 300X_2$. For the graphical technique, which is based on the relationship between two variables, X_1 and X_2, how does one handle a three-variable relationship? The "graph" of $P = 200X_1 + 300X_2$ is a family of lines, that is, an infinite number of parallel lines, one for each value of P. Figure 4–7 shows this relationship for three particular values of P. These lines are sometimes called *iso-profit lines*. Notice that the larger the value of P (the higher the total profit), the farther away from the origin is the associated line.

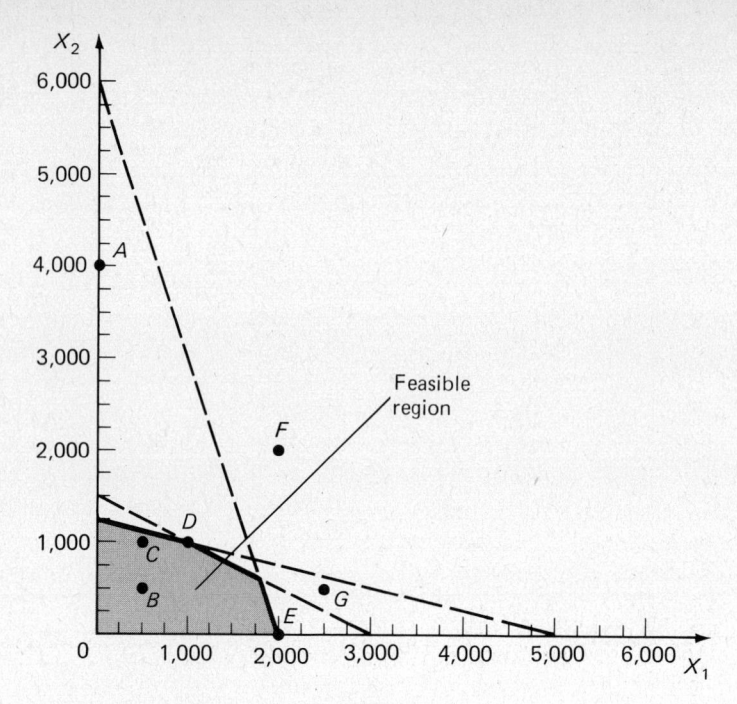

Figure 4–6. Combined feasible region.

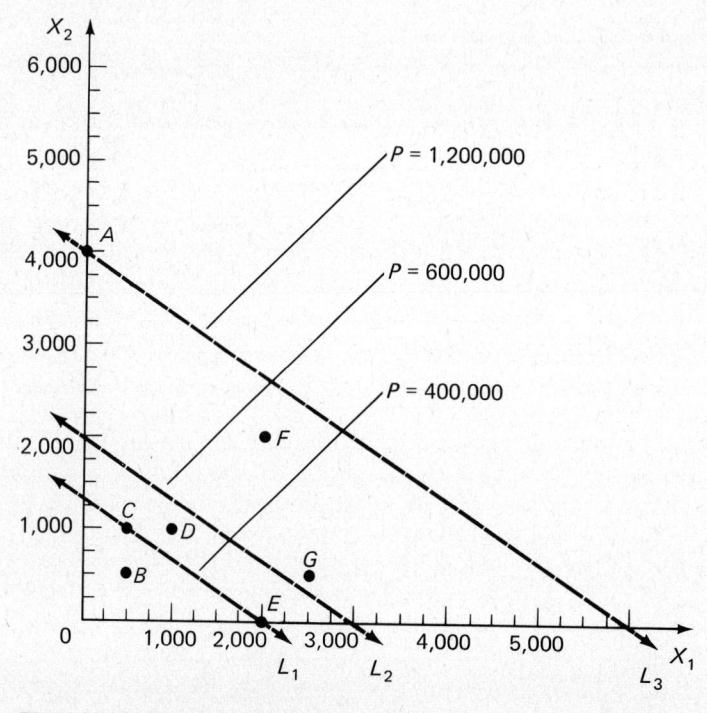

Figure 4–7. Graph of objective functions.

106

Recalling our trial-and-error results in Table 4–1, we can note several similarities. The P values of both points C and E were calculated in Table 4–1 to be 400,000, and in Figure 4–7 these points lie on the same iso-profit line (P = 400,000). Point A, the point in our trial-and-error approach with the highest P value (ignoring feasibility), lies on the iso-profit line farthest from the origin (0, 0). Thus, graphically, to find the optimal solution point we search for a solution point that lies on the iso-profit line farthest from the origin, but yet is still feasible.

Constructing iso-profit lines is very similar to our method for constructing boundary lines for constraints. Remember that all iso-profit lines are parallel, so we only have to graph one and we have the rest. To obtain a particular iso-profit line, we have to reduce the number of variables from three to two. By setting P to an arbitrary value, we can then solve for the X_1 and X_2 intercepts in the same manner as for constraints. We can make a propitious choice, however, for a value of P, so that the graphing becomes easier. By using a common multiple of the coefficients of the iso-profit line, we can readily find integer X_1 and X_2 intercept values. In our particular example, a common multiple of 200 and 300 (the coefficients of X_1 and X_2) is 600,000. Setting P = 600,000 yields the following line equation:

$$600{,}000 = 200X_1 + 300X_2$$

Setting $X_1 = 0$ yields $X_2 = 2000$, and setting $X_2 = 0$ yields $X_1 = 3000$; connecting these intercepts produces iso-profit line L_2. Now that a standard iso-profit line has been established, and because all other lines are parallel for different values of P, say, P', the associated X_1 and X_2 intercepts are proportionate to the ratio P'/P. For example, for P' = 1,200,000, the X_2 intercept for P' is (1,200,000/600,000) = 2 times the X_2 intercept for P, that is, (6000, 0). Similarily, for P' = 400,000, the X_1 intercept for P' is (400,000/600,000) = 2/3 times the X_1 intercept for P; that is, (0, 1333).

Thus, we have answered, separately, our two questions concerning the graphical solution of a linear programming model: feasibility and optimality. To find the set of feasible alternative points, we determine the intersection of the feasible regions of all our constraints. To determine optimality we look for the iso-profit line farthest from the origin. To determine the optimal, feasible solution, obviously we must combine the two graphical techniques. This is the subject of the next section.

4.4 The Graphical Solution

To find the optimal solution we first start with the feasible region (see Figure 4–8), because the solution must be a member of this area. We

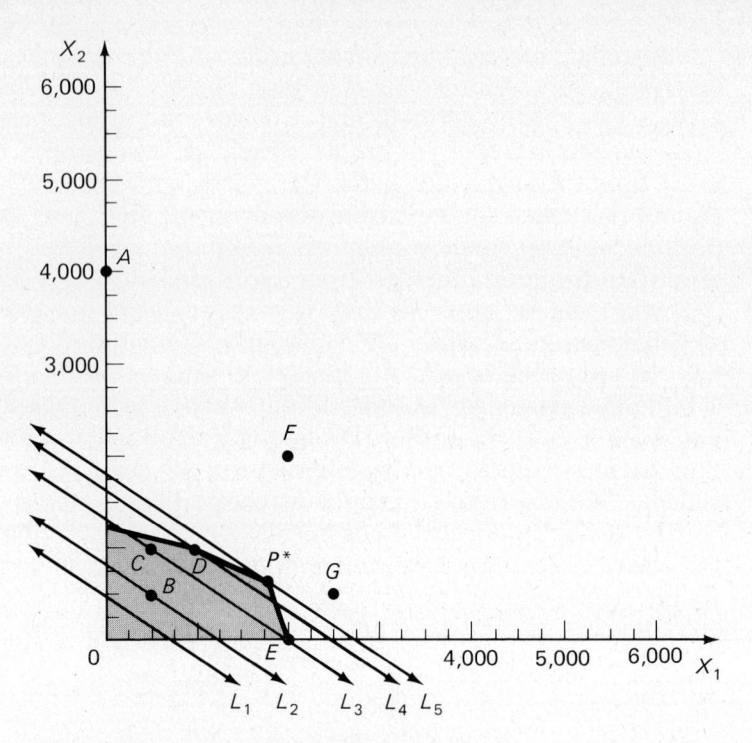

Figure 4–8. Finding the optimal solution.

then plot a representative iso-profit, say, L_1. Recalling that the optimal iso-profit line is farthest from the origin, we begin to move an imaginary iso-profit line away from the origin to positions L_2, L_3, and so on. As these lines move farther out, we note several relationships. As the line goes through interior points such as B (feasible points not on a boundary line), we can see that there are other points in the feasible region that have higher P values. In fact, at L_3, which goes through both points C and E, for each point in the interior (C) there is another point on that same iso-profit line that lies on a boundary line (such as E). Therefore (and this is borne out mathematically), the points we should be concerned with are those on the boundary of the feasible region. Furthermore, it is a consequence of linear algebra and geometry that not only should the points be boundary points but extreme points (corner points) as well.

Thus, from an initial infinite number of possible solutions, we have narrowed it down to a finite set of corner points of our feasible region. Now, the optimal solution via the graphical method is easy. We keep pushing our imaginary iso-profit line out from the origin until it intersects a corner point beyond which there is no feasible region or no

4.4 / The Graphical Solution

other corner points. L_3 intersects a corner point at E, but there is at least one corner farther out than E (D), which thus has a higher profit. L_4 again goes through a corner point D, but there is still one more corner point remaining. L_5, then, intersects the final corner point beyond which there are no more feasible alternatives. This is then the optimal solution, P^*, for our decision problem. Note that this differs from our trial-and-error optimum, which was point D.

Unfortunately, the value of P for the iso-profit going through P^* is not obvious from Figure 4–8, nor are the corresponding values of X_1 and X_2. To determine these values we note that all corner points of the feasible region are the intersection points of the boundary lines of the limiting constraints. In the case of P^*, it is the intersection of the boundary lines of the assembly and machining constraints. To find the value of P^* we must solve the equations for these two lines:

$$10X_1 + 20X_2 = 30{,}000$$
$$15X_1 + 5X_2 = 30{,}000$$

There are a number of ways to solve these two linear equations for X_1, X_2 values. We shall use a procedure of elimination. Multiply the assembly constraint through by 4. We then have

$$60X_1 + 20X_2 = 120{,}000$$

Now, take the machining constraint and multiply it by -1:

$$-10X_1 - 20X_2 = -30{,}000$$

Now, take these two modified constraints and add them term by term.

$$-10X_1 - 20X_2 = -30{,}000$$
$$\underline{60X_1 + 20X_2 = 120{,}000}$$
$$50X_1 = 90{,}000$$
$$X_1 = 1{,}800$$

Substituting $X_1 = 1800$ into the original machining constraint, we have

$$10(1{,}800) + 20X_2 = 30{,}000$$
$$20X_2 = 12{,}000$$
$$X_2 = 600$$

Thus, the optimal solution is to produce

$X_1 = 1800$ unicycles

and

$X_2 = 600$ bicycles

For these two values of X_1 and X_2, the profit is then

$$P = 200(1,800) + 300(600)$$
$$= 360,000 + 180,000$$
$$= \$540,000$$

This is the *optimal solution* for our decision problem.

We have thus determined the optimal solution to our linear programming decision problem via a graphical technique. Obviously it applies only to the two-variable case, but there are several insights to be gained from the general linear programming solution. The requirements of the constraint must be satisfied at all times to maintain feasibility. The points of intersection to optimality are only the corner points of the resultant feasible region. And, finally, the corner point that lies on the iso-profit lines farthest from the origin is the optimal solution. These factors will reappear in the next chapter, which describes the mathematical solution approach, the simplex method. This method systematically calculates the corner points of the feasible region until it finds the optimal corner point.

The steps in the graphical approach can be summarized as follows:

1. From a verbal description of the decision problem, construct a mathematical linear programming model.
2. Graph each of the constraints.
3. Determine the intersection of all of the constraints to form the feasible region.
4. Plot a representative objective function (iso-profit lines).
5. Find the iso-profit line that intersects the feasible region at a corner point farthest from the origin.
6. Determine the constraints that form that corner point.
7. Solve the boundary-line equations for those constraints to determine the values for X_1 and X_2.
8. Substitute the derived X_1 and X_2 values into the objective function to determine the optimal value of P.

4.5 Variations

The above discussion has presented the basic linear programming model: profit maximation, all constraints "less than or equal to," and a single optimal solution. Each of these characteristics can easily be altered through the events of the business environment. The power of linear programming is consequently demonstrated as linear programming can easily handle each case. Because we have been approaching

4.5 / Variations

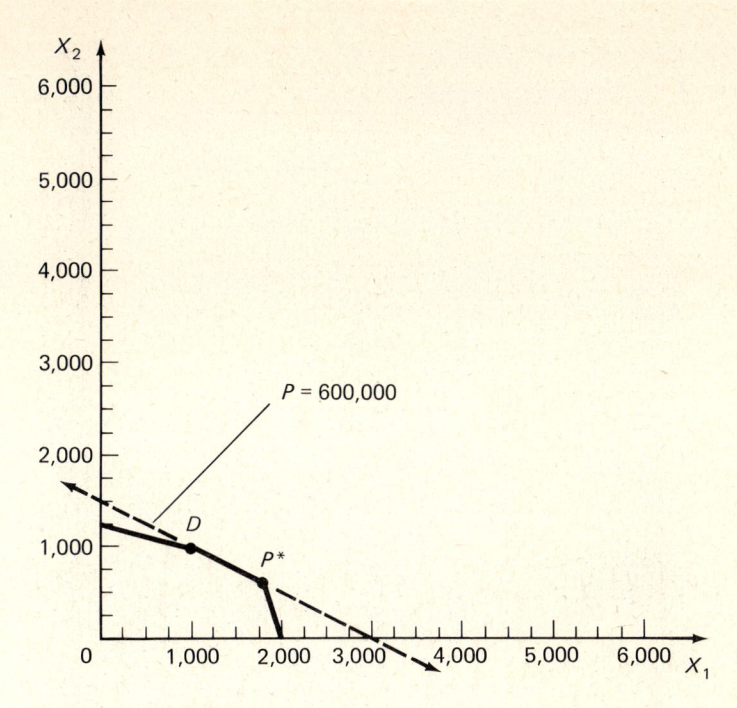

Figure 4–9. Multiple optimal solutions.

the solution of linear programming decision problems graphically, we shall illustrate these variations graphically also.

First consider the possibility of having more than one optimal solution. This occurs when the slope of the iso-profit line equals the slope of the farthest boundary line. In our example, if P had been equal to $200X_1 + 400X_2$, the iso-profit lines would have been parallel to the limiting machining constraint. As Figure 4–9 demonstrates, this produces optimal solutions at both points D and P^*. Furthermore, all points on the boundary line between D and P^* have the same iso-profit value and thus are also optimal solutions. This situation produces a *multiple optimal solution*.

Second, not all constraints are of the form "less than or equal to." In our example we could have a production situation where a union contract requires at least 10,000 hr of machine time per month. This constraint would be formulated as

$$10X_1 + 20X_2 \geq 10{,}000$$

One graphs this inequality like the "$\leq$" inequalities by plotting the boundary line first, but now the feasible region lies above the

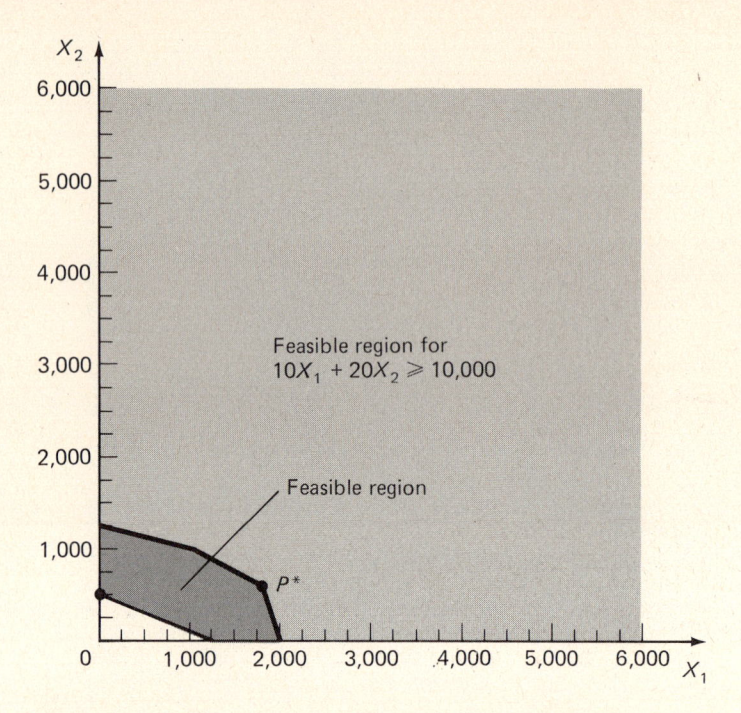

Figure 4–10. Effect of greater-than production constraint.

boundary line (see Figure 4–10). When this is intersected with the original feasible region in Figure 4–6, the darkened feasible region in Figure 4–10 results. Note that it does not change the optimal solution.

We could have also had a greater-than-or-equal-to marketing constraint. Assume that by prior contract the firm had to produce and sell 800 bicycles (X_2). The constraint is of the form

$$X_2 \geq 800$$

We cannot use the same approach for graphing this inequality, because it has no X_1 intercept. But the boundary line is simply $X_2 = 800$—easy enough to graph. Figure 4–11 shows how this constraint affects the original feasible region. It moves the previous optimal point from P^* to the point (1,400, 800). (The reader should verify that $X_1 = 1400$.) The new P value is $520,000. Note that this is less than the original optimal solution. The procedure for determining the feasible region and the optimal solution, however, has not changed.

The combination of "$\leq$" constraints and "$\geq$" constraints in the same linear programming model can provide an unfortunate result, namely,

4.5 / Variations

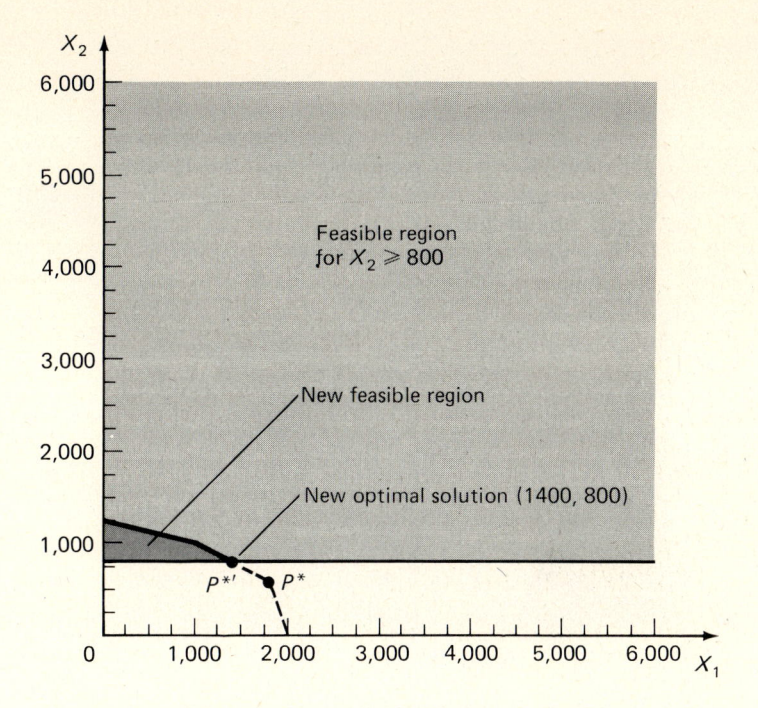

[Figure: graph showing feasible region for $X_2 \geq 800$, new feasible region, new optimal solution (1400, 800), with points $P^{*'}$ and P^* marked]

Figure 4–11. Effect of greater-than marketing constraint.

an infeasible situation. Consider the following linear mathematical model of a business decision:

$$\begin{aligned}
\text{Max:} \quad & P = 500X_1 + 200X_2 \\
\text{Subject to:} \quad & 20X_1 + 20X_2 \geq 100{,}000 \\
& 40X_1 + 20X_2 \geq 80{,}000 \\
& 10X_1 \geq 30{,}000 \\
& X_1 \geq 0 \quad X_2 \geq 0
\end{aligned}$$

Figure 4–12 illustrates the graphical interpretation of these constraints. Unfortunately, there is no intersection of the feasible regions of all three constraints. If there is no feasible region, there obviously cannot be an optimal solution. This situation, where the constraints are contradictory, produces an *infeasible* solution.

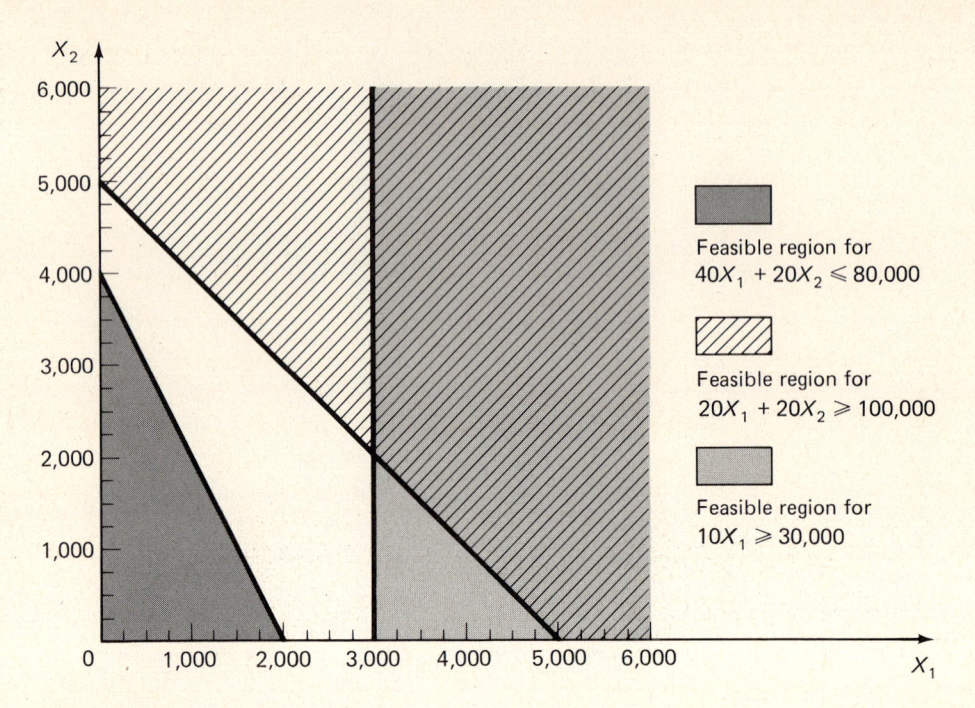

Figure 4-12. An infeasible solution.

4.6 Marginal Values at the Optimal Solution

After finding the optimal output for X_1 and X_2 within a given system of constraints, we consider questions concerning these constraints. By studying Figure 4-8 carefully, we can see that if we had either more assembling or machining hours available, we could increase our present optimal profit. We now ask ourselves by how much would our profits increase if we did add 1 hr first to our machining time and afterward to our assembly time. This increased profit is the *marginal value*.

From Figure 4-8, it is clear that painting does not limit the production at the optimal production quantities. There are unused painting hours, and we can say that painting is inoperative as a constraint. What does this mean in terms of economics? What is the value of another hour of painting time? Another hour of painting time has value only if it changes profits, that is, increases the value of the objective function:

$$P = 200X_1 + 300X_2$$

where the optimal value is \$540,000 for $X_1 = 1800$ and $X_2 = 600$. Such an increase is possible only if we can increase the value of X_1 and/or

4.6 / Marginal Values at the Optimal Solution

X_2. The present production of unicycles and bicycles is constrained by the available machining and assembly hours. Increasing painting capacity, therefore, will in no way affect present optimal output. Hence we can conclude that the value of another hour of painting time is zero. In economics terminology, painting is called a *free good*. This is not the case for the machining and assembly departments, however, whose current capacities are fully utilized.

MARGINAL VALUE OF ANOTHER HOUR OF MACHINING

The marginal value is the increase in profits if we had another hour (30,000 + 1 hr) of time available in machining. One way to find the marginal value is to calculate the profits with 30,001 hr available in machining. Note that we do not do a complete reformulation of the problem, but we can proceed directly to a solution. This is possible because we know that painting is inoperative in both cases; that is, point P^* remains optimal even if we move the machining constraint a small amount. See Figure 4–8.

To find the new value of P^*, we perform the same solution process of boundary lines as before.

$$10X_1 + 20X_2 = 30{,}001$$
$$15X_1 + 5X_2 = 30{,}000$$

This results in

$$X_1 = 1{,}799.98$$
$$X_2 = 600.06$$

and, therefore,

$$P' = 200 \times 1{,}799.98 + 300 \times 600.06$$
$$= 359{,}996 + 180{,}018 = 540{,}014$$

The change in profits due to one additional hour of machining is the new profit minus the old profit; that is,

$$P' - P = \$540{,}014 - \$540{,}000 = \$14$$

This marginal value is often referred to as the *shadow price* by economists. Accountants use the term *opportunity value* for the same idea. In both cases, it is the marginal value of an additional unit of a scarce resource. For notational simplicity, let us call this marginal value of an additional machine hour U_1. We then have

$$U_1 = \$540{,}014 - \$540{,}000 = \$14$$

MARGINAL VALUE OF ANOTHER UNIT OF ASSEMBLING

Similarly, we want to know the value of another hour of assembling time:

$$10X_1 + 20X_2 = 30{,}000$$
$$15X_1 + 5X_2 = 30{,}001$$

Solving:

$$X_1 = 1{,}800.08$$
$$X_2 = 599.96$$

and

$$P'' = 200 \times 1{,}800.08 + 300 \times 599.96$$
$$= 360{,}016. + 179{,}988. = 540004.$$

Let the shadow price be

$$U_2 = P'' - P$$

Then

$$U_2 = \$540{,}004 - \$540{,}000 = \$4$$

We now have two quantities, U_1 and U_2, which are the marginal values of machining and assembling, respectively. An additional hour of machining time will increase profits by U_1 or \$14. And an additional hour of assembling will increase profits by U_2 or \$4. (Remember that we have already established that the marginal value of painting is zero).

We shall now calculate the total value of our scarce resources. There are 30,000 hr per month of available machining time. If we let its price (or value) be U_1, that is, the marginal worth, then the total value to the firm of machining (evaluated at the margin) is $30{,}000 \times U_1 = 30{,}000 \times 14 = \$420{,}000$. Similarly, we have 30,000 hr per month of assembly time. Letting U_2 be its price, we find that the total value (to the firm) is $30{,}000 \times U_2 = 30{,}000 \times \$4 = \$120{,}000$. So the total value (evaluated at the margin) of the operating constraints is $\$420{,}000 + 120{,}000 = \$540{,}000$. This is the same as the maximum profit we calculated previously. Coincidence? No, it is a fundamental property of all linear programs.

Let us repeat what we have just indicated. At the optimum, *the total profit is the same as the total value of the operative constraints valued at their marginal value.* In this problem we have

$$200(1{,}800) + 300(600) = 30{,}000(14) + 30{,}000(4) + 6{,}250(0)$$

Or, in general notation, at the optimum,

$$P_1X_1 + P_2X_2 = C_1U_1 + C_2U_2 + C_3U_3$$

where P_i is the profit coefficient of X_i (the ith product), and U_j is the marginal value of the jth constraint, of which there is a quantity C_j.

4.7 The Dual Formulation

For every *primal* formulation of a *linear program* there is a corresponding *dual*. The dual is simply another way to view the same linear program. For our problem, we shall arbitrarily refer to the previous linear program as the primal. Its dual yields additional information about marginal values that is not readily available from the primal solution. We now present the dual of our problem and its solution. In discussing the dual we shall, however, refer to the preceding marginal analysis in order to point out the primal-dual relationship.

THE DUAL PROBLEM

Recall that our problem is given as

Maximize:	$P = 200X_1 + 300X_2$		Objective function
Subject to:	$10X_1 + 20X_2$	$\leq 30{,}000$	Machining constraint
	$15X_1 + 5X_2$	$\leq 30{,}000$	Assembly constraint
	$1.25X_1 + 5X_2$	$\leq 6{,}250$	Painting constraint
	$X_1 \geq 0 \quad X_2 \geq 0$		Nonnegativity constraint

This is the primal linear program. There are a number of primal/dual relations that are important:

1. If the primal is a maximation problem, then the dual is a minimization problem (or vice versa).
2. For every structural constraint in the primal, there is a dual variable; in this case we have U_1, U_2, and U_3, corresponding to the machining, assembly, and painting constraints, respectively.
3. For every variable in the primal, there is a constraint in the dual; in this example we have two constraints in the dual, corresponding to X_1 and X_2 in the primal.

For our situation, the goal of the primal formulation is to maximize profits using the resources available; that is, we want to find the production of unicycles and bicycles that yields the maximum profit. The goal of the associated dual formulation is a costing or value problem; that is, we want to find the prices or marginal values for each of the fixed and limited resources of machining, assembly, and painting that yields a total minimum cost. Thus, in the primal we maximize profits for production, and in the dual we minimize costs for limited resources. For each limited resource in the primal, there is a cost variable U_i in the dual, and for each production variable X_i in the primal, there is a cost constraint in the dual.

The dual problem objective function is to minimize total costs. The total cost is the sum of the resources multiplied by their dual variables.

Min: $\quad P' = 30{,}000U_1 + 30{,}000U_2 + 6{,}250U_3$

The first constraint is the sum of the permitted resource use of each resource (machining, assembly, and painting) multiplied by its corresponding unit cost (the dual variables), for each product.

The first constraint, then, is that the cost of the first product is equal to or greater than its profit:

$$10U_1 + 15U_2 + 1.25U_3 \geq 200$$

Similarly, the second constraint states that the cost of the second product, a bicycle, is equal to or greater than its profit:

$$20U_1 + 5U_2 + 5U_3 \geq 300$$

As in the primal, we have nonnegativity conditions for the dual variables:

$$U_1 \geq 0 \quad U_2 \geq 0 \quad U_3 \geq 0$$

Writing the dual compactly, we have

Min: $\quad P' = 30{,}000U_1 + 30{,}000U_2 + 6{,}250U_3 \quad$ Total cost
$\qquad\qquad 10U_1 + 15U_2 + 1.25U_3 \geq 200 \quad$ Unicycle cost
$\qquad\qquad 20U_1 + 5U_2 + 5U_3 \geq 300 \quad$ Bicycle cost
$\qquad\qquad U_1 \geq 0 \quad U_2 \geq 0 \quad U_3 \geq 0$

Note carefully the symmetry of the primal and dual problems.

SOLUTION TO THE DUAL

The dual problem has three variables: U_1, U_2, and U_3. Three variable problems are not convenient to graph, but we can use what we already know to reduce the problem to a two-variable problem. Recall from Figure 4–8 that painting is an inoperative constraint, and its marginal value is zero. Therefore the value of U_3 is zero. Thus we reduce the dual problem to a two-dimensional one, namely:

Min: $\quad P' = 30{,}000U_1 + 30{,}000U_2$
Subject to: $\qquad 10U_1 + 15U_2 \geq 200$
$\qquad\qquad\quad\; 20U_1 + 5U_2 \geq 300$
$\qquad\qquad\quad\; U_1 \geq 0, \quad U_2 \geq 0$

4.7 / The Dual Formulation

This is the dual problem in which U_3 is known to be zero, and thus it does not appear in the equations.

The graphical solution for the dual is similar to the graphical solution of the primal, except that we are now minimizing cost rather than maximizing profit. Consider first a plot of the feasible area is given by the constraints, as given in Figure 4–13.

The first constraint for unicycles is

$$10U_1 + 15U_2 \geq 200$$

We graph the boundary equation $10U_1 + 15U_2 = 200$ by setting $U_1 = 0$ and finding that $U_2 = 13.33$ for the U_2 intercept. The U_1 intercept is found similarly by setting $U_2 = 0$ and then $U_1 = 20$. The resulting unicycle constraint is shown in Figure 4–13 as L_1. The feasible area is to the right of the line because the constraint is greater to or equal to. Similarly, the second constraint for bicycles is

$$20U_1 + 5U_2 \geq 300$$

which produces the boundary line L_2 and its associated feasible region.

Putting the two constraints together, the feasible area is to the right of both constraint lines. This is to the right of lines that connect

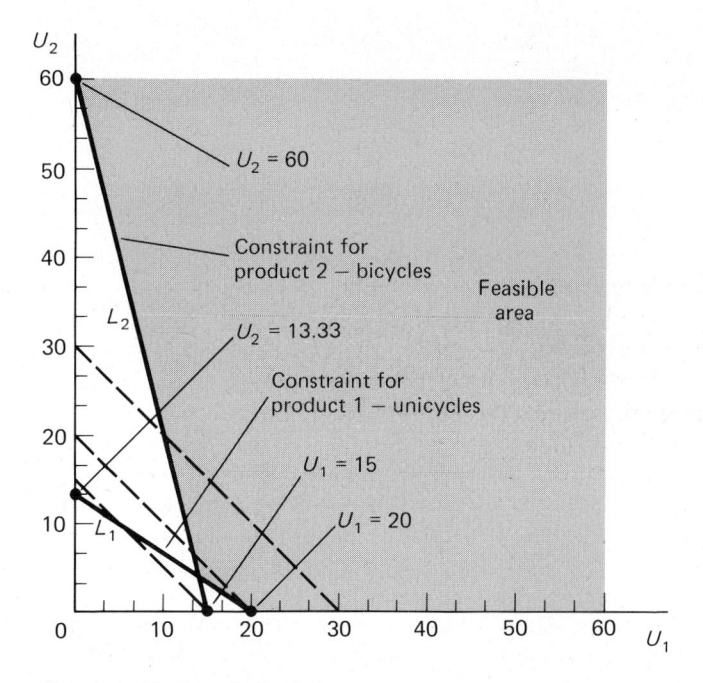

Figure 4–13. The dual solution.

$U_1 = 0$, $U_2 = 60$, the intersection of the two constraint lines, and $U_1 = 15$, $U_2 = 0$.

The objective function in the dual produces iso-cost lines as opposed to the iso-profit lines of the primal. An iso-cost line is a line that yields the same total cost for the resources. The dashed lines in Figure 4–13 are iso-cost lines. In this case, the iso-cost lines are of the form

$$P' = 30{,}000 U_1 + 30{,}000 U_2$$

To find a solution to our dual problem, we reverse the procedure used for maximization problems. Instead of the objective function line farthest from the origin, for minimization we look for the point where the two constraint lines intersect on a iso-cost line closest to the origin in the feasible area. Thus, P' is the minimal point, and we need to find values for U_1 and U_2 at the intersection point. These U_1, U_2 values are given by again solving two constraint equations simultaneously:

$$10U_1 + 15U_2 = 200$$
$$20U_1 + 5U_2 = 300$$

Multiplying the second equation by -3 and adding to the first equation, we have

$$\begin{aligned} 10U_1 + 15U_2 &= 200 \\ -60U_1 - 15U_2 &= -900 \\ \hline -50U_1 &= -700 \end{aligned}$$

or

$$U_1 = 14$$

Letting $U_1 = 14$ in the first equation, we have $10(14) + 15U_2 = 200$ or $U_2 = 4$. The solution is $U_1 = 14$, $U_2 = 4$.

Now, putting the values for U_1 and U_2 into P', we find that

$$P' = 30{,}000 \times 14 + 30{,}000 \times 4$$
$$= \$420{,}000 + \$120{,}000 = \$540{,}000$$

This is the same solution as we found earlier for the marginal values of the machining and assembly resources. The demonstrated relation between the primal and dual formulations is fundamental in linear programming. If the primal solves for the best production levels, then the dual values the scarce resources to minimize costs used in the production. The dual problem is another approach to finding the value of scarce resources.

4.8 A Comprehensive Problem

We present the solutions to the following sequence of business decisions to reinforce our basic understanding of linear programming.[1]

> Girth, Inc., makes two kinds of men's suede leather belts. Belt A is a high-quality belt, whereas belt B is of somewhat lower quality. The company earns $7 for each unit of belt A that is sold, and $2 for each unit sold of belt B. Each unit (belt) of type A requires twice as much manufacturing time as is required for a unit of type B.
>
> Further, if only belt type B is made, Girth has the capacity to manufacture 1000 units per day. Suede leather is purchased by Girth under a long-term contract that makes available to Girth enough leather to make 800 belts per day (A and B combined). Belt A requires a fancy buckle, of which only 400 per day are available. Belt B requires a different (plain) buckle, of which 700 per day are available. The demand for the suede leather belts (A and B) is such that Girth can sell all that it produces. The graph in Figure 4–14 displays the constraint functions based on the facts presented.
>
> a. Using the graph, determine how many units of belt A and belt B should be produced to maximize daily profits.

With the graph we are a long way toward a solution. First, note that the problem uses A and B as variables, where we have used X_1 and X_2 in our development. There is no standard notation for linear programs. Various symbols are used: X_1, X_2, X_3; X, Y, Z; A, B, C, and so on. Next let us review where each constraint on the graph is derived from the problem statement:

1. "Each unit of type A requires twice as much manufacturing time as is required for a unit of type B. Further, if only belt type B is made, Girth has the capacity to manufacture 1000 units per day."

    Thus, in equation form,

    $2A + B \leq 1000$

    This is a requirement for feasibility.

    It should be clear from the above verbal and algebraic statements that if only belt type A is made, the maximum output is 500 belts. On the graph we find the straight line marked $2A + B = 1000$, which denotes the equation; the feasible region is to the left and below the line.

[1] This problem was adapted from a CMA examination.

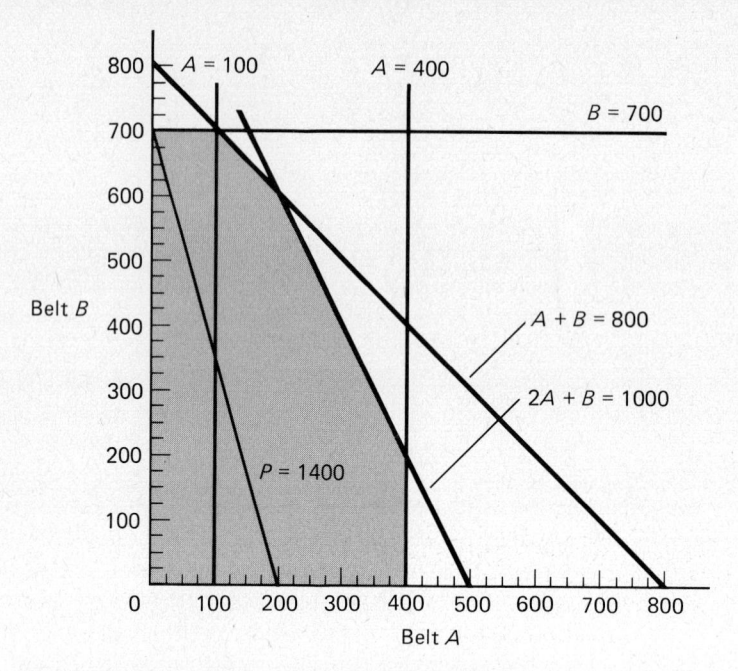

Figure 4–14. Graphical representation of problem.

2. "Suede leather . . . available to Girth . . . to make 800 belts per day (A and B combined)." This is stated as

   $A + B \leq 800$

3. "Belt A requires a fancy buckle, of which only 400 per day are available." Thus we can state that

   $A \leq 400$

4. "Belt B . . ., of which 700 buckles per day are available."

   $B \leq 700$

This completes the constraint set, which is indicated on the graph. The feasible area lies to the "left and below" all constraints, as the feasible area boundary is hatched.

The objective function follows from the statement: "The company earns $7 for each unit of belt A that is sold, and $2 for each unit sold of belt B." Assuming that these are profit margins, we have

Max: $P = 7A + 2B$

To obtain a solution, we construct an iso-profit line for $P = 1400$ (chosen arbitrarily), which intersects the A axis at 200 and the B axis at 700 as shown. It is clear that the parallel iso-profit line that maxi-

4.8 / A Comprehensive Problem

mizes P and is within the feasible region goes through the point where $A = 400$ and $B = 200$; that is, it is at the intersection of the lines

$$A = 400$$
$$2A + B = 1000$$

The optimal daily profit P is

$$P = 7 \times 400 + 2 \times 200 = \$3200$$

Furthermore, the constraints that limit production are the supply of fancy belt buckles ($A \leq 400$) and the manufacturing capacity ($2A + B \leq 1000$).

This is more than sufficient information to answer the question in part a. The answer is simply $A = 400$, $B = 200$, or produce 400 belts of type A and 200 belts of type B daily.

> b. Assume the same facts as above except that the sole supplier of buckles for belt A informs Girth, Inc., that it will be unable to supply more than 100 fancy buckles per day. How many units of each of the two belts should be produced each day to maximize profits?

The supplier of fancy belt buckles has dropped the supply from 400 to 100 daily. We want to investigate how that affects the solution. In equation form, we replace $A \leq 400$ with

$$A \leq 100$$

On the graph this is denoted by the straight line labeled $A = 100$. The feasible region is considerably reduced, and the best operating level is now

$$A = 100 \quad \text{and} \quad B = 700$$

This solution occurs at the intersection of

$$A = 100$$
$$A + B = 800$$

and then

$$B = 700$$

Note there are three equations and two variables, and one of the equations can be eliminated. The new profit level is

$$P = 7 \times 100 + 2 \times 700 = \$2100$$

The loss of the fancy buckle supply of 300 daily (400 − 100) gives an opportunity loss for Girth, Inc., of $3200 − $2100 or $1100 daily.

> c. Assume the same facts as in part b, except that Texas Buckles, Inc., could supply Girth, Inc., with the additional fancy buckles it needs. The price would be $3.50 more than Girth, Inc., is paying for such buckles. How many, if any, fancy buckles should Girth, Inc., buy from Texas Buckles, Inc.? Explain how you determined your answer.

This question suggests that there is a possible change in a constraint ($A \leq 100$), and we want to know if changing the constraint is worth $3.50 per unit. This involves the dual formulation, as we are determining the value of changing a constraint. For completion we quickly write the primal with the corresponding dual variables on the right side:

Maximize: $7A + 2B$ Dual Variables
Subject to: $2A + B \leq 1000$ U_1
$A + B \leq 800$ U_2
$A \leq 100$ U_3
$B \leq 700$ U_4
$A \geq 0 \quad B \geq 0$

The dual can then be written as

Minimize: $1000U_1 + 800U_2 + 100U_3 + 700U_4$
Subject to: $2U_1 + U_2 + U_3 \geq 7$
$U_1 + U_2 + U_4 \geq 2$
$U_1 \geq 0 \quad U_2 \geq 0 \quad U_3 \geq 0 \quad U_4 \geq 0$

The dual has four variables and only two constraints. From our knowledge of the primal solution, we can select an optimal dual solution. For part b, we found three binding constraints, but it takes only two constraints to determine a point, and we have one extra or redundant constraint. Now, as the constraint on buckles is increased (e.g., $A \leq 101$), we note that the optimal solution is determined by the constraint

$A + B \leq 800$
$A \leq 100 + 1$

The corresponding dual variables are U_2 and U_3. The constraints corresponding to U_1 and U_4 are not limiting, and we can then set $U_1 = U_4 = 0$. To find the optimal solution for U_2 and U_3, we solve

$U_2 + U_3 = 7$
$U_2 = 2$

This yields $U_2 = 2$ and $U_3 = 5$.

As we have discussed previously, this means that the profit can be increased by $5 for at least one additional fancy belt buckle. Therefore, it would be profitable to pay $3.50 for a buckle and obtain a net profit of $1.50 per belt buckle.

Thus, to answer the question partially, Girth should buy at least one belt buckle. Further, from the graph it is clear that Girth should by at least 100 buckles, with the corresponding solution that $A = 200$, $B = 600$. Note that the optimal solution moves along the line $A + B = 800$ from $A = 100$, $B = 700$ to $A = 200$, $B = 600$. Now, should Girth buy more than 100, or should A be increased beyond 200? Note that as the availability of buckles moves beyond 200, the optimal solution is now determined by the first and third primal constraints, namely,

$$2A + B = 1000$$
$$A = 200 + 1$$

The corresponding dual involves $U_2 = U_4 = 0$ and

$$2U_1 + U_3 = 7$$
$$U_1 = 2$$

Here, $U_1 = 2$ and $U_3 = 3$.

Now, at this point, the extra belt buckle is only worth $3, and it still costs $3.50. We should buy no more. The complete answer is that Girth, Inc., should buy 100 buckles from Texas Buckles, Inc. The analysis necessary to solve part c is usually called sensitivity analysis. In the next chapter we shall take up sensitivity analysis involving more general techniques based on the simplex method.

4.9 Summary

In this chapter we have introduced linear programming as an effective method for allocating scarce resources. Using a simple example, we developed a graphical method for a solution. The most important steps were the graphing of the constraint equations, the determination of the feasibility region, the inclusion of the objective function, and the testing of the corner points for optimality. At the conclusion of the chapter we calculated the marginal values of the scarce resources at the optimal solution and introduced the dual formulation of a linear program.

Glossary

Constraint. A linear mathematical statement that the use of a resource cannot exceed its availability for a profit-maximization problem. There are usually many such statements—one for each limited resource. For a cost-minimization problem, a constraint relates the cost of the resources to the product's profit.

Dual linear program. A different representation of the *primal linear program*. If the primal linear program chooses production quantities to maximize profits, then the dual linear program chooses marginal values to minimize the cost of the resources used in production.

Extreme point solution. A solution at the intersection of two or more constraints. At least one feasible extreme point will be an optimal solution.

Feasible area. The set of all feasible solutions.

Feasible solution. A solution that does not violate any constraint.

Linear program. A program that has an objective to maximize (or minimize) subject to the availability of resources. It has only linear relationships.

Linear programming. A mathematical technique to solve managerial decision problems.

Marginal value. The economic value of a scarce resource. The dual variables of the dual linear program represent marginal values. They are also called opportunity values or shadow prices.

Nonnegativity constraint. A constraint which states that all variables can take on only zero or positive values.

Objective function. A linear mathematical statement of the goal—for example, profit—to be maximized (or costs to be minimized).

Optimal solution. A feasible solution that has the highest possible value for the objective function for a maximization problem. It has the lowest possible value for a minimization problem.

Primal linear program. The original formulation of a linear program.

Shadow price. The value of an additional unit of a resource associated with an operative constraint.

Problems

1. Solve these two linear equations for X_1 and X_2:

    $2X_1 + X_2 = 10$
    $X_1 + X_2 = 8$

2. Solve the following linear program using the graphical approach:

    Max: $500X_1 + 1000X_2$
    Subject to: $60X_1 + 70X_2 \leq 4200$
    $80X_1 + 50X_2 \leq 4000$
    $X_1 \geq 0 \quad X_2 \geq 0$

3. Solve the following two simultaneous linear equations for X_1, X_2:

    $7X_1 + 8X_2 = 56$
    $2X_1 + 3X_2 = 24$

Problems

4. Solve the following linear program using the graphical approach:

   Min: $14U_1 + 7U_2$
   Subject to: $U_1 + U_2 \geq 3$
                  $12U_1 + 5U_2 \geq 36$
                  $U_1 \geq 0 \quad U_2 \geq 0$

5. Write the dual linear program for the following primal linear program:

   Max: $3X_1 + 4X_2 + 5X_3$
   Subject to: $X_1 + X_2 + X_3 \leq 7$
                  $2X_1 + 3X_2 + X_3 \leq 8$
                  $X_1 \geq 0 \quad X_2 \geq 0 \quad X_3 \geq 0$

   Then solve the dual linear program using the graphical approach.
6. Managers sometimes refer to limiting resources as "bottlenecks." Explain why the word "bottlenecks" is appropriate here.
7. For the example problem, if overtime costs $5.00/hour in assembly, would it be profitable for the firm to engage overtime labor? Why or why not?
8. Solve the following linear program using the graphical approach.

   Max: $4X_1 + 3X_2$
   Subject to: $2X_1 + X_2 \leq 10$
                  $X_1 + X_2 \leq 8$
                  $X_1 \geq 0 \quad X_2 \geq 0$

9. (CPA) In a linear programming maximization problem for business problem solving, the coefficients of the objective function usually are
   a. Marginal contributions per unit
   b. Variable costs
   c. Profit based upon allocations of overhead and all indirect costs
   d. Usage rates for scarce resources
   e. None of the above
10. (CPA) The constraints in a linear programming problem usually model
    a. Profits
    b. Variable costs
    c. Dependent variables
    d. Goals
    e. None of the above
11. Linear programming is used most commonly to determine
    a. That mix of variables which will result in the largest quantity
    b. The best use of scarce resources
    c. The most advantageous prices
    d. The fastest timing
    e. None of the above
12. (CPA) The Ball Company manufactures three types of lamps, labeled A, B, and C. Each lamp is processed in two departments—I and II. Total available labor hours per day for departments I and II are 400 and 600, respec-

tively. No additional labor is available. Time requirements and profit per unit for each lamp type is as follows:

	A	B	C
Labor hours required in department I	2	3	1
Labor hours required in department II	4	3	2
Profit per unit (sales price less all variable costs)	$5	$4	$3

The company has assigned you as the accounting member of its profit planning committee to determine the numbers of types of A, B, and C lamps that it should produce in order to maximize its total profit from the sale of lamps. The following questions relate to a linear programming model that your group has developed. Pick the best answer and indicate why it is correct.

a. The coefficients of the objective function would be
   (1) 4, 2, 3
   (2) 2, 3, 1
   (3) 5, 4, 3
   (4) 400, 600

b. The constraints in the model would be
   (1) 2, 3, 1
   (2) 5, 4, 3
   (3) 4, 2, 3
   (4) 400, 600

c. The constraints imposed by the available labor hours in department I could be expressed as
   (1) $4X_1 + 2X_2 + 3X_3 \leq 400$
   (2) $4X_1 + 2X_2 + 3X_3 \geq 400$
   (3) $2X_1 + 3X_2 + 1X_3 \leq 400$
   (4) $2C_1 + 3X_2 + 1X_3 \geq 400$

d. The most types of lamps that would be included in the optimal solution would be
   (1) 2
   (2) 1
   (3) 3
   (4) 0

The answer to part d is (1). For this problem there are two constraints and there can be no more variables in the optimal solution than there are constraints. This result will be clearer in the next chapter.

13. (CPA) The ABC Company has three departments and manufactures three products. However, product 3 can be made in two ways: (1) manufactured entirely at ABC, or (2) a partially completed product 3 can be purchased from an outside vendor. The partially completed product 3 does not require any time in department 1—but requires the same amount of time in departments 2 and 3 as a unit of product 3 made entirely at ABC. ABC wants to know how many of the three products it should make and how many of the partially completed units to buy from the vendor.

Problems

The following data are given for ABC's internally manufactured products:

	Product 1	Product 2	Product 3	
Profit margins	$51	$76	$100	
Selling price	$5000	$200	$600	
Usage of department 1	5.0	10.2	4.2	min/unit
Usage of department 2	0.8	1.2	2.0	hr/unit
Usage of department 3	10.5	4.8	1.9	min/unit

There are 2200 min available in department 1, 450 hr in department 2, and 2600 min in department 3.

A partially completed unit of product 3 (as described above) costs $535 each from the vendor.

a. Set up the problem as a linear programming problem for profit maximization. That is, define variables carefully; indicate objective function, the constraints and nonnegativity conditions. *Hint:* Treat product 3 as two separate products.

b. State the dual problem.

c. What is the meaning for each dual variable? Be sure to indicate its dimensional units.

14. (CPA) (In addition to picking the correct multiple-choice answer, indicate why it is correct.) A company markets two products, Alpha and Gamma. The marginal contributions per gallon are $5 for Alpha and $4 for Gamma. Both products consist of two ingredients, D and K. Alpha contains 80 percent D and 20 percent K, whereas the proportions of the same ingredients in Gamma are 40 percent and 60 percent, respectively. The current inventory is 16,000 gal of D and 6,000 gal of K. The only company that produces D and K is on strike and will neither deliver nor produce them in the foreseeable future. The company wishes to know the numbers of gallons of Alpha and Gamma that it should produce with its present stock of raw materials in order to maximize its total revenue.

a. The objective function for this problem could be expressed as
   (1) $f \max = 0X_1 + 0X_2 + 5X_3 + 5X_4$
   (2) $f \min = 5X_1 + 4X_2 + 0X_3 + 0X_4$
   (3) $f \max = 5X_1 + 4X_2 + 0X_3 + 0X_4$
   (4) $f \max = X_1 + X_2 + 5X_3 + 4X_4$
   (5) $f \max = 4X_1 + 5X_2 + X_3 + X_4$

b. The constraint imposed by the quantity of D on hand could be expressed as
   (1) $X_1 + X_2 \geq 16{,}000$
   (2) $X_1 + X_2 \leq 16{,}000$
   (3) $0.4X_1 + 0.6X_2 \leq 16{,}000$
   (4) $0.8X_1 + 0.4X_2 \geq 16{,}000$
   (5) $0.8X_1 + 0.4X_2 \leq 16{,}000$

c. The constraint imposed by the quantity of K on hand could be expressed as
   (1) $X_1 + X_2 \geq 6{,}000$
   (2) $X_1 + X_2 \leq 6{,}000$
   (3) $0.8X_1 + 0.2X_2 \leq 6{,}000$
   (4) $0.8X_1 + 0.2X_2 \geq 6{,}000$
   (5) $0.2X_1 + 0.6X_2 \leq 6{,}000$

d. To maximize total revenue, the company should produce and market
   (1) 106,000 gal of Alpha only
   (2) 90,000 gal of Alpha and 16,000 gal of Gamma
   (3) 16,000 gal of Alpha and 90,000 gal of Gamma
   (4) 18,000 gal of Alpha and 4,000 gal of Gamma
   (5) 4,000 gal of Alpha and 18,000 gal of Gamma
   Develop your answer using graphical technique for solving linear programs.

e. Assuming that the marginal contributions per gallon are $7 for Alpha and $9 for Gamma, the company should produce and market
   (1) 106,000 gal of Alpha only
   (2) 90,000 gal of Alpha and 16,000 gal of Gamma
   (3) 16,000 gal of Alpha and 90,000 gal of Gamma
   (4) 18,000 gal of Alpha and 4,000 gal of Gamma
   (5) 4,000 gal of Alpha and 18,000 gal of Gamma
   Develop your answer using graphical technique for solving linear programs.

15. Solve the following linear program using the graphical technique:

    Max: $X_1 + X_2$
    Subject to: $6X_1 + 7X_2 \leq 42$
    $6X_1 + 5X_2 \leq 30$
    $X_1 \geq 0 \quad X_2 \geq 0$

16. Solve the following linear program using the graphical technique:

    Min: $X_1 + X_2$
    Subject to: $6X_1 + 7X_2 \geq 42$
    $2X_1 + X_2 \geq 10$
    $X_1 \geq 0 \quad X_2 \geq 0$

17. Solve the following linear programming problem:

    Max: $P = 2X_1 + 3X_2 + 1X_3$
    Subject to: $2X_1 + 1X_2 + 7X_3 \leq 7$
    $1X_1 + 4X_2 + 13X_3 \leq 6$
    $X_1 \geq 0 \quad X_2 \geq 0 \quad X_3 \geq 0$

Hint: You may be able to solve the problem graphically, but the easier way is to formulate the dual problem, which has only two variables, and solve the dual graphically. From a solution to the dual, you can then indicate the primal solution.

Problems

18. The XYZ Corporation manufactures products E and L. The marginal income for the products is 80¢ and 90¢, respectively. The total hours of skilled labor required for the manufacture of these two products is 900 hr. Product L requires 1.5 hr per unit, and product E requires 1 hr per unit. Product L also has to go through a dipping process where $\frac{1}{10}$ hr is required for each unit. Forty dipping hours are available. Both products go through a painting process. Total painting hours are 37.5, and the painting time for each product is 0.05 hr per unit. The total shipping capacity is limited to 800 units for both products. Find an optimal solution for the mix of these two products by the graphical method.

19. *(SMA)* Consider the following minimization problem as a primal problem:

$$\begin{aligned}
\text{Min:} \quad & 30{,}000Z_1 + 30{,}000Z_2 + 6{,}250Z_3 \\
\text{Subject to:} \quad & 10Z_1 + 15Z_2 + 1.25Z_3 \geq 200 \\
& 20Z_1 + 5Z_2 + 5Z_3 \geq 300 \\
& Z_1 \geq 0 \quad Z_2 \geq 0 \quad Z_3 \geq 0
\end{aligned}$$

Using complementary rules to those presented in the text, devise the dual maximization problem. Note that the dual here is the primal example problem used in this chapter.

20. *(SMA)* Minicomp Inc. is considering producing four different models of minicomputers that will yield the following per unit profits:

Model	A	B	C	D
Net profit ($)	14,000	7,000	10,000	5,000

The company has $800,000 capital to invest in production and a capacity of 8500 working days.

The capital and labor requirements for each model are given as follows:

Model	Required Capital per Unit ($ thousands)	Required per Unit Working Days
A	18	175
B	13	110
C	15	145
D	11	100

Formulate two linear programming models, one to maximize profits and one to maximize the number of units produced.

21. *(SMA)* Having just purchased a new home, Jacques Ross is busily engaged in landscaping the property. He intends to plant grass over an area of 1000 m² (square meters) and has spent many hours in preparing the soil. He is now ready to purchase the seed.

The provincial department of agriculture recommends using at least 1 kg of seed mixture per 250 m². The recommended mixture for this neighborhood consists of three types of grass seed in the following proportions: a minimum of 20 percent bluegrass, a maximum of 40 percent bentgrass, and the rest ryegrass.

Unfortunately, commercially prepared mixtures satisfying these requirements are not available. Ross has decided to purchase two commercial mixtures, EX and WY, and to mix them himself to obtain a satisfactory mixture.

Brand EX is priced at $5/kg and consists of 35 percent bluegrass, 30 percent bentgrass and 35 percent ryegrass. Brand WY, priced at $4/kg, consists of 15 percent bluegrass, 45 percent bentgrass and 40 percent ryegrass.

Because of his high mortgage payments, Ross wants to spend as little as possible for seed while ensuring that he has a mixture satisfying the department of agriculture's recommendations.

REQUIRED

Letting x and y represent the number of kilograms of brands EX and WY, respectively, formulate this problem as a linear programming problem. *Do Not Solve.*

22. (SMA) The Tiberian Transformation Company was formed in 68 B.C., during a relative slump in the Roman conquests. A tent was set up on the north bank of the Tiber River and the company commenced work turning swords into plowshares. Thousands of soldiers are unemployed, therefore, large numbers of swords are available at a reasonable price.

Tiberian plans to produce two models of plowshares. Each regular model is produced from 20 swords and requires four man-hours of forming and two man-hours of assembly. Twenty-four swords are required for the heavy-duty plowshare, along with five man-hours for forming and four man-hours for assembly. Swords are purchased from the war surplus store in Rome at a price of 10 shekels each. (The shekel is a unit of currency.) This price is not expected to change. Tiberian's work force consists of 20 skilled formers earning 8 shekels per hour and 12 semiskilled assemblers earning 6 shekels per hour. Each employee works a maximum of 80 hr a week.

Regular plowshares will sell for 225 shekels, and heavy-duty plowshares for 300 shekels. Tiberian believes that no more than 150 heavy-duty plowshares can be sold in a week, while demand for regular plowshares is unlimited.

REQUIRED

a. Let x be the number of regular plowshares produced (and sold) and y the number of heavy-duty plowshares. If Tiberian wishes to maximize sales in shekels, formulate the problem as a linear program.

b. Solve graphically, determining production of each type of plowshare in units and maximum sales in shekels. Your graph should be fully labeled and the feasible area clearly indicated.

c. If Tiberian wishes to maximize the total number of plowshares sold rather than sales in shekels, how many plowshares of each type should be produced?

Problems

    d. If Tiberian wishes to maximize profits, how many of each type should be produced?

23. *(SMA)* The Sleep-E Mattress Company assembles a standard mattress which is called Posture-ONE and a very firm mattress called Posture-PLUS. Each Posture-ONE requires 0.5 hr for basic assembling (binding together the springs) and 1.0 hr for finishing (adding foam and padding and covering the unit with a cover). Each Posture-PLUS requires 1.2 hr for basic assembling and 0.8 hr for finishing. The current labor force available at the plant provides 3600 hr for basic assembling and 3120 hr for finishing. The profit on the Posture-ONE mattress is $17.50 and on the Posture-PLUS $32.50, and the Marketing Department has stipulated that at least 1800 Posture-ONE mattresses must be manufactured each week.

REQUIRED
    a. Formulate the above problem in a linear programming framework, specifying the objective function and all constraints.
    b. Using the graphical approach, determine how many mattresses of each type should the Sleep-E Mattress Company produce each week to maximize its profit within the specified constraints?

24. *(SMA)* The Antique Furniture Company manufactures two models of rocking chairs: Applewood and Bentwood. Each sells for $120 although variable costs are different: $85 for Applewood and $70 for Bentwood. Each unit of Applewood requires 2 machine hr and 3 hr of assembly labor; Bentwood requires 3 machine hr and 2 hr of assembly labor. Plant capacity is 1200 machine hr and 1400 assembly labor hr.

    Because of a shortage of Applewood, the company has materials to produce a maximum of 400 Applewood chairs. Materials for the Bentwood model are available in unlimited quantities. The company is committed to fill existing orders for 50 Bentwood chairs.

REQUIRED
    a. Letting A represent the number of units of the Applewood model produced and B represent the number of units of the Bentwood model produced, and assuming that Antique Furniture Company wishes to maximize total contribution margin (sales minus variable costs), formulate the above problem as a linear program.
    b. Solve graphically.
    c. Because of the popularity of Bentwood chairs, Antique is considering increasing the price of Bentwood to $125. All other figures would remain unchanged. Determine the change in optimum total contribution margin.
    d. Refer to the original problem using a $120 selling price for both models. How much should Antique be willing to pay to increase machine hour capacity from 1200 hr to 1500 hr?

25. *(SMA)* Gemini Publications produces a hardcover edition of a specialized textbook that sells for $15 and a paperback edition of the same text that sells for $8. Variable costs to Gemini are $12 and $6 per book, respectively, in addition to weekly fixed costs of $2000. Both editions require 4 min of printing time; however, the hardcover edition requires 5 min of binding time versus only 1 min per paperback version.

Printing facilities and binding facilities are *each* available for 120 machine hr per week. Gemini is required by contract to print at least 200 paperback copies weekly and wishes to find the product mix that maximizes profits.

REQUIRED

    a. Formulate the above problem in a linear programming framework, specifying the objective function and all constraints. *Be sure to define all variables.*

    b. How many of each version of the text should be produced weekly in order to maximize profits?

       (1) Solve graphically

       (2) Solve algebraically

26. *(CMA)* The following data apply to items a to c. Items a to c should be treated as completely independent of one another.

The Marlan Metal Products Company has just established a department for the production of two new products—metal trays and storage devices. This department is ready to begin operations with five metal forming machines and five metal cutting machines that have been rented for $300 each per month from a local machine company. Both products require production time on both machines. Each of the machines is capable of 400 hr of production per month. No additional machines can be obtained.

	MACHINE HOURS PER UNIT		
	Trays	Storage Devices	Total Available Machine Hours per Month
Metal cutting machines	1	2	2000
Metal forming machines	2	2	2000

The controller's department has summarized expected costs and revenues as follows:

	Trays	Storage Devices
Selling price per unit	$18	$27
Variable cost per unit	14	20

Demand for the storage devices is unlimited but Marlan believes that no more than 800 units of the trays can be sold per month.

Problems

The following linear programming formulation and accompanying graph represent the facts described above. Marlan must operate within the specified constraints as it tries to maximize the contribution margin from this new operation. Marlan intends to operate at the optimal level that it has determined to be the point labeled "OP" on the graph below.

LINEAR PROGRAMMING FORMULATION

Maximize

$$Z = \$4T + \$7S$$

Subject to:

$$T + 2S \leq 2000$$
$$2T + 2S \leq 2000$$
$$T \leq 800$$
$$T, S \geq 0$$

where

T = number of units of trays produced
S = number of units of storage devices produced
Z = contribution margin

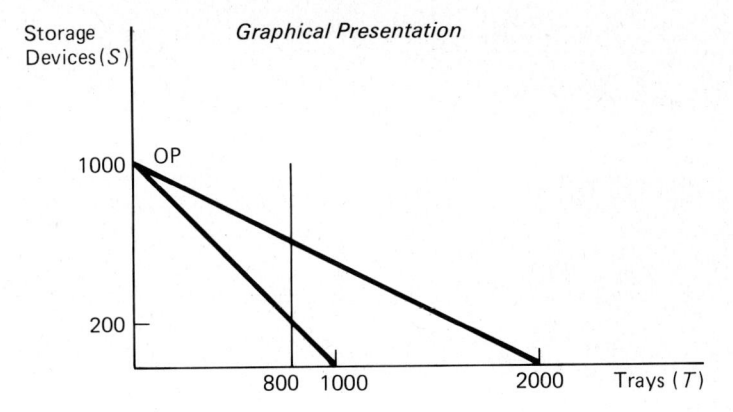

Graphical Presentation

REQUIRED

a. If the selling price of storage devices is lowered from $27 to $23, the maximum total contribution margin Marlan could earn would
  (1) Decrease by $3800
  (2) Decrease by $4000
  (3) Increase by $4000
  (4) Decrease by $3200
  (5) Not be expected to change

b. The maximum amount Marlan should be willing to spend on advertising in order to increase the demand for trays to 1000 units per month would be
   (1) $0
   (2) $600
   (3) $1400
   (4) $5400
   (5) $7000

c. If one metal forming machine is returned to the rental agency and the rent can be avoided on the returned machine, Marlan's total profit would
   (1) Be unaffected
   (2) Increase by $300
   (3) Decrease by $1100
   (4) Decrease by $1400
   (5) Decrease by $4300

d. Marlan has just realized that a material needed for the production of both products is in short supply. The company can obtain enough of this material to produce 1200 trays. Each tray requires $\frac{2}{3}$ as much of this material as the storage devices. Which of the following constraints will incorporate completely and correctly this additional information into the formulation of the problem?
   (1) $T \leq 1200$
   (2) $\frac{2}{3}S \leq 1200$
   (3) $T + \frac{2}{3}S \leq 1200$
   (4) $\frac{2}{3}T + 1S \leq 800$
   (5) $T - \frac{3}{2}S = 0$

27. *(CMA)* Excelsion Corporation manufactures and sells two kinds of containers—paperboard and plastic. The company produced and sold 100,000 paperboard containers and 75,000 plastic containers during the month of April. A total of 4000 and 6000 direct labor hr were used in producing the paperboard and plastic containers respectively.

    The company has not been able to maintain an inventory of either product, due to the high demand; this situation is expected to continue in the future. Workers can be shifted from the production of paperboard to plastic containers and vice versa, but additional labor is not available in the community. In addition, there will be a shortage of plastic material used in the manufacture of the plastic container in the coming months due to a labor strike at the facilities of a key supplier. Management has estimated there will be only enough raw material to produce 60,000 plastic containers during June.

    The income statement for Excelsion Corporation for the month of April is shown below. The costs presented in the statement are representative of prior periods and are expected to continue at the same rates or levels in the future.

Problems

Excelsion Corporation
Income Statement
For the month ended April 30, 1978

	Paperboard Containers	Plastic Containers
Sales	$220,800	$222,900
Less: Returns and allowances	$ 6,360	$ 7,200
Discounts	2,440	3,450
	$ 8,800	$ 10,650
Net sales	$212,000	$212,250
Cost of sales		
Raw material cost	$123,000	$120,750
Direct labor	26,000	28,500
Indirect labor (variable with direct labor hours)	4,000	4,500
Depreciation—machinery	14,000	12,250
Depreciation—building	10,000	10,000
Cost of sales	$177,000	$176,000
Gross profit	$ 35,000	$ 36,250
Selling and general expenses		
General expenses—variable	$ 8,000	$ 7,500
General expenses—fixed	1,000	1,000
Commissions	11,000	15,750
Total operating expenses	$ 20,000	$ 24,250
Income before tax	$ 15,000	$ 12,000
Income taxes (40%)	6,000	4,800
Net income	$ 9,000	$ 7,200

REQUIRED

    a. The management of Excelsion Corporation plans to use linear programming to determine the optimal mix of paperboard and plastic containers for the month of June to achieve maximum profits. Using data presented in the April income statement, formulate and label the
        (1) Objective function
        (2) Constraint functions
    b. Identify the underlying assumptions of linear programming.
    c. What contribution would the management accountant normally make to a team established to develop the linear programming model and apply it to a decision problem?

28. *(CMA)* Leastan Company manufactures a line of carpeting that includes a commercial carpet and a residential carpet. Two grades of fiber—heavy-duty and regular—are used in manufacturing both types of carpeting. The

mix of the two grades of fiber differs in each type of carpeting with the commercial grade using a greater amount of heavy-duty fiber.

Leastan will introduce a new line of carpeting in 2 mo to replace the current line. The present fiber in stock will not be used in the new line. Management wants to exhaust the present stock of regular and heavy-duty fiber during the last month of production.

Data regarding the current line of commercial and residential carpeting are presented at the top of the next column.

	Commercial	Residential
Selling price per roll	$1000	$800
Production specifications per roll of carpet:		
Heavy-duty fiber	80 lb	40 lb
Regular fiber	20 lb	40 lb
Direct labor hours	15 hr	15 hr
Standard cost per roll of carpet:		
Heavy-duty fiber ($3/lb)	$240	$120
Regular fiber ($2/lb)	40	80
Direct labor ($10/DLH)	150	150
Variable manufacturing overhead (60% of direct labor cost)	90	90
Fixed manufacturing overhead (120% of direct labor cost)	180	180
Total standard cost per roll	$700	$620

Leaston has 42,000 lb of heavy-duty fiber and 24,000 lb of regular fiber in stock. All fiber not used in the manufacture of the present types of carpeting during the last month of production can be sold as scrap at $0.25 a pound.

There are a maximum of 10,500 direct labor hr available during the month. The labor force can work on either type of carpeting.

Sufficient demand exists for the present line of carpeting so that all quantities produced can be sold.

REQUIRED
a. Calculate the number of rolls of commercial carpet and residential carpet Leastan Company must manufacture during the last month of production to exhaust completely the heavy-duty and regular fiber still in stock.

b. Can Leastan Company manufacture these quantities of commercial and residential carpeting during the last month of production? Explain your answer.

c. A member of Leastan Company's cost accounting staff has stated that linear programming should be used to determine the number of rolls of commercial and residential carpeting to manufacture during the last month of production.
   (1) Explain why linear programming should be used in this application.
   (2) Formulate the objective and constraint functions so that this application can be solved by linear programming.

29. The Farnsworth Company makes two products, Alfas and MGs, from two fixed inputs, polishing and rubbing, and wants to plan for 3 periods. Farnsworth has $30,000 cash balance now and no accounts receivable. The company wants to maximize the sum of the cash balance and accounts receivable at the end of the third period. Ending inventory has no value. Product 1, Alfas, can be inventoried and sold at a later date. Product 2, MGs, must be sold in the period when they are produced. The technology is invariant overtime and the input-output coefficients are given as follows:

	Product 1, Alfas	Product 2, MGs
Input 1, polishing	7 hr/unit	6 hr/unit
Input 2, rubbing	8 hr/unit	3 hr/unit

During each planning period there are 160 hr of polishing available and 182 hr of rubbing. Each Alfa has a cash flow expenditure of $2000 in the period produced. An MG has a cash flow of $1500 if produced in the first period, $1600 in the second, and $1800 in the third. Similarly, the product period demands are given as

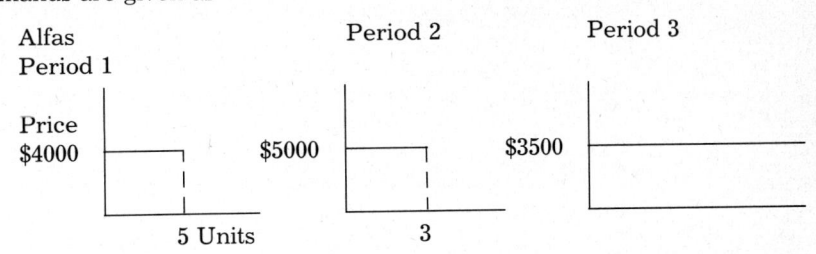

Alfas
Period 1: Price $4000, 5 Units
Period 2: $5000, 3
Period 3: $3500

MGs can be sold for $3500 in unlimited amounts in any period. Cash expenditures are incurred during the period of production. Revenues from sales are realized for use during the period after the sale has taken place.

a. Set up a linear programming formulation (ignore integer restrictions) that would yield the optimal production and sales plan.

b. Interpret and give the meaning of the dual variables for the above linear program. (You need not write out the dual program.)

30. *(CPA)* The following schedule provides data for product A, which is processed through processes 1 and 2, and product B, which is processed through process 1 only:

	Product A	Product B
Raw material cost per gallon	$ 4	$ 9
Process 1 (500 gal input capacity per hour)		
Processing cost per hour	$60	$60
Loss in processing	30%	20%
Process 2 (300 gal input capacity per hour)		
Processing cost per hour	$50	
Loss in processing	10%	
Selling price per gallon	$20	$40

If the objective is to maximize profit per 8-hr day, the objective function of a profit-maximizing linear programming problem is

a. $20A + 40B - 4A - 4B$
b. $20A + 40B - 4A - 4B - 60(A + B) - 50A$
c. $20(0.63A) + 40(0.80B) - 4(0.63A) - 9(0.8B)$
$-60\left(\dfrac{A + B}{500}\right) - 50\left(\dfrac{0.7A}{300}\right)$
d. $20(0.63A) + 40(0.80B) - 4A - 9B$
$-60\left(\dfrac{A}{500} + \dfrac{B}{500}\right) - 50\left(\dfrac{0.7A}{300}\right)$
e. None of the above

Justify your selection.

31. Assuming the same facts as in Problem 30, a constraint of the problem is

a. $0.63A \leq 2400$
b. $0.8A \leq 2400$
c. $0.7A + 0.8B \leq 4000$
d. $0.9A \leq 4000$
e. None of the above

32. *(CPA)* A linear programming model is being used to determine for two products having different profitabilities per unit the quantities of each to produce to maximize profit over a 1-yr period. One component of cost is raw materials. If both products use the same amount of the same raw material:

a. This cost may be ignored because it is the same for each product.
b. This cost must be ignored because it is the same for each product.
c. This cost must be included in the objective function because it varies with the independent variables in the model.
d. More information about the products and the other components of the objective function is needed to determine whether to include this cost.
e. None of the above

33. The *portfolio problem* is to choose a set of investments (for example, stocks, bonds, and real estate) that yield a maximum return to the investor and yet

meets the risk constraint of not "putting all one's eggs in one basket." Assume that there is $1 million to invest in a combination of the 10 securities listed in the table below. To minimize risk the total investment in airlines is limited to 15 percent, the total investment in state or city bonds is limited to 10 percent, and at least 25 percent of the investment is in utilities.

Security Number	Name	Price	Expected Return
1	Power Company	$ 60	$ 3.50
2	Telephone Company	50	4.00
3	Life Insurance	120	8.00
4	Ohio Bonds	1015	45.00
5	New York City Bonds	980	43.00
6	Gas Company	95	6.00
7	Brown Industries	24	2.00
8	Dixie Airlines	70	7.00
9	Northern Airlines	125	10.00
10	World Airlines	44	4.00

REQUIRED

Formulate a linear programming model that maximizes the return to the investor but still meets the risk requirements.

34. The cycle manufacturing problem in Chapters 4 and 5 has been treated as a single-period production planning problem. We will now expand it to a multiperiod production situation. Assume that the cycle shop is planning for 3 mo. The profit contributions for each product are as follows:

	X_1	X_2
January	$200	$300
February	300	300
March	300	500

The manufacturer believes it is advantageous to produce some items before they are needed, that is, to maintain an inventory between months. There are no inventories at the beginning of the 3-mo period. Note, this implies that although there can be no sales in January, there can be production.) The productive constraints previously applied to a single period now apply to each of the three periods for each product.

REQUIRED

Formulate the linear program to maximize profit contribution for the 3-mo period. (*Hint:* To handle inventory, note that for a given production a given month's beginning inventory plus that month's production equals sales plus the ending inventory.)

35. **CMA**
   a. The Witchell Corporation manufactures and sells three grades, A, B, and C, of a single wood product. Each grade must be processed through three phases—cutting, fitting, and finishing—before it is sold.

   The following unit information is provided:

	A	B	C
Selling price	$10.00	$15.00	$20.00
Direct labor	5.00	6.00	9.00
Direct materials	0.70	0.70	1.00
Variable overhead	1.00	1.20	1.80
Fixed overhead	0.60	0.72	1.08
Materials requirements in board feet	7	7	10
Labor requirements in hours			
Cutting	$3/6$	$3/6$	$4/6$
Fitting	$1/6$	$1/6$	$2/6$
Finishing	$1/6$	$2/6$	$3/6$

   Only 5000 board feet can be obtained per week. The cutting department has 180 hr of labor available each week. The fitting and finishing departments each have 120 hr of labor available each week. No overtime is allowed.

   Contract commitments require the company to make 50 units of A per week. In addition, company policy is to produce at least 50 additional units of A, 50 units of B, and 50 units of C each week to remain active in each of the three markets. Because of competition, only 130 units of C can be sold each week.

   REQUIRED

   Formulate and label the linear objective function and the constraint functions necessary to maximize the contribution margin.

   b. The graph provided presents the constraint functions for a chair manufacturing company whose production problem can be solved by linear programing. The company earns $8 for each kitchen chair sold and $5 for each office chair sold.

   REQUIRED
   (1) What is the profit-maximizing production schedule?
   (2) How did you select this production schedule?

   Hint: To determine the points of potential optimality, you should use the procedure of elimination demonstrated in Section 4.4. To check your progress, the line through the point (0, 4000) is $y = -\frac{1}{3}x + 4{,}000$.

36. (*CMA*) The Elon Company manufactures two industrial products—X-10 which sells for $90 a unit and Y-12 which sells for $85 a unit. Each product

Problems

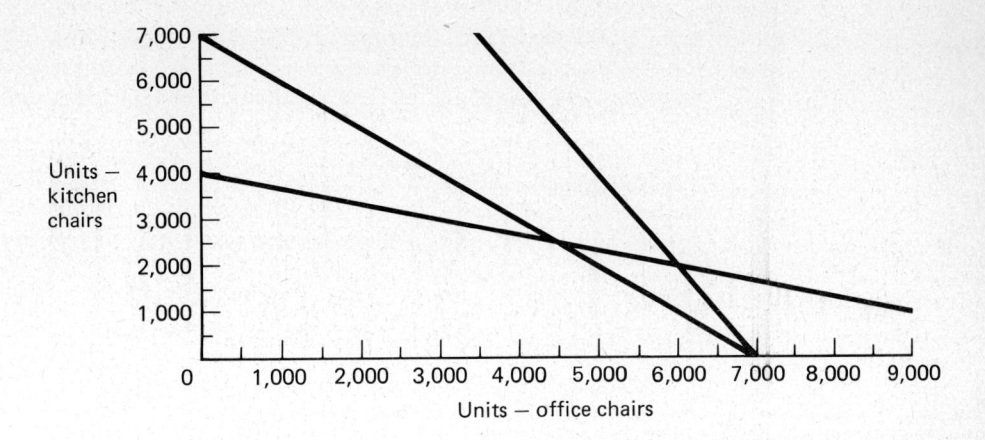

[Graph: Units — kitchen chairs (y-axis, 0 to 7,000) vs Units — office chairs (x-axis, 0 to 9,000)]

is processed through both of the company's manufacturing departments. The limited availability of labor, material, and equipment capacity has restricted the ability of the firm to meet the demand for its products. The production department believes that linear programming can be used to routinize the production schedule for the two products.

The following data are available to the production department.

	AMOUNT REQUIRED PER UNIT	
	X-10	Y-12
Direct material: weekly supply is limited to 1800 lb at $12/lb	4 lb	2 lb
Direct labor:		
Department 1—weekly supply limited to 10 people at 40 hr each at an hourly cost of $6	$\frac{2}{3}$ hr	1 hr
Department 2—weekly supply limited to 15 people at 40 hr each at an hourly rate of $8	$1\frac{1}{4}$ hr	1 hr
Machine time:		
Department 1—weekly capacity limited to 250 hr	$\frac{1}{2}$ hr	$\frac{1}{2}$ hr
Department 2—weekly capacity limited to 300 hr	0 hr	1 hr

The overhead costs for Elon are accumulated on a plantwide basis. The overhead is assigned to products on the basis of the number of direct labor hours required to manufacture the product. This base is appropriate for overhead assignment because most of the variable overhead costs vary as a function of labor time. The estimated overhead cost per direct labor hour is:

Variable overhead cost	$ 6
Fixed overhead cost	6
Total overhead cost per direct labor hour	$12

The production department formulated the following equations for the linear programming statement of the problem.

A = number of units of X-10 to be produced
B = number of units of Y-12 to be produced

Objective function to minimize costs:
minimize

$$Z = 85A + 62B$$

Constraints:
material

$$4A + 2B \leq 1800 \text{ lb}$$

Department 1 labor

$$\tfrac{2}{3}A + 1B \leq 400 \text{ hr}$$

Department 2 labor

$$1\tfrac{1}{4}A + 1B \leq 600 \text{ hr}$$

nonnegativity

$$A \geq 0, B \geq 0.$$

REQUIRED
    a. The formulation of the linear programming equations as prepared by Elon Company's production department is incorrect. Explain what errors have been made in the formulation prepared by the production department.
    b. Formulate and label the proper equations for the linear programming statement of Elon Company's production problem.
    c. Explain how linear programming could help Elon Company determine how large a change in the price of direct materials would have to be to change the optimum production mix of X-10 and Y-12.
37. How would you use accounting data to generate the profit coefficients of the objective function? For example, the coefficient of the first product is $200. How would you calculate this figure from accounting records?
38. How would you use accounting data to generate the coefficients of the constraints?

39. Do the dual values in linear programming have any relation to standard costs? If so, what is it?
40. Can you relate the answers to the example linear program to a budget plan as used in accounting?

References

Anderson, David R., Sweeney, D. J., and Williams, T. A. *An Introduction to Management Science, Quantitative Approaches to Decision Making.* St. Paul, Minn.: West, 1979.

Baumol, W. J. *Economic Theory and Operations Analysis,* 4th ed. Englewood Cliffs, N.J.: Prentice-Hall, 1977.

Dopuch, Nicholas. "Mathematical Programming and Accounting Approaches to Incremental Cost Analysis." *The Accounting Review* 38, no. 4 (October 1963) 745–753.

Vatter, Paul A., Bradley, Stephen P., Frey, Sherwood S., Jr., and Jackson, Barbara. *Quantitative Analysis in Management: Text and Cases.* Homewood, Ill.: Irwin, 1978.

CHAPTER 5
Linear Programming—The Simplex Method

5.1 **Introduction**
5.2 **The Simplex Method**
　　Standard Form
　　The Initial Tableau—Step 0
　　Can We Do Better?—Is It Profitable to Produce Different Products?—Step 1
　　Choosing Which Product to Produce—Step 2
　　How Much Can We Produce?—Step 3
　　How Much of Other Products to Produce—Step 4
　　What Are the New Technological Rates of Substitution?—Step 5
　　Can We Do Better?—Step 6
5.3 **The Second Iteration**
5.4 **The Third Iteration**
5.5 **The Optimal Solution—Primal and Dual**
5.6 **Variations**
　　Unbounded Solutions
　　Degenerate Solutions
　　Multiple Optimal Solutions
5.7 **Extensions**
　　Artificial Variables
　　Surplus Variables
　　Minimization
5.8 **Sensitivity Analysis and the Limits of the Solution**
　　Changes in Profit Coefficients
　　Changes in the Availability of Resources
5.9 **Summary**
Glossary
Problems
Artificial variable
Basic solution or basis
Degenerate solution
Iteration
Minimization problem
Multiple optimum
Pivot element
Sensitivity analysis
Key Applications
Costing constraints
Larger resource allocation problems

References
Key Concepts
Simplex criterion
Simplex method
Simplex tableau
Slack variable
Standard form
Surplus variable
Technological rate of substitution
Unbounded solution

Managerial accounting
Production planning

5.1 Introduction

The *simplex method* permits us to solve very large linear programs. It is an algebraic method employing principles of matrix algebra. Obviously, it has practical advantages over the graphical approach, as most real-world problems involve many more than two variables—frequently hundreds, if not thousands. These real-world problems are generally solved on a computer using some form of the simplex method.

The question remains: Why should anyone develop a knowledge of the simplex method when these problems are generally solved on a computer? The reasons are many. A good understanding of the simplex method:

1. Aids in problem formulation. Practical problems are seldom formulated correctly the first time, and a knowledge of the simplex method helps one find the formulation error(s).
2. Helps develop a better understanding of the primal-dual relationship. The simplex method illustrates these relations and their meaning, and sensitivity analysis exploits these relations for the planning process.
3. Formalizes marginal reasoning arguments used in managerial accounting and managerial economics. The explanation of the simplex method developed here is a formalization of the ad hoc marginal analysis used in managerial accounting and managerial economics.
4. Provides a better foundation for reading the management literature which uses linear programming.

This presentation of the simplex method is not meant to provide the reader with the most efficient approach to solving linear programming problems by hand, but one that facilitates understanding of the implications of linear programming for business decisions.

We begin with a development of the simplex method, using the same example as in the previous chapter. It permits us to reference our algebraic approach of the simplex method to the graphical presentation of Chapter 4. The important issue of sensitivity analysis is then presented. Sensitivity analysis begins with the optimal solution to the original problem and considers the effects and the implicit value of changes in constraints and objective function coefficients.

5.2 The Simplex Method

Applying the simplex method to the same problem used in the previous chapter, we find that in solving the primal problem, we have also solved the dual problem as a by-product. The primal problem is:

$$\begin{aligned} \text{Max:} \quad & P = 200X_1 + 300X_2 \\ \text{Subject to:} \quad & 10X_1 + 20X_2 \leq 30{,}000 \\ & 15X_1 + 5X_2 \leq 30{,}000 \\ & 1.25X_1 + 5X_2 \leq 6{,}250 \\ & X_1 \geq 0 \\ & X_2 \geq 0 \end{aligned}$$

This form of the problem was convenient for the graphical solution, but we need to rewrite the problem in an equivalent algebraic form to apply the simplex method.

STANDARD FORM

The standard form is an equivalent form where all inequalities ($\leq$ or $\geq$) have been changed to equalities ($=$), by introducing new additional variables. For our example we introduce three additional variables.

$$\begin{aligned} \text{Max:} \quad & P = 200X_1 + 300X_2 + 0X_m + 0X_e + 0X_p \\ \text{Subject to:} \quad & 10X_1 + 20X_2 + 1X_m \quad\quad\quad\quad\quad\quad = 30{,}000 \\ & 15X_1 + 5X_2 \quad\quad + 1X_e \quad\quad\quad = 30{,}000 \\ & 1.25X_1 + 5X_2 \quad\quad\quad\quad + 1X_p = 6{,}250 \\ & X_1 \geq 0 \quad X_2 \geq 0 \quad X_m \geq 0 \quad X_e \geq 0 \quad X_p \geq 0 \end{aligned}$$

where

X_m = the unused amount of machining time
X_e = the unused amount of assembly time
X_p = the unused amount of painting time

Each variable is restricted to be nonnegative.

These variables are called *slack variables*, as they denote the slack or unused resources. Consider the first constraint again. It says that the machining time used for product 1, unicycles, plus the machining time for product 2, bicycles, plus the unused machining time, X_m, must equal the machining time available, 30,000 hr. Note that the coefficient of X_m is 1 in the constraint and 0 in the objective function (unused machining time cannot be sold or used elsewhere). The second and third constraints are constructed in similar fashion.

We have added three nonnegative variables and replaced three inequalities with equalities. Looking at the new set of constraints (ignoring the nonnegativity constraints), we find that there are three equations in five unknowns. There are an infinite number of solutions for this set of equations. We want to choose a feasible solution that maximizes P (exactly what we did graphically in the previous chapter).

The simplex method is an efficient search technique that permits us to find an optimal solution in a systematic fashion. We start by finding a feasible extreme point (i.e., a corner point) and proceed to an adjacent extreme point with a higher value of P until the best solution is found. Previously, we argued intuitively that an extreme point will be an optimal solution (although not necessarily the only optimal solution), and now we shall be able to support that intuition.

The constraint set above involves three equations in five variables. A solution can be found for which, at most, three variables are at the positive level, whereas the other two variables are zero. Each such solution is called a *basic solution* or a *basis*. It involves no more positive variables than there are constraints. A basic feasible solution is represented graphically as an extreme point. For example, $X_1 = X_2 = 0$, $X_m = 30,000$, $X_e = 30,000$, and $X_p = 6,250$ is a basic solution. The simplex method systematically moves from one basic feasible solution to another, more profitable one.

Figure 5–1 provides a convenient diagram that outlines the conceptual basis for the simplex method in a step-by-step fashion. In solving our problem, we shall follow the diagram through to a solution. Read through the diagram to observe the intuitive rationale of the approach and the questions to be answered.

THE INITITAL TABLEAU—STEP 0

Although not mandatory, it is convenient to put the linear program information in table or a tableau form. It provides a logical way to organize the information. It is identical in content to the standard form of the problem, though much more compact. For our example, the initial *simplex tableau* is given as

Profit Coefficients (C_j)	Solution Variables	C_j 200 X_1	300 X_2	0 X_m	0 X_e	0 X_p	Available Resources Current Solution Values (RHS)
0	X_m	10	20	1	0	0	30,000
0	X_c	15	5	0	1	0	30,000
0	X_p	1.25	5	0	0	1	6,250

5.2 / The Simplex Method

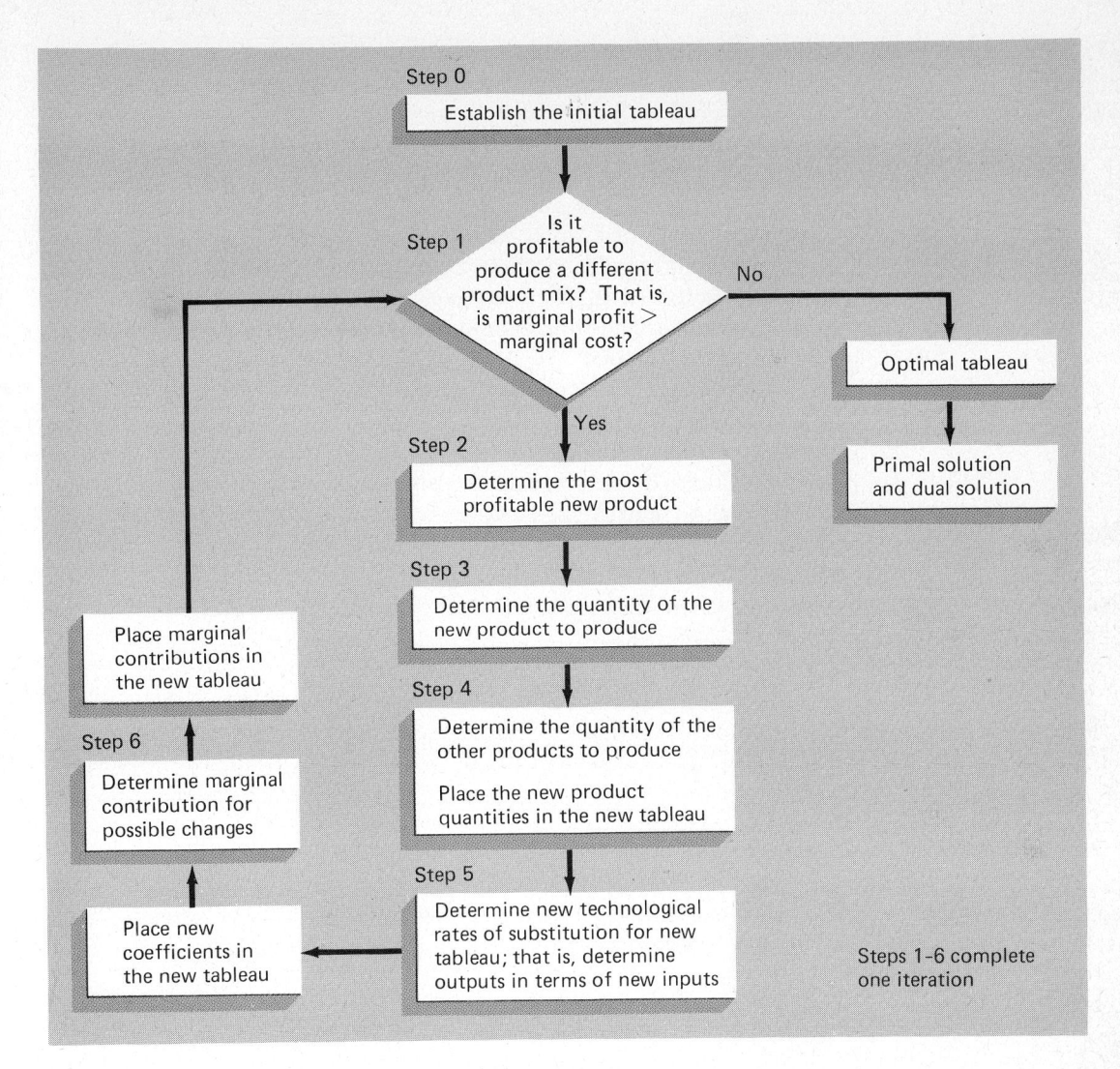

Figure 5-1. The simplex method for maximization problems.

The construction of the initial tableau involves identifying each column with a variable (including slacks) by placing the variable name at the top of the column and the corresponding objective function coefficient, C_j, above the name. Each row of the tableau is an abstraction of a constraint equation in its standard form. For example, the first constraint, $10X_1 + 20X_2 + 1X_m + 0X_e + 0X_p = 30{,}000$, becomes the first row, with values 10, 20, 1, 0, 0, and 30,000. These are, respectively, the coefficients of X_1, X_2, X_m, X_e, X_p and the availability of machining [or the right-hand side (RHS) of the equation]. The second and third rows represent the same coefficients and RHS values for the second and third constraints.

Down the left-hand side of the tableau we indicate the variables in the current solution. For the initial solution and tableau of our example we start at the origin. This places the slack variables in the basic solution. These variables are listed down the left-hand side of the tableau with their associated profit coefficients from the top of the tableau. The "1s" in the columns with the headings X_m, X_e, and X_p indicate that these variables are in the basic solution. This solution is $X_1 = X_2 = 0$, $X_m = 30{,}000$, $X_e = 30{,}000$, $X_p = 6250$. Notice that this solution corresponds to the corner point a (0, 0) in the feasible region (see Figure 5–2). This is a worst-case situation in that the iso-profit line intersecting this corner point has the least value ($P = 0$). In general, our initial basic solutions will take a worst-case assumption, although not always at the origin. Because X_1 and X_2 are zero, we do not produce any unicycles or bicycles. The values of the slack variables X_m, X_e, and X_p indicate that none of our production capacity is utilized with this initial solution; that is, all resources have maximum slack.

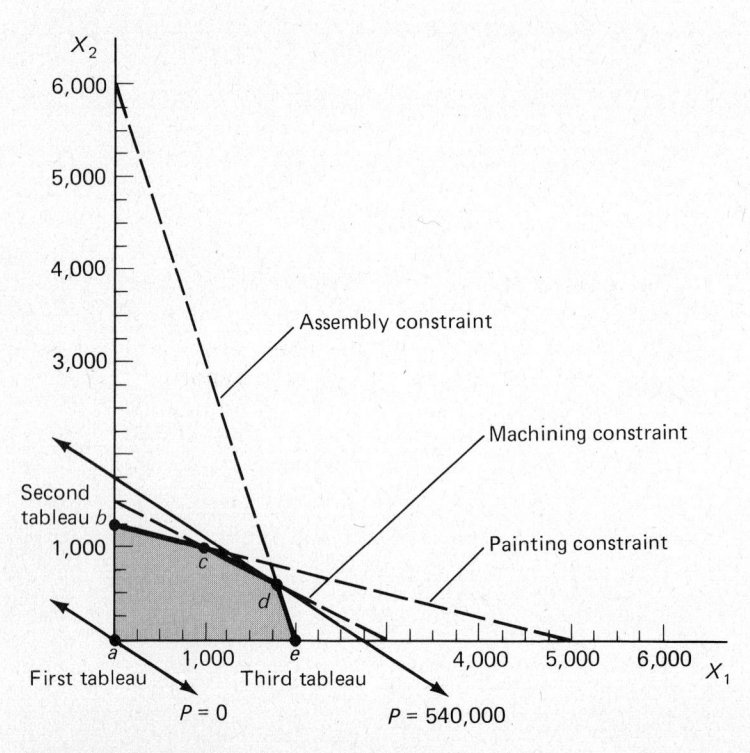

Figure 5–2. Graphical solution to problem.

5.2 / The Simplex Method

The reader is warned that simplex tableaux come in variations. Some authors will include the objective function as a row in the tableau itself; omit the left-hand-side variables; rearrange the order of the variables, for example, put the slack variables first; or label the slack variables X_3, X_4, and X_5 for this problem. Whatever the particular format, the tableau will contain the same information as we have given.

CAN WE DO BETTER—IS IT PROFITABLE TO PRODUCE DIFFERENT PRODUCTS?—STEP I

To do better requires that we obtain more profit than the current solution yields. For the initial tableau the current solution is $X_1 = X_2 = 0$, $X_m = 30,000$, $X_e = 30,000$, and $X_p = 6,250$, and the current profit is $P = 200(0) + 300(0) + 0(30,000) + 0(30,000) + 0(6,250) = 0$. To find P in a tableau, for each row we multiply the C_j entry times the RHS entry and sum. We know from our graphical analysis that we can do better, because there are extreme points beyond the iso-profit line $P = 0$. We need to systematize our approach, however. We can do so by formalizing a familiar question from managerial accounting or managerial economics: Can we find an alternative for which the marginal profit is greater than the marginal opportunity cost? This is the *simplex criterion*. For this example, let us consider what we gain (marginal profit) and what we give up (marginal opportunity lost) by producing one unicycle. We gain additional profit of $200, but to produce this one unit, we must give up:

10 hr of machining time (X_m)
15 hr of assembling time (X_e)
1.25 hr of painting time (X_p)

These values are called the *technological rates of substitution* by input for an output. In the first tableau, we find these coefficients in the X_1 column. What is the opportunity cost of each of these inputs for a new solution? We have assumed that we cannot sell machining, assembling, or painting directly into the market, and have included 0 as their objective function coefficient. The total marginal opportunity cost is then

$$10(0) + 15(0) + 1.25(0) = 0$$

So the marginal profit minus the marginal opportunity cost—that is, the marginal return—is $200 - 0 = $200. Therefore it would be to our advantage to produce at least one unit of X_1. But are there other products that are advantageous as well? Yes, one bicycle would yield $300 marginal profit at zero opportunity cost, producing a $300 marginal return.

We shall now formalize these calculations in the tableau at the bottom of the X_1 and X_2 columns as shown.

	Solution	C_j	200	300	0	0	0	
C_j	Variables		X_1	X_2	X_m	X_e	X_p	RHS
0	X_m		10	20	1	0	0	30,000
0	X_e		15	5	0	1	0	30,000
0	X_p		1.25	5	0	0	1	6,250
	C_j		200	300				
			− 10(0)	− 20(0)				
	$-Z_j$		− 15(0)	− 5(0)				
			− 1.25(0)	− 5(0)				
	$C_j - Z_j$		= 200	= 300				

(marginal return)

1. The simplex criterion is sometimes referred to as the "$C_j - Z_j$" calculation, where C_j is the marginal profit and Z_j is the marginal opportunity cost for the jth variable.
2. The C_j row beneath the constraint is merely a subset of the appropriate C_j values above the tableau.
3. To find Z_j, for each variable in the current solution, we multiply their technological rates of substitution (found in the nonsolution variable column) times their C_j value, found in the left-most column, and subtract.
4. The result of $C_j - Z_j$, the marginal return, is shown as the bottom row.
5. This calculation is done for all variables not in the current solution, namely, X_1 and X_2 here.
6. If, for any column, the resultant marginal return is positive, then the current solution is not optimal, because bringing the associated variable into the solution will increase the objective function.
7. Thus, in this case, both X_1 and X_2 should become part of the solution.
8. For maximation problems we have found an optimal solution when

   $$C_j - Z_j \leq 0$$

   for all decision variables and all slack variables; that is, when the marginal opportunity cost exceeds or equals the marginal profit for each variable, this is maximum profit production.

CHOOSING WHICH PRODUCT TO PRODUCE—STEP 2

Both unicycles and bicycles are profitable, but because only one variable can enter at a time, we must make a choice. Either one will lead us to a more profitable solution, but as a general rule, we select the one with the higher marginal return per unit. In our example, this is X_2, with a net marginal profit of 300.

The reader may consider this systematization a bit laborious to obtain results that seem rather obvious. This is usually the situation for the initial tableau. But the procedure is general, and on subsequent tableaux, the selection of an appropriate variable will not always be obvious. We need a clearly defined procedure as given above.

HOW MUCH CAN WE PRODUCE?—STEP 3

It is intuitive that we want to produce as much as possible of product X_2. We therefore move to the nearest extreme point along the X_2 axis. To help our intuition, reexamine the graph of the feasible region in Figure 5–2. From the origin, move along the X_2 axis. There are three constraint lines that intercept the X_2 axis, but only one represents a feasible solution. The assembly constraint establishes a corner point at $X_2 = 6000$, but is not feasible for machining and painting. Machining establishes a corner point at $X_2 = 1500$, but it violates the painting constraint. Painting establishes a corner point at $X_2 = 1250$ that is feasible for all constraints. This extreme point is a basic feasible solution. Therefore, we shall introduce 1250 units of X_2 into the next solution.

This calculation can be systematized using the tableau. Consider the X_2 column and the right-hand column (RHS) of available resources as shown in the partial initial tableau.

C_j		X_1	X_2	X_m	X_e	X_p	RHS	Ratio
0	X_m		20				30,000	1500
0	X_e		5				30,000	6000
0	X_p		5				6,250	1250

Pivot Row → Pivot Column ↑ Pivot Element

The ratio of the right-hand-side value over the X_2 column value for each row yields the extreme points established above. From the above graphical illustration, we should choose the minimum positive ratio[1] to maintain feasibility. Thus we calculate:

$$\text{Min}\left\{\frac{30{,}000}{20}, \frac{30{,}000}{5}, \frac{6{,}250}{5}\right\} = 1{,}250$$

By bringing X_2 into the solution at a level of 1250, we are using up all available painting hours. Thus, X_p will be zero in the new tableau and not in the solution. The column associated with the variable identified to enter the solution is called the *pivot column*. The row identified

---

[1] If there are negative rates of substitution, they are ignored for this calculation. A negative rate of substitution would mean that you gain the resource and thus it is not limiting in determining feasibility.

by the ratio analysis that is associated with the variable leaving the solution is called the *pivot row*. The intersection of the pivot column and pivot row is called the *pivot element*. In the new tableau this pivot element will be 1 and all other entries in the pivot column will be 0, just as is the case in the initial tableau for X_m, X_e, and X_p.

HOW MUCH OF OTHER PRODUCTS TO PRODUCE—STEP 4

The right-hand column indicates how much of each product to produce in the current solution. To develop the second tableau further, we want to consider how much of X_m and X_e we have remaining as unused available resources, or slack resources. (We already know that $X_p = 0$, and $X_2 = 1{,}250$.) Recall that we have a total availability of 30,000 hr of machining. Each unit of X_2 requires 20 hr of machining. Therefore, the 1,250 units of X_2 require 20(1,250) or 25,000 hr of machining. Thus, we have 5,000 hr left over or unused; that is, $X_m = 5{,}000$. We can rewrite the first constraint to obtain

$$X_m = 30{,}000 - 10X_1 - 20X_2$$

where

$$X_1 = 0$$

and

$$X_2 = 1{,}250$$

Thus,

$$X_m = 5{,}000$$

In terms of the tableau, we take the right-hand-side entry for X_m and subtract from it the new level of X_2 times its technological coefficient:

$$X_m = 30{,}000 - 1{,}250(20) = 5{,}000$$

Similarly,

$$X_e = 30{,}000 - 1{,}250(5) = 23{,}750$$
$$X_p = 6{,}250 - 1{,}250(5) = 0$$

This is as expected; however, X_2 now uses all of X_p.

The profit coefficients on the left-hand side now include 300 for X_2. This says that if we give up one unit of X_2, there is an associated opportunity cost of 300. We can readily fill in the column under X_2, X_m, and X_e, as we know that they are the variables in the new basic solution. Each variable has a 1 in the matching row and column, with 0s in all other column entries; for example, the column for X_2 can be read that for this solution it takes 0 units of X_m, 0 units of X_e, and 1 unit of X_2; that is, X_2 is a perfect substitute for itself.

5.2 / The Simplex Method

With this information we can begin the second tableau. So far we have developed the following information:

C_j		200 X_1	300 X_2	0 X_m	0 X_e	0 X_p	RHS
0	X_m		0	1	0		5,000
0	X_e		0	0	1		23,750
300	X_2		1	0	0		1,250

The tableau indicates the new basic solution involves $X_1 = X_p = 0$, $X_m = 5{,}000$, $X_e = 23{,}750$, and $X_2 = 1{,}250$, and the objective function value is \$375,000, that is, $1{,}250 \times \$300$.

Referring back to Figure 5–2, this second tableau corresponds to point b on the graph. The other columns X_1 and X_p must be developed in order to complete the tableau.

WHAT ARE THE NEW TECHNOLOGICAL RATES OF SUBSTITUTION?—STEP 5

To complete the second tableau we use the information from the initial tableau and apply matrix algebra manipulations. Recall that the last line of the initial tableau came from the third equation of the standard form,

$$1.25X_1 + 5X_2 + 0X_m + 0X_e + 1X_p = 6250$$

We can multiply this equation by a constant without changing its content. We already know that we want the coefficient of X_2 to be 1, as X_2 is a basic variable in the new solution. Thus, we multiply this equation by $\frac{1}{5}$ and we have

$$\frac{1.25}{5}X_1 + \frac{5}{5}X_2 + \frac{0}{5}X_m + \frac{0}{5}X_e + \frac{1}{5}X_p = \frac{6250}{5}$$

or

$$0.25X_1 + 1X_2 + 0X_m + 0X_e + 0.2X_p = 1250$$

Thus, 0.25, 1, 0, 0, 0.2, and 1250 are the entries in the third row of the second tableau. We already knew some of these values from above, but we now have completed the third row with the coefficients of X_1 and X_p.

To obtain the second row of the second tableau, we return to the second row of the first tableau and the standard form. The second equation is

$$15X_1 + 5X_2 + 0X_m + 1X_e + 0X_p = 30{,}000$$

Now, for the second tableau we want the coefficient of X_2 to be 0. How do we obtain this result? We can multiply one linear equation by a constant and add it to another equation. So we can take the third-row equation of our second tableau:

$$0.25X_1 + 1X_2 + 0X_m + 0X_e + 0.2X_p = 1250$$

Multiplying by -5, we have

$$-1.25X_1 - 5X_2 + 0X_m + 0X_e - 1X_p = -6250$$

We now add this equation to the second equation:

$$-1.25X_1 - 5X_2 + 0X_m + 0X_e - 1X_p = -6250$$
$$\underline{15X_1 + 5X_2 + 0X_m + 1X_e + 0X_p = 30{,}000}$$
$$13.75X_1 + 0X_2 + 0X_m + 1X_e - 1X_p = 23{,}750$$

We have obtained the "zero" coefficient of X_2 as desired. Thus, for the second row of the second tableau, the entries are 13.75, 0, 0, 1, -1, and 23,750.

To obtain the entries for the first row, we proceed in the same way. We want to obtain a "zero" coefficient for X_2. From the first tableau and the standard form, we have

$$10X_1 + 20X_2 + 1X_m + 0X_e + 0X_p = 30{,}000$$

Take the third row equation of the second tableau and multiply by -20. We have

$$-5X_1 - 20X_2 + 0X_m + 0X_e - 4X_p = -25{,}000$$

We then add the two equations:

$$-5X_1 - 20X_2 + 0X_m + 0X_e - 4X_p = -25{,}000$$
$$\underline{10X_1 + 20X_2 + 1X_m + 0X_e + 0X_p = 30{,}000}$$
$$5X_1 + 0X_2 + 1X_m + 0X_e - 4X_p = 5{,}000$$

The first-row entries are then 5, 0, 1, 0, -4, and 5,000 for the second tableau.

We can now write the complete second tableau as

C_j		X_1	X_2	X_m	X_e	X_p	RHS
0	X_m	5	0	1	0	-4	5,000
0	X_e	13.75	0	0	1	-1	23,750
300	X_p	0.25	1	0	0	0.2	1,250

The right-hand-side entries were obtained in two different ways, both ways yielding the correct answer. Our initial explanation for the RHS

5.3 / The Second Iteration

entries related the approach directly to the graph in Figure 5–2. This completes one iteration of the simplex method.

CAN WE DO BETTER?—STEP 6

We have completed one *iteration*. The second tableau can now be completed. Again, we must ask ourselves: "Can we do better?" To answer this question, we calculate the marginal returns for adding either X_1 or X_p to our solution.

C_j		200 X_1	300 X_2	0 X_m	0 X_e	0 X_p	RHS
0 X_m		5	0	1	0	−4	5,000
0 X_e		13.75	0	0	1	−1	23,750
300 X_2		0.25	1	0	0	0.2	1,250
	C_j	200				0	
	−Z_j	− 5(0)				− (−4)(0)	
		− 13.75(0)				− (−1)(0)	
		− 0.25(300)				− 0.2(300)	
	$C_j - Z_j$	= 125				= −60	

From this we note that this second tableau is not optimal, as the marginal return for X_1 is positive, $125. Further, to recover one unit of X_p (unused painting time) would "cost" $60, even if used in the current, nonoptimal fashion. Thus, this iteration is complete and we must go back to step 1 and continue our analysis.

5.3 The Second Iteration

Analysis of the $C_j - Z_j$ values (step 1) indicates that the current solution is not optimal, because $C_j - Z_j$ for X_1 is positive. Thus, X_1 should be brought into the solution as the pivot column, because each unit will increase profit P by $125. We must now determine how much of X_1 we can produce (step 3). To determine this limit we perform another analysis of the current RHS values over the X_1 column values as shown in the partial tableau.

		X_1	X_2	S_m	X_e	X_p	Ratio
X_m	Pivot row	5				5,000	1,000
X_p	Pivot element	13.75				23,750	1,727.27
X_2		0.25				1,250	5,000
		Pivot Column					

Thus, the X_m row is the pivot row and 5 is the pivot element. We can now proceed to steps 4 and 5. We know 1, 0, 0 as column entries in the X_1 column for the third tableau. To find the first row of the third tableau, we first write the first row of the second tableau in equation form as

$$5X_1 + 0X_2 + 1X_m + 0X_e - 4X_p = 5000$$

To obtain a coefficient of 1 or X_1, we multiply by $\frac{1}{5}$:

$$\tfrac{1}{5} \times 5X_1 + 0X_2 + \tfrac{1}{5}X_m + 0X_e - \tfrac{1}{5} \times 4X_p = \tfrac{1}{5} \times 5000$$

or

$$1X_1 + 0X_2 + .2X_m + 0X_e - 0.8X_p = 1000$$

Thus, the first-row entries are 1, 0, 0.2, 0, -0.8, and 1000.

To find the second row, we begin with the equation form of the second tableau:

$$13.75X_1 + 0X_2 + 0X_m + 1X_e - 1X_p = 23{,}750$$

Multiplying our new first equation by -13.75, we have

$$-13.75X_1 + 0X_2 - 2.75X_m + 0X_e + 11X_p = -13{,}750$$

We then add these two equations:

$$
\begin{aligned}
-13.75X_1 + 0X_2 - 2.75X_m + 0X_e + 11X_p &= -13{,}750 \\
13.75X_1 + 0X_2 + 0X_m + 1X_e - 1X_p &= 23{,}750 \\
\hline
0X_1 + 0X_2 - 2.75X_m + 1X_e + 10X_p &= 10{,}000
\end{aligned}
$$

Thus, the second-row entries are 0, 0, -2.75, 1, 10, and 10,000.

The third row is developed in the same way. The third row from the second tableau in equation form is

$$0.25X_1 + 1X_2 + 0X_m + 0X_e + 0.2X_p = 1250$$

Multiplying the new first equation by -0.25 and adding gives

$$
\begin{aligned}
-0.25X_1 + 0X_2 - 0.05X_m + 0X_e + 0.2X_p &= -250 \\
0.25X_1 + 1X_2 + 0X_m + 0X_e + 0.2X_p &= 1250 \\
\hline
0X_1 + 1X_2 - 0.05X_m + 0X_e + 0.4X_p &= 1000
\end{aligned}
$$

The third-row entries are then 0, 1, -0.05, 0, 0.4, and 1000.

The third tableau can now be written as

	X_1	X_2	X_m	X_e	X_p	RHS
X_1	1	0	0.2	0	-0.8	1,000
X_e	0	0	-2.75	1	10	10,000
X_2	0	1	-0.05	0	0.4	1,000

5.4 / The Third Iteration

To complete the third tableau we add the simplex criterion evaluations. The completed third tableau is

C_j		C_j 200 X_1	300 X_2	0 X_m	0 X_e	0 X_p	RHS
200	X_1	1	0	0.2	0	−0.8	1,000
0	X_e	0	0	−2.75	1	10	10,000
300	X_2	0	1	−0.05	0	0.4	1,000
	C_j		0	0		0	
	−Z_j			− 0.2(200)		− (−0.8)200	
				− (−2.75)(0)		− 10(0)	
				− (−0.05)300		− 0.4(300)	
	$C_j - Z_j$			= −25		= 40	

This tableau corresponds to point c in Figure 5–2. It is not an optimal solution, because the $C_j - Z_j$ value for X_p is positive. Therefore, according to our step 1, we must proceed to a third iteration.

5.4 The Third Iteration

The only choice for entering variable is X_p, because it has the only positive $C_j - Z_j$ value. The amount of X_p that can be introduced into the solution is

$$\text{Min}\left\{\frac{10{,}000}{10}, \frac{1{,}000}{0.4}\right\} = 1{,}000$$

(Note that we do not include negative technological coefficients such as −0.8 in this calculation.) This also identifies X_e as the pivot row and, consequently, the 10 in the X_p column as the pivot element. Repeating the third tableau partially, we have

	X_1	X_2	X_m	X_e	X_p		Ratio
X_1					−0.8	1,000	
X_e Pivot Row					(10)	10,000	1,000
X_2					0.4	1,000	2,500

Pivot Element   Pivot Column

Thus, the X_p column entries are 0, 1, 0 for the fourth tableau. To find the second row, we first write the equation form of the second row from the third tableau.

$$0X_1 + 0X_2 - 2.75X_m + 1X_e + 10X_p = 10{,}000$$

Multiplying by $\frac{1}{10}$, we have

$$0X_1 + 0X_2 - 0.275X_m + 0.1X_e + 1X_p = 1000$$

Thus, the second-row entries are 0, 0, -0.275, 0.1, 1, and 1000 for the fourth tableau. To find the first row, we write the first row from the third tableau.

$$1X_1 + 0X_2 + 0.2X_m + 0X_e - 0.8X_p = 1000$$

Multiplying the new second row by .8, we have

$$0X_1 + 0X_2 - 0.22X_m + 0.08X_e + 0.8X_p = 800$$

and adding, we obtain

$$\begin{array}{r} 0X_1 + 0X_2 - 0.22X_m + 0.08X_e + 0.8X_p = 800 \\ 1X_1 + 0X_2 + 0.2X_m + 0X_e - 0.8X_p = 1000 \\ \hline 1X_1 + 0X_2 - 0.02X_m + 0.08X_e + 0X_p = 1800 \end{array}$$

The first-row entries are 1, 0, -0.02, 0.08, 0, and 1800. Proceeding in the same way, the third row of the third tableau in equation form is

$$0X_1 + 1X_2 - 0.05X_m + X_e + 0.4X_p = 1000$$

We take our new second row and multiply by -0.4 to obtain

$$0X_1 + 0X_2 + 0.11X_m - 0.04X_e - 0.4X_p = -400$$

Adding these two equations, we have

$$0X_1 + 1X_2 + 0.06X_m - 0.04X_e + 0X_p = 600$$

The third-row entries are then 0, 1, 0.06, -0.04, 0, and 600. The fourth tableau is then

	X_1	X_2	X_m	X_e	X_p	
X_1	1	0	-0.02	0.08	0	1800
X_p	0	0	-0.275	0.1	1	1000
X_2	0	1	0.06	-0.04	0	600

To complete this tableau, we need to add the simplex criterion evaluations. The completed fourth tableau is

5.5 / The Optimal Solution—Primal and Dual

C_j		200 X_1	300 X_2	0 X_m	0 X_e	0 X_p	RHS
200	X_1	1	0	−0.02	0.08	0	1800
0	X_p	0	0	−0.275	0.1	1	1000
300	X_2	0	1	0.06	−0.04	0	600
	C_j			0	0		
	$-Z_j$			− (−0.02)(200) − (−0.275)0 − 0.06(300)	− 0.08(200) − 0.1(0) − (−0.04)300		
	$C_j - Z_j$			= −14	= −4		

This fourth tableau is optimal by our criterion. That is, none of the variables not included in the solution (X_m and X_e) would increase the value of our objective function if they were included. The solution corresponds to point d of Figure 5–2. Our algebraic solution is the same as the graphical solution, but the algebraic approach is more general.

Note that the second tableau used all of painting, that is, $X_p = 0$. But the final optimal tableau has X_p in the basis at a positive level. In general, a variable may enter and leave the basis a number of times in the process of finding an optimal solution.

5.5 The Optimal Solution—Primal and Dual

The fourth tableau is the optimal tableau and contains the optimal solutions for both the primal and the dual problems. We have solved both problems with a single approach. We shall now review the tableau and interpret these solutions.

The primal solution is given in the right-hand column with the corresponding variables down the left-hand side. Namely, we have

$$X_1 = 1800 \quad X_p = 1000 \quad X_2 = 600$$

This is the optimal basic solution. Further, it is implied that $X_m = 0$ and $X_e = 0$. (Some authors omit the listing of the variable names on the left; thus the optimal solution can be identified with the corresponding column that contains a 1 and the remainder 0.) The optimal solution profit is 1,800 × $200 + 600 × $300 = $540,000. The above solution indicates that the products X_1 and X_2 are produced and there is some excess painting (X_p) capacity of 1000 hr. The slack variables for machining and assembling are zero, and these resources are therefore fully consumed.

If we now apply our fundamental marginal return question to the optimal tableau, that is, step 1, we find that it is not profitable to introduce either X_m or X_e into the solution. But let us ask: "What would be the cost if we did?" The calculations at the bottom of columns X_m and X_p give the answer. It would cost $14 to recover one unit of machining and $4 for assembling. That is, there is an opportunity cost of $14 if someone took away 1 hr of machine time, and $4 for 1 hr of assembly time. Now consider the question; "What do we gain if we have an additional unit of machining or assembling?" The answer is $14 for machining and $4 for assembling. This means that by adding or subtracting 1 hr to the available machining hours, we would increase or decrease the value of our objective function by $14. The corresponding change in the objective function resulting from the addition or subtraction of one assembly hour would be $4. That is, $14 is the marginal value of machining, and $4 is the marginal value of assembling. Indeed, these are the shadow prices or dual variable values we derived in the previous chapter.

The dual linear program was given in the previous chapter

$$\begin{aligned}
\text{Min:} \quad & 30{,}000 U_1 + 30{,}000 U_2 + 6{,}250 U_3 \\
\text{Subject to:} \quad & 10 U_1 + 15 U_2 + 1.25 U_3 \geq 200 \\
& 20 U_1 + 5 U_2 + 5 U_3 \geq 300 \\
& U_1 \geq 0 \quad U_2 \geq 0 \quad U_3 \geq 0
\end{aligned}$$

From the optimal tableau, we find the solution for the dual variables in the $C_j - Z_j$ row:

$$U_1 = 14 \quad U_2 = 4 \quad U_3 = 0$$

The optimal solution is given as $30{,}000(14) + 30{,}000(4) + 6{,}250(0) = \$540{,}000$. The dual objective function value is the same value as the primal objective function value at optimality.

5.6 Variations

Not every linear program has a unique finite primal and dual solution as does our illustrative problem. An *unbounded solution* exists when there is no finite solution. This is evident in a tableau when a proposed entering primal variable is not limited. A *degenerate solution* occurs when a basic variable value in the finite tableau is zero. *Multiple optimal solutions* imply that more than one basic solution has the highest objective function. This occurs in the simplex method when a nonbasic

5.6 / Variations

variable can enter without changing the objective function value. Let us consider each situation in more detail.

UNBOUNDED SOLUTIONS

An *unbounded solution* occurs when a proposed entering X_{10} basic variable is not bounded, or is unlimited. For example, consider variable X_{10} in the following tableau.

3

X_{10}	X_{11}	RHS	Ratio Q/Pivot
0		100	∞
0		20	∞
−1		10	—
−8		1000	—
0		48	∞

According to Figure 5–1, we should try to apply our rule for choosing the leaving variable. First, the negative numbers (-1, -8) do not apply, as they represent complements of X_{10}, that is, their availability increases as X_{10} increases. They are not limiting. Further, the ratio of the right-hand-side numbers to zero is not finite—indicating X_{10} can enter at any value, or it is unbounded. We now restate the unbounded solution criterion. Any column that has only zeros or negative coefficients in its technology column implies an unbounded solution. For all resource-allocation problems, an unbounded solution indicates a formulation error. Because no resource is of infinite capacity, we have simply omitted a limiting resource, mistakenly changed a sign, or in general, misspecified the problem.

To illustrate, let us take our example problem and assume that we made several formulation errors in the primal linear program with respect to the technological coefficients of X_2. Assume that the primal formulation is

$$\text{Max:} \quad P = 200X_1 + 300X_2$$
$$\text{Subject to:} \quad 10X_1 - 20X_2 \leq 30{,}000$$
$$15X_1 + 0X_2 \leq 30{,}000$$
$$1.25X_1 - 5X_2 \leq 6{,}250$$
$$X_1 \geq 0 \quad X_2 \geq 0$$

Applying the usual procedure, the initial tableau, including the simplex criterion evaluation and the ratios, is

C_j			200 X_1	300 X_2	0 X_m	0 X_e	0 X_p	RHS	Ratio
0	X_m		10	−20	1	0	0	30,000	—
0	X_e		15	0	0	1	0	30,000	∞
0	X_p		1.25	−5	0	0	1	6,250	—
		C_j $-Z_j$ $C_j - Z_j$	200 − 10(0) − 15(0) − 1.25(0) = 200	300 + 20(0) + 0(0) + 5(0) = 300					

Pivot
Column

The simplex criterion indicates that X_2 is the entering variable. But there is no leaving variable because the ratio calculations indicated that X_2 is not restricted. It has an unbounded solution.

Our formulation error involved the signs on the use of resources to make bicycles. The negative signs indicate a supply of additional resources rather than a usage of resources, which is clearly incorrect. This can be seen directly if one considers the dual linear program. It is

$$\text{Min:} \quad P' = 30{,}000U_1 + 30{,}000U_2 + 6{,}250U_3$$
$$\text{Subject to:} \quad 10U_1 + 15U_2 + 1.25U_3 \geq 200$$
$$-20U_1 + 0U_2 - 5U_3 \geq 300$$
$$U_1 \geq 0 \quad U_2 \geq 0 \quad U_3 \geq 0$$

The second constraint presents an impossible situation. For this constraint to be satisfied, either U_1 or U_3 must take on a negative value. This would violate, however, the nonnegativity conditions, $U_1 \geq 0$ and $U_3 \geq 0$. Thus, there is no feasible solution to the formulation.

DEGENERATE SOLUTIONS

A *degenerate solution* occurs when a basic variable has a zero value for the RHS coefficient in the simplex tableau. For example, let us assume that there were only 5250 hr of painting time available in our example. This is 1000 hr fewer than in the original problem, and as the optimal solution has 1000 unused hours of painting time, the optimal solution for the modified problem has $X_p = 0$, but with X_p as a basis variable.

5.6 / Variations

The primal linear program would be

$$\text{Max:} \quad P = 200X_1 + 300X_2$$
$$\text{Subject to:} \quad 10X_1 + 20X_2 \leq 30{,}000$$
$$15X_1 + 5X_2 \leq 30{,}000$$
$$1.25X_1 + 5X_2 \leq 5{,}250$$
$$X_1 \geq 0 \quad X_2 \geq 0$$

The initial tableau is then

C_j		200 X_1	300 X_2	0 X_m	0 X_e	0 X_p	RHS
0	X_m	10	20	1	0	0	30,000
0	X_e	15	5	0	1	0	30,000
0	X_p	1.25	5	0	0	1	5,250

Applying the simplex method, we would obtain the optimal tableau as

C_j		X_1	X_2	X_m	X_e	X_p	RHS
200	X_1	1	0	−0.02	0.08	0	1800
0	X_p	0	0	−0.275	0.1	1	0
300	X_2	0	1	0.06	−0.04	0	600
$C_j - Z_j$				−14	−4		

The solution is $X_1 = 1800$, $X_p = 0$, and $X_2 = 600$. X_p is a basic solution variable at the zero level. The graphical solution to this problem, with the painting hours reduced by 1000, is shown in Figure 5–3. The painting constraint now passes through point d, that is, all three constraints pass through point d, and all are exactly consumed at the optimal solution. As is clear from the graph, any two of the constraints are sufficient to determine point b. Thus, it is also possible to include X_m or X_e as a basic variable. Any one of the three can be basic at the zero level, and an optimal solution results. However, note that a different dual solution results for each of the three choices. The result is that the dual solution is not unique; and we obtain a family of solutions for the dual values, which causes difficulties for the usual marginal analysis.

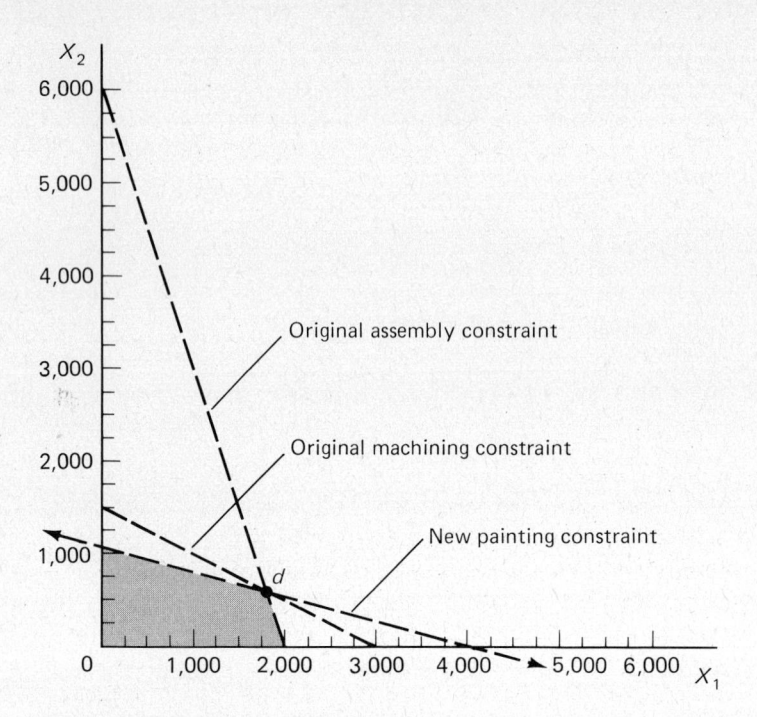

Figure 5–3. Graphical representation of a change in the painting constraint.

MULTIPLE OPTIMAL SOLUTIONS

Multiple optimal solutions occur when a nonbasic variable can enter from an optimal solution without decreasing the optimal function value. Let X_{11} be a nonbasic variable in the following partial tableau:

			C_j	20
C_j				X_{11}
1	X_1			1
20	X_2			0
10	X_3			1
		C_j		20
				$-$ 10(1)
		$-Z_j$		$-$ 0(20)
				$-$ 1(10)
		$C_j - Z_j$		$= 0$

where 0 is the simplex criterion-marginal profit minus marginal cost calculation. Clearly, X_{11} can enter the solution without changing the objective function value. Recall from Chapter 4 that we argued that

5.7 / Extensions

multiple optimal solutions result when the objective function has the same slope as a binding constraint. In more general terms, the algebraic identification is when a nonbasic variable can enter the solution without changing the objective function, and thus, there are two alternative basic optimal solutions. This change in basis is like moving from one corner-point optimal solution to another corner-point optimal solution.

5.7 Extensions

ARTIFICIAL VARIABLES

Linear programs can include equality and greater-than constraints as well as less-than constraints. Also, we can minimize the objective function as well as maximize. As the name suggests an *artificial variable* is a variable created for the convenience of the simplex method; that is, it makes the method work without having any real meaning on its own. Consider an equality constraint as

$$25X_1 + 6X_2 = 20{,}000$$

This is a perfectly reasonable statement and constraint, but there is no slack variable to add on the left to be in the first set of basic variables. But the simplex method requires an initial basic variable in the first basic solution, represented by a positive "one." Therefore, we add an artificial variable, call it X_a. Then we have

$$25X_1 + 6X_2 + 1X_a = 20{,}000$$

Now, X_a can be in our first basic solution. But we know that it must be zero in the final optimal solution, so we assign a very high negative profit to this variable in the objective function for maximization, say, $-1000.^2$ X_a is artificially created to obtain a desired result.

SURPLUS VARIABLES

Similarly, greater-than constraints require some modification to make the simplex method work. Let

$$30X_1 + 40X_2 \geq 10{,}000$$

be a constraint. Now, we must subtract a positive term from the left to yield an equality constraint. Namely,

$$30X_1 + 40X_2 - X_s = 10{,}000$$

---

[2] For a minimization problem, we would assign a high positive cost in the objective function, i.e., $+1000$.

where X_s is a nonnegative variable. It is called a *surplus variable*. X_s cannot be in the first tableau, because $X_s = -10{,}000$ if $X_1 = X_2 = 0$, and a negative X_s is not permitted. Thus, we must add an artificial variable, and proceed as above. Thus,

$$30X_1 + 40X_2 - X_s + X_b = 10{,}000$$

where X_b is an artificial variable. Again, we assign a high negative profit coefficient in the objective function.

Let us now take our example problem and add these two constraints, and then state a new initial tableau.

$$\text{Max:} \quad 200X_1 + 300X_2$$
$$\text{Subject to:} \quad 10X_1 + 20X_2 \leq 30{,}000$$
$$15X_1 + 5X_2 \leq 30{,}000$$
$$1.25X_1 + 5X_2 \leq 6{,}250$$
$$25X_1 + 6X_2 = 20{,}000$$
$$30X_1 + 40X_2 \geq 10{,}000$$
$$X_1, X_2 \geq 0$$

Adding slack variables, surplus variables, and artificial variables to the constraints and objective function, the standard form is then

Max:
Subject to:
$$200X_1 + 300X_2 + 0X_m + 0X_e + 0X_p - 1000X_a + 0X_s - 1000X_b$$
$$10X_1 + 20X_2 + 1X_m \qquad\qquad\qquad\qquad\qquad\qquad = 30{,}000$$
$$15X_1 + 5X_2 \qquad + 1X_e \qquad\qquad\qquad\qquad\qquad = 30{,}000$$
$$1.25X_1 + 5X_2 \qquad\qquad\qquad + 1X_p \qquad\qquad\qquad = 6{,}250$$
$$25X_1 + 6X_2 \qquad\qquad\qquad\qquad\qquad + 1X_a \qquad\qquad = 20{,}000$$
$$30X_1 + 40X_2 \qquad\qquad\qquad\qquad\qquad\qquad - 1X_s + 1X_b = 10{,}000$$
$$X\text{'s} \geq 0$$

Now, the initial tableau is

C_j		C_j 200 X_1	300 X_2	0 X_m	0 X_e	0 X_p	−1,000 X_a	0 X_s	−1,000 X_b	RHS
0	X_m	10	20	1	0	0	0	0	0	30,000
0	X_e	15	5	0	1	0	0	0	0	30,000
0	X_p	1.25	5	0	0	1	0	0	0	6,250
−1,000	X_a	25	6	0	0	0	1	0	0	20,000
−1,000	X_b	30	40	0	0	0	0	−1	1	10,000

Then we proceed in the usual manner. The reader should verify that the simplex criterion calculation for X_1 is

$$200 + 1{,}000(25) + 1{,}000(30) = 55{,}200$$

and for X_2 is

$$300 + 1{,}000(6) + 1{,}000(40) = 46{,}300$$

with X_1 as the entering variable. The ratio calculation is

$$\text{Min}\left[\frac{30{,}000}{10}, \frac{30{,}000}{15}, \frac{6{,}250}{1.25}, \frac{20{,}000}{25}, \frac{10{,}000}{30}\right] = 333.3$$

The minimum is associated with X_b, and it is the leaving variable.

We continue to calculate the optimal tableau, which must have X_a and X_b as nonbasic variables.

MINIMIZATION

Minimization problems can be handled in two ways. First, slack variables, surplus variables, and artificial variables are added in the usual manner. Then, one method of solving a minimization problem is to convert it to an equivalent maximization problem:

$$\text{Min } Z \equiv -\text{Max}(-Z)$$

or, for as an example,

$$\text{Min } Z = 2X_1 + 3X_2 = \text{Max}(-Z) = 2X_1 - 3X_2$$

That is, for minimization, change the sign on all coefficients in the objective function, and proceed to maximize. The sign of the resulting objective function value must be changed to obtain the correct sign.

Another approach is to change the criterion for choosing the entering variable. Recall that for maximization we choose the variable with the largest marginal revenue minus marginal cost. Then, for minimization, we choose the variable with the largest negative cost (or largest negative value). The stopping criterion is to determine when all dual variable values are nonnegative.

5.8 Sensitivity Analysis and the Limits of the Solution

Sensitivity analysis involves a continuing analysis of the primal and the dual relationships at the optimal solution. In general, the idea is to find, for one variable at a time, the limits of possible changes that can be made in the profit coefficients and input resources for the current optimal solution to remain optimal. We have already performed similar analysis in Chapter 4 on Girth, Inc., the belt manufacturer. There we found the limits of the optimal solution graphically. We now want to pursue the same ideas using an algebraic approach, beginning with the optimal tableau. We continue our analysis with the same example used previously in this chapter.

For easy reference, we repeat the optimal tableau.

C_j		200 X_1	300 X_2	0 X_m	0 X_e	0 X_p	RHS
200	X_1	1	0	−0.02	0.08	0	1800
0	X_p	0	0	−0.275	0.1	1	1000
300	X_2	0	1	0.06	−0.04	0	600
	$C_j - Z_j$			−14	−4		

Recall that machining and assembling are completely used in the optimal solution. Further, we know that one more unit of machining time has a marginal value of $14 per hour. Similarly, assembly time is worth $4 per hour.

CHANGES IN PROFIT COEFFICIENTS

We want to answer the question: How much can we change the profit coefficient of X_1 unicycles and have the current optimal solution remain optimal? Let the $200 profit coefficient in the optimal tableau be replaced by $200 + \Delta$, as shown in the following tableau. This solution can remain *optimal* if the *profitability calculations* for X_m and X_e remain nonpositive.

C_j		C_j 200 + Δ X_1	300 X_2	0 X_m	0 X_e	0 X_p	RHS
200 + Δ	X_1	1	0	−0.02	0.08	0	1800
0	X_p	0	0	−0.275	0.1	1	1000
300	X_2	0	1	0.06	−0.04	0	600
				−14	−4		

For X_m, the simplex criterion calculation is

$$
\begin{array}{l}
C_j \\
-Z_j \\
C_j - Z_j
\end{array}
\quad
\begin{cases}
0 \\
-(200 + \Delta)(-0.02) \\
+ 0(-0.275) \\
- 300(0.06) \\
\leq 0
\end{cases}
$$

or

$$0.02\Delta - 14 \leq 0$$

or

$$\Delta \leq 700$$

5.8 / Sensitivity Analysis and the Limits of the Solution

That is, the coefficient of X_1 can be increased by \$700 and the current solution remains optimal. For X_e, the calculation is

$$C_j \quad\quad 0$$
$$-Z_j \quad \begin{cases} -(200+\Delta)(0.08) \\ -(0)(0.1) \\ -(300)(-0.04) \end{cases}$$
$$C_j - Z_j \quad \leq 0$$

or

$$-0.08\Delta - 4 \leq 0$$

or

$$\Delta \geq -50$$

That is, the coefficient of X_1 can be decreased by \$50 and the current solution remains optimal.

In summary,

$$-50 \leq \Delta \leq 700$$

or, for the profit coefficient, we have the following range on the profit coefficient for X_1, P_1:

$$150 \leq P_1 \leq 900$$

The profit coefficient for X_1 can be any value between \$150 and \$900 and the current optimal solution remains optimal. Thus we do not need very accurate profit information for X_1 to make an optimal production decision. A manager would not be concerned about an accurate estimate for P_1—only that it is between \$150 and \$900.

For bicycles, X_2, we proceed in the same way. Let the profit coefficient for bicycles be $300 + \Delta$ in the optimal tableau.

C_j		C_j	200 X_1	300 + Δ X_2	0 X_m	0 X_e	0 X_p	RHS
200	X_1		1	0	−0.02	0.08	0	1800
0	X_p		0	0	−0.275	0.1	1	1000
300 + Δ	X_2		0	1	0.06	−0.04	0	600

The simplex criterion evaluation for X_m is

$$C_j - Z_j \quad \begin{cases} 0 \\ -200(-0.02) \\ -0(-0.275) \\ -(300+\Delta)(0.06) \end{cases} \leq 0$$

or

$$-0.06\Delta - 14 \leq 0$$

or

$$\Delta \geq -233.33$$

That is, the profit coefficient for bicycles can be decreased by $233.33 without changing the optimal basic solution.

For X_e the simplex criterion evaluation is

$$C_j - Z_j \quad \begin{cases} 0 \\ -200(0.08) \\ -0(0.1) \\ -(300+\Delta)(-0.04) \end{cases} \leq 0$$

or

$$0.04\Delta - 4 \leq 0$$
$$\Delta \leq 100$$

That is, the profit coefficient for bicycles can be increased by 100 without changing the optimal basic solution.

Thus, for $-233.33 \leq \Delta \leq 100$, the profit coefficient limits are $66.67 \leq P_2 \leq \$400$.

Sensitivity analysis to obtain the limits on the profit coefficients requires the current optimal solution to remain optimal.

CHANGES IN THE AVAILABILITY OF RESOURCES

We want to answer the question: How much can we change (increase or decrease) machining time, for example, and have the current optimal basic solution remain feasible? Why is this question important? If someone offers to rent us machining time at less than $14 per hour (or assembling at less than $4 per hour), it is advantageous to rent the machine, but for how many hours? Thus, we have to find the limits of the current solution, where the solution values may change but the

5.8 / Sensitivity Analysis and the Limits of the Solution

same variables remain in the basis; that is, X_1, X_p, and X_2 remain in the basis. These variables must remain feasible for any changes, that is, $X_1 \geq 0$, $X_p \geq 0$, and $X_2 \geq 0$. Thus, the question now becomes: What are the limits on machine time availability such that $X_1 \geq 0$, $X_p \geq 0$, and $X_2 \geq 0$?

Consider the slack variable, X_m, associated with machining time. If we had not used 1 hr of machining time, we have a new solution. This is the optimal solution, where each variable decreases by the amount required to gain one unit of X_m:

$$X_1 = 1800 - 0.02$$
$$X_p = 1000 - 0.275$$
$$X_2 = 600 + 0.06$$

Note that these are all positive and therefore feasible.

Now we want to determine a value of Δ hours of machining time and maintain feasibility. The conditions are that each optimal solution value remain nonnegative:

$$X_1 = 1800 - 0.02\Delta \geq 0$$
$$X_p = 1000 - 0.275\Delta \geq 0$$
$$X_2 = 600 + 0.06\Delta \geq 0$$

All three of the relations must be satisfied. They can be reduced to

$$90{,}000 \geq \Delta$$
$$3{,}636.36 \geq \Delta$$
$$-10{,}000 \leq \Delta$$

or

$$-10{,}000 \leq \Delta \leq 3{,}636.36$$

Thus, the original 30,000 hr of machining time can be decreased to 20,000 hr, or increased to 33,636.36 hr, and the current optimal solution remains feasible; that is,

$$20{,}000 \leq b_1 \leq 33{,}636.36$$

where b_1 is the original number of machine hours available. Note these calculations require feasibility of the current optimal solution as the fundamental criterion.

Similarly, we can determine the limits on assembly time. The required Δ must satisfy

$$X_1 = 1800 + 0.08\Delta \geq 0$$
$$X_p = 1000 + 0.1\Delta \geq 0$$
$$X_2 = 600 + 0.04\Delta \geq 0$$

All three relations must be satisfied. They reduce to

$$\Delta \geq -22,500$$
$$\Delta \geq -10,000$$
$$\Delta \leq 15,000$$

or $-10,000 \leq \Delta \leq 15,000$. Thus, the assembly time can be decreased to 20,000 hr or increased to 45,000 hr without changing the optimal basic solution.

This information is very important in assessing whether to increase the availability of resources. Here, if it were possible to lease up to 3636.36 hr of machining time at less than \$14 per hour, the company should do it. Similarly, if additional assembly hours are available at less than \$4 per hour, they should lease up to 15,000 hr.

Sensitivity analysis information is as important for management as knowing the optimal solution. Frequently, prices change or contracts are renegotiated, and management wants to know the impact. Re-

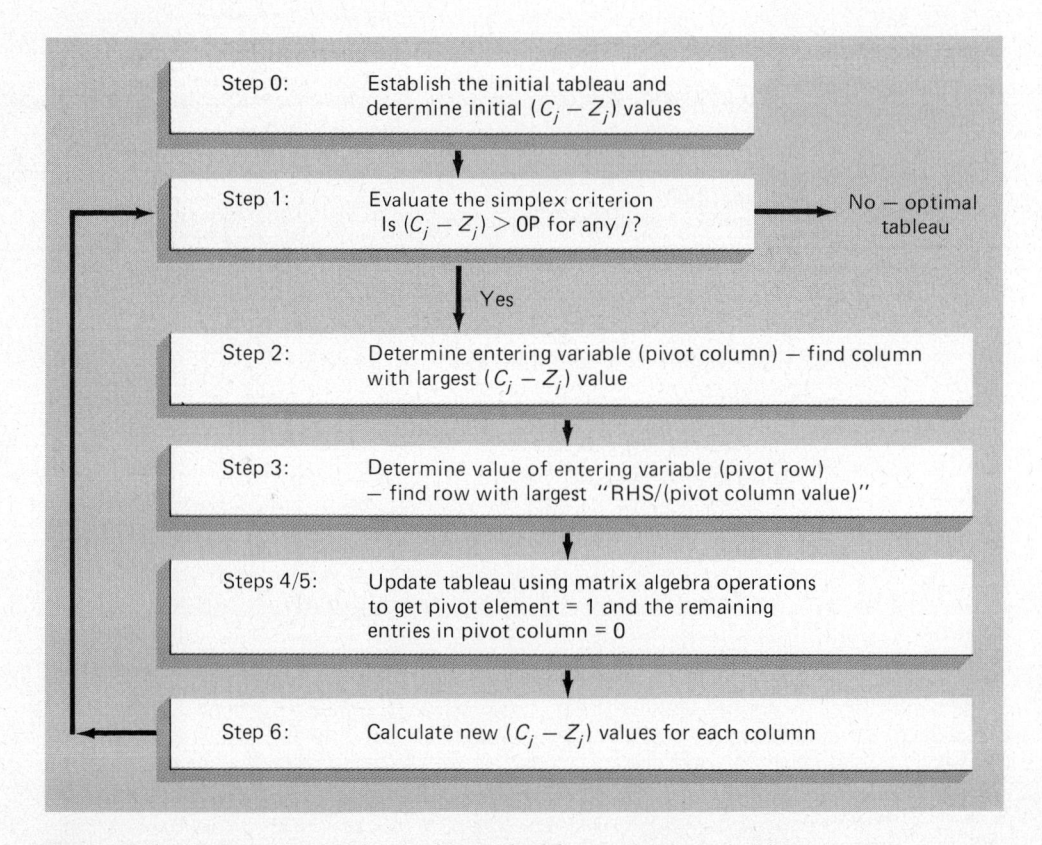

Step 0:	Establish the initial tableau and determine initial $(C_j - Z_j)$ values
Step 1:	Evaluate the simplex criterion. Is $(C_j - Z_j) > 0$ for any j? → No — optimal tableau
	↓ Yes
Step 2:	Determine entering variable (pivot column) — find column with largest $(C_j - Z_j)$ value
Step 3:	Determine value of entering variable (pivot row) — find row with largest "RHS/(pivot column value)"
Steps 4/5:	Update tableau using matrix algebra operations to get pivot element = 1 and the remaining entries in pivot column = 0
Step 6:	Calculate new $(C_j - Z_j)$ values for each column

Figure 5–4. Algebraic steps in the simplex method for maximization problems.

source availability can be changed through renting, leasing, or new investment. The value of the additional resource is given by the dual values, and sensitivity analysis gives the range for which this value is correct.

5.9 Summary

This chapter has presented the simplex method to solve linear programs. The following were covered:

1. Solving any linear program by the simplex method
2. Interpreting primal/dual relations in the optimal tableau
3. Finding the limits of the current optimal solution using sensitivity analysis based on the simplex method
4. Figure 5–4 presents a summary of the algebraic manipulations employed in the simplex method.

Glossary

Artificial variable. A nonnegative variable added to the left-hand side of an equality constraint to obtain a basic solution for the simplex method. For example, $2X_1 + 3X_2 - X_4 = 7$ is converted to $2X_1 + 3X_2 - X_4 + X_a = 7$, where X_a is an artificial variable.

Basic solution. A solution to a linear program that chooses the same number of nonnegative variables (ordinary and slack) as constraints with the remaining variables being necessarily zero. At least one basic solution will be optimal. Each simplex tableau represents a basic solution. In Chapter 3, a corner-point solution is a basic solution.

Degenerate solution. A solution that has a basis variable of value zero.

Iteration. One complete application of the simplex method.

Minimization problem. A linear program for which the objective function is to be set at its lowest possible value.

Multiple optimum. When there is more than one basic solution that yields the highest objective function for maximization. In the simplex tableau, alternative optima are identified by a zero marginal revenue for at least one nonbasic variable.

Pivot element. In the simplex tableau, the intersection of the variable that leaves the basis, that is the pivot row, and the variable that enters the basis, that is, the pivot column.

Sensitivity analysis. The determination of the limits on the range of each profit coefficient, and each limited resource, for which the optimal solution remains optimal at the current basis.

Simplex criterion. A solution that evaluates, for each variable not in the current solution, its marginal profit minus its marginal opportunity cost. When no variable has a positive marginal return, an optimal solution has been found.

Simplex method. An algebraic method to solve a linear program of any given size. It involves a stepwise iterative procedure, which continually finds a better solution and finds the optimal solution in a finite number of steps.

Simplex tableau. A convenient table for performing the simplex method. Each tableau represents one solution in the iterative procedure.

Slack variable. A nonnegative variable added to the left-hand side of a "less-than" constraint to convert it to an equality. For example, $2X_1 + 3X_2 \leq 7$ is changed to $2X_1 + 3X_2 + X_3 = 7$, where X_3 is the slack variable.

Standard form of a linear program. A form that changes all inequality and equality constraints to equality constraints by adding the required slack variables, surplus variables, and artificial variables such that there is either a slack variable or artificial variable in each constraint. This permits easy identification of an initial basic solution for applying the simplex method.

Surplus variable. A nonnegative variable subtracted from the left-hand side of a "greater-than" constraint to convert it to an equality. For example, $2X_1 + 3X_2 \geq 7$ is converted to $2X_1 + 3X_2 - X_4 = 7$, where X_4 is a surplus variable.

Technological rate of substitution. The use of a resource to make a unit of output. It is sometimes called an input-output ratio.

Unbounded solution. A solution that exists when there is no finite solution to the linear program. It is identified in the simplex tableau when a proposed entering variable is infinite.

Problems

1. Using the simplex method, solve the Girth, Inc., problem stated in Chapter 4. Read and interpret both the primal and dual solutions. Relate to the graph for the problem given in Chapter 4. Write out the dual problem completely.
2. Using the simplex method, find the optimal solution to Problem 2 of Chapter 4. Write out the dual problem.
3. Using the simplex method, find the optimal solution to Problem 4 of Chapter 4.
4. Using the simplex method, solve:

$$\begin{aligned}
\text{Max:} \quad & 100X_1 + 200X_2 + 300X_3 \\
\text{Subject to:} \quad & 1X_1 + 1X_2 \leq 200 \\
& 3X_1 + 4X_2 + X_3 \leq 400 \\
& X_1, X_2, X_3 \geq 0
\end{aligned}$$

5. A manufacturer of lawn furniture makes three products: lawn chairs, benches, and tables. Processing of these products is done on a tube-bending machine and a drilling machine. A table requires 1 hr of time on the tube-bending machine and 2 hr on the drill; the contribution to profit and overhead per table is $5. A lawn chair requires 1 hr on the tube bender

Problems

and 1 hr on the drill; the contribution to profit and overhead per chair is $3. A bench requires 1 hr on the tube bender and no time on the drill. The contribution to profit and overhead per bench is $3. There are 10 hr of time per day available on the tube bender and 12 hr on the drill.

a. Find the optimal solution for the production of lawn chairs, benches, and tables, using the simplex method.
b. Indicate the values of the dual variables, that is, the shadow prices.
c. Verify your solution by a graphical solution. Hint: Find the graphical solution to the dual.

6. *(CPA)* Choose the best answer and justify.
   a. A final tableau[3] for a linear programming profit-maximization problem is shown below:

	X_1	X_2	X_3	S_1	S_2	
X_1	1	0	4	3	−7	50
X_2	0	1	−2	−6	2	60
	0	0	5	1	9	1200

If X_1, X_2, and X_3 represent products, S_1 refers to square feet (in thousands) of warehouse capacity, and S_2 refers to labor hours (in hundreds), the number of X_2 that should be produced to maximize profit would be
(1) 60
(2) 50
(3) 1
(4) 0
(5) None of the above

b. Assuming the same facts as in part a, the contribution to profit of an additional 100 hr of labor would be
(1) 9
(2) 2
(3) 1
(4) −7
(5) None of the above

c. Assuming the same facts as in part a, an additional 1000 ft² of warehouse space would
(1) Increase X_1 by 3 units and decrease X_2 by 6 units
(2) Decrease X_2 by 6 units and increase X_1 by 2 units
(3) Decrease X_1 by 7 units and increase X_2 by 2 units
(4) Increase X_1 by 3 units and decrease X_2 by 7 units
(5) Do none of the above

---

[3]This tableau is different than the format of the text. Nonetheless, the student can make the necessary correspondence to read this format.

7. The following problem appeared as a case study situation found in the article by Alfred Rappaport, "Sensitivity Analysis in Decision Making," *The Accounting Review*, July 1967, p. 443.

> Assume that during the recent surge of demand for color television sets, a manufacturing company was considering how best to utilize its production facilities to maximize profits. The company produces three styles of black-and-white sets (standard, deluxe, and super) and a color set. The company confidently believes it can sell as many sets as it can produce. Each set goes through the plant's three departments—subassembly, assembly, and testing. The number of man-hours of labor required in each department is as follows:
>
> | | Standard | Deluxe | Super | Color |
> | --- | --- | --- | --- | --- |
> | Subassembly | 12 | 15 | 15 | 25 |
> | Assembly | 10 | 12 | 13 | 30 |
> | Testing | 0.5 | 0.6 | 0.6 | 2.0 |
>
> The capacity of the plant allows no more than 3500, 3000, and 240 daily man-hours in the subassembly, assembly, and testing departments, respectively. Due to existing contractual agreements, at least 10 standard and 10 deluxe models must be produced daily. The profit contribution (revenue minus variable costs) from the sale of each set is as follows:
>
> | | Standard | Deluxe | Super | Color |
> | --- | --- | --- | --- | --- |
> | Profit contribution | $25 | $30 | $40 | $100 |
>
> a. Formulate the appropriate linear program. Write both the primal and the dual.
> b. Develop the second tableau of the simplex method.
> c. If available, use a standard computer routine to find the optimal solution. If it is an available option, ask for a complete printout of all tableaux used to find the solution. Compare the second tableau with part b.
> d. If available, request a sensitivity-analysis printout. Verify some of the numerical results to enhance your understanding of the results.

8. A company with two major products (A and B) must make a product-mix decision for a year. The company is in a seller's market and expects to sell all it can produce of either product. Product A goes through a machining process and is stored waiting for distribution to field warehouses. Product B must, in addition to the steps required for A, be painted. The following information is available:

… Problems

	Machining, hr/piece	Painting, hr/piece	Warehousing, ft²/piece	Profit Margin/piece
Product A	2	0	4	$1
Product B	3	1	3	$3
Capacities	36,000 hr/yr	6,000 hr/yr	36,000 ft²	

The tableau for the optimal solution is

		0 X_m	0 X_p	0 X_w	1 X_A	3 X_B	C
0	X_m	1	$-\frac{3}{2}$	$-\frac{1}{2}$	0	0	9,000
3	X_B	0	1	0	0	1	6,000
1	X_A	0	$-\frac{3}{4}$	$\frac{1}{4}$	1	0	4,500
		0 $- 0\times(1)$ $- 3\times(0)$ $- 1\times(0)$ $= 0$	0 $- 0\times(\frac{3}{2})$ $- 3\times(1)$ $- 1\times(-\frac{3}{4})$ $= -2\frac{1}{4}$	0 $- 0\times(\frac{1}{2})$ $- 3\times(0)$ $- 1\times(\frac{1}{4})$ $= -\frac{1}{4}$			

where the subscript letters (A, B, m, p, and w) correspond to the obvious variables in the problem.

A new painting machine can be purchased at a cost of $20,000. This machine will change the painting constraint from 6,000 hr/yr to 9,000 hr/yr. The cost of capital is 10 percent. Using the above information:

a. What is the annual profit under existing conditions?
b. What would be the annual profits if the new machine is purchased?
c. Assuming a continuing market and that there is no change in basis variables with the new machine (i.e., the same constraints are operative), what is the payback period? That is, how many years are required for the firm to recoup its investment in the new painting machine? (Do not ignore the time value of money.)
d. Show that the optimal basis does not change with the new painting machine.

9. *(SMA)* Sleep-Easy Waterbeds Limited manufactures two nicely finished models of bed frames, the Contemporary and the Colonial. The gross profit is $85 for the Contemporary model and $125 for the Colonial model. Both products must go through three distinct job-shop processes for cutting, assembling, and final finishing. The shops are also used for other small products, but are exclusively available for the two models of bed frames for a maximum of 300, 210, and 336 man-hours per week, respectively. The Co-

lonial and the Contemporary bed frames require the following job-shop time, in man-hours:

Job-shop	Contemporary	Colonial
Cutting	3	2
Assembling	1.5	3
Final finishing	3	4

The marketing department has stipulated that not *more* than 70 Contemporary models should be produced each week. Also, *at least* 20 Colonial models must be produced weekly.

Sleep-Easy Waterbeds Limited wishes to maximize its weekly gross profits.

REQUIRED
a. Formulate the above problem in a linear programming framework, specifying the *objective function* and all *constraints*. Be sure to define *all* variables.
b. How many of each type of bed frame should Sleep-Easy manufacture weekly in order to maximize gross profits?
(1) Solve graphically
(2) Solve using the simplex method algebraically

10. (CPA) Choose the best answer and indicate why it is correct.
The following is the final tableau of a linear programming profit-maximization problem:

	X_1	X_2	S_1	S_2	
X_1	1	0	−5	3	125
X_2	0	1	1	−1	70
	0	0	5	7	500

The marginal contribution to profit is 5 for each added resource unit. S_1 can be maintained if the added resource units do not exceed
a. 125
b. 100
c. 70
d. 25
e. None of the above

11. Complete the simplex method solution for the surplus variable problem stated in Section 5.7.

12. Solve:

Minimize: $7X_1 + 8X_2$
Subject to: $X_1 + X_2 \geq 3$
$4X_1 + 3X_2 \geq 12$
$X_1, X_2 \geq 0$

Problems

13. Identify each of the following solutions as a unique optimal solution, unbounded solution, multiple optima solution, or degenerate solution. Indicate the solution in each case.

a.

	X_1	X_2	X_e	X_p	X_e	
X_2	0	1	0.04	0	16	1700
X_1	1	0	0.4	0	1.7	300
X_p	0	0	−1.4	1	−0.6	40
$C_j - Z_j$			−2	0	−1	

b.

	X_1	X_2	X_3	X_p	X_e	
X_1	1	−0.4	−0.2	0	0.6	60
X_p	0	−0.6	0.1	1	−0.03	40
$C_j - Z_j$	6	−1	0		−4	

c.

	X_1	X_2	X_3	X_e	X_q	X_f	
X_1	1	1.7	0	0.3	0	−0.1	42
X_3	0	0	1	−1	0	0.1	31
X_f	0	−0.6	0	0.6	1	0.2	11
$C_j - Z_j$	−1	0		−4	0	−2	

d.

	X_1	X_2	X_f	X_g	X_q	
X_1	1	0.6	−0.2	0.67	0	0
X_q	0	−0.1	0.1	0.13	1	2
$C_j - Z_j$	−1	−0.5	−0.1			

e.

	X_1	X_2	X_3	X_f	X_e	
X_2	−0.1	1	0	−0.1	−0.2	10
X_3	0	0	1	0.2	0.1	12
$C_j - Z_j$	2	0	0	−1	1	

f.

	X_1	X_2	X_f	X_g	
X_2	−0.1	1	0	−0.1	0
X_f	0.2	0	1	0	2
$C_j - Z_j$	−1	0	0	2	

14. First, using the graphical approach and then applying the simplex method, solve:

$$\begin{aligned} \text{Max:} \quad & X_1 + 2X_2 \\ \text{Subject to:} \quad & X_1 \geq 15 \\ & X_1 + X_2 \leq 40 \\ & X_1 \geq 0 \quad X_2 \geq 0 \end{aligned}$$

15. Write out the dual linear problem for Problem 14. First, solve the dual by the graphical approach, and then apply the simplex method to find the optimal solution.
16. Wentworth Construction builds houses and condos in Durham, North Carolina. The two most important constraints are the availability of plumbers and carpenters. For this construction season, Wentworth has contracted (and guaranteed payment) for 18,000 hr from plumbers, and 22,000 hr from carpenters. Each house requires 300 plumbing hours and 700 carpenter hours. Each condo requires 250 plumbing hours and 350 carpenter hours. The profit margins on houses and condos are $40,000 and $30,000, respectively.

REQUIRED
   a. Find the optimal combination of houses and condos for Wentworth.
   b. Wentworth is negotiating with a plumber to work more hours. What is the maximum amount per hour that Wentworth should pay for additional plumbing hours?

17. Refer to Problem 16:

REQUIRED:
   a. Find the profit-margin increase required on houses such that Wentworth would build only houses and not build any condos.
   b. One of Wentworth's carpenters quit and left town. This decreases the availability of carpenter hours to 20,500 hr. How does this change Wentworth's plans? *Hint:* Do not resolve Wentworth's problem, but use a sensitivity analysis approach.

18. There are 80 hr available per week in the operating room of a local hospital. The nursing staff provides 1800 hr per week. Medical doctors perform three kinds of operations: appendectomies, open-heart surgery, and kidney transplants. Because of local conditions, the hospital board requires at least 20 percent of the operations to be appendectomies, although the hospital can choose any mix it wants because of its excellent reputation. The hospital manager wants to maximize profits, within the constraints, where $1000, $5000, and $3000, respectively, are the profits per operation. Each appendectomy requires $\frac{1}{2}$ hr in the operating room and 10 hr of nursing. Each open-heart surgery case requires 5 hr in the operating room and 15 hr of nursing. And each kidney transplant requires 3 hr in the operating room and 20 hr of nursing.

Problems

REQUIRED:

a. If the hospital board did not impose its policy on operations, what is the maximum number of different kinds of operations that the hospital should perform to maximize its profits?

b. Find the optimal profit-maximizing combinations of operations, taking into account all the constraints.

19. *(CMA)* Jenlock Mill Company produces two grades of interior plywood from fir and pine lumber. The fir and pine lumber can be sold as saw lumber or used in the plywood.

To produce the plywood, thin layers of wood are peeled from the logs in panels, the panels are glued together to form plywood sheets, and then they are dried. The peeler can peel enough panels from logs to produce 300,000 sheets of plywood in a month. The dryer has a capacity of 1.2 million min for the month. The amount of lumber used and the drying time required for each sheet of plywood by grade is shown below.

	Grade A Plywood Sheets	Grade B Plywood Sheets
Fir (in board feet)	18	15
Pine (in board feet)	12	15
Drying time (in minutes)	4	6

The only restriction on the production of fir and pine lumber is the capacity of the mill saws to cut the logs into boards. These saws have a capacity of 500,000 board feet per month regardless of species.

Jenlock has the following quantities of lumber available for July production.

| Fir | 2,700,000 board feet |
| Pine | 3,000,000 board feet |

The contribution margins for each type of output are as follows.

Fir lumber	$0.20 per board foot
Pine lumber	$0.10 per board foot
Grade A plywood	$2.25 per sheet
Grade B plywood	$1.80 per sheet

The demand in July for plywood is expected to be a maximum of 80,000 sheets for grade A and a maximum of 100,000 sheets for Grade B. There are no demand restrictions on pine and fir lumber.

Jenlock Mill Company uses a linear programming model to determine the production quantities of each product. The correct formulation of the linear programming model is presented below and a summary of the solution of the model follows.

FORMULATION

F = board feet of fir lumber to be sold
P = board feet of pine lumber to be sold
A = number of sheets of Grade A plywood to be sold
B = number of sheets of Grade B plywood to be sold

Maximize:

$$0.20F + 0.10P + 2.25A + 1.80B$$

Subject to:

Amount of fir available	F			$+$	$18A$	$+$	$15B$	$\leq$ 2,700,000
Amount of pine available			P	$+$	$12A$	$+$	$15B$	$\leq$ 3,000,000
Peeler capacity					A	$+$	B	$\leq$ 300,000
Dryer capacity					$4A$	$+$	$6B$	$\leq$ 1,200,000
Saw capacity	F	$+$	P					$\leq$ 500,000
Maximum demand:								
Grade A plywood					A			$\leq$ 80,000
Grade B plywood							B	$\leq$ 100,000

SUMMARY OF SOLUTION
SUMMARY OF THE PRIMAL PROBLEM

Solution Variables	Solution Values
Pine lumber to be sold	500,000 board feet
Grade A plywood to be sold	80,000 sheets
Grade B plywood to be sold	84,000 sheets
Slack items:	
Pine available	280,000 board feet
Peeler capacity	136,000 sheets
Dryer capacity	376,000 minutes
Demand for Grade B plywood	16,000 sheets

Nonsolution Variables	Opportunity Costs
Fir lumber to be sold	$0.02
Constraining items:	
Fir available	$0.12
Saw capacity	$0.10
Demand for Grade A plywood	$0.09

Problems

Ranges of the Restraining Values of the Constraints
(000 omitted)

Constraints	Initial Constraint Value	Lower Limit	Upper Limit
Amount of fir available	2700	1440	2940
Amount of pine available	3000	2720	Infinity
Peeler capacity	300	164	Infinity
Dryer capacity	1200	824	Infinity
Saw capacity	500	-0-	780
Demand for plywood			
Grade A	80	67	150
Grade B	100	84	Infinity

Ranges of Objective Function Coefficients

Objective Coefficient	Initial Value	Lower Bound	Upper Bound
Fir lumber	$0.20	Negative Infinity	$0.22
Pine lumber	$0.10	$0.08	Positive infinity
Grade A plywood	$2.25	$2.16	Positive infinity
Grade B plywood	$1.80	$1.50	$1.875

REQUIRED

Refer to the Summary of Solution to answer each of the following requirements. The requirements are independent of each other.

    a. How much fir, pine, Grade A plywood, and Grade B plywood should Jenlock Mill Company produce and what is the total contribution margin of this mix?

    b. Will Jenlock Mill Company use all of its resources to their capacities during July if it follows the solution derived from the linear programming model? Explain your answer.

    c. Two items regarding *fir* lumber appear under nonsolution variables: fir lumber to be sold with an opportunity cost of $0.02 and fir available as a constraining item with an opportunity cost of $0.12. Explain what these two items mean.

    d. Assuming there is no change in price, should Jenlock Mill Company attempt to acquire any more fir for use during July, and if so, how much should be acquired? Explain your answer.

    e. Jenlock Mill Company has been approached by one of its competitors asking Jenlock to sell it some drying time. How much, if any, drying time should Jenlock sell to its competitor? Explain your answer.

    f. Jenlock Mill Company can acquire the use of additional mill saw capacity at the rate of $1800 for an 8-hr day. The additional saw capacity can

process 20,000 board feet of lumber in an 8-hr day. Should Jenlock acquire the use of extra saw capacity, and if so, how much time should it acquire? Explain your answer.
g. What is the range within which the contribution of the Grade B plywood can fluctuate before the optimal solution changes?

References

Anderson, David R., Sweeney, Dennis J., and Williams, Thomas A. *An Introduction to Management Science: Quantitative Approaches to Decision Making*, 2d ed. St. Paul, Minn.: West.

Baumol, W. J. *Economic Theory and Operations Analysis,* 4th ed. Englewood Cliffs, N.J.: Prentice-Hall, 1977.

Bierman, Harold, Jr., Bonini, Charles P., and Hausman, Warren H. *Quantitative Analysis for Business Decisions*. Homewood, Ill.: Irwin, 1978.

Bowman, Edward H., and Fetter, Robert B. *Analysis for Production and Operations Management*. Homewood, Ill.: Irwin, 1967.

Dantzig, George B. *Linear Programming and Extensions*. Princeton, N.J.: Princeton University Press, 1963.

Dinkel, John J., Kochenberger, Gary A., and Plane, Donald R. *Management Science: Text and Applications*. Homewood, Ill.: Irwin, 1978.

Dorfman, Robert, Samuelson, Paul A., and Solow, Robert M. *Linear Programming and Economic Analysis*. New York: McGraw-Hill, 1958.

Gass, S. I. *Linear Programming*, 4th ed. New York: McGraw-Hill, 1975.

Hadley, George. *Linear Programming*. Reading, Mass.: Addison-Wesley, 1962.

Hillier, Fred, and Lieberman, Gerald J. *Introduction to Operations Research*, 3d ed. San Francisco: Holden-Day, 1980.

Rappaport, Alfred. "Sensitivity Analysis in Decision Making." *The Accounting Review* (July 1967): 441–456.

Vatter, Paul A., Bradley, Stephen P., Frey, Sherwood, C. Jr., and Jackson, Barbara. *Quantitative Analysis in Management: Text and Cases*. Homewood, Ill.: Irwin, 1978.

Wagner, Harvey M. *Principles of Operations Research*. Englewood Cliffs, N.J.: Prentice-Hall, 1975.

CHAPTER 6
The Transportation Model

6.1 Introduction
A Transportation Problem
A Graphical Basis

6.2 A Simplex Approach
The Initial Tableau—The Northwest Corner Rule
The Initial Tableau—Vogel's Approximation Method
Can We Do Better?—The Simplex Criterion (Stepping-stone Method)

6.3 Dummy Distributors and Factories

6.4 A Special Situation: Degeneracy

6.5 Applications

6.6 The General Linear Programming Formulation of the Transportation Model

6.7 Summary

Glossary

Problems

References

Key Concepts
Basic solution
Degenerate solution
Demand constraint
Dummy distributor
Dummy factory
Feasible solution
Northwest corner rule
Redundant constraint
Supply constraint
Transportation model
Vogel's approximation method

Key Application
Combined production and distribution planning
Large-scale distribution
Oil tanker shipments
Plant location
Shipping problems

6.1 Introduction

The objective of a transportation model is to determine the lowest-cost combination of shipments from a given number of origins to a given number of destinations. This problem can be solved by the simplex method described in Chapter 5, but it is more convenient to consider the problem anew and to devise a special method for finding a solution.

The transportation problem occurs in many real-world situations. For example, a major oil company has a number of oil fields (origins) and a number of refineries (destinations), and the company wants to find the least-cost shipping schedule. Or a manufacturer has a number of factories and a number of distributors as customers for the product. The manufacturer is also interested in obtaining the least-cost shipping schedule. In this chapter we develop the transportation model using the manufacturer's factory-distributor example. Later in the chapter we comment on some other applications.

As before, we are concerned with developing an understanding of the transportation model and its applications. The solution method is intuitive and relates easily to the simplex method of Chapter 5, but it is not the most efficient technique, and is not the basis for standard packages for most computers.

A TRANSPORTATION PROBLEM

To illustrate the *transportation model,* consider a manufacturer with three factories from which he can ship to four distributors (see Figure 6–1). The level of supply available at each factory is 10, 15, and 6, respectively. The level of demand by the four distributors is 8, 4, 12, and 7, respectively. The total supply is equal to the total demand of 31. Assume that it is possible to ship from each factory to each distributor; that is, there are 12 (4 × 3) possible routes. The quantity shipped along each route is the set of unknown variables of our problem, usually denoted by X_{ij}, where i is the index of the factory and j is the index of the distributor. For example, X_{23} is the quantity to be shipped from the

6.1 / Introduction

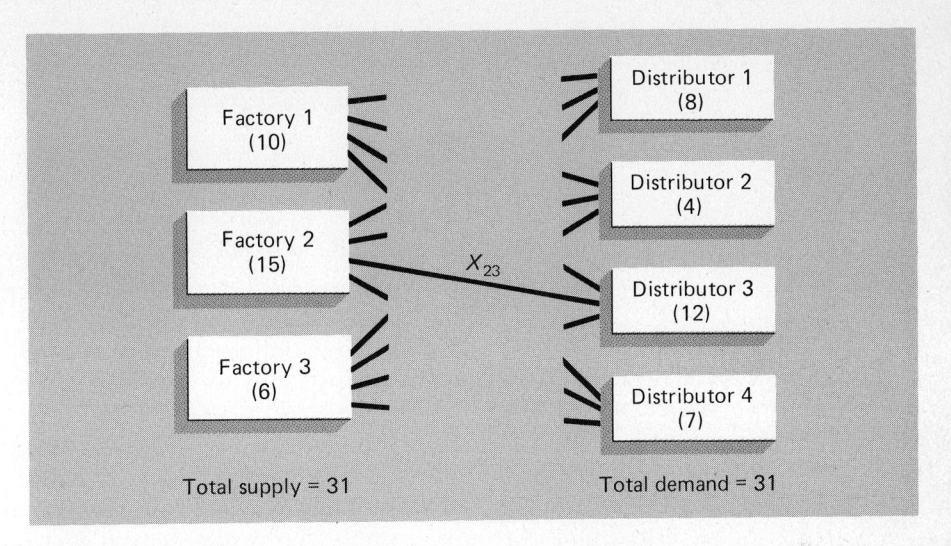

Figure 6–1. A transportation problem.

second factory to the third distributor. We now have a statement of the physical problem.

The economic problem is to choose the shipments X_{ij} such that the overall cost of transportation is minimized. To have a complete statement of the problem, we need to know the unit cost of shipping from each factory i to each distributor j, C_{ij}. Assume that the cost accounting department has determined a table of such unit costs as given in Table 6–1. For example, it costs \$7 to ship 1 unit of the product from the second factory to the third distributor, or $C_{23} = 7$. The costs are linear;

TABLE 6–1. Unit Shipping Costs

Factory	Distributor 1	2	3	4
1	3	8	6	5
2	12	3	7	9
3	8	12	1	10

for example, it costs \$14 to ship 2 units. A statement of the problem as an ordinary linear program is as follows:

$$\begin{aligned}\text{Min:} \quad & 3X_{11} + 8X_{12} + 6X_{13} + 5X_{14} \\ & + 12X_{21} + 3X_{22} + 7X_{23} + 9X_{24} \\ & + 8X_{31} + 12X_{32} + 1X_{33} + 10X_{34}\end{aligned}$$

Subject to:
$$X_{11} + X_{12} + X_{13} + X_{14} = 10$$
$$X_{21} + X_{22} + X_{23} + X_{24} = 15$$
$$X_{31} + X_{32} + X_{33} + X_{34} = 6$$
$$X_{11} + X_{21} + X_{31} = 8$$
$$X_{12} + X_{22} + X_{32} = 4$$
$$X_{13} + X_{23} + X_{33} = 12$$
$$X_{14} + X_{24} + X_{34} = 7$$
$$X_{ij} \geq 0 \quad i = 1, 2, 3; j = 1, 2, 3, 4$$

There are 12 variables; one for each possible factory-distributor combination. The objective function is formed by taking each variable X_{ij} and multiplying it by its unit cost C_{ij}, and then summing over both i and j. The first three constraints are *supply constraints*, which indicate that the amount supplied from each factory is equal to the amount available. The first constraint says that the shipments from factory 1 to all distributors are equal to 10, the production at factory 1. Similarly, the second and third constraints relate to the second and third factories. The last four constraints are *demand constraints*, which indicate that the amount received by each distributor is equal to the amount demanded. The first demand constraint states that the shipments to distributor 1 must equal its demand of 8. Similarly, the last three constraints state the demand requirement for distributors 2, 3, and 4, respectively. Note that there are seven constraints, the number of factories plus the number of distributors. A solution that meets these constraints is a *feasible solution*. The general linear programming model is given in Section 6.6.

We could consider this problem as an ordinary linear program and proceed with the simplex algorithm. But you can see that it has a special form; for example, all the coefficients in the constraint matrix are 0 or 1. It is interesting to consider it as a special linear program. We begin that development with the simplest possible graphical analysis.

A GRAPHICAL BASIS

Consider a very simple problem with one factory and two distributors (Figure 6–2). Writing the constraint set, we have

$$X_{11} + X_{12} = 10$$
$$X_{11} = 6$$
$$X_{12} = 4$$

Graphically, in $X_{11} \times X_{12}$ space, the constraints are as given in Figure 6–3.

The obvious solution, independent of any economic criterion of cost minimization, is $X_{11} = 6$ and $X_{12} = 4$. The problem is simple, but

6.2 / A Simplex Approach

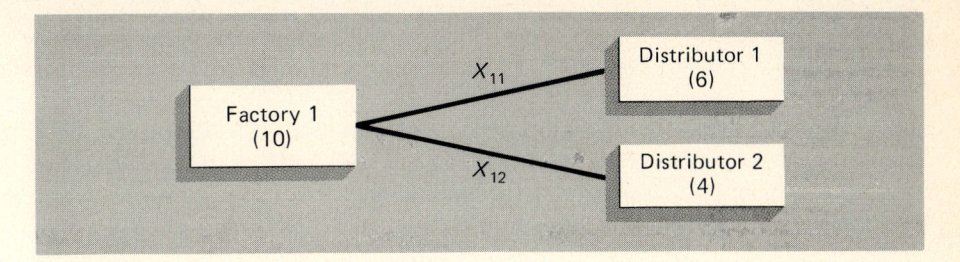

Figure 6-2. One factory, two distributors.

it does illustrate very clearly one general result for the transportation problem—namely, one of the supply and demand constraints is a *redundant constraint*. For this example, if $X_{11} + X_{12} = 10$ and $X_{11} = 6$, then X_{12} must equal 4, and there is no new information in the third constraint. The implication of this result is that there will be two variables in a basic solution, as there are two independent constraints.

6.2 A Simplex Approach

To present a more general procedure, we return to our original example with three factories and four distributors. Refer to the blank tableau in Table 6-2. We want to establish an initial tableau—which represents a basic solution. This is similar in approach to the simplex method for any linear program.

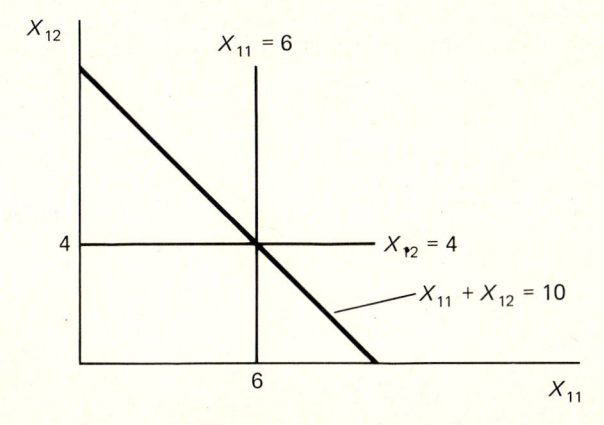

Figure 6-3. One-factory, two-distributor graphical solution.

THE INITIAL TABLEAU—THE NORTHWEST CORNER RULE

As in the ordinary simplex method, the initial tableau must represent a basic feasible solution. A procedure called the *northwest corner rule* gives us an initial basic feasible solution. Let us use our factory distributor problem of Section 6.1 to demonstrate.

Consider a tableau (see Table 6–2) where the rows represent shipments from origins (e.g., factory) and the columns represent shipments to destinations (e.g., distributor). The levels of supply at each origin are indicated along the right hand edge of the tableau and the levels of demand are shown along the bottom of the tableau. The variables representing the amount shipped across a given route, X_{ij}, are places in the cells of the tableau. Note that total demand equals total supply.

TABLE 6–2. A Tableau with the Variables Identified

Factory	Distributor 1	2	3	4	Supply
1	X_{11}	X_{12}	X_{13}	X_{14}	10
2	X_{21}	X_{22}	X_{23}	X_{24}	15
3	X_{31}	X_{32}	X_{33}	X_{34}	6
Demand	8	4	12	7	

To establish the initial tableau (see Table 6–3) we start with the upper left entry (northwest corner) and fill in the maximal amount that can be shipped from the first factory to the first distributor, X_{11}, without violating a row or column constraint. Here the entry is 8; note that the first distributor is completely served. The remaining two units from factory 1 are sent to the second customer, or $X_{12} = 2$. This satisfies the first-row constraint. We then consider the second factory in a similar manner.

To satisfy the second-column constraint without violating the second-row constraint, we set X_{22} equal to 2. In column 3, we can receive the maximal amount ($X_{23} = 12$) and still not exhaust factory 2. Thus, moving to the fourth column (distributor), we can first exhaust our stock at factory 2, $X_{24} = 1$. Then, to satisfy the last distributor's remaining demand of 6 units, we ship all our stock from factory 3; that is, $X_{34} = 6$. This is a feasible solution, as all of the factory (row) constraints and all of the distributors (column) constraints are satisfied.

6.2 / A Simplex Approach

TABLE 6-3. The Initial Tableau

Factory	Distributor 1	2	3	4	
1	8 →2				10
2		2 →12 →1			15
3				6	6
	8	4	12	7	

For any linear program, the number of basic variables is equal to the number of independent constraints. In the transportation model there are m origin (factories) constraints and n destination (distributor) constraints, which is a total of $m + n$ constraints. But one constraint is *redundant;* that is, it contains no additional information. In applying the northwest corner rule, the last entry, $X_{34} = 6$, can be determined in two ways, either from the last row constraint or the last column constraint. It is also given from the total demand equal total supply constraint. As either condition is sufficient to determine X_{34}, one constraint is redundant. And so there are 6 ($m + n - 1 = 3 + 4 - 1$) independent constraints. This condition makes this particular solution also a basic solution. (This assumes nondegeneracy, which will be considered later.)

THE INITIAL TABLEAU—VOGEL'S APPROXIMATION METHOD

The northwest corner rule is a naive method to find an initial feasible solution. It uses no cost information, and it is arbitrary, as we could have used a southwest corner rule as well. The northwest corner rule would give a different initial solution if we simply switched names on factories 1 and 2. Vogel's approximation method (VAM) is not an arbitrary rule. It uses the cost information together with the feasibility requirements to find an initial tableau that is more likely to be near the eventual optimal solution. That is, Vogel's initial tableau usually requires fewer iterations to the optimal than the northwest corner rule. In terms of the time to find an optimal solution, it is a more efficient method. The disadvantage, however, is that it requires more calculations than the northwest corner rule.

The conceptual idea of Vogel's approximation rule is straightforward. The initial tableau allocations, or transport assignments, are made by first calculating an opportunity cost, or penalty, for each factory and for each distributor. Then one chooses the transport assignment that incurs the largest penalty, or the largest opportunity cost if it were not chosen. That is, for each initial assignment, we minimize the opportunity cost. To illustrate the method, we again consider the three-factory, four-distributor example.

In Table 6–4 the problem statement is repeated from Table 6–2 and now the unit cost parameters are included from Table 6–1. The costs are shown in the upper left corner of each cell.

TABLE 6–4. Blank Tableau with Unit Cost Parameters

Factory	Distributor 1	Distributor 2	Distributor 3	Distributor 4	Supply
1	3	8	6	5	10
2	12	3	7	9	15
3	8	12	1	10	6
Demand	8	4	12	7	

Now, we want to determine the row penalties and the column penalties. Consider row 1 for the first factory. The lowest cost element is 3, the unit cost to distributor 1. The next lowest cost is 5 to distributor 4. Thus, if we ship from factory 1 to distributor 4 rather than distributor 1, we incur a (marginal) opportunity cost, or penalty, of 2 (5 − 3). For row 2, the minimum unit cost is 3, and the next smallest is 7, yielding a row penalty of 4.

TABLE 6–5. Beginning Vogel's Approximation Method

Factory	Distributor 1	Distributor 2	Distributor 3	Distributor 4	Supply	Row Penalty
1	3	8	6	5	10	2
2	12	3	7	9	15	4
3	8	12	1	10	6	7
Demand	8	4	12	7		
Column Penalty	5	5	5	4		

6.2 / A Simplex Approach

For the column penalties, we proceed in a similar fashion. For column 1, the minimal element is 3, and the next smallest is 8. This yields a penalty of 5 (8 − 3). Similarly, the penalties for columns 2, 3, and 4 are 5, 5, and 4, respectively. Table 6–5 summarizes these calculations in tableau form.

Considering all row and column penalties, we choose the largest, as it indicates the maximal opportunity cost that would be incurred if it were not chosen. Here, row 3 has the highest penalty of 7. It would occur if we did not ship from factory 3 to distributor 3. In order to avoid this cost, we ship as much as possible from factory 3 to distributor 3. In order not to violate the row 3 feasibility constraint, we can ship only 6 units as shown in Table 6–5. Thus, factory 3 shipments are determined for the initial tableau.

The next step is to repeat the procedure with the 6 units from factory 3 to distributor 3 given. Table 6–6 shows a line through factory 3 to indicate that its origin is already satisfied. Also, distributor 3 needs only an additional 6 units as shown (12 − 6 shipped from factory 3). The new row supply and column demand totals are now 25. To determine the new row and column penalties, we proceed as before. The penalties for rows 1 and 2 are unchanged. The penalty for column 1 is 12 − 3 = 9; for column 2, 8 − 3 = 5; for column 3, 7 − 6 = 1; and for column 4, 9 − 5 = 4. The maximal penalty for the tableau is 9 from column 1, and we thus set X_{11} as large as possible at 8. The first distributor is now complete.

TABLE 6–6. Vogel's Approximation Method—Step I

Factories	Distributors 1	Distributors 2	Distributors 3	Distributors 4	Supply	Row Penalty
1	3 [8]	8	6	5	10	2
2	12	3	7	9	15	4
3	8	12	1 [6]	10	6	
Demand	8	4	~~12~~ 6	7		
Column Penalty	9	5	1	4		

The next step is to draw a line through column 1 as shown in Table 6–7. With this new situation, we now calculate the new row and column penalties. The maximal element is 5 associated with column 2, which yields a shipment of 4 units from factory 2 to distributors.

TABLE 6–7. Vogel's Approximation Method—Step 2

Factory	Distributor 1	Distributor 2	Distributor 3	Distributor 4	Supply	Row Penalty
1	3 / 8	8	6	5	~~10~~ 2	1
2	12	3 / 4	7	9	15	4
3	8	12	1 / 6	10	6	
Demand	8	4	~~12~~ 6	7		
Column Penalty		5	1	4		

The next step is to create Table 6–8, which shows column 2 with a line through it. The new row and column penalties are shown, and the maximum is 4 for column 4, associated with factory 1. Thus, X_{14} is set to 2 in order not to violate the row 1 constraint.

TABLE 6–8. Vogel's Approximation Method—Step 3

Factory	Distributor 1	Distributor 2	Distributor 3	Distributor 4	Supply	Row Penalty
1	3 / 8	8	6	5 / 2	~~10~~ 2	1
2	12	3 / 4	7 / 6	9 / 5	~~15~~ 11	2
3	8	12	1 / 6	10	6	
Demand	8	4	~~12~~ 6	7		
Column Penalty			1	4		

At this point, it is obvious that the only feasible way to satisfy the constraints is by shipping from factory 2 to distributors 3 and 4, 6 and

6.2 / A Simplex Approach

5 units, respectively. Thus, again, the redundant constraint makes the final allocation automatic.

To review our initial tableau, put the solution back in a blank tableau as shown in Table 6–9. All of the factory and distributor constraints are satisfied by this initial solution. Further, it is a basic solution with 6 ($m + n - 1$) strictly positive elements.

TABLE 6–9. Initial Tableau by Vogel's Approximation

Factory	Distributor				Supply
1	3	8	6	5	10
	8			2	
2	12	3	7	9	15
		4	6	5	
3	8	12	1	10	6
			6		
Demand	8	4	12	7	

Although requiring more calculations, this initial tableau given by Vogel's approximation method will usually require fewer iterations toward an optimal solution than the initial tableau given by the northwest corner rule. Next, we consider how to move from an initial tableau (however determined) to an optimal solution.

CAN WE DO BETTER?—THE SIMPLEX CRITERION (THE STEPPING-STONE METHOD)

Having developed an initial solution, we need to evaluate it with respect to optimality. The first step in that process is to determine the current value of our objective function. The goal of the transportation model is to minimize $\Sigma_i \Sigma_j C_{ij} X_{ij}$. Recalling the cost values from Table 6–1, the total cost of the initial solution by the northwest corner method is $8(3) + 2(8) + 2(3) + 12(7) + 1(9) + 6(10) = 199$. The total cost of the initial solution by VAM is $8(3) + 2(5) + 4(3) + 6(7) + 5(5) + 6(1) = 139$. Thus, the northwest corner method did not produce an optimal solution, but did VAM? In either case, we need to determine optimality and if need be, modify our initial solution toward that optimal solution (see Table 6–10).

TABLE 6–10. The Initial Tableau with Costs

Factory	Distributor 1	Distributor 2	Distributor 3	Distributor 4	
1	3 / 8	8 / 2	6	5	10
2	12	3 / 2	7 / 12	9 / 1	15
3	8	12	1	10	6
	8	4	12	7	

To determine if the current solution is optimal, we use the simplex criterion of the previous chapter: We evaluate the marginal returns of each nonbasic variable. To take advantage of the unique form of the transportation model, the method of analysis may appear different, but, in actuality, it is identical. Any open cell is a nonbasic variable in the transportation tableau. Marginal analysis answers the question: What is the effect of shipping 1 unit of goods through an unused route (i.e., a nonbasic variable) and not through the currently identified routes (i.e., the basic variables)?

Consider some initial possibilities. There is no shipment from the second factory to the first distributor, or $X_{21} = 0$. Is it desirable to ship any goods over this route? Assuming that we do ship 1 unit across X_{21} (see Table 6–11), to maintain the demand constraint for distributor 2, which is 8, this 1 unit must come from somewhere, namely, from the current shipping order over route X_{11}. In order not to violate the supply constraints of factories 1 and 2, we must add 1 unit to X_{21} and subtract 1 unit from X_{22}. Notice that, as a result, the demand constraint for distributor 1 is still attained. To each of these marginal unit changes, we can apply their associated cost value to determine the marginal return of this possibility, yielding:

$$(+1)(12) + (-1)(3) + (+1)(8) + (-1)(3) = +14$$

Because our objective is cost minimization, this implies that each unit shipped across route X_{21} costs the company $14 *more*—an undesirable result.

Consider another unused route, X_{33}. As Table 6–11 shows, again, the assumed additional unit across route X_{33} sets off a chain reaction of

6.2 / A Simplex Approach

TABLE 6–11. Marginal Analysis of Routes X_{21} and X_{33}

Factory	Distributor 1	Distributor 2	Distributor 3	Distributor 4	Supply
1	3 8(−1)	8 2(+1)	6	5	10
2	12 +1	3 2(−1)	7 12(−1)	9 1(+1)	15
3	8	12	1 +1	10 6(−1)	6
Demand	8	4	12	7	

potential supply and demand constraint violations that must be avoided. Applying the resultant assignments of +1 and −1 to the associated cost values produces the following marginal return: (+1)(1) + (−1)(7) + (+1)(9) + (−1)(10) = −7. In this, each unit shipped across route X_{33} would decrease total shipping costs by 7, a desirable shift in shipping routes.

There are several points to notice about the above analysis. For each unassigned route that was being evaluated, its effect on some, but not necessarily all, of the currently assigned routes was crucial. To maintain feasibility, (+1)'s and (−1)'s were assigned in an alternating pattern. And finally, the marginal return was the cost value of the affected routes (assigned and unassigned) times the assigned (±1) value.

This heuristic method for determining marginal returns is commonly called the "stepping-stone" method. The analogy is that the tableau is a pond and that the currently assigned routes ($X_{ij} > 0$) are "stones" in this pond. To evaluate an unassigned route, we put a temporary "stone" in that cell and then, *only* by "stepping on stones" and only by going straight or making 90° turns, we attempt to walk through the pond and return to our original unassigned stone (cell). As Table 6–12 shows, the analyses of both X_{21} and X_{33} adhere to this rule. The resultant sequence of "stones" is called a *closed path*.

Once we have found a closed path for a particular unassigned cell, we assign (+1)'s and (−1)'s to each cell in that path, alternating signs, starting with (+1) for the unassigned cell we are evaluating. Thus, the sequence for X_{21} is $X_{21}(+1)$, $X_{11}(−1)$, $X_{12}(+1)$, and $X_{22}(−1)$. Because these (+1)'s are essentially units of goods, we can apply them to the cost values of the affected cells to produce the total marginal return.

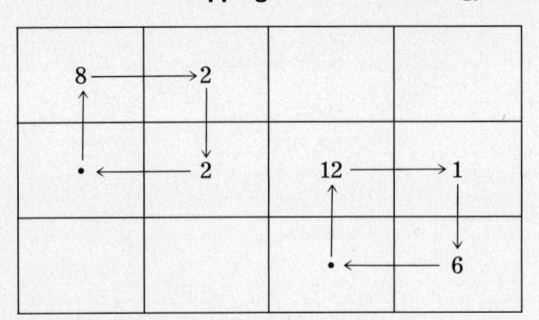

TABLE 6–12. Stepping-Stone Path for X_{21} and X_{33} Routes

This stepping-stone method can be applied to each of the remaining unassigned cells. Table 6–13 shows their associated paths.

TABLE 6–13. Stepping-Stone Analysis of Remaining Cells

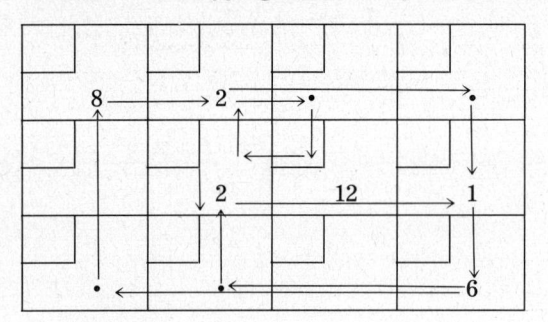

Several other points are evident here. In the routes for X_{14}, X_{31}, and X_{32}, an assigned cell was skipped over. Whenever the closed path stops on an assigned cell, it must make a 90° turn, left or right, to another assigned cell. The cell continually skipped over, X_{23}, does not have any assigned cells in its column, and thus it cannot be stepped on. The closed path for X_{31} is also instructive in that it shows that not all closed paths are squares or rectangles, but may be quite involved.

By applying the rest of the stepping-stone method, the calculations of the marginal returns for the unassigned cells in Table 6–14 are

$X_{31}:(+1)(8) + (-1)(3) + (+1)(8) + (-1)(3) + (+1)(9) + (-1)(10) = 9$
$X_{32}:(+1)(12) + (-1)(3) + (+1)(9) + (-1)(10) = 8$
$X_{13}:(+1)(6) + (-1)(7) + (+1)(3) + (-1)(8) = -6$
$X_{14}:(+1)(5) + (-1)(9) + (+1)(3) + (-1)(8) = -9$

We can now fill in our initial tableau with all the relevant data to determine optimality and, if we are not optimal, to determine what our next solution should be.

6.2 / A Simplex Approach

TABLE 6–14. Complete Marginal Analysis of Initial Tableau

Factory	Distributor 1	Distributor 2	Distributor 3	Distributor 4	Supply
1	3 / 8	8 / 2	6 / (−6)	5 / (−9)	10
2	12 / (14)	3 / 2	7 / 12	9 / 1	15
3	8 / (9)	12 / (8)	1 / (−7)	10 / 6	6
Demand	8	4	12	7	

Because our goal is cost minimization, it is clear that if any one of these cost calculations produces a negative change (i.e., a negative $C_j - Z_j$), we do not have an optimal solution. The current solution is optimal if *all* of the possible cost changes are nonnegative. "Zero" values indicate alternate optimal solutions as they did in the simplex criterion in the previous chapter. We can choose to introduce any shipment that has a cost savings, but it is logical to choose the shipment with the greatest marginal savings. For our example, the greatest savings is the (−9) associated with X_{14}, or shipping from the first factory to the fourth distributor.

We would like to ship as much as possible across this new route but still maintain feasibility of our column and row totals. The closed path we found for route X_{14} helps us here. Table 6–15 reproduces the relevant aspects of the current nonoptimal tableau.

TABLE 6–15. Analysis of Incoming Route

Factory	Distributor 1	Distributor 2	Distributor 3	Distributor 4	Supply
1		8 / 2(−1)		5 / 0(+1)	10
2		3 / 2(+1)		9 / 1(−1)	15
3					
Demand		4		7	

The closed path identifies those row and column constraints that will be affected (row 1, row 2, column 2, and column 4), those routes that will be affected (X_{12}, X_{14}, X_{22}, and X_{24}), and how they will be affected (+1). To find the amount of goods that can be shifted, identify the cells on the closed path that have been assigned (−1)'s, and then determine the minimum X_{ij} value of these cells. For our example, these cells are X_{12} and X_{24}, with current X_{ij} values of 2 and 1. Thus, the amount that can be shifted is 1 unit. (Note: If 2 units are shifted, the demand constraint in column 4 is violated). To generate the new tableau, multiply the just-determined shift amount times the assigned (±1) value and then add to the current amount. For our example, the calculations are

X_{12}: $2 + (-1)(1) = 1$
X_{14}: $0 + (+1)(1) = 1$
X_{24}: $1 + (-1)(1) = 0$
X_{22}: $2 + (+1)(1) = 3$

Table 6–16 shows the new, second tableau. The assigned cells not on the closed path for X_{14} are not affected, and therefore do not change.

TABLE 6–16. The Second Tableau

Factory	1	2	3	4	Supply
1	8	$2 + (-1)(1) = 1$		$0 + (+1)(1) = 1$	10
2		$2 + (+1)(1) = 3$	12	$1 + (-1)(1) = 0$	15
3				6	6
Demand	8	4	12	7	

(Distributor across columns 1–4)

This new tableau is a basic solution; there are six positive variables, and note that we have maintained the row and column totals, that is, feasibility. The total cost of this solution ($\Sigma_i \Sigma_j X_{ij} C_{ij}$) is $190. Our marginal analysis told us each unit of X_{14} saved us $9. Because we shifted 1 unit, we should have saved $9. Our initial solution was $199, which verifies that our marginal analysis and second tableau are accurate. In this new tableau we can test for optimality in the same fashion as for the initial tableau.

Tables 6–17 through 6–19 show the complete analysis of this transportation problem resulting in an optimal solution. The marginal analysis of unassigned routes are in parentheses. The new route to enter the solution in each tableau is circled, and the minimum shift amount is underlined. Note that the current cost minus the marginal improve-

6.2 / A Simplex Approach

ment always equals the current cost of the next tableau. Also, in Table 6–19, note that all marginal analyses are nonnegative, indicating optimality. The reader should verify each value in Tables 6–17 through 6–19.

TABLE 6–17. Evaluation of Second Tableau

Factory	Distributor 1	2	3	4	
1	3 / 8	8 / 1	6 / (−6)	5 / 1	
2	12 / (+14)	3 / 3	7 / 12	9 / (+9)	Current Cost 190
3	8 / (0)	12 / (−1)	1 / ⊖−16⊖	10 / 6	Marginal Improvement (1)(−16) − 16 / New Cost 174

TABLE 6–18. Evaluation of the Third Tableau

Factory	Distributor 1	2	3	4	
1	3 / 8	8 / (+16)	6 / (+10)	5 / 2	
2	12 / (−2)	3 / 4	7 / 11	9 / ⊖−7⊖	Current Cost 174
3	8 / (0)	12 / (+15)	1 / 1	10 / 5	Marginal Improvement (5)(−7) − 35 / New Cost 139

TABLE 6–19. Optimal Shipping Schedule

Factory	Distributor 1	2	3	4	
1	8	(+9)	(+3)	2	Current Cost 139
2	(+5)	4	6	5	Marginal Improvement 0
3	(+7)	(+15)	6	(+7)	New Cost 139

6.3 Dummy Distributors and Factories

For some problems there is an imbalance between total supply and total demand. For example, let the supply at factory 1 be 14 units. This creates an imbalance, as there are now 35 units available at the three factories, and only 31 units demanded at the four distributors. This creates a problem, as the northwest corner rule or VAM will not give us a basic feasible solution. We must use an alternative form to bring total demand in balance with total supply in order to use our transportation simplex method. That alternative is a *dummy distributor*. We create a new distributor who has a demand of 4 (the excess of total supply over total demand). Call the dummy distributor d. The initial tableau using the northwest corner rule is given in Table 6–20.

TABLE 6–20. The Initial Tableau with Distributor d

Factory	1	2	3	4	d	Supply
1	8	4	2			14
2			10	5		15
3				2	4	6
Demand	8	4	12	7	4	

To find an optimal solution with the simplex approach, one further modification is required. We must construct a unit cost table. The new cost table is identical to the original cost given in Table 6–1, except that we must include the costs from each factory to d. Those unit costs are zero since the dummy distributor does not exist. Thus, the new cost table is as shown in Table 6–21. Now we have all the information required in an appropriate format to proceed with the simplex method.

TABLE 6–21. Unit Costs Including Distributor d

Factory	1	2	3	4	d
1	3	8	6	5	0
2	12	3	7	9	0
3	8	12	1	10	0

The analogous situation arises if the total demanded by the distributors exceeds the total supplied by the factories. In this case we create a *dummy factory* with zero unit costs. Consider the example where the demand at distributor 2 is 6. This creates an imbalance, as the total demand is 33 and the total supply is 31. We bring the total supply and total demand into balance by creating a "dummy factory" with a supply of 2 units. The new initial tableau as established by the northwest corner rule is given in Table 6–22.

TABLE 6–22. The Initial Tableau with Factory d

Factory	Distributor 1	2	3	4	Supply
1	8	2			10
2		4	11		15
3			1	5	6
d				2	2
Demand	8	6	12	7	

The new cost table is given in Table 6–23. The cost from factory d to each distributor is zero. This guarantees that the dummy factory supply will be allocated at minimum cost, or the undersupply distributor will be incurred at minimum cost. Note that only one of these forms is applicable at a time; one cannot have both excess supply and excess demand simultaneously.

TABLE 6–23. Unit Cost with Factory d

Factory	Distributor 1	2	3	4
1	3	8	6	5
2	12	3	7	9
3	8	12	1	10
d	0	0	0	0

6.4 A Special Situation: Degeneracy

Degeneracy occurs when the number of strictly positive basic variables is less than $m + n - 1$. In our original example, if the number of positive basis variables was less than 6 the solution would be degenerate.

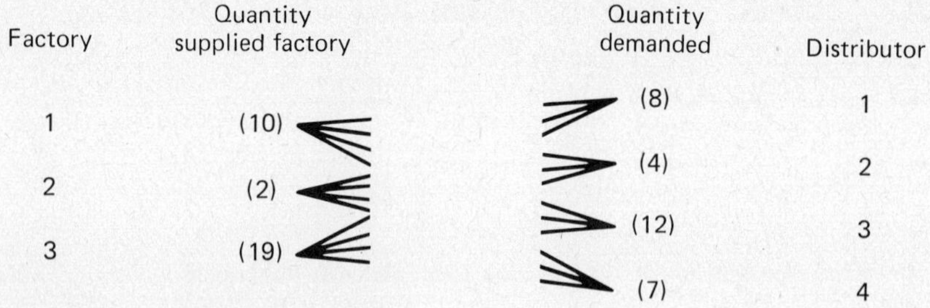

Figure 6–4. A degenerate situation.

Factory	Quantity supplied factory		Quantity demanded	Distributor
1	(10)		(8)	1
2	(2)		(4)	2
3	(19)		(12)	3
			(7)	4

Degeneracy occurs frequently in transportation problems, but is not a serious issue, and most computer routines handle it automatically.

To illustrate degeneracy, let us change our basic example as shown in Figure 6–4. Applying the northwest corner rule to this problem, we have the initial tableau as given in Table 6–24. All of the feasibility conditions are met, but there are only five positive variables. The difficulty arises because in calculating the marginal cost changes, there will be no closed path to follow in some of the calculations. Consider, for example, the possibility of shipping 1 unit from factory 1 to distributor 3, or X_{13}. It is not possible to complete the path. A basic solution for this problem requires six variables—thus, one of the zero variables must be made positive. But which one? If either X_{23} or X_{32} were positive, it would be possible to construct a path for all nonbasis variables. Thus we can create a basis of six positive variables by letting either X_{23} or X_{32} be positive, but very small. Call it ϵ. (Note: ϵ will be set to zero if it occurs in the final tableau.) One tableau would appear as Table 6–25. Note that ϵ is added to the row total for row 2 and the column total for column 3 to maintain feasibility.

It is now possible to construct the path cost calculation for all nonbasis variables. In essence, we have created a nondegenerate solution, and we proceed in the normal manner. However, note that if X_{23} were to enter on the next tableau, it could enter only at ϵ value. Degeneracy

TABLE 6–24. Initial Tableau for Degenerate Situation

Factory	Distributor 1	2	3	4	Supply
1	8	2			10
2		2			2
3			12	7	19
Demand	8	4	12	7	

6.5 / Applications

TABLE 6–25. A Created Nondegeneracy

Factory	\multicolumn{4}{c}{Distributor}	Supply
	1	2	3	4	
1	8	2			10
2		2	ϵ		$2 + \epsilon$
3			12	7	19
Demand	8	4	$12 + \epsilon$	7	

can appear in any tableau, not only the initial tableau. Furthermore, it can disappear at any time. The reader should verify that if X_{32} enters the solution at a value of 2, the next tableau will not be degenerate. It will have six positive variables in the basis.

6.5 Applications

The transportation model is applied by large oil companies to optimize shipping schedules from oil fields to refineries, and then from refineries to distributors. A similar application is the shipping schedule of a large electrical public utility of its coal shipments. A local utility has several coal-fired generating plants scattered over two states. Its coal sources are located over an even wider area and, in general, some distance away. The utility was able to achieve a savings of several hundred thousand dollars per year by applying a transportation model. The actual model had some additional constraints, but the basic form is the same as presented.

Another transportation model application involves the selection of a location for a new plant. Several possible plant locations are selected for testing in the model. Each alternative location is optimized, and then the lowest-cost site is chosen. This application is interesting in that it involves more than the optimization of existing facilities, but the larger question of choosing the proper location. Once the location is chosen, potential savings may be quite limited. The lesson here is that the transportation model (and other models) can be used to solve problems beyond the optimization of existing facilities, and the student should try to imagine various ways to use the model.

With the advent of deregulation in trucking, one more application becomes possible. Consider again the example of the manufacturer who wants the least-cost shipping schedule from factories to distributors. Further, let us assume that a trucker has none of the business, but would like to. The manufacturer then tells the trucker, "If you lower your costs to, say, $3, then I will use your route." The trucker does a sensitivity analysis. The manufacturer not only has a model to optimize shipping, but also to negotiate better unit costs. Similarly, the oil companies apply the model to negotiate tanker rates.

6.6 The General Linear Programming Formulation of the Transportation Model

The general formulation of the transportation model follows the format of the example given in the second section of this chapter. Let:

$i = 1, \ldots, m$ = the index for origins (factories)
$j = 1, \ldots, n$ = the index for destinations (distributors)
X_{ij} = the quantity shipped from origin i to destination j
C_{ij} = the unit cost of shipping from origin i to destination j
S_i = the supply at origin i
D_i = the demand at destination j

The linear programming formulation for total cost minimization is

$$\text{Min:} \quad \sum_{ij} C_{ij} X_{ij}$$

$$\text{Subject to:} \quad \sum_j X_{ij} \leq S_i \quad \text{for } i = 1, \ldots, m$$

$$\sum_i X_{ij} \geq D_j \quad \text{for } j = 1, \ldots, n$$

$$X_{ij} \geq 0 \quad i = 1, \ldots, m; j = 1, \ldots, n$$

The objective function is to minimize total costs. The first set of constraints states that the total amount shipped from each origin i is equal to or less than the supply at origin i. These are the row constraints in the tableau. The second set of constraints states that the total amount shipped to destination j is equal to or greater than the demand at distributor j. These are the column constraints in the tableau. Finally, there are the nonnegativity constraints for each variable.

Any transportation problem can be formulated in this fashion. It can be converted to standard form as discussed in the previous chapter and solved by the ordinary simplex method as given in the previous chapter. Of course, this is much longer and more involved than the special transportation simplex method developed in this chapter. This general formulation is given to demonstrate that the transportation model is a linear programming model.

6.7 Summary

In this chapter we have considered the transportation model—a special linear programming problem. The chapter includes:

    An example formulation

    A graphical approach for a one-origin, two-destination problem

    A general approach (a special simplex algorithm) for a problem of any size

    Dummy distributors and dummy factories

    A brief consideration of degeneracy

    A discussion of applications

    A presentation of the general transportation model

Glossary

Basic solution. A solution that has $m + n - 1$ strictly positive variables, where $m + n$ is the number of factories plus the number of distributors. (This is a nondegenerate solution. For a degenerate solution, there are less than $m + n - 1$ strictly positive variables.)

Degenerate solution. A solution in which one basic variable is zero. To avoid degeneracy, let the variable take on a very small value, ϵ, and proceed in the usual manner.

Demand constraint. A constraint that states the quantity required by a distributor that must be shipped from the factories.

Dummy distributor. A created distributor who takes the excess by which supply exceeds demand.

Dummy factory. A created factory that supplies the deficient supply to meet total demand.

Feasible solution. A solution that meets all supply and demand constraints.

Northwest corner rule. A procedure to find a basic and feasible solution for a transportation problem.

Redundant constraint. A constraint that contains no additional information. For the transportation model, one supply or demand constraint is redundant.

Supply constraint. A constraint that gives the quantity available at a factory that can be shipped to any distributor.

Transportation model. A special linear program to determine the minimum-cost combination of routes from a number of factories (origins) to a number of distributors (destinations).

Vogel approximation method. A procedure for the transportation model that uses opportunity costs or penalties to establish an initial basic feasible solution.

Problems

1. Solve the following transportation problem. There are three factories with supplies of 13, 8, and 9, respectively, which ship to three distributors with demands of 11, 7, and 12, respectively. The cost table is

Factory	Distributor 1	2	3
1	8	9	3
2	4	8	7
3	5	9	5

2. The transportation problem could also be a maximization problem. For example, let the unit costs be unit profits on products. For the example in the text, assume that the costs C_{ij} are profits P_{ij}, and then find the maximum-profit solution to the problem. Hint: Devise a method to calculate marginal profit for the nonbasic variables and then select the one of higher marginal profit to enter the basis.

3. Using the marginal savings/marginal cost rule for optimality, verify that the graphical solution given for the one-origin, two-destination problem in the text is indeed optimal.

4. Solve the following transportation problem. There are two factories with supplies of 13 and 10, respectively, which ship to three distributors with demands of 7, 8, and 8, respectively. The cost table is given as

Factory	Distributor 1	2	3
1	7	1	2
2	12	3	8

5. Solve the problem given in Section 6.4. Assume the cost figures in Table 6–1.

6. Discuss the issue of determining the cost table from a firm's accounting records.

7. A brewer is considering whether to build a second brewery of capacity 12 in Champaign or Durham. Currently, the brewer has one brewery in New Orleans. There are three beer markets: South, Midwest, and Mideast. The supplies and demands are as follows:

Brewery	Supplies	Demands by Market
New Orleans	18	10 Midwest
		15 South
Durham or Champaign	12	5 Mideast

Problems

After some research, the accounting department has determined that the cost table for Champaign is

	Midwest	South	Mideast
New Orleans	5	3	4
Champaign	2	4	5

and the cost table for Durham is

	Midwest	South	Mideast
New Orleans	5	3	4
Durham	3	2	1

Assuming that all other factors are equal, should the brewer build in Champaign or Durham?

8. The Jones Company has two factories, Alpha and Beta, with capacities of 18 and 19, respectively. The unit manufacturing cost at Alpha is $9 per unit, and it is $7 at Beta. The unit shipping costs for Alpha and Beta to markets 1, 2, and 3 are given as

	Markets		
	1	2	3
Alpha	3	4	2
Beta	1	2	5

The market demand at markets 1, 2, and 3 are 11, 9, and 13, respectively. Find the optimal manufacturing and shipping schedule for Jones Company.

9. The price for crude oil is the same in the Middle East, Nigeria, and Venezuela, with supplies of 20, 5, and 10, respectively. Normal Oil has two large refineries in Gulfport and Eastport, with capacities of 18 and 13, respectively. It wants to minimize total transportation costs. Because the price is the same at each supplier, this will also minimize overall costs. Find the minimum-cost shipping scheduling for the following cost table. Note: You will need to augment the refineries with a dummy refinery.

	Refinery	
Source	Gulfport	Eastport
Middle East	10	9
Nigeria	7	6
Venezuela	4	7

10. A typewriter manufacturer can sell in the United States, Canada, or Mexico. The maximum demand in each country is 10, 4, and 3, respectively. It has two factories in Texas and South Dakota, which can produce 8 and 3, respectively. After considering manufacturing costs, shipping costs, and tariffs, the cost accounting department has determined the following unit *profit* table.

Plant	U.S.	Country Canada	Mexico
Texas	5	3	6
South Dakota	4	4	2

Find the maximum-profit production and distribution plan. Note: A dummy plant will be required to find a solution.

11. A Midwestern grain elevator can ship by water, rail, or truck, with respective capacities of 18, 10, and 6, respectively, to two equal-price markets: Chicago and New Orleans. Chicago has a limited capacity of 21, but New Orleans can take any amount. For the following cost table:

Transportation Mode	Chicago	Destination New Orleans
Water	8	6
Rail	12	14
Truck	16	11

Find the optimal combination of transportation modes and destinations to minimize the elevator's total shipping costs.

12. Consider Problem 4. Formulate the problem as an ordinary linear program, state the problem in standard form, develop the initial tableau, and do one ordinary simplex iteration.
13. If you did not use Vogel's approximation method, find an initial tableau for Problems 1, 8, 9, 10, and 11, using this technique.
14. For the initial tableaux established in Problem 13, find an optimal solution for each problem.
15. For the initial tableau for the "dummy distributor" case in Table 6–20, solve using the simplex transportation method.
16. For the "dummy distributor" problem in the text, redo the initial tableau using Vogel's approximation method and solve.
17. For the initial tableau of the "dummy factory" case in Table 6–22, solve using the simplex transportation method.
18. For the "dummy factory" problem in the text, redo the initial tableau using Vogel's approximation method and solve.

References

Anderson, David R., Sweeney, Dennis J., and Williams, Thomas A. *An Introduction to Management Science: Quantitative Approaches to Decision Making.* St. Paul, Minn.: West, 1979.

Buffa, Elwood S., and Dyer, James S. *Essentials of Management Science/Operations Research.* New York: Wiley, 1978.

Dantzig, George B. *Linear Programming and Extensions.* Princeton, N.J.: Princeton University Press, 1963.

Dinkel, John J., Kochenberger, Gary A., and Plane, Donald R. *Management Science: Text und Applications.* Homewood, Ill.: 1978.

CHAPTER 7
Inventory Models with Deterministic Demand

7.1 Introduction

7.2 Cycle Inventories—Economic Order Quantity (EOQ) Model

7.3 Data, Errors, and Sensitivity

7.4 Economic Production Lot Size Model
An Example

7.5 Quantity Discounts and the EOQ Model

7.6 Inventory Models with Stockouts and Backorders

7.7 Summary

Glossary

Problems

References

Appendix
Derivation of Optimal Order Size Q and Optimal Shortage V

Key Concepts
Buffer inventories
Carrying costs
Cycle inventories
Economic lot size
Economic order quantity
Ordering costs
Quantity discount
Seasonal inventory
Stockout
Stockout cost

Key Applications
Optimal ordering quantities
Optimal production lot sizes
Adjustments for quantity discounts
Adjustments for stockout costs

7.1 Introduction

Inventories constitute one of the most important assets of business organizations. It is therefore not surprising that mismanagement of inventories is one of the most frequently cited causes of business failures. In this chapter and the next we analyze the economic factors that should be considered in arriving at decision rules for efficient inventory management. Before analyzing these economic factors, let us look briefly at the functions that different inventories serve in the economy.

Inventories perform a decoupling function between the demand system for a good and the supply system for that good. When these two systems operate asynchronously, or at least at different rates, problems can occur for both systems and for organizations as a whole.[1] The inventory system can provide a buffer or cushion between these two systems, so that aberrations in one system have a diminished effect on the operation of the other system and on the larger organization.

To illustrate this concept, consider a factory that produces wooden cases out of plywood (see Figure 7–1). The production rate for finished plywood cases necessitates 1000 ft^2 of plywood a day. One method of supplying this need is to procure exactly 1000 ft^2 of plywood each day. Assuming that the vendor does supply the factory with the needed 1000 ft^2 each day, the factory can then produce the wooden cases. In this situation, there is no inventory—no excess square feet of plywood maintained at the factory.

Let us consider the benefits and costs of this situation. If the plywood is delivered, then the production of wooden cases can proceed; that is, the supply system gets the job done. Because there is no excess plywood at the factory, there is no need for storage costs, additional

---

[1]Pipeline or transit inventories (also referred to as movement stocks) are quantities of raw materials, goods in process, and finished goods en route (on trains, ships, or trucks) from a supplier to a customer, or flowing through the manufacturing process (e.g., the crude oil in the pipes of a refinery). The amount of these inventories is determined largely by technological factors (e.g., speed of flow and capacity), and usually cannot be changed in the short run. They are therefore not discussed in these chapters.

7.1 / Introduction

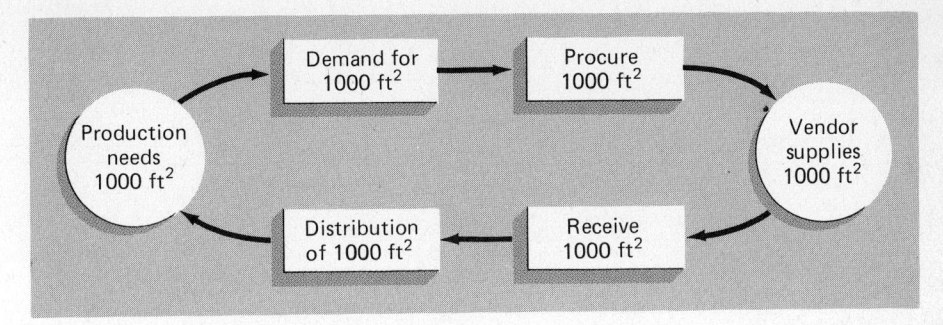

Figure 7–1. Uncoupled/noninventory system.

insurance, and additional operations personnel to manage the inventory. On the cost side, however, there are equally significant concerns. The daily procurement process suggested above requires daily ordering, transportation, receiving, and bookkeeping costs. Because the factory does not order in bulk, that is, more than 1000 ft^2, it will probably have to pay premium prices. In this coupled system, if the demand on a given day is 1100 ft^2 and the vendor cannot supply the additional 100 ft^2, a sale may be lost. Of a more catastrophic nature, if the vendor cannot supply any of the daily demand because of a strike, fire, or cancellation of the contract, the entire factory may have to be shut down. It is to these costs of a coupled supply-demand system that inventories are aimed.

In order to allow the supply and the demand systems to be uncoupled, the inventory system must operate between them (see Figure 7–2). Ideally, it must be able to react to the vagaries of the demand system in such a way as to be transparent to the demand system. That is, the demand system should be able to operate as if it were still in the coupled daily procurement system. On the other side of the inventory system, the supply system would ideally like to operate in response to regular requests for goods as opposed to daily dynamic requests. It is the job of the inventory system to match these two rates of operation.

Within the inventory system, several key questions must be answered (see Figure 7–3). As the demand for the 1000 ft^2 arrives at the inventory system, the first question to be asked is "Are there 1000 ft^2 in inventory?" If there are not, then a *stockout* has occurred, and the insufficient amount of inventory must be ordered immediately. (This is the daily occurrence in the coupled system.) When the order is filled by the vendor, the units ordered are added to the current inventory. Once there is enough inventory on hand to handle the demand, the 1000 ft^2 (or n, in general) are then removed from inventory. The second question that must be addressed concerns the amount of inventory left after removing the current demand. It is a forward-looking question: Is

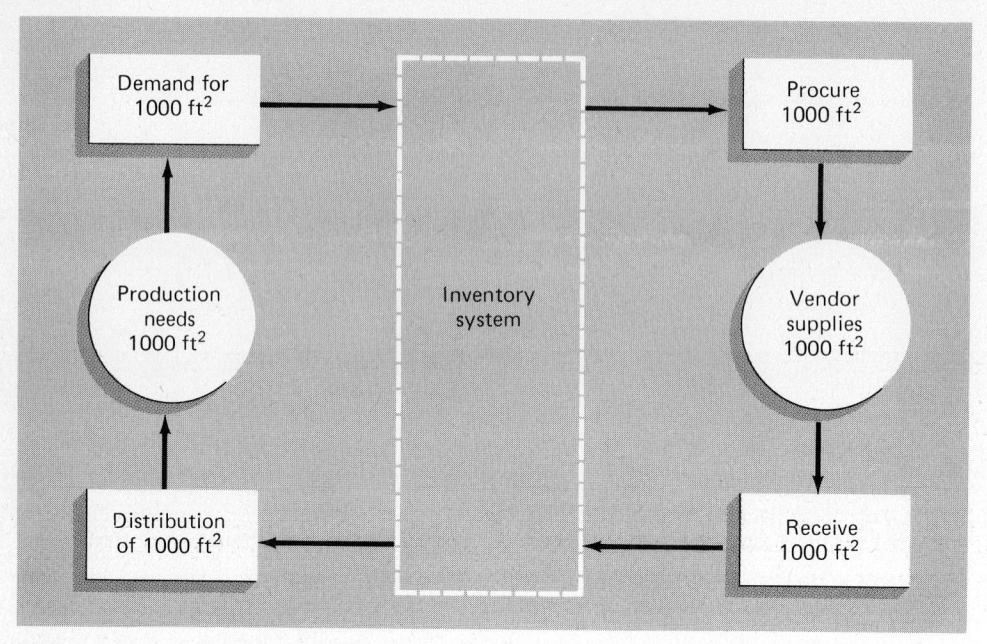

Figure 7–2. Role of inventory system.

there enough inventory left to handle future demand? This question is the *reorder point* question. This value depends on the demand rate, the supply rate, and timing. Along with this question there is a third question: How much should be ordered when the *reorder point* is reached? This last question is the *economic order quantity* question. Through the continual asking and appropriate answering of these three questions, the inventory system can function as the intermediary between supply and demand. We can classify inventories into three major categories:

1. *Cycle inventories* are constituted whenever the rate of supply of an item is not synchronized with the rate at which it is demanded. Assume that a grocery store has a daily demand for 30 dozen quarts of orange juice; wholesalers, however, will ship only in cases containing 60 dozen quarts. There is a mismatch of possible supply and desired usage.
2. *Buffer inventories* (also referred to as *safety stock*) serve to protect against excessive stockouts due to random fluctuation in the demand rate and/or supply rate.
3. *Seasonal inventories* occur usually because of seasonal fluctuations in the demand rate and a fairly constant rate of output. The analysis of seasonal inventories is left for more advanced study.

7.2 / Cycle Inventories—Economic Order Quantity (EOQ) Model

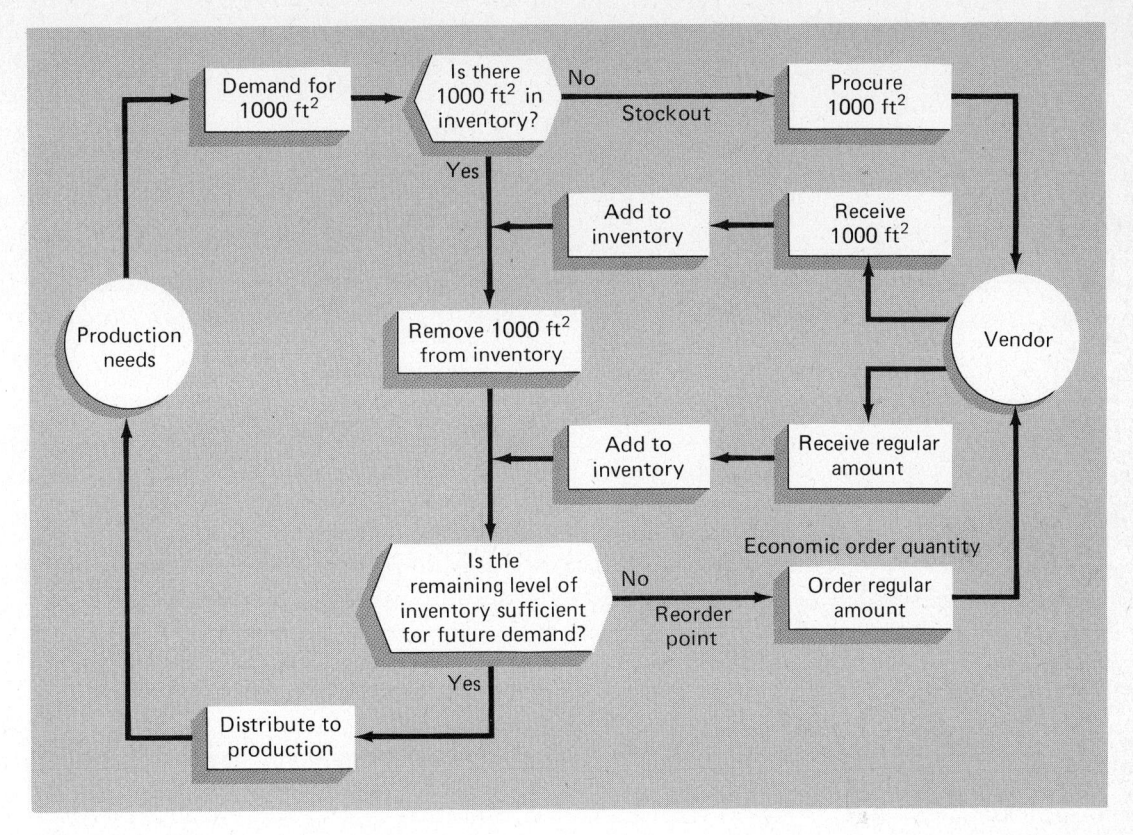

Figure 7-3. Key questions in inventory systems.

7.2 Cycle Inventories—Economic Order Quantity (EOQ) Model

In this section we discuss how much of an item should be ordered. In Chapter 8 we describe and analyze quantitative tools that help managers answer the question "when to order."

The economic order quantity model is the oldest and most widely known inventory model. The model helps us to determine the most economic *quantity* that we should *order* to be purchased or to be produced. The most economic quantity is defined as the quantity that minimizes all costs related to the placing of orders and the subsequent carrying of stocks (inventories).

In the following discussion we assume certainty about all relevant factors; models developed under the assumption of certain knowledge are called deterministic models. In developing the economic order quantity model we make a number of assumptions that are very important for understanding the model and its limitations:

1. The variable cost of placing an order (referred to as *ordering costs*), C_s, is established by an analysis of the relevant cost factors. These costs can include costs incurred in preparing requisitions, inviting and processing bids, issuing and following up on purchase orders, costs of receiving, and costs of processing and paying invoices. Given a fixed order size for a certain item, it follows that the total cost of ordering will depend on the number of times an order is placed.
2. The *cost of carrying inventory, c,* is also determined through cost analysis. These costs include the outlay costs of storing inventories, insurance, taxes, obsolescence, shrinkage and spoilage, and the important opportunity cost of tying up capital in inventory. These costs are frequently expressed as a percentage of the unit cost of purchasing or manufacturing an item carried in inventory.
3. The annual demand, D, for the item in question is known with certainty and assumed to occur at a constant rate; that is, the number of items needed per day, week, or month does not change.
4. The unit cost, b, is assumed to be constant, that is, there are no price changes and no quantity discounts. For purchased items, the unit cost is the purchase price per unit.
5. The objective of our analysis is to determine *how much* we should order each time; that is, each order throughout the year will always be for the quantity Q. This quantity Q is assumed to arrive whenever the quantity on hand drops to zero; thus we do not permit stockouts. Given the assumed constant demand rate, the inventory quantity on hand will follow a sawtooth pattern as shown in Figure 7–4.

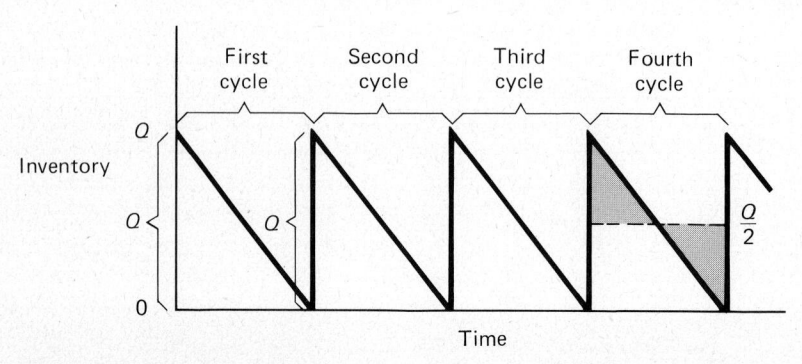

Figure 7–4. Inventory cycle.

7.2 / Cycle Inventories—Economic Order Quantity (EOQ) Model

Given the above assumptions and symbols, we can now develop a total annual cost, *TC*, for any item that is to be purchased and stocked:

$$TC = \text{annual purchase cost} + \text{annual reorder cost} + \text{annual carrying cost} \quad (7\text{–}1)$$

From assumptions 3 and 4 above, the purchase cost is constant and equals (annual demand in units) × (cost/unit) or $D \times b$. The annual reorder cost is (number of orders per year) × (cost/order). C_s has been defined as the cost per order. To determine the number of orders per year, one recognizes that total demand D must equal (number of order/year) × (quantity ordered = Q), and then the number of orders equals D/Q. Thus, the annual reorder cost is $C_s(D/Q)$.

The annual carrying cost for the inventory is (carrying cost/unit stocked) × (number of units stocked in inventory). From assumption 2, the carrying cost per unit is frequently expressed as a percentage c of the unit cost b, that is, bc. From Figure 7–4 we see that the level of inventory goes from Q at order arrival time to 0 just before the next order arrives. Thus, assuming a constant demand rate, the number of units in inventory is $(Q + 0)/2 = Q/2$.[2] This yields an annual carrying cost of $cb(Q/2)$.

Thus, the total annual cost to purchase and stock an item is

$$TC = Db + C_s\left(\frac{D}{Q}\right) + bc\left(\frac{Q}{2}\right) \quad (7\text{–}2)$$

Note that Db, the total cost of purchasing the item for the year, is independent of Q, the quantity to be purchased. That means the Q can be increased or decreased and will not affect Db. We can therefore ignore it in determining an optimal value for Q. Thus, the total inventory cost attributable to (and controllable by) the quantity ordered is

$$TC_Q = C_s\frac{D}{Q} + bc\left(\frac{Q}{2}\right) \quad (7\text{–}3)$$

Figure 7–5 shows a graph of this total cost function in terms of Q. The first term, the ordering cost, is hyperbolic. As Q increases, the ordering cost drops. The second term, the inventory holding cost, is linear in Q. It rises constantly as Q increases. The sum of the two, the total annual cost attributable to quarterly ordered, is a U-shaped function.

---

[2] Average inventory could be determined by adding up the inventory level for each day of the year and dividing by the number of days. For the geometrically minded, the average inventory can be determined by drawing a horizontal line through one of the sawtooths at $Q/2$ (see Figure 7–4). The little triangle on the top will fit perfectly into the space on the right side of the sawtooth. Now one has a rectangle of height $Q/2$, thus the average inventory.

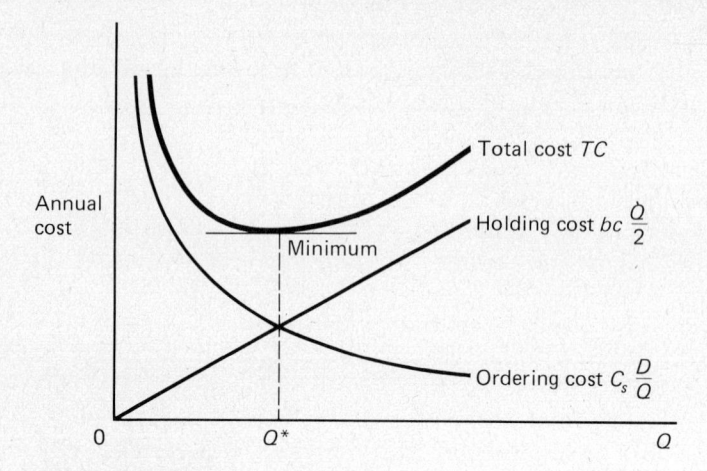

Figure 7–5. Variable inventory costs.

The optimal order quantity is that value for Q for which the total cost, TC_Q, is minimal. Applying calculus, we differentiate the total cost function and set the derivative equal to zero.[3]

$$\frac{d(TC)}{dQ} = -\frac{C_s D}{Q^2} + \frac{bc}{2} = 0$$

This is the first-order condition for a minimal solution. From Figure 7–5, we are quite certain that there is only one point for which the derivative is zero, and it is a minimum.[4] Solving the equation $-(C_s D/Q^2) + (bc/2) = 0$, we obtain the optimal Q, usually referred to as the *optimal order quantity* or the *economic order quantity*, or EOQ.

$$Q_{opt} = \sqrt{\frac{2C_s D}{bc}} \tag{7-4}$$

We shall now use an example to illustrate the application of the EOQ model. Assume that a big-city wholesaler of beauty shop supplies has an item that, over the last few years, has had a fairly constant demand of an average of 1,000 units per week, that is, about 52,000 units per year or $D = 52,000$. During the last year, the unit cost of the item was $4, and no change in this cost is expected in the foreseeable

---

[3]Students not familiar with calculus will note that the lowest point of the total cost curve occurs where $bc(Q/2) = C_s(D/Q)$. Solving for Q:

$$Q^2 = \frac{2C_s D}{bc} \qquad Q = \sqrt{\frac{2C_s D}{bc}}$$

[4]Analytically, we note that the second-order condition for a minimum is also satisfied, i.e., $d^2(TC)/dQ^2 = 2C_s D/Q^3 > 0$ for $Q > 0$, $C_s > 0$, $D > 0$. This assures that the positive value for the optimal Q will yield the minimal total cost.

7.2 / Cycle Inventories—Economic Order Quantity (EOQ) Model

future. An analysis of the inventory holding costs showed that carrying an item for a year would cost about 15 percent of its dollar value, that is, $bc = \$4\,(0.15) = \$0.60$ per unit.

An analysis of our order-placing costs, which included such items as purchasing salaries, telephone expense, and postage expense, revealed that placing an order would cost about $13.50. We can now state the total annual cost *(TC)* equation for this item as follows:

$$TC = D \times b + C_s \times \frac{D}{Q} + bc\left(\frac{Q}{2}\right)$$

$$= 52{,}000(4) + 13.5\left(\frac{52{,}000}{Q}\right) + 0.60\left(\frac{Q}{2}\right)$$

Again we see that the first expression, the annual purchasing cost (52,000 × 4) is not influenced in any way by the quantity ordered (Q). We also see that $C_s(D/Q)$ will decrease as Q increases; on the other hand, $bc(Q/2)$ will increase as Q increases (see Figure 7–5). We now use our model to determine the economic order quantity (EOQ) or Q_{opt}. We have

$$Q_{opt} = \sqrt{\frac{2C_s D}{bc}}$$

$$= \sqrt{\frac{2 \times 13.5 \times 52{,}000}{0.60}} = 1{,}530$$

According to our model, we should therefore order 1,530 units whenever an order is placed. Using D/Q or $52{,}000/1{,}530 = 34$, we find that we shall order the item about 34 times a year or roughly every eleventh day. The average inventory quantity carried is 1,530/2 or 765 units. Under our assumption 5, the maximum quantity on hand will be 1,530 units.

We can now also calculate the optimal total annual cost (TC_{opt}) for the item in question by replacing Q with Q^*:

$$TC_{opt} = Db + 13.5\left(\frac{D}{Q^*}\right) + 0.6\left(\frac{Q^*}{2}\right)$$

$$= 52{,}000 \times 4 + 13.5\left(\frac{52{,}000}{1{,}530}\right) + 0.60\left(\frac{1{,}530}{2}\right) = \$208{,}918$$

In Table 7–1 we show the ordering and holding costs for different order quantities. Again we want to note that the total purchase cost for the year is independent of the order quantity. The ordering cost decreases at a decreasing rate, and the carrying cost increases linearly as Q increases. Also note that at the economic order quantity, the annual carrying cost equals the annual ordering cost. Figure 7–6 further illustrates the relationship between TC and Q, yielding the familiar flattened U shape.

TABLE 7–1. Inventory Ordering and Carrying Costs for Various Order Quantities

Q	No. of Order (D/Q)	Annual Ordering Cost	Average Inventory Q/2	Annual Carrying Cost	Purchasing Cost	Total Annual Cost
500	104	1,404	250	150	$208,000	$209,554
1,000	52	702	500	300	$208,000	$209,002
1,530	34	459	765	459	$208,000	$208,918
2,000	26	351	1,000	600	$208,000	$208,951
3,000	19	234	1,500	900	$208,000	$209,134

7.3 Data, Errors, and Sensitivity

In most mathematical models one should consider the effect that errors in data may have on the decision criteria (in our case, total costs). Accurate data are often expensive to obtain, and inaccurate data may lead to poor solutions. The most advantageous models are those for which errors (real or potential) in the data do not seriously affect the solution. Fortunately, the basic inventory model is reasonably insensitive to data inaccuracies. In mathematical terms, because both the optimal Q and the optimal TC are square-root functions of the parameters, a given error in these parameters will lead to a smaller

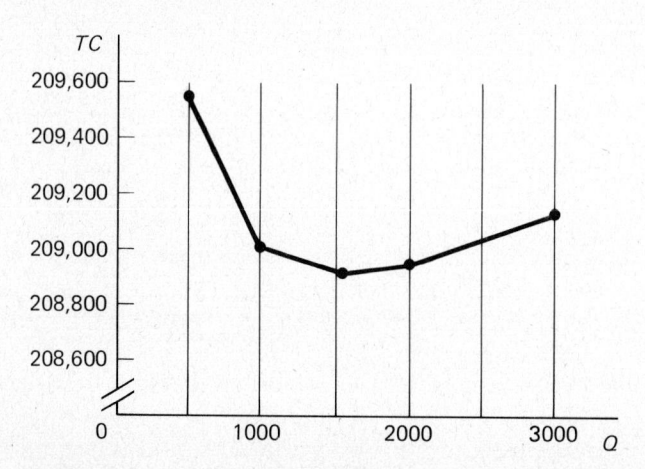

Figure 7–6. Total inventory cost for various order quantities.

7.3 / Data, Errors, and Sensitivity

percentage error in Q and TC. Thus, one can obtain good answers even when the data may be somewhat inaccurate. This can be easily demonstrated by an example.

Consider an inventory situation where the constant demand, D, is 50 units, the purchase price of a unit of this product, b, is \$5, the cost to place an order, C_s, is \$1, and the carrying costs per item stocked, c, is 20 percent of the purchase price.

Using the optimal order quantity formula,

$$Q_{opt} = \sqrt{\frac{2(1)(50)}{0.2(5)}} = 10$$

Using Eq. (8–2), we now calculate the optimal total cost (TC_{opt}).

$$TC_{opt} = 50(5) + 1\left(\frac{50}{10}\right) + 1\left(\frac{10}{2}\right) = 260$$

For the following data error scenarios, we demonstrate the effect on Q and TC and discuss their impact on decision making.

1. Assume that we made a 20 percent error in estimating demand, and D actually equals 60. Let us first calculate optimal Q using $D = 60$.

$$Q = \sqrt{\frac{2(1)(60)}{0.2(5)}} = 10.95$$

Then

$$TC_{opt} = 60(5) + 1\left(\frac{60}{10.95}\right) + 1\left(\frac{10.95}{2}\right) = 310.94$$

To determine our actual cost we use our original order quantity of 10 but the "true" demand level of 60. Thus,

$$= 60(5) + 1\left(\frac{60}{10}\right) + 1\left(\frac{10}{2}\right) = 311.00$$

Thus, a 20 percent error in demand estimation, D, leads to only a 9.5 percent error [(10.95 − 10.0)/10] in Q, and less than 1 percent error in total cost [(311 − 310.94)/310.94].

2. Assume that we overestimated the cost of placing an order, and that the actual cost is \$0.90 per order. Then

$$Q_{opt} = \sqrt{\frac{2(0.9)(50)}{0.2(5)}} = 9.5$$

and

$$TC_{opt} = 50(5) + 0.9\left[\frac{50}{(9.5)}\right] + 1\left[\frac{(9.5)}{2}\right] = 259.48$$

3. Assume an error in the estimate of opportunity cost for money, and that the correct value for c is 30 percent. What is the impact?
   The optimal Q should be:

$$Q_{opt} = \sqrt{\frac{2(1)(50)}{0.3(5)}} = 8.17$$

The optimal cost TC should be

$$TC_{opt} = 50.5 + 1\left(\frac{50}{8.17}\right) + 1.5\left(\frac{8.17}{2}\right) = 262.25$$

The actual total cost will be

$$TC_{actual} = 50.5 + 1\left(\frac{50}{10}\right) + 1.5\left(\frac{10}{2}\right) = 262.5$$

The 50 percent error in c led to an 18.3 percent [(10 − 8.17)/10.0] error in Q, and an insignificant (0.25/262.5) error in TC.

4. Finally, assume that the unit price was in error by $2 (40 percent): the actual unit price was $7. Then

$$Q_{opt} = \sqrt{\frac{2(1)(50)}{0.2(7)}} = \frac{500}{7} = 8.45$$

and

$$TC_{opt} = 50(7) + 1\left(\frac{0.56}{8.45}\right) + 1.5\left(\frac{8.45}{2}\right) = 362.26$$

$$TC_{actual} = 50(7) + 1\left(\frac{50}{10}\right) + 1.5\left(\frac{10}{2}\right) = 362.5$$

Thus, a large error in b (40 percent) caused only a 15.5 percent error in Q [(10 − 8.45)/10] and a very insignificant error [(362.5 − 362.26)/362.5] in TC.

Summarizing, we find that our model has a relatively low sensitivity to errors. Intuitively we can see this by studying the inventory cost functions in Figure 7–5 and 7–6. The curve is very flat bottomed around its minimum, and we note that the rate of increase or slope of the total cost function is more gradual to the right of the minimum then to the left. This means that errors producing a Q that is too large impact on total cost somewhat less than errors that produce a smaller-than-optimal Q.

7.4 Economic Production Lot Size Model

The preceding economic order quantity model applies to purchases where, under the stated assumptions, the entire quantity Q arrives whenever the stock level drops to zero.

We now examine an environment where inventory is obtained via a production process. The items in question have a constant demand rate of d. When the available stock level drops to zero, a production run for Q units begins. The total quantity Q is not produced at one time, however, but at a constant rate of p units per time period for T_p time periods. For example, if the level of Q desired is 2000 units, and the production rate p equals 250 units per day, then an 8-day production period T_p is required. Furthermore, if the demand rate d for the same manufactured unit is 100 units per day, then during the production run, inventory will increase $(250 - 100)$ units per day, reaching a maximum of $(150)(8) = 1200$ units. Note that this is less than the production quantity of 2000 units. After the production ends, the 1200 units in inventory are depleted at the constant rate $d = 100$ until the level is zero, and the production period begins again. This example is illustrated in Figure 7–7.

To analyze this situation from an inventory cost perspective, we have to modify the five assumptions made earlier for the EOQ model:

1. The notion of an order-placing cost must now be viewed in a manufacturing setting. The costs incurred in a factory when we pre-

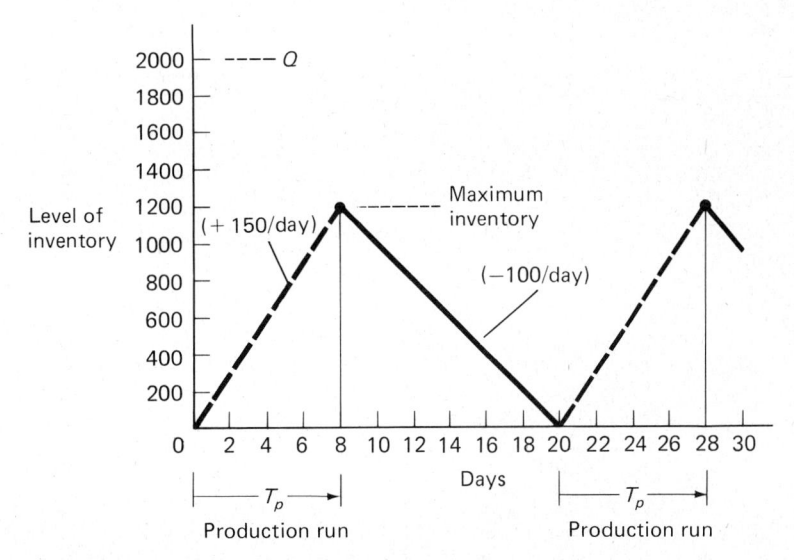

Figure 7–7. Example of production-generated inventory.

pare for the production of an item consist of the cost of preparing the production order (bill of materials, routing sheets, and operations lists) and, more important, the cost of adjusting and setting up the machines involved to produce a different product. This cost is commonly referred to as *setup cost*. Again, we assume that cost accountants have analyzed the relevant costs and can furnish us with a reasonable estimate.
2. The cost of carrying inventory is identical to our previous EOQ assumption, except that the unit cost of an item is now the unit cost of manufacturing as determined by a cost accounting system.
3. The assumption concerning demand is unchanged; that is, we assume that the annual demand is known and occurs at a constant rate d.
4. As already mentioned, the unit cost for items is now a unit cost of manufacturing. It is assumed to be constant throughout the year.
5. Again, our objective is to determine the optimal quantity Q to be produced in one production run. Inventory will no longer arrive all at once, but will gradually increase at a rate $(p - d)$ as long as production of the item continues, and decrease at a rate of d between production periods. Note that this requires that $p > d$; otherwise, for $p < d$, production cannot meet demand, and for $p = d$, we have the coupled, no-inventory system again.

The production lot model is similar to the economic order quantity model in that the total cost is the sum of the cost of carrying inventory and the cost of obtaining that inventory. In the EOQ model the carrying cost was relatively easy to determine, because all of the requested Q units, the maximum inventory level, arrived at the same time. Therefore, the average inventory was simply $Q/2$, and the total carrying cost was $Q/2$ annual times carrying cost per unit.

The economic production lot size model presents a different situation, however. Because the inventory does not arrive all at one time but at a constant rate p, and is simultaneously being depleted at a rate d, the full production quantity Q is never attained. Instead, as shown in Figure 7–7, the maximum inventory attained is the inventory accumulated during the production period, T_p, at the marginal supply/annual rate, $(p - d)$, that is, $(p - d)T_p$. But T_p is a function of the production quantity Q and the production rate p, namely, $T_p = Q/p$. Therefore, the maximum inventory equals $(p - d)(Q/p)$, and the average inventory is $\frac{1}{2}(p - d)(Q/p)$. We can now state the carrying cost for the production lot model as

$$\frac{bc(p - d)(Q)}{2p}$$

where bc is the carrying cost per unit.

7.4 / Economic Production Lot Size Model

The annual ordering cost, or, in this case, the annual setup cost is very similar to that of the EOQ model.

Annual setup cost = number of product runs per year × setup cost per run

Assuming again that D is the total annual demand, and defining C_s as the set-up cost,

$$\text{Annual setup cost} = \frac{D}{Q}(C_s)$$

Therefore the total annual cost function is

$$TC = Db + bc(Q)\left(\frac{p-d}{2p}\right) + C_s\left(\frac{D}{Q}\right) \quad (7\text{--}5)$$

To obtain the optimal Q, the quantity that should be produced, we differentiate TC with respect to Q and set it equal to zero.

$$\frac{d(TC)}{dQ} = \frac{bc(p-d)}{2p} - \frac{C_s D}{Q^2} = 0$$

$$Q^2 = \frac{2pC_s D}{bc(p-d)}$$

$$Q^* = \sqrt{\frac{2C_s D}{bc}\left(\frac{p}{p-d}\right)} = \sqrt{\frac{2C_s D}{bc}}\sqrt{\frac{p}{p-d}} \quad (7\text{--}6)$$

This is the *economic lot size* formula. Except for the expression $\sqrt{p/(p-d)}$, the equation is identical to the basic EOQ model for purchasing. The factor $\sqrt{p/(p-d)}$ will reduce the carrying cost for average inventory because of use during the production cycle.

AN EXAMPLE

Assume that we have a production process that produces 60 units per day of a product for which the annual demand is 6500 units, or about 25 units per day. The setup cost for a production run is $180, the manufacturing cost per unit is $5.50 per unit, and the annual inventory carrying cost is 18 percent of inventory investment. On average, it takes a week to set up. What is the recommended production lot size? Using Eq. (7–6), we have

$$Q^* = \sqrt{\frac{2(180)(6500)}{0.18(5.50)}\left(\frac{60}{60-25}\right)} = 2013$$

Dividing Q^* by p, we obtain the number of days needed to produce Q^*. In our case, 2013/60 = 34 days. Our maximum inventory will be 34(60 − 25) = 1190 units. Dividing these units by the demand rate of 25 per day, that is, 1190/25 = 48, we find that it takes about 48 days to use up the inventory when no production takes place. The entire cycle is about 34 + 48 = 82 days, and there will be 6500/2013 = 3.2 such cycles a year.

Now we want to investigate the relation between the EOQ model and the economic lot size model in more detail. Take the previous EOQ example where $D = 50$, $C_s = \$1$, $b = \$5$, and $c = 20$ percent; further assume that the production rate is twice the consumption rate, that is, $p = 2$ and $d = 1$. Then the optimal production quantity Q and the average inventory will be as follows:

$$Q = \sqrt{\frac{2(1)(50)}{0.2(5)}} \sqrt{\frac{2}{(2-1)}} = 10(1.414) = 14.14$$

$$I_{av} = \frac{Q}{2}\left(\frac{p-d}{p}\right) = \frac{14.14}{2}\left(\frac{2-1}{2}\right) = 3.54$$

As expected, the order quantity Q increased (from 10 to 14.14) and the average inventory dropped (from 5 to 3.54). Intuitively, if we use an item as it is being produced, we save on inventory costs, but we also need to order more. The new balance between inventory costs and ordering costs results in fewer orders per year and larger order quantities. We also note that as d gets smaller and approaches zero, or as p gets larger and approaches infinity, the fraction $p/(p-d)$ approaches unity. We are left with the economic lot size for purchasing developed in the preceding section. As d approaches p, the economic lot size Q gets larger, and at the point where $p = d$, we reach the point where no inventory is accumulated. This would, of course, imply continuous production, because supply rate and demand rate are equal.

7.5 Quantity Discounts and the EOQ Model

Many suppliers offer lower unit prices in the form of *quantity discounts* as an incentive for the purchase of larger order quantities. Whereas we assumed at the beginning of this chapter that the purchase price would not change in Q, we now include such changes. The basic variable values are annual demand of 500, setup costs C_s of 50, and carrying costs of 2 percent of unit cost. The following schedule of discounts is also assumed:

Order Size Q	Discount, %	Unit Price
0–99	0	10
100–249	2	9.80
250 and over	5	9.50

7.5 / Quantity Discounts and the EOQ Model

Because of the price breaks in the unit cost, we have three different total cost functions, which are discontinuous at the point where the quantity discounts become effective. Our total basic cost function is

$$TC = Db + C_s\left(\frac{D}{Q}\right) + bc\left(\frac{Q}{2}\right)$$

where b is the unit purchase cost. Because we now have three unit costs, we need three total cost functions of the form

$$TC_i = Db_i + C_s\left(\frac{D}{Q_i}\right) + b_iC\left(\frac{Q}{2}\right) \quad \text{for } i = 1, 2, 3$$

Figure 7–8 illustrates these cost functions. Note that the current ordering cost C_s (D/Q) is not affected by the price breaks.

As the graph suggests, we must analyze all three sections of the total cost function to find the minimum cost. We do this by first calculating an optimal Q for each cost function.

$$Q_1 = \sqrt{\frac{2(500)(50)}{0.2(10)}} = 158$$

$$Q_2 = \sqrt{\frac{2(500)(50)}{0.2(9.8)}} = 159$$

$$Q_3 = \sqrt{\frac{2(500)(50)}{0.2(9.5)}} = 160$$

Given the small differences in the unit cost, it is not surprising that the three order quantities do not differ significantly. We do note that Q_1

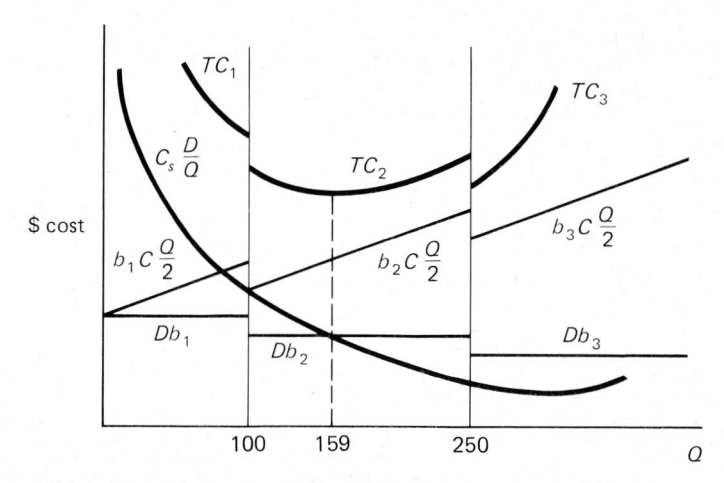

Figure 7–8. Total costs with price breaks.

and Q_3 result in quantities outside their assumed discount range; the $10 unit cost used in calculating Q_1 is valid only for order quantities up to 99 units, and the $9.50 unit cost applies only to quantities over 250. Therefore, both Q_1 and Q_3 represent invalid optima.

We now make the invalid optima valid. Q_3, which was too small to qualify for the applicable discount, is increased to the quantity needed for the price break (in this case, 250). Similarly, Q_1, which was too large is decreased to the value of its price break. Using the total cost formula, we now calculate the total annual cost for Q_1, Q_2, and Q_3:

$$TC_1 = 500(10) + 50\left(\frac{500}{99}\right) + 10(0.2)\left(\frac{99}{2}\right) = \$5351.53$$

$$TC_2 = 500(9.80) + 50\left(\frac{500}{159}\right) + 9.80(0.2)\left(\frac{159}{2}\right) = \$5213.05$$

$$TC_3 = 500(9.50) + 50\left(\frac{500}{250}\right) + 9.50(0.2)\left(\frac{250}{2}\right) = \$5087.50$$

Thus the total annual cost is minimized when we order 250 units at a price of $9.50. This can be easily verified by studying Figure 7–8.

In terms of differential calculus, we first test each segment of the total cost function for a valid optimum; we find only one, for TC_2. We then calculate the total cost of both TC_2 and TC_3 at their end points. Comparing these results, we find the minimum-cost solution to be the price break between Q_2 and Q_3.

7.6 Inventory Models with Stockouts and Backorders

Excessive *stockouts* or inventory shortages are usually not desirable because of the high cost they entail. These costs include, for example, profit margins on lost sales and the costs connected with production stoppages. In this section we assume that there is only a relatively small cost incurred when we are out of stock and that our customers are willing to wait. We therefore assume that stockouts do not affect our annual demand. In terms of our basic EOQ model, we are now changing the assumption of no stockouts. We let stockouts occur and assume that they are associated with a small stockout cost. We define d as the *cost of stockout* per unit per year.

In the basic EOQ situation we developed earlier, by admitting no stockouts, we implicitly imputed infinite stockout costs. Further, we ordered in such a way that there was no inventory on hand when a new order was received. We must now establish the level of shortage to be tolerated in addition to establishing the optimal order quantity. The

7.6 / Inventory Models with Stockouts and Backorders

new inventory cycle to include the possibility of shortages is shown in Figure 7–9.

For additional notation, let

d = stockout cost per unit per year
V = shortage amount per cycle
Q = order quantity

Figure 7–9 can be used to determine the relevant costs in this situation. Periods T_1 and T_2 should be thought of as fractions of a year. During the period of time labeled T_1, there is a positive inventory level varying linearly between $(Q - V)$ and 0. The average inventory level during this period is $(Q - V)/2$. Because this average inventory is carried for the time period T_1, the inventory carrying cost for one cycle is

$$bc\left(\frac{Q-V}{2}\right)(T_1)$$

Similarly, we can see that during period T_2, there is a shortage. The average shortage is $V/2$, and the shortage cost for one cycle is

$$d\left(\frac{V}{2}\right)(T_2)$$

Because there will be one order during the cycle to procure Q units, the order cost is C_s. The total cost per cycle is the sum of these three costs and is written as

$$C = \frac{dVT_2}{2} + bc\left(\frac{Q-V}{2}\right)(T_1) + C_s$$

Now $T_1 + T_2 = Q/D$, that is, the reciprocal of the number of cycles per year; therefore $T_1 = (Q - V)/D$ and $T_2 = V/D$; that is, we express both time segments of the cycle as fractions of the annual demand. Substituting for T_1 and T_2, we can now rewrite the cost per cycle:

$$C = \frac{dV^2}{2D} + bc\left[\frac{(Q-V)^2}{2D}\right] + C_s$$

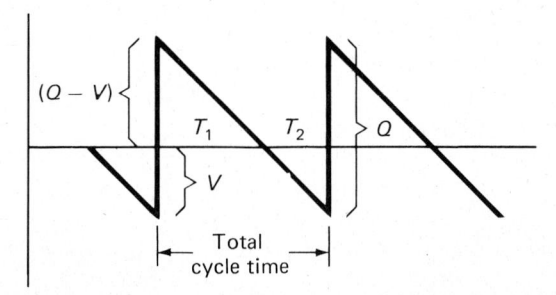

Figure 7–9. Inventory cycle with shortages permitted.

The total annual cost can be found by multiplying the cost per cycle (C_1) by the average number of cycles per year (D/Q) to obtain

$$TC = \left[\frac{dV^2}{2D} + bc\left[\frac{(Q-V)^2}{2D}\right] + C_s\right]\frac{D}{Q}$$

or

$$TC = \frac{dV^2}{2Q} + bc\left[\frac{(Q-V)^2}{2Q}\right] + \frac{C_s D}{Q} \tag{7-7}$$

This equation is the resulting annual cost model and is expressed in terms of the two controllable decision variables, Q and V. To find the optimum values of Q and V, we use the first-order conditions:

$$\frac{\delta TC}{\delta Q} = -\frac{dV^2}{2Q^2} + \frac{bc}{2}\left[2Q\frac{(Q-V)-(Q-V)^2}{Q^2}\right] - \frac{C_s D}{Q^2} = 0$$

and

$$\frac{\delta TC}{\delta V} = \frac{dV}{Q} - \frac{bc(Q-V)}{Q} = 0$$

Solving simultaneously,[5] we obtain

$$Q^* = \sqrt{\frac{2C_s D}{bc}}\sqrt{\frac{d+bc}{d}} \tag{7-8}$$

$$V^* = \sqrt{\frac{2C_s D}{d}}\sqrt{\frac{bc}{d+bc}} \tag{7-9}$$

These relationships express the optimal order size Q and the optimal amount of shortages V for the assumed situation.

The results of this model can be compared directly with those of the basic model. The basic model yielded

$$Q = \sqrt{\frac{2C_s S}{bc}}$$

$$V = 0$$

Remember that the only difference between the present model and the basic model is the assumption concerning stockout cost. In the basic model, the stockout cost (d) was infinite (stockouts are not tolerated); here it is assumed to be finite (stockouts do not cost too much, and thus are permitted). Note that when $d \to \infty$, the stockout model yields the

---

[5]The details of the algebra are given in the appendix to this chapter.

7.6 / Inventory Models with Stockouts and Backorders

results for the basic models. Thus, we can see that as stockout costs become extremely high, the stockout model approaches the basic model. On the other hand, when carrying costs are high, as is the case with items that have an extremely high unit cost, V increases. This explains why in many business situations high-cost items are frequently backordered.

To illustrate the stockout model, let us use the same assumptions used for our basic EOQ example: $D = 50$, $C_s = \$1$, $b = \$5$, $c = 20$ percent, and $d = 3$. In the stockout situation, we get

$$Q^* = \sqrt{\frac{2(1)(50)}{1}} \sqrt{\frac{3+1}{3}} = 11.55 \quad \text{or} \quad 12 \text{ units}$$

$$V^* = \sqrt{\frac{2(1)50}{3}} \sqrt{\frac{1}{3+1}} = 2.887 \quad \text{or} \quad 3 \text{ units}$$

If this model is applied, we obtain the following characteristics for the system:

Maximum inventory $= Q - V = 12 - 3 = 9$ units

$$\text{Total cycle time} = T_1 + T_2 = \left(\frac{Q}{D}\right)(365) \text{ days} = \left(\frac{12}{50}\right)365$$

$$= 88 \text{ days}$$

The part of the cycle when inventory is carried is

$$T_1 = \frac{Q-V}{D} = \frac{12-3}{50}(365 \text{ days}) = 0.18(365) = 66 \text{ days}$$

The part of the cycle when we are out of stock is

$$T_2 = \frac{V}{D}(365 \text{ days}) = \frac{3}{50}(365) = 22 \text{ days}$$

The total annual cost [refer to Eq. (7–7)] is

$$\text{Shortage cost} = \frac{dV^2}{2Q} = \frac{3(3)^2}{2(12)} = \frac{27}{24} = \$1.13$$

$$\text{Carrying cost} = bc\left[\frac{(Q-V)^2}{2Q}\right] = \frac{9^2}{24} = \frac{81}{24} = \$3.38$$

$$\text{Ordering cost} = C_s\left(\frac{D}{Q}\right) = 1.00\left(\frac{50}{12}\right) = \underline{\$4.17}$$

$$\underline{\$8.68}$$

Had we used the basic model, our EOQ would have been

$$Q^* = \frac{2(1)(50)}{1} = 10 \text{ units}$$

Our total cost [using Eq. (7–1) but ignoring Db, the total purchasing cost] would have been

$$TC = C_s\left(\frac{D}{Q}\right) + bc\left(\frac{Q}{2}\right)$$

$$= 1\left(\frac{50}{10}\right) + 1\left(\frac{10}{2}\right) = 5 + 5 = \$10.00$$

7.7 Summary

In this chapter we introduced the basic economic order quantity (EOQ) model. We assumed certain knowledge of demand, and by analyzing the relevant cost functions, developed a model that helps us to answer the question of how much to order. After discussing a simple purchasing situation, we expanded our analysis and developed a model that can be applied to production processes, furnishing an answer to the question of how much to produce. The impact of quantity discounts on the EOQ model necessitates an analysis of discontinuous total cost functions. Stockouts and backorders were introduced, and a modified EOQ model was developed. The very important question of *when* an order should be placed is discussed in the next chapter.

Glossary

Buffer inventories or **Safety stock.** Additional units of stock carried to avoid excessive stockouts and the costs associated with them.

Carrying costs. Costs associated with holding inventories; examples are the costs of receiving, storing, and the cost of the capital invested in the inventory.

Cycle inventories. Inventories carried because the rate at which a product is needed is smaller than the rate at which it is supplied.

Economic lot size. The optimal production quantity to be produced in a lot when there is usage of items while it is being produced.

Economic order quantity (EOQ). The quantity of goods to be ordered that will minimize the total annual cost of ordering (placing orders) and carrying inventories.

Ordering costs. Costs incurred when placing an order to purchase goods from a supplier or to produce goods in a factory.

Problems

Quantity discount. A reduction in the per-unit price when a large quantity of the item is ordered.
Seasonal inventory. Inventory that experiences increases and decreases due to seasonal fluctuations in demand.
Stockout. Occurs when an item is required but none is available.
Stockout cost. Per-unit cost due to stockout.

Problems

1. In developing the basic inventory decision rule,

   $$Q = \sqrt{\frac{2DC_s}{bc}}$$

   where

   Q = optimal lot size
   C_s = setup cost
   D = annual sales rate
   bc = holding cost per unit per year

   numerous assumptions were made. We used the model

   $$TC = \frac{D}{Q} + bc\left(\frac{Q}{2}\right)$$

   to obtain this decision rule. Identify and discuss *two* of these assumptions that you consider limit the rule's usefulness in practical inventory problems. Also, discuss the effects on the above model if these assumptions are replaced with more realistic ones.

2. Identify and *discuss* a criterion for determining the appropriate costs to consider when analyzing an inventory problem. Define all concepts used in this criterion.

3. The Skidless Tire Company purchases a line of radial tires for small imported automobiles. The manufacturer's selling price to Skidless is $25.86 each, and they purchase 135,000 of this line per year in order to meet their excellent sales record. The purchasing department at Skidless has determined that it costs $125 to place an order for tires and that the minimum total cost for this line of tires is achieved by ordering 45 times per year.

   REQUIRED
   a. Calculate the total inventory costs per year associated with this line of radial tires.
   b. Assuming that the demand for these tires increases to 160,000 per year, that the ordering costs also increase to $150 per order, but that the purchase cost decreases to $25.25 per tire, how will this affect the economic order quantity (EOQ)? Justify your answer by calculating the new EOQ.

4. What functions can inventories serve for a business enterprise? Discuss in some detail each function identified, giving examples where possible.

5. Westcoast Industries purchases a microswitch from a large supplier. The switch can be bought at the following prices:

   For quantities of 1 − 4999 $5.40 per unit
   For quantities of 5000 − 9999 $5.30 per unit
   For quantities of 10,000 or more $5.25 per unit

   Westcoast purchases 40,000 switches per year. The cost of placing one order is $80 and the cost of capital is 15 percent per year. Five percent of the switches are either stolen or destroyed by Westcoast during production and are discarded.

   REQUIRED
   Determine the optimum purchasing policy for Westcoast Industries.
   Be sure to indicate the:
   a. Size of the order
   b. Comparison of total annual cost of inventory for alternative policies

6. A frequent criticism leveled against the use of mathematical inventory models is that the parameters that must be used in them are subject to errors of estimation, and therefore the value of using such models is questionable. Do you agree or disagree with this criticism? Defend your position, using examples where possible.

7. The forecasted annual requirement for a certain spare part is 15,000 units, with a carrying cost of 20 percent and ordering costs of $40 per order. The average inventory shrinkage is 5 percent. The purchase cost is $20 per unit; however, if the order size is for 750 or more units, a 15 percent quantity discount is applied to the order.

   REQUIRED
   Based on the above information, calculate the optimum order size.

8. Write a paragraph indicating what happens to the EOQ model and its solution as usage occurs during production.

9. Jones and Hamilton, a local men's store, observes that its sales of white shirts total 6000 shirts per year. Further, it notes that this demand is distributed evenly through the year. Jones and Hamilton pay $5 for each shirt. Their ordering cost (paperwork and shipping) is $15 per order, and the carrying cost on inventory is 12 percent per year. Jones and Hamilton want to know how many shirts they should order each time.

10. a. As an inventory expert, you are given the following problem by your supervisor. He tells you that

    Ordering cost = $6 per order
    Annual demand = 1000 units
    Carrying cost = $30 per unit per year

    Also, he tells you that the warehouse cannot hold more than 18 units of the product at a time. He asks you to determine the most economical and feasible purchase lot. Support your answer with analysis. Make any necessary assumptions.

    b. Your company is considering the purchase of a machine that will make its product. Thus, units produced are immediately available for use. The machine has an annual capacity of 3000 units. Your supervisor wants to know if the optimal internal production lot is the same as the optimal order quantity. If it changes, he wants to know by how much.

11. *(CMA)* The Robney Company is a restaurant supplier that sells a number of products to various restaurants in the area. One of their products is a special meat cutter with a disposable blade. The blades are sold in packages of 12 blades for $20 per package. After a number of years, it has been determined that the demand for the replacement blades is at a constant rate of 2000 packages per month. The packages cost the Robney Company $10 each from the manufacturer, and require a 3-day lead time from date of order to date of delivery. The ordering cost is $1.20 per order, and the carrying cost is 10 percent per annum. Robney is going to use the economic order quantity formula

$$EOQ = \sqrt{\frac{2(\text{annual requirements})(\text{cost per order})}{(\text{price per unit})(\text{carrying cost})}}$$

REQUIRED
  a. Calculate:
    (1) The economic order quantity
    (2) The number of orders needed per year
    (3) The total cost of buying and carrying blades for the year
  b. Assuming that there is no reserve (i.e., safety stock) and that the present inventory level is 200 packages, when should the next order be placed? (Use 360 days = 1 year.)
  c. Discuss the problems that most firms would have in attempting to apply this formula to their inventory problems.

12. For the basic EOQ model, one can obtain the optimal order quantity Q by equating the total ordering costs to the total annual inventory carrying costs. That is, let

$$C_s\left(\frac{D}{Q}\right) = bc\left(\frac{Q}{2}\right)$$

REQUIRED
  a. Verify that the optimal EOQ is determined by equating either total or average costs as shown above.
  b. Is it a general concept that one can optimize decision models by equating average costs, or is this only a special result of the EOQ model?

13. Consider a situation in which you want to minimize cost and have the following model:

$$TC = ax - bx^3$$

where a, b are parameters, x is a controllable variable, and TC is total cost. Your best guess is that a and b have about the same value, even though both are subject to errors of estimation. Because of limited funds, you can obtain a better estimate of a or b, but not both. On which parameter would you spend the funds in order to gain a better estimate? Give reasons for your answer.

14. Assume an annual demand of 250 units, an ordering cost of $40 per order, and an inventory carrying cost of 25 percent. The following quantity discounts are available:

Quantity Ordered	Discount, %	Unit Cost
0–99	0	$60.00
100–199	5	$57.00
200 and over	10	$54.00

REQUIRED
Determine the order quantity that will minimize total annual cost.

15. Gruen Manufacturing Company estimates it will require 600,000 kg of raw material J-101 during the next year. This material is purchased from a single supplier, who has guaranteed a price of $20 per kg throughout the year. Costs of placing each order amount to $30, while the cost of carrying this material in inventory is 15 percent of the purchase price.

REQUIRED
   a. Determine the economic order quantity.
   b. What are the minimum total inventory costs?
   c. Suppose that the annual requirements decrease next year by 20 percent to 500,000 kg. What is the percentage decrease in total inventory costs?
   d. Comment on the result in part c.

16. *(CMA)* Hermit Company manufactures a line of walnut office products. Hermit executives estimate the demand for the double walnut letter tray, one of the company's products, at 6000 units. The letter tray sells for $80 per unit. The costs relating to the letter tray are estimated to be as follows for 1977:

   1. Standard manufacturing cost per letter tray unit: $50
   2. Costs to initiate a production run: $300.00
   3. Annual cost of carrying the letter tray in inventory: 2 percent of standard manufacturing cost.

In prior years, Hermit Company has scheduled the production for the letter tray in two equal production runs. The company is aware that the economic order quantity model can be employed to determine optimum size for production runs. The EOQ formula as it applies to inventories for determining the optimum order quantity is

$$\text{EOQ} = \sqrt{\frac{2(\text{annual demand})(\text{cost per order})}{(\text{cost per unit})(\text{carrying cost})}}$$

REQUIRED
Calculate the expected annual cost savings that Hermit Company could experience if it employed the EOQ model to determine the number of production

runs that should be initiated during the year to manufacture the double walnut letter trays.

17. *(CMA)* Pointer Furniture Company manufactures and sells office furniture. In order to compete effectively in different quality and price markets, it produces several brands of office furniture. The manufacturing operation is organized by item produced rather than by furniture line. Thus, the desks for all brands are manufactured on the same production line. For efficiency and quality control reasons, the desks are manufactured in batches. For example, 10 high-quality desks might be manufactured during the first 2 weeks in October and 50 units of a lower-quality desk during the last 2 weeks. Because each model has its own unique manufacturing requirement, the change from one model to another requires that the factory's equipment be adjusted.

The management of Pointer wants to determine the most economical production run for each of the items in its product lines. The manager of the cost accounting department is going to adapt the EOQ inventory model for this analysis.

One of the cost parameters that must be determined before the model can be employed is the setup cost incurred when there is a change to a different furniture model. The cost accounting department has been asked to determine the setup cost for the desk (model JE 40) in its junior executive line as an example.

The equipment maintenance department is responsible for all of the changeover adjustments on production lines in addition to preventive and regular maintenance of all production equipment. The equipment maintenance staff has a 40-hr work week; the size of the staff is changed only if there is a change in the workload that is expected to persist for an extended period of time. The equipment maintenance department had 10 employees last year, and they each averaged 2000 hr for the year. They are paid $9 an hour, and employee benefits average 20 percent of wage costs. The other departmental costs, which include such items as supervision, depreciation, insurance, and others total $50,000 per year.

Two men from the equipment maintenance department are required to make the change on the desk line for model JE 40. They spend an estimated 5 hr in setting up the equipment as follows:

Machinery changes	3 hr
Testing	1 hr
Machinery readjustments	1 hr
Total	5 hr

The desk production line on which model JE 40 is manufactured is operated by five workers. During the changeover these workers assist the maintenance workers when needed and operate the line during the test run. However, they are idle for approximately 40 percent of the time required for the changeover.

The production workers are paid a basic wage rate of $7.50 per hour. Two overhead bases are used to apply the indirect costs of this production line, because some of the costs vary in proportion to direct labor hours whereas others vary with machine hours. The overhead rates applicable for the current year are as follows:

	Based on Direct Labor Hours	Based on Machine Hours
Variable	$2.75	$ 5.00
Fixed	2.25	15.00
	$5.00	$20.00

These department overhead rates are based on an expected activity of 10,000 direct labor hours and 1,500 machine hours for the current year. This department is not scheduled to operate at full capacity, because production capability currently exceeds sales potential at this time.

The estimated cost of the direct materials used in the test run totals $200. Salvage material from the test run should total $50.

REQUIRED

a. Prepare an estimate of Pointer Furniture Company's setup cost for desk model JE 40 for use in the economic production run model. For each cost item identified in the problem, justify the amount and the reason for including the cost item in your estimate. Explain the reason for excluding any cost item from your estimate.

b. Identify the cost items that would be included in an estimate of Pointer Furniture Company's cost of carrying the desks in inventory.

18. Subgum Manufacturing Company produces transistorized cassette recorders. The Model XY-243 transistor is purchased at a unit cost of $1.50, regardless of quantity. Incremental costs of placing an order are $40.50. Subgum expects to produce 60,000 recorders next year, and three of the Model XY-243 transistors are required for each recorder. The firm's cost of funds is 12 percent and inventory shrinkage is negligible.

REQUIRED

a. (1) Determine the order size that leads to minimum total inventory costs for Model XY-243 transistors.

(2) Determine the total inventory cost associated with the order size in part 1.

b. Suppose that the supplier of Model XY-243 transistors allows a 2 percent discount in price on orders of 20,000 or larger. Should Subgum order in lots of 20,000 units? Explain.

19. A small plastics manufacturer purchased an expensive injection molding machine primarily to manufacture cabinets for television sets for a large electronics manufacturer. About 40 percent of the machine's capacity, however, was not required for the TV cabinet production, and the plastics manufacturer used this time to make a variety of items for other customers. The standard time to produce a TV cabinet was 1.5 min. The injection

Problems

molding machine was operated two shifts or a total of 80 hr per week. The contract with the electronics firm called for deliveries at the rate of 2000 cabinets per week.

When a setup change was made to produce the cabinet, a considerable number of adjustments were needed because of the mold's complexity. The standard time for such a setup (including cleaning, setup, trial production, inspection, and takedown at end of run) was 6 hr. One man was involved; he was paid $3.50 per hour. The plastics manufacturer had storage space available, but because the cabinets were bulky items to store and they were exposed to a certain amount of damage in handling, he estimated that the cost of storage (including cost of capital, space, insurance, etc.) was $6 per cabinet per year.

REQUIRED
   a. What is the economic production lot size for producing the TV cabinet?
   b. What would be the economic production lot size if demand increased to 4000 cabinets per week?

20. Assume the following characteristics for an important inventory item:

   Annual demand for the item is 400 units.

   Cost of placing an order is $60.

   The estimated annual carrying cost is $3 per unit.

REQUIRED
   a. Calculate the economic order quantity.
   b. For scheduling purposes, depending on the size of the company's backlog, it is often desirable to schedule production of lots that are somewhat larger or smaller than the economic lot size. Assuming that the company wishes to limit the extra costs incurred by not adhering strictly to the economic lot size to 12 percent of the optimum total costs, determine the range of lot sizes that might be used. (*Hint:* Use the total cost equation.)

21. An automotive spare parts distributor would like to reduce the inventory of carburetor assemblies for imported cars. He thinks that the assumptions for the backorder model apply and gives you the following information:

   Annual demand $D = 2000$ units.

   Unit purchasing costs are $100.

   Carrying cost is estimated at 10 percent of the cost of an item carried, the backordering cost per unit per year, d, is $30, and the cost of placing an order is $25.

REQUIRED
   a. Calculate the economic order quantity Q^* and the backorder quantity V^*.
   b. Using your answers, determine:
      (1) The maximum inventory level
      (2) The cycle times T_1 and T_2

c. (1) Calculate the total annual cost using the backorder model, and (2) compare it with the total annual cost under the basic EOQ model to show the cost savings that might be realized under the new policy.

22. Assume the following for the ABC Company: Annual demand for material X is 10,000 units; usage is at a constant rate throughout the year; the cost of ordering C_s is $36 per order; the cost of carrying is 20 percent; the unit price is $2.50; lead time is 3 days; backorder costs are estimated at $4 per unit; and the company operates during 50 weeks.

REQUIRED
   a. Find the economic lost size Q.
   b. Find the maximum number of backorders.
   c. Find the maximum inventory level.
   d. Find the number of inventory cycles and their length.
   e. Find the reorder point (ROP). Explain why the ROP is different from the example at the beginning of the chapter, where we permitted no stockouts.
   f. Draw an inventory graph for this problem.

23. A job forge landed a contract covering 3 yr to supply a large earth-moving equipment manufacturer located in the same city with a forged part. The parts are to be delivered at a rate of 80 units per day during each of 250 working days per year. The part can be produced at the rate of 240 units per day. The setup cost is estimated at $56, and the annual carrying cost is $2 per part per year.

REQUIRED
   a. Calculate the optimal production quantity.
   b. Calculate the length of the total production cycle and the length of the production run.
   c. Calculate the maximum inventory.
   d. Calculate the average inventory.
   e. Calculate the total inventory carrying cost for a year.

References

American Accounting Association. Report of Committee on Managerial Decision Models. "II-B Inventory Models" and "II-B Appendix." *The Accounting Review*, Supplement to vol. XLIV (1969):64–72.

Brown, R. G. *Decision Rules for Inventory Management.* New York: Holt, Rinehart and Winston, 1970.

Buffa, E. S., and Taubert, W. H. *Production-Inventory Systems: Planning and Control*, rev. ed. Homewood, Ill.: Irwin, 1972.

Greene, J. H. *Production and Inventory Control Handbook.* New York: McGraw-Hill, 1970.

Hadley, G., and Whitin, T. M. *Analysis of Inventory Systems.* Englewood Cliffs, N.J.: Prentice-Hall, 1963.

Lewis, C. D. *Scientific Inventory Control.* New York: American Elsevier, 1970.
Starr, M. K., and Miller, D. W. *Inventory Control: Theory and Practice.* Englewood Cliffs, N.J.: Prentice-Hall, 1962.
Wagner, H. M. *Principles of Operations Research.* Englewood Cliffs, N.J.: Prentice-Hall, 1969.

APPENDIX. Derivation of Optimal Order Size Q and Optimal Shortage V

$$TC = \frac{dV^2}{2Q} + \frac{bc(Q-V)^2}{2Q} + \frac{C_s D}{Q}$$

$$= \frac{dV^2}{2Q} + \frac{bcQ}{2} - bcV + \frac{bcV^2}{2Q} + \frac{C_s D}{Q}$$

$$\frac{\delta TC}{\delta V} = \frac{dV}{Q} - bc + \frac{bcV}{Q}$$

$$= \frac{V}{Q}(d + bc) - bc = 0$$

$$\frac{\delta TC}{\delta Q} = \frac{-dV^2}{2Q^2} + \frac{bc}{2} - \frac{bcV^2}{2Q^2} - \frac{C_s D}{Q^2}$$

$$= \frac{V^2}{Q^2}\left(\frac{-d-bc}{2}\right) + \frac{bc}{2} - \frac{C_s D}{Q^2} = 0$$

Solving for V:

$$\frac{V}{Q}(d + bc) = bc$$

$$\frac{V}{Q} = \frac{bc}{d + bc}$$

$$V = \frac{Qbc}{d + bc}$$

Substituting this for V in the equation $\delta TC/\delta Q = 0$,

$$\frac{\delta TC}{\delta Q} = \frac{V^2}{Q^2}\left(\frac{-d-bc}{2}\right) + \frac{bc}{2} - \frac{C_s D}{Q^2} = 0$$

$$= \frac{[Qbc/(d+bc)]^2(-d-bc)}{2Q^2} + \frac{bc}{2} - \frac{C_s D}{Q^2} = 0$$

$$= \frac{(Qbc)^2(-d-bc)}{2Q^2(d+bc)^2} + \frac{bc}{2} - \frac{C_s D}{Q^2} = 0$$

$$= \frac{-Q^2 b^2 c^2 (d+bc)}{2Q^2(d+bc)^2} + \frac{bc}{2} - \frac{C_s D}{Q^2} = 0$$

$$= \frac{-b^2 c^2}{2(d+bc)} + \frac{bc}{2} - \frac{C_s D}{Q^2} = 0$$

$$= \frac{-b^2 c^2}{2(d+bc)} + \frac{bc}{2} = \frac{C_s D}{Q^2}$$

$$Q^2 = \frac{C_s D}{[-b^2 c^2/2(d+bc)] + bc/2}$$

$$= \frac{C_s D}{(bc/2[-bc/(d+bc)] + 1)}$$

$$= \frac{C_s D}{(bc/2)[(d+bc-bc)/(d+bc)]}$$

$$= \frac{C_s D}{(bc/2)[d/(d+bc)]} = \frac{2C_s D(d+bc)}{bc(d)}$$

Substituting this value for Q into $V = Qbc/(d+bc)$:

$$V = \frac{Qbc}{d+bc} = \frac{bc}{d+bc} \sqrt{\frac{(2C_s D)(d+bc)}{(bc)(d)}}$$

$$= \sqrt{\frac{(2C_s D)(d+bc)(bc)^2}{(bc)(d)(d+bc)^2}}$$

$$= \sqrt{\frac{(2C_s D)(bc)}{(d)(d+bc)}}$$

CHAPTER 8
Inventory Models with Probabilistic Demand

8.1 **Introduction**

8.2 **When to Order: An Example**

8.3 **Reorder Point and Safety Stock**

8.4 **Optimal Levels of Safety Stock**
Assuming Independence Between Safety Stock and Order Quantity
Assuming Dependence of *ROP* and *EOQ*

8.5 **Note on Normally Distributed Demand During Lead Time**

8.6 **Safety Stock When Stockout Costs Are Unknown**

8.7 **Constant Order Cycle Systems and Periodic Review Systems**

8.8 **Some General Remarks**

8.9 **ABC Inventory Systems**

8.10 **Summary**

Glossary

Problems

References

Appendix
Derivation of Optimal *Q* and *ROP* Under Uncertainty (Shortages Backordered)

Key Concepts
ABC inventory systems
Constant order cycle systems
Expected stockouts
Lead time
Periodic inventory review systems

Reorder point
Safety stock
Service level
Stockout
Stockout costs

Key Applications
Adjustments for uncertain demand
Optimal order quantities
Optimal safety stocks
Risk avoidance with inventory

8.1 Introduction

One of our assumptions in the preceding chapter was that demand is known with certainty and not subject to any unexpected fluctuations. Implicitly, we also assumed that the time elapsed between placing an order and receiving it, commonly referred to as lead time, l, is also deterministic. "When to order" is thus obvious; given our perfect knowledge of demand and lead times, we place orders so that the order quantity Q always arrives exactly when needed, that is, either when the stock level has dropped to zero or when the number of back-ordered items has reached the predetermined optimum level. In the following sections we examine the question of when to order when we are no longer certain about the demand during lead time.

8.2 When to Order: An Example

Assume that the supplier of a raw material used in a manufacturing process guarantees a 3-working-day delivery. The cost of the material is $2.50 per unit, and the carrying cost b equals 20 percent of the unit price. Usage of the raw material in the factory occurs at a constant rate of 200 units per day, and we assume that the factory operates during 50 weeks of the year; the annual demand is thus 50,000 units. The cost of placing an order is estimated at $36 per order. What is the economic order quantity, and at what inventory level must we place an order if we are to avoid running out of stock? Using the lot-size model from the preceding chapter, we calculate

$$Q = \sqrt{\frac{2(50{,}000)36}{0.20(2.50)}} = 2683 \text{ units}$$

The lead time l is 3 working days, and demand during this lead time, S, is $3 \times 200 = 600$ units. Figure 8–1 illustrates these relationships.

We now define the *reorder point (ROP)* as the inventory level at which an order must be placed if stockouts are to be avoided. In Fig-

8.3 / Reorder Point and Safety Stock

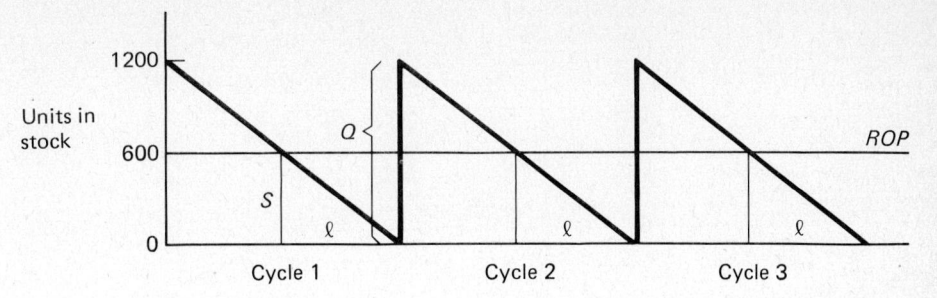

Figure 8–1. Reorder point.

ure 8–1 we assume that $ROP = 600$ units $= S$, which is the demand during lead time. The number of cycles and reorder periods during the year is given by D/Q or $50,000/2,683 = 18.6$ cycles or lead times per year. Assuming that we want to avoid stockouts, we can summarize these relationships as follows. When we *are certain* about the *length of the delivery period (l)* and *the demand during that period,* the reorder point *(ROP)* is reached (i.e., an order must be placed) when the inventory level drops to the point where it is equal to the demand during lead time, that is, when $ROP = S$.

If we had used the model that permits stockouts and backorders discussed in the preceding chapter, the *ROP* again would be determined such that the ordered quantity *Q* arrives exactly when the backordered quantity (the stockouts) reaches the predetermined optimal level.

8.3 Reorder Point and Safety Stock

Let us now continue our discussion of the reorder point by dropping our assumption of certainty about the demand during lead time. Throughout the discussion in this chapter, we assume a *constant* lead time. We again use the example of the preceding section, in which we assumed a demand during lead time of 200 per day or 600 for a lead time of 3 days. We now assume that the 600 units are the mean or average of the demand during lead time. In addition, we assume that demand during lead time is normally distributed with a standard deviation of 100 units. These facts are illustrated in the inventory graph of Figure 8–2.

An inspection of Figure 8–2 reveals that if we place the replenishment order at the old *ROP* of 600 units, we shall be out of stock, on the average, half the time, or somewhat more than nine times a year (recall that we had 18.6 cycles per year). The *stockout* probability is given by the entire area under the shaded right half of the curve; the short-

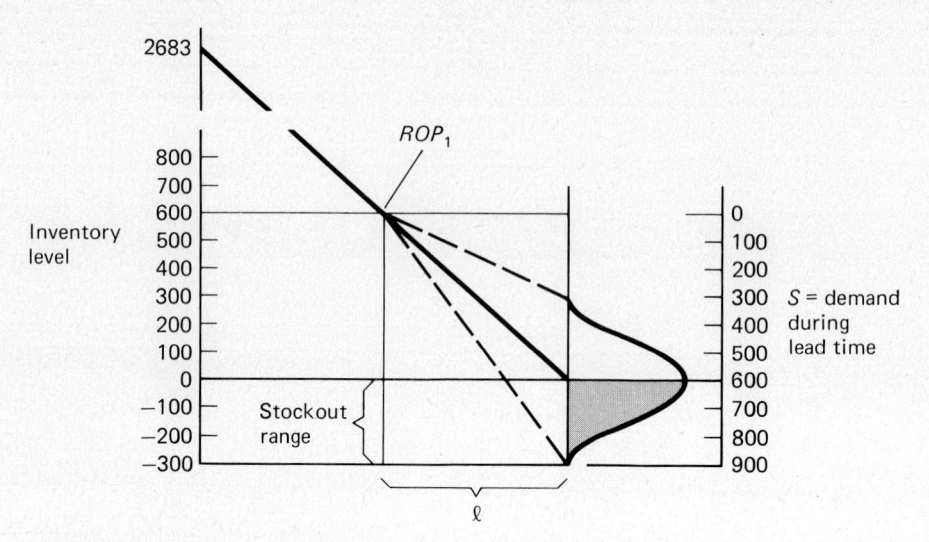

Figure 8–2. Probabilistic lead times.

ages will vary from one to more than 300 units. On the other hand, we observe that on average during every other lead time, we still have units on hand when the ordered lot size Q arrives (the number of units on hand will also be between zero and 300).

Can we reduce the number of stockouts? The answer, of course, is yes. We can, for example, raise the ROP to 800 units, as indicated in the right part of Figure 8–3 (labeled ROP_2). By placing the order when

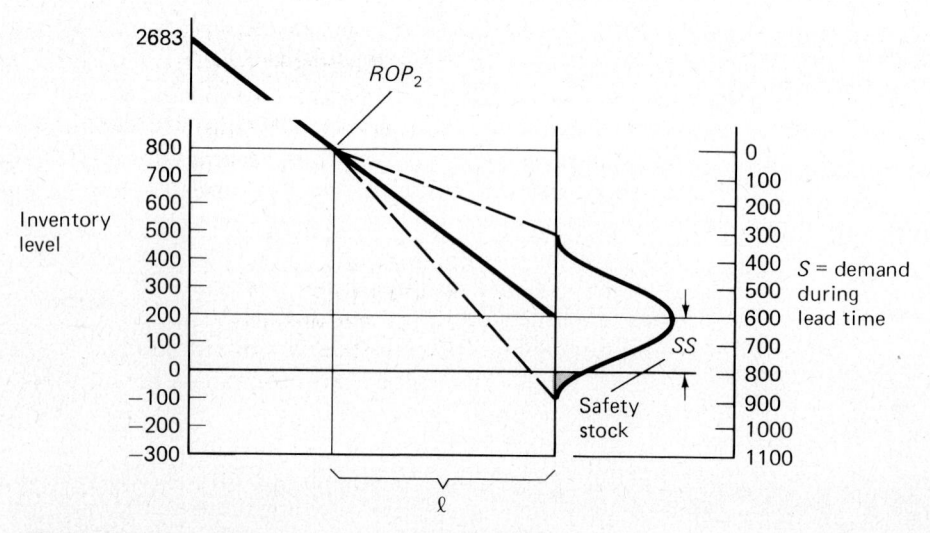

Figure 8–3. Probabilistic lead times with safety stock.

8.3 / Reorder Point and Safety Stock

the inventory level is at 800, we drastically reduce the probability of stockouts, from 50 percent to about 2.3 percent. This probability is represented by the shaded area in the right tail (the demand level of 800 is 2 standard deviations (2 × 100) from the mean of 600). But this was achieved at a price. On average we shall now have 200 units on hand when our order arrives, whereas with $ROP = 600$ we had, on average, zero units on hand when the shipment arrived. In fact, we have added 200 units permanently to our inventory. These additional units are called safety stock. *Safety stock* is defined as additional (units of) stock carried to avoid excessive stockouts. Assuming that we shall carry at least some additional units of safety stock, we can redefine the reorder point as

$$ROP = E(S) + SS$$

where $E(S)$ stands for the expected or average demand during the lead time and ROP now is equal to the average demand during lead time plus safety stock. Thus, safety stock can be defined as

$$SS = ROP - E(S)$$

that is, reorder point less average demand. We have seen that the amount of safety stock depends on the reorder point. The higher the ROP, the higher the amount of safety stock. But how much safety stock should we carry? To determine the optimal amount of safety stock, we must analyze the cost factors involved.

As indicated earlier, every unit of safety stock represents a permanent addition to our inventory; that is, on the average, we must carry it during the entire year. All the costs associated with carrying inventories must be considered. These costs were discussed and defined in the preceding chapter.

The second set of cost factors deals with the cost of stockouts. What are these costs? Let us simply enumerate some of the consequences of running out of stock and describe some of the costs they entail:

Consequence of Inventory Shortages	Associated Costs
Special orders	Overtime, rescheduling costs, loss of customer goodwill
Production stoppage	Cost of idleness, subsequent overtime, loss of customer goodwill
Lost sales	Loss of contribution margins, loss of goodwill

Obviously, these costs are not easily quantifiable, yet many inventory models require their quantification. Thus, a reasonable effort must be made to estimate these costs. Students should realize that a precise measurement of stockout costs is practically impossible in most cases, and that these estimates necessarily involve judgment.

In the following section we analyze these two cost factors in developing the notion of optimal safety stock levels.

8.4 Optimal Levels of Safety Stock

ASSUMING INDEPENDENCE BETWEEN SAFETY STOCK AND ORDER QUANTITY

We now introduce an analysis of cost factors aiming at the determination of optimal levels of safety stock. Let us now assume that demand for a stock item during a lead time of 2 days is subject to random fluctuations[1] as illustrated in Table 8–1.

TABLE 8–1. Probablistic Demand During Lead Time

Demand During Lead Time in Units (x)	Probability of Demand $P(S = X)$	Cumulative Greater Than $P(S > x)$	Cumulative Equal to or Less Than $P(S < x)$
0	0.01	0.99	0.01
1	0.02	0.97	0.03
2	0.14	0.83	0.17
3	0.20	0.63	0.37
4	0.26	0.37	0.63
5	0.20	0.17	0.83
6	0.14	0.03	0.97
7	0.02	0.01	0.99
8	0.01	0.0	1.00
9	0		

Mean demand $E(s)$ = 4 units

Assume that we reorder when our stock level reaches 4 units; that is, we set the reorder point *(ROP)* at 4 units, which is the mean of the demand. From Table 8–1, we can see that we shall experience stockouts 37 percent of the time, that is, 37 percent of the time that actual demand is greater than 4. If we set *ROP* at 5 units, we can reduce the probability of a stockout to 0.17; with *ROP* at 6, it will be 0.03; *ROP* at

---

[1] Such a distribution can be derived from empirical data. For example, we can tabulate orders received during the last 100 reorder periods. Assuming that demand does not change, we can readily construct the demand distribution of Table 8–1.

8.4 / Optimal Levels of Safety Stock

7 reduces it to 0.01; and finally, *ROP* at 8 eliminates all stockouts. Recall that safety stock *(SS)* is defined as the difference between the *ROP* and the average demand during lead time, or

$$SS = ROP - E(S)$$

Thus, in our example, a *ROP* at 5 units gives us 1 unit of safety stock. Now let us assume that we have 50 reorder periods or lead times during a year; that is, *Q*, the economic order quantity, has already been determined, and $D/Q = 50$.

Let us also assume, for the moment, that the safety stock can be determined independently from the economic order quantity *(EOQ)* developed in the previous chapter. To establish an appropriate level of safety stock, we must first analyze the cost of carrying safety stock. As mentioned earlier, every unit of safety stock represents an addition to our inventory. When we add safety stock *(SS)*, the average number of units carried in inventory will be $(Q/2) + SS$, and the total cost of carrying inventory will be $c_s [(Q/2) + SS]$. Second, we must make assumptions about the cost of stockouts, where *d* is the unit stockout cost. Whatever that cost, it should be clear that the total stockout cost will decline with each additional unit of safety stock carried and will finally approach zero when enough units are carried to eliminate practically all stockouts. Figure 8–4 shows the declining *stockout cost,* the increasing cost of carrying additional units of safety stock, and the sum of both cost functions. This total cost function shows that there should be an optimal level of safety stock. We shall illustrate these relationships by applying marginal analysis to our example.

Assume that the cost of carrying a unit of safety stock is $30 (i.e., $bc = \$30$) and that the cost of a stockout (lost contribution margin, lost goodwill, backorder, and expediting costs) has been estimated at $20

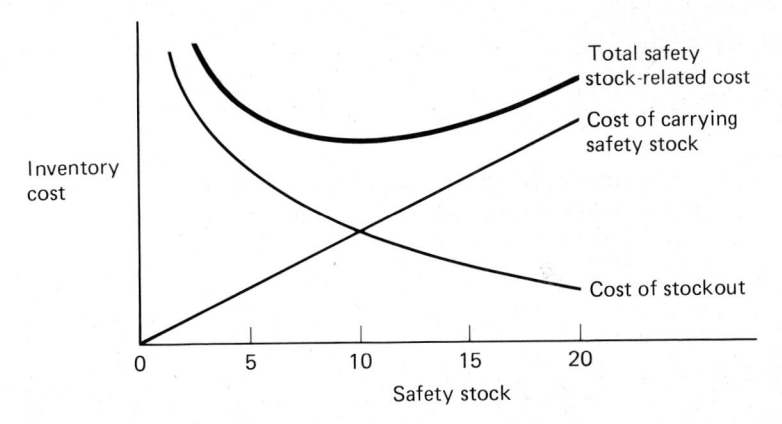

Figure 8–4. Safety stock related costs.

per stockout. Using these assumptions and the information given in Table 8–1, we can develop the analysis shown in Table 8–2.

TABLE 8–2. Marginal Analysis of Carrying Costs and Stockout Costs

(1) Safety Stock	(2) Annual Stockouts Eliminated $P(S = SS)D/Q$	(3) Annual Reduction in Stockout Costs (2) × $20	(4) Annual Increase in Carrying Costs	(3) + (4) Net Increase (Decrease) in Annual Inventory Cost
1st unit	0.2 × 50 = 10.0	$(200)	$30	$(170)
2nd unit	0.14 × 50 = 7.0	(140)	30	(110)
3rd unit	0.02 × 50 = 1.0	(20)	30	10
4th unit	0.01 × 50 = 0.5	(10)	30	20
5th unit	0	0	30	30

The first column is based simply on our definition of safety stock. Recall that the mean demand during lead time $E(S) = 4$; if we set $ROP = 5$, we get 1 unit of safety stock $[SS = ROP - E(S)]$. Then a $ROP = 6$ gives us 2 units of safety stock, and so on. The probabilities in the second column are simply the demand probabilities $P(S)$ from Table 8–1 for the fifth, sixth, seventh, and eighth units. To calculate the annual stockouts eliminated, we multiply the demand probability for the fifth unit (0.2) by the number of lead times during the year (50). Column (3) indicates the varying slope of the cost of stockout in Figure 8–4. Similarly, column (4) indicates the slope of safety stock cost.

The last column represents points on the total cost function of Figure 8–4. Our analysis shows that the first 2 units of safety stock effectively reduce total inventory cost. Beginning with the third unit, total costs begin to increase. Under the assumption of our example, it is therefore best to carry 2 units of safety stock, or to set the ROP at 6 units (4 units average demand during lead time plus 2 units safety stock).

The approach used in our example can be developed in more general terms. Our marginal analysis shows that we should keep adding units of safety stock until the cost of stockouts equals the annual carrying cost of the added unit. We have a stockout whenever the units demanded are more than the available stock, where x denotes the nth unit of stock carried; that is, $P(s > x)$. This may occur during each lead time. The number of lead times is the same as the number of orders per year and can be expressed as D/Q; the cost of a stockout is d. The expected annual stockout costs incurred when not adding the nth unit to our safety stock can now be stated as $P(s > x) \times d \times D/Q$. To find

8.4 / Optimal Levels of Safety Stock

the optimal safety stock level, we equate it with the annual carrying cost per unit, yielding

$$P(s > x) \times d \times \frac{D}{Q} = bc \tag{8-1}$$

Rearranging, we get

$$P(s > x) = \frac{(bc)(Q)}{(d)(D)} \tag{8-2}$$

Because $P(s > x) = 1 - P(s \leq x)$, by substituting into Eq. (8-1) we have

$$1 - P(s \leq x) = \frac{bc}{d}\left(\frac{Q}{D}\right)$$

or

$$P(s \leq x) = 1 - \frac{bc}{d}\left(\frac{Q}{D}\right) \tag{8-3}$$

Applying this to our example, we get (Q was not given, but we know that $D/Q = 50$)

$$P(s \leq x) = 1 - \frac{30}{20}\left(\frac{1}{50}\right) \qquad P(s \leq x) = 1 - 0.03 = 0.97$$

To find the *ROP* that corresponds to this probability, we refer to the cumulative probabilities in Table 8–1 to find an optimal reorder point of 6 units, including safety stock of 2 units. (Note that the preceding marginal analysis assumes a continuous distribution. Examples with discrete distributions will often give only an approximation of an optimal *ROP*.) Figure 8–5 shows the graph for the incremental cost analysis

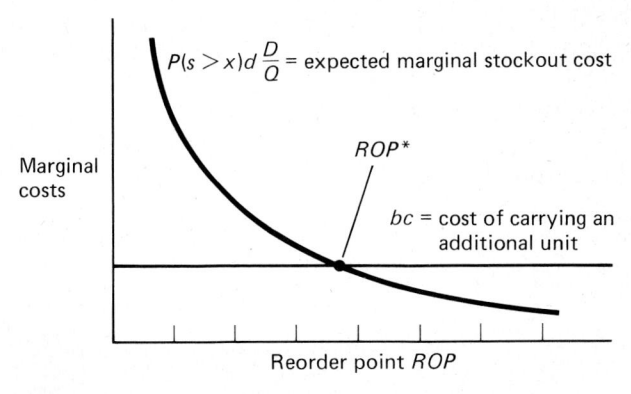

Figure 8–5. Marginal costs.

that underlies Eq. (8–1). The function labeled expected marginal stockout cost shows that the expected stockout cost will decline for each additional unit of safety stock. It will eventually approach zero when we carry enough units of safety stock to eliminate all stockouts, that is, when $P(s > x) = 0$. The optimal ROP^* is obtained when the cost of carrying the additional unit bc is equal to the incremental stockout cost.

ASSUMING DEPENDENCE OF ROP AND EOQ

In the foregoing analysis we have determined the reorder point ROP independently of the economic order quantity Q. This will often give satisfactory solutions, even though this assumption of independence between ROP and Q is incorrect. We now show that Q and ROP are not independent by developing a total cost equation for an example similar to the ones discussed so far in this chapter. Let us assume that our estimated expected demand for the year D is not affected by any stockouts we experience. When stockouts do not affect demand, the units that were demanded but not available during the lead time will be backordered. That means that the unfilled sales orders received during the lead time will be filled as soon as the order quantity Q arrives.

In the preceding section we defined safety stock as $SS = ROP - E(S)$, or safety stock minus expected demand during lead time. The average inventory can now be expressed as

$$\text{average inventory} = \frac{Q}{2} + ROP - E(S)$$

The total annual inventory carrying cost then becomes

$$\text{annual carrying cost} = bc \left[\frac{Q}{2} + ROP - E(S) \right]$$

where bc is the unit carrying cost per year. The ordering cost is defined as in Chapter 7:

$$\text{annual ordering cost} = C_s \frac{D}{Q}$$

where C_s is the cost per order placed and D is the expected annual demand. Because demand is now considered as a random variable, D is viewed as the mean of the annual demand. The third element of our total equation is the annual stockout cost. We express it as

$$\text{annual stockout cost} = d\, E(SPL)\, \frac{D}{Q}$$

where d is the cost per stockout, $E(SPL)$ is the expected or mean number of stockouts per lead time, and D/Q is the number of orders per

8.4 / Optimal Levels of Safety Stock

year (i.e., the number of lead times per year). The expected number of stockouts $E(SPL)$ will, of course, depend on the amount of safety stock, which, in turn, depends on where we set the reorder point ROP.

We can now state the total cost equation as

$$TC = C_s \frac{D}{Q} + bc \left[\frac{Q}{2} + ROP - E(S) \right] + d\, E(SPL) \frac{D}{Q} \qquad (8\text{--}4)$$

It is important to note the total cost now depends not only on the order quantity Q but also on the reorder point ROP. We therefore seek the combination of values for Q and ROP that will minimize the total cost function. We now illustrate the calculation of the total annual cost for different values of Q and ROP.

Let us consider the following scenario. A sporting goods store in a small college town estimates the annual demand for squash rackets to be 225 units. The cost of placing an order is estimated at \$5, the stockout cost is estimated at \$6 per unit, and inventory carrying cost is estimated at \$2.50 per unit. A careful study of the demand during the 2-day lead time resulted in the distribution given in Table 8–3. $P(S = X)$ can be read as a stockout probability for a given reorder point ROP indicated by the x units in the first column. For example, if we select the ROP at 2 units, the *probability* of running out of stock is 0.16.

TABLE 8–3.

Demand During Lead Time (x) units/2 days	$P(S)$	$P(S > X)$	
0	0.25	0.75	
1	0.27	0.48	
2	0.32	0.16	
3	0.11	0.05	Mean demand during
4	0.05	0.00	lead time $E(S) =$
	1.00		1.44

We now calculate the *expected number of stockouts* per lead time $E(SPL)$ for each possible ROP, in our example 0 to 4. We do this in Table 8–4. We start with a ROP of zero. In the second column we list the number of units that can possibly be demanded when not available given the ROP in column 1. For example, with $ROP = 0$, it is possible that we shall be short by 4, 3, 2, or 1 units. For the ROP of 1, possible shortages are 3, 2, and 1 units. The third column, labeled $P(S = X)$, shows the probability for each possible value of demand during the lead time. For example, the column labeled $P(S = X)$ for $ROP = 0$ should be read as: The probability that a fourth unit is demanded is 0.05; the probability that the third unit is demanded is 0.11; and so on.

The number of units demanded and not available, in other words, the number of units by which we are short (column 2), are then multiplied by their associated probabilities [column labeled $P(S = X)$] to give us the fourth column. The sum of the products in the fourth column gives us the *expected* number of shortages per lead time [$E(SPL)$] for each *ROP*.

TABLE 8–4. Computation of Expected Stockouts per Lead Time E(SPL) for Each Reorder Point (ROP)

ROP	Units Demanded (x) Minus ROP	P(S = X)	(x − ROP) [P(S = X)]	
0	(4 − 0)	0.05		0.20
	(3 − 0)	0.11		0.33
	(2 − 0)	0.32		0.64
	(1 − 0)	0.27		0.27
			E(SPL)	1.44
1	(4 − 1)	0.05		0.15
	(3 − 1)	0.11		0.22
	(2 − 1)	0.32		0.32
			E(SPL)	0.69
2	(4 − 2)	0.05		0.1
	(3 − 2)	0.11		0.11
			E(SPL)	0.21
3	(4 − 3)	0.05	E(SPL)	0.05
4	(4 − 4)	0.05	E(SPL)	0

To find the optimal inventory policy, we have to determine the best order quantity (Q) and the best safety stock level (i.e., *ROP*). We have both Q and *ROP* under our control, but not in one comprehensive model. We can determine an initial Q from our EOQ model in the previous chapter. Recall that the EOQ model is relatively insensitive to error, and thus provides a good starting point. Using our model yields

$$Q = \sqrt{\frac{2(225)(5)}{2.5}} = 30 \text{ units}$$

We now arbitrarily select a *ROP* of 3. The total cost equation is

$$TC = C_s \frac{D}{Q} + bc \left[\frac{Q}{2} + ROP - E(S) \right] + d\, E(SPL) \frac{D}{Q}$$

By inserting $Q = 30$, and $E(SPL) = 0.05$, $E(S) = 1.44$, and the other values given, we can readily calculate the total annual cost (using $Q = 30$ and $ROP = 3$) to be 81.15. Because Q and *ROP* are the only decision variables, we can test the cost equation for many different combina-

8.4 / Optimal Levels of Safety Stock

tions of *Q* and *ROP*. The combination that yields the lower total cost would probably be close to the optimal solution. In Table 8–5 we do this for several selected values of *Q* and *ROP*. We find that from the values for *Q* and *ROP* analyzed, *Q* = 31 and *ROP* = 3 yield the minimum cost solution. We also note again that the total cost is not very sensitive to changes in the order quantity *Q*.

In the appendix to this chapter we develop, by the use of differential calculus, the following models for determining optimal values for *Q* and *ROP*:

$$Q^* = \sqrt{\frac{2D[C_s + d\, E(SPL)]}{bc}} \qquad (8\text{--}5)$$

$$P(S > X)^* = \frac{bcQ}{dD} \qquad (8\text{--}6)$$

TABLE 8–5. Total Annual Cost for Different Values of *Q* and *R*.

Q	ROP	Order Cost $C_s \dfrac{D}{Q}$	Inventory Carrying Cost $bc\left[\dfrac{Q}{2} + ROP - E(S)\right]$	Stockout Cost $d\, E(SPL) \dfrac{D}{Q}$	Total Cost TC
29	4	38.75	42.65	0.00	81.40
	3	38.75	40.15	2.33	81.23
	2	38.75	37.65	9.78	86.18
	1	38.75	35.15	32.12	106.02
30	4	37.5	43.90	0.00	81.40
	3	37.5	41.40	2.25	81.15
	2	37.5	38.90	9.45	85.85
	1	37.5	36.40	31.05	104.95
31*	4	36.29	45.15	0.00	81.44
	3*	36.29	42.65	2.18	81.12
	2	36.29	40.15	9.14	85.58
	1	36.29	37.65	30.04	103.98
32	4	35.16	46.40	0.00	81.56
	3	35.16	43.90	2.11	81.17
	2	35.16	41.40	8.85	85.41
	1	35.16	38.90	29.11	103.17
33	4	34.09	47.65	0.00	81.74
	3	34.09	45.15	2.05	81.29
	2	34.09	42.65	8.59	85.33
	1	34.09	40.15	28.23	102.47

*Policy yielding lowest total cost.

$P(S > X)^*$ is the optimal stock out probability that enables us to find the optimal *ROP* by referring to Table 8–5. These two equations cannot be solved independently. We solve them by using a trial-and-error procedure; that is, we have to assume a value for Q^* and solve for $P(S > X)^*$. Having obtained a value for $P(S > X)^*$, we again solve for Q^*, noting that $P(S > X) = E(SPL)$. We repeat this procedure until we find a value for both Q^* and $P(S > X)^*$ that will satisfy both equations.

Let us begin with $Q^* = 30$, the value we obtained using the square-root model for the EOQ introduced in Chapter 7. We use this value in Equation (8–6) to obtain:

$$P(S > X)^* = \frac{2.5(30)}{6(225)} = 0.0556$$

We now continue the trial-and-error method by updating Q^* with the value of $E(SPL)$:

$$Q^* = \sqrt{\frac{2(225)[5 + 6(0.0556)]}{2.5}} = 30.98$$

Because this yields a different Q^* value than the previous iteration, we must recalculate $P(S > X)^*$.

$$P(S > X)^* = \frac{2.5(30.98)}{6(225)} = 0.0574$$

Again, substituting in the equation for Q^* yields

$$Q^* = \sqrt{\frac{2(225)[5 + 6(0.0574)]}{2.5}} = 31.02$$

Once again, a new Q^* forces recalculation of $P(S > X)^*$, with the new value for Q^*, yielding

$$P(S > X)^* = \frac{2.5(31.02)}{6(225)} = 0.0574$$

Because this is the same value as we obtained in the preceding iteration, we have obtained a solution for both equations. We find the optimal *ROP* by referring to Table 8–4, where we note that $P(S > X)^* = 0.0574$ indicates a *ROP* of 3 units. The minimum total cost solution is therefore given by $ROP = 3$ and $Q = 31$ units; using these values, we calculate the total cost using Eq. (8–4).

$$TC = 5\left(\frac{225}{31}\right) + 2.5\left(\frac{31}{2} + 3 - 1.44\right) + 6(0.05)\frac{D}{Q} = 81.12$$

8.5 / Note on Normally Distributed Demand During Lead Time

This result is identical with the minimum cost solution obtained in Table 8–5.

Earlier in the chapter we developed, by means of marginal analysis, Eq. (8–2) for obtaining an optimal *ROP* independent of the reorder point. This equation,

$$P(S > X) = \frac{bc}{d}\left(\frac{Q}{D}\right)$$

is identical to the one developed by means of differential calculus. If we determine *Q* using the square-root model of Chapter 7 and *ROP* using the above formula, we get

$$Q = \sqrt{\frac{2(225)(5)}{2.5}} = 30$$

$$P(S > X) = \frac{2.5(30)}{6(225)} = 0.0556$$

This also indicates an *ROP* of 3. The total cost for *ROP* = 3 and *Q* = 30 has already been calculated in Table 8–5. It amounts to $81.15 and is therefore only insignificantly higher than the one obtained by the correct model, in which the total cost depends on both *Q* and *ROP*. We can conclude that under the given assumptions, calculating *ROP* and *Q* independently will usually give a close approximation to the optimal solution.

8.5 Note on Normally Distributed Demand During Lead Time

In many inventory systems it is appropriate to represent the demand during lead time by a continuous distribution. If the normal distribution can be used as a realistic representation of the demand during the lead time, only minor modifications are needed for the *ROP* and EOQ models presented earlier.

The major difference concerns the manner in which we calculate the expected number of stockouts per lead time *E(SPL)*. Figure 8–6 shows the normal distribution for the demand during lead time *E(S)* and the reorder point *ROP*. The distance between *E(S)* and *ROP* can be expressed in numbers of standard deviations or Z (σ). A shortage will occur whenever demand during lead time exceeds *ROP*. The increase in number of units short can be plotted as a straight line with a slope of 1. The area under the normal curve beyond the *ROP* repre-

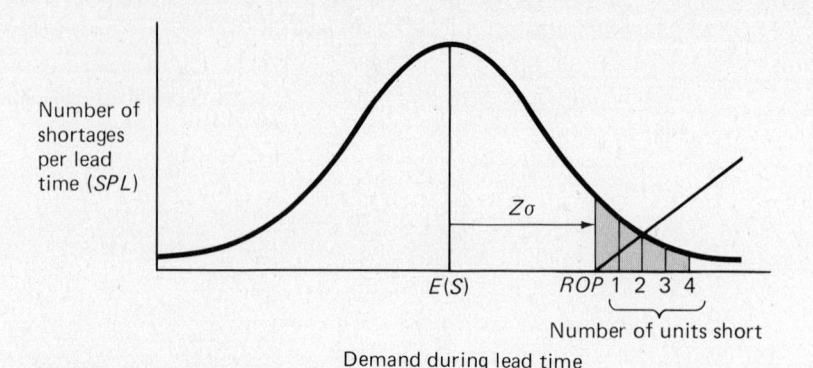

Figure 8-6. Normal distribution for $E(S)$

sents the stockout probability. By dividing the area into small intervals, we can see how probabilities could be assigned to each number of units short and the expected number of units short $E(SPL)$ may then be calculated. In the case of the normal distribution, the expected number of stockouts per lead time is

$$E(SPL) = \sigma N(Z)$$

where $N(Z)$ is the so-called normal loss function given in Table 5 at the back of the book. Assume that we have a $ROP = 2.14$, with $\sigma = 30$, to the right of $E(S)$. We go to Table 5 at the end of the book and find $N(Z)$ for 2.14 as 0.005788, giving us $E(SPL) = 30(0.00588) = 0.1764$.

We now use an example to illustrate these calculations. Assume that the expected annual demand $D = 2000$. The cost of placing an order $C_s = \$10$; annual cost of carrying a unit $bc = \$0.80$; there is a guaranteed lead time of 10 days and average demand during that lead time of 100 units; the standard deviation of that demand $\sigma = 30$ units, and the cost of being out of stock is estimated to be \$5 per unit. We first calculate the economic lot size using the EOQ formula of Chapter 7.

$$Q = \sqrt{\frac{2(10)(2000)}{(0.8)}} = 224$$

Using Eq. (8-6), we calculate $P(S > X)^*$.

$$P(S > X) = \frac{(0.8)(224)}{(5)(2000)} = 0.01792$$

Referring to Table 2 at the end of the book, we find that this probability corresponds to a distance of approximately 2.1 standard deviations from $E(S)$. Referring to Table 5, we find $N(Z) = 0.006468$, giving

$$E(SPL) = 30(0.006468) = 0.19404$$

We can now use Eq. (8–5) to calculate Q^*.

$$Q^* = \sqrt{\frac{2(2000)[10 + 5(0.19404)]}{0.8}} = 234$$

substituting 234 into Eq. (8–6) yields

$$P(S > X) = \frac{0.8(234)}{5(2000)} = 0.01872$$

which corresponds to 2.08 standard deviations. Referring to Table 5, we find $N(Z)$ to be (0.006835), which gives us

$$E(SPL) = 30(0.006835) = 0.2051$$

substituting 0.2051 into Eq. (8–5) yields

$$Q^* = \sqrt{\frac{2(2000)[10 + 5(0.2051)]}{0.8}} = 237$$

which, when substituted into Eq. (8–6), gives us

$$P(S > X)^* = \frac{0.8(237)}{5(2000)} = 0.01896$$

corresponding to about 2.08 standard deviations; referring to Table 5, we find $N(Z)$ to be 0.006835, giving us $E(SPL) = 0.2051$, as before. The minimal total cost will be achieved with an order quantity $Q = 237$ and $ROP = 2.08(30) = 62$ units.

8.6 Safety Stock When Stockout Costs Are Unknown

In determining the optimal level of safety stock in the preceding sections, we consistently assumed that we could reasonably estimate the stockout cost. In many cases such costs can be estimated, although a special cost study must be made because management accounting systems are not designed to furnish such information on a routine basis. Such a study would involve estimating stockout-related costs over a given period. Such costs include costs of following up on customer inquiries and costs of expediting production and deliveries, including overtime, additional shipping charges, and lost contribution margins. After determining the total of these costs, we could divide them by the total number of units backordered or not sold due to stockouts in the same period to arrive at a reasonable stockout cost per unit of stockout.

Especially in manufacturing firms, it is often almost impossible to develop a reasonable estimate. A temporary shortage of raw materials or spare parts may interrupt production for only a few minutes, or in extreme cases for several days or longer. This makes the estimation of a stockout cost per unit of stockout extremely difficult. In cases where it is considered impossible to estimate stockouts, many firms adopt a so-called *service-level* policy. A *service level* is simply a subjective probability estimate for stockouts that management is willing to tolerate. For example, a 95 percent service level means that we are willing to accept only a 5 percent probability of being out of stock. Because, under the economic lots size system, for all practical purposes we risk being out of stock only during the lead time, a 95 percent service level implies that we shall be out of stock on average only once during 20 inventory cycles. If we have five cycles per year, this means one stockout during 4 years, on the average.

Establishing a reasonable service level assumes that we have a reasonable idea of the demand probability distribution during the lead time and that the costs of carrying additional units of safety stock have been carefully considered. An example will illustrate the basic concepts involved.

Assume that the average demand during the lead time $s = 100$ with a standard deviation $\sigma = 20$ and an annual cost of carrying a unit of safety stock of \$5. Annual demand D is 3000, and Q has been calculated as 300 units. In Table 8–6 we show the safety stock requirements and costs for selected service levels.

TABLE 8–6. Inventory Service Level

(1) Service Level (%)	(2) Approximate Z Value	(3) Units of Safety Stock Needed*	(4) Annual Carrying Cost for Safety Stock
50	0	0	0
75	0.67	13	65
90	1.28	26	130
95	1.65	33	165
96	1.75	35	175
97	1.88	38	190
98	2.06	41	205
99	2.33	47	235
99.9	3.09	62	310

*Rounded to the nearest unit.

Column (2) of Table 8–6 contains approximated Z values obtained from Table 2 at the back of the book. They are multiplied by 20, the standard deviation of the demand, to obtain the units of safety stock required to assure the service level indicated in column (1). Column (4) shows the annual carrying cost, which is obtained by multiplying the safety stock units by 5.

The table shows that assuring higher service levels requires increases in safety stock and, consequently, increased carrying costs. Conceptually, the increased cost of higher service levels should be justified by the equivalent benefits of avoiding stockouts and their related costs, which under a service-level policy are assumed to be impossible to estimate.

Let us now refer again briefly to Eq. (8–3):

$$P(S \leq X) = 1 - \frac{bc}{d}\left(\frac{D}{Q}\right)$$

Recall that $P(S \leq X)$ was the probability that demand during lead time was less than or equal to the ith unit on the cumulative less than probability distribution of Table 8–3. We used Eq. (8–3) to establish an optimal ROP and with it an optimal level of safety stock. In fact, $P(S \leq X)$ indicated the *optimal service level* for the example discussed.

We can now use Eq. (8–3) to evaluate service-level policies. The left side of the equation represents the given service level. On the right-hand side the only unknown is d, the stockout cost per unit. All other factors are assumed known when we establish a service-level policy. We can therefore use this to compute the stockout cost implicit in a given service-level policy. Applying this to our example and evaluating a service-level of 99 percent, we have

$$0.99 = 1 - \frac{5}{d}\left(\frac{3000}{300}\right)$$

$$d = 5000$$

This implicit cost per unit of stockout can therefore be used to evaluate the reasonableness of a given service-level policy.

8.7 Constant Order Cycle Systems and Periodic Review Systems

The inventory systems discussed in the preceding sections using a constant order quantity are sometimes referred to as Q systems. These systems react to fluctuations of demand by changing the time period between reorders. Other systems, called *constant order cycle systems* or *periodic inventory review systems* have fixed reorder dates; that is, the time between reorders is constant, and Q depends on usage since the previous replenishment order. In the following we refer to periodic review systems simply as P systems. P systems may be preferable when several items are bought from the same supplier, because joint ordering may significantly reduce transportation costs (carload freight rates). There may also be situations where the managerial cost of constant surveillance, as required for the Q systems, is considered too high. The cost of operating a P system tends to be lower than that for the Q system. However, the average inventory level in the constant order system tends to be higher than under the Q system to obtain the same service level. The tradeoff is between more information and operating costs versus the cost of carrying more inventory. Obviously, it is a complex problem to choose between the two approaches.

In general, we can say that Q systems are preferable for relatively high-cost items with high stockout costs, such as expensive parts that are part of a larger assembly. The constant order cycle, or P system, is preferable in situations where inventory costs are low (i.e., high inventory levels are not expensive) and stockout costs are reasonably low (e.g., items with low unit costs, short lead times, long shelf lives, and low storage costs). Here we trade off higher inventory costs against a lower cost of managing the system. Later in this chapter we discuss briefly other tradeoffs in inventory systems.

The logic and mathematical derivations of constant order cycle systems are more difficult than the basic EOQ model and are beyond the scope of this book.

8.8 Some General Remarks

For the constant order cycle system we discussed some of the issues and basic tradeoffs. In practice, the cost of managing the inventory system itself becomes important. The total costs of an inventory system are the costs we considered in explaining the basic models *plus* the cost of managing the system.

A crucial aspect of the EOQ model is the assumption concerning the nature of demand (or usage). For the deterministic model we assumed a constant, known, and uniform usage; for example, every day we use 3 units. Even for the stochastic models we assume a regularity of usage on average, or over the long term; we cannot predict exactly how many items will be used on a given day, but we can forecast quite accurately the annual demand. For some items, this is appropriate. In either case, we have assumed a reasonably constant and known demand for the item. This is a basic assumption of the model. Where the assumption is appropriate, the EOQ is a reasonable model. When this assumption is not met, for example, when demand is random and in small quantities, the EOQ model is inappropriate. These situations include stand-by generators for power plants, jet engines for a small fleet of planes, or transmissions for a small fleet of trucks. These situations involve high-priced items with infrequent, random demand, and the EOQ simply will not fit—we must return to a more basic analysis, starting with probability models. Such situations often require a unique probability model to obtain a reasonable answer. However, given the cost of the inventory, this investment in analysis may well be worth the effort.

8.9 ABC Inventory Systems

As pointed out in the preceding section, a company's inventories usually consist of a large number of different items. Some may be very important because they require large investments in terms of dollars, others are important because they account for a major part of sales; still others, such as critical spare parts for automated manufacturing equipment, may be important because a stockout situation may cause costly stoppages of a manufacturing process. Obviously management wants a system that controls more important items more effectively than others. In order to identify these important items, we need a measure of importance.

The most commonly used system to identify inventory items that need tight controls is the so-called *ABC* classification system. Under this system, inventory items are grouped into three classifications called *A*, *B*, and *C* on the basis of some measure of relative importance. One such measure would be the usage value of inventory items. Usage value is defined as unit cost times annual usage. The usage value for each item is determined, and all items are then listed in descending order of usage value. Figure 8–7 shows a graph resulting from such an analysis.

In Figure 8–7 we assume that a company has a 3000-item inventory. After listing them in descending order of their usage value, we assign the top 10 percent of the items to group *A*, thus accounting for about 75 percent of the total usage value. Group *B* consists of the next 15 percent of the items, constituting 20 percent of total usage value, whereas group *C* includes the remaining 75 percent of the items, which account for only 5 percent of total usage value. Table 8–7 also illustrates these *ABC* classifications.

It should be emphasized that the classification scheme illustrated is only an example, and the grouping is, of course, somewhat arbitrary. Companies may use two, three, four, or even five classifications, and the cutoffs between the classifications will also vary. The dividing line between *A* and *B* items is usually set such that a small percentage of

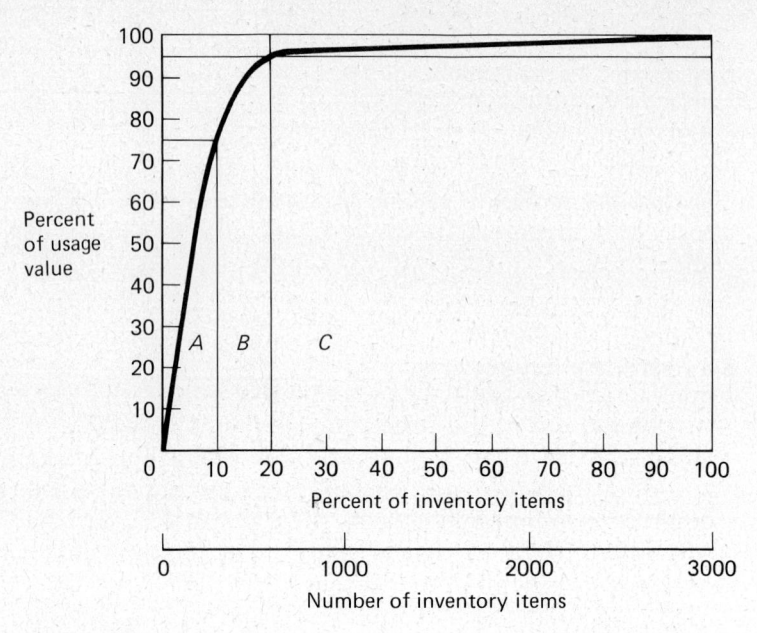

Inventory Models with Probabilistic Demand / Chapter 8

Figure 8–7. Inventory usage and valuation under an ABC classification system.

items, say, 10 percent, will account for 50 to 80 percent of usage value. Instead of usage value, sales value or some other measure may be used as a measure of importance.

The *A* group of items, representing the most important portion of our stocks, should be monitored very closely. Obviously it is very important to have a supply available. Carrying costs are high and should be balanced against ordering cost and the cost of stockouts. Given a relatively constant demand, an EOQ system, even though the most costly to operate, is probably appropriate.

The *B*-group items are less important but do require a reasonable amount of managerial attention. These items are relatively less expensive, and stockout costs are in many cases less important. It is probably worthwhile to trade off higher average inventories and higher stockout

TABLE 8–7. ABC Inventory Classifications

Inventory Classification	Number of Items	Percent of Items	Percent of Usage Value
A	300	10	75
B	450	15	20
C	2250	75	5
Total	3000	100	100

probabilities against the lower operating costs of a periodic review system.

The C-group items constitute only a minor investment. They should require only minimal controls, because the potential savings usually do not justify the expense of an elaborate control system. Rules of thumb may be used to establish reorder points, and relatively large quantities are usually ordered and carried.

8.10 Summary

In this chapter we tried to answer the important question of "when to order." We have dropped the assumptions of certainty with respect to demand, but we continued to assume a fixed lead time. Using a given discrete probability distribution and marginal analysis of stockout costs and the cost of carrying safety stock, we determined an optimal reorder point *(ROP)* and an optimal level of safety stock. We also introduced the notion of *service levels* for a situation where it is difficult or impossible to estimate stockout costs.

We then compared constant order, or Q cycle, systems with periodic inventory review, or P, systems. We found that P systems require a higher level of safety stock but may be less expensive than Q systems in terms of system operating costs. We also pointed out the limitations of the models discussed, especially with respect to assumptions of a reasonably constant demand. At the conclusion of the chapter, we introduced the *ABC* inventory system, under which inventory items are classified into groups according to their importance. Obviously, management efforts for planning and controlling inventory items will concentrate on the most important items.

Glossary

ABC inventory systems. Systems that classify inventory items into three groups according to their importance. Management will concentrate its control efforts on the most important items.

Constant order cycle system. An inventory system that uses a constant reorder quantity. Also called economic lot-size model.

Expected stockouts during lead time. The average number of units by which we will be short during a lead time.

Lead time. The time, usually in days or weeks, that elapses between the placing of an order and the arrival of the goods.

Periodic inventory review system. An inventory system with a constant time period between reorders and a variable reorder quantity.

Reorder point. The inventory level at which we place a new order to replenish the stock.

Safety stock. Additional units of stock carried in order to avoid an excessive number of stockouts. Also called buffer stock.
Service level. The percentage of time during a replenishment cycle for which all arriving orders can be satisfied.
Stockout. A situation that arises when an item is demanded or needed but not in stock.
Stockout cost. The unit cost due to a stockout.

Problems

1. Compare the inventory models under certainty with those that assume uncertainty. State all assumptions and explain all the differences in the functions we try to minimize. Also discuss how we can go about estimating the parameters required by the models.
2. In the chapter we assumed that stockouts would not affect our expected demand for the planning period. What would happen if sales lost due to stockouts were permanently lost?

   REQUIRED
   a. The impact on our estimated demand D
   b. The impact on Q, ROP, and the safety stock
   c. The impact on the total cost function TC
   d. An attempt to modify the total cost function TC, the models for Q^* and ROP to reflect the fact that stockouts result in a permanent loss of sales.
3. The owner of a small bakery must decide on how many dozen of a special sweet roll to bake every day. Estimated variable cost per unit is 15¢ per dozen, and they can be sold on the same day for 35¢. Any rolls not sold during the day are sold the next day for 10¢ per dozen. The baker assesses the probability of demand for these rolls as follows:

Demand (Dozen per Day)	Probability
Less than 4	0
4	0.15
5	0.35
6	0.40
7	0.10

   REQUIRED
   a. How many rolls should be baked each day?
   b. Now assume that the local village witch is willing to go into a trance every night to predict the exact demand for sweet rolls for the next day. How much of a fee should the baker be willing to pay for this information? Note that it is not exactly the same as the safety stock problem.
4. (CPA) This question can be answered with very little knowledge of inventory theory. You can answer the question with a careful reading, and ap-

plication of basic concepts in probability that were developed in an earlier chapter.

As the accounting consultant for Leslie Company, you have compiled data on the day-to-day demand rate from Leslie's customers for product A and the lead time to receive product A from its supplier. The data are summarized in the following probability tables:

Demand for Product A

Unit Demand per Day	Probability of Occurrence
0	0.45
1	0.15
2	0.30
3	0.10
	1.00

Lead Time for Product A

Lead Time in Days	Probability of Occurrence
1	0.40
2	0.35
3	0.25
	1.00

Leslie is able to deliver product A to its customers the same day that product A is received from its supplier. All units of product A demanded but not available, due to a stockout, are backordered and are filled immediately when a new shipment arrives.

a. The probability of the demand for product A being 9 units during a 3-day lead time for delivery from the supplier is
   (1) 0.00025
   (2) 0.10
   (3) 0.025
   (4) 0.25

b. If Leslie reorders 10 units of product A when its inventory level is 10 units, the number of days during a 360-day year that Leslie will experience a stockout of product A is
   (1) 0.75 days
   (2) 36 days
   (3) 10 days
   (4) 0 days

c. Leslie has developed an inventory model based on the probability tables and desires a solution for minimizing total annual inventory costs. Included in inventory costs are the costs of holding product A, ordering

and receiving product A, and incurring stockouts of product A. The solution would state:
  (1) At what inventory level to reorder and how many units to reorder
  (2) Either at what inventory level to reorder or how many units to reorder
  (3) How many units to reorder but not at what inventory level to reorder
  (4) At what inventory level to reorder but not how many units to reorder

5. Currently, the ABC Company is reviewing its inventory decision on item #ABC-017. At present, ABC is satisfied with the order quantity, but needs a clarification on the inventory level for reorder. The following data are available:

   1. The order quantity is 600 units per order.
   2. Annual demand is 7200 units per year.
   3. The lead time on an order is 15 calendar days, i.e., $\frac{1}{2}$ month or $\frac{1}{24}$ yr.
   4. The holding cost is $1 per unit per cycle.
   5. The stockout cost is $3 per unit per cycle.
   6. The demand over the lead time is probabilistic, and takes the distribution shown in the accompanying diagram.

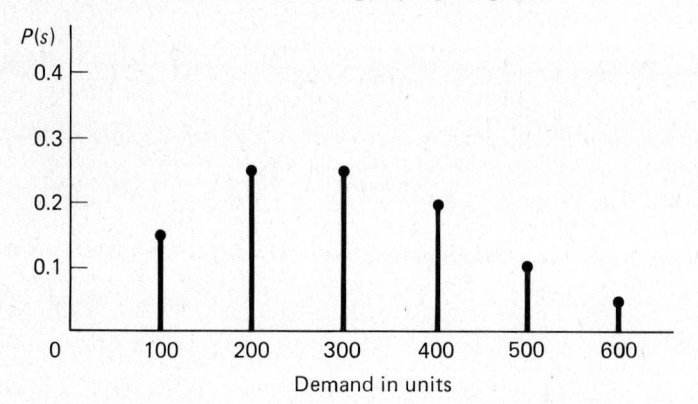

These data were collected from the inventory clerk who notes every request for #ABC-017, whether it is filled or not.
   The ABC managers have a number of questions:
a. If, at present, ABC reorders this item when there are 200 in inventory, what is the probability of stockout during any cycle? What are the total expected inventory and stockout costs for a cycle?
b. If the probability of stockout must be 0.05 or less, what will be the reorder point? What are the total expected inventory and stockout costs for a cycle?
c. Using the data given, what is the reorder point that will balance the ordering cost against the stockout cost in an optimal manner? What are the total expected inventory and stockout costs for a cycle?
d. If ABC assumes an infinite stockout cost, what is the reorder point? What are the total expected inventory and stockout costs for a cycle?

Problems

e. The lead time may be changed to 20 days. Can you answer the above questions for this case? Why or why not?
f. You have been asked to work with inventory control and the computer department to put inventory records on the computer and to use EOQ models for control. To begin, you have been asked to devise a flowchart of the computer information system for the inventory control. Your manager has suggested the system must do, at least, the following:
   (1) Use EOQ models for inventory quantities and times.
   (2) Provide relevant accounting data so that we know where we are, i.e., inventory levels, back orders, orders outstanding, etc., at any point in time.
   (3) Provide data that will make inventory easily audited by the external auditor.
   (4) Provide management with details concerning "errors and what went wrong," with answers for each mistake (management is particularly interested in this information so that the system can be modified and improved). On a separate page, indicate how your system as flow charted addresses your manager's concern.

6. A large sporting goods store in California specializing in tennis equipment has enjoyed a fairly regular demand for a popular racket. During the next year, the store expects to sell 7200 of these rackets. The rackets cost $50 per unit, delivery included. Inventory carrying cost is estimated at 20 percent of unit cost. The cost of placing an order is $12. The company is the only distributor for this brand in the area, and does not think it will lose a customer on the few occasions when it is out of stock. The store makes every effort to deliver the racket to the customer as soon as the next shipment arrives. The cost of these efforts is estimated to be about $3 per occurrence. The store operates 360 days a year. It takes only 3 days from the time an order is placed until delivery. Based on careful analysis of past sales during these 3-day replenishment periods, management developed the following probability distribution for the sale of rackets during a replenishment period:

Estimated Sales During Lead Time

Number of Rackets Sold per Lead Time	Probability of Sale $P(S)$
18	0.15
19	0.20
20	0.30
21	0.20
22	0.10
23	0.05
	1.00

REQUIRED
Using the square-root formula for the economic lot size and Eq. (8–4) calculate:
   a. The economic order quantity

b. The number of lead times per year
c. The reorder point and the safety stock
d. The annual inventory-related total cost

Recalculate a, b, c, and d using Eqs. (8–6) and (8–7), then compare the results and explain the differences.

7. A manufacturer of kitchen appliances finds that a gear assembly that had been purchased on the outside could be produced internally at a standard price that is identical to the purchase cost per unit. The annual demand for the part is 26,000 units, or about 500 units per week on average. The standard cost includes all variable manufacturing costs but does not include the setup cost of $200 per setup. The gear assembly can be produced internally at a rate of 2000 per week. When purchasing the gear, an ordering cost of $40 is incurred in addition to the purchase price. When manufacturing the part internally, there is practically no lead time. When buying, the lead time is 20 days. Demand during this lead time is normally distributed, with a mean of 2000 units and a standard deviation of 400 units. The cost of carrying a unit of inventory is $0.20 per unit per year. The shortage cost is estimated at $2 per unit.

REQUIRED

a. Based on the information given, do you think that the firm should make or buy the assembly?
b. What additional information would you request before making a decision?

8. An automotive parts dealer carries transmission gears in inventory that yield a contribution margin of $20 per unit when sold. Expected sales are 90 units per year, the cost to carry one such gear in inventory is estimated at $5 per year, and the reorder quantity Q has been calculated at 30 units. If management decided to carry sufficient safety stock to assure a service level of 95 percent at all times, what is the imputed stockout cost per unit of management's policy?

9. In analyzing the expected demand for the supply of a certain lubricant used in a factory, the purchase-order quantity was determined by the EOQ formula of Chapter 7. This resulted in eight replenishment cycles per year. The demand during lead time is based on the following distribution:

Demand x in Units	$P(S = X)$
4	0.04
5	0.08
6	0.10
7	0.40
8	0.18
9	0.10
10	0.06
11	0.04

Problems

The carrying cost is estimated at $20 per year. Assume that the safety stock is 2 units.

REQUIRED
a. What is the ROP?
b. What is the expected number of stockouts per lead time E(SPL)?
c. What is the stockout probability?
d. What is the implicit stockout cost?

10. Assume that a liquor store estimates that next year's demand for a little-known brand of beer, brewed by a small local brewery in a neighboring state, will be 4000 cases. The purchase cost is $2.50 per case, including shipping. The lead time for delivery is exactly 10 days. Ordering costs are $10, and carrying cost is estimated at 20 percent of unit cost. Demand during lead time period is normal, with a standard deviation of 30 units; stockouts are backordered at an estimated cost of $5.

REQUIRED
a. Compute Q using the EOQ model developed in Chapter 7. Also calculate ROP independent of your calculation of Q. Calculate the total annual cost.
b. Compute Q and ROP using the appropriate models from this chapter. Calculate total cost and compare with the results obtained in part a.

11. (CPA) The Polly Company wishes to determine the amount of safety stock that it should maintain for product D that will result in the lowest cost. The following information is available:

Stockout cost	$80 per occurrence
Carrying cost of safety stock	$2 per unit
Number of purchase orders	5 per year

The available options open to Polly are as follows:

Units of Safety Stock	Probability of Running Out of Safety Stock (%)
20	40
40	20
50	10
55	5

What is the optimal number of safety stock?

12. (CPA) Harrington & Sons, Inc., would like to determine the safety stock to maintain for a product, so that the lowest combination of stockout cost and carrying cost would result. Each stockout will cost $75; the carrying cost for each safety stock unit will be $1; the product will be ordered five times a year. The following probabilities of running out of stock during an order period are associated with various safety stock levels:

Safety Stock Level (units)	Probability of Stockout (%)
10	40
20	20
40	10
80	5

Using the expected value approach, determine the safety stock level.

13. *(CMA)* SaPane Company is a regional distributor of automobile window glass. With the introduction of the new subcompact car models and the expected high level of consumer demand, management recognizes a need to determine the total inventory cost associated with maintaining an optimal supply of replacement windshields for the new subcompact cars introduced by each of the three major manufacturers. SaPane is expecting a daily demand for 36 windshields. The purchase price of each windshield is $50.

Other costs associated with ordering and maintaining an inventory of these windshields are as follows:

The historical ordering costs incurred in the Purchase Order Department for placing and processing orders is shown below:

Year	Orders Placed and Processed	Total Ordering Costs
1978	20	$12,300
1979	55	12,475
1980	100	12,700

Management expects the ordering costs to increase 16 percent over the amounts and rates experienced the last 3 yr.

The windshield manufacturer charges SaPane a $75 shipping fee per order.

A clerk in the Receiving Department receives, inspects, and secures the windshields as they arrive from the manufacturer. This activity requires 8 hr per order received. This clerk has no other responsibilities and is paid at the rate of $9 per hour. Related variable overhead costs in this department are applied at the rate of $2.50 per hour.

Additional warehouse space will have to be rented to store the new windshields. Space can be rented as needed in a public warehouse at an estimated cost of $2500 per year plus $5.35 per windshield.

Breakage cost is estimated to be 6 percent of the average inventory value.

Taxes and fire insurance on the inventory are $1.15 per windshield.

The desired rate of return on the investment in inventory is 21 percent of the purchase price.

Six working days are required from the time the order is placed with the manufacturer until it is received. SaPane uses a 300-day work year when making economic order quantity computations. The economic order quantity formula is:

$$EOQ = \sqrt{\frac{2(\text{annual demand})(\text{ordering cost})}{\text{storage cost}}}$$

REQUIRED
a. Calculate the following values for SaPane Company.
   (1) The value for ordering cost that should be used in the EOQ formula.
   (2) The value for storage cost that should be used in the EOQ formula.
   (3) The economic order quantity.
   (4) The minimum annual relevant cost at the economic order quantity point.
   (5) The reorder point in units.
b. Without prejudice to your answer to Requirement a, assume the economic order quantity is 400 units, the storage cost is $28 per unit, and the stockout cost is $12 per unit. SaPane wants to determine the proper level of safety stock in order to minimize its relevant costs. Using the following probability schedule for excess demand during the reorder period, determine the proper amount of safety stock.

Number of Units Short Due to Excess Demand During Reorder Period	Probability of Occurrence
60	0.12
120	0.05
180	0.02

14. *(SMA)* A discount retail store estimates that the demand for an item will be 12,000 units per year. Each item costs the store $13. Ordering costs are $60 per order and the carrying costs are 12 percent per year. Four percent of the stock is either stolen or damaged after receipt by the store and cannot be sold.

REQUIRED
a. (1) Determine the economic order quantity.
   (2) Calculate the total annual cost of ordering and carrying the required inventory.
b. The retail store operates 250 days per year and the required ordering lead time is 10 days.
   (1) At what inventory level should reordering take place?
   (2) How does this affect the total annual cost of ordering and carrying the required inventory?

c. How much buffer stock should the retail store carry in order to maintain a 98 percent service level? (It is known that the standard deviation of the demand over a 10-day period is 20 units.)

References

American Accounting Association Report of Committee on Managerial Decision Models. "II-B Inventory Models" and "II-B Appendix." *The Accounting Review*, Suppl. to vol. 44 (1969): 64–72.

Brown, R. G. *Decision Rules for Inventory Management*. New York, Holt, Rinehart and Winston, 1970.

Buffa, E. S., and Taubert, W. H. *Production-Inventory Systems: Planning and Control*, rev. ed. Homewood, Ill.: Irwin, 1972.

Greene, J. H. *Production and Inventory Control Handbook*. New York, McGraw-Hill, 1970.

Hadley, G., and Whitin, T. M. *Analysis of Inventory Systems*. Englewood Cliffs, N.J.: Prentice-Hall, 1963.

Lewis, C. D. *Scientific Inventory Control*. New York: American Elsevier, 1970.

Lorber, H. W. "Coping with Fluctuating Demand for Professional Staff: A Prescription and Examples." *Interfaces* 9, no. 5 (November 1979).

Starr, M. K., and Miller, D. W. *Inventory Control: Theory and Practice*. Englewood Cliffs, N.J.: Prentice-Hall, 1962.

Wagner, H. M. *Principles of Operations Research*. Englewood Cliffs, N.J.: Prentice-Hall, 1969.

Appendix. Derivation of Optimal Q and ROP Under Uncertainty (shortages backordered)

$$TC = C_s \frac{D}{Q} + bc\left[\frac{Q}{2} + ROP - E(S)\right] + d\, E(SPL) \frac{D}{Q}$$

$$\frac{\delta TC}{\delta Q} = \frac{-C_s D}{Q^2} + \frac{bc}{2} - \frac{d\, E(SPL)\, D}{Q^2} = 0$$

$$Q^* = \sqrt{\frac{2D[C_s + d\, E(SPL)]}{bc}}$$

$$\frac{\delta TC}{\delta ROP} = bc - \frac{dD}{Q} P(S > X) = 0$$

$$P(S > X)^* = \frac{bc(Q)}{d(D)}$$

Appendix

Because $E(SPL)$, the expected number of stockouts, is

$$E(SPL) = \sum_{S=ROP}^{si} (S - ROP) P(S)$$

$$\frac{d\,E(SPL)}{dROP} = \frac{d\left[\sum_{S=ROP}^{si}(S - ROP) P(S)\right]}{dROP}$$

$$= \sum_{P(S=ROP)}^{si} P(S)$$

= stockout probability designated as $P(S = X)$ in the text

CHAPTER 9
Project Scheduling and Control Using CPM and PERT

9.1 **Introduction**

9.2 **The Project Structure**
An Example: Test Marketing of New Products

9.3 **The Project Network**

9.4 **A Dummy Task**

9.5 **PERT**

9.6 **PERT/Cost**

9.7 **CPM with Limited Resources**
Limited Resources Approach

9.8 **A Comprehensive Example for CPM with Limited Resources**

9.9 **Summary**

Glossary

Problems

References

Key Concepts

CPM
CPM under limited resources
Critical path
Dummy task
Earliest completion time
Earliest start time
Expected project time
Immediate predecessor
Latest completion time

Latest start time
PERT
PERT/cost
Project
Project network
Resource conflict
Sequencing constraint
Slack time
Task or activity

Key Applications
Development of new technology, e.g., aerospace, electronics, etc.
Large highway and building construction
Large project scheduling, e.g., a large audit review
Project management

9.1 Introduction

Managers are frequently faced with the problem of managing activities that can be labeled as programs or *projects*. Examples of such projects are the construction of a bridge or a new factory, the development of a new product, the installation of a new computer system, or the implementation of an audit of a major corporation. All such projects consist of a large number of *tasks* or *activities*, some of which may have to be implemented in sequence (for example, the walls of a house must be finished before one can start the roof) and others that may be carried out simultaneously (a furnace in the basement may be installed while the roof is being finished). Both time and cost are very important factors in the implementation of the tasks making up a project. The techniques discussed in this chapter are designed to assist managers in planning and controlling the timing and the cost of project implementation.

The critical path method (CPM) is widely used in the scheduling and control of large projects or highway and building construction. CPM was first used by E. I. duPont de Nemours & Co. in 1957 to improve scheduling of new plant construction. Program evaluation and review technique (PERT) is more widely used in aerospace, among defense contractors, and governmental projects. PERT was introduced by the U.S. Navy in 1958 in the management of the Polaris weapon system. Today both techniques are widely applied in both business and government. The two techniques are fundamentally the same, and differ only in their assumptions concerning the knowledge of time required for each task. CPM is a deterministic model; PERT, a probabilistic model. Other variations on CPM and PERT include (1) PERT/cost, and (2) CPM under limited resources, where the resource requirements for each task are given explicit consideration.

9.2 The Project Structure

When planning the implementation of complex projects, it is usually advisable to break up the total project into logical components. These logical subdivisions of a project are referred to as *tasks* or activities. Suppose that the project involves the construction of a home. Logical tasks would probably include excavation, construction of walls, installation of plumbing, electrical wiring, and so on. The construction of a house could be a project by itself, but it could also constitute a subtask within a larger project, for example, within the development of a neighborhood. Tasks should be viewed as organizational subunits of a project. Each task requires resources and time, and implementation should be carefully planned.

Once tasks have been identified, we must analyze the relationships among them. In building a house, it is necessary to put in the foundation before the electrical system. A task that must be completed before another task can start is called an *immediate predecessor*. However, not all tasks are sequential; for example, the plumbing system and the electrical system can be put in simultaneously or one before the other, in either order. In these cases, there is no *sequencing constraint*. For most projects, the set of tasks is a combination of those that are sequenced and those that are not sequenced. A project that is composed of tasks and sequencing constraints can be represented graphically as a *project network*. We begin with CPM, and consider PERT as a CPM variation. CPM, PERT, and their important variations are developed in the context of simple examples.

AN EXAMPLE: TEST MARKETING OF NEW PRODUCTS

Suppose that a firm wants to establish a schedule for the development, initial production, and test marketing of a new product. After careful analysis, the project is broken down into a set of tasks or activities. These tasks are shown in Table 9–1. Each task is given a code name for convenience: for example, D is the code name for the task of designing and preparing the package. Some of the tasks can be started only after another task is complete. For example, task D, the design and preparation of the package, can be started only after task A, the initial analysis of market and cost data, has been completed. Task A is said to be the immediate predecessor of task D. Or task D has task A as its immediate predecessor. The third column of Table 9–1 lists the immediate predecessors for the tasks in this project. A given task may have more than one immediate predecessor; for example, task H has both tasks E and G as immediate predecessors. For each task we must estimate the time required for its completion. This information is also included in Table 9–1. Defining the tasks, their immediate predecessors, and the estimation of completion times, as shown in Table 9–1, are very important parts of the analysis. This is not a simple mechanical process, but requires a thorough understanding of the project.

TABLE 9–1. The Tasks and Immediate Predecessors for the New Product Test Marketing Project

Code	Task	Immediate Predecessor	Estimated Completion Time for Each Task (wks)
A	Initial analysis of market and cost data		2
B	Devise test market plan and procedure for data gathering	A	5
C	Prepare production setup for new product	A	4
D	Design and prepare package	A	6
E	Set up and organize test market data collection	B	4
F	Initial production run	C	4
G	Distribute product to test market	D, F	2
H	Test market—gather and analyze data	E, G	6

9.3 The Project Network

One major objective of analyzing a project is the determination of the time required to complete the project. For this purpose a graphical network or CPM chart is introduced. The information in Table 9–1 is converted to a network representation for the new product as shown in Figure 9–1.

In the network, tasks are represented by arrows. Each arrow has a small circle or node at its start and its completion. These nodes represent so-called events. An event is defined as the beginning or completion of a task. The node following task A marks the completion of task A. At the same time it denotes the beginning of tasks B, C, and D. Task A, the first task on the left-hand side of Figure 9–1, is represented by the arrow labeled A. Tasks B, C, and D all have task A as immediate predecessors, and their three arrows all leave from the node marking the completion of task A. Task E has only task B as an immediate

9.3 / The Project Network

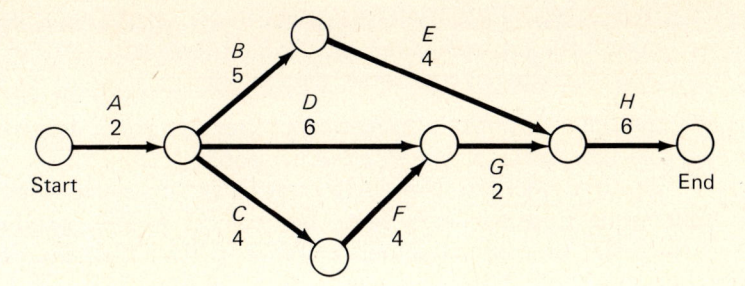

Figure 9-1. CPM network.

predecessor. Similarly, tasks *F* and *E* also have only one immediate predecessor. Tasks *H* and *G* are the only other tasks with two immediate predecessors. Another way of identifying tasks is by numbering the circles or the nodes. Each task is then identified by the number of the nodes at its beginning and its end. The estimated completion times for each task are shown above or below each arrow.

A path through the network is a sequence of connected tasks from the start of the project to its completion. In our example we have three paths: *A–B–E–H*, *A–D–G–H*, and *A–C–F–G–H*. We now calculate the total time required for each path by adding the times for each task on the path. Thus, the length of path *A–B–E–H* is 2 + 5 + 4 + 6 = 17, and the lengths of paths *A–D–G–H* and *A–C–F–G–H* are 16 and 18, respectively. The longest path through the network is called the *critical path*. The length of the critical path indicates the estimated minimum time required for the completion of the project. The tasks or activities on the critical path are referred to as critical tasks. These tasks are critical because any delay in their completion will delay the entire project. We now define the *slack* of an activity as the amount of time a task can be delayed without delaying the timely completion of the entire project. Critical tasks obviously have zero slack, because any delay in their completion will delay the project.

Identification of the critical path by adding estimated completion times for all possible paths through a network is both cumbersome and impractical as networks become more complicated. Some projects include thousands of tasks; therefore an efficient algorithm is used for the identification of the critical path and slack times for noncritical tasks. The following variables are used in this procedure:

ES_i = earliest possible start time for task i, assuming that all predecessor tasks were also started at their earliest possible starting times.
EF_i = earliest possible finish or completion time for activity i.
LF_i = latest possible finish for task i; exceeding this latest possible finish time means delay of the project's completion.

LS_i = latest possible start time for task i; if the task is started after LS_i, the project's completion will be delayed.

t_i = estimated completion time for activity i.

We shall illustrate the application of this algorithm using the new product test marketing project as our example.

We first calculate the early start (ES_i) and early finish (EF_i) times. Early start time for A is zero, because A has no predecessors. The early finish time for any task is its early start time plus the estimated completion time, or

$$EF_i = ES_i + t_i$$

For task A we have $EF_A = 0 + 2 = 2$; we enter these times for activity A on Figure 9–2. For task B, ES_B is given by A's early finish time; therefore $ES_B = 2$ and $EF_B = 2 + 5 = 7$. The early start and finish times for tasks C, D, E, and F are computed in the same manner. Task G depends on the completion of tasks D and F; its earliest possible starting time is therefore $EF_D = 8$, versus $EF_F = 10$, week 10. Task H, which depends on E and G, has week 12 as its earliest possible start time. The completion time for the entire project coincides with the finish time of the last task H and is 18 weeks.

To calculate the latest finish and latest start times, we begin at the project's end and move toward the project's start. For H the latest finish time is 18; therefore the latest start time to finish the project with no delay is $18 - 6 = 12$. The latest finish times for both E and G are thus week 12. We obtain the latest starting times by subtracting the respective estimated completion times from the latest start time of the immediate successor task. When there is more than one successor activity, such as for A, we take the smallest latest starting time of all immediate successor tasks. Thus, for task A the latest finish time is the

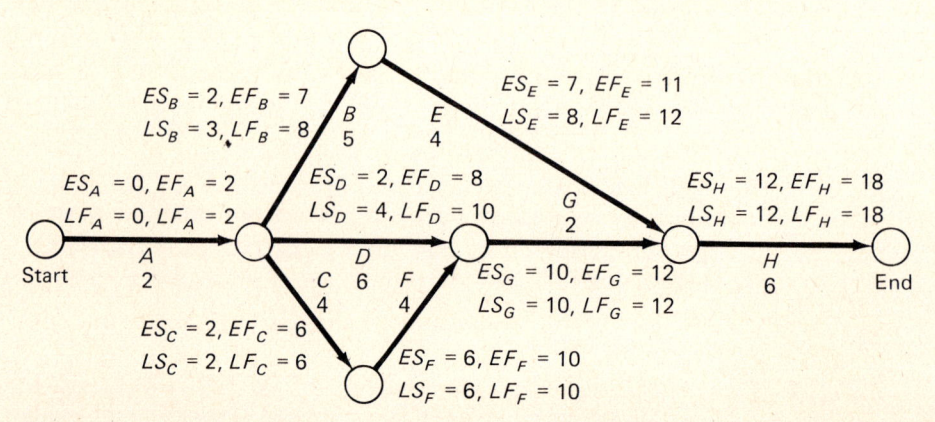

Figure 9–2. CPM network.

smallest of the latest start times of *B*, *D*, and *C*, that is, week 2. If more than 2 weeks are needed for task *A*, the entire project will be delayed. In general terms, we have

$$LS_i = \min(LS_{i+1} - t_i)$$

We can now calculate the slack of each task by subtracting the earliest finish time from the latest finish time:

$$\text{slack of task}_i = LF_i - EF_i$$

When the slack is zero, the task is on the critical path. Any positive slack indicates the number of weeks by which the activity can be extended without delaying the project's total completion time. In Table 9–2 we summarize the results of our analysis and identify tasks *A*, *C*, *F*, *G*, and *H* as the tasks that constitute the critical path. The slack we calculate for tasks *B*, *D*, and *F* assumes that all other activities are completed on time. The slack for any consecutive activities, in our example, *B* and *E*, is shared by both activities; the slack of *E* depends on the timely completion of task *B*. *E*'s slack will be reduced or eliminated by any delay of *B*.

TABLE 9–2. Summary of New Product Test Marketing Project Analysis

Task	Immediate Predecessor	Estimated Completion Time (weeks)	ES_i	EF_i	LS_i	LF_i	Slack
A		2	0	2	0	2	0
B	A	5	2	7	5	10	1
C	A	4	2	6	2	6	0
D	A	6	2	8	4	10	2
E	B	4	7	11	8	12	1
F	C	4	6	10	6	10	0
G	D, F	2	10	12	10	12	0
H	E, G	6	12	18	12	18	0

9.4 A Dummy Task

A *dummy task* is a task that takes zero time but whose sequencing restriction must be met. Suppose that the new product test marketing project task *C*, "design and prepare the package," must be completed before task *E*, "set up and organize test market data collection," can start. In Table 9–1 we would add *C* as an immediate predecessor to *E*. In Figures 9–1 and 9–2 we would add an arrow to reflect this additional constraint as shown in Figure 9–3. Dummy tasks cause no complica-

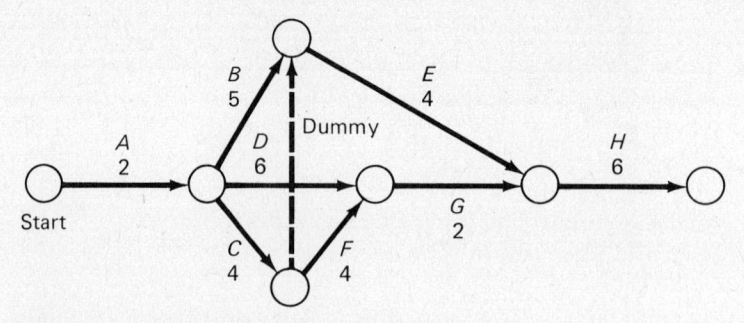

Figure 9–3. CPM network with dummy activity.

tion. They enter into the network as ordinary tasks, and the calculations, such as those in Table 9–2, then include an additional task with a zero time duration.

In large real-world projects, dummy tasks are frequent. They also enter in CPM under limited resources, as we shall see later in this chapter.

9.5 PERT

PERT is similar to CPM, the only difference being the assumption concerning the estimated task times, that is, the t_i's. In CPM each task is assumed to have a definite known time; that is, it is a parameter. In PERT, each task time t_i is probabilistic, that is, a random variable with an associated probability distribution. Otherwise the network calculations of earliest start times, and so on, are identical.

Under PERT each task time t_i is assumed to be a random variable described by a beta distribution.[1] For each task, we obtain from knowledgeable sources three estimates of the time required to complete the task. They are

a_i = the optimistic time estimate
m_i = the most likely time estimate
b_i = the pessimistic time estimate

Using our example from the previous section, we now ask the test marketing manager to give us these three estimates for task H. Suppose that the manager responds: $a_H = 5$, $m_H = 6$, $b_H = 7$. With these three

---

[1]The beta distribution is a complex probability distribution that has desirable statistical properties for this application. An in-depth analysis of this distribution is not required for application, and we state only some simple results. The beta assumption is so widespread that it is usual to make the assumption without stating it explicitly.

estimates we can then calculate the mean or expected time and the variance. The general equation for the expected time for a task is

$$\bar{t}_i = \tfrac{1}{6}(a_i + 4m_i + b_i)$$
$$\bar{t} = \tfrac{1}{6}[5 + 4(6) + 7] = 6 \text{ weeks}$$

The general equation for the variance of a task is given as

$$\text{VAR}(t_i) = \tfrac{1}{36}(b_i - a_i)^2$$

For task H we get

$$\text{VAR}(t) = \tfrac{1}{36}(7 - 5)^2 = \tfrac{4}{36} = 0.111 \text{ week}$$

The task's expected time and the task variance are important data for all subsequent calculations.

The task mean $\bar{t}_i$ is used as if it were a deterministic t_i, as in CPM, for the calculation of all network times, that is, earliest start time, earliest finish time, latest finish time, slack, and the identification of the critical path. Thus Figure 9–2 becomes a PERT diagram if we assume that the task times are the mean times that were calculated from pessimistic, most likely, and optimistic times.

Using the mean or average times and variances for all the activities on the critical path, we can establish a probability distribution for the completion time of the entire project. We can then determine probabilistic estimates for the completion of the project as follows:

1. Determine the critical path using the usual CPM calculations.
2. The *expected project time* μ_p is determined as the sum of the means of the task times along the critical path; that is,

$$\mu_p = \Sigma \bar{t}_i$$

3. The project variance is determined as the sum of the variances along the critical path,

$$T_p^2 = \Sigma \text{ VAR}(t_i)$$

The project time is then assumed to be normally distributed with mean μ_p and variance T_p^2.

To justify the assumption of normality, certain requirements should be met. First, the number tasks should be large (larger than 30) and the task completion times should be *independent* of each other. When these requirements are satisfied we can then apply the *central limit theorem* and state that the project completion time is approximately normal.[2] Finally, we use only the critical path based on means to calculate the probability distribution for the project's completion time.

[2]The requirement of a large number of tasks is ignored in the illustrations and problems of the chapter in order to keep the calculations manageable.

To illustrate these calculations, let us assume that Figure 9–2 is a PERT network. The times given are the expected task times, that is, $\bar{t}_i$. Then the critical path is the sequence of tasks (A, C, F, G, and H). Let us assume that this information was generated from the three time estimates given in Table 9–3. The critical path has already been identified as consisting of tasks A, C, F, G, and H. The expected project completion time of 18 weeks is obtained by adding the $\bar{t}_i$'s for each activity on the critical path. To obtain the variance T_p^2, we add the variances for the same activities. For A, C, F, G, and H we have 0.25 + 0.4444 + 0.4444 + 0.0278 + 0.1111 = 1.25.

TABLE 9–3. PERT Time Estimates

Task	Immediate Predecessor	a_i	m_i	b_i	$\bar{t}_i$	VAR(t_i)
A		1	2	4	2	$\frac{9}{36}$ = 0.2500
B	A	4	5	6	5	$\frac{4}{36}$ = 0.1111
C	A	2	4	6	4	$\frac{16}{36}$ = 0.4444
D	A	4	6	8	6	$\frac{16}{36}$ = 0.4444
E	B	3	4	5	4	$\frac{4}{36}$ = 0.1111
F	C	2	4	6	4	$\frac{16}{36}$ = 0.4444
G	D, F	1.5	2	2.5	2	$\frac{1}{36}$ = 0.0278
H	E, G	5	6	7	6	$\frac{4}{36}$ = 0.1111
					18	

The project completion time is now assumed to be normally distributed with mean 18 and variance 1.25. The standard deviation is therefore $\sigma_p = \sqrt{1.25} = 1.118$. Assume that we want to know the probability that the completion time will exceed 20 weeks (see Figure 9–4). The Z value is given as

$$Z = \frac{20 - 18}{1.118} = 1.789$$

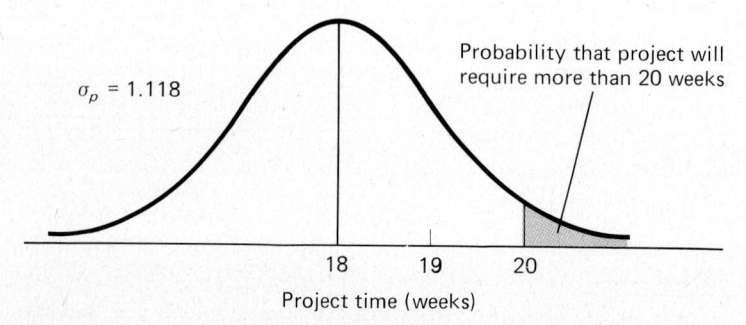

Figure 9–4. The project time probability distribution.

Then, from the table at the back of the book, we find that there is less than a 3 percent chance that the project will take more than 20 weeks.

In the same manner, we can calculate the distribution of expected completion times for all presently noncritical paths. In the case of our project we have two additional paths, namely, A–B–E–H and A–D–G–H. The expected completion times and variances for these two paths are as follows:

	Completion Time	Variance	Standard Deviation
A–B–E–H	17	0.25 + 0.1111 + 0.1111 + 0.1111 = 0.5833	0.764
A–D–G–H	16	0.25 + 0.4444 + 0.0278 + 0.1111 = 0.8333	0.913

Let us calculate for both of these paths the probability that project completion time will be less than 18 weeks. For A–B–E–H we have

$$Z = \frac{18 - 17}{0.764} = 1.309$$

or a probability of 0.905, and for A–D–G–H we get

$$Z = \frac{18 - 16}{0.913} = 2.19$$

or a probability of 0.986. If we consider only the critical path A–C–F–G–H, the probability that the project will be completed in 18 weeks or less is 0.5. Because there is a chance that the noncritical paths may become critical and delay the project beyond 18 weeks, they must also be considered. If we assume that the completion times of all paths are independent random variables, we can calculate the joint probability of completing the project in 18 weeks or less. If the independence assumption is justified, we get a probability of (0.5)(0.905)(0.986) = 0.446.

If the required assumptions for the preceding calculations (number of tasks and independence) cannot be satisfied, it is often possible to obtain satisfactory solutions through the use of simulation models (see Chapter 11).

9.6 PERT/Cost

PERT/cost is a variation that includes cost considerations in the analysis. The cost of each task is assumed to be a function of the task time. The usual assumption is that the task cost is a linear function between a normal time and a crash time as shown in Figure 9–5. Crash time is usually defined as the shortest possible time for the completion of a

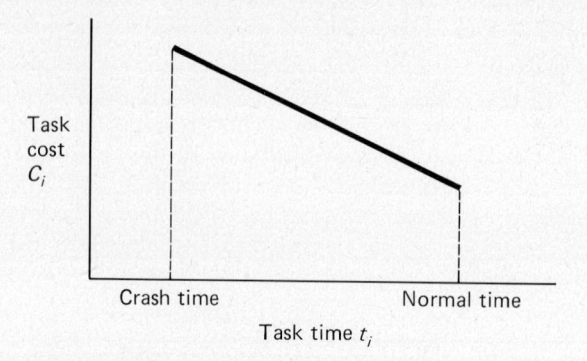

Figure 9–5. The cost function for a task.

task. Shortening the completion time of a task naturally involves additional costs.

The model assumes that the normal time is a minimum-cost solution—regular time for labor, normal material deliveries, and so on. As the task time is reduced, overtime rush shipments, and so on, drive the cost up. The (negative) slope of the cost function represents the marginal cost of reducing the task time. The crash time represents a lower bound on the task time. In PERT/cost we investigate the cost of reducing the project time—for example, how much it would cost to have a school building available on September 1 rather than on November 1. In addition to determining the cost, we want to determine a "new" schedule that will permit us to meet a shorter project completion time. Not all tasks have the same time importance for the project, and not all tasks have the same cost of time reduction.

For PERT/cost the (marginal) cost of reducing the project time by 1 week (day) may be of crucial importance. We want to reduce completion times of tasks in the network with the following two properties: (1) The tasks must be on the critical path, and (2) they should be the least costly of those tasks. Continuing in this fashion, it is possible to construct a project variable cost function as shown in Figure 9–6. This is a *piecewise-linear* function with the minimum cost occurring where all tasks are performed at normal cost and time. The costs increase as the project time is reduced. There exists some minimal time for the project, called the project crash time. The project crash time need not have all network tasks at crash time, but it should be intuitive that the critical path tasks will be "crashed."

We now present a method to generate the project variable cost function from the network and the task cost functions.

1. Assume that all tasks are performed at normal time. Calculate the network times and identify the critical path. This is the normal

9.6 / PERT/Cost

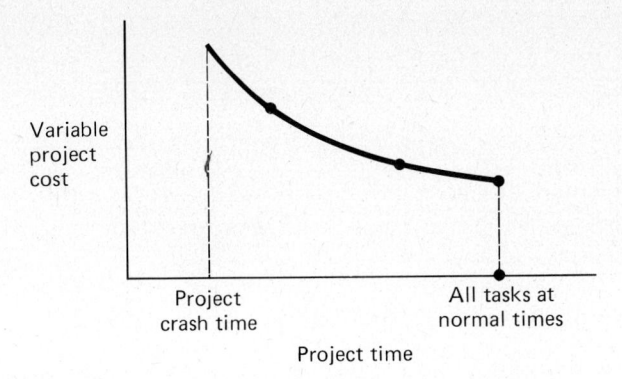

Figure 9–6. The project cost function.

project time, and the sum of the normal task costs determines the project cost. This is the minimum point on the project cost graph in Figure 9–6.

2. Now we ask how we can reduce the project time by 1 week at minimum cost.

   a. Investigate the tasks on the critical path. Pick that task which has the minimal cost (i.e., minimum absolute value of the slope) and reduce it by 1 week. (Assume that the original critical path remains critical.) Add this cost to the original normal project cost; it determines the project cost for the project normal time minus 1 week. Note that the slope of the project cost function is the same as that of the task being reduced.

   b. Continue as in step a until:
      (1) Either the reduced task is at crash time and another task (on the critical path) must be chosen;
      (2) Or another path becomes critical, and a new task is chosen to be reduced (more than one path may be critical).

      In either case, we must choose the reduction at a higher cost—which explains the breakpoint on the project cost function or the piecewise linearity.

   c. Continue until it is not possible to reduce the project, or until no additional task can be reduced. This occurs when a critical path is totally crashed.

The above is a systematic, logical process, but it is extremely tedious. This process can be computerized, and it is not unusual to find a PERT/cost algorithm as part of the standard computer software. In passing, we note that PERT/cost can be modeled as a linear program. We ask the reader to model one PERT/cost problem in the problem section.

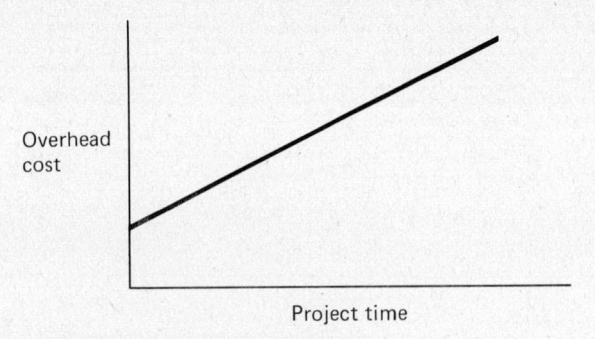

Figure 9-7. Project overhead cost.

PERT/cost may also involve the additional consideration of project overhead costs that are a function of the project time. In most projects, there are costs of management that are a function of the total project time, but that cannot be allocated to individual tasks as we assumed above. For example, the overhead cost appears in Figure 9-7. Total project cost is then the sum of the variable cost and the overhead cost. Putting both costs from Figure 9-6 and 9-7 on a single graph, we have the function depicted in Figure 9-8. The optimal project time is associated with the minimal project cost, that is, the low point on the total cost function. Note that this is generally a time between the project crash time and the normal project time.

Reducing the total completion time of a project does not only in-

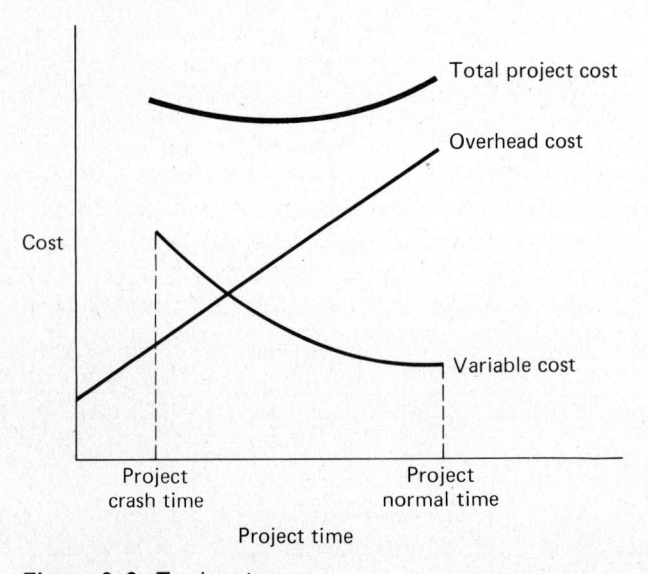

Figure 9-8. Total project cost.

crease completion cost, but it will frequently make possible savings due to an earlier completion of the project. For example, the earlier completion time of a factory would make an earlier startup possible. Associated benefits include the earlier realization of revenues and contribution margins from the production and sale of the product. These benefits of early project completion can in many situations justify the increased cost due to shortening the completion of critical tasks.

9.7 CPM with Limited Resources[3]

In the previous discussions of CPM and PERT, it is implicit that there are limited resources at any point in time. CPM under limited resources explicitly accounts for limitation. The t_i for CPM is only the time requirement for the tasks, not an explicit statement about the required resources. For example, saying that digging a hole in the ground requires 3 hr is an incomplete statement without adding that 4 men are required. In this section we shall take explicit account of the fact that each task requires resources as well as time and that available resources are limited.

For this generalization, we require that each task be assigned a known time t_i, and a statement concerning the required resources, such as that a task requires 3 men, 4 bulldozers, and a crane, all for 14 hr. Further, we require that the available quantity of each resource be stated for each point in time of the project.

LIMITED RESOURCES APPROACH

There are many variations in approach to the limited resource problem, and no one method has been found to be better than others. All methods follow a general pattern:

1. Establish a threshold of resource availability for all points in time. These quantities are based on the resources that a project contractor has or may procure; for example, a contractor may have 3 bulldozers and can hire up to 100 men.
2. Attempt to schedule all tasks in the network at their earliest start time.
   a. If no *resource conflict* results, schedule all tasks at their earliest start time. A resource conflict is defined as a situation that exists at a point in time where the resources available are less than the resources desired, for example, a contractor who has 2 bulldozers but needs 3 at a given time.

---

[3]This is a more advanced topic, which can be omitted without loss of continuity.

b. If a conflict results (at a point in time):
   (1) Assign priorities to the tasks involved in the conflict.
   (2) Schedule as many tasks as possible (to start at this time) subject to the resources available and according to the priority list.
   (3) Schedule the remaining tasks at a later date when resources become available.
3. Repeat step (2) until all tasks are scheduled.

The variations in this general approach depend on the method of priority rankings suggested in (1) above. Some choose the priority arbitrarily, some at random; other writers suggest more reasonable methods. One such method is called the resource scheduling method (RSM).

As a first step, calculate the delay caused in total project time due to conflict:

$$Q_{ij} = \max(EF_i - LS_j)$$

where task i has the smallest EF (earliest completion time) among those in the conflict, and task j is the task with the largest LS (latest start time). Remember that Q_{ij} is the delay caused in total project time due to the conflict.

We shall use an example to illustrate this. Suppose that we have two parallel tasks, S and D, that overlap in time as shown in Figure 9-9. S is the digging of a ditch for sewer pipes, and D is the digging of a ditch for a cable. Both tasks require a ditch-digging machine, but only one is available. What is the total delay in project time due to the conflict? We have $Q_{S,D} = (EF_S - LS_D) = (11 - 10) = 1$ day as the maximum delay due to the conflict. In the given example we can start task S on day 6 and finish it on day 11; the start of the critical task D must therefore be delayed by 1 day. If we started task D before task S, the delay would be even greater.

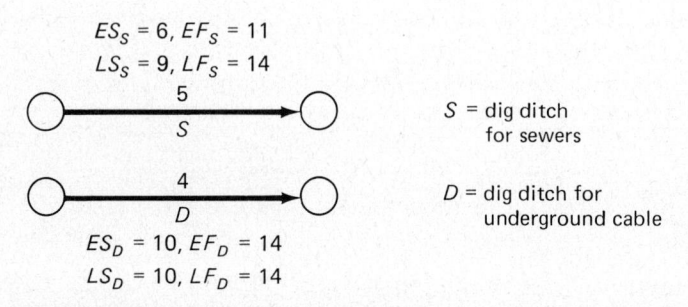

$ES_S = 6, EF_S = 11$
$LS_S = 9, LF_S = 14$

```
        5
O ————————————→ O        S = dig ditch
        S                    for sewers

        4
O ————————————→ O        D = dig ditch for
        D                    underground cable
```

$ES_D = 10, EF_D = 14$
$LS_D = 10, LF_D = 14$

Figure 9-9. Two parallel, overlapping tasks.

9.8 / A Comprehensive Example for CPM with Limited Resources

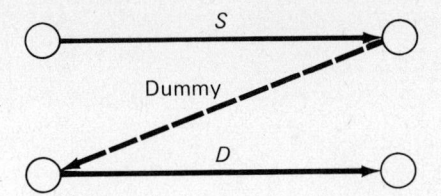

Figure 9–10. Synchronizing overlapping tasks with a dummy task.

For step 2, a sequencing restriction must be inserted between these two tasks such that task i precedes task j, or j follows i. For our example this means that task S must be completed before D if the project is not to be delayed by more than 1 day. Figure 9–10 shows this new relationship by the insertion of a dummy task. Finally, using this additional sequencing restriction, we recalculate the earliest start times, and so on, for all tasks and attempt to schedule the tasks.

For our example this means that task S will no longer have any slack, because it has to be started on day 6 and completed on day 11. Task D will be delayed by 1 day, as will all subsequent critical tasks. Critical tasks preceding D may gain some slack.

The rationale behind this method is that it sequences the tasks so that total project time is delayed minimally by the new sequence, ignoring other conflicts that may exist in the network. It is well to note that this method may or may not give an optimal solution to the problem of completing the project in the minimal total project time subject to the resources available. It is a workable solution that yields a feasible schedule.

9.8 A Comprehensive Example for CPM with Limited Resources

Consider the network given in Figure 9–11. The task times, resource requirements, and resources available are identified in Table 9–4. The task times and the identification of the critical path in Figure 9–11 are carried out without regard to potential conflicts due to limited resource availability.

At time zero, it is possible to start tasks A and B. Together they require $1 + 0 = 1$ pipefitters and $2 + 3 = 5$ ironworkers, which implies a conflict because there are only 3 ironworkers available.

Now task B has a minimum EF_B of 2
and task A has a maximum LS_B of 4

$ES_C = 4, EF_C = 6$
$LS_C = 8, LF_C = 10$

$ES_A = 0, EF_A = 4$
$LS_A = 4, LF_A = 8$

$ES_F = 6, EF_F = 14$
$LS_F = 10, LF_F = 14$

Start

A
4

C
2

F
4

D
8

$ES_D = 2, EF_D = 10$
$LS_D = 2, LF_D = 10$

B
2

E
4

$ES_B = 0, EF_B = 2$
$LS_B = 0, LF_B = 2$

$ES_E = 2, EF_E = 6$
$LS_E = 10, LF_E = 14$

▬▬▬ Critical path

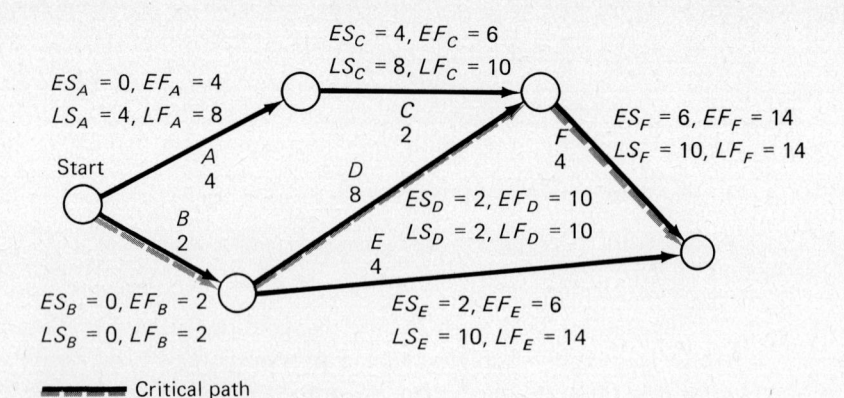

Figure 9–11. Initial project data.

TABLE 9–4.

Task	Time t_i	Pipefitters Required	Ironworkers Required
A	4	1	2
B	2	0	3
C	2	2	0
D	8	1	0
E	4	3	0
F	4	1	2
Total resources available for the project		4	3

Thus,

$$Q_{AB} = \max(0, 2-4) = 0$$

which implies that the required sequence will not delay the total project time. Thus, the conflict is resolved by sequencing task B before task A. We need to modify the network to incorporate this sequence. The fact that no delay for the project results is due to the available slack for task A. The network with the new sequencing constraint in the form of dummy task X is shown in Figure 9–12. Note that the new early start and finish times for tasks A and C have been calculated and inserted in the network. All other task times are not affected. Note also that the slack for both A and C has been reduced by 2 days.

There now exists a potential conflict for pipefitters if A, D, and E start at the same time. Because task D requires only 1 pipefitter, 3

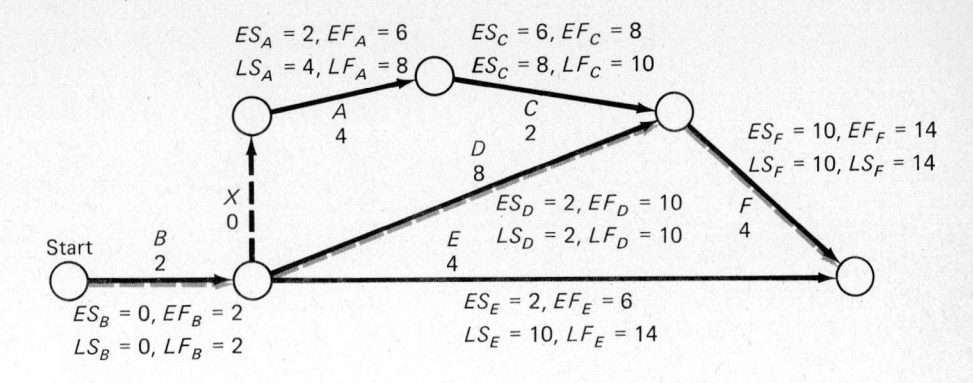

9.8 / A Comprehensive Example for CPM with Limited Resources

Figure 9–12. Resolving resource conflict between tasks A and B with a dummy task.

could be available for task E when A is completed. To show clearly this new sequencing constraint, we use two dummy tasks Y and Z as shown in Figure 9–13. We need two dummy tasks in order to show that task D is not affected by the new sequencing constraint. Had we drawn the arrow for dummy Z directly to the node following B, it could have implied that D could start only after the completion of A, which, of course, is not true. Note that this sequencing constraint changes only the task times for E; it reduces E's slack from 8 to 4.

Now, on day 6, task A is complete and task D is in process, and tasks C and E may be started. D, C, and E together require:

$1 + 2 + 3 = 6$ pipefitters $\Rightarrow$ conflict
$0 + 0 + 0 = 0$ ironworkers

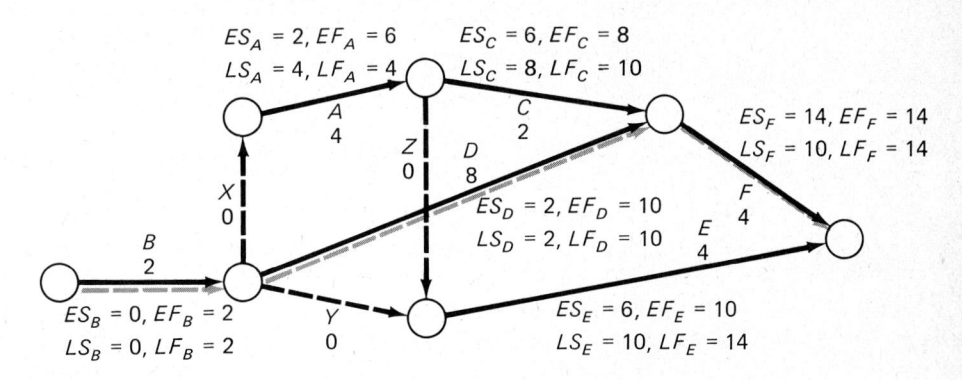

Figure 9–13. Resolving potential resource conflict between tasks A and E with two dummy tasks.

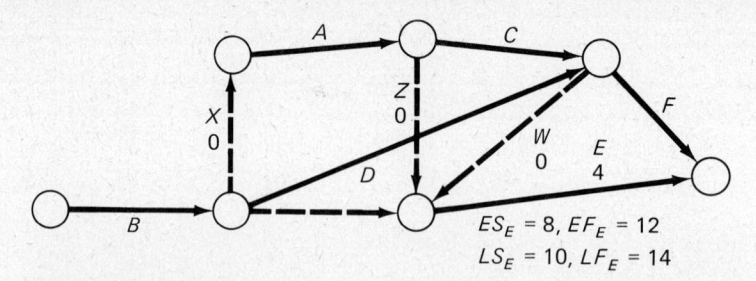

Figure 9-14. Resolving resource conflict between tasks C and E with a dummy task.

For this conflict, task *C* has the smallest *EF* of 8, and task *E* has the largest *LS* of 10.

$$Q_{DCE} = \max(0, 8-10) = 0 \Rightarrow \text{no project time increase}$$

The required sequence is completion of task *C* before task *E*.

In Figure 9-14 we show this by inserting the dummy task *W*. The task times for *E* are changed. All other task times are not affected. At time equal to 8, task *C* has been completed and task *D* is in process. Task *D* and task *E* overlap. Together they require:

1 + 3 = 4 pipefitters
0 + 0 = 0 ironworkers

which involves no conflict. At time equal to 10, task *D* is complete and tasks *E* and *F* may be done. Together they require:

3 + 1 = 4 pipefitters
0 + 2 = 2 ironworkers

which involves no conflict. Thus, we have a feasible schedule that does not violate the resources given. Note that for this problem, all the conflicts are resolved without delaying the total project time.

9.9 Summary

In this chapter we considered CPM/PERT project scheduling and some variations. Topics discussed were the relation among the project, its tasks, and sequencing restrictions, that is, the construction of the project network; the calculation of usual CPM project times, earliest start times, earliest finish times, latest starting and finish times, slack, and the critical path; the PERT variation on CPM, which permits task and project times to be probabilistic; the PERT/cost model, where task and project times are functions of cost; and CPM under limited resources, where there is explicit consideration of the fact that resources are limited at a point in time.

Glossary

CPM (critical path method). A technique to schedule large projects, such as a new building.

CPM under limited resources. A variation of CPM that explicitly considers the task resource requirement and the project resource availability.

Critical path. The longest time sequence through the network when all tasks are completed as early as possible. It is the minimal project completion time.

Dummy task. A task that takes zero time to complete but whose sequencing constraint must be met.

Earliest completion time. The earliest possible moment to complete a task.

Earliest start time. The earliest possible moment a task can begin.

Expected project time. The average time required to complete a project.

Immediate predecessor. A task that must be completed just prior to the given task.

Latest completion time. The last moment possible to complete a task without increasing the project completion time.

Latest start time. The last moment to begin a task without increasing the project completion time.

PERT (project evaluation review technique). A probablistic version of CPM. Each task time is probablistic.

PERT/Cost. A variation of PERT and CPM where each task has a variable completion time that decreases as the task cost increases.

Project. A set of tasks to be completed.

Project network. A graphical representation of the project stated in terms of the tasks and the sequencing restriction.

Resource conflict. A conflict that occurs when two or more tasks may be started, but there are insufficient resources available and one or more tasks must be delayed.

Sequencing constraint. A constraint gives the necessary time order of two tasks, for example, that the foundation must be in place prior to beginning the sidewalls.

Slack time. The length of time that a task can be delayed without delaying the project.

Task. A part of the project, frequently called an activity; for example, the installation of plumbing is a task in the project of completing a new building.

Problems

1. For the CPM example given in the text, add the dummy task (4, 6) with $t_{46} = 0$. Then complete the calculations to establish the earliest start times, earliest completion times, and latest completion times. Calculate the activity slacks and identify the critical path.

2. For the accompanying network, establish the earliest start times, earliest completion times, and latest completion times. Note that task (3, 6) requires no time, but its sequencing restriction must be honored.

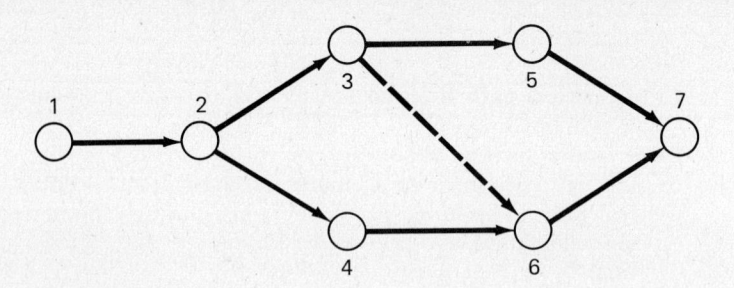

TASKS (i, j) t_{ij}
1, 2   3
2, 3   4
2, 4   2
3, 6   0
4, 6   1
3, 5   3
5, 7   2
6, 7   6

3. *(SMA)* Hometools Limited, a public company, has decided to produce a revolutionary new tool for the handyman, one that is flexible and can be adapted to a large number of household carpentry chores. In planning the project, management establishes the various activities that must be accomplished and estimates the time that it will take to complete each of them with the available resources. A formal written report must be made to the Board of Directors for final production approval. The required activities are listed below. All times are presented in weeks.

Activity	Description	Immediate Predecessor	Expected Time to Complete
A	Product design	—	6
B	Market research	—	4
C	Working product model	F	3
D	Product testing	C	5
E	Production analysis	A	3
F	Component delivery	A	2
G	Cost accounting	E	1
H	Sales literature	A	4
I	Sales survey	B, H	8
J	Demand analysis	I	1
K	Preparation of report for Board of Directors	D, G, J	2

REQUIRED
   a. Draw a PERT network and calculate the earliest and the latest allowable event times. Show them on your network.
   b. List the activities that are on the critical path.

c. Management would like to present their formal report to the Board of Directors 28 weeks after the start of the project. Calculate the *latest* time that the working product model must be *started* in order to accomplish this. (Assume that all time estimates are quite conservative and will be easily met.)

4. For Problem 2, assume that the task times given are the mean task times for a PERT network.
   a. Given that $a_{12} = 2$, is it possible that $b_{12} = 3.5$?
   b. Assume an error in estimation, $\bar{t}_{35} = 5$. Does this change the critical path?
   c. Ignoring the changes in parts a and b, what is the probability that the project completion time will exceed 13?
   d. Can you determine the probability that the project completion will exceed 14?

5. *(CMA)* Dryfus Company specializes in large construction projects. The company management regularly employs the program evaluation and review technique (PERT) in planning and coordinating its construction projects. The following schedule of separable activities and their expected completion times have been developed for an office building that is to be constructed by the Dryfus Company.

Activity Description	Predecessor Activity	Expected Activity Completion Time (in weeks)
Excavation	—	2
Foundation	a	3
Underground utilities	a	7
Rough plumbing	b	4
Framing	b	5
Roofing	e	3
Electrical work	f	3
Interior walls	d, g	4
Finish plumbing	h	2
Exterior finishing	f	6
Landscaping	c, i, j	2

REQUIRED
   a. Identify the critical path for this project and determine the expected project completion time in weeks.
   b. Briefly discuss how the "expected activity completion times" are derived in the PERT method and what the derived value for the expected activity completion time means in the PERT method.

6. *(CMA)* A construction company has contracted to complete a new building and has asked for assistance in analyzing the project. Using the program evaluation review technique (PERT), the accompanying network has been developed.

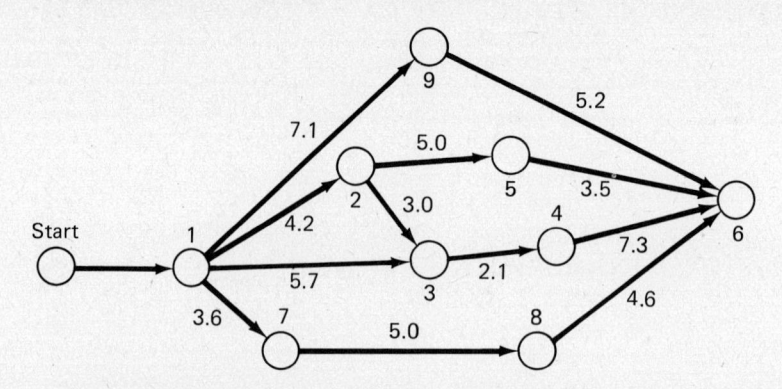

All paths from the start point to the finish point, event 6, represent activities or processes that must be completed before the entire project, the building, will be completed. The numbers above the paths or line segments represent expected completion times for the activities or processes. The expected time is based on the commonly used, 1–4–1, three-estimate method. For example, the three-estimate method gives an estimated time of 4.2 to complete task (1, 2).

a. The critical path (the path requiring the greatest amount of time) is
  (1) 1–2–5–6
  (2) 1–2–3–4–6
  (3) 1–3–4–6
  (4) 1–7–8–6
  (5) 1–9–6

b. Slack time on path 1–9–6 equals
  (1) 4.3
  (2) 2.8
  (3) 0.9
  (4) 0.4
  (5) 0

c. The latest time for reaching event 6 via path 1–2–5–6 is
  (1) 20.8
  (2) 19.3
  (3) 17.4
  (4) 16.5
  (5) 12.7

d. The earliest time for reaching event 6 via path 1–2–5–6 is
  (1) 20.8
  (2) 16.9
  (3) 16.5
  (4) 12.7
  (5) 3.5

e. If all other paths are operating on schedule but path segment 7–8 has an unfavorable time variance of 1.9:
  (1) The critical path will be shortened.
  (2) The critical path will be eliminated.

Problems

(3) The critical path will be unaffected.
(4) Another path will become the critical path.
(5) The critical path will have an increased time of 1.9.

7. *(SMA)* Listed below are data concerning a project that consists of eight activities:

Activity	Immediate Predecessor	Estimated Completion Time (days)		
		Optimistic	Most Probable	Pessimistic
A	—	2	3	4
B	A	2	3	10
C	B	1	2	3
D	C	3	4	5
E	A	7	8	15
F	A	3	4	11
G	F	3	4	5
H	D, E, G	6	8	16

REQUIRED

a. Determine the expected completion time and variance for each activity.
b. Determine the expected completion time for the project.
c. What is the probability of the project being completed by the end of 25 days?
d. Give two reasons why the probability calculated in part c may, at best, be only approximately correct. Explain your reasons.

8. Some authors use a complementary network notation to the one used in this text. This CPM graph gives the tasks (indicated by circles) and the sequencing constraints (indicated by arrows) necessary to complete a project. In this graph, the letters A, B, C, and so on, give each task a name, and the arabic numbers 7, 17, and so on, give the time required to complete

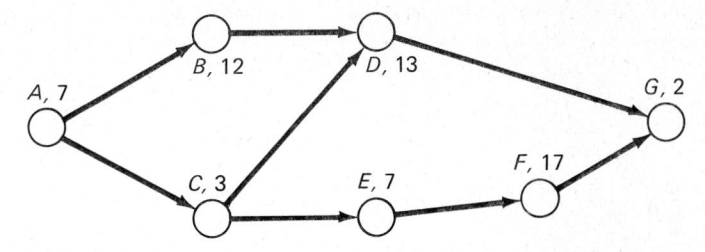

the corresponding task. Using these basic ideas, establish the earliest start times and earliest completion times for each task in the project. (Note: You cannot apply the exact calculation rules given in the text, as they are developed for the other network representation—but use your intuition.)

9. For the general scheduling problem:
a. Formulate (but do not solve) a linear program that will establish the earliest start time for each task.

b. For your linear program, give an interpretation for the corresponding dual variable for each constraint.
c. Indicate a relationship between the dual program and the critical path for the graph.

10. *(CMA)* Whitson Company has just ordered a new computer for its financial information system. The present computer is fully utilized and no longer adequate for all financial applications Whitson would like to implement. The present financial system applications must all be modified before they can be run on the new computer. Additionally, new applications that Whitson would like to have developed and implemented have been identified and ranked according to priority.

Sally Rose, Manager of Data Processing, is responsible for implementing the new computer system. Rose listed the specific activities that had to be completed and determined the estimated time to complete each activity. The activity list follows.

REQUIRED
a. Determine the number of weeks that will be required to implement fully Whitson Company's financial information system (i.e., both existing and new applications) on its new computer and identify the activities that are critical to completing the project.
b. The term *slack time* is often used in conjunction with network analysis.
   (1) Explain what is meant by slack time.
   (2) Identify an activity that has slack time and indicate the amount of slack time available for that activity.
c. Whitson Company's top management would like to reduce the time necessary to begin operation of the entire system.
   (1) Which activities should Sally Rose attempt to reduce in order to implement the system sooner? Explain your answer.
   (2) Discuss how Sally Rose might proceed to reduce the time of these activities.
d. The General Accounting Manager would like the existing financial information system applications to be modified and operational in 22 weeks.
   (1) Determine the number of weeks that will be required to modify the existing financial information system applications and make them operational.
   (2) What is the probability of implementing the existing financial information system applications within 22 weeks?

Activity	Description of Activity	Expected Time Required to Complete (in weeks)	Variance in Expected Time (in weeks)
AB	Wait for delivery of computer from manufacturer	8	1.2
BC	Install computer	2	0.6
CH	General test of computer	2	0.2
AD	Complete an evaluation of manpower requirements	2	0.8
DE	Hire additional programmers and operators	2	1.6
AG	Design modifications to existing applications	3	1.2
GH	Program modifications to existing applications	4	1.4
HI	Test modified applications on new computer	2	0.4
IJ	Revise existing applications as needed	2	0.6
JN	Revise and update documentation for existing applications as modified	2	0.4
JK	Run existing applications in parallel on new and old computers	2	0.4
KP	Implement existing applications as modified on the new computer	1	0.6
AE	Design new applications	8	3.2
GE	Design interface between existing and new applications	3	1.8
EF	Program new applications	6	2.6
FI	Test new applications on new computer	2	0.8
IL	Revise new applications as needed	3	1.4
LM	Conduct second test of new applications on new computer	2	0.6
MN	Prepare documentation for the new applications	3	0.8
NP	Implement new applications on the new computer	2	0.8

11. For the PERT modifications of Figure 9–2 given in the text assume that the project is now 8 weeks old. Task (1, 2) is complete. Task (2, 3) is just started now. Task (2, 5) is 75 percent complete. No other tasks have begun. Devise a new project network for this "new" project. Calculate the usual times involved and indicate the critical path. Calculate the probability that the project completion will exceed 24 weeks (i.e., 16 weeks for this new project). Compare your results with the original schedule given in the text.

12. A project consisting of seven independent activities is to be analyzed by using PERT. The following information is given (time estimates are in days):

Activity	Immediate Predecessor	t_o	t_m	t_p
A	—	0	4	14
B	—	3	4	5
C	A	2	2	2
D	B, C	1	3	5
E	D	6	6	6
F	A	7	9	17
G	E, F	1	8	9

REQUIRED
  a. (1) Construct a network diagram for the project. Be sure to label all activities and number all events.
  (2) Calculate the earliest and latest allowable times for each event, and show them *clearly* on your network. Identify the critical path.
  (3) What is the expected duration of this project?
  b. (1) If you were required to reduce the expected project duration by 3 days and you knew that any of the seven activities could be reduced by a maximum of 1 day each, which activities would you reduce? List the activities by letter, and *briefly* justify your choices.
  (2) What activities are now critical?

13. Consider the accompanying PERT project network modified from a problem by Allan McMasters.

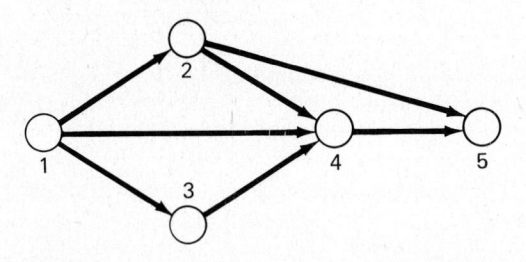

	Normal		Crash	
Activity	$	days	$	days
(1, 2)	50	3	100	2
(1, 3)	25	2	50	1
(1, 4)	140	6	260	4
(2, 4)	100	5	180	3
(2, 5)	115	7	175	5
(3, 4)	80	2	80	2
(4, 5)	100	4	240	2

Problems

REQUIRED
a. Using normal times, calculate the usual network times. Specify the critical path.
b. Determine the normal project completion time and the associated total project cost.
c. Calculate the cost of reducing the project time by 1 day. Which task's time is reduced?
d. Continue part c to determine the total project cost versus the project time.
e. What is the critical path for the crashed project time? Are all activities crashed?
f. If the overhead cost is given at $100 per day, find the total project time that minimizes total project cost.

14. *(SMA)* Your company has the opportunity to participate in a project that will sell for $77,000. This project consists of eight activities *(A through H)* with completion times and costs given below:

Activity	Immediate Predecessor	Normal Time Weeks	Normal Time Cost	Crash Time Weeks	Crash Time Cost
A	—	5	$ 6,000	4	$10,000
B	—	2	3,000	1	8,000
C	—	3	5,000	2	8,000
D	B	4	9,000	3	15,000
E	B	5	10,000	4	13,000
F	B	4	12,000	3	16,000
G	A, D	4	8,000	3	14,000
H	C, F	4	6,000	3	9,000

Under normal conditions, activity A, for example, will be completed in 5 weeks at a cost of $6,000; this activity can, however, be completed in 4 weeks at a total cost of $10,000.

REQUIRED
a. Determine the time required and the total cost of the project under normal conditions.
b. If the customer requires completion of the project in 8 weeks, should the project be undertaken? Support your answer with appropriate calculations.

15. Discuss how you would do a cost study to determine the cost function for a PERT/cost network. Keep in mind that the most important data are the task normal time and the *slope* of the cost function for each task (and, particularly, those on the critical path).

16. a. Formulate the PERT/cost problem in Problem 13 as a linear program.
    b. If available, solve your formulation on a standard linear programming routine.

c. Investigate the dual solution. Interpret the meaning of each dual variable. What is the relation between the critical path and the dual variables?

17. *(SMA)* You are given the following PERT network.

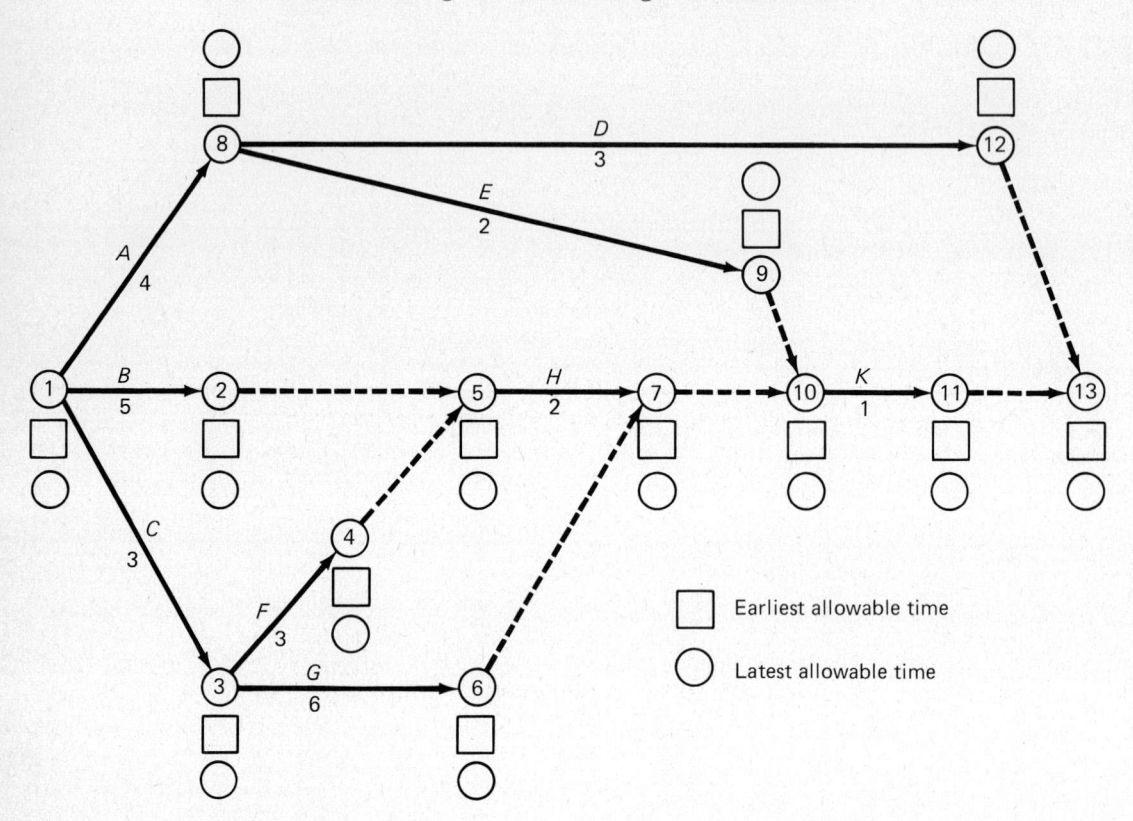

■ Earliest allowable time

○ Latest allowable time

REQUIRED

a. Calculate the normal duration of the project and indicate clearly the critical path. Compute the earliest and the latest allowable event times.

b. A bonus of $500 per day will be paid to the contractor for each day he completes the schedule ahead of the schedule agreed to in part a. Applying the following additional data, calculate the maximum *net* bonus that the contractor should schedule to gain.

Activity	t_e	t_e Can Be Cut by (days)	At an Additional Cost of ($)
A	4	1	100
B	5	2	500
C	3	2	600
D	3	2	150
E	2	1	100
F	3	1	250
G	6	2	600
H	2	1	300
K	1	—	—

    c. List the activities reduced and at what total additional cost.
    d. Indicate your revised critical path. Compute the earliest and the latest allowable event times.

18. Consider the accompanying project network. The nodes and tasks follow the usual notation. The numbers in parentheses near each arrow represent the task time in weeks and the task resource in men, respectively, that is, (T_{ij}, r_{ij}), where r_{ij} is the required task resource. For example, task (2,3) requires 4 weeks for 6 men to complete.

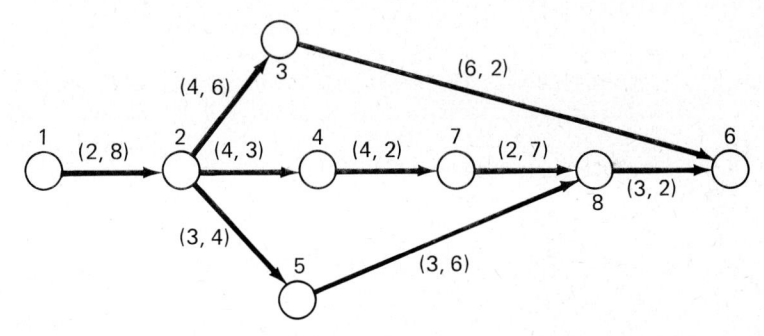

REQUIRED
    a. Calculate the usual network times assuming that there are no resource restrictions.
    b. Using the RSM method given in the text, devise a schedule for the project assuming that there are 10 men available.
    c. Make up a scheduling rule of your own (to replace RSM) and apply it to this problem. Compare your results with the RSM schedule. Which yields the minimum project completion time?

19. "PERT/cost estimates are a new way of looking at the expense budgets. If properly conceived, they can become an integral part of the comprehensive budget program. Yet they differ from conventional expense budgeting in certain respects" (DeCoster, 1964). Develop and explain some of these differences.

20. For the project in Problem 2, formulate a linear program that will minimize the project cost for a project time of 12. The activity cost time relations are as follows:

	Time		Cost	
Task (i, j)	Normal	Crash	Crash	Normal
(1, 2)	4	3	$400	$300
(2, 3)	6	4	$800	$400
(2, 4)	3	2	$500	$400
(3, 6)	0	0	0	0
(4, 6)	3	1	$100	$ 50
(3, 5)	4	3	$1000	$800
(5, 7)	3	2	$300	$200
(6, 7)	8	6	$600	$400

References

Dane, C. W., Gray, C. F., and Woodworth, B. M. "Factors Affecting the Successful Application of PERT/CPM Systems in a Government Organization." *Interfaces* 9, no. 5 (November 1979).

DeCoster, Don T. "The Budget Director and PERT." *Business Budgeting* (March 1964): 13–17. (Reprinted in Don T. DeCoster et al. *Accounting for Managerial Decision Making*. Los Angeles: Melville, 1974).

DeCoster, Don T. "PERT/COST: The Challenge." *Management Services* (May/June 1964).

Levy, F. K., Thompson, G. L., and Wiest, J. D. "The ABC's of the Critical Path Method." *Harvard Business Review* (September/October 1963): 98–108.

Ross, W. R. "PERT/Cost Resource Allocation." *The Accounting Review* (July 1966): 464–473. (Reprinted in Donald L. Anderson and Donald L. Raun. *Information Analysis in Management Accounting*. Santa Barbara, Calif.: Wiley/Hamilton, 1978, pp. 481–495).

Shaffer, L. R., Ritter, J. B., and Meyer, W. L. *The Critical-Path Method*. New York: McGraw-Hill, 1965.

Weist, J. D., and Levy, F. K. *A Management Guide to PERT/CPM*, 2d ed. Englewood Cliffs, N.J.: Prentice-Hall, 1977.

CHAPTER 10
Forecasting and Cost Estimation

10.1 Introduction

10.2 Extrapolations of Historical Observations (Time Series)
The Simple Average
The Moving Average
The Weighted Average
Exponential Smoothing
Estimation of Linear Trends

10.3 Prediction Models
Regression Analysis
Coefficient of Determination
Testing the Significance of the Regression Coefficient
Confidence Intervals for the Regression Coefficient b
Confidence Intervals for the Expected Value of y'

10.4 Multiple Regression

10.5 Learning Curves and Cost Estimation

10.6 Summary

Glossary

Problems

References

Appendix
Development of the Normal Equations from Least Squares

Key Concepts
Coefficient of correlation
Coefficient of determination
Exponential smoothing
Judgmental forecasting
Learning curve
Learning index
Learning ratios
Least-squares method

Moving average
Prediction model
Quantitative forecast
Regression model
Simple average
Standard error of the estimate
Standard error of the regression coefficient
Trend estimation
Weighted average

Key Applications
Adjusting cost for learning
Cost estimation
Managerial accounting

Sales forecasting
Statistical analysis

10.1 Introduction

Forecasting may be defined as the estimation or prediction of some future event or variable. In a business context we use the term to describe management's systematic effort to estimate quantities, such as product sales or costs. This chapter presents an introduction to some of the more widely used techniques.

Forecasts may be classified into *judgmental* and *quantitative* forecasts. Judgmental forecasts are based on the subjective judgment of "experts" or "specialists." One such method is the Delphi technique. It involves the obtaining of opinions from individual experts. Questioning is repeated until a majority of the experts are in agreement. Under another method a sample of a firm's most important customers is requested to furnish an estimate of their needs for our products. These estimates are helpful in developing an overall forecast of sales. Although these judgmental methods are frequently used—many times in conjunction with other methods—they will not be discussed.

Quantitative forecasting approaches can be classified into those that are based entirely on historical observations (i.e., an extrapolation of the past into the future) and methods that attempt to establish a functional relationship between the variable to be predicted (the dependent variable) and one or more other independent variables, for example, sales as a function of price. In our discussion we shall use the term *prediction model* for this approach.

10.2 Extrapolations of Historical Observations (Time Series)

The collection of historical data over successive time intervals is generally referred to as *time series*. The basic assumption when employing these methods is that historical observations have predictive value. They all involve various kinds of averaging of past values. Changes in the fluctuations or pattern of a time series are usually classified into four basic types of variations:

1. The trend (also referred to as secular trend)
2. Cyclical variations
3. Seasonal variations
4. Random or irregular variations

A *trend* is a generally smooth pattern of the variable observed, usually over a fairly long time period. Trends may be increasing or decreasing at various rates; they may remain fairly constant or may change from growth to decline.

Cyclical variations are fluctuations of the observed values that occur over longer periods. They are generally thought to be a result of business cycles—the repeated general movements in economic activity from prosperity to recession.

Seasonal variations are fluctuations in the value of the variable observed during a fixed period, usually a year, that repeat themselves regularly over each consecutive period.

Random or irregular variations include all fluctuations that are not due to trend, seasonal, or cyclical influences. Because they show no systematic pattern, they are thought to be caused by usually unidentifiable chance factors, hence the term random variations.

In all time series models the prediction of the variable in question is based on an analysis of past observations over a time period. Past patterns are modeled and used for estimating the future. In classical time series analysis, any particular value of the variable to be estimated is assumed to be the product of the four basic types of variations discussed earlier. The objective of the analysis is to identify each component and to produce a forecast by combining their projected impact in the future. In this chapter we introduce some of the simpler forecasting methods. The most common ones are the simple average, the moving average, the weighted average, exponential smoothing, and linear trend estimation. Each approach attempts to remove random variations to uncover a basically stable underlying pattern. All of these methods use some form of averaging or smoothing techniques. They are useful for short-term forecasting when there are no pronounced cyclical or seasonal variations. For a more complete discussion of forecasting techniques, the reader is referred to the textbooks and articles listed in the references.

THE SIMPLE AVERAGE

We find the simple average by summing a number n of observed values and dividing the sum by n. In algebraic terms we have

$$\bar{x} = \frac{\sum_{i=1}^{n} x_i}{n}$$

where $\bar{x}$ is the simple average of our observations, the x_i's are the individual observation and n is the number of observations. Assume that we want to predict the quantity of next week's sales of an item on the basis of the sales during the past 5 weeks, which were 22, 23, 20, 21, and 24, respectively. The simple average is

$$\bar{x} = \frac{22 + 23 + 20 + 21 + 24}{5} = 22 \qquad (10\text{--}1)$$

Next week's sales would therefore be estimated as 22 units. If the variations around this average, or mean value, are small, this method will give satisfactory results. The principal advantage of the method is its minimal cost and its ease of use. The simple average assumes implicitly that sales vary about the same constant "base" or average level of sales and that the variations or deviations from that average are due to irregular or random factors. Conceptually, the more numbers we average, the closer we come to the "true" average. However, if the base level should ever change during the time period covered, the simple average will be very slow in responding to such a change.

THE MOVING AVERAGE

Under the moving-average method, we calculate a new average whenever a new observation becomes available; that is, we use only the most recent observations. The general expression for this method is

$$\bar{x}_t = \sum_{i=t-k}^{t-1} \frac{x_i}{k}$$

where $\bar{x}_t$ is the estimate for the period t, the x_i's are the individual observations, and k is the number of periods included in calculating the average. Assume that the monthly sales of a commodity in units are as shown in Table 10–1. In calculating the moving average we use only a fixed number k of the most recent observations. Suppose that experience has shown that using the most recent 4 months as basis produces a satisfactory forecast. Then

$$\bar{x}_{\text{Aug.}} = \frac{63 + 64 + 58 + 62}{4} = 61.75 \qquad (10\text{--}2)$$

10.2 / Extrapolations of Historic Observations (Time Series)

TABLE 10–1. Sales (in 000 Units)

January	52
February	55
March	53
April	63
May	64
June	58
July	62

gives us the forecast for the month of August. Assuming that actual sales for August were 65,000 units, we calculate the forecast for September by again using the actual sales of the most recent 4 months:

$$\bar{x}_{\text{Sept.}} = \frac{64 + 58 + 62 + 65}{4} = 62.25$$

The same procedure is then used for any future month.

Care should be taken in selecting k, the number of time periods. With larger k's the model will be more stable and less sensitive to random variations. It will, however, also be slower in responding to the underlying trend. Small k's, on the other hand, will respond quickly to the underlying trend. At the same time, there is a greater risk of being misled by random variations. We must realize that the influence of random variability distracts from the underlying trend. Many firms experiment with different numbers of periods before selecting the one that gives the best results.

THE WEIGHTED AVERAGE

In the moving average, each period used in the base is given equal weight. Given an underlying trend, any such moving average, even one using only a small number of recent periods in the base, will always lag behind the trend. To eliminate this lag, at least partially, we assign more weight to more recent periods. There is an infinite number of possible weighting schemes. Again, various weighting schemes ought to be experimented with before choosing one that promises the best results.

The general expression for this method is

$$\bar{x}_t = \sum_{i=t-k}^{t-1} W_i x_i$$

where

$$\sum_{j=1}^{k} W_j = 1.0$$

The W_j's are the weights assigned to the different observations; their sum must be equal to 1. In Table 10–2 we compare a 3-months moving average with a 3-months weighted average. The values for the weighting scheme are developed as follows: $\frac{3}{6}$ for the latest period, $\frac{2}{6}$ for the preceding one, and $\frac{1}{6}$ for the oldest period used. Table 10–2 shows that the weighted average responds more quickly than the moving average to the underlying trend. A scheme weighting recent observations more than the one employed in Table 10–2 would, of course, be even more responsive. However, when the variable observed is also subject to large random fluctuations, it may also result in a highly variable estimate.

TABLE 10–2. Comparing Forecasting Methods

Time Period (Month)	Actual Sales (Units)	Three-Months Moving-Average Forecast	Three-Months Weighted-Average Forecast
1	60		
2	60		
3	60	60	60
4	65	61.7	62.5*
5	70	65.0	66.67
6	75	70	71.67
7	60	68.3	66.67
8	60	65.0	62.5
9	60	60	60
10	60	60	60

$$*\bar{x}_5 = \frac{65(3) + 60(2) + 60(1)}{6} = \frac{195 + 120 + 60}{6} = 62.5.$$

EXPONENTIAL SMOOTHING

Exponential smoothing is also a moving-average forecasting method that has the advantage that only a single number need be stored for the variable being forecast. An additional advantage is that we need only a single weighting factor, called α. The formula employed is

$$F_{t+1} = \alpha A_t + (1 - \alpha) F_t \tag{10-3}$$

where F_{t+1} is the smoothed forecast for $t + 1$, the next period; α is the smoothing constant, which is usually between zero and one; A_t is the actual value of the variable being forecast in the period immediately preceding the forecast period; and F_t is the forecast for the previous period.

At first glance it seems that the forecast F_{t+1} depends only on the actual value for period t, A_t, and the forecast for the same period, F_t.

10.2 / Extrapolations of Historic Observations (Time Series)

This, however, is not true. The continuous influence of older observations can be shown as follows.
We have, from Eq. (10–3),

$$F_{t+1} = \alpha A_t + (1 - \alpha)F_t$$

The forecast for the previous period was

$$F_t = \alpha A_{t-1} + (1 - \alpha)F_{t-1} \tag{10–4}$$

Substituting Eq. (10–4) into Eq. (10–3), we get

$$\begin{aligned} F_{t+1} &= \alpha A_t + (1 - \alpha)[\alpha A_{t-1} + (1 - \alpha)F_{t-1}] \\ &= \alpha A_t + \alpha(1 - \alpha)A_{t-1} + (1 - \alpha)^2 F_{t-1} \end{aligned} \tag{10–5}$$

The forecast for F_{t-1} was

$$F_{t-1} = \alpha A_{t-2} + (1 - \alpha)F_{t-2} \tag{10–6}$$

Substituting Eq. (10–6) into Eq. (10–5) yields

$$\begin{aligned} F_{t+1} &= \alpha A_t + \alpha(1 - \alpha)A_{t-1} + (1 - \alpha)^2 [\alpha A_{t-2} + (1 - \alpha)F_{t-2}] \\ &= \alpha A_t + \alpha(1 - \alpha)A_{t-1} + \alpha(1 - \alpha)^2 A_{t-2} + (1 - \alpha)^3 F_{t-2} \end{aligned} \tag{10–7}$$

We could continue this expansion, but to illustrate the influence of older observations we need not go any further. Let us assume that $\alpha = 0.5$. Note the weighting of the actual observations A as we move further into the past:

$$\alpha A_t = 0.5 A_t$$
$$\alpha(1 - \alpha)A_{t-1} = 0.25 A_{t-1}$$
$$\alpha(1 - \alpha)^2 = 0.125 A_{t-2}$$

We see, therefore, that F_{t+1} depends on A_t, A_{t-1}, A_{t-2}, and F_{t-2}. We could continue this process by writing out the formula for F_{t-2} and substituting it in Eq. (10–7). Exponential smoothing thus does take previous observations into account, although the weight assigned to older observations diminishes exponentially with time. The rate of this decay in the weights is more rapid the closer α is to unity. A simple example will illustrate the method.

A large discount store needs to estimate the monthly demand for a popular portable television set. In recent months sales had been erratic but increasing. In the past they had used a simple moving-average method to forecast monthly sales. The forecast for last September had been 220 units. Actual sales for September and October had been 280 and 320, respectively. They now want to use exponential smoothing to estimate their November sales using a smoothing coefficient of $\alpha = 0.8$.

First let us calculate what the forecast for October would have been (t = September, $t + 1$ = October); for F_t we use the old September forecast of 220 units.

$$F_{t+1} = \alpha(A_t) + (1 - \alpha)F_t$$
$$= 0.8(280) + (1 - 0.8)220 = 224 + 44 = 268$$

The forecast for November would be

$$F_{t+2} = 0.8(320) + 0.2(268) = 256 + 54 = 310$$

We see that the November forecast is very close to the actual sales for October. This is due to our use of a smoothing constant of 0.8, which is very close to 1.

In Table 10–3 we show a more detailed example of an exponentially smoothed forecast, first beginning with the series of calculated forecasts using an α of 0.3. Note in column 6 that the first value of 22 had to be assumed to begin the series of calculated forecasts.

Using a smoothing constant of $\alpha = 0.03$, we can see in Figure 10–1 that the forecast is rather slow in responding to the increases in sales and that it reacted to the decrease in sales only 1 month after the fact. A large α results in behavior similar to a moving average with just a few values; a small α is similar to a moving average with a large number of terms. In the last column we show the forecast values obtained when using a smoothing constant of $\alpha = 0.8$. Note the much quicker response to both increases and decreases in sales in Figure 10–1.

There are many variations of exponential smoothing. Whatever procedure is used, care must be taken to select an appropriate value for α. This can be done by experimenting with varying values of α and determining the resulting forecast error as measured by the variation between the forecast and the actual values. The best α would be the

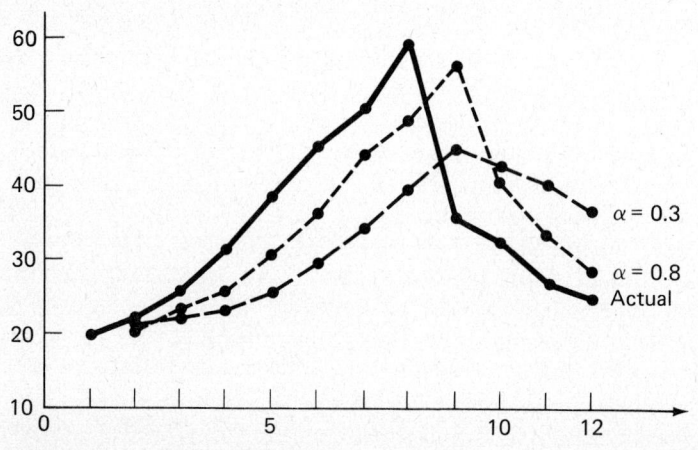

Figure 10–1. Comparison of smoothed forecasts.

TABLE 10–3. Exponentially Smoothed Forecast of Sales ($\alpha = 0.3$) and ($\alpha = 0.8$)

Time Period Month ①	Actual Sales ②	Last Month's Sales ③	α ④	$\alpha \times$ Last Month's Sales ③ × ④	$(1 - \alpha)$ ⑤	Forecast Made for the Previous Period ⑥	$(1 - \alpha) \times$ ⑥ ⑤ × ⑥	Smoothed Forecast for This Month ③ × ④ + ⑤ × ⑥	Smoothed Forecast for This Month Using $\alpha = 0.8$
1	20								
2	23	20	0.3	6	0.7	22*	15.4	21.4	20.4
3	26	23	0.3	6.9	0.7	21.4	15.0	21.9	22.5
4	32	26	0.3	7.8	0.7	21.9	15.3	23.1	25.3
5	38	32	0.3	9.6	0.7	23.1	16.2	25.8	30.7
6	46	38	0.3	11.4	0.7	25.8	18.1	29.5	36.5
7	50	46	0.3	13.8	0.7	29.5	20.7	34.5	44.1
8	58	50	0.3	15.0	0.7	34.5	24.2	39.2	48.8
9	36	58	0.3	17.4	0.7	39.2	27.4	44.8	56.2
10	32	36	0.3	10.8	0.7	44.8	31.4	42.2	40.0
11	27	32	0.3	9.6	0.7	44.2	31.0	40.6	33.6
12	25	27	0.3	8.1	0.7	40.6	28.4	36.5	28.3

*Assumed.

one that results in the smallest historical variation. When a satisfactory α has been chosen, there will still be a need to monitor forecasting errors and to consider a revision of α or the entire forecasting procedure whenever the errors exceed acceptable limits.

ESTIMATION OF LINEAR TRENDS

One final approach to forecasting based on historical observations deals with the projection of a linear trend using the method of least squares. This method is often employed to find a linear trend equation on the basis of past observations. The equation is then used to develop forecasts for future periods. A simple example illustrates the process.

Assume that a firm's sales during the last 8 years are as given in Table 10–4. This information can be plotted on a scatter diagram as

TABLE 10–4. Historical Sales

Year	Sales (Million $)
1971	8.6
1972	9.2
1973	10.5
1974	11.5
1975	13.6
1976	14
1977	16
1978	16.5

shown in Figure 10–2. The trend line equation is

$$y' = a + bx$$

To find the equation for the line of the "best fit," which minimizes the sum of the square of the differences between the points on the line and the actual observations, we use the normal equations:[1]

$$\Sigma y = na + b \Sigma x$$
$$\Sigma xy = a \Sigma x + b \Sigma x^2$$

where b is the slope, a is the intercept with the y axis, x is the independent variable (time), and Σ represents the sum for n observations. The sum is frequently written more completely as $\Sigma_{i=1}^{n}$. To find the num-

---

[1] The derivation of the normal equations is given in the appendix to this chapter.

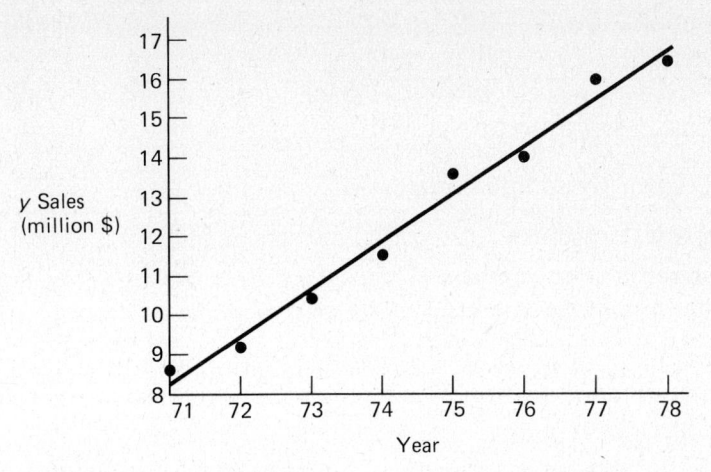

10.2 / Extrapolations of Historic Observations (Time Series)

Figure 10–2. A plot of sales.

bers necessary to solve these simultaneous equations for a and b, we use Table 10–5.[2]

TABLE 10–5. Calculations for the Normal Equations

(yr)	Observations (x)	Sales (y)	(x)(y)	x^2
1971	1	8.6	8.6	1
1972	2	9.2	18.4	4
1973	3	10.5	31.5	9
1974	4	11.5	46.0	16
1975	5	13.6	68.0	25
1976	6	14.0	84.0	36
1977	7	16.0	112.0	49
1978	8	16.5	132.0	64
	$\Sigma x = 36$	$\Sigma y = 99.9$	$\Sigma xy = 500.5$	$\Sigma x^2 = 204$

Using the totals from Table 10–5 in our normal equations, we get

$$99.9 = 8a + 36b$$
$$500.5 = 36a + 204b$$

[2] For computational convenience, we can also use the following formulas:

$$\sum_{i=1}^{n} x_i = \frac{n(n+1)}{2} \quad \text{and} \quad \sum_{i=1}^{n} x_i^2 = \frac{n(n+1)(2n+1)}{6}, \text{ when } x_i = i$$

$$= \frac{8 \times 9}{2} = 36 \qquad = \frac{8 \times 9 \times 17}{6} = 204$$

These are two linear equations in two unknowns, which are solved to yield

$b = 1.212$
$a = 7.03$

Our trend line equation is

$y' = a + bx$

or

$y' = 7.03 + 1.212x$

We have plotted this equation in Figure 10–2 as a dashed line. Using this equation we can now forecast sales for 1980 (the tenth year, as 1971 is year 1) as

$y' = 7.03 + 1.212(10) = \$19.15$ million

In the following section, when discussing regression analysis, we shall have more to say about the assumptions and the validity of this kind of analysis. (Also, see any statistics text for discussion of time series analysis and trend projection). We should, however, stress that we do not assume *any* direct functional link between sales and time. The basic underlying assumption is that history partially repeats itself, time is a surrogate for the many factors that influence sales, and the overall process is regular over time. In other words, sales and time are correlated, but we cannot say anything about the causal factors that determine sales.

10.3 Prediction Models

Contrary to the time series approaches discussed in the preceding section, the prediction models try expressly to establish a *functional relationship* between the variable to be forecast (the dependent variable) and one or more independent variables. These models are often referred to as "causal" models. Under causal forecasting we must, first of all, establish economically plausible relationships between variables. The models themselves do not prove causality. An independent variable can affect the value of a dependent variable. In contrast, an independent variable's value is not influenced by the dependent variable's value. It is a one-way causality. Examples are that ice cream sales *depend* on the weather (weather is not influenced by ice cream sales), attendance in outdoor swimming pools depends on temperature, and the demand for plumbing sales of fixtures and repairs depends on housing starts and the number of existing homes.

Changes in independent variables that are concurrent with changes of the dependent variable (e.g., the number of parking spaces used in a shopping center and the sales of an individual store vary the same way, day by day) are not very useful for forecasting. We want *leading* variable indicators. Their fluctuations precede the changes of the dependent variable by one or more periods. For example, the number of building permits granted for the construction of family dwellings is a variable that precedes or *leads* the demand for household appliances. Movements up or down in the number of building permits over time *lead* movements in the same or opposite direction of the demand for household appliances. A *regression model* for forecasting sales of kitchen appliances would therefore link sales to such independent variables as number of building permits issued and the size of the units to be built. More sophisticated models make future sales dependent on advertising, prices, and competitors' actions, in addition to some leading economic indicators (see also Chapter 12 on corporate modeling). The most commonly used causal models are simple and multiple regression models, econometric models, and input-output models.[3]

In this section we discuss regression analysis as a planning tool and the use of established learning rates in forecasting costs and labor requirements.

REGRESSION ANALYSIS

Regression analysis is a statistical method of analysis that measures the relationship between a dependent variable and one or more independent variables. The objective of regression analysis is to obtain an equation that can be used for predicting future values for the dependent variable. In making predictions, we assume that there is an actual relationship between the dependent and independent variables. Regression measures this relationship, but even though the relationship may be very strong, it *does not imply* any *causal relation* between the variables. *Simple regression analysis* measures the relationship between a dependent variable and one independent variable. *Multiple regression analysis* is the term used when two or more independent variables are involved. In the following we discuss simple linear regression analysis; multiple regression will be introduced briefly at the end of the chapter.

Assume that a recently established small firm installed neither a costing system nor time-keeping procedures. The bookkeeper keeps track of labor costs per month, and the factory manager has a record of the units produced (see Table 10–6). A significant increase in demand is almost certain, and an estimate of the labor cost for various production levels is essential for planning and budgeting purposes.

---

[3]For an excellent comprehensive discussion of forecasting models, see Chambers (1971).

Based on the information given in Table 10–6, we shall develop a linear estimating equation for the cost of labor.

Table 10–6. Direct Labor Costs Observed in Output Range of 3 to 10 Units

Observation (per Month) No.	Units Produced x	Labor Costs y
1	5	$ 60
2	4	45
3	7	75
4	6	65
5	4	55
6	8	100
7	7	90
8	3	35
9	6	80
10	10	105

Let us first do the regression analysis and then discuss the underlying assumptions and limitations.

Using the same normal equations as in the previous section,

$$\Sigma y = na + b \Sigma x$$
$$\Sigma xy = a \Sigma x + b \Sigma x^2$$

where n is the number of data points and each sum refers to the total observations over the n points, we tabulate the available information in Table 10–7 to obtain the necessary totals.

TABLE 10–7. Least Squares Calculations

Observation No.	Units Produced x	Labor Costs y	x^2	xy	y^2
1	5	$ 60	25	$ 300	3,600
2	4	45	16	180	2,025
3	7	75	49	525	5,625
4	6	65	36	390	4,225
5	4	55	16	220	3,025
6	8	100	64	800	10,000
7	7	90	49	630	8,100
8	3	35	9	105	1,225
9	6	80	36	480	6,400
$n = 10$	10	105	100	1,050	11,025
$\Sigma =$	60	$710	400	$4,680	55,250

10.3 / Prediction Models

Entering this information in our normal equation, we get

$$710 = 10a + 60b$$
$$4680 = 60a + 400b$$

These are two linear equations in two unknowns, a and b. Their solution is

$$b = 10.5 \quad a = 8$$

where b is the regression coefficient and a is the y-axis intercept. The equation of the regression line is then

$$y' = 8 + 10.5x$$

This equation represents the least-squares line or line of best fit and can now be used for forecasting the cost of labor for various levels of output.[4]

Our analysis rests on the assumption that there is a persistent and ongoing relationship between cost and production quantities. In other words, we assume that the underlying process is stable over time and not subject to significant changes. Unusual changes, such as a sudden increase in inflation or significant new changes in labor and material costs, must be adjusted for.

It is important to keep in mind that the following four assumptions must be satisfied in order to arrive at valid conclusions.

First, there is a linear relationship between X and Y. This linear relationship for the population can be stated as $E(y) = A + Bx$, where $E(y)$ is the expected value of y and A and B are the parameters of the population that specify the linear relationship. Because A and B are not known, we take a sample of the population (i.e., the observations in the foregoing example represent a sample) and obtain values for A and B that are estimates of the true population parameters.

Second, any deviation of our observations y from the true regression line is referred as an error. It is defined $y - y'$, where y' is the calculated value of y on the regression line. We assume that the average or *expected value of all error terms is zero*. In addition, we assume that the variance or the mean-square error [given by $\Sigma(y - y')^2/(n - 2)$] is constant. A constant variance will exist only when the error terms are evenly distributed around the regression line (see Figure 10–3). The right part of Figure 10–3 indicates that the assumption of a constant variance is not justified.

Third, the deviations from the true regression line are independent of each other; that is, the error included in an observation is assumed to be independent of the errors of all other observations. When they

---

[4]See Chapter 11 on simulation for the incorporation of a cost estimation equation into an accounting simulation model.

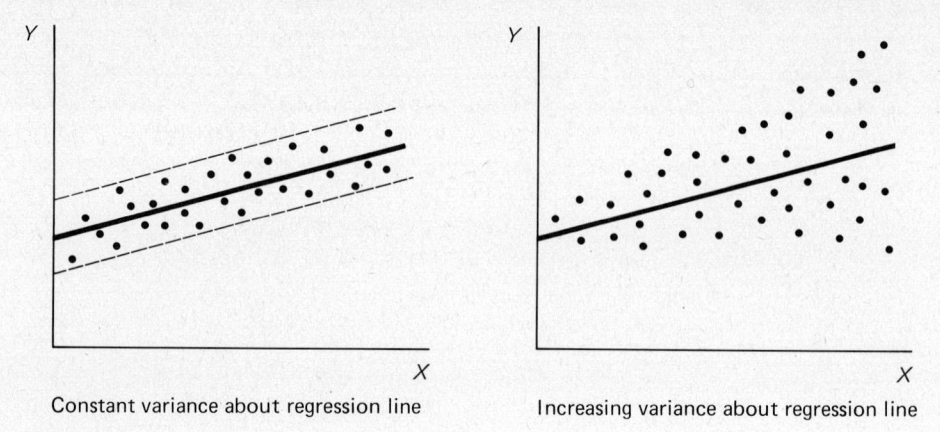

Figure 10-3. Variance about regression line.

Constant variance about regression line

Increasing variance about regression line

are not independent, there is serial correlation. Fourth, the error terms around the true regression line are assumed to be normally distributed.

It should be noted that the first and second assumptions can often be checked by visual inspection of the scattergrams. This is possible when we use only one independent variable. Computer programs are also available to check the validity of our assumptions. It is possible to fit a regression line to any set of data, whether the assumptions are met or not. But if the regression line is to be interpreted intelligently, these assumptions must be met.

Regression analysis in itself does not permit any conclusion as to cause and effect. Also, the estimated cost function is valid only for a certain range. If we go beyond the range of the observations, the relationship may no longer hold (see Figure 10-4). Using the equation in our example to estimate labor costs for an output of 20 units (twice the current maximum) may not be possible, because overtime costs and new equipment may have changed the underlying process.

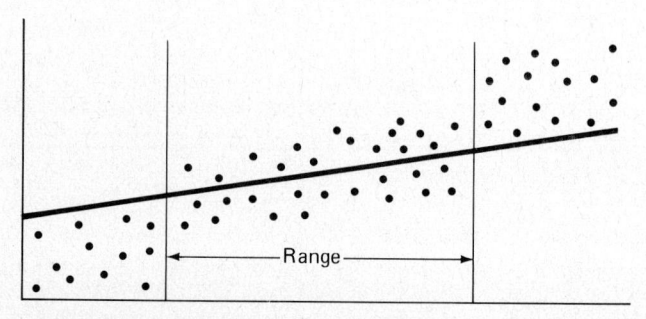

Figure 10-4. Valid range of regression line.

10.3 / Prediction Models

COEFFICIENT OF DETERMINATION

We obtain a measure of closeness of fit by calculating the difference between observed values of Y and Y' calculated by the regression equation. This amount is then compared with the difference between the observed Y and the mean of the observations $\overline{Y}$ (see Figure 10–5). $(Y' - \overline{Y})$ is the portion of the difference (the deviation from the average value) that is explained by a variation of X. And $(Y - Y')$ is the portion of the difference that is not explained. It is assumed to be due to random factors and/or omitted variables.

The sum of the unexplained differences squared, $\Sigma(Y - Y')^2$, which obviously would be equal to zero if we had a perfect fit and the sum of the square of the total differences, $\Sigma(Y - \overline{Y})^2$, are used to develop the coefficient of determination. The ratio $(Y - Y')^2/(Y - \overline{Y})^2$ yields the percentage of the total variation that is not explained; deducting it from one gives us the *coefficient of determination* r^2:

$$r^2 = 1 - \frac{\Sigma(Y - Y')^2}{\Sigma(Y - \overline{Y})^2}$$

As above, $\Sigma(Y - Y')^2$ is the squared sum of the unexplained deviations from the computed line, and $\Sigma(Y - \overline{Y})^2$ the total squared variations from the average value of our observations. Our expression for r^2 has the first term in the numerator and the second in the denominator.

This relationship, $\Sigma(Y - Y')^2/\Sigma(Y - \overline{Y})^2$, is influenced by two factors:

Numerator. $(Y - Y')^2$ represents the scatter around the regression line; it approaches zero the closer we get to a perfect fit (regardless of the value for b) and r^2 approaches one.

Denominator. Deviations from the average value of our observations, $(Y - \overline{Y})^2$; it will tend to zero the closer the observations are

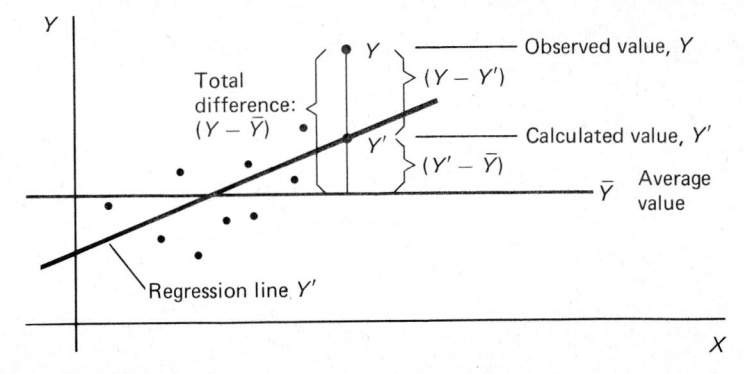

Figure 10–5. Average, calculated, and observed values.

scattered around $\overline{Y}$, the average value. This sum will approach zero when we have a perfect fit to the line $\overline{Y}$, that is, when all the observations are on the horizontal line representing $\overline{Y}$. But when all observations tend toward a perfect fit, the numerator will also approach zero, the fraction will therefore approach unity, and r^2 will get smaller and smaller.

The possible values of r^2 are therefore between zero and one, or $0 \leq r^2 \leq 1$.

Referring back to our example (Table 10–7), we first calculate $\Sigma(Y - \overline{Y})^2$. We have $\Sigma y = 710$, therefore $\overline{Y} = 710/10 = 71$; we now calculate the squared difference from $\overline{Y}$ for each observation in Table 10–8. The variations from the computed line $(Y - Y')^2$ are given in the last column. To find Y', we use the equation of the regression line $Y' = 8 + 10.5x$. Thus, for the first observation we have $8 + 10.5(5) = 60.5$; for the second, $8 + 10.5(4) = 50$; and so on.

TABLE 10–8. Coefficient of Determination Calculations

Observation	Y	$(Y - \overline{Y})^2$	Y'	$(Y - Y')^2$
1	60	121	60.5	0.25
2	45	676	50.0	25.0
3	75	16	81.5	42.25
4	65	36	71.0	36.0
5	55	256	50.0	25.0
6	100	841	92.0	64.0
7	90	361	81.5	72.25
8	35	1296	39.5	20.25
9	80	81	71.0	81.0
10	105	1156	113.0	64.0
		$\Sigma(Y - \overline{Y})^2 = 4840$		$\Sigma(Y - Y')^2 = 430.0$

For our example,

$$r^2 = 1 - \frac{430}{4840} = 0.911$$

The coefficient of determination therefore indicates that about 91 percent of the variance is explained by changes in the production level (the independent variable x) and about 9 percent is due to random variations and/or omitted variables.

The square root of r^2 is called the *coefficient of correlation r*. It measures the relationship between the variables x and y. The sign of r

10.3 / Prediction Models

is that of the regression coefficient b in the regression equation. In our example,

$$r = \pm\sqrt{1 - \frac{430}{4840}} = +0.95$$

Possible values for r vary from -1 to $+1$, or $-1 \leq r \leq +1$. The closer it is to $+1$ or -1, the better the regression line is. Positive values for r mean that y increases with increases in x, and negative values for r mean that y decreases when x increases.

Our set of observations represent only a sample of many possible observations. If we made another set of observations, we would not expect to obtain exactly the same regression equation, and our values for a and b would be different. (All sample statistics are subject to chance variations.) All of our observations yielding equations in the form of

$$Y' = a + bX$$

are only estimates of the true regression equation $E(y) = A + Bx$. To assess the accuracy of our regression line, we need a measure of the dispersion of our observations around the computed line. *The standard error of the estimate* S_{yx} is one such measure. It is given by

$$S_{yx} = \sqrt{\frac{\Sigma(Y - Y')^2}{n - 2}}$$

We have to divide by $(n - 2)$ because there are $10 - 2 = 8$ degrees of freedom. Two constants a and b had to be calculated on the basis of the given observations.

The reader will recall that $(Y - Y')^2$ is simply the squared sum of the unexplained deviations from the computed line. A more convenient computational formula is

$$S_{yx} = \sqrt{\frac{\Sigma y^2 - a \Sigma y - b \Sigma xy}{n - 2}}$$

In our example we obtain a standard error

$$S_{yx} = \sqrt{\frac{55{,}250 - 8(710) - 10.5\,(4{,}680)}{8}} = 7.33$$

If our assumption concerning the normal distribution of error terms around the regression line is justified, we can use the standard error of the estimate to obtain a *level of confidence* in our predictions.

Because we are uncertain about the estimated line itself we must modify S_{yx} by the expression $[1 + (1/n) + ((x - \bar{x})^2/(\Sigma x^2 - \bar{x}\Sigma x))]^{1/2}$. We can now state that the average total hours required for 10 units $[y' = 8 + 10.5(10) = 113]$ will be within the interval of 113 ± 8.94 about 68 percent of the time (see Figure 10–6). Recall that for the normal distribution, the value of the random variables lies within ± one standard deviation from the mean with probability of 0.68. This "prediction interval" is analogous to the estimate of confidence intervals; that is, for a large sample we can expect about 68 percent of the points to be within this interval. For a 95 percent confidence interval, we have

$$113 \pm 2(8.94) = 113 \pm 17.88$$

This approach is analogous to setting a confidence interval for estimates on the mean from a sampling distribution.[5]

TESTING THE SIGNIFICANCE OF THE REGRESSION COEFFICIENT

Obtaining a measure for the reliability of the regression coefficient is very important. In many business applications we need estimates of the variability of a functions, that is, marginal costs and marginal revenue. The regression coefficient b of 10.5 indicates that, on the average, we shall observe a change in our total cost of 10.5 whenever we increase our activity measure x by 1 unit. Our observations (our Ys) represent only a sample; b is an estimate of the population parameter B. If there were no relationships between X and Y, then B would be zero. We can test the hypothesis that $B = 0$ with the alternative $B \neq 0$ by calculating the standard error of the regression coefficient b and finding out how

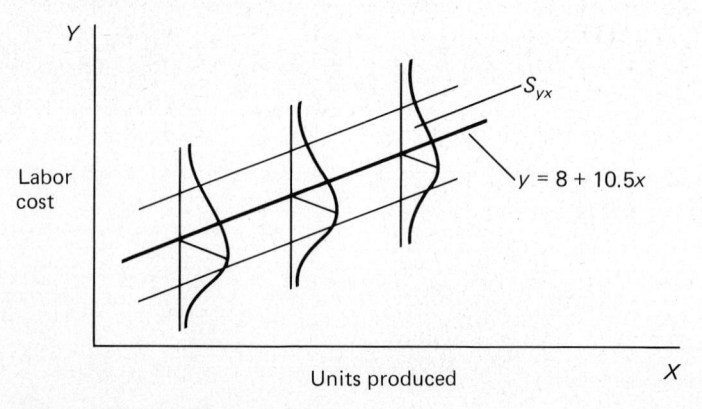

Figure 10–6. Prediction interval.

[5]Theoretically, this statement is true only when the sample size is relatively large; however, it will give an approximation of the correct interval (see section on "Confidence Intervals for the Expected Value of y'").

10.3 / Prediction Models

many standard errors b (the 10.5) is removed from the hypothesized value of zero. The *standard error of regression coefficient* S_b is given by

$$S_b = \frac{S_{yx}}{\sqrt{\Sigma(x - \bar{x})^2}} \quad \text{or} \quad S_b = \frac{S_{yx}}{\sqrt{\Sigma x^2 - \bar{x} \Sigma x}}$$

where S_{yx} is the standard error of the estimate. Because we are dealing with a small sample, the t distribution applies. Here S_b measures the relationship between the standard error of the estimate and the variations of x around its mean. The wider the range of observations is, the smaller S_b is, and vice versa.

In our example, we have

$$S_b = \frac{7.33}{\sqrt{400 - 6(60)}} = 1.1589$$

We now calculate a t value by dividing b by S_b to determine its distance from the hypothesized B.

$$t = \frac{10.5}{1.1589} = 9.06 \quad \text{where} \quad t = \frac{b - 0}{S_b}$$

Because b is more than 9.06 standard errors from the hypothesized B of zero, we can safely reject the hypothesis that $B = 0$. High t values increase the reliability of the coefficient as predictor, whereas low t values (as a rule of thumb, less than 2.00) indicate low reliability. More precisely, for $t < 2.306$ (8 degrees of freedom), we can reject the hypothesis $B = 0$ with 0.95 confidence.

The choice of independent variables is, of course, very important. Should we regress costs against machine hours, direct labor hours, units of output, or a combination of two or all three? (Multiple regression is discussed briefly below.) We may run several regressions and should select one that has a high r^2 and significant t values. We should also test for the validity of the basic four assumptions (computer programs are available for these tests). These tests of significance for regression parameters are, of course, very useful in evaluating the forecasting models discussed in the earlier sections of this chapter.

CONFIDENCE INTERVALS FOR THE REGRESSION COEFFICIENT b

Using a table for t values, we can also establish confidence intervals for b. In our example we have a sample size 10 with eight degrees of freedom; we enter a table on the 8 d.f. line to determine a confidence interval. For example, for a 95 percent confidence interval, we obtain

$$b = 10.5 \pm 2.306(1.1589)$$

Therefore, we are 95 percent confident that the "true" value for b marginal cost will be within $7.828 and $13.172. The width of the confidence interval depends on the relative size of S_b (which, in turn, depends on S_{yx} and the range of observed values for x) and the number of degrees of freedom, that is, the sample size.

CONFIDENCE INTERVALS FOR THE EXPECTED VALUE OF y'

At the end of the section on the coefficient of determination in this chapter, we referred briefly to the confidence intervals around our predicted value for y'. Because the illustrative example of this chapter used a small sample, we should have used the student's t distribution to estimate the confidence intervals. Recall that, using the equation of the regression line, the estimated labor cost for the units of output was

$$y' = 8 + 10.5(10) = 113$$

The standard error of the estimate was

$$S_{yx} = 7.33$$

If we use the student's t statistic for a 95 percent confidence interval for $n - 2$, that is, $10 - 2 = 8$ degrees of freedom is 2.306 (See Table 3 in the Appendix), and using the modified S_{yx} we get

$$\begin{aligned} y' &= 113 \pm 7.33(2.306) \\ &= 113 \pm 16.9 \\ &= 96.1\text{--}129.9 \end{aligned}$$

There are further statistical requirements of this estimate, which are beyond the scope of this chapter. The interested student is referred to any standard introductory text on statistical analysis.

Summarizing the preceding discussion, we now state the following. Regression analysis can be a useful technique for predicting the future value of a variable such as sales or costs. For the technique to be valid, four basic assumptions must be satisfied: (1) the existence of a meaningful, linear relationship between the dependent and the independent variable; (2) a constant variance, that is, the variations from the line of "best" fit (the computed Y') are evenly distributed; (3) the deviations from the regression line must be independent of each other (no serial correlation); and (4) the error terms around the regression line should be normally distributed. Computer programs exist to test the validity of these assumptions.

Even if these assumptions are satisfied, we should not use the resulting equation until we have obtained the following measures for its reliability:

1. The coefficient of determination r^2 (it should be near 1)
2. The standard error of the estimate s_{yx} (the smaller the better)
3. The standard error of the coefficient s_b ($t = b/s_b$ should be larger than 2)

Additional requirements for obtaining valid results are that the process from which the data observations were collected must be *stable* over the time periods included in the observations. For example, in estimating the cost for a production process, none of the cost factors (machine, quality of materials, productivity of labor) should change during the observation. If any important factor changes, we are dealing with a new process. Furthermore, there must also be an adequate number and range of observations. To come up with sound conclusions, we need a sufficient number of observations, and they should cover a sufficient range of values for the independent variable that is of interest, for example, the possible levels of production. The reader should recall that the estimating equation is valid only for the range of observed values.

10.4 Multiple Regression

So far we have discussed only models involving a single independent variable. As already mentioned, the variable to be estimated, say, sales, may depend on two or more independent variables, such as advertising, some leading economic indicator, and market growth. In estimating sales we may find that the inclusion of additional variables may improve our forecast. This applies also to the estimation of cost functions. Costs may be functionally related not only to the quantity of output but also to such variables as machine hours, product mix, type of raw material, types of machines used, and so forth. As we add variables, our analysis will, of course, become more complex. However, with the availability of packaged computer programs, computational complexity presents no problems.

The general equation used in multiple linear regression is

$$y' = a + b_1 x_1 + b_2 x_2 + b_3 x_3 + \cdots + t_n x_n + \epsilon$$

where $x_1, x_2, \ldots, x_n$ are the independent variables; a again is the y intercept; $b_1, b_2, \ldots, b_n$ are the regression coefficients; and ϵ is the error term, which is again assumed to be normally distributed with an expected value (mean) of zero and a constant variance. Multiple linear regression is an extension of simple linear regression. Programs for performing the calculations will usually include tests for validity of the underlying assumptions. In multiple regression analysis, we must satisfy one additional assumption. We assume that the independent variations (those due to changes in x_1 and those due to variations in x_2, etc.) are not related to each other. If they are, it is called collinearity. If two independent variables move in the same direction, their coefficients are no longer reliable estimates for their individual variability. A simple example illustrates the observations, the regression equation, and its use for predicting sales.

Mr. Miller, the manager of a supermarket located in a suburban shopping center, wants better estimates of his sales, which recently were subject to unexpected fluctuations. This, in turn, caused lost sales on some items and overstocking of others. After discussing the problem with a marketing specialist, he believes that his sales for a given week are strongly influenced by the newspaper advertising of a department store next door on preceding Sundays. Information about the department store's advertising would be available to Mr. Miller at least a week before placement. He also feels that the weather may have an influence. On extremely cold and nasty days, his sales are higher than average because many shoppers living in the vicinity seem to prefer to do their shopping nearby rather than going to the more distant supermarkets belonging to national and regional chains. The information available to Mr. Miller is tabulated in Table 10–9.

TABLE 10–9. Mr. Miller's Supermarket Sales During the Last 10 Weeks

Week	Sales in 000s	Department Store Advertising on the Preceding Sunday in 000s	Degrees Below Average Daily Temperature
1	$ 60	$10	3
2	40	2	0
3	50	5	2
4	75	8	7
5	80	12	8
6	60	2	5
7	80	8	7
8	45	2	0
9	100	12	8
10	80	8	3
Variables	y	x_1	x_2

A multiple regression analysis of this problem gives us the following results:

$$y' = 38.62 + 1.95x_1 + 3.46x_2$$

The r^2 is 0.827. The t values for the three coefficients are 6.5, 1.76, and 2.47, respectively. The first and third are significant at the 0.05 level, where the null hypothesis is that the parameters are zero.

Assume Mr. Miller knows that the neighboring department store placed a $15,000 newspaper advertisement this Sunday, and from the weather service he learns that they expect an unusually cold, windy, and wet week, with temperatures averaging 10 degrees below normal. Using the multiple regression equation, he would obtain the following forecast:

$$y' = 38.62 + 1.95(15) + 3.46(10) = 102{,}470$$

He then estimates his sales for the next week to be about \$102,470. Mr. Miller uses r^2 and the t values to assess the reliability of his estimating equation. We note that the t values for the y intercept and x_2 are satisfactory, whereas the one for x_1 is not significant at the 0.05 level and therefore indicates that the coefficient of x_1 may not be very reliable. Mr. Miller may want to use only one independent variable, namely, the weather (see Problem 26).

A thorough discussion of multiple regression is not required here. We have presented an example to show how the technique may be used for forecasting sales. The technique is also often used to estimate cost functions, for example, when production cost depends not only on volume, but also on product mix, machines used, temperature, and other factors.

10.5 Learning Curves and Cost Estimation

Learning is a phenomenon that occurs not only in schools. It is an important factor not only in the life of an individual but also in business organizations. In many production processes we observe a reduction in costs when they are repeated. This is due to the fact that workers and supervisors "learn" how to do their jobs more efficiently. The effect of this learning is increased productivity in terms of output per machine or labor hours. Such learning effects can continue for quite some time; for example, when a new factory is started up, it may take months or even years before the employees "learn" to operate at the level of efficiency for which the plant was designed. If the learning effect occurs with observable regularity, it may be anticipated and used for planning when new products are introduced or new processes started up.[6]

The effect of learning on labor cost can be expressed as a learning or improvement ratio as follows:

$$\text{learning ratio } r = \frac{\text{average labor hours per unit for } n \text{ units}}{\text{average labor hours per unit for } 2n \text{ units}}$$

---

[6] See Baloff and Kennelly (1967).

For example, if 6.25 hr per unit were needed for 100 units and this average drops to 5 hr per unit when we produce 200 units, we have a learning ratio of 5/6.25 or 80 percent. That is, we measure the reduction in labor hours in terms of a percentage reduction in the labor hours per unit that occurs whenever production doubles. Table 10–10 gives an illustration of such an 80-percent learning ratio. Figure 10–7 shows the graph for this 80-percent learning ratio. The curve in the graph is referred to as a learning curve.

TABLE 10–10. Eighty-percent Learning Ratio

PRODUCTION	HOURS		
Cumulative	Marginal Average per Unit	Cumulative	Cumulative Average per Unit
1	100	100	100
2	60	160	80 (100 × 0.8)
4	48	256	64 (80 × 0.8)
8	38.4	409.6	51.2 (64 × 0.8)
16	30.72	655.36	40.96 (51.2 × 0.8)

The learning curve shows that the average labor hours per unit decline sharply at first and then decline more gradually as production increases. If the curve were extended further to the right the decline in average hours per unit would eventually become insignificant. In the case of a new factory, we would say that the "breaking-in" phase is over and we now operate at a "steady" level of productivity. The learning curve was first recognized in the aircraft industry, when it was dis-

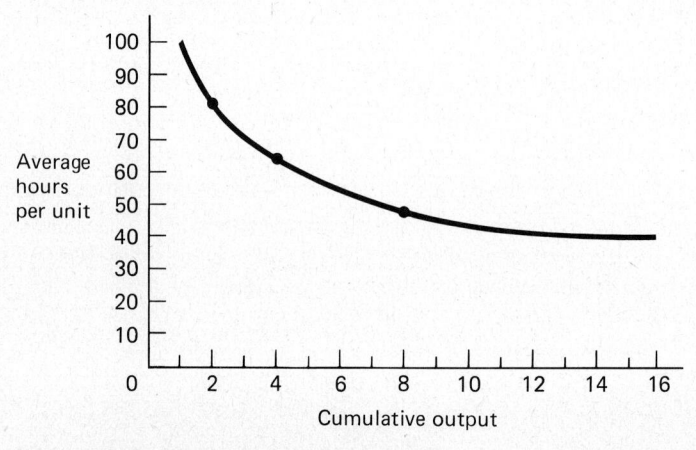

Figure 10–7. Eighty-percent learning curve.

10.5 / Learning Curves and Cost Estimation

covered that there was a fairly constant relationship between labor input per airplane and the number of airplanes produced. In our example we used labor hours to measure inputs of labor; these hours can be readily translated into dollars to give us cost estimates for planning, budgeting, and pricing purposes.

The relationships shown in Table 10–10 and Figure 10–7 can be expressed by the following exponential function:

$$Y = kX^n \qquad (10\text{--}8)$$

where

Y = cumulative average labor hours
k = hours required to complete the first unit
X = number of completed units
n = learning index (This exponent will always be between -1 and 0). When graphed, we see Y as an exponentially decreasing function as X increases.

Assuming a learning rate r whenever production doubles, we have for the second unit rk, using Eq. 10–8,

$$rk = k2^n \qquad (10\text{--}9)$$

Using natural logarithms[7] to solve for n, we get

$$\ln r + \ln k = \ln k + n \ln 2$$
$$\ln r = n \ln 2$$

Therefore

$$n = \frac{\ln r}{\ln 2} \qquad (10\text{--}10)$$

This expression can be used to find n, the *learning index*, for any percentage reduction due to learning.[8]

For an 80-percent learning effect, for example, the learning index is

$$n = \frac{\ln 0.8}{\ln 2} = \frac{-0.223143}{0.693147} = -0.32193$$

---

[7] To facilitate the calculations in this section, students are advised to use calculators equipped with natural logarithmic functions ($\ln x$).

[8] Linear regression can be applied to learning curves, because they can be readily converted to an equivalent linear form. We simply take the logarithm of Eq. (10–8):

$$\ln y = \ln k + n \ln x$$

This is a linear equation in the form $y = a + bx$. All values on both sides of the equation must be converted to their logarithmic equivalents before performing the regression analysis.

To compute the average hours per unit required for the 16 units of Table 10–10, we proceed as follows:

$$Y = 100(16)^{-0.32193}$$
$$\ln Y = \ln 100 - 0.32193 \ln 16$$
$$= 4.60517 - [0.32193(2.77288)]$$
$$= 4.60517 - 0.892666$$
$$= 3.712504$$
$$Y = 40.96$$

Sometimes we know the learning rate and the index that are applicable, but because our records are kept on a job-lot basis, we do not know k, the number of hours required to produce the first unit. The value for k can be readily determined as follows: Assume that the average hours per unit required for a first lot of 30 units was 30 hr and that there is an 80 percent learning effect. How many hours were required for the first unit?

In this case Y is equal to 30 hr, and we can state that

$$30 = k(30)^{-0.32193}$$
$$\ln 30 = \ln k - 0.32193 \ln 30$$
$$\ln k = \ln 30 + 0.32193 \ln 30$$
$$= 4.49615$$

Therefore $k = 89.67$ hr.

By definition, $y = kx^n$ is an average (cost) hours per unit function. To obtain the total hours (cost) required, we multiply by x, the number of units produced. Thus

$$TH = kx^n x = kx^{n+1} \qquad (10\text{–}11)$$

Applying this to our example on Table 10–10 and determining the total hours required for 16-units, we get

$$TH = 100(16)^{0.67807}$$
$$\ln TH = \ln 100 + 0.67807 \ln 16$$
$$= 4.6052 + 1.8801$$
$$TH = 655.36$$

We can obtain incremental labor-hour requirements by examining Table 10–10. The table shows that cumulative hours increased by 60 hr when output went from 1 to 2 units (average hours per unit went from 100 to 80 hr). For all subsequent increments on Table 10–10, average marginal cost per unit is 80 percent of the unit cost of the preceding increment.

To obtain a marginal function for labor requirements of 1 additional unit, we take the function for total labor hours,

$$TH = kX^n X = kX^{n+1} \qquad (10\text{–}12)$$

and taking its derivative, we obtain

$$TH' = (n + 1)kX^n \qquad (10\text{--}13)$$

where TH' is the marginal hours required for an additional unit. It is important to note that we took the derivative of the total hours function TH and not of the function for average Y. It also should be pointed out that the marginal hours differ from the cumulative average hours by the factor $(n + 1)$.

For example, the marginal hours required for the sixteenth unit in Table 10–10 may be determined as follows:

$$\begin{aligned}
TH'(\text{16th unit}) &= (-0.32193 + 1)100(16)^{-0.32193} \\
&= (0.67807)(100)(16)^{-0.32193} \\
\ln TH' &= \ln 67.807 - 0.32193 \ln 16 \\
&= \ln(3.52408)
\end{aligned}$$

Therefore, $TH' = 27.7736$ hr. Note that $27.7736 \div 0.67807 = 40.96$ hr; that is, the marginal average hours for the sixteenth unit are exactly by the factor $(n + 1)$ less than the cumulative average hours per unit.

Knowledge of the learning curve is useful for planning costs and labor requirements and their subsequent control. Ideally, the applicable learning ratio should be based on historical observations. When no directly comparable historical products are available, learning ratios experienced with similar products can often be used. If learning is known to be an important cost factor, a reasonable effort should be made to estimate its expected impact on costs.

10.6 Summary

In this chapter we introduced some quantitative forecasting methods. Our discussion started with methods that extend historical observations, such as the simple, moving, and weighted averages. Exponential smoothing was covered in more detail. Although the method uses only two inputs (the actual value of the variable being forecast in the immediately preceding period, A_t, and the forecast for the same period, F_t) older observations continue to influence the forecast. Trend estimation, using the least-squares method, was the last of the extrapolation methods discussed.

In the section on prediction models we based our estimates on one or more independent variables that help us estimate the value of a dependent variable. As examples we discussed the use of regression analysis in cost estimating and sales forecasting. The importance of the underlying assumptions (linearity, constant variances, independence, and normality) for the validity of estimates was stressed. The coefficient of determination and the coefficient of correlation were developed in the context of the first example. We then introduced the standard error of the estimate and its use in estimating prediction intervals. Tests of significance and estimates of confidence intervals for the regression coefficient concluded the example on simple regression analyses. Multiple regression analysis was introduced with an illustrative example. The chapter ended with a discussion of the use of learning curves for cost estimates.

Glossary

Coefficient of correlation. The square root of r^2; possible values vary from -1 to $+1$; the sign is that of the regression coefficient b; it is a relative measure of the relationship between the variables x and y.

Coefficient of determination. The percentage of the squared sum of the total variations from $\bar{y}$, the mean of the observations, that is not explained by the computed line y',

$$r^2 = 1 - \frac{\Sigma(y - y')^2}{\Sigma(y - \bar{y})^2}$$

Possible values vary from zero to one.

Exponential smoothing. A moving-average forecasting method that uses only a single weight factor, called α. The formula is as follows:

$$F_{t+1} = \alpha(A_t) + (1 - \alpha)F_t$$

where F_{t+1} is the smoothed forecast for the next period and α is the smoothing constant, which is usually between zero and one.

Judgmental forecasting. Forecasting based on the subjective judgment of experts or a panel of specialists. The delphi method represents one such approach.

Learning curve. A model used for forecasting labor requirements in industries where the learning effect can be measured and anticipated with reasonable certainty.

Learning index. The exponent n in the learning function $y = kx^n$, which is used to estimate cumulative average labor hours (or costs) per unit of output.

Learning ratio. A measure of the learning effect on labor requirements or costs when production doubles.

Least-squares method. A method of fitting a line that minimizes the sum of squares of the difference between observed values and the calculated line.

Moving average. An average calculated by using only a fixed number of the most recent observations.

Prediction model. A forecasting method that expressively tries to establish causal relationships between the variable to be forecast (the dependent variable) and one or more independent variables.

Problems

Quantitative forecast. The analysis of numerical data using a mathematical model to forecast.

Regression model. A model of forecasting that links a dependent variable (e.g., refrigerator sales) to one or more leading independent variables (e.g., building permits).

Simple average. A forecast calculated by summing a number of n observed values and dividing the sum by n.

Standard error of the estimate. A measure of the dispersion of the observed values of y around the regression line.

Standard error of the regression coefficient. A measure of the variability of the regression coefficient b.

Trend estimation. A method of forecasting based on historical observations, often employing the least-squares method to determine a linear trend.

Weighted average. A calculation of the average by assigning more weight to recent observations. For example, in a 3-months moving average, we could assign a weight of $\frac{3}{6}$ for the latest month, $\frac{2}{6}$ for the preceding one, and $\frac{1}{6}$ for the oldest period used.

Problems

1. A newsboy notes that the demand for newspapers has been 17, 18, 12, 13, 15, 21, 18 for the last week, where the numbers represent demand Sunday, Monday, ...
    a. Determine a simple forecast for Sunday using a 7-day simple average.
    b. Determine a moving average for Sunday that uses only the demand for Thursday, Friday, and Saturday.
    c. Determine a weighted average for Sunday that uses only Thursday, Friday, and Saturday, but weights the weekend demand twice as much as the weekday demand.
2. An automobile dealer has 4 yr of auto sales history for the month of August: 80, 75, 97, 107.
    a. Using a simple average, calculate a sales forecast for next August, using all 4 yr data; the last 3 yr; the last 2 yr; and last year's demand.
    b. A new salesperson suggests that exponential smoothing is better than a simple average. The salesperson uses $\alpha = 0.8$, and the forecast for last year was 92.8 cars. Find the forecast for this year.
    c. Another salesperson has argued that the method is not important, but that the appropriate historical sales data is April, May, June, July of this year; and not August sales of the last 4 yr. Comment.
3. A third salesperson has argued that a linear trend forecast using least-squares is superior to a moving average, or exponential smoothing. Find the forecast for August auto sales using a least-squares forecast based on August sales of the last 4 yr.
4. Find the least-squares forecast for Sunday newspapers using answers given in Problem 1.
5. The ABC Company is attempting to forecast the price of gasoline for its

fleet for next year. The average cost per year for the last 6 yr has been $0.43, $0.72, $0.52, $0.60, $0.72, and $1.11. Determine the simple average forecast; the weighted-average forecast with weights $\frac{1}{18}, \frac{1}{18}, \frac{1}{18}, \frac{2}{18}, \frac{6}{18}$, and $\frac{7}{18}$; an exponential smoothing forecast with $\alpha = 0.6$ and the last forecast of $0.92; and a linear trend line.

6. *(SMA)* Watski Limited produces and sells water skis throughout northern Canada. Because of the relatively short season for waterskiing in this area, most sales are made late in the first half of each year. Unit sales for the last six periods (3 yr) were:

Period	Sales (units)
Jan.–June 1977	1200
July–Dec. 1977	200
Jan.–June 1978	1500
July–Dec. 1978	300
Jan.–June 1979	2000
July–Dec. 1979	300

a. Using a smoothing constant of 0.1, calculate single exponentially smoothed moving averages for this time series.
b. Repeat part a using a smoothing constant of 0.8.
c. Which of the two series of moving averages appears to be more useful in predicting sales for January to June 1980? Why?
d. In your own words, interpret S_t when $\alpha = 1$.

7. *(SMA)* The monthly TV sales of the Acme Electronics Company are given in the table below. To facilitate calculations, data are given for only 7 mo.

Month—1977	Sales
January	140
February	110
March	80
April	80
May	110
June	125
July	155

REQUIRED
Please display your answers to parts a and b on one table.
a. Compute the 3-mo moving average of sales for the period shown when $M = 3$.
b. Using an exponential smoothing constant $\alpha = 0.1$, calculate the exponentially smoothed values for each month. (Answer should be carried to one decimal place.)
c. Plot three curves depicting the raw data, moving average data, and exponentially smoothed data. *Label* the three lines.

Problems

8. The ABC Company is considering using a different approach to gasoline price forecasting. The new approach suggests that the price of gasoline is a function of previous year's mean average temperature in Saudi Arabia. The data are as follows:

Year	Gasoline Price	Temperature
0		100
1	0.43	120
2	0.72	98
3	0.52	131
4	0.60	120
5	0.72	118
6	1.11	128

Determine a least-squares forecasting equation for the price of gasoline. There is a 1-yr lag in the function. What is the forecasted price of gasoline for next year?

9. (CMA) Regression analysis is a procedure used to measure the relationship of one variable with one or more other variables. Regression provides a rational statement rather than a causal statement with regard to the relationship. The basic formula for a regression equation is:

$$Y_i = \alpha + \beta_1 x_{i1} + \beta_2 x_{i2} + E_i$$

For a regression equation to provide meaningful information, it should comply with the basic criteria of goodness-of-fit and specification analysis. Specification analysis is determined by examining the population relationships for (1) linearity within a relevant range, (2) constant variance (homoscedasticity), (3) independence of observations (serial correlation), (4) normality, and (5) multicollinearity.

REQUIRED
   a. Explain what is meant by the phrase "regression provides a rational statement rather than a causal statement."
   b. Explain the meaning of each of the following symbols that appear in the basic formula for a regression equation.
      (1) Y_i
      (2) α
      (3) β_1
      (4) X_{i1}
      (5) E_i
   c. Identify the statistical factors that are used to test a regression equation for goodness-of-fit and, for each item identified, indicate whether a high or low value describes a "good" fit.
   d. Explain what each of the following terms means with respect to regression analysis.
      (1) Linearity within a relevant range
      (2) Constant variance (homoscedasticity)

(3) Serial correlation
(4) Normality
(5) Multicollinearity

10. The chief cost accountant of a large jobbing plant wants to establish realistic overhead rates for the machining department. As a first step she wants to get an idea as to the variability of all indirect costs in the department. She had a clerk prepare the tabulation below, showing machine hours and total indirect costs for each of the past 12 months.

	Month	Machine Hours (in 000s)	Total Overhead Costs (in 000s)
	1	52	$65
	2	88	92
	3	64	83
	4	82	93
	5	60	68
$N = 12$	6	83	98
	7	58	72
	8	90	95
	9	72	88
	10	85	95
	11	76	78
	12	78	82

REQUIRED

Prepare a regression analysis using the least-squares method, find the coefficient of determination, and give a thorough evaluation of your results.

11. *(CMA)* The following annual sales data have been collected for Fiberglass Marine Products Limited over the last 10 yr:

Year	1969	1970	1971	1972	1973	1974	1975	1976	1977	1978
Sales ($10,000)	60	65	70	58	61	68	72	77.5	65	72

REQUIRED
  a. Plot the original data on the supplied graph paper, using as large a scale as possible.
  b. (1) Calculate the 4-yr moving average. Use three places of decimals.
     (2) Plot this moving average on the same graph.
  c. (1) Use exponential smoothing, with $\alpha = 0.10$ to smooth the original data. Show your calculations to three places of decimals.
     (2) Plot your results on the same graph.
     (3) Discuss what effect the application of $\alpha = 0.50$ (instead of $\alpha = 0.10$) would have on the data. Do not calculate or plot.

Problems

Note: Your graphs should be drawn neatly and properly labeled and titled.

12. *(CMA.)* The controller of the Connecticut Electronics Company believes that the identification of the variable and fixed components of the firm's costs will enable the firm to make better planning and control decisions. Among the costs the controller is concerned about is the behavior of indirect supplies expense. He believes that there is some correlation between the machine hours worked and the amount of indirect supplies used. A member of the controller's staff has suggested that a simple linear regression model be used to determine the cost behavior of the indirect supplies. The regression equation shown below was developed from 40 pairs of observations using the least-squares method of regression. The regression equation and related measures are as follows:

$$S = \$200 + \$4H$$

where

S = total monthly costs of indirect supplies
H = machine hours per month

Standard error of estimate: $S_e = 100$
Coefficient of correlation: $r = 0.87$

REQUIRED
Answer the following questions.
   a. When a simple linear regression model is used to make inferences about a population relationship from sample data, what assumptions must be made before the inferences can be accepted as valid?
   b. Assume that the assumptions identified in part a are satisfied for the indirect supplies expense of Connecticut Electronics Company.
      (1) Explain the meaning of "200" and "4" in the regression equation $S = \$200 + \$4H$.
      (2) Calculate the estimated cost of indirect supplies if 900 machine hours are to be used during a month.
      (3) In addition to the estimate for the cost of indirect supplies, the controller would like the range of values for the estimate if a 95 percent confidence interval is specified. He would use this range to judge whether the estimated costs indicated by the regression analysis was good enough for planning purposes. Calculate, for 900 machine hours, the range of the estimate for the cost of indirect supplies with a 95 percent confidence interval.
   c. Explain briefly what the
      (1) Coefficient of correlation measures.
      (2) Value of the coefficient of correlation ($r = 0.87$) indicates in this case if Connecticut Electronics Company wishes to predict the total cost of indirect supplies on the basis of estimated machine hours.
13. *(CMA)* Beccal Corporation is a manufacturer of equipment for several different sports. Although Beccal's revenue does not fluctuate greatly from

one month to the next, the sales of the individual products are very seasonal. For instance, the actual sales for the baseball bat product-line over the last 18 mo (the current estimate for June 1982 is based upon the sales made during the first 10 days of June) have been as follows:

1981	Sales in Units
January	14,000
February	18,000
March	30,000
April	45,000
May	70,000
June	63,000
July	54,000
August	36,000
September	18,000
October	45,000
November	15,000
December	12,000

1982	
January	15,000
February	21,000
March	36,000
April	45,000
May	81,000
June (estimated)	72,000

The company has had difficulty in scheduling its production properly due to problems in estimating monthly product demand. The Profit Planning Department has been studying this problem, and one member of the staff suggested that a sales/production model in units could be developed.

The model based upon seasonal unit sales levels and sales growth was proposed. The coming month's sales demand would be a function of the budgeted annual sales in units for a product multiplied by the proportion that actual sales in units for the same month last year is to the total sales in units for the prior 12 mo. This result would then be adjusted for the growth in the current year-to-date unit sales over the same period of months as the prior year-to-date unit sales, that is, the sum of the unit sales for the first n months of the current year would be divided by the sum of the unit sales for the first n months of the prior year. The quantity produced for the coming month would be the coming month's sales demand in units (as determined above) plus 30 percent of the second coming month's unit sales demand (determined similarly to the coming month unit sales demand) minus the inventory on hand for the current month. The mathematical representation of the model is presented below:

$$D_t = B \left(\frac{S_{-12}}{\sum_{n=-1}^{-12} S_n} \right) \left(\frac{\sum_{n=-1}^{(-t+1)} S_n}{\sum_{n=-13}^{(-t-12+1)} S_n} \right)$$

$$D_{t+1} = B \left(\frac{S_{-11}}{\sum_{n=-1}^{-12} S_n} \right) \left(\frac{\sum_{n=-1}^{(-t+1)} S_n}{\sum_{n=-13}^{(-t-12+1)} S_n} \right)$$

$$P_t = D_t + 0.3 D_{t+1} - I_{t-1}$$

where

D_t = sales demand in units for month t
D_{t+1} = sales demand in units for month $t + 1$
B = budgeted annual sales in units
S_n = actual (or estimated if actual data are not available) sales volume in units for month n
P_t = proposed production in units for month t
I_{t-1} = projected ending inventory in units for month $t - 1$

The annual budgeted sales for the baseball bat product-line for 1982 is 500,000 units. The projected inventory of baseball bats at the end of June is 15,000 units. Beccal uses a calendar year for reporting purposes.

REQUIRED

a. Using the proposed model developed by Beccal Corporation's Profit Planning Department and the sales data for the past 18 mo, calculate for the baseball bat product-line:
   (1) The sales demand in units for July 1982 (i.e., $D_t = D_7$).
   (2) The proposed production in units for July 1982 (i.e., $P_t = P_7$).
b. One member of Beccal's profit planning staff suggested that a 3-mo moving average be used for the factors S_{-12} and S_{-11} in the formula for D_t and D_{t+1} respectively; for example, S_{-12} would be replaced by the factor $(S_{-12} + S_{-11} + S_{-10}) \div 3$. Should a 3-mo moving average be used in the model rather than a single-month figure? Explain your answer.
c. Evaluate the model proposed by Beccal's Profit Planning Department including an identification of:
   (1) Its strengths
   (2) Its weaknesses
   (3) Other factors, if any, Beccal should incorporate into the model
d. If Beccal Corporation decides to use a model (either the one presented

or another model of some kind) to solve its production scheduling problem, explain how the company should proceed to determine if the model is feasible before it is implemented.

14. *(CMA)* The Lockit Company manufactures door knobs for residential homes and apartments. Lockit is considering the use of simple and multiple linear regression analysis to forecast annual sales because previous forecasts have been inaccurate. The sales forecast will be used to initiate the budgeting process and to identify better the underlying process that generates sales.

Larry Husky, the controller of Lockit, has considered many possible independent variables and equations to predict sales and has narrowed his choices to four equations. Husky used annual observations from 20 prior years to estimate each of the four equations.

Following is a definition of the variables used in the four equations and a statistical summary of these equations:

S_t = forecasted sales (in dollars) for Lockit in time period t
S_{t-1} = actual sales (in dollars) for Lockit in time period $t-1$
G_t = forecasted U.S. gross national product in time period t
G_{t-1} = actual U.S. gross national product in time period $t-1$
N_{t-1} = Lockit's net income in time period $t-1$

Statistical Summary of Four Equations

Equation	Dependent Variable	Independent Variable (s)	Dependent Variable (Intercept)($)	Independent Variable (rate)($)	Standard Error of the Estimate($)	Coefficient of Correlation	t Value
1	S_t	S_{t-1}	+ 500,000	+ 1.10	500,000	+0.97	5.50
2	S_t	G_t	+1,000,000	+ 0.00001	510,000	+0.95	10.00
3	S_t	G_{t-1}	900,000	+ 0.000012	520,000	+0.90	5.00
4	S_t		+ 600,000		490,000	+0.98	
		N_{t-1}		+10.00			4.00
		G_t		+ 0.000002			1.50
		G_{t-1}		+ 0.000003			3.00

REQUIRED

a. Write equations 2 and 4 in the form $y = a + bx$.
b. If actual sales are $1,500,000 in 1981, what would be the forecasted sales for Lockit in 1982?
c. Explain the meaning and significance of the coefficient of correlation.
d. Why might Larry Husky prefer equation 3 to equation 2?
e. Explain the advantages and disadvantages of using equation 4 to forecast annual sales.

Problems

15. *(SMA)* Engine Rebuilders Limited is in the process of negotiating a penalty charge for defective components supplied by their only auto parts supplier. Management believes that the time lost in disassembling and reassembling an engine (or part thereof), in which the components are used, is a linear function of the number of defective components encountered. A random sample of eight engine rebuilds revealed the following information:

Job Number	Number of Defective Components (x)	Time Lost Due to Disassembly and Reassembly (in hours) (y)
12	2	4.0
171	1	2.5
316	3	6.9
204	4	10.1
142	3	7.0
71	2	4.8
96	2	5.1
248	1	2.6
	18	43.0

REQUIRED
a. Calculate the equation of the least-squares regression line. (Use three places of decimals.)
b. On the enclosed graph paper (using an appropriately large scale) accurately plot the actual data and the regression line calculated in part a.
c. Is there sufficient evidence to indicate that the number of defective components is linearly related to the time lost due to disassembly and reassembly? ($\alpha = 0.10$)
d. Engine Rebuilders Limited charges $22 per hour for shop time. Management intends that their policy concerning defective components be based on expected lost shop time. Their auto parts supplier will be charged a penalty of a fixed base amount if any defectives are encountered and a variable charge for each defective component that must be replaced.
   (1) What should the fixed base amount be?
   (2) What should the variable charge per defective component encountered be?

16. *(CMA)* The Alpha Company, which produces several different products, is making plans for the introduction of a new product, which it will sell for $6 a unit. The following estimates have been made for manufacturing costs on 100,000 units to be produced the first year:

   Direct materials: $50,000

   Direct labor: $40,000 (The labor rate is $4 per hour.)

Overhead costs have not yet been estimated for the new product, but monthly data on total production and overhead cost for the past 24 months have been analyzed using simple linear regression. The following results were derived from the simple regression and will provide the basis for overhead cost estimates for the new product.

Simple Regression Analysis Results (y = a + bx)

Dependent variable (y): factory overhead costs
Independent variable (x): direct labor hours
Computed values:

y intercept	$40,000
Coefficient of independent variable	$2.10
Coefficient of correlation	0.953
Standard error of estimate	$2,840
Standard error of regression coefficient	0.42
Mean value of independent variable	$18,000
Coefficient of determination	0.906

REQUIRED
Answer the following questions.
  a. What percentage of the variation in overhead costs is explained by the independent variable?
  b. Using the table of values for the student's t distribution, what is the 95 percent confidence interval for the t values?
  c. What would be the total overhead cost for an estimated activity level of 20,000 direct labor hours?
  d. What is the expected contribution margin per unit (unit selling price minus variable cost per unit) during the first year on 100,000 units of the new product?

17. (SMA) Management wishes to prepare a flexible budget relating expected revenues and costs to production volume. No great problems arise with variable cost items such as material and labor cost, but overhead costs are somewhat more difficult to handle.

Data concerning overhead costs for certain levels of production are given below:

Production (units × 10,000)	3	5	6	9
Overhead ($ × 1000)	8	10	12	14

REQUIRED
(All calculations should be to three decimal places.)
  a. Using the method of least squares, fit a regression line relating overhead to production volume.
  b. The method of least squares produces a regression line that minimizes SSE. Why do we choose to minimize the sum of the squared deviations rather than the sum of the deviations themselves?

Problems

c. Calculate s^2 for the data.
d. Calculate the coefficient of determination and comment on its significance.
e. Find a 95 percent confidence interval for the variable overhead cost (β_1).

18. *(CMA)* Brown Company employs 20 salespeople to market its products in well-defined sales territories. The company has analyzed the weekly sales order-getting costs for the past year using regression analysis. The following was derived from the regression analysis:

$$C = \$6{,}000 + \$0.50M + \$6.00S$$

where

C = weekly sales order-getting costs
M = number of miles driven per week by the sales force
S = number of sales calls completed per week
The standard error of the estimate for C given the values for M and S is 400

REQUIRED
Answer the following questions.

a. The sales department has estimated that the sales force will drive 10,000 miles and make 500 calls during the first week in July.
  (1) Calculate the estimated sales order-getting costs for the week.
  (2) What criteria should be met before Brown's sales department relies on the estimate derived in part a(1)?
b. What does the value for the standard error of the estimate for C (400) mean, and how might it be used in cost estimation?

19. *(CMA)* The Kelly Company plans to manufacture a product called Electrocal which requires a substantial amount of direct labor on each unit. Based upon the company's experience with other products that required similar amounts of direct labor, management believes that there is a learning factor in the production process used to manufacture Electrocal.

Each unit of Electrocal requires 50 ft^2 of raw material at a cost of $30 per square foot for a total material cost of $1500. The standard direct labor rate is $25 per direct labor hour. Variable manufacturing overhead is assigned to products at a rate of $40 per direct labor hour. The company adds a markup of 30 percent on variable manufacturing costs in determining an initial bid price for all products.

Data on the production of the first two lots (16 units) of Electrocal are as follows:

The first lot of eight units required a total of 3200 direct labor hours.

The second lot of eight units required a total of 2240 direct labor hours.

Based upon prior production experience, Kelly anticipates that there will be no significant improvement in production time after the first 32 units. Therefore, a standard for direct labor hours will be established based upon the average hours per unit for units 17 to 32.

REQUIRED
  a. What is the basic premise of the learning curve?
  b. Based upon the data presented for the first 16 units, what learning rate appears to be applicable to the direct labor required to produce Electrocal? Support your answer with appropriate calculations.
  c. Calculate the standard for direct labor hours that Kelly Company should establish for each unit of Electrocal.
  d. After the first 32 units have been manufactured, Kelly Company was asked to submit a bid on an additional 96 units. What price should Kelly bid on this order of 96 units? Explain your answer.
  e. Knowledge of the learning curve phenomenon can be a valuable management tool. Explain how management can apply the learning curve in the planning and controlling of business operations.
20. Assuming that there is a constant reduction of labor hours of 90 percent whenever production doubles:
  a. Calculate the learning index n for use in the learning curve formula.
  b. Do the same thing for learning effects of 75 percent and 85 percent.
  c. Show mathematically the economic consequences of a 100 percent and a 50 percent learning effect.
21. The ABC Aerospace Company controller is in the process of preparing a bid on an order of 300 units of a special subassembly for NASA. Previous experience shows that the first lot of 8 units required 300 direct labor hours. Assume a learning effect of 90 percent whenever production doubles.

REQUIRED
You are to answer the following questions:
  a. What is the estimated *total* labor hours required for the 300 units?
  b. What is the number of *average cumulative hours* required for the 300th unit?
  c. What is the number of marginal average hours required to produce the 300th unit?
  d. What is the total number of hours required to produce units 100 through 200?
22. Refer to Problem 21. The controller of the ABC Aerospace Company now wants an estimate of the total cost for the contract, and also wants you to evaluate the proposed selling price of $450 per unit. You are furnished the following cost information:

  Direct labor: $10 per hour

  Material: $30 per unit

  Direct labor-related overhead: $5 per hour

  Other variable overhead: $2.50 per unit

  Assignable fixed cost: $500,000

REQUIRED
  a. What is the total cost for the 300 units? What is the expected contribution to fixed cost and profit?
  b. What is the cumulative average cost for the 300th unit?

Problems

    c. What is the cost of the 300th unit?
    d. Calculate a breakeven point on an average-cost basis.

23. The Galexplo Company has just completed the assembly of 150 units of a guidance system. The company is now considering a new order for 100 additional units. Management has noted that the number of direct labor hours worked on each unit seems to be declining. For the first 50 units produced, the average hours per unit were 580. For the assembly of 150 units, however, the average hours per unit dropped to 398. These two observations imply a learning-curve function of the form $y = ax^{-l}$

REQUIRED
    a. Using these two points on the curve, derive the values for a and l so that the average hours for 250 units can be determined.
    b. Using your values from part a, calculate the total hours required to assemble 250 units.
    c. Suppose that labor rates average $5 per hour. What would be the incremental labor costs if the new order were accepted?

24. *(CMA)* Horace Company employs a standard cost system in the manufacturing of all its products. Based on past experience, the company considers the effect of an 80 percent learning factor when developing standards for direct labor costs. Horace Company is planning for the production of an automatic electrical timing device requiring the assembly of purchased components. Production is planned in lots of 5 units each. A steady-state production phase with no further increases in labor productivity is expected after the eighth lot. The first production lot of 5 units required 90 hr of direct labor time at a standard rate of $6 per hour.
    a. Determine the standard amount Horace Company should establish for the total direct labor costs required for the production of the first eight lots of the automatic electrical timing devices.
    b. Discuss the factors that should be considered in establishing the direct labor standards for each unit of output produced beyond the first eight lots.

25. The ABC Company, a frequent contractor for NASA, is preparing cost estimates for a bid on 300 units of a navigation device. One hundred units of an identical device had just been completed for another government agency. For this and similar components, the company has experienced an 80 percent learning curve for assembly and testing-related costs. The company controller has prepared the following summary of costs incurred for the completed contract:

Materials and components	$36,000
Assembly and testing	72,000
Setup and special tooling	9,000
Variable overhead	9,000
Total costs	$126,000

    1. Tooling can be reused, even though its total cost has already been charged to the completed contract.
    2. Variable overhead is related directly to assembly and testing.

REQUIRED
a. Prepare a cost estimate for the contract of 300 units.
b. What is your average direct labor cost per unit included in part a?

26. Mr. Miller, the supermarket manager in the section on multiple regression, has decided to use a simple regression model with sales as a function of temperature. Thus, his "new" model is

$$y = a + bx$$

where y is sales and x is the degrees below the average daily temperature. Using data given in Table 10–9, find estimates for a and b. Test their significance. For this situation, is multiple regression or simple regression the better model?

References

Baloff, Nicholas, and Kennelly, John W. "Accounting Implications of Product and Process Start-Ups." *Journal of Accounting Research* vol. 5, no. 2 (Autumn 1967): 131–143.

Benston, George J. "Multiple Regression Analysis of Cost Behavior." *The Accounting Review* vol. 41 (October 1966): 657–672.

Chambers, John S., Mullik, Sotmider K., and Smith, Donald D. "How to Choose the Right Forecasting Technique." *Harvard Business Review* 49, no. 4 (July/August 1971): 55–64.

Dupoch, Nicholas, Birnberg, Jacob C., and Demski, Joel. *Cost Accounting: Accounting Data for Management's Decisions.* New York: Harcourt Brace Jovanovich, 1974.

Gillespie, Jackson F. "An Application of Learning Curves to Standard Costing." *Management Accounting* vol. 63 (September 1981): 63–65.

Hubbard, Charles L., Mohn, N. Carroll, and Reid, John C. "The Backcast: A Sales Performance Evaluation Tool at Coca-Cola." *Interfaces* 9, no. 4 (August 1979): 38–45.

Jensen, Robert E. "A Multiple Regression Model for Cost Control—Assumptions and Limitations." *The Accounting Review* vol. 42 (April 1967): 265–273.

Kallina, Carl. "Development and Implementation of a Simple Short Range Forecasting Model—A Case Study." *Interfaces* 8, no. 3 (May 1978): 32–39.

Neter, John, Wasserman, William, and Whitmore, G. A. *Applied Statistics.* Boston: Allyn & Bacon, 1978.

Spurr, William A., and Bonini, Charles P. *Statistical Analysis for Business Decisions*, rev. ed. Homewood, Ill.: Irwin, 1963.

Wheelwright, Steven, and Makridakis, Spyros. *Forecasting Methods for Management.* New York: Wiley, 1973.

Winkler, Robert L., and Hayes, William L. *Statistics: Probability, Inference, and Decision.* 2d ed. New York: Holt, Rinehart and Winston, 1975.

Appendix

Appendix. Development of the Normal Equations from Least Squares

We want to develop the value of the slope b and the y intercept a for a linear equation that has the property that the sum of the squared deviations from that line is minimized for the data given. Let us consider it step by step using Figure 10–8.

1. A data set that is represented by the stars on the graph. Each point has an (X, Y) value.
2. A point on the regression line has the (X, Y) relation $Y' = a + bX$.
3. Any datum point is represented by Y, and thus the difference between Y and Y' is an error; that is, $Y - Y'$ is the deviation of that point from the regression line. And the squared deviation is $(Y - Y')^2$.
4. The sum of the squared deviations is then

    $$\Sigma(Y - Y')^2$$

    where the sum is taken over all data points, or

    $$\sum_{i=1}^{n}(Y_i - a - bx_i)^2$$

    for n data points and with the substitution $Y' = a + bx$.
5. Now, to minimize the sum of the squared deviations, we apply differential calculus. Taking partial derivatives of the sum with respect to the unknown parameters a and b, we have

    $$\frac{\delta}{\delta a} = \sum_{i=1}^{n} 2(Y_i - a - bx_i)(-1) = 0$$

    $$\frac{\delta}{\delta b} = \sum_{i=1}^{n} 2(Y_i - a - bx_i)(-x_i) = 0$$

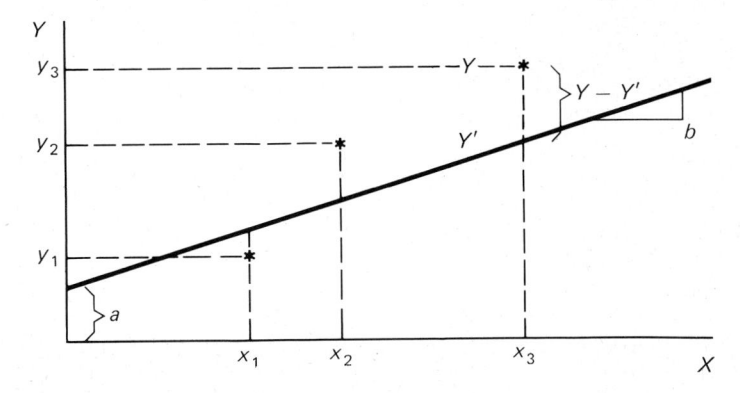

Figure 10–8. Least squares line.

Rewriting:

$$\Sigma Y_i - \Sigma a - \Sigma bx_i = \Sigma Y - na - b\Sigma x = 0$$
$$\Sigma Y_i x_i - \Sigma ax_i - \Sigma bx_i^2 = \Sigma xy - a\Sigma x - b\Sigma x^2 = 0$$

These are the normal equations used in the text.

To illustrate, consider the following three points.

X	Y
2	5
3	6
5	11

The deviation for the three points, respectively, is

$$Y_1 - a - bX_1$$
$$Y_2 - a - bX_2$$
$$Y_3 - a - bX_3$$

or

$$5 - a - b(2)$$
$$6 - a - b(3)$$
$$11 - a - b(5)$$

The sum of the squared deviations is then

$$(5 - a - 2b)^2 + (6 - a - 3b)^2 + (11 - a - 5b)^2$$

Then, take the partial derivatives, and setting each equal to zero:

$$\frac{\delta}{\delta a} = -2(5 - a - 2b) - 2(6 - a - 3b) - 2(11 - a - 5b) = 0$$

$$\frac{\delta}{\delta b} = -4(5 - a - 2b) - 6(6 - a - 3b) - 10(11 - a - 5b) = 0$$

Simplifying, we have

$$22 - 3a - 10b = 0$$
$$83 - 10a - 38b = 0$$

Solving these two linear equations simultaneously, we have

$$a = 0.43$$
$$b = 2.07$$

The least-squares equation is then

$$Y = 0.43 + 2.07X$$

The interested reader should verify that the normal equations yield the same result.

CHAPTER 11
Introduction to Simulation

11.1 **Introduction**

11.2 **An Accounting Model: A Deterministic Simulation**
Concepts and Issues in Simulation
Validation of a Model
Expanding the Basic Model

11.3 **Monte Carlo Simulation**
Using a Random Number Table
Sampling and Inference
Confidence Intervals
Hypothesis Testing
The Sample Size: How Many Trials to Perform

11.4 **Simulation of Analytic Models**
An Inventory Application
Variations on the Inventory Model
A Queuing Application

11.5 **Summary**

Glossary

Problems

References

Key Concepts
Confidence interval
Definitional relation
Flow chart
Model
Monte Carlo simulation
Random number

Sample size
Sampling
Simulation
State variable
System
Transition variable
Validation

Key Applications
Accounting
Financial planning

Inventory management
Queuing

11.1 Introduction

Simulation is becoming a more widely used approach in business analysis and decision making. An area of most rapid growth of simulation is accounting and financial planning for corporations. For this reason, we present the basic concepts and ideas using accounting and financial planning as illustrations. Applications to inventory management and queuing, more traditional applications, are also discussed.

In contrast to most other quantitative techniques in this text, simulation is not an optimization approach such as linear programming. Simulation is a technique that describes the behavior of a system and attempts to obtain better understanding of the system from this description. The word "simulation" has its origin in Latin, and the dictionary meaning is to "imitate." The U.S. Corps of Engineers has a physical model of the Mississippi River Basin, where they perform experiments to obtain a better understanding of how the river will behave under varying circumstances such as flooding. Through this model they can effectively manage river use.

In a modern decision-making context, simulation may be defined as a numerical technique to conduct experiments that describe the behavior of economic systems over many periods.[1] Using a simulation model, we can predict better the firm's income, profits, inventory position, and so on. The purpose is not only better prediction, but also better decision making and better performance for the firm.

Simulation offers some advantages over other approaches. A simulation model can be built for complex systems for which optimization models such as linear programming are not feasible or are unrealistic. Because simulation models are frequently more like the real world, business managers can more readily understand and contribute to their conception and construction. This contributes to the expanding application of models in financial and corporate planning. On the negative side, however, there are several considerations. Simulation mod-

---

[1]The definition is based on one given by Naylor and Vernon (1969).

els are costly to devise. The statistical issues in design and interpretation require a good understanding of statistics if one is not to be misled. Finally, nearly all simulation models of real-world relevance require the use of a computer. On balance, simulation is a powerful quantitative technique that continues to grow in popularity and use.

The basic approach of simulation follows the concepts of experimentation, sampling, and inference from statistics. Once we have a model that adequately describes the behavior of the firm's finances, inventory, or whatever, we can run a "paper" experiment using a mathematical model to describe the behavior of the firm. That is, the simulation model is run many times to generate a statistical sample of observations for analysis. There are many important issues to consider: the simulation model, the experimental design, the statistical analysis of the data, the interpretation of the analyses, and the determination of the sample size for the experiment. Although most simulation models involve the use of a computer, the basic concepts employed in the construction of simulation models do not rely on a computer. In this chapter we present these basic concepts using the traditional accounting model, an inventory model, and queuing as examples.

11.2 An Accounting Model: A Deterministic Simulation

Consider a medium-sized firm that manufactures and sells only one product. In Figure 11–1 we show the firm's balance sheet as of December 31, 1984. A projected income statement for the year 1985 is presented in Figure 11–2. Contrary to the income statement in Figure 11–1, which is based on last year's transactions, and therefore presents historical data, a projected or pro forma income statement shows management's reasonable expectations for next year. Such a statement can be called a simulation of the firm's income producing activities for the next year.

Balance Sheet as of December 31, 1984			
Assets *(A)*		Liabilities and Equity *(LE)*	
Cash *(Ca)*	$100,000	Accounts Payable *(AP)*	$200,000
Inventory *(I)*	200,000		
Plant and Equipment *(PE)*	500,000	Stockholder's Equity *(SE)*	600,000
Total	$800,000		$800,000

Figure 11–1. Balance Sheet as of December 31, 1984.

> Pro Forma Income Statement for Year 1985
> Sales (S) $1,000,000
> Costs of Goods Sold (C)   500,000
> Gross Profit (GP) $ 500,000
> Administrative Expense (AE)   100,000
>
> Depreciation* (D)   100,000
> Net Operating Income (NOI) $ 300,000
> Taxes (T)   150,000
>
> Net Income (NI) $ 150,000
>
> *Straight line, assuming 5-yr life and zero salvage value.

Figure 11–2. Income Statement for 1984.

As a pro forma statement, it is based on many assumptions concerning future events. For example, sales depend on a prediction of sales quantities and prices for all the firm's products. Many assumptions are made in the projections of the cost of manufacturing and the cost of goods sold. For example, we can say that the projected cost and revenue figures depend externally on developments in the firm's markets, and internally on the efficiency of the manufacturing process. Some quantities, however, such as depreciation and taxes, depend on known relationships, that is, established formulas for their calculation. The resulting net income figure is not an actual figure of what happened, but a simulated result of what might reasonably occur.

In a similar fashion, it is possible to construct a pro forma or simulated balance sheet for the firm. Given the balance sheet for December 31, 1984, in Figure 11–1, the projected income statement for 1985 shown in Figure 11–2 produces the pro forma balance sheet as of December 31, 1985, in Figure 11–3. The model is specified as follows:

$$A = Ca + I + PE$$
$$LE = AP + SE$$
$$NI = S - C - AE - D - T$$

CONCEPTS AND ISSUES IN SIMULATION

With this example we can now introduce some fundamental concepts and definitions of simulation.

System. The entity to be studied and simulated. In the above example, it is the firm—not a part of the firm, or the entire economy, but the firm as a whole.

11.2 / An Accounting Model: A Deterministic Simulation

Pro Forma Balance Sheet as of December 31, 1985

Assets* *(A)*		Liabilities and Equity *(LE)*	
Cash *(Ca)*	$250,000	Accounts Payable *(AP)*	$200,000
Inventory *(I)*	300,000		
Plant and Equipment (net)	400,000	Stockholder's Equity *(SE)*	750,000
Total	$950,000		$950,000

*From the information given, we don't know the unique distribution between cash and inventory. If inventory remained at $200,000, then cash would be $350,000. However, we are sure that cash plus inventory = $550,000. To be more precise, we must specify the annual production rate and recall that beginning inventory plus production = cost of sales plus ending inventory.

Figure 11-3. Pro Forma Balance Sheet as of December 31, 1985.

Model. The abstract description and analysis of the system. Here, the model is the well-known accounting model.

State variables. Variables that measure the state (or level) of behavior of the system at a point in time. Quantities in the balance sheet are state variables. They measure the state of the firm at a given date, for example, December 31.

Transition variables. Variables that measure changes in the system over a period of time. Income statement items are transition variables linking variables between two states.

VALIDATION OF THE MODEL

What can we conclude from a simulation model? This is the most difficult and, at the same time, the most important issue. Intuitively, simulation gives the manager a notion about the future and what is likely to happen. How good is this notion? It is rhetorical to say that the projections are no better than the model. So, how good is the model? The accounting model incorporated into our simulation model is identical to the accounting model that will be used for recording the actual events. That is, we used the same accounting rules to generate the income statement as will be used for future real events. Thus, the validation of this aspect of the simulation model follows the normal process of validation of any accounting model.

Another aspect of the validation process is the relationships between variables in our example—how good the cost model is and how valid the pricing predictions and the sales estimates are. This issue is crucial and goes beyond the usual accounting model notions of validation. Clearly, if the cost model is not correct, then the resulting net income prediction will be wrong—even if we use generally accepted accounting rules. Thus, the cost model must be shown to be reasonably correct.

This is a difficult issue. As in all such models, the past should be a good predictor of the future. Nonetheless, sales forecasting and price prediction can be subject to considerable error. The manager must remember that the accounting simulation model must be consistent with accepted accounting rules. This is necessary but does not guarantee that the model will be useful and practical.

Another approach to validation is sensitivity analysis. The emphasis here is more on the usefulness of the results than the process of obtaining the results. The approach is the same as in previously discussed sensitivity analyses. To illustrate, we investigate the change in net income as we change the price, sales, or costs. That is, how sensitive is the resulting item of interest to changes in one of our basic variables or parameters? If it is very insensitive, there may be little need to obtain a more accurate estimate of the input. If the result is very sensitive, then we should be reasonable sure that the input quantity is correct.

However, we must not add false accuracy to the model. If the price is known to be very uncertain, then simulation can deal with the uncertainty. But if we add certainty artificially, just for our convenience, we create a false certainty about how much we know. For example, if the costs are known to be probabilistic over a wide range, artificially reducing or eliminating this uncertainty will make the information incorrect.

EXPANDING THE BASIC MODEL

Simulation becomes an important technique for management when it is expanded beyond the above model definition. It can be expanded in numerous ways to yield more realistic and more practical predictions. One possibility is to construct a more complete and detailed model. Conceptually, it should be possible to simulate each and every accounting transaction and associated accounting entry for the firm. However, this is probably not practical, because the simulation cost would most likely far exceed the benefits obtained. On the other hand, the income statement should not be too aggregated and, at least, the most important assumptions should be stated explicitly. For example, the sales figure involves a sales quantity and a price figure for each of the firm's products. These figures should be examined for accuracy. Furthermore, a more detailed model permits management to examine the effects of a price and/or a quantity change through sensitivity analysis.

A second extension involves building a multiperiod model. Frequently, managers and accountants are interested not only in the next period, but many periods in the future for planning purposes. Clearly, if we can specify reasonable revenue and cost figures for several peri-

11.2 / An Accounting Model: A Deterministic Simulation

ods, we can generate the associated income statements and balance sheets.

A More Detailed Model. A more detailed accounting model can be developed. Let us first consider a more refined sales submodel and a model for the cost of goods sold. Total sales (S) are given by selling price (P) times the quantity sold (Q). Let

$$S = PQ$$

or sales equal price times quantity. In our income statement model for the first period, we simply stated sales as $S = \$1$ million without specifying P or Q. Obviously, there are many feasible combinations. One of these is that $P = \$20$ and $Q = 50{,}000$ units. The advantage of this more detailed model is that we can now more easily investigate the validity of the $20 price and 50,000 units of sales. Further, we can investigate the effects of changes in price and quantity separately or jointly, using sensitivity analysis. For example, what is the percentage change in stockholders' equity for a $2 decrease in selling price?

The cost of goods sold could be determined from a statistical cost model. Such a model could be developed using linear regression analysis, which was discussed in Chapter 10. The total cost of goods sold is the sum of fixed cost and variable cost. Figure 11–4 gives a graphical representation of the equation

$$C = C_F + C_V Q$$

where C is total cost, C_F is fixed cost, C_V is unit variable cost, and Q is quantity sold.

For example, in our model, C is given as $500,000 for the first period. We now add that this was derived from

$$C_F = \$125{,}000$$
$$C_V = \$7.50$$

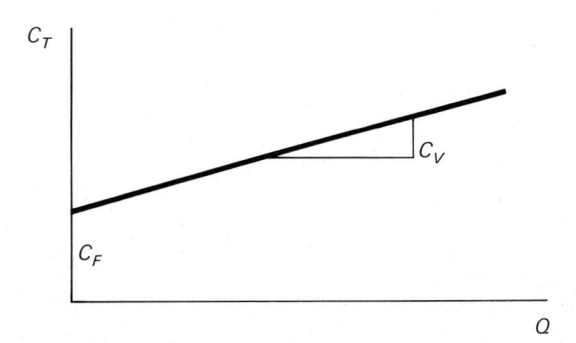

Figure 11–4. Cost model using linear regression.

or

$$C = \$125{,}000 + 7.50Q = \$125{,}000 + \$7.50(50{,}000) = \$500{,}000$$

To demonstrate the advantage of the more detailed approach, assume that the sales quantity Q is predicted to be 55,000 units, whereas the price P remains at \$20. Then

$$S = PQ = 20 \times 55{,}000 = \$1{,}100{,}000$$

The corresponding cost of goods sold is then

$$C_T = \$125{,}000 + \$7.50(55{,}000) = \$537{,}500$$

Using the same accounting rules as before, we then prepare the income statement shown in Figure 11–5.

Other relations we can break down include the measure of depreciation expense. In our example model, we first assumed depreciation to be \$100,000. We can also express it as

$$D = \frac{\text{acquisition cost of plant and equipment} - \text{salvage value}}{\text{useful life}}$$

$$= \frac{\$500{,}000}{5} = \$100{,}000$$

that is, depreciation expense is constant unless there are changes in either the cost of our plant and equipment, its useful life, or salvage value. We have assumed a zero salvage value. There are, of course, other possible formulas for depreciation expense, and they depend on accepted accounting rules.

Similarly, for taxes, we assumed that tax is at 50 percent of net operating income,

$$T = 0.5 \times \text{net operating income}$$

Pro Forma Income Statement	
Sales	$1,100,000
Cost of Goods Sold	537,500
Gross Profit	$ 562,500
Administrative Expense	100,000
Depreciation	100,000
Net Operating Income	$ 362,500
Taxes	181,250
Net Income	$ 181,250

Figure 11–5. Pro Forma Income Statement.

Depending on the size and industry of a given firm, other tax levels may apply. These relations could be further divided into those that may require statistical validation, such as the cost model, and those that follow directly from specification, such as the tax law and depreciation formulas.

A Multiperiod Model. The multiperiod model simply extends the single-period model one or more periods into the future. That is, a two-period model would be for next year and the year after. The limitation on the number of periods comes from the availability and accuracy of the projections for sales, prices, and costs. There is no limitation in the accounting model itself.

Consider again our example where the following year's projected income statement (represented in Figure 11–2) produces the corresponding ending balance sheet in Figure 11–3. Continuing in this manner, we can generate statements for any number of periods into the future.

The multiperiod simulation is the single period repeated in time sequence a number of times. As with the single-period simulation, we begin with the actual existing balance sheet and generate the income statement and the ending balance. The ending balance sheet for period t is the beginning balance sheet for the next period, $t + 1$, for which we require an income statement and an ending balance sheet. These are recursive relationships. We continue in this fashion for as many periods as desired. Given its repetitiveness, it is desirable, if not necessary, to use the digital computer. A flow chart for the multiperiod situation illustrates the idea (see Figure 11–6).

This flow chart begins by initializing the period counter, $T = 1$, and the initial balance sheet. Then, we enter the income statement and ending balance sheet loop for the desired number of periods. For the period being calculated, the income statement and balance sheet are derived and printed out. (Note: This flowchart gives these instructions in general, not details.) If all the periods have been calculated, we stop. If not, we continue for the next period. It is noted that the calculations for each period are procedurally identical, although they can be complex and tedious. For such situations, the computer is a particularly practical and cost efficient tool.

To generate a sample of N trials of the multiperiod simulation requires repeating the multiperiod program N times, where each trial begins with the current balance sheet values. That is, we repeat the program in Figure 11–6 N times. This yields N different sequences of balance sheets and income statements, or N possible futures.

We have presented an accounting model of the firm and discussed issues in modeling as well as basic concepts and terminology in simu-

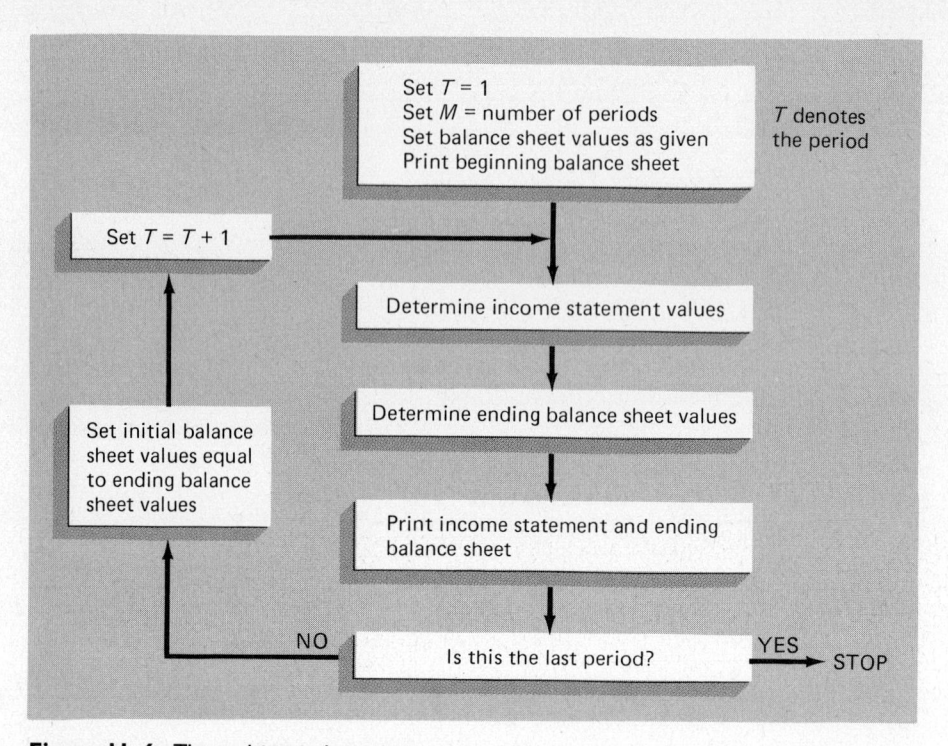

Figure 11-6. The multiperiod simulation.

lation. The accounting simulation model of the firm as the system has the balance sheet entries as state variables and the income statement variables are transition variables. Simulation models can be aggregated or detailed, single period or multiperiod. Detailed models are more costly, but frequently more valid, as they usually replicate the firm's behavior more accurately. Multiperiod models serve longer-term planning but become less valid for the more distant future. In validation, it is important to distinguish definitional relations and behavioral relations that require empirical validation of the parameter values. All of these issues are very important to establish a simulation model. We now consider how to do a Monte Carlo simulation using the accounting model for the experiment.

11.3 Monte Carlo Simulation

Monte Carlo simulation introduces probabilistic elements into the model. For example, let us assume that there is an even chance that price will be either $20 or $25, with the sales quantity Q remaining at 50,000 units.

11.3 / Monte Carlo Simulation

Let us follow through one trial solution of the Monte Carlo simulation. The probability distribution is

$$P(P = \$20) = P(P = \$25) = 0.5$$

We can now use a coin to generate the price randomly. We associate heads with the $20 price and tails with the $25 price. We toss the coin and it comes up tails. Thus, the price P is $25 for this trial. The simulation model is

$$S = PQ = \$25 \times 50{,}000 = \$1{,}250{,}000$$

The cost of goods sold is

$$C_T = \$125{,}000 + \$7.50 \times 50{,}000 = \$500{,}000$$

Then

$$\begin{aligned}
\text{Gross profit} &= \text{sales} - \text{cost of goods sold} \\
&= \$1{,}250{,}000 - 500{,}000 = \$750{,}000 \\
\text{Net operating income} &= \$750{,}000 - \$100{,}000 - \$100{,}000 = \$550{,}000 \\
\text{Net income} &= \text{net operating income} - \text{taxes} \\
&= \$550{,}000 - \$275{,}000 = \$275{,}000
\end{aligned}$$

We could have written this as a standard income statement, but we chose the above form to illustrate that the calculation can be reduced to a set of well-specified mathematical relations that are readily programmable on the computer. Now, the other possible outcome is a price of $20, for which we have already determined a net income of $150,000 (see Figure 11–1). Thus, we can state that if the price is probabilistic as given above, then the probability distribution on net income is

$$P(\text{net income} = \$150{,}000) = 0.5$$
$$P(\text{net income} = \$275{,}000) = 0.5$$

Net income is therefore a function of price. As price is a random variable, net income is also a random variable with an associated probability distribution. Expected net income is

$$E(\text{net income}) = (0.5) \times 150{,}000 + (0.5) \times 275{,}000 = 212{,}500$$

USING A RANDOM NUMBER TABLE

The above Monte Carlo simulation illustrates the basic approach. Let us now assume more complex probabilistic conditions, with four possible prices and associated probabilities as follows:

$$P(P = 20) = 0.1$$
$$P(P = 21) = 0.2$$
$$P(P = 23) = 0.3$$
$$P(P = 25) = 0.4$$

Further, the sales quantity is subject to the random fluctuations:

$P(Q = 50,000) = 0.6$
$P(Q = 55,000) = 0.4$

Assume that price and sales are independent.

We now have to determine net income under a number of possible conditions for which the probability of occurrence is given. To generate the price and quantity for each trial, we require a more sophisticated *random number* generator than a coin. One approach is to use a table of random numbers. Refer to Table 1 at the back of the book. Such a table permits us to generate the outcome by associating the probabilities with a random number of the table.

Consider the set of 100 random numbers between 0 and 99. Because the probability of price = 20 is 0.1, 10 of those random numbers should be assigned to $P = 20$. For $P = 21$, with 0.2 probability, 20 random numbers should be assigned. Similarly, for $P = 23$, 30 numbers should be assigned, and for $P = 25$, 40 numbers. Then, if we randomly choose one number from our set of 100, we will have 0.1, 0.2, 0.3, and 0.4 probability of getting P equal to 20, 21, 23, and 25, respectively. To make the mechanics easier, we can assign each value of P a consecutive set of numbers as follows.

Price	20	21	23	25
Random number	00–09	10–29	30–59	60–99
Probability	0.1	0.2	0.3	0.4

For example, take a pencil and point to the table. The number under your pencil is, say, 15. Thus, for this trial, the associated price is $21. Similarly, for the possibilities of quantity Q, we have

Quantity	50,000	55,000
Random number	00–59	60–99
Probability	0.6	0.4

With these ideas in mind, let us generate 10 trials for net income. Using the random number table to generate prices and quantities, and the same behavioral and definitional relations, we have 10 resulting net income values. Table 11–1 summarizes this simulation. Note that many of the intermediate calculations have been omitted from the table. The reader should verify three to five of the calculations in Table 11–1.

TABLE 11-1. Monte Carlo Income Statement Simulation

Trial	Random Number	Price	Random Number	Quantity Q (000s)	Sales (000s)	Cost of Goods Sold COS (000s)*	G.P. (000s)	Net Income Before Tax (000s)	Income Tax (000s)	Net Income (000s)
1	21	21	61	55	$1155	$412.5 + 125 = 537.5	$617.5	$417.5	208.75	208.75
2	95	25	17	50	1250	$375 + 125 = 500	750	550	275	275.00
3	09	20	10	50	1000	$375 + 125 = 500	500	300	150	150.00
4	62	25	35	50	1250	$375 + 125 = 500	750	550	275	275.00
5	46	23	35	50	1150	$375 + 125 = 500	650	450	225	225.00
6	45	23	01	50	1150	$375 + 125 = 500	650	450	225	225.00
7	79	25	70	55	1370	$412.5 + 125 = 537.5	837.5	637.5	318.75	318.75
8	74	25	11	50	1250	$375 + 125 = 500	750	550	275	275.00
9	02	20	78	55	1100	$412.5 + 125 = 537.5	562.5	362.5	181.25	181.25
10	64	25	27	50	1250	$375 + 125 = 500	750	550	275	275.00

Average net income $240.88

$C_{OS} = C_F + C_v Q$.
*$COS = 125 + 7.5Q$.

373

Intuitively, the results of the Monte Carlo simulation give the accountant a better feel for what could happen to net income for next year. It could go as high as $318,750 or as low as $150,000, with an expected value of about $240,880. We can add considerable precision to our statements by considering these 10 trials as a data set, on the basis of which we can calculate confidence intervals and test hypotheses.

SAMPLING AND INFERENCE

Each trial of a Monte Carlo simulation can be considered as a sample value from a population of possible outcomes. Thus, we can treat a simulation of n trials as a sample of n values for the phenomenon under study. Then all of the statistical techniques of parameter estimation, confidence intervals, and hypothesis testing are at our disposal.

Consider our Monte Carlo simulation of the example firm. We did 10 trials. Let us consider these as a sample of size 10. That is, the simulation model is a sampling from possible future outcomes. Now the item of interest is the probable net income. We have 10 observations (see Table 11–1). We have already calculated the sample mean and the sample variance. The sample mean is

$$\overline{X} = \tfrac{1}{10} \sum_{i=1}^{10} x_i = \$240{,}880$$

where x_i are the observed net income values. This is a sample of 10 independent observations. However, the simulation of the firm over time—for example, 10 years—generates a related time sequence of net incomes. Simple averages can be used as good estimates of mean values.

The sample variance is

$$S^2 = \tfrac{1}{10} \sum_{i=1}^{10} (x_i - \overline{X})^2 = 2{,}407{,}200{,}000$$

or the sample standard deviation is

$$S = \$49{,}060$$

CONFIDENCE INTERVALS

Based on the Monte Carlo simulations, the expected net income is $240,880. To obtain some notion about the level of belief in this number, we can establish a confidence interval for this estimate. If we assume that the estimator of net income is normally distributed (this is reasonable for a large number of trials, say, 30, but we accept 10 to illustrate the approach), then the t statistic is the appropriate statistic with $n - 1 = 9$ degrees of freedom. For a two-tailed test, the random interval is

$$\overline{X} \pm t_{90\%} \sqrt{\frac{S}{n-1}} = 240{,}880 \pm 1.833 \left(\frac{49{,}060}{3}\right) = 240{,}880 \pm 29{,}980$$

$$= \$210{,}900 - \$270{,}860$$

This is a 90 percent confidence interval for the mean net income. That is, if we were to repeat the experiment 100 times, the calculated interval would contain the true mean about 90 times on the average. The above interval either contains the mean or not. So our confidence is in the rule; that is, the rule is correct with probability 0.9.

HYPOTHESIS TESTING

This does not exhaust the possible statistical investigations. For example, one accountant might state that the true mean net income is $250,000; another says it is not. More formally, we can test the hypothesis:

$H_0:$ $\mu = \$250{,}000$
$H_1:$ $\mu \neq \$250{,}000$

For a test at the 0.05 level (two-tail), the critical region is outside:

$$\mu \pm t_{95\%} \sqrt{\frac{S}{n-1}} = \$250{,}000 \pm 2.262 \left(\frac{49{,}060}{3}\right)$$

$$= \$250{,}000 \pm \$36{,}991.24$$

$$= \$213{,}008 \text{ to } \$286{,}991$$

The expected value $240,880 lies within these limits, and thus we cannot reject the hypothesis, $\mu = \$250{,}000$. That is, there is not sufficient evidence to consider the assertion wrong.

The statistical analysis of Monte Carlo simulations is a very useful technique. It permits us to say more precisely what is likely to happen and how strongly we can argue. That is, we can state both the confidence and the limits of our predictions. Sometimes we can be rather sure about what will happen; other times we are very uncertain. It is important to know the difference.

THE SAMPLE SIZE: HOW MANY TRIALS TO PERFORM

In the accounting experiment, we performed 10 trials of the Monte Carlo simulation. The statistical *sample size* of 10 was chosen arbitrarily. A basic question is "How large should the sample size be?" Logically, it is a question we should ask before running the experiment. So, let us assume we are about to perform a new experiment and determine an appropriate sample size. An excessive sample wastes resources, and a sample that is too small will not achieve the experimentation goals.

Basically, there are two questions to be answered. First, how precise do you want the result? And second, how probable do you want the precision to be? A greater precision clearly requires a larger sample size, and a greater probability for the desired precision also requires a larger sample. Thus, the experimenter, or manager, must decide these issues before the sample size is determined and the experiment is performed.

The basic formula for determining the sample size is given by the relation between the variance of the mean of the sample and the population variance. By definition,

$$\sigma_{\bar{x}}^2 = \frac{\sigma^2}{n} \quad \text{or} \quad \sigma_{\bar{x}} = \frac{\sigma}{\sqrt{n}}$$

where σ^2 is the population variance, $\sigma_{\bar{x}}^2$ is the variance of the mean of the sample, and n is the sample size.

Rewriting, we have

$$n = \frac{\sigma^2}{\sigma_{\bar{x}}^2} \quad \text{or} \quad \sqrt{n} = \frac{\sigma}{\sigma_{\bar{x}}}$$

Now we must choose σ^2 and $\sigma_{\bar{x}}^2$ in terms of a desired precision, and the probability that the precision will obtain.

An approach is first to determine a value for σ^2, the population variance. This value is not a statistical estimate, but an intuitive, intelligent guess. One approach is to use the range of past observed values divided by 6. That is, we assume that all past observed values fall within 3σ of the true mean. For our experiment, $\sigma = (300,000 - 150,000)/6 = 25,000$. Now assume that we want a probability of 0.997 that the interval contains the true mean or a value within 3 standard deviations of that mean. Further, we assume a normal distribution for the sample mean. We want the mean within $\pm\$10,000$. The \$10,000 is the desired precision, and the 0.997 is the probability of that precision.

$$3\sigma_{\bar{x}} = \$10,000$$

or

$$3\frac{\sigma}{\sqrt{n}} = \$10,000$$

$$\sqrt{n} = \frac{3 \times 25,000}{10,000} = 7.5$$

or

$$n = 57$$

That is, a sample size of 57 is required to obtain the desired precision and at a probability of 0.997. To affirm your intuition, what happens if the precision of $10,000 is increased to $5,000? From the above, the sample size must increase to 225. Further, if the probability of 0.997 is decreased to 0.954 or 2σ, then the sample size is decreased to 25.

We have just considered how to do a Monte Carlo simulation, the issue of validation via statistical analyses, and the determination of the sample size. In actual practice, the appropriate sequence is to determine the sample size, run the validation experiment, and analyze the resulting data.

11.4 Simulation of Analytic Models

Simulation has the advantage of being able to replicate or extend analysis from other quantitative methods techniques. The same assumptions of other models, such as independence of arrivals in queuing models (see Chapter 14), can be maintained in verifying these techniques. Many assumptions are made in other quantitative techniques to keep the mathematics feasible—for example, linearity, independence, and finite populations. This can greatly limit the applicability of techniques such as linear programming, queuing theory, and scheduling algorithms. Similarly, however, models can be so designed to incorporate these types of relationships and provide insight into the behavior of such dynamic systems. To demonstrate this capability, we reexamine a situation we investigated before only mathematically. The basic inventory model is reassessed and then some of the typical real-life variations to inventory control are addressed. Second, a waiting line application is analyzed with simulation.

AN INVENTORY APPLICATION

Inventory management is an important managerial issue for the firm. Simulation offers an alternative approach to the techniques presented in Chapters 7 and 8 when the behavior of the inventory system is more complex and analytical solutions are not possible. Situations in which demand and lead time are probablistic are very difficult to solve, but straightforward to simulate. We begin with a probabilistic demand and certain lead time to illustrate the approach. More complex situations can be easily built into the approach.

Consider a retailer who sells television sets. He buys TVs from a wholesaler in lots of 8. The firm reorders when the number of TVs on hand drops to 3. This is the inventory policy for the store—an order quantity of 8 and an order point of 3. The daily demand for TVs is probabilistic as shown in Table 11–2.

TABLE 11–2 Daily Demand for TVs

Number of TVs Demanded per Day	Probability	Random Numbers
1	0.25	00–24
2	0.50	25–74
3	0.25	75–99

The cost of placing an order (including shipping) is $20. The holding cost is $1 per day per TV on the average of starting and ending inventory, but ignoring negative inventories in that period. If a customer arrives at the store to buy a TV and none is available, the sale is made but it costs the store $3 to make the delivery. And the lead time for TV orders, that is, the time between order by the store and delivery to the store, is 2 days.

Now, the store wants to know what its costs will be under this policy. First, we assign appropriate random numbers for the demands in Table 11–2 as shown. Second, the inventory policy is simulated as shown in Table 11–3. For a 10-day period, the total inventory cost is $99, or an average of $9.90 per day.[2] The store is interested in the question: Is there a better inventory policy? For example, should we order fewer TVs each time, or when the inventory on hand is smaller, say, one TV? To answer, the approach is to take a different policy and try it, that is, simulate its behavior. The policy that yields the lowest average daily inventory cost is considered best.

VARIATIONS ON THE INVENTORY MODEL

For many real situations the periodic review model is preferable to the basic inventory model. In the previous model we assumed that an order could be placed any day, which requires a daily (or continuous) review of the inventory level. An alternative approach is a periodic review—for example, review on Mondays. (It is less costly to manage.) Then, if inventory exceeds a minimum level, order nothing. If the inventory level is less than the minimum, order some maximum level minus current inventory. Using simulation, we can choose the best

---

[2] Note that this period's inventory levels and costs are dependent on the previous period's, and the usual t test would be inappropriate to determine a confidence interval. More advanced techniques are required. However, the mean is an unbiased estimate of the daily cost.

TABLE 11-3. Inventory Simulation

Day	R.N.	Demand	Starting Inventory	Ending Inventory	Number Ordered	Number Received	Number Backordered	Holding Cost	Stockout Cost	Ordering Cost	Total Cost
1	45	2	4*	2	0	0	0	3	0	0	3
2	11	1	2	1	8	0	0	1.5	0	20	21.5
3	28	2	1	−1	0	0	0	0.5	3	0	3.5
4	05	1	−1	6	0	8	1	3	0	0	3
5	45	2	6	4	0	0	0	5	0	0	5
6	83	3	4	1	0	0	0	2.5	0	0	2.5
7	32	2	1	−1	8	0	1	0.5	3	20	23.5
8	81	3	−1	−4	0	0	4	0	12	0	12
9	35	2	−4	2	0	8	0	1	0	0	1
10	88	3	2	−1	8	0	0	1	3	20	4

Sum is 99
Average per day is $9.90

*Arbitrarily chosen as a beginning point.

from among the periodic review policies. Usually, a periodic review is used on low-cost items with low stockout costs or low backorder costs.

Backorders and Lost Sales. If a customer comes to buy an item and there is none available, the sale is delayed, or lost. If lost, we call it a lost sale. If delayed, there is a backorder. Usually, the lost sale incurs the larger (opportunity) cost; thus, if lost sales are probable, larger average inventories are required.

Probabilistic Lead Times. In most situations, the time between placing an order and receiving it is known within limits. As demand is probabilistic, the lead time is also frequently probabilistic. This creates no difficulty in simulation. Using the probability distribution on the lead time and the associated random numbers, we sample to find the lead time for a given order, and proceed as shown in the previous example.

Optimization Models. In Chapters 7 and 8, we studied inventory models to determine optimal order points and optimal order quantities. The analytic approach is preferred to simulation in that the optimization is defined over a larger set of policy choices—for example, all order quantity levels from zero to infinity. Simulation is limited to test those particular policies that we can make up. Clearly, the optimization approach is preferred when it can be applied. However, optimization models are extremely difficult to solve, except in the simpler situations. Simulation is readily adaptable to complex situations of probabilistic demand and probabilistic lead times. The issue between optimization and simulation is not that one is preferred over the other, but that both are useful depending on the nature of the problem.

A QUEUING APPLICATION[3]

Queuing problems, or waiting-line problems, occur frequently. As customers, we wait at supermarket checkout counters, doctors' offices, and government offices, to name just a few. In industry, partially completed orders wait for machines. Or sometimes, machines wait for orders on which to work. Accounting vouchers wait until someone is available to process them. Or a clerk may wait on vouchers to process. In all of these situations, there are tradeoffs to be made.

Let us consider a supermarket situation. There is a cost to the customer for waiting in line. This time is lost, and it is frustrating if the waiting time becomes excessive. If long waiting times continue, the customer will shop elsewhere. This is costly to the supermarket. Why not eliminate these costs by having a checkout counter available im-

---

[3] See Chapter 14 on mathematical queuing models.

11.4 / Simulation of Analytic Models

mediately for each customer? This is also costly to the supermarket, and will result in many checkers being idle for much of the time. Idle checkers must be paid. This cost eventually must be recovered in higher grocery prices, which will also encourage customers to go elsewhere. Thus, there is a tradeoff between excessive customer waiting time and excessive idle checker time. Just how to strike this balance is a difficult problem. This begins with a better understanding of the behavior of queues. Here we consider a simulation approach to queues.

Consider a small supermarket with one checkout counter. From past observations we know that the time between customer arrivals at the checkout counter is given by

Probability	Time Between Arrivals in Minutes	Random Number
0.3	3	0–29
0.5	4	30–79
0.2	7	80–99

And the time required for the checker to service a customer is given by

Probability	Service Time	Random Number
0.5	2	0–49
0.4	3	50–89
0.1	6	90–99

We are interested in describing the queuing system in order to find some measures of interest to management. What are those quantities? The average customer waiting time is of interest. The average total service time, waiting plus service time, is also important to the supermarket manager, as is the amount of checkout counter idle time. We can now simulate the checkout counter to generate data to determine estimates of these quantities. Table 11–4 summarizes the arrival and service of 10 customers. Let us follow two calculations through. Take the seventh customer, who arrives at 9:28. He goes immediately to the idle checker and is serviced in 6 min, departing at 9:34. The check out counter was idle from 9:26 to 9:28, or 2 min. The seventh customer did not wait in line, and the total service time is 6 min. The eighth customer arrives at 9:31 and must wait in line for 3 min, until 9:34. She is completed at 9:36. So she spent 3 min in line, plus 2 min at the checkout counter, for a total service time of 5 min.

TABLE 11–4. Queuing Simulation

Random Number	Time Between Arrivals	Random Number	Service Time	Clock Time at Arrival	Clock Time to Begin Service	Clock Time at End of Service	Time Checkout Counter Idle	Waiting Time	Total Service Time
51	4	32	2	9:04*	9:04	9:06	0	0	2
69	4	87	3	9:08	9:08	9:11	2	0	3
37	4	10	2	9:12	9:12	9:14	1	0	2
61	4	78	3	9:16	9:16	9:19	2	0	3
35	4	69	3	9:20	9:20	9:23	1	0	3
46	4	01	2	9:24	9:24	9:26	1	0	2
59	4	91	6	9:28	9:28	9:34	2	0	6
18	3	46	2	9:31	9:34	9:36	0	3	5
86	7	59	3	9:38	9:38	9:41	2	0	3
33	4	12	2	9:42	9:42	9:44	$\frac{1}{12}$	$\frac{0}{3}$	$\frac{2}{31}$
						Sums			

*Determined arbitrarily.

With the data from Table 11–4, we can calculate quantities of interest. The average waiting time is

$$\frac{3 \text{ min waiting}}{10 \text{ customers}} = 0.3 \text{ min per customer}$$

The average total service time is

$$\frac{31 \text{ min}}{10 \text{ customers}} = 3.1 \text{ min per customer}$$

The checkout counter idle time is 12 min of the 44 min of operation, or 27.3 percent of the time. Now, how can management use this information? Idle time is costly. At $3 per hour, idle time costs the supermarket $0.82 per hour. Customer waiting time is also costly, and the manager estimates that the loss to the supermarket is $5 per hour. So the supermarket incurred a customer cost of $.25 for one customer for 3 min. The supermarket manager wants to keep these costs in balance. (However, balance does not imply that the two costs should be equal. We discuss these issues more fully in Chapter 14.)

The supermarket manager has several options. First, he could leave an idle counter without a checker, by letting the checker stock inventory during idle time. That would decrease idle time, but it would also increase the service time for customers, as a customer arriving at the idle counter must wait for a clerk as well as be checked out. The supermarket manager might hire a less talented checker at a lower cost, but who would require longer service times. Perhaps the most obvious alternative is to adjust the number of checkout counters and checkers. A slightly modified simulation experiment is required for two checkers, but the modification is straightforward if one keeps in mind that there is one line and two checkout counters. Problem 31 asks the student to work through an example.

The simulation of queuing situations follows the general approach of describing the behavior of the queuing in an experimental situation. The analysis of these data produces information that management can use to make tradeoffs between waiting times and idle service times.

11.5 Summary

In this chapter we introduced simulation without the necessary use of a computer. Simulation is a very useful quantitative technique for modern management.

We began the development of simulation by reference to the familiar pro forma income statement and balance sheet. This establishes the base for accounting simulation to multiperiod models, detailed models, and Monte Carlo models. Multiperiod models are simply an extension of the single-period model. Detailed models involve the specification of more fundamental accounting transactions and measures. Monte Carlo simulations permit some input variables, such as price or quantity, to be random variables.

Simulation models are very helpful, but considerable care must be exercised in their construction and use. They must be validated, and their results carefully analyzed. Validation includes the verification that generally accepted rules have been used to generate statements. Further, sales, price, and cost projections must be statistically valid in order to obtain reasonable results from the simulation. Finally, the analysis of simulation results is considerably enhanced by the use of statistical techniques of parameter estimation, confidence intervals, and hypothesis testing.

Simulation can be used to help set inventory policies for the firm, how much to order, and when. We considered an inventory model with a probabilistic demand for the product under continuous review. The main question is to determine the order quantity and the order point. Other inventory models use a periodic review. Probabilistic lead time further complicates the inventory issue. These more complex inventory models are straightforward to simulate, but optimization is usually quite difficult. Thus, simulation can be used effectively to set inventory policy under rather complex circumstances.

Simulation can be used to describe the behavior of queues, or waiting-line situations. The simulation generates experimental data that the manager can use to determine if there is an appropriate balance between customer waiting time and idle time for the service facility.

Glossary

Confidence interval. An interval that has a given probability of containing the true parameter value. For example, there is a 0.9 probability that the interval 17 to 22 contains the true mean value.

Definitional relation. A statement that is true for all systems; for example, profit = revenue − costs.

Flowchart. A statement of the computer model logic, order, and content. It is a communication document.

Model. A description of a system.

Monte Carlo simulation. A simulation where some of the variables are probabilistic.

Random number. A number that permits one to generate outcomes from a probability distribution.

Sample size. The number of trials in a simulation experiment.

Sampling. A statistical technique to generate data to learn about a general system.

Simulation. A numerical technique to examine policy alternatives.

State variable. A variable that measures the system's position at a point in time.

System. The entity to be simulated, for example, the firm, or an inventory item.

Transition variable. A variable that measures the change in the system from one point in time to another.

Validation. A consideration of how well a model represents the system.

Problems

1. Work out an income statement and pro forma balance sheet for the example firm where the cost of goods sold is $420,000.
2. *(SMA)* Classic Used Cars estimates that there is a 20 percent chance of selling 80 units, a 55 percent chance of selling 100 units, and a 25 percent chance of selling 120 units. The profit per unit is $450.

   REQUIRED
   - a. Use simulation to find the average profit. (Use 12 trials: random numbers: 86, 64, 71, 58, 84, 28, 07, 38, 33, 10, 55, 46.)
   - b. (1) Compare your answer in part a to the results of the expected value.
     (2) Explain why a difference, if any, exists.
3. Work out a cash flow statement for the example firm for the first year.
4. *(SMA)* Heavy Construction Limited has a long-term contract at a remote site and must stock a special bearing required for a conveyor system. The weekly demand for the bearings is according to the following distribution:

Demand	Probability
6	0.2
7	0.4
8	0.3
9	0.1

   The bearings are flown in and arrive on Saturday mornings. Since maintenance is only done during the week (Monday to Friday), the bearings are put into inventory. The bearing supplier always ships the bearings either in packages of 5 (40 percent of the time) or packages of 9 (60 percent of the time).

   REQUIRED
   Simulate 10 weeks of the bearing maintenance operation to determine:
   - a. The average inventory of bearings on hand (at the beginning of the week).
   - b. The probability of a stockout (i.e., when unsatisfied demand exceeds zero).

c. The inventory at the end of 10 weeks (before the last shipment arrives). Assume for all questions above
   (1) Current inventory at the beginning of week 1 is 5.
   (2) Unsatisfied demand is provided from stock whenever a supply arrives.
   (3) Use the following random numbers:

   For demand: 5, 3, 8, 6, 9, 7, 4, 9, 5, 3
   For arrivals: 5, 9, 9, 3, 8, 4, 7, 1, 4, 2

5. Work out the example firm's third-year income statement and balance sheet where net sales are $1,100,000 and cost of goods sold is $525,000.
6. *(SMA)* A contract calls for 2000 pieces of copper tubing with a length of 2500 ± 30 mm. These pieces are produced on a machine that cuts tubing in lengths that are normally distributed with a mean of 2500 mm and a standard deviation of 20 mm.

   The initial cost of producing a unit is $21.60. If an item is too short, it is reworked (soldered and recut) at an additional cost of $3. Items too long for specifications (greater than 2530 mm) are reworked (recut) for an additional $0.40. A piece that has been reworked does not necessarily meet specifications. The contract specifies that the cost of rework may be included in the cost of good items produced.

REQUIRED
   a. Using the following random numbers, simulate the length of eight pieces produced on the cutting machine: 7580, 1492, 9922, 5910, 0401, 8238, 3300, 9750.
   b. On the basis of the simulation, determine the costs (including rework) of producing the 2000 pieces specified in the contract.
7. For the example firm and the more detailed model, what is the percentage change in net income if the fixed cost C_F increases by 10 percent? The variable cost C_V increases by 10 percent? Both increase by 10 percent simultaneously?
8. *(SMA)* Weekly demand for bananas at George's Groceteria is normally distributed with a mean of 1000 kg and a standard deviation of 100 kg. Bananas are purchased in 100 kg lots for $0.50 per kilogram and sold for $0.70 per kilogram. George receives one shipment each week from his banana supplier. Any bananas on hand by the end of the week are sold for $0.20 per kilogram.

REQUIRED
   a. Using the following five random numbers, simulate demand for 5 weeks: 0968, 7291, 4522, 8023, 1587.
   b. On the basis of the simulated demand in part a, how many 100 kg lots should George's Groceteria stock weekly in order to maximize profits for the 5-week period?
9. Write a short paragraph describing how the detailed model could be further disaggregated. What would be the usefulness of your more disaggregated model?

Problems

10. *(SMA)* Sophisticated Retailers Ltd. has observed that the daily demand for a product depends, in part, upon the number of units on display. The following table shows the probabilities of various demands given the number of units on display.

Units on Display	Daily Demand (units)			
	100	200	300	400
0–200	0.6	0.3	0.1	0
201–400	0.5	0.2	0.2	0.1
more than 400	0.2	0.3	0.3	0.2

Sophisticated earns a profit of $0.20 on each item sold, experiences a stockout cost of $0.35 per unit when demand cannot be satisfied (unfilled orders are lost orders), and is faced with a fixed replenishment cost of $50 (independent of amount) each time the display is replenished. Holding costs are not consequential, but shelf space limitations preclude the stocking of more than 1000 units. There are currently 1000 units on hand.

Two restocking policies are under consideration.

Policy X—restock overnight with 800 or more units whenever units on display drop below 201 to restore total to 1000 units.

Policy Y—Restock after every 3 days with whatever amount is required to bring units on display up to 1000 units.

Use the following 10 random numbers to simulate 10 days of demand:

8, 7, 9, 3, 8, 0, 8, 1, 4, 5

REQUIRED
a. Over a period of 10 days, simulate Policy X and Policy Y, indicating the following for each policy:
   (1) Total units sold
   (2) Total number of replenishments
   (3) Total units short
   (4) Total profit
   Be sure to show clearly how you arrived at your answers; a tabular format would be desirable.
b. (1) Which policy would you select? Why?
   (2) List at least two limitations of drawing such a conclusion from your simulation model.

11. For practical simulations, the most difficult issue is the validation of the behavioral relations. Comment.

12. Monte Carlo simulation is made more accurate by using random number tables rather than flipping coins to generate the outcomes for random variables. Comment.

13. For the example problem, generate 10 trial outcomes for net income where

$$P(\text{price} = 20) = 0.5$$
$$P(\text{price} = 22) = 0.5$$

and

$$P(\text{quantity} = 50{,}000) = 0.3$$
$$P(\text{quantity} = 55{,}000) = 0.7$$

14. For the example problem, generate 10 trial outcomes for net income where

$$P(C_V = \$7.50) = 0.8$$
$$P(C_V = \$10.00) = 0.2$$

Other quantities are as originally given.

15. For the data of Problems 13 and 14, find the sample mean value of net income, and the sample variance.
16. Find a 95 percent confidence interval for net income for the data in Problems 13 and 14.
17. For the example problem, determine the appropriate sample size when there is a probability of 0.95 that the sample mean ±$5,000 contains the true mean income.
18. For Problem 17, how does the sample size change if the probability is 0.9? How does the sample size change if the precision is changed to ±$10,000? Answer these questions intuitively. Then perform the calculations to find the appropriate sample size for each situation.
19. For your data in Problem 13, calculate an associated stockholders' equity figure for each net income figure. Find the average stockholders' equity. Establish a 90 percent confidence interval for stockholders' equity.
20. Using the accounting simulation model[4] on your local computer, do Problems 13 through 17 for a sample size of 20 in each case.
21. Harry runs a Hotdog Hutch. His rent is $1200 for the day, and it does not vary with sales. Harry sells hotdogs for $1 each. The raw hotdogs, buns, and mustard cost $0.25 per hotdog. Harry buys the number of hotdogs today that were *demanded* yesterday. If any hotdogs are left over, they are thrown out. After some research, Harry has determined that demand will be 2000 with probability 0.3, 2200 with probability 0.5, or 2500 with probability 0.2.

REQUIRED
  a. Find the theoretical expected demand.
  b. Simulate HHH's profits over 10 days.
  c. Find a 90 percent confidence interval for the expected profit for HHH based on the 10 trials in part b.
22. For the example inventory problem,[5] simulate a 10-day period under the policy of ordering four TVs when one, or no, TV is on hand. Compare this policy with the one in the text. Which is better?

[4]A version of the model written in BASIC is available from the authors upon request, and is also reproduced in the accompanying Solutions Manual.
[5]See footnote 4.

Problems

23. The store manager of the TV example in the text has noticed that buyers no longer backorder TVs for later delivery. If there are no TVs in stock, the customer goes elsewhere. This is a lost sale. The opportunity cost on each lost sale is $35, that is, the selling price less the cost. Given this change, the store manager is considering two policies:

	Order Quantity	Order Point
Policy 1	8	2
Policy 2	4	4

Using a 15-day simulation, which policy is better?

24. The store manager is considering a periodic review on a new line of plastic gloves. Backorders are not allowed, and a lost sale has an opportunity cost of $0.25 per pair. A pair of gloves costs $0.01 per day to hold in inventory. The lead time on an order is 3 days, and each order costs $10. The manager is considering two periodic review policies:

	Maximum Inventory	Reorder Point
Policy 1	20	2
Policy 2	15	3

Simulate the behavior of each policy for 20 periods, and suggest the better policy.

25. Using the inventory example from the text, simulate a 10-day period where the lead time is probabilistic as follows:

1	0.1
2	0.6
3	0.3

26. The XYZ Corporation uses a periodic review for a class of small nuts and bolts. As a prototype, you are asked to simulate the behavior of one small item—an R2XQ transistor. The inventory level is reviewed every Friday, and if the inventory is 10 or less, an order is placed for up to 30; that is, if 3 are on hand, order 27. If there are more than 10 available, then don't order. The demand for a week is probabilistic as follows:

Demand	Probability
3	0.1
4	0.2
5	0.3
6	0.4

The lead time for an order is probabilistic:

Lead Time	Probability
1	0.1
2	0.3
3	0.4
4	0.2

Each order costs XYZ $25. The holding cost is $0.20 per week per transistor. If a customer asks for an R2XQ and it is unavailable, the sale is lost, but without deterring further sales. However, XYZ views such opportunity losses as costing $2 per transistor.

Using a 30-week simulation, XYZ wants an estimate of the weekly cost for this policy.

27. Consider again the situation in Problem 24 and your answer. Propose a different policy (one that you think would be better). Simulate its behavior and see if it is better.
28. The XYZ Company makes one product and uses two inputs. The production function is the Cobb-Douglas function

$$X = x_1^{1/2} x_2^{1/2}$$

where X is the output quantity and x_1, x_2 are the input quantities.
The selling price for the output product is probabilistic:

$P(P = 200) = 0.3$
$P(P = 250) = 0.4$
$P(P = 300) = 0.3$

The buying price for the first input is probabilistic:

$P(P_1 = 10) = 0.5$
$P(P_1 = 12) = 0.5$

The buying price for the second input is constant at 8. XYZ operates at a level where $x_1 = 49$ and $x_2 = 36$.

REQUIRED
  a. Write an equation for the profit for XYZ, first in general notation and then specifically.
  b. Find the expected profit for XYZ.
  c. Simulate the profit behavior of XYZ for 5 trials. (Set up your experiment clearly and label all tables. Explain what you are doing in some detail.)
  d. Using the data generated in part c, what is a good estimate for XYZ's average profit?
  e. Find an 80 percent (two-tailed) confidence interval for the average profit.

Problems

    f. Give *one* behavioral relation that is contained in the total simulation model.

    g. Give *one* definitional relation.

29. Perform another simulation for the supermarket example in the text. Beginning at 9:00, simulate the queue behavior for 20 customers. Calculate the average waiting time, the average total service time, and checkout counter idle time. How do your results compare with the results given in the text?

30. The supermarket manager of the example in the text anticipates an increased demand next week and wants to know whether the present one checker can handle the increased business. The anticipated customer arrivals are given by:

Probability	Time Between Arrivals in Minutes
0.3	2
0.4	3
0.3	6

Simulate the behavior of the anticipated queue for the first 25 customers. Is the queue behavior acceptable or is the situation out of control? Give reasons.

31. Next year, the supermarket manager anticipates further increased demand with anticipated customer arrivals given by:

Probability	Time Between Arrivals in Minutes
0.4	1
0.3	2
0.2	6

Assuming that *two* checkers (identical to one already there) are employed, what is the average waiting time for each customer, the average total service time, and the percentage of idle check time? Hint: You may assume that there is one waiting line, and the first person in line will proceed to the first available checker. Your simulation may describe the line and each of the two checkers. You will need to devise a modification to Table 11–4 to describe this enlarged system.

32. a. For the following project, establish the earliest start time, earliest finish time, latest start time, latest finish time, and slack for each activity.[6]

---

[6]The student may want to review the first sections on CPM calculations in Chapter 9 before attempting this problem.

Note that activity (3, 6) requires no time, but its sequencing restriction must be honored (it is a dummy activity).

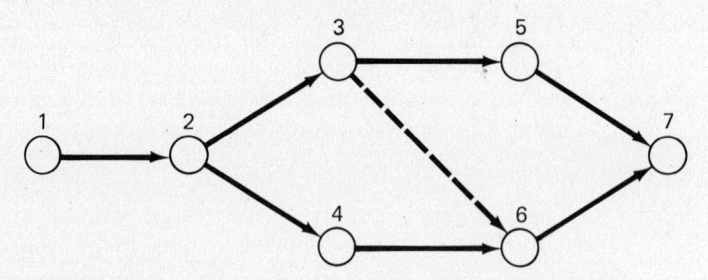

For the above project, assume that each activity time, t_{ij}, is a random variable with distributions given as follows:

	PROBABILITY		
Task (i, j)	0.3	0.4	0.3
1, 2	1	3	6
2, 3	3	4	5
2, 4	1	2	4
3, 6	0	0	0
4, 6	1	1	3
3, 5	2	3	6
5, 7	1	2	3
6, 7	3	6	7

b. For 10 trials, simulate the time required to complete the project.
c. Find a 90 percent confidence interval on the projects' completion time.

References

Bonini, C. P. *Computer Models for Decision Analysis*. Palo Alto, Calif.: Scientific Press, 1980.

Gordon, G. *Systems Simulation,* 2d ed. Englewood Cliffs, N.J.: Prentice-Hall, 1978.

Hillier, F., and Lieberman, G. J. *Introduction to Operations Research,* 3d ed. San Francisco: Holden-Day, 1980.

Maisel, H., and Gnugnoli, G. *Simulation of Discrete Stochastic Systems*. Chicago: Science Research Associates, 1972.

Meier, R. C., Newell, W. T., and Pazer, H. L. *Simulation in Business and Economics*. Englewood Cliffs, N.J.: Prentice-Hall, 1969.

Naylor, T. H. *Computer Simulation Experiments with Models of Economic Systems*. New York: Wiley, 1971.

———. *Corporate Planning Models*. Reading, Mass.: Addison-Wesley, 1979.

References

———, Balintfy, J. L., Burdick, D. S., and Chu, K. *Computer Simulation Techniques*. New York: Wiley, 1966.

Schmidt, J. W., and Taylor, R. E. *Simulation and Analysis of Industrial Systems*. Homewood, Ill., Irwin, 1970.

Shannon, R. E. *Systems Simulation*. Englewood Cliffs, N.J.: Prentice-Hall, 1975.

Wagner, H. M. *Principles of Operations Research,* 2d ed. Englewood Cliffs, N.J.: Prentice-Hall, 1975.

CHAPTER 12
Simulation: Corporate Modeling and Implementation

12.1 Introduction

12.2 Steps in Corporate Simulation Modeling
 1. Creating the Data Base
 2. Constructing the Corporate Model
 3. Using the Model for Managerial Reports

12.3 An Example of a Corporate Model

12.4 Expanding the Corporate Model: Cash Flow

12.5 What Are "What If" Questions?

12.6 The "What If?" Response Matrix

12.7 Corporate Modeling on Spreadsheets

12.8 The Combination of Simulation and Optimization Techniques
 Optimization as an Idea Generator for Simulation
 Optimization as a Submodel in the Larger Simulation Model

12.9 Reviewing the Simulation Technique

12.10 Summary

Glossary

Problems

References

Key Concepts
Corporate planning model
Definitional relation
Empirical relation
Recursive relation
"What if?"
"What if?" response matrix

Key Applications
Corporate planning
"What if?" questioning

12.1 Introduction

Corporate planning using computer-based simulation models is a natural extension of the previous chapter. Further, corporate modeling for planning is one of the most significant business applications of simulation today. Many simulation models build on the traditional financial and accounting model such as that explained in the previous chapter. What are the advantages of simulation models? In reporting the experience of one large corporation, Naylor (1977, p. 88) put it succinctly:

> To be sure, all of these questions could be answered manually by the accountants and financial analysts at United Airlines. But every time the Treasurer asked a different "What If?" question, it would literally take days to crank out the answers.

With computer simulation models, answers that might require days can be given in minutes, even seconds. "What If?" questions may be related to the energy crisis, other shortages, tight money and inflation, international competition, and economic uncertainty. Examples are "What if" there is another energy crisis of the 1973 magnitude?; "What if" the inflation rate is 18 percent?; "What if" interest rates go to 25 percent?; and "What if" the dollar falls to 1.5 Deutsch marks? What are the outcomes of interest? We want to know the effect on net income, stockholders' equity, cash flow, short-term debt requirements, long-term equity requirements, cash flows for capital investment evaluation, and so on.

These are the concerns of the planner, managerial accountant, and manager, all of whom are involved both in planning and in making data and models relevant for management. Today we are in the midst of tremendous growth in the development and implementation of these simulation models for corporations. The operations research/management information systems/controller staffs find the need for these models, develop the models, and program the models for managerial use. In addition, there are many external consulting firms and individuals who work with internal staffs, and most important, with corporate management, to develop and implement simulation models. To name a few, Deloitte, Haskins and Sells, Arthur Andersen, and Ernst and Whinney, of the Big Eight, have such models available through their management service activities. Several management consulting firms specialize in simulation models for corporate planning.

12.2 Steps in Corporate Simulation Modeling

The following steps, among others, are necessary in corporate modeling.

1. CREATING THE DATA BASE

Recall that our accounting/financial planning model in Chapter 11 required last year's balance sheet, a sales forecast or product demand function, and historical data for the cost function. These data must be gathered and stored in the computer for convenient use by the planning model. In more general terms, a library of data files must be created and stored inside the computer. The exact data and their form are determined by the model. They may include the following: past internal data on costs; past data on sales, inventories, production, and productivity; and external data on the national economy if it is used to predict sales, inflation rates, and so on. If the model requires the data for relevant relations, such as product cost or product demand, then these data must be available in the data base.

2. CONSTRUCTING THE CORPORATE MODEL

There are a wide variety of corporate models in use today. Practically all of them are simulation models, and most are deterministic financial models. Leading applications of corporate simulation models include cash flow analysis, financial forecasting, balance sheet projections, financial analysis, and profit planning. Models are used mainly to evaluate policy alternatives, to provide financial projections, and to facilitate long-term and short-term planning and decision making.

All these models should reflect some cause-and-effect relationships (either definitional or behavioral). These relationships are defined in terms of dependent variables, independent variables, and constants, where the independent variables may be internal, external, or lagged. Constants or parameters may be fixed by nature, policy, or for reasons of simplification.

Definitional relations are mathematical or accounting definitions. The following are examples:

Closing inventory = opening inventory + purchases − issues
Cash = beginning cash + accounts receivable receipts + loan receipts − loan repayments − payments of accounts payable

Empirical relations reflect some expected response of individuals, a market, or the economy that can be verified empirically. An example is the following relationship for the collection of accounts receivable:

Collection of accounts receivable = $0.1S_m + 0.8S_{m-1} + 0.08S_{m-2}$

where S_m is sales in month m. This is an expected pattern of collections and 2 percent uncollectable sales. This relationship is a hypothesis that can be tested empirically.

Another example is

$S_t = \$10{,}000{,}000 - 10P_t + 5A_t$

where S_t is sales, P_t is price, and A_t is advertising.

Recursive relations are relations that tie the model together over time, either definitionally or empirically. A definitional recursive relation is

$I_t = I_{t-1} + P_t - S_t$

where I = inventory, P = production, and S = sales. In each period t, the ending inventory is equal to the beginning inventory, plus the quantity produced, minus the quantity sold. The multiperiod financial model is a recursive model, as the model logic is the same for each year, and the output of any year depends on the previous year's results and the model.

An empirical recursive relation is

$S_t = S_{t-1} + \alpha \, \Delta P_t$

where S = sales, P = price, and α is a parameter. Current sales is the same as last period's sales, except modified by a price change, ΔP_t.

Variables can also be classified as follows:

1. External variables (also exogenous or independent variables) are determined outside the firm's control. Examples are gross national product, competition prices, wage rates, tax rates, and so on.
2. Internal variables (also controllable, endogenous, or decision variables) are set by management. Examples are advertising, R&D expenditures, capital expenditures, and so on.
3. Lagged dependent variables depend on the values of variables in

preceding time periods. For example, current sales may depend on sales in a previous period, $S_t = S_{t-1} - \alpha \Delta P_t$, where ΔP_t is a change in price; α may be a coefficient determined by regression analysis.

3. USING THE MODEL FOR MANAGERIAL REPORTS

Corporate models can generate great masses of numbers and printouts. The issue is to determine what the user wants and needs, and attempt to generate those results. Many corporate models have failed because they generated too much irrelevant output, which engulfed the few pieces of important information. Managers can use a few pieces of relevant information, and they frequently get a mass of unusable and unused printouts. The important lesson is that the corporate model must be, in part, designed by the manager who wants a question answered. If the manager is interested in the cash availability for corporate reinvestment for the next 5 yr, it should be a list of five numbers—not 300 pages of balance sheets, income statements, depreciation schedules, and so on. The easiest mistake in building a corporate model is to generate too much output. In designing model outputs, work with management; keep the formats simple. Create different reports for different users from the same model results.

12.3 An Example of a Corporate Model

A firm has a small corporate model that is used primarily to predict profits. Consequently, the two primary relations are (1) a definitional relation for profits, and (2) an empirical relation to predict sales. Profits are defined as revenue minus fixed cost and variable costs:

$$P = R - F - VC \qquad (12\text{--}1)$$

where

P = profit
R = revenue
F = fixed costs
VC = variable costs

Revenue can be disaggregated as

$R = pn$

where

p = unit sales price
n = quantity sold

The variable costs VC can be stated as

$$VC = Cn + A$$

where

C = standard unit cost of production
A = advertising expenditure

Substituting these last two definitional relations into the profit relation yields

$$P = pn - F - Cn - A \quad \text{or} \quad P = (p - C)n - F - A \tag{12-2}$$

Thus, profits are equal to sales n times the profit contribution $(p - C)$ minus the fixed costs and advertising.

The second primary relation is an empirical relation to explain the quantity sold, or sales n:

$$n = a_1 - a_2 p + a_3 A \tag{12-3}$$

where a_1, a_2, and a_3 are empirically determined parameters. Assume that we used the regression forecasting techniques discussed in Chapter 10 and have determined the sales relation as $n = 2000 - 1p + 0.1A$. This two-equation corporate model can be reduced to a simple equation model by substituting Eq. (12-3) into Eq. (12-2). The result is

$$P = (p - C)(a_1 + a_3 A - a_2 p) - F - A \tag{12-4}$$

For the particular sales equation, the profit is

$$P = (p - C)(2000 - 1p + 0.1A) - F - A$$

This latter equation can be specified numerically. From internal accounting data, we determine

$c = \$300$ and $F = \$1{,}000{,}000$

Thus,

$$P = (p - \$300)(2000 - 1p + 0.1A) - \$1{,}000{,}000 - A$$

Now we have a model that has incorporated the definitional and behavioral relations together with parameter estimates. The price p and the advertising budget A are internal variables, or decisions to be set by management. With a price of $500 and an advertising budget of $50,000, the profit is $250,000.

12.4 Expanding the Corporate Model: Cash Flow

The income statement and balance sheet are fundamental financial statements. The cash flow statement is of major importance for cash

Sources	Uses
1. Cash collected on accounts receivable	1. Cash payments on accounts payable
2. Cash collected on current sales	2. Cash operating expenses
3. New loans	3. Cash payments on new machines and equipment
4. New equity issues	4. Interest paid
	5. Loan repayment
	6. Dividends paid

Figure 12–1. Sources and uses of funds.

planning, debt planning, capital investment analysis, and many other decisions. For management, it is an equally important statement.

The cash flow statement can exist in many forms. We can derive the net cash inflow figure in a fashion similar to the income statement, or we can make up two lists: sources of cash and expenditures of cash for the current period. Taking the former approach, the determination of net cash inflow can be calculated as equal to net income plus depreciation expense. However, this approach is not very instructive for the manager. The manager is more concerned with the sources and uses of cash in some detail so that items for investigation, evaluation, and possible change can be pinpointed. This is a more detailed statement. Figure 12–1 is a representative cash flow sources and uses statement. Cash flow statements are frequently integrated into the multiperiod simulation. For the multiperiod simulation, or the N-trial Monte Carlo simulation, it is more efficient to calculate all the desired statements during a single pass through the program than to have separate programs for each statement.

12.5 What Are "What If" Questions?

If the future is very much like the present, there is little reason to plan. But "what if" something is different? There are two "What if?" questions here: The first is "What if" the future is different? The second is how to transform the "What if?" question for the real world into a "What if?" question for the corporate planning model.

The important "What if?" real-world questions are endless, and thus, we must limit ourselves to those that (1) are reasonably likely, and (2) we think would impact important outcomes. These are some likely "what if?" questions: the inflation rate jumps to 30 percent, worker productivity increases 5 percent, the OPEC price of oil goes down 50 percent, labor costs go up 10 percent, and so on. These factors usually enter as parameter values or empirical relations in the corporate planning model. This brings us to the second question of how to modify the model for a "What if?" question. Let us return to the profit model, which states that

$$P = (p - 300)(2000 - 1p + 0.1A) - F - A$$

What if the variable cost of production goes up by 10 percent, to $330? This new increased value is substituted into the model, and a new P value is calculated. This gives a measure of the sensitivity of profits to a change in variable cost.

12.6 The "What If?" Response Matrix

The initial goal in "What if?" questioning is to determine the effect on our current solution of changes in the environment of that solution, that is, changes in parameter values or definitional, empirical, or recursive relations. As a by-product, we can determine the stability of our current solution, gain insight into the strength of our internal relationships, find the limits to our current solution, or even find a better solution. In a formal sense, the current solution yields a point value on a multidimensional response function, and the approach is to explore the nature of the function in the neighborhood of the point by generating the gradient.

Consider a company with an operating corporate model. The "What if?" question is "What if we increase production quantity by 10 percent?" Is this a better solution? It is a better solution if it adds to a goal of interest, say, profit. If it actually did occur, what would be the effect on our firm? The calculation for comparison is

profit (+ 10% production) − profit (base production)

This is a marginal profit calculation, and economic theory suggests that production should be increased until marginal profit becomes zero. We can also put this result in ratio form (using Table 12–1):

$$\frac{\text{profit (+ 10\% production)} - \text{profit (base production)}}{1.1 \text{ base production quantity} - \text{base production quantity}}$$

$$= \frac{\text{change in profit}}{\text{change in production quantity}} = \frac{\Delta Y_3}{\Delta Z_1}$$

This resulting ratio is a marginal measure. Economic theory suggests that we would increase production by 10 percent if the marginal profit were positive, that is,

$$\frac{\Delta Y_3}{\Delta Z_1} > 0$$

12.6 / The "What If" Response Matrix

This proposed solution would be better. This result and others are summarized in Table 12-1, the "What if?" response matrix. The important "What if?" issues are listed down the left side and important responses are suggested across the top.

TABLE 12-1. The "What If?" Response Matrix

	OUTPUT RESPONSES		
"What If?" Questions	ΔY_1 Inventory Levels	ΔY_2 Sales	ΔY_3 Profit, Cash Flow, ROI
ΔZ_1 Input quantities, Production quantities			$\dfrac{\Delta Y_3 \text{ (profit)}}{\Delta Z_1 \text{ (output)}}$
ΔZ_2 Price, advertising			
ΔZ_3 Short-term debt			
ΔX_1 Productivity, technology capacity			$\dfrac{\Delta Y_3}{\Delta X_1}$
ΔX_2 Competitors' price		$\dfrac{\Delta Y_2}{\Delta X_2}$	
ΔX_3 Prime interest rate, inflation, price of oil			$\dfrac{\Delta Y_3}{\Delta X_3}$

Two other questions concern technological and input balance. Again, "What if?" search can be used:

1. What if the firm increases its production capacity by one machine? Using the corporate model, the marginal product is

$$\frac{\Delta Y_3}{\Delta X_1}$$

2. What if the rate of inflation is 20 percent? What is the impact on cash flow and sales?

$$\frac{\Delta Y_3}{\Delta X_3}, \quad \frac{\Delta Y_2}{\Delta X_2}$$

The result is quite simple. An efficient "What if?" search follows the economic theory of the firm—both by supplying the questions to ask on prices, costs, and technology, and by supplying the criterion for a better solution, namely, is the marginal profit positive? This oversimplifies the search and the analysis. It supplies the dimensions of the questions, and the form of the answers. In more complex, real situations, the questions must be operational, and the answers multidimensional.

The "What if?" response matrix in Table 12–1 suggests that any questions will have a multidimensional response impact. Usually, the impact will be mixed—a good impact on some variables, and a bad one on others; for example, a 10 percent price increase will usually decrease sales volume and force layoffs, but may increase profits. The appropriate action is not clear. How does one weigh the relative impact and make the appropriate tradeoffs? The answer must depend on the preferences and the risks of the decision makers. Complex issues do not have simple answers. The model permits us to develop implications of alternatives quickly, but there is no easy single variable maximization.

12.7 Corporate Modeling on Spreadsheets

Spreadsheet software is useful for modeling and simulation in corporate planning. "What if?" questions can be examined through the use of equations relating different submodels (sales, accounts receivable, inventory, fixed assets, capital structure, etc.) to the financial statements. Effects of changes in basic conditions can be seen through models of the income statement, balance sheet, and cash budget. The continued growth in the use of microcomputers will make spreadsheet modeling almost a requirement for managers of the future.

An electronic spreadsheet is an empty matrix until variables and labels are input into the cells. The rows are referenced by numbers running down the left-hand side and the columns are referenced by either numbers or letters across the top. The intersection of a row and column is a cell. A variable, or a formula to calculate the variable, can be input into each cell. By referencing several cells in a formula, one can use definitional relationships to specify the balance sheet, cash budget, and income statement. The solution of all problems at the end of this chapter, with exception of number 9, can be greatly facilitated through the use of one of the popular spreadsheet programs.

For example:

	A	B	C
1	Sales	2000	2400
2	Variable cost	1000[A]	1200[B]
3	Fixed cost	500	500
4	Net income	500[C]	700

A: +B1 * 0.5
B: +C1 * 0.5
C: +B1 − B2 − B3

12.8 The Combination of Simulation and Optimization Techniques

Many people consider simulation and optimization techniques as substitute, if not rival approaches. The pro-simulation group argues that simulation models can be built at low cost to replicate (even duplicate) the real-world phenomena under study, and thus the projections into the future are very accurate. For them, optimization models such as linear programming are necessarily too aggregative and naive to be of much use, and much of the real-world relevance is lost in the mere task of formulating the model. Thus, optimization models are interesting theoretical mathematical models but of little, if any, practical relevance. For them, the final damning characteristic of optimization is its costs of formulation, programming, and of use in answering relevant questions.

The counter-argument for the pro-optimization group is that optimization models truly search for efficiency in a global sense; they are not merely a replication of existing approaches. Further, only with optimization models can one control the model with a necessary sense of economy. They refute the approach whereby possible future outcomes are sampled, arguing that predictions from such an approach are mere creations. For us, both arguments are nonsensical in their extreme form, and not very enlightening or useful in any form. Simulation and optimization are complements, not rivals. Thus, the question of interest is how to use them in concert—not which side to join in the wrong war.

In our discussion, we take as given that optimization models are more costly than simulation models for the same level of detail; optimization models consider simultaneously large numbers of possible tradeoffs, whereas simulation models consider only limited numbers of tradeoffs; stochastic optimization models are more difficult to formulate and solve than Monte Carlo simulations. With these premises, we suggest two possible joint procedures: optimization as an idea generator for simulation; and optimization as a submodel in the larger simulation model.

OPTIMIZATION AS AN IDEA GENERATOR FOR SIMULATION

The procedure is as follows. Assume that there is a relatively aggregate optimization model and a larger, more detailed simulation model for the real-world situation. The optimization model is used to yield optimization solutions from which policies are developed for testing on the simulation model. For example, the optimization model may suggest a change in product mix 3 yr hence. This policy is then tested on the simulation model for its more detailed implications.

The advantage here is that this alternative may not be generated by management, particularly, if there is no a priori notion that 3 yr is better than 4 yr, or 5 yr, or 2 yr. Another advantage is that from a near infinite number of possible policies to test by simulation, the optimization model can be used to select a more reasonable subset for further investigation.

OPTIMIZATION AS A SUBMODEL IN THE LARGER SIMULATION MODEL

The notion is straightforward. Some part of the large simulation model may lend itself to optimization. Consider our multiperiod income sheet and balance sheet simulations of this chapter. For each year, one must develop the income statement for proposed policies and predicted situations. Rather than use a known policy, we could incorporate an optimization model that would develop the best annual policy under the conditions.

Both of these joint optimization-simulation approaches permit the user to capture possibilities for better planning that are not possible if either approach is used alone. Yet these developments are not widely implemented. In their survey, Naylor and Schauland (1976, p. 928) mention only two firms that use linear programming as minimum-cost subroutines. "The important point to realize is that while many firms (particularly the petroleum industry) make extensive use of mathematical programming models to run their refineries, relatively few of the mathematical programming models are linked into a corporate model."

12.9 Reviewing the Simulation Technique

Simulation is a very powerful technique. But it must be used with care and knowledge. Naylor et al. (1966, 23–42) have developed a checklist of issues that must be considered for any simulation model and program. In one way or another, we have considered each point, but it would be useful to state the issues more formally and discuss each one. Naylor and Vernon (1969, pp. 331–352) list the issues:

1. Formulation of the problem
2. Formulation of a mathematical model
3. Formulation of a computer program
4. Validation
5. Experimental design
6. Data analysis

As ever, we must begin with the questions of interest to the user. The manager and the investor are interested in the financial health of the corporation. In accounting, the income statement, the balance sheet, the cash flow statement, and so on, answer questions of interest. But it is frequently appropriate to probe further with the user. For example, a tax accountant and a brokerage firm analyst want different responses, different levels of detail, different forms, different variable values, and so on. Without a focus on questions, there is no guidance on the appropriate level of detail, variables of interest, notions of required accuracy, and so on. To state it simply, simulation is purposeful. Without the questions, the purpose is veiled, and we are flying blind.

The corporate planning model can be formulated and stated in mathematical notation, but it is usually sufficient to state the model in an equivalent form as a well-defined, step-by-step procedure. An unambiguous and complete flowchart is a sufficient mathematical expression. Whatever the exact form, it must be an expression of the logic of the corporate model. It must contain and incorporate:

1. The accepted accounting rules for measure of definitional relations, aggregation, and transformation, stated in state and transactional variables.
2. Estimates of empirical relations and parameters. These involve both endogenous factors as standard usages and exogenous factors as price predictions. Our earlier illustrations of sales projections and statistical cost equations are examples. The latter includes both endogeneous and exogeneous factors, as it incorporates both a measure of efficient use of resources as well as their cost.

When the model has been stated, it is then transformed into a computer program. The computer program should be an exact image of the model—no more, no less. It is a restatement in a different language. There is an abundance of programming languages—FORTRAN, ALGOL, PL/1, and so on. These are general scientific languages, and it frequently involves considerable cost and time to program the model in these languages. More recently, a number of user-oriented languages have become available, such as SIMPLAN, GPSS, and SIMSCRIPT. These languages are specially devised to make the programming of simulation relatively easy and inexpensive. With the general availability of these special languages, the user will want to investigate their use because of their programming ease, user orientation, and potentially lower cost.

Validation is the most important and the most difficult aspect of simulation. Basically, the question is "Is the simulation any good?" or "Can we use it to answer the original managerial or research questions with reasonable confidence?" The easiest approach is to ask oneself what could go wrong to cause the simulation to produce inappropriate answers to the questions. Clearly, many things can go wrong, each of which can lead to poor results:

1. The accounting model and rules are not followed, both in the mathematical model and the computer program.
2. Empirical relations can be in error; the cost equation could have both the wrong variables and wrong cost parameters. Sales predictions, price predictions, cost estimates, productivity estimates, and so on must all be checked. Statistical tests of confidence intervals and hypothesis testing are appropriately helpful.
3. The model itself—does the composite of accounting rules and appropriate empirical relations make sense in total? Is it a representation of the total system? To answer "yes," the model builder must understand the real situation and the simulation process in some detail.

Briefly, this gives a checklist. Of course, the final aspect of validation is the continuing relationship between the user and the model. Does the intended user ever use it? If he uses it one time, then the test of experience will make itself evident. But what about the first time? One final validation test is the use of the past as the future. Move yourself back 2 yr and start from there. Did the simulation predict what actually happened? Or would the results of the simulation have permitted one to do better? Even here, validation does not absolutely guarantee that the model is right, or useful for the decision makers. These checks are necessary, but unfortunately, not sufficient.

The design of simulation experiments involves two issues: What is the question, and how do we know when we have an answer? Usually, the question involves whether a change in a policy decision is advisable or not. Is it profitable to increase advertising, raise prices, increase production, and so on? Sometimes, the language of factor and response is used. A factor can be controlled, like production level; or observed, like market price. The response is the result of interest, such as profit, net income, and so on. The ideal simple design is to vary one factor and observe the response of interest. With a valid simulation, the results are straightforward to interpret. For the deterministic model, one trial is sufficient. For Monte Carlo simulation, the sample size becomes important, and sampling theory helps. For discussion of the design of simulation experiments, see Naylor et al. (1966). They discuss many issues of more complex designs, including the multiple-factor experiment.

The final question concerns the analysis of simulation results: Have we answered the question? Statistical techniques of confidence intervals, hypothesis testing, and regression analysis are appropriate aids to data analysis. These techniques, together with the validity of the simulation, permit us to say that we have answered the question.

12.10 Summary

The computer-based corporate simulation model is an important practical application of simulation. Such a model permits managers to obtain answers to important policy issues in a matter of minutes. In this chapter, we considered three important steps in building a corporate planning model: the creation of the data base; the creation of the model; and finally, the design of the managerial reports. The corporate model was then expanded to include cash flow. "What if?" questions are an important managerial technique to help determine important issues and their implications. The pseudo-battle between optimizers and simulators was discussed and we concluded that we need a synthesis of the two. Finally, we reviewed the steps in simulation modeling and use. This chapter provides a general framework for simulation in the context of corporate planning.

Glossary

Corporate planning model. A computer-programmed mathematical model that includes important corporate relations. It is used to predict corporate results under various circumstances.

Definitional relation. A relation based on a given, unprovable, mathematical or accounting definition.

Empirical relation. A relation that reflects a relationship between variables that can be determined or tested empirically.

Recursive relation. A relation that ties today's activities to future activities.

"What if?" question. A managerially relevant question concerning the effects of changes in controllable or predictable behavioral parameters.

"What if?" response matrix. A table that shows the impact on important system outcomes as a function of varying inputs—for example, the effect of a changed interest rate on profit.

Problems

1. For the example corporate model given in the text,

$$P = pn - \$10{,}000 - \$300n - A$$
$$n = 2000 - 1p + 0.1A$$

Determine a "What if?" response matrix of the form

	Outputs	
	Δn	Δp
Inputs (increase by 10%) Δp		
ΔA		

where the base level of $p = \$500$ and $A = \$50,000$.

2. *(CMA)* Shotz Company is a major producer and distributor of a regional brand of beer. The beer is marketed in 13 states along the East Coast of the United States. Recent decisions by some states to ban nonreturnable bottles and cans and the expectation that more states will do the same have led the Shotz management to reappraise its bottling function. Shotz has automatic bottling and canning facilities that can handle three sizes of nonreturnable bottles and two sizes of cans.

Demand for beer in cans and nonreturnable bottles will be reduced drastically in the next few years as a result of the ban of nonreturnables. However, demand for beer in returnable bottles is expected to increase sufficiently to offset the reduced sales of beer in nonreturnables. The present canning equipment cannot be adapted for use in the returnable container environment. The bottling equipment can be adapted for use in bottling returnable bottles. Therefore, the company will have to acquire more automated bottling equipment to replace the capacity lost from the discarded canning equipment. The new equipment should enable the company to have adequate capacity for 5 yr. Should returnable cans be developed, the company would be prepared to invest in the necessary equipment 5 yr from now.

The company's largest bottling plant, which is located in New Jersey, produces approximately 75 percent of the firm's total output, split evenly between bottles and cans. The present canning equipment will be replaced by new automated bottling equipment. The new equipment is technologically superior to the present automated bottling equipment. The major decision that plant management must now make is how large the New Jersey plant's maintenance and repair staff should be to keep both the new and adopted automated equipment running efficiently.

The maintenance and repair staff is responsible for both preventive maintenance conducted according to a planned schedule and repairs arising from any breakdowns. Comprehensive accounting records regarding the maintenance and repair function exist for the past 5 yr of operations. Records on the number of breakdowns for each 3-month quarter during the past 5 yr are classified by kind, length of time, and type of product being processed (bottle or can identified by size). Total costs of the maintenance and repair department, consisting of labor, supplies, equipment, and an allocation of general factory overhead, have averaged $500,000 a year for the past 5 yr.

Two separate, 10-person maintenance and repair staffs have been used to service the bottling and canning operations for each of the two 8-hr shifts. The total staff has averaged 40 persons for the past 5 yr.

There no longer will be a need for two separate maintenance and repair staffs on each shift, because the canning equipment is to be replaced by new bottling equipment. Further, management believes that it may be able to reduce the size of the maintenance and repair staff on each shift to fewer than 20 persons. However, the staff will not be reduced unless operations can be maintained as efficiently as in the past. The plant will not be able to hire temporary service persons, because the servicing of the automatic bottling equipment requires a relatively high level of skill.

Because a great deal of uncertainty is associated with this decision, plant management has decided to use a simulation model in its analysis. Simulation models have been used by the company in the past to analyze other problems, and they have proved very useful.

REQUIRED
  a. The use of a simulation model to analyze the size of the maintenance and repair staff for the New Jersey plant requires the accumulation of certain costs.
   (1) Identify the different types of costs that should be included in the simulation model and briefly justify their inclusion.
   (2) Indicate the source for each of the cost inputs identified.
  b. Assuming that the decision problem can be adequately simulated, explain the typical types of information that will be generated from the simulation model to assist the New Jersey plant management in its decision regarding the appropriate size for the maintenance and repair staff.

  Note: The following problems assume that the example problem of Chapter 11 is extended for 5 yr. The base problem assumes that the parameter value in Chapter 11 remains the same for the 5-yr period. Unless stated otherwise, all comparisons are made with the base situation.
3. What if the variable cost increases at 10 percent per year for the next 5 yr? The effect on net income and stockholders' equity are of interest. Run the model 10 times and use averages. Make up a "What if?" response matrix for each year.
4. What if the fixed cost of production decreases at 5 percent per year for 5 yr? Make up a "What if?" response matrix similar to the one in Problem 3. Run the model 10 times and use averages.
5. What if the price distribution increases at 10 percent per year for 5 yr? Make up a "What if?" response matrix. Run the model 10 times and use averages.
6. Rerun Problem 5 with all parameters set at their average values. This is a single run of the model. Make up a "What if?" response matrix. Compare the results with the results in Problem 5. Are they as expected? Why?
7. Shippy's Retail Outlet specializes in one family of products. The retail firm has been profitable in the past. The balance sheet for December 31, 1983 is shown here:

Cash	$ 1,000
Accounts receivable	5,800

Allowance for doubtful accounts	(290)
Inventory	22,500
Land	5,000
Building	22,500
Accumulated depreciation—building	(7,500)
Equipment	5,000
Accumulated depreciation—equipment	(1,000)
Total assets	$53,010
Accounts payable—purchases	$23,000
Accounts payable—expenses	1,550
Short term notes payable	500
Taxes payable	500
Long-term notes payable	10,000
Common stock	10,000
Retained earnings	7,460
Total liabilities and stockholders equity	$53,010

Joe (Mr. Shippy) has forecasted a stable sales rate continuing in 1984. Previous year's sales revenues and predictions for future years are as follows:

Past		Future	Unit Sales	Sales Price ($)	Total Sales ($)
1980:	$28,500	1984:	300	95	28,500
1981:	28,700	1985:	302	95	28,690
1982:	28,800	1986:	299	95	28,405
1983:	29,000	1987:	301	95	28,595
		1988:	303	95	28,785
		1989:	300	95	28,500
		1990:	300	95	28,500

The cost of goods sold was 82 percent of the sales price and collections of sales were 90 percent which were made in the year of sale and 10 percent in the year after the sale. Bad debts ran at 0.5 percent of yearly sales. Ending inventory was set as 100 percent of next year's sales. Joe wishes to know how his business will look with this forecast.

Some additional information collected by Joe's assistants follows:

Tax rate	42%
Short-term interest rate (annual)	9%
Long-term interest rate (annual)	6%

Problems

Asset life: building	15 yr
equipment	5 yr
Remaining life of existing assets: building	10 yr
equipment	4 yr
Payback period of long-term notes	6 yr
Remaining life of existing long-term notes	6 yr
Beginning number of common stock outstanding	2000 shares
Dividend payments each year	$500

No asset purchases or stock sales were considered. This problem is designed for use with spreadsheet software (developed on Lotus 123).

REQUIRED

a. Produce the income statement, cash budget, and balance sheets for Shippy's Retail Outlet for 1984 through 1988. Additional information needed is:

	1984	1985	1986	1987	1988	1989
Equipment purchase			2500			
Administrative salaries	200	200	200	200	200	200
Salesmen salaries	500	500	500	500	500	500
Advertising	475	475	475	475	475	475
Utilities	375	375	375	375	375	375

b. Joe's newest assistant John Walters believes that the economy will take another dive in 1984. John's forecasted sales are as follows:

	Units	Price ($)	Total Sales ($)
1984:	290	95	27,550
1985:	275	95	26,125
1986:	274	95	26,030
1987:	280	95	26,600
1988:	285	95	27,075
1989:	293	95	27,835
1990:	300	95	28,500

John believes that accounts receivable collections will slow to 80 percent collected in the year of sale and 20 percent collected the year after. Bad debts should increase to 1 percent of sales. Interest rates should also increase, long-term to 7.5 percent and short-term to 10 percent.

Can Shippy's weather this type of recession? Produce the income statements, cash budgets, and balance sheets for 1984 through 1988.

c. Joe's sales manager, Bill Duff believes that he has a product that will bring the company out of its doldrums. Bill's product is a technological advance applied to the old products. Shippy's would have a jump on the market if it were to market the product immediately.

The product is an improvement on the existing product, so Bill thinks it should be priced at the higher end of the product line. He also thinks Shippy's should keep the price as low as possible to encourage people to try the new product. Bill's strategy would be to price the new product so that the average sales price would be $95.5 in 1984. Bill believes the product should be priced on the higher end of the quality spectrum because it is advanced technology, even though the process is less expensive.

Bill's strategy leads to the following forecast:

	1984	1985	1986	1987	1988	1989	1990
Unit sales	300	350	390	420	440	450	455
Avg. sales price	95.5	96	96.5	97	97.5	98	98

As unit sales of the new product comprise a higher percentage of total unit sales, the average sales price increases.

Produce the income statement, cash budget, and balance sheet under this forecast and the following assumptions:

COGS = 0.80 of $ sales
A/R collection: period of sale (t) = 0.70
$(t + 1)$ = 0.30
Equipment purchase: $2500 in 1984
2500 in 1986

Is this pricing strategy feasible for Shippy's? How much of a loan would Shippy's need at the beginning of 1984 to finance this product?

Is the project feasible if there is a lesser increase in demand such as:

	1984	1985	1986	1987	1988	1989	1990
Sale units	300	340	370	390	400	405	408
Price	95.5	95.8	96.25	96.5	97	97.5	98

8. Nubbins, Inc. (by James Jeck) Art Tosco was a newly minted MBA from a fine southern business school. He was convinced that the production department of Nubbins, Inc. had developed a profitable line extension for their famous "Nubbins" line of sporting goods. Mr. Tosco had presented his convictions about the new item earlier today. Several members of upper management had expressed concern about the robustness of the conclusions under various market conditions. He was instructed to answer a

Problems

long series of questions as basis for a discussion and consequent decision at a meeting of the Product Approval Committee tomorrow. Nubbins had established itself as a widely distributed brand. The very existence of the companies label on a new product, it was believed, would result in a sizable number of customers at least "trying out" the new product. However, only 65 percent of the new products marketed in the firms history had been profitable.

Tosco's original estimates assumed a unit sales volume of 46,000 in the first year with an increase of 16 percent each year thereafter. A price of $8.52 was expected upon introduction with increases of $.55/unit/year. Variable costs were predicted to be the only area subject to inflation rates of 6.5 percent, 8.0 percent, and 6 percent for each of the first 3 yr.

Materials	$3.10
Labor (direct)	$1.90
Packaging labor	$0.20
Packaging materials	$0.33
Distribution charges	$0.70

Plant and equipment would require an immediate investment of $210,000. It could be depreciated (straight line) over 4 yr with no scrap value. The firms marginal tax rate was 28 percent. Maintenance under a fixed 4-yr contract totaled $60,000 paid out in four equal amounts.

Prior experience suggested that working capital requirements would run at 14 percent of dollar sales. Lastly, the firm's cost of capital was 12 percent.

REQUIRED
The following concerns were to be addressed:
   a. Assuming cash flows take place only at the end of the year, what would each year's net income and cash flow look like? What would be the net present value (NPV) of a 4-yr product life? What would be the internal rate of return (IRR)?
   b. Would the product still be profitable if inflation were actually level at 9 percent? How about all integer inflation values between 9 percent and 20 percent. Furnish NPV and IRR of cash flows for each rate.
   c. What if the firm sold 6 percent more units initially, unit volume increases 20 percent each subsequent year, and unit price increases at 0.71 per unit per year? Give NPV and IRR of cash flows. *Note:* Use original inflation values.
   d. What would be the effect on NPV and IRR of cash flows from changing projected units sold over a range from −10 percent to +8 percent of the original assumption? *Note:* Use original yearly unit price and volume increases.
   e. If the competition responded to the new product introduction with a drastic price cut, what would be the lowest initial price at which the product could still break even (NPV 0)? *Note:* Use all original assumptions.

9. **DST, INC.** (by Professor Frederick Winter) Colin W. Matthew, marketing manager of Dynamic Systems Technology (DST) was trying to decide on the optimal pricing schedule to charge for DST's newest product, a laser cutting device used in orthopedic surgery. Matthew was aware that marketing could commence in 1 mo and that four major competitors were near the development of a technology that did not utilize technology protected by DST's patent. Each of the four potential competitors has a probability of having the necessary technology to enter the market of 10 percent within the next 4 mo, 50 percent in the next 7 mo, 80 percent in the next 10 mo, and 95 percent in the next 13 mo, and virtually 100 percent in the next 16 mo.

DST can expect to be the price leader and any competitor can be expected to match DST's price with a probability of 0.7. The probability of any competitor in the market pricing 10 percent below DST's price is 0.2 and 10 percent above DST's price is 0.1.

DST is considering a sale price as high as $30,000 per unit but no lower than $18,000. The cost to produce, market, and service the unit is $9000 direct cost.

There are 7400 health-care units, each of which is a potential customer of one of the laser cutting devices. Twenty percent of these units are not price sensitive and the probability they would buy in a given quarter (assuming they have not purchased to date) is the following:

Price ($)	Probability
30,000–27,000	0.30
26,999–24,000	0.40
23,999–21,000	0.60
20,999–18,000	0.90

Eighty percent of these units are price sensitive and their probability of buying in any quarter is the following:

Price	Probability
$30,000–27,000	0.05
26,999–24,000	0.08
23,999–21,000	0.10
20,999–18,000	0.70

DST believes that the probability of any competitor choosing to enter (assuming they have the technology) the market in a given quarter is related to remaining expected potential (equal to number of units that have not been purchased multiplied by selling price). They believe the probabilities are the following:

Problems

Remaining Potential ($)	Probability of Competitor Entering
222 MM–155 MM	0.95
154.99 MM–108 MM	0.80
107.99 MM–76 MM	0.50
77.99 MM–53 MM	0.40
52.99 MM–37 MM	0.20
36.99 MM–0	0

When DST is the only firm in the market, market share will, of course, be 100 percent. With competitors, DST expects to have the following market share.

$$MS_1 = \frac{1.1}{n} \frac{\sum_{i=2}^{n} P_i}{P_1}$$

where

MS_1 = market share of firm 1 (DST)
n = total number of firms in the market
P_1 = DST price
P_i = price of firm i

REQUIRED

Try alternative pricing strategies for each quarter and pick the optimum strategy, using discounted cash flow to compare strategies. Do not allow DST's price from one quarter to the next to increase or do not allow price decreases to be more than 10 percent below the previous period.

10. The Controller of XYZ Company asks you to develop a simple model on the basis of an econometric model supposedly simulating market behavior for one of the firm's products. The behavioral relationship of the particular product is assumed to be as follows:

$$(1) \quad n = a_1 - a_2 p + a_3 A$$

Where n is the number of units sold per period, a_1 the total market, a_2 the competition's portion of the market, p the unit price, a_3 advertising by the competition, and A the advertising effort by the company. Only A and p are decision variables.

Assume the following for developing your model:

$a_1 = 2000$
$a_2 = 50$
$a_3 = 0.1$
$p = 20$
$A = 1000$

XYZ company's variable manufacturing and distribution cost $v = 10$ per unit, total fixed costs $F = \$3000$.

REQUIRED

Develop a simple profit model that incorporates the behavioral and definitional variables. Through simulation determine the impact on profit of changes in the decision variables. For example, you may wish to consider the following changes:

Changes in advertising: $A-400$, $A-200$, $A+100$, $A+200$
Changes in price : $p-2$, $p+2$
Changes in both : $p+4$ and $A+10\%$, $p+4$ and $A-10\%$
$p-4$ and $A+10\%$, $p-4$ and $A-10\%$.

Determine the profit for the base assumptions and each change.

References

Ackoff, Russell L. "Management Misinformation Systems." *Management Science* 14, no. 4 (December 1967): B147–B156.

Burton, Richard M., and Naylor, Thomas H. "An Economic Theory of Corporate Planning." *Strategic Management Journal* 1 (1980).

Cunningham, A. A., and Swirles, J. "Modeling the Great Canadian Oil Sands Operation: The Politics of Implementation." *Interfaces* 10, no. 5 (October 1980).

Dupoch, Nicholas, Birnberg, Jacob G., and Demski, Joel. *Cost Accounting: Accounting Data for Management's Decisions*. New York: Harcourt Brace Jovanovich, 1974.

Gershefski, George. "Building a Corporate Financial Model." *Harvard Business Review* (July–August 1969): 61–72.

Golovin, Lewis. "Product Blending: A Simulation Case Study in Double-Time." *Interfaces* 9, no. 5 (November 1979).

Gray, Paul. "Practice of Management Science." *Interfaces* 10, no. 1 (February 1980).

Krueger, Donald A., and Kohlmeier, John M. "Financial Modeling and 'What If' Budgeting." *Management Accounting* (May 1972): 25–30.

Mattessich, Richard. "Budgeting Models and Systems Simulation." *Accounting Review* 36, no. 3 (July 1961): 384–397.

Naylor, Thomas H. *Corporate Planning Models*. Reading, Mass.: Addison-Wesley, 1978.

Naylor, Thomas H. "Why Corporate Planning Models." *Interfaces* 8, no. 1 (November 1977): 87–94.

Naylor, Thomas H. "The Future of Corporate Planning Models." *Managerial Planning* (March/April 1976): 1–10.

Naylor, Thomas H., Balintfy, Joseph L., Burdick, Donald S., and Chu, Kong. *Computer Simulation Techniques*. New York: Wiley, 1966.

References

Naylor, Thomas H., and Vernon, John M. *Microeconomics and Decision Models of the Firm.* New York: Harcourt, Brace & World, 1969.

Parker, Lloyd. "The Hydro Configuration Modeling System: Its Application on the Ottawa River." *Interfaces* 10, no. 4 (August 1980).

Peck, Stephen C. "Communicating Model Based Information for Energy Debates: Two Case Studies." *Interfaces* 10, no. 5 (October 1980).

Rosenkranz, Friederich. *An Introduction to Corporate Modeling.* Durham, N.C.: Duke University Press, 1979.

Schreiber, Albert, Ed. *Corporate Simulation Models.* Seattle: Graduate School of Business, University of Washington, 1970.

CHAPTER 13
Dynamic Programming

13.1 **Introduction**

13.2 **Stages and State Variables**

13.3 **The Shortest-Route Problem**

13.4 **An Investment Problem**

13.5 **A Purchasing Problem**

13.6 **A Production Planning Problem**
Stage I
Stage II

13.7 **Summary**

Glossary

Problems

References

Key Concepts
Dynamic programming
Principle of optimality
Recursive relationship
Stage
State variable

Key Applications
Pricing
Production management
Purchasing problems
Risk management
Sequential investment problems
Shortest-route problems

13.1 Introduction

Dynamic programming is a mathematical optimization technique that can be applied to decision problems of a sequential nature. The technique involves the division of a larger problem into a number of smaller problems. Each subproblem should then be solved in such a way that an overall optimal solution is obtained.

In contrast to linear programming, there is no standard form for dynamic programming models. The mathematical formulation of dynamic programs therefore will usually differ from case to case, although it is possible to classify them into prototypes in terms of computational procedure. The student may think of dynamic programming as a systematic approach to solving large and complex problems.

13.2 Stages and State Variables

The basic approach to dynamic programming problems involves the following steps:

1. We must define the *stages* of the problem. A stage may be viewed as a group of subproblems.
2. Once the problem has been divided into stages, we find optimal solutions for each subproblem within each stage. We do this for one stage after another, usually beginning at the logical end of a problem. In finding the optima for subproblems, we take the solutions of succeeding stages into account. We do this by recording the payoffs from that stage to the logical end of the problem. In solving the subproblems within a stage, we employ *state variables*. The state variables describe the condition or the states of the system within each stage.
3. When all the interrelated stages have been solved, we backtrack to find the overall optimal solution.

13.3 / The Shortest-Route Problem

We shall illustrate these steps and the application of the concepts with a simple problem involving the identification of an optimal route. This class of problems is sometimes referred to as the "shortest-route problem."

13.3 The Shortest-Route Problem

A shipping company in Milwaukee has to ship a large, dismantled generator to Brazil, where it is to be installed in the outskirts of the new capital, Brasilia. There are three possible ports where the shipment can be transferred to an ocean freighter to Brazil: Quebec (Q) (via the St. Lawrence Seaway); Baltimore (B) (via rail); and New Orleans (NO) (by inland waterways via the Mississippi River); from each of these ports there are three Brazilian ports (RJ, S, R) to which the generator can be shipped. From these ports, shipment can go to two alternative intermediate terminals by rail (T_1, T_2). The last leg to the final destination is by road. Figure 13–1 shows these various routes and their associated costs (in thousands). We are to find the routing for the shipment that will minimize total shipping costs.

The reader should note that the problem can be divided into stages (labeled I, II, III, and IV). Within each stage we have to make decisions; for example, at the origin of our shipment, labeled AOS, we must decide whether to ship to Q, B, or NO. Obviously, the decision at AOS

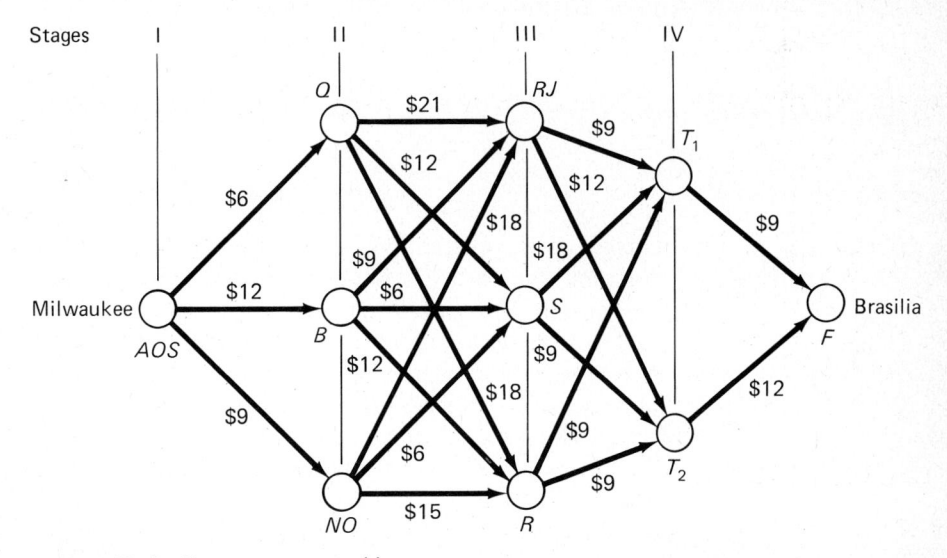

Figure 13–1. Shortest route problem.

influences the decisions at subsequent decision points; that is, we are dealing with a sequential decision problem.

We now develop a solution following the three steps outlined earlier. The stages are as follows:

I. Factory to shipping ports
II. Shipping ports to receiving ports
III. Receiving ports to rail terminals
IV. Rail terminals to destination

The state variables are the ports and terminals as labeled beside the circles. Note that for any stage and state, there is always an optimal solution (route) to the problem's logical end (destination). We start our analysis at the beginning of the final stage. At stage IV we have T_1 and T_2 as input states. Because there are no alternative routes to our destination, no decisions are necessary and we simply record the costs of the two routes.

$$\text{Stage IV} \quad T_1 \to F = \$9$$
$$T_2 \to F = \$12$$

We now move backward to the preceding stage III. For each input variable (RJ, S, and R), we examine the possible routes to F and record their total costs. (We already know the costs from T_1 and T_2 to F.)

Stage III
$$RJ \to T_1 = \text{⑱}$$
$$RJ \to T_2 = 24$$
$$S \to T_1 = 27$$
$$S \to T_2 = \text{㉑}$$
$$R \to T_1 = \text{⑱}$$
$$R \to T_2 = 21$$

Optimal routes for RJ, S, and R, respectively

The choice of an optimal route for each input variable represents the solution of a subproblem within each stage. We identify the optimal route by circling the one with the least cost. (Note that we have three subproblems, each designated by an input variable; the possible destinations are referred to as output variables.)

We now move to stage II and consider all the possible routes from shipping to receiving ocean ports.

We again have three input (Q, B, and NO) and three output state variables (RJ, S, and R). Note that in calculating the total costs to F for the various routes, we use only the optimal routes identified in our analysis of stage III.

13.3 / The Shortest-Route Problem

Stage II

input state variable   output state variable

$$Q \to RJ = 18 + 21 = 39$$
$$Q \to S = 21 + 12 = \textcircled{33}$$
$$Q \to R = 18 + 18 = 36$$
$$B \to RJ = 18 + 9 = \textcircled{27}$$
$$B \to S = 21 + 6 = \textcircled{27} \quad \text{optimal routes}$$
$$B \to R = 18 + 12 = 30$$
$$NO \to RJ = 18 + 18 = 36$$
$$NO \to S = 21 + 6 = \textcircled{27}$$
$$NO \to R = 18 + 15 = 33$$

For example, if at Quebec (Q) we ship to S from S via T_2 to the final destination, our total cost is $33,000.

Again we need to consider only the optimal routes Q, B, NO to F identified in the analysis of stage II. We now analyze stage I.

Stage I

$$AOS \to Q = 33 + 6 = 39$$
$$AOS \to B = 27 + 12 = 39$$
$$AOS \to NO = 27 + 9 = 36 \quad \text{optimal solution}$$

We can now backtrack to stages II, III, and IV to identify the overall optimal routing as

$$AOS \to NO \to S \to T_2 \to F \quad \text{at a total cost of 36.}$$

The student should note that as we established an optimal route for any state in stages III and II, we ignored alternative nonoptimal routes identified in the analysis of the subsequent stage. Although we had to analyze several paths at each stage, we did not have to consider all possible paths from the origin to the final destination. This is a definite advantage of dynamic programming.

We now state the *principle of optimality*: *An optimal policy has the property that, whatever the initial state and the initial decision, the re-*

maining decisions must constitute an optimal policy with regard to the state resulting from the first decision.[1]

Applying this to our problem, we see that our analysis gives us for each state (regardless at which stage) an optimal routing to the final destination. The optimal routing from state *AOS* (also the first stage) to *F* represents, of course, the solution for the entire problem.

13.4 An Investment Problem

Another class of problems that can be solved by the dynamic programming approach is the so-called knapsack problem. Here we are faced with the problem of the limited capacity (in terms of volume, weight, or funds) of a "knapsack," where each item that can be carried in a knapsack has a different profit (contribution) margin. The objective is to carry that combination of items that will maximize the total profit.

The problem can be formulated as follows: Let

x_n = number of items of type n to be carried
N = number of item types
v_n = profit contribution of one type n item
w_n = weight of one type n item
W = total weight or other quantitative constraints

Our objective can now be expressed as

$$\text{Maximize:} \quad \sum_{n=1}^{N} v_n x_n$$

$$\text{Subject to:} \quad \sum_{n=1}^{N} w_n x_n \leq W$$

(13–1)

The following example illustrates the use of the dynamic programming approach to a "knapsack" problem in the capital budgeting area.

Assume that a big manufacturing division of a large national corporation has been assigned $100 million for the replacement of plant and equipment. In Table 13–1 we show a summary of the investment proposals submitted by the department heads. The objective is to find that combination of the proposed investments in each department that will maximize net present value within the given budgeting constraint of $100 million.

[1]Bellman (1957), p. 83.

13.4 / An Investment Problem

TABLE 13–1. Summary of Departmental Investment Proposals*

Department	(Stage)		INVESTMENT Total (Million $)	INVESTMENT Per Unit (Million $)	NET PRESENT VALUE Total (Million $)	NET PRESENT VALUE Per Unit (Million $)
A	(I)	Replace 5 generator units at an installed cost of $20 million each	$100	$20	$54	$10.8
B	(II)	Replace 4 automatic machining units (at $25 million each)	100	25	42	10.5
C	(III)	Replace 2 assembly lines (at $40 million each)	80	40	53	26.5
D	(IV)	Install 2 new induction heating units for steel treatment (at $50 million each)	100	50	54	27.0
E	(V)	Automate 3 presently semimechanized materials-handling units (at $30 million each)	90	30	55	18.33

*These investments are divisible in terms of units, i.e., with respect to department A, we could install 1, 2, 3, 4, or 5 generators, and the net present value for each generator is one-fifth of the total.

Algebraically, we could state this as:

Max: $18.33x_5 + 27.0x_4 + 26.5x_3 + 10.5x_2 + 10.8x_1$
Subject to: $20x_1 + 25x_2 + 40x_3 + 50x_4 + 30x_5 \leq 100$

In applying the dynamic programming approach, we treat the possible investments in each department as a separate stage, where the unused budget dollars are the input states for each stage. We arbitrarily begin our analysis with department E (see Table 13–2) and label it as stage 5.

As input states we have all possible levels of funds available for department E listed under S. Output states are possible investments, that is, 0, 1, 2, or 3 materials-handling lines (labeled x_5). There is no logical end to this problem, therefore we can start with any stage. Many, if not most, dynamic problems deal with sequential interrelated problems over time, and therefore have a logical ending.

TABLE 13–2. Stage 5: Department E

$18.33 x_5$ (x_5 = NUMBER OF NEW MATERIALS-HANDLING UNITS)

S Input States (Amount Available for Investments in Department E)	Output States x_E 0	1	2	3	Max. $f_5(S)$	Optimal Decision
0	0	0	0	0	0	$x_5 = 0$
10	0	0	0	0	0	$x_5 = 0$
20	0	0	0	0	0	$x_5 = 0$
30	0	18.33	0	0	18.33	$x_5 = 1$
40	0	18.33	0	0	18.33	$x_5 = 1$
50	0	18.33	0	0	18.33	$x_5 = 1$
60	0	18.33	36.67	0	36.67	$x_5 = 2$
70	0	18.33	36.67	0	36.67	$x_5 = 2$
80	0	18.33	36.67	0	36.67	$x_5 = 2$
90	0	18.33	36.67	55	55.00	$x_5 = 3$
100	0	18.33	36.67	55	55.00	$x_5 = 3$

Note in Table 13–2 that the input states represent the unused portion of the $100 million available for the investments proposed by department E;[2] the functional relationship can be stated as

$$f_5(S) = v_5 x_5 \quad \max(18.33 x_5; \max)$$

Subject to: $30 x_5 \leq 100$ where 30 is the required investment; x_5 is the number of new materials handling lines; and v_5 is the net present value per line ($18.33)

In other words, we explore the possible investments in department E (1, 2, or 3 materials handling lines) assuming all the possible levels of funds available (from 0 to $100 million in increments of $10 million). In the last column we indicate the optimal of x_5 for each row.

We now continue our analysis at stage IV (department D), again exploring the possible investments (1 or 2 induction heating units) at the different levels of available capital funds (varying between 0 and $100 million), but now we assume that any funds available and not used by department D will, to the extent possible, be used optimally in department E.

---

[2] Output states are the possible values for x_5 (0, 1, 2, or 3).

13.4 / An Investment Problem

TABLE 13-3. Stage 4: Department D

S Input	X_4 = 0	$f_4(S) = 27x_4 + f_5(S - 50x_4)$ 1	2	Max. $f_4(S)$	Optimal Decision
0	0	0	0	0	$x_4 = 0$
10	0	0	0	0	$x_4 = 0$
20	0	0	0	0	$x_4 = 0$
30	18.33	0	0	18.33	$x_4 = 0$
40	18.33	0	0	18.33	$x_4 = 0$
50	18.33	27	0	27	$x_4 = 1$
60	36.67	27	0	36.67	$x_4 = 0$
70	36.67	27	0	36.67	$x_4 = 0$
80	36.67	45.33*	0	45.33	$x_4 = 1$
90	55.00	45.33	0	55.00	$x_4 = 0$
100	55.00	45.33	54	55.00	$x_4 = 0$

*If only one x_4 is installed (at cost of $50 million), $30 million will be left for one x_5 in department E, and the combined payoffs are 27 + 18.33 = 45.33.

The function in Table 13-3 determines the amounts in the columns under 0, 1, and 2; it should be read as follows:

$$f_4(S) = 27x_4 + f_5(S - 50x_4)$$

In words, the net present value of our function $f_4(S)$ in stage IV is determined by the number and present value of the units of x_4 *plus* the optimal net present value of funds left over for investments in stage V. The student is asked to verify carefully all the numbers in Tables 13-3 through 13-6. In making these calculations, the student should always refer to the recursive function at the top of each table.

Note in the column under zero x_4, if no investment is made in department D and $30 million or more is still available, the funds will be invested in department E (see Table 13-2 for all values in the $x_4 = 0$ column).

We can now state this *recursive relationship* for our analysis in general terms as

$$f_n(S) = \text{Max}[v_n x_n + f_{n+1}(S - w_n x_n)] \tag{13-2}$$

where n denotes the stage (1, 2, 3, 4 or 5, in our case the department); v_n is the net present value of an investment unit, and x_n is the investment unit of a given department.

Equation (13-2) states that the value of the function S at stage n is the maximum of the number of units we invest at that stage times their net present value + the optimal value of $f(S)$ at the succeeding stage $(n + 1)$ after considering the capital funds used in the current stage $(S - w_n x_n)$.

For example, see Table 13–3, where $S = 100$:

The max for $f_{(4)}S = 100$ is the maximum of:
$$x_4 = 0;\ 27(0) + 18.33(3) = 55.00$$
$$x_4 = 1;\ 27(1) + 18.33(1) = 45.33^3$$
$$x_4 = 2;\ 27(2)\ \ \ \ \ \ \ \ \ \ \ \ \ = 54$$

Table 13–4 shows the analysis of investments in Department C, Table 13–5 the analysis for Department B, and Table 13–6 the analysis for Department A.

We now backtrack through the preceding stages to find our optimal policy:

Stage 1 gives us the optimum when $x_1 = 1$; therefore, 80 million are available in stage 2. Entering stage 2 at $S = 80$, we find that $x_2 = 0$; therefore, $80 million are still left intact. Entering stage 3 at $S = 80$, we find that $x_3 = 2$; here $10 million are left, but because we have no investments for $10 million available, we have to return them to the treasurer.

TABLE 13–4. Stage 3: Department C

$$f_3(S) = 26.5x_3 + f_4(S - 40x_3)$$

S	0	1	2	Max. $f_{(3)}(S)$	Optimal Decision
0	0	0	0	0	$x_3 = 0$
10	0	0	0	0	$x_3 = 0$
20	0	0	0	0	$x_3 = 0$
30	18.33	0	0	18.33	$x_3 = 0$
40	18.33	26.5	0	26.5	$x_3 = 1$
50	27.00	26.5	0	27.0	$x_3 = 0$
60	36.67	26.5	0	36.67	$x_3 = 0$
70	36.67	44.83	0	44.83	$x_3 = 1$
80	45.53	44.83	53	53.0	$x_3 = 2$
90	55.00	53.5*	53	55.0	$x_3 = 0$
100	55.00	63.17**	53	63.17	$x_3 = 1$

*Max of 26.5(1) + 27(1)   = 53.5
      26.5(1) + 18.33(1) = 44.83
**Max of 26.5(1) + 18.33(2) = 63.17
       26.5(1) + 27(1)   = 53.5

[3] This is determined by the second part of the recursive function; we go back to stage 5 and find the optimal value when $50 million are left is 18.33.

13.4 / An Investment Problem

TABLE 13-5. Stage 2: Department B

$$f_2(S) = 10.5x_2 + f_3(S - 25x_2)$$

S	0	1	2	3	4	Max. $f_2(S)$	Optimal Decision
0	0	0	0	0	0	0	$x_2 = 0$
10	0	0	0	0	0	0	$x_2 = 0$
20	0	0	0	0	0	0	$x_2 = 0$
30	18.33	10.5	0	0	0	18.3	$x_2 = 0$
40	26.5	10.5	0	0	0	26.5	$x_2 = 0$
50	27.0	10.5	21.0	0	0	27.0	$x_2 = 0$
60	36.67	28.83	21.0	0	0	36.67	$x_2 = 1$
70	44.83	36.5	21.0	0	0	44.83	$x_2 = 0$
80	53.0	37.5*	39.33	31.5	0	53.0	$x_2 = 0$
90	55.0	47.16**	47.5	31.5	0	55.0	$x_2 = 0$
100	63.17	55.3†	48.0	31.5	42	63.17	$x_2 = 0$

$$
\begin{array}{ll}
 & \quad x_2 \quad\quad x_3 \quad\quad x_4 \quad\quad x_5 \\
\text{*Maximum of} & 10.5(1) + 26.5 \quad\quad\quad\quad\quad = 37 \\
 & 10.5 \quad\quad\quad\quad 27(1) \quad\quad\quad = 37.5 \\
 & 10.5(1) \quad\quad\quad\quad\quad 18.33(1) = 28.83 \\
\text{**Maximum of} & 10.5(1) + 26.5 \quad\quad\quad\quad\quad = 37 \\
 & 10.5(1) + \quad\quad 27(1) \quad\quad\quad = 37.5 \\
 & 10.5(1) + \quad\quad\quad\quad 18.33(2) = 47.16 \\
\text{†Maximum of} & 10.5(1) + \quad\quad\quad\quad 18.33(2) = 47.16 \\
 & 10.5(1) + 26.5(1) + \quad 18.33(1) = 55.33
\end{array}
$$

TABLE 13-6. Stage 1: Department A

$$f_1(S) = 10.8x_1 + f_2(S - 20x_1)$$

S	0	1	2	3	4	5	Max. $f_1(S)$	Optimal Decision
10	63.17	63.8*	58.27*	58.9*	43.2	54.00	63.8	$x_1 = 1$

```
*   53.00    36.67    26.5
  + 10.8     21.6     32.4
    63.8     58.27    58.9
```

Best policy: The following investments should be made:

1. Two assembly lines at a cost of $80 million and a NPV of $53.0
2. One generator unit at a cost of $10 million and a NPV of   10.8

For a total of $63.8

This problem illustrates the application of dynamic programming to a particular investment problem and the application of the general dynamic programming approach.

13.5 A Purchasing Problem

The dynamic programming examples discussed so far were of a deterministic nature. We now present a simple problem involving price as a probabilistic variable.

Assume that a buyer must have a certain quantity of raw materials available within 5 weeks. The materials can be ordered at the beginning of each week and will be delivered at the latest on Friday of the same week. The weekly price of this material is subject to the following fluctuations:

Price	Probability
$18	0.4
16	0.3
14	0.3

Each Monday the buyer must decide whether he wants to buy the commodity during the current week or postpone the purchase by one more week. Of course, on the fifth Monday he must purchase regardless of price. What would be the buyer's optimum purchasing strategy?

We can break this problem up into *five* stages. At the beginning of each of the first 4 weeks we must decide whether to purchase or to wait.

We begin our analysis with stage 5, that is, Monday of the fifth week. The decision is simple—if we have not yet purchased the raw material, we must buy it regardless of the prevailing price.

At the beginning of the fourth week, that is, stage 4, if we have not yet made the purchase, we face the following situation: The expected price on Monday of the fifth week is

$$E_5 = 0.4(18) + 0.3(16) + 0.3(14) = 16.2$$

The $16.2 are the expected price if we delay our purchase to the fifth week. At the beginning of the fourth week, we therefore make our purchase only when the price is either 14 or 16.

Now we consider the situation on the third Monday, that is, stage 3. For the fourth week we calculate the expected price as

$$E_4 = 0.4(16.2) + 0.3(16) + 0.3(14) = 15.48$$

Note that we use the expected price of the fifth period (and not $18), because that is the average price we shall experience if we wait until the fifth period. Therefore as we enter the *third week,* the buyer's decision is as follows: Buy if the price is $14, otherwise wait. On the second Monday (stage 2), we must calculate the expected value for the third week:

$$E_3 = 0.4(15.48) + 0.3(15.48) + 0.3(14) = 15.036$$

Our decision on Monday of the second week is the same as at the beginning of the third week.

On the first Monday we now get

$$E_2 = 0.4(15.036) + 0.3(15.036) + 0.3(14) = 14.7252$$

We shall therefore buy only when the price is $14. The expected price for the first Monday and therefore also the long-run average purchasing price is given by

$$E_1 = 0.7(14.7252) + 0.3(14) = 14.50764$$

If we want to follow an optimal policy, we shall buy during the first 3 weeks only when the price is $14 and buy during the fourth week only when the price is $14 or $16, and, of course, during the fifth week whatever the price.

13.6 A Production Planning Problem

The final example[4] of dynamic programming illustrates the application to a production situation. It is more complex than the preceding ones, but is ideally suited to reinforce the basic concepts illustrated with the preceding problems.

A plant has three different production processes, any of which can produce product A. Process 1 is the oldest and least efficient; processes 2 and 3 although modern, differ in efficiency over different rates of output as shown in Table 13–7. Note the different productivity of workers per week in the different processes. Thus workers employed in P_1 are always less productive than when employed in either P_2 or P_3. Thus, when $L_i = 3$, $P_1(L_1) = 15 < P_2(L_2) = 24 < P_3(L_3) = 30$. Marginally, however, $P_1(MPPL_i)$[5] is more productive than either $P_2(MPPL_2)$ or $P_3(MPPL_3)$ at some points of the production function. For example when L_i increases from 2 to 3, $MPPL_1 = 10$; when L_i increases from 5 to 6, $MPPL_2 = 4$, and $MPPL_3 = 2$. This means that although P_1 is less efficient overall, at some point it may be best to allocate a marginal unit

---

[4]This problem has been adapted from an article by Albert J. Simone, "A Dynamic Programming Approach to the Maximization of Output from Production Processes of Varying Efficiencies," in *Academy of Management Journal* (June 1967): 33–38, reprinted in Efraim Turba and N. Paul Lomba, *Readings in Management Science*, Business Publications, Inc., Dallas, Texas, 1976, pp. 183–195.

[5]$MPPL_i$ = marginal productivity per L_i.

of labor to P_1 in order to maximize output when available workers are limited.

TABLE 13–7. Production Function for Processes 1, 2, and 3

Average Number of Workers Employed per Week L_i	Process $P_1(L_1)$	OUTPUT $P_2(L_2)$	$P_3(L_3)$
1	2	4	5
2	5	12	14
3	15	24	30
4	23	44	42
5	29	54	48
6	32	58	50

Assume now that only 12 workers are available, that is, $L_T = 12$, and that we want to allocate labor to the three processes in such a way as to maximize output per week Q. We can state this as follows:

$$\text{Max:} \quad Q = P_1(L_1) + P_2(L_2) + P_3(L_3)$$
$$\text{Subject to:} \quad L_T = L_1 + L_2 + L_3 = 12 \quad (13\text{--}3)$$
$$L_1, L_2, L_3 \geq 0$$

We want to select values for L_1, L_2, and L_3 that will maximize Q. The problem could be solved by enumeration. Dynamic programming, however, provides a much more efficient and systematic computational procedure.

Again, we have to divide the problem into three separate stages, each requiring a number of decisions. The optimality principle will be applied to each stage and an optimal solution will be obtained at the final stage. We do this by first considering just one production process, say, P_1, and maximize output. Then we consider P_1 and P_2 combined, again optimizing output, and finally we combine all three processes. We have three stages denoted by n, that is, $n = 1, 2, 3$.

Within each stage we have $L_T + 1 = 13$ possible allocations (state variables) of labor L available. L is therefore an integer in the range $0 \leq L \leq L_T = 12$. $M_i L$ is the maximum output obtainable from allocating L to the first i processes (i is an integer, $1 \leq i \leq n$). In dynamic programming terms we can state[6]

---

[6]This should be read as find the maximum output of all possible allocations in process P_i and the allocations made to the preceding processes (M_{i-1}).

13.6 / A Production Planning Problem

$$M_i L = \text{Max } \{P_i L_i + M_{i-1}(L - L_i)\} \quad (13\text{--}4)$$

$0 \leq L_i \leq L$ [i.e., the allocations to a process lie within a stage range from 0 to L]

$i = 1, 2, 3, \ldots, n$ (there will be n primary allocations or stages)

$0 \leq L \leq L_T$ (L, the number of workers, varies from 0 to L_T)

STAGE I

First we allocate all L units to process 1. Table 13–8 shows the secondary allocations at $M_1(L)$. Obviously, the maximum output is 32; $M_1(L) = P_1(L)$, $0 \leq L \leq L_T = 12$.

TABLE 13–8. First-Stage Allocations

Number of Workers Available per Week L	Maximum Output Obtainable from Allocation of L to P_1 $M_1(L)$	Number of Workers Allocated to P_1 at $M(L_1)$ L_1
0	0	0
1	2	1
2	5	2
3	15	3
4	23	4
5	29	5
6	32	6
7	32	7
8	32	8
9	32	9
10	32	10
11	32	11
12	32	12

STAGE II

We can now use $M_1(L)$ to determine $M_2(L)$ as follows:

$$M_2(0) = \text{Max } \{P_2(L_2) + M_1(0 - L_2)\}$$
$$= \text{Max } \{P_2(0) + M_1(0)\} = \text{Max } \{0 + 0 + 0\} = 0$$

$M_2(0)$ means that we allocate zero workers between P_1 and P_2; maximum output is zero.

$$M_2(1) = \text{Max }\{P_2(L_2) + M_1(1 - L_2)\} = \text{Max}\begin{Bmatrix} P_2(0) + M_1(1) \\ P_2(1) + M_1(0) \end{Bmatrix}$$

$$= \text{Max}\begin{Bmatrix} 0 + 2 = 2 \\ 4 + 0 = 4 \end{Bmatrix} = 4$$

$M_2(1)$ means that we allocate one worker between P_1 and P_2; maximum output is 4.

$$M_2(2) = \text{Max}\{P_2(L_2) + M_1(2 - L_2)\} = \text{Max}\begin{Bmatrix} P_2(0) + M_1(2) \\ P_2(1) + M_1(1) \\ P_2(2) + M_1(0) \end{Bmatrix}$$

$$= \text{Max}\begin{Bmatrix} 0 + 5 \\ 4 + 2 \\ 12 + 0 \end{Bmatrix} = 12$$

$M_2(2)$ means that we allocate three workers between P_1 and P_2. Enumerating all possible allocations, we find a maximum output of 12, so we now proceed to allocate 3, 4, 5, . . ., 12 workers between the two processes, establishing the maximum output for each level of labor.

$$M_2(3) = \text{Max}\{P_2(L_2) + M_1(3 - L_2)\} = \text{Max}\begin{matrix} P_2(0) + M_1(3) \\ P_2(1) + M_1(2) \\ P_2(2) + M_1(1) \\ P_2(3) + M_1(0) \end{matrix}$$

$$= \text{Max}\begin{matrix} 0 + 15 = 15 \\ 4 + 5 = 9 \\ 12 + 2 = 14 \\ 24 + 0 = 24 \end{matrix} = 24$$

$$M_2(4) = \text{Max}\{P_2(L_2) + M_1(4 - L_2)\} = \text{Max}\begin{matrix} P_2(0) + M_1(4) \\ P_2(1) + M_1(3) \\ P_2(2) + M_1(2) \\ P_2(3) + M_1(1) \\ P_2(4) + M_1(0) \end{matrix}$$

$$= \text{Max}\begin{matrix} 0 + 23 = 23 \\ 4 + 15 = 19 \\ 5 + 12 = 17 \\ 24 + 2 = 26 \\ 44 + 0 = 44 \end{matrix} = 44$$

We shall skip the second-stage allocations from $M_2(5)$ to $M_2(10)$ and show $M_2(11)$.

13.6 / A Production Planning Problem

$$M_2(11) = \text{Max } \{P_2(L_2) + M_1(11 - L_2)\}$$

$$= \text{Max} \begin{vmatrix} P_2(0) + M_1(11) \\ P_2(1) + M_1(10) \\ P_2(2) + M_1(9) \\ P_2(3) + M_1(8) \\ P_2(4) + M_1(7) \\ P_2(5) + M_1(6) \\ P_2(6) + M_1(5) \\ P_2(7) + M_1(4) \\ P_2(8) + M_1(3) \\ P_2(9) + M_1(2) \\ P_2(10) + M_1(1) \\ P_2(11) + M_1(0) \end{vmatrix} = \text{Max} \begin{vmatrix} 0 + 32 = 32 \\ 4 + 32 = 36 \\ 12 + 32 = 44 \\ 24 + 32 = 56 \\ 44 + 32 = 76 \\ 54 + 32 = 86 \\ 58 + 29 = 87 \\ 58 + 23 = 81 \\ 58 + 15 = 73 \\ 58 + 5 = 63 \\ 58 + 2 = 60 \\ 58 + 0 = 58 \end{vmatrix} = 87$$

Note again that we enumerate all possible allocations of 11 workers between P_1 and P_2. In Problem 3 the student is asked to make the computations for the second-stage allocation of 12 workers. The maximum values obtainable from all second-stage allocations of L to P_1 and P_2 are given in Table 13–9.

TABLE 13–9. Second-Stage Allocations

Number of Workers Available per Week L	Maximum Output Obtainable from Allocation of L to P_1 and P_2	Number of Workers Allocated per Week to Process 2 at $M_2(L)$
0	0	0
1	4	1
2	12	2
3	24	3
4	44	4
5	54	5
6	58	6
7	60	6
8	69	5
9	77	5
10	83	5
11	87	6
$L_T = 12$	90	6

$M_2(L)$ is now used to determine $M_3(L)$ as follows [We shall show only $M_3(5)$ and $M_3(7)$; the allocations for $M_3(4)$ and $M_3(12)$ are given as problems at the end of the chapter.]

$$M_3(5) = \text{Max}\{P_3(L_3) + M_2(5 - L_3)\}$$

$$= \text{Max} \begin{vmatrix} P_3(0) + M_2(5) \\ P_3(1) + M_2(4) \\ P_3(2) + M_2(3) \\ P_3(3) + M_2(2) \\ P_3(4) + M_2(1) \\ P_3(5) + M_2(0) \end{vmatrix} = \text{Max} \begin{vmatrix} 0 + 54 = 54 \\ 5 + 44 = 49 \\ 14 + 24 = 38 \\ 30 + 12 = 42 \\ 42 + 4 = 46 \\ 48 + 0 = 48 \end{vmatrix} = 54$$

Note that we refer back to Table 13–9 to obtain the output figures for $M_2(5 - L_3)$; for example, $M_2(5) = 54$; $M_2(3) = 24$, and so on. This process is repeated for $M_3(7)$ below. The reader should be sure to verify all calculations.

$$M_3(7) = \text{Max} \begin{vmatrix} P_3(0) + M_2(7) \\ P_3(1) + M_2(6) \\ P_3(2) + M_2(5) \\ P_3(3) + M_2(4) \\ P_3(4) + M_2(3) \\ P_3(5) + M_2(2) \\ P_3(6) + M_2(1) \\ P_3(7) + M_2(0) \end{vmatrix} = \text{Max} \begin{vmatrix} 0 + 60 = 60 \\ 5 + 58 = 63 \\ 14 + 54 = 68 \\ 30 + 44 = 74 \\ 42 + 24 = 66 \\ 48 + 12 = 60 \\ 50 + 4 = 54 \\ 50 + 0 = 50 \end{vmatrix} = 74$$

The calculations for $M_3(L)$ are summarized in Table 13–10. This table shows that 111 units is the maximum output available with 12 workers per week. The allocation of workers to P_1, P_2, and P_3 can be determined by examining Tables 13–8, 13–9, and 13–10.

TABLE 13–10. Third-Stage Allocations

Number of Workers Available per Week L	Maximum Output Obtainable from Allocation of L to P_1, P_2, and P_3.	Number of Workers Allocated per Week to Process 3 at M_3L
0	0	0
1	5	1
2	14	2
3	30	3
4	42	0
5	54	0
6	59	1
7	74	3
8	86	4
9	96	4
10	102	5
11	106	5
$L_T = 12$	111	4

Table 13–10 shows that for the output of 111 units, four workers are assigned to P_3. Because four workers are assigned to P_3, eight workers (12 − 4) must be assigned to P_1 and P_2. In Table 13–9 we can readily find how eight workers allocated optimally to P_1 and P_2; five will work in P_2 and three will be assigned to P_1. Therefore we have $L_1 = 3$, $L_2 = 5$, and $L_3 = 4$. This is summarized in Table 13–11.

TABLE 13–11. Optimal Assignment of 12 Workers and Optimal Output of P_1, P_2, and P_3 per Week

Process	Number of Workers	Output
P_1	3	15
P_2	5	54
P_3	4	42
		111

13.7 Summary

Dynamic programming is used to model decision systems where the decision process is sequential. Many of these problems are of a multiperiod nature, such as our purchasing problem. The basic objective of dynamic programming is to develop an *optimal policy* that will tell the decision maker, given the condition of and the stage within the system, what action to take. There is no standardized mathematical format for dynamic programming. The developing of a model requires breaking down the model into *stages* and finding optimal solutions for each stage, usually beginning at the logical end of the problem. When all stages have been solved, we find an overall optimal solution. Four illustrative problems were presented to introduce the basic concepts and their application.

Glossary

Dynamic programming. A mathematical technique for solving certain kinds of sequential decision problems. It can be applied to large problems that can be decomposed into a sequence of smaller problems (stages), which are usually easier to solve. Frequently the sequence of decisions occurs over time, hence dynamic programming. Because the procedure requires that one work backward from the logical end of the problem to its beginning, it may also be called recursive programming.

Principle of optimality. An optimal policy that has the property that, whatever the initial state and initial decisions, the remaining decisions must constitute all optimal policy with regard to the state resulting from the first decision.

Recursive relationship. A mathematical expression defining the optimal solution at a given stage.

Stage. A sequential arrangement of subproblems of the overall problem requiring separate decisions.

State variable. A variable whose value completely defines the state or condition of a process or a system.

Problems

1. A company wants to develop a pricing strategy problem for a new product for the next 5 yr. On the basis of a market survey that included a careful analysis of pricing patterns for competitive products, it is decided that the price could vary between $18 and $27 per unit, but should never be changed by more than $3 from one year to the next. Under these assumptions, the following table of *estimated contribution margins* has been prepared for the next 5 yr:

Price/Year	\multicolumn{5}{c}{CONTRIBUTION MARGIN IN 000s}
	1	2	3	4	5
18	51	15	24	30	48
21	42	24	48	12	24
24	33	21	54	42	18
27	51	45	15	36	21

REQUIRED

Using dynamic programming, develop an optimal pricing strategy.

2. Figure 13-2 shows a map of the United States with different possible stagecoach routes available for travel from the New York City to San Francisco. The square boxes and the letters above them represent necessary rest stops along the way. You may refer to them as *states* at which a traveler may find himself. Note that at each state (except L and M), a traveler has various routes from which to choose. The rest stops have been arranged in such a way that, regardless of the route chosen, only four stops are necessary in order to reach San Francisco. The arrows represent the available routes, and the numbers above the arrows the cost of travel between the different states. The remaining numbers designate the five *stages* into which we divide the problem.

Problems

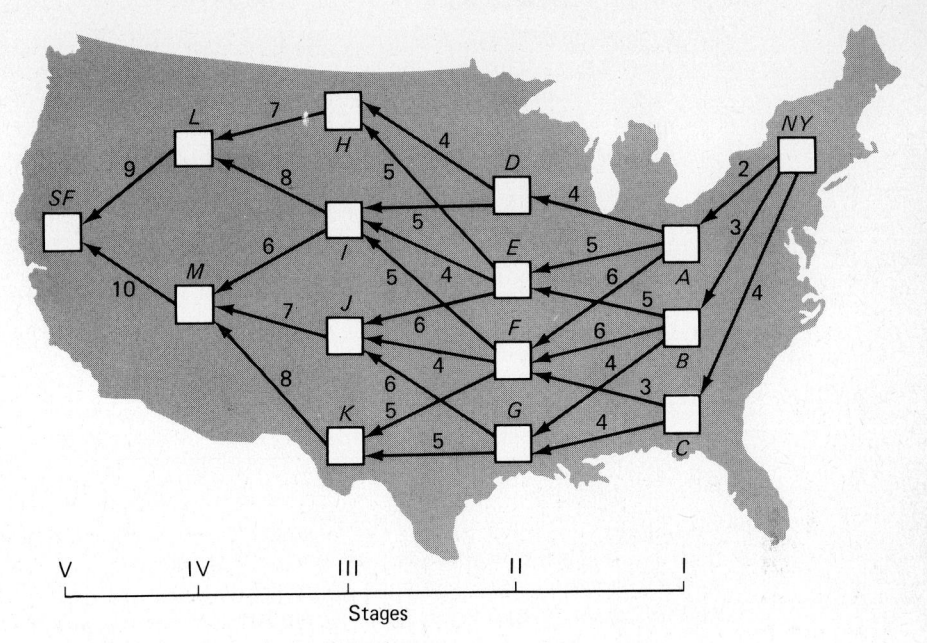

Figure 13-2. Stagecoach routing problem.

REQUIRED

Using dynamic programming, find the least-cost route from New York to San Francisco. Hint: You may find it helpful to do your analysis of the various stages using the format outlined below where each cell is $C_{si} + f_5(S)$.

Input States S	Output States j L	M	Least Cost to SF	Optimal Decision	
H	16		16	to L	
I	17	16	16	to M	
J		17	17	to M	
K		18	18	to M	etc.

3. **a.** Calculate the optimal second-stage allocation for 12 workers $[M_2(12)]$ in the labor-allocation problem of the text.
   b. Calculate the third-stage optimal allocation for 4 $\{[M_3(4)]\}$ and 12 workers $\{[M_3(12)]\}$.
4. You are a student, notoriously short of cash, but with a strong urge to spend a summer in Europe. Through fellow students who were there last year, you learn that certain American-made items can be sold readily in

Europe at a fairly good profit without violating any laws (given that you don't take too many). Below is a list of such items, including their weight and the potential profit (from fairly accurate estimates by friends who have done this before). The estimated maximum weight available for all items you can take is 20 lb.

		Profit per Unit
a. U.S.-made blue jeans (top-quality brand)	2 lb	$ 50
b. MBA calculator (Texas Instruments)	1 lb	22
c. Guitar	5 lb	135
d. Transistor radio	3 lb	82
e. Tennis racket (including metal press)	4 lb	106

REQUIRED

This is the classical knapsack problem. You are to find the optimal combination of items to take using a dynamic programming approach. (*Hint:* Use the format and approach of the second problem in the text.)

5. A large European electronics manufacturer is developing a revolutionary small computer. They feel confident that if the project is successfully completed on time, there will be a good chance to get a slice of an extremely profitable market. Presently, three teams of top researchers are working *independently* on the development of an extremely critical assembly. Management assesses the probability of failure for each team of scientists as follows:

	P(failure)
Team A	0.4
Team B	0.6
Team C	0.8

The probability that all three will fail is therefore 0.4 × 0.6 × 0.8 = 0.192. Management considers this too risky, and will assign two top specialists in the area to one of the teams. After careful analysis, they have developed the following revised failure probabilities:

Assign New Specialists	P(team failure)		
	A	B	C
0	0.4	0.6	0.8
1	0.2	0.40	0.50
2	0.15	0.20	0.30

Problems

REQUIRED

Use a dynamic programming approach to find that assignment of the two specialists that will minimize the probability of failure.

6. The Cryogenic Technology Company (CTC) manufactures highly sophisticated electrical components that must be made under extremely low temperatures. To produce such temperatures, CTC requires a large number of cannisters of liquid nitrogen. The requirements for these cannisters, the associated costs of obtaining the cannisters, and the costs of storing excess cannisters are shown below.

Month	Number of Cannisters Required	Cost per Cannister Purchased at Start of Month	Storage Costs for Excess Cannisters Purchased but Not Required During the Month (per Cannister)
1	150	100	60
2	200	150	50
3	100	160	40

At the start of any month, management can either purchase enough cannisters for the current month only, or purchase exactly enough for all months to the end of month 3. CTC has zero cannisters on hand at the start of month 1. Use dynamic programming to determine the number of cannisters to be purchased at the start of each month to minimize total costs.

7. Referring to the previous problem of purchasing cannisters of liquid nitrogen, assume that you now know that the purchase price is going to explode in month 3 to $300 per unit. You wonder if you should stockpile the cannisters early on. Use dynamic programming to determine how many cannisters should be purchased at the start of each month to minimize total costs.

8. A large construction firm has won a bid on a 40-story building for the city government. They have received a partial payment of $5 million to begin initial construction. Because of torrential rains and subsequent flooding of the site, construction cannot begin for 2 months. The financial officer of the firm cannot let the $5 million sit idle for this time, and is therefore investigating several short-term investment possibilities. At the end of 2 months, however, all the $5 million must be available. The following investments are available:

Investment*	When Investment Can Be Made*	Amount That Can Be Invested	Months to Maturity	Interest Rate
I(1)	Start of month 1	$3 million	1*	4
I(2)	Start of month 1	$5 million	2	2**
I(3)	Start of month 1	$2 million	1	1
I(4)	Start of month 2	(Any amount available)	1	3

*Any principal plus interest earned in month 1 can be reinvested in month 2.
**Compounded monthly.

Use dynamic programming to determine a cash-management program for the construction firm that maximizes the interest earned on the short-term investments.

9. In the previous cash-management problem, assume that a fifth investment opportunity has become available for month 1: $4 million at 2.5 percent interest, maturing in 2 months, but it is *not* compounded at the end of the first month. Use dynamic programming to determine if the financial officer should invest in this opportunity.

10. Commercial Satellite Corporation designs and launches satellites for world communications. A current design calls for three components to be placed in series; that is, all three components must work for the satellite to operate. In general, more reliable—a higher probability of proper operation—components cost more. The following table lists three components of receiver, transmitter, and emitter with their reliability and cost functions:

Receiver		Transmitter		Emitter	
r_1	c_1	r_2	c_2	r_3	c_3
0.9	3	0.99	4	0.95	3
0.8	2	0.92	3	0.9	2
		0.8	2		

The corporation has a budget of 8 and wants to maximize the reliability of satellite design. Find the optimal design and state the reliability cost of each component.

Hint: You will want to maximize the system reliability $R = r_1 \cdot r_2 \cdot r_3$.

11. Solve problem 10 for:
   a. A total budget of 9
   b. A total budget of 7

12. For the situation described in Problem 10, Commercial Satellite has found an alternative transmitter design. It is a redundancy design where only one unit must work for successful operation. A transmitter has a reliability of 0.8. At a cost of 1 make up a table of $r_2 \cdot c_2$ for $c_2 = 1, 2, 3, 4$. Then, using this new transmitter design, find the optimal satellite design. Compare this solution with the solution for Problem 10.

Hint: The reliability of a single transmitter unit is 0.8. For a two-unit transmitter the reliability is $1 - (1 - 0.8)^2 = 0.96$, and so on.

13. The General Landing Company designs landing gear for returning space vehicles. The landing gear requires all four independent subsystems work for a successful landing. They are: (1) landing gear, (2) braking subsystem, (3) parachute retarder, and (4) cross-wind stabilizer. General wants to build a system where the probability of a successful landing, that is, system reliability, is maximized. The contract has a budget of 10. Each subsystem has a reliability, cost function as given on page 445.

Landing Gear		Braking Subsystem		Parachute Retarder		Cross-wind Stabilizer	
r_1	c_1	r_2	c_2	r_3	c_3	r_4	c_4
0.9	3	0.95	3	0.99	4	0.95	6
0.8	2	0.9	2	0.90	3	0.94	3
0.7	1	0.85	1	0.85	2	0.93	2

REQUIRED
Use dynamic programming to determine the design that maximizes reliability.

References

Bellman, Richard. *Dynamic Programming*. Princeton, N.J.: Princeton University Press, 1957.

Burton, R. M., and Howard, G. T. "Optimal System Reliability for a Mixed Series and Parallel Structure." *Journal of Mathematical Analysis and Applications* 28, no. 2 (November 1969): 370–382.

Hadley, G. *NonLinear and Dynamic Programming*. Reading, Mass.: Addison-Wesley, 1964.

Nemhauser, George L. *Introduction to Dynamic Programming*. New York: Wiley, 1966.

Wagner, Harvey M. *Principles of Operations Research: With Applications to Managerial Decisions*. Englewood Cliffs, N.J.: Prentice-Hall, 1969.

CHAPTER 14
Queuing Theory

14.1 **Introduction**

14.2 **Waiting-Line Systems**
The Population
The Waiting Line
The Service Facility
Served Units
Steady-State Versus Transient-Stage Operating Characteristics
Definitions and Notations of Operating Characteristics

14.3 **The Single-Channel Model**

14.4 **Multiple-Channel Waiting Lines**

14.5 **Other Queuing Models**

14.6 **Summary**

Glossary

Problems

References

Appendix
The Poisson Process and Distribution; The Exponential Distribution

Key Concepts
Arrival rate
Exponential probability distribution
Operating characteristics
Poisson probability distribution
Population to be served

Queue discipline
Queuing theory
Service rate
Steady-state
Transient stage

Key Applications
Bank teller's counters
Doctor's office
Loading docks
Port facilities

Restaurants
Supermarket checkout counters
Toll roads
Tool cribs

14.1 Introduction

Waiting lines or *queues* are frequent occurrences in today's societies. Students have to stand in line during registration, to get tickets for a concert or a movie; housewives stand in line at supermarket checkout counters. Traveling salespeople have to line up with their cars when getting on or off toll roads; even top executives occasionally have to wait in line when registering in hotels or checking in for business trips at airline counters.

Waiting in line is an unpleasant experience for those in the line. Understandably, people feel that they are wasting their time because everybody can think of better things to do. Waiting lines are also undesirable for most businesses that render a service or offer goods for sale. Excessive waiting lines may produce disgruntled customers and eventually lead to loss of customers.

Waiting could, of course, be eliminated or reduced considerably by increasing the capacity of the service-rendering units. In a supermarket we could install additional checkout counters and staff them with additional clerks. Additional staff could be hired to run reception desks in hotels and at airports. Whenever we increase our service-rendering capacity, however, we necessarily incur additional costs. Unfortunately, the added capacity will not only reduce waiting lines but will frequently be idle. Thus there is a need to balance the benefits of better service against the additional costs involved. In this chapter we introduce "queuing theory," which is concerned with the study of waiting lines or queues.

Queuing theory is concerned with the mathematical analysis of *queuing* or *waiting-line systems*. The analysis of waiting lines with the aid of queuing models is not an optimization technique. Its objective is to describe important operating characteristics of queuing systems. Examples of some operating characteristics of the system are the average number of units in the waiting line (e.g., customers waiting to be served, cars waiting at toll booths), the average waiting time, and the

14.2 / Waiting-Line Systems

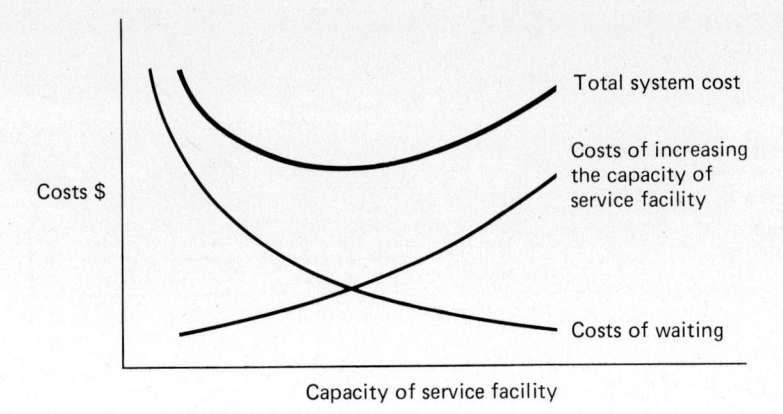

Figure 14–1. Costs of a waiting-line system.

percentage of idle time for the service facility. These operating characteristics that *describe* how the system works are the outputs of mathematical queuing models.

These outputs, once obtained, are then used by management to analyze the costs associated with the operation of the system with a view of finding an optimal or at least a satisfactory solution. These costs can be broken down into costs associated with the time units spent waiting in line and the costs associated with increasing the capacity of the service facility (see Figure 14–1). The costs of waiting decreases as we increase the capacity of the service facility, but there are also increased costs associated with that increased capacity. Given an arrival rate of units demanding service and the costs of waiting, management would increase the capacity of the service facility to the point where the total system costs is minimized.

14.2 Waiting-Line Systems

A simple waiting-line system can be broken down into four parts:

I. The population to be served (also referred to as calling population or input source)
II. The waiting line
III. The service facility
IV. The units served

Figure 14–2 illustrates these four parts. Each of them is discussed in the following section.

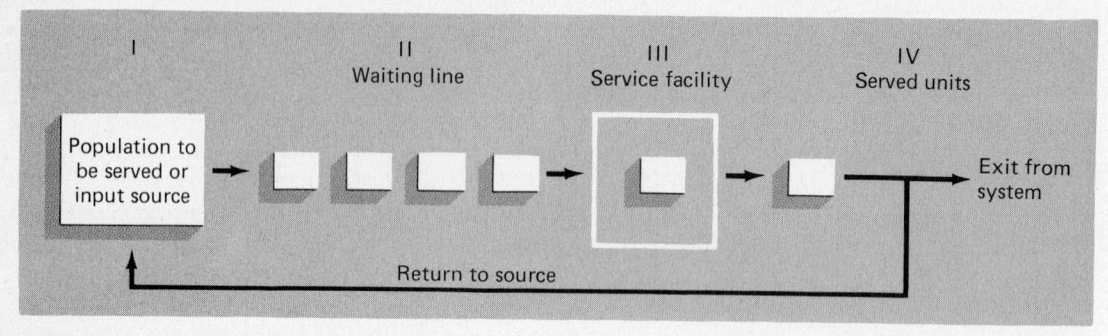

Figure 14-2. A simple waiting-line system.

THE POPULATION

The population to be served or input source may consist, for example, of all potential customers of a supermarket, cars on a toll road, or the number of computers to be serviced by a maintenance crew. Three properties of the input source must be considered, however, before the selection of an appropriate queuing model can be considered.

The Size of the Population. The primary distinction here is between finite and infinite population or sources. When the number of potential clients for the service is definitely limited, we deal with a finite population or source. For example, assume that the repair and maintenance department of the public bus system in a small town is responsible for a fleet of 10 buses. The 10 buses constitute a finite population. The number of potential customers of a supermarket in a large city, on the other hand, is considered an infinite population.

The key criterion for distinguishing between finite and infinite populations is whether the probability of an arrival changes when a unit is being serviced. Suppose that the population to be served by a repair center consists of 10 buses. When 1 unit is in the service center, the population to be served is significantly reduced, thus reducing the probability for the arrival of another unit. On the other hand, if one customer enters a supermarket in a city of 500,000 people, the effect on the probability of another arrival is insignificant.

Arrival Pattern. Units to be served may arrive according to a predetermined schedule, for example, by appointment. Or they may arrive randomly. If they arrive randomly, the probability distribution of the times between arrivals must be determined. If these interarrival times can be represented realistically by a theoretical probability distribution, the use of mathematical queuing models is possible. In our introduction to queuing theory, we limit ourselves to situations where interarrival times can be represented by the exponential probability distribution. Mathematically, it can be shown that when interarrival times are distributed exponentially, the arrivals will follow the Poisson process (to be discussed in a subsequent section of this chapter).

In-Line Behavior. Units arriving and entering the waiting-line system may be willing to wait, regardless of the length of the line, or may leave the system when the line is too long. In this chapter we assume that arriving units will remain in the system regardless of queue length.

THE WAITING LINE

The length of the waiting line depends not only on the behavior of arriving units, but possibly on physical constraints (storage space, room for waiting customers, etc.). When a waiting line has reached the physical limit of its capacity, arriving units cannot enter the system. In our introduction to queuing, we assume that no such limitations of queue length exist.

THE SERVICE FACILITY

The following characteristics of the service facility are important.

1. Structure of the service facility. A service facility may be single channel or multichannel. The seven checkout counters of a supermarket represent a multichannel service facility. If there was only one checkout counter, it would be a single-channel facility.

    Services rendered to arriving units may be performed in one or more stages. The stall of an automatic car washing facility would be a single-stage service facility. If there is another stall in which washed cars are waxed, we would have a two-stage-service facility. Note that we now have the possibility of two waiting lines, one before the car wash (stage 1) and the other before the waxing stall (stage 2). In our introduction we discuss only single-stage waiting-line systems.
2. Duration of service. The time required to perform the service may be constant or variable, that is, subject to fluctuations. If the service times constitute random variables, it may be possible to represent them by a theoretical probability distribution. We limit our discussion to those situations where service times can be realistically represented by the exponential probability distribution.
3. Queue discipline. Another important characteristic of the service facility concerns the order in which arriving units are being serviced. In many waiting-line systems, arrivals are served on a first-come, first-served (FCFS) basis. Other queuing disciplines provide a random selection for service from the units in the waiting line. In some systems, certain arriving units are given preferential treat-

ment; for example, in first aid centers, serious cases will be treated immediately regardless of the number of less serious cases that are already waiting for service. In general terms, we speak of ranking arrivals by priorities.

SERVED UNITS

Served units that originate from a finite population to be served will, in most cases, again become a part of that population. Such waiting-line systems are sometimes referred to as closed systems. In many systems with infinite populations, the units served will leave the system (e.g., cars exiting a toll road). These are referred to as open systems. Large systems can safely be considered as open systems, even though served units may rejoin the population to be served.

The parts of a waiting system and their important characteristics are summarized in Table 14–1.

TABLE 14–1. Characteristics of Queuing Systems

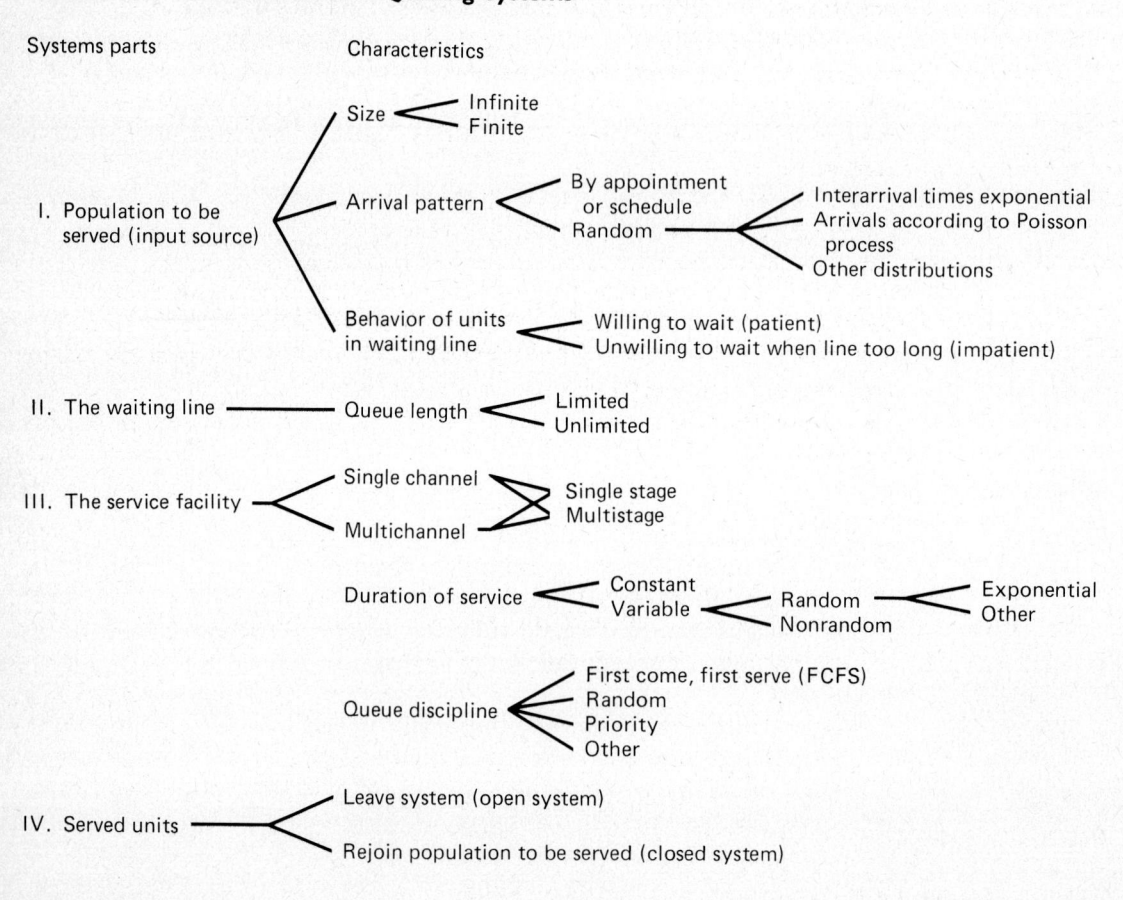

Systems parts — Characteristics

I. Population to be served (input source)
- Size: Infinite / Finite
- Arrival pattern:
  - By appointment or schedule
  - Random: Interarrival times exponential / Arrivals according to Poisson process / Other distributions
- Behavior of units in waiting line:
  - Willing to wait (patient)
  - Unwilling to wait when line too long (impatient)

II. The waiting line — Queue length: Limited / Unlimited

III. The service facility
- Single channel / Multichannel
- Single stage / Multistage
- Duration of service: Constant / Variable — Random (Exponential / Other) / Nonrandom
- Queue discipline: First come, first serve (FCFS) / Random / Priority / Other

IV. Served units
- Leave system (open system)
- Rejoin population to be served (closed system)

14.2 / Waiting-Line Systems

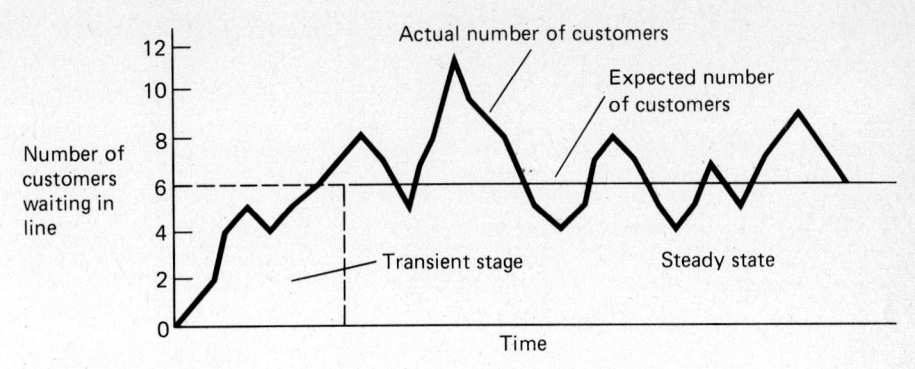

Figure 14–3. Number of customers in the waiting line.

STEADY-STATE VERSUS TRANSIENT-STAGE OPERATING CHARACTERISTICS

Most of the models used for the analysis of waiting lines assume that the operation of the system has already reached its so-called *steady state*. The operating characteristics mentioned earlier, such as average number of units waiting for service, the expected number of units in the system, and the average waiting time, represent the system's behavior only after the system has been operating for a certain time. Usually, at the start of its operation a queuing system goes through what is called a *transient stage*. During this transient stage, the operating characteristics do not reflect the long-term expected values. For example, when the drive-in teller of a bank opens for business at 9:00 A.M., there may be no waiting line, and therefore no customers will be in the system. As time elapses, customers begin to arrive, and eventually the system will reach its steady state. During the transient stage the system's operating characteristics change with the time elapsed. During the steady state they are independent of the time elapsed (see Figure 14–3).

DEFINITIONS AND NOTATIONS OF OPERATING CHARACTERISTICS

In the following we define the most important operating characteristics used in the analysis of waiting lines and introduce the notation used in the discussion of the models in this chapter.

OPERATING CHARACTERISTICS	NOTATIONS
The expected or average number of units in the system. This includes the number of units in the waiting line plus the number of units being serviced.	$E(n)$

The expected or average number of units in the waiting line or queue.	$E(nq)$
The expected or average time a unit spends in the system (waiting time plus service time).	$E(w)$
The expected or average time a unit spends waiting in line.	$E(wq)$
The average arrival rate per unit of time (lambda).	λ
The average service rate per unit of time (mu).	μ
The probability of having n units in the system.	P_n
The service utilization factor, that is, the proportion of time the service facility is expected to be busy (equals λ/μ)	p

The models in the following section are presented by using an example that may represent a real-world problem. The mathematics involved in deriving queuing models is unnecessarily rigorous for our purposes. Emphasis is placed on the assumptions of the models, on obtaining the data necessary for using the model, and on the use of the results for decision-making purposes.

14.3 The Single-Channel Model

We begin our introduction of the "basic" queuing model with a simple example of a single-channel model. The problem: A regional automotive parts distribution center belonging to the ABC chain has only one dock available for company trucks arriving with shipments from a central warehouse (see Figure 14–2). One man who operates a forklift truck has been hired full-time to unload trucks and place shipments in the warehouse. Recently there have been complaints from the company's truck dispatcher. Some of the trucks had been considerably delayed because they had to wait to be unloaded at the parts distribution center. Hiring an additional man and leasing a second forklift truck would probably reduce truck waiting time considerably. On the other hand, it was also obvious that both men would often be idle when there was no truck to be unloaded. The question is whether ABC should lease another forklift truck and hire a second man.

The problem described is a straightforward case of a single-chan-

14.3 / The Single-Channel Model

nel, single-stage, waiting-line system. Before we can analyze the characteristics of the system, we must know more about the distribution of the arrival times of the trucks and the unloading (service) time. The single-channel model we are about to introduce requires that interarrival times of the trucks be exponentially distributed so that arrivals will follow the Poisson distribution. To make sure that interarrival times and unloading times can be realistically represented be the exponential probability distribution, we would have to collect a sufficient number of actual arrival and unloading times and perform appropriate statistical tests. For our example we assume that the following assumptions are justified:

1. Trucks will be unloaded on a first-come, first-served basis (FCFS).
2. We assume that arrivals are independent of each other, follow the Poisson distribution, and that the average arrival rate is constant.
3. Unloading times are also independent, and the exponential probability distribution can be used to describe their distribution.

The *Poisson probability distribution* is as follows (see the appendix of this chapter for a more detailed discussion):

$$P(X = x) = \frac{\lambda^x e^{-\lambda}}{x!} \qquad (x = 0, 1, 2, \ldots) \qquad (14\text{--}1)$$

where X is the number of arrivals during the specified time interval; λ is the average number of arrivals during the same period of time; $e = 2.71828$, and x is a random variable.

We now comment on the second and third assumptions. Concerning the arrival rate, we find out that 32 trucks must be unloaded during every 8-hr working day; thus the average number of trucks arriving in an hour is four ($x = 4$). We use the Poisson distribution to calculate the probabilities for the arrival of varying numbers of trucks per hour.

In Table 14–2 we obtain the probabilities for the arrivals of 0, 1, 2, 3, 4, and 5 trucks as follows during the same time period, given that the average x is 4. (The necessary calculations can be verified on any hand calculator with scientific functions.) This analysis shows that, on the average, approximately 62.3 percent of the time no more than 4 trucks will arrive per hour. There is only a very small probability of 0.0183 that no trucks will arrive during any given hour. We can also see that the probability of more than 5 trucks arriving is about 0.21.

We now continue our analysis by calculating probabilities for service times, that is, the time it takes to unload the trucks. Because the trucks are loaded with varying quantities and kinds of parts, the unloading times vary. As mentioned, we assume that the exponential probability distribution provides us with a good description of the real-

TABLE 14–2. Truck Arrival Probabilities with Poisson Distribution

		Cumulative "Equal to or Less Than" Probabilities
$P(X = 0) = \dfrac{4^0 e^{-4}}{0!}$	$= 0.0183$	0.0183
$P(X = 1) = \dfrac{4^1 e^{-4}}{1!}$	$= 0.0733$	0.0916
$P(X = 2) = \dfrac{4^2 e^{-4}}{2!}$	$= 0.1465$	0.2381
$P(X = 3) = \dfrac{4^3 e^{-4}}{3!}$	$= 0.1954$	0.4335
$P(X = 4) = \dfrac{4^4 e^{-4}}{4!}$	$= 0.1954$	0.6289
$P(X = 5) = \dfrac{4^5 e^{-4}}{5!}$	$= 0.1563$	0.7852

world distribution of unloading times. The *exponential distribution* is (again, see the appendix to this chapter for a discussion)

$$f(t) = \mu e^{-\mu t} \qquad (t \geq 0) \tag{14–2}$$

where $f(t)$ is the service time, μ is the average number of units handled during a specified time interval, also called the mean service rate, and t is the random variable.

Let us assume that we studied the present one-man unloading operation over a long period of time. Taking the different composition of truck loads into account, we estimate that an average of 5 trucks can be unloaded during 1 hr ($\mu = 5$). We now define T as service time and note the probability of completing the unloading of a truck within a specified period of time as[1]

$$P(T \leq t) = 1 - e^{-\mu t} \tag{14–3}$$

In Table 14–3 we calculate these probabilities for some arbitrarily selected time intervals. Assuming that the exponential probability distribution is a realistic description of unloading times, we see that it almost always takes less than 1 hr ($t \leq 1$), about 92 percent of the time less than $\frac{1}{2}$ hr. ($t \leq 0.5$), 71 percent of the time less than 15 min ($t = 0.25$), and so on.

We now calculate the operating characteristics of the waiting-line system. These operating characteristics include:

---

[1] $\displaystyle\int_t^\infty \mu e^{-\mu t}\, dt = -e^{-\mu t}\Big|_t^\infty = 0 + e^{-\mu t} = P(T > t)$, therefore, $P(T \leq t) = 1 - e^{-\mu t}$.

TABLE 14–3. Service Time Calculations

$$P(T \le 1) = 1 - e^{-5(1)} = 1 - 0.00674 = 0.99326$$
$$(T \le 0.75) = 1 - e^{-5(0.75)} = 1 - 0.02352 = 0.97646$$
$$(T \le 0.5) = 1 - e^{-5(0.5)} = 1 - 0.08209 = 0.91791$$
$$(T \le 0.25) = 1 - e^{-5(0.25)} = 1 - 0.28651 = 0.71349$$
$$(T \le 0.20) = 1 - e^{-5(0.20)} = 1 - 0.36788 = 0.63212$$
$$(T \le 0.10) = 1 - e^{-5(0.10)} = 1 - 0.60653 = 0.39347$$
$$(T \le 0.05) = 1 - e^{-5(0.05)} = 1 - 0.77880 = 0.2212$$

1. The expected number of trucks in the system, that is, either being serviced or waiting in the queue, denoted by the symbol $E(n)$
2. The expected number of trucks in the queue, denoted by $E(nq)$
3. The probability of having n units in the system, P_n
4. The waiting time w, that is, the time an arriving truck must wait in line and in service $E(w)$

Using our assumptions of Poisson arrivals and exponention service times, the following relationships hold:

$$P_0 = 1 - \frac{\lambda}{\mu} \tag{14-4}$$

where P_0 is the probability of having zero trucks in the system, that is, the expected idle time percentage of the system. Therefore, $1 - P_0$ is the expected percent of time the system is occupied; λ/μ is often called the service utilization factor p. The average service rate μ must exceed the average *arrival rate* λ; otherwise the queue would increase without limit.

$$P_n = \left(\frac{\lambda}{\mu}\right)^n P_0 = \left(\frac{\lambda}{\mu}\right)^n \left(1 - \frac{\lambda}{\mu}\right) \tag{14-5}$$

where P_n is the probability of n trucks in the system.

$$E(n) = \frac{\lambda}{\mu - \lambda} \tag{14-6}$$

where $E(n)$ is the expected or average number of trucks in the system.

$$E(w) = \frac{1}{\mu - \lambda} \tag{14-7}$$

where $E(w)$ is the expected or average time a truck spends in the system (waiting time plus service time).

$$E(nq) = \frac{\lambda^2}{\mu(\mu - \lambda)} \tag{14-8}$$

where $E(nq)$ is the average number of trucks waiting for service.

$$E(wq) = \frac{E(nq)}{\lambda} \qquad (14\text{-}9)$$

where $E(wq)$ = the average time a truck spends waiting for service.
For our example,

$$\frac{\lambda}{\mu} = \frac{4}{5} = 0.80$$

$$P_0 = 1 - 0.80 = 0.20$$

$$E(n) = \frac{\lambda}{\mu - \lambda} = \frac{4}{5 - 4} = 4 \text{ trucks}$$

$$E(w) = \frac{1}{\mu - \lambda} = \frac{1}{5 - 4} = 1 \text{ hr}$$

$$E(nq) = \frac{\lambda^2}{\mu(\mu - \lambda)} = \frac{4^2}{5(5 - 4)} = \frac{16}{5} = 3.2 \text{ trucks}$$

$$E(wq] = \frac{E(nq)}{\lambda} = \frac{3.2}{4} = 0.8 \text{ or } 0.8 \text{ hr} = 48 \text{ min}$$

The above information can now be used to analyze the desirability of increasing the capacity of the unloading operation. We can summarize as follows:

1. Twenty percent of the time the single forklift truck and its operator are idle.
2. The average number of trucks being unloaded or waiting in line is 4 (therefore they spend, on average, one full hour in the system).
3. There are, on average, 3.2 trucks waiting in line.
4. The average waiting time for each truck is 48 min.

Having each truck and driver idle on average during 48 min of each hour may be too long. Management will therefore weigh the costs of adding another operator and forklift truck against the benefits in terms of reduced waiting and unloading times for the trucks. A careful analysis reveals that by leasing a second forklift truck, an average of 8 trucks per hour can be unloaded ($\mu = 8$). The capacity cannot be doubled, because space limitations sometimes make it difficult for the two forklifts to operate simultaneously.

With two forklift trucks, we have unchanged arrival times; therefore $\lambda = 4$ but an increased service rate $\mu = 8$. The operating characteristics of the new system are as follows:

$$\frac{\lambda}{\mu} = \frac{4}{8} = 0.50$$

14.3 / The Single-Channel Model

$$P_0 = 1 - 0.5 = 0.5$$

$$E(n) = \frac{\lambda}{\mu - \lambda} = \frac{4}{8 - 4} = 1 \text{ truck}$$

$$E(w) = \frac{1}{\mu - \lambda} = \frac{1}{8 - 4} = 0.25 \text{ hr} = 15 \text{ min}$$

$$E(nq) = \frac{\lambda^2}{\mu(\mu - \lambda)} = \frac{4^2}{8(8 - 4)} = 0.5 \text{ truck}$$

$$E(wq) = \frac{E(nq)}{\lambda} = \frac{0.5}{4} = 7.5 \text{ min}$$

Table 14–4 summarizes the data for comparison between the one-man and the two-man unloading operation. Adding another forklift truck will considerably reduce unloading and waiting times. On the other hand, the unloading crew will be idle 50 percent of the time. To conclude our analysis, we must study the relevant costs of the two alternatives.

TABLE 14–4. Queue Comparisons

	One-Man, One Forklift	Two Men, Two Forklifts
1. Average unloading capacity, μ	5	8
2. Service utilization factor, λ/μ	0.8	0.5
3. Average number of trucks in system, $E(n)$	4	1
4. Average time a truck spends in system, $E(w)$	1 (60 min)	0.25 (15 min)
5. Average number of trucks waiting in line, $E(nq)$	3.2	0.5
6. Average waiting time for each truck, $E(wq)$	48 (min)	7.5 (min)

Suppose that the accounting department tells us that the relevant variable operating costs of trucks are $35 per hour and the operating costs of the leased forklift truck is $15 per hour. The savings in truck operating costs would be

Reduction in waiting time and unloading time: (48 − 7.5) + (12 − 7.5) = 45 min
Cost savings per hour: 45 min or 0.75 hr × $35   = $26.25
Additional cost per hour for operating second forklift = 15.00
Net savings in operating costs per hour   = $11.25

The analysis suggests that it may be advantageous to lease a second forklift truck and to hire a second operator. Of course, we might consider purchasing the forklift truck rather than leasing it. This would require additional analysis. What is important is that the queuing model enabled us to develop the data needed for a meaningful analysis of the alternatives.

We have introduced queuing theory by applying it to a single-channel or single-service problem. We have shown that a queuing model provides a useful *description* of a situation where a service facility is faced with a fluctuating demand. The model is *descriptive* and *does not* by itself suggest a better or an *optimal* solution. To arrive at such a solution, additional analysis of the economic factors (investment, cost, and/or revenue) is required. It should again be pointed out that the usefulness of queuing models depends on the validity of the assumptions, especially those concerning the probability distributions for arrivals and service times.

14.4 Multiple-Channel Waiting Lines

There is a large variety of different waiting-line models, some of which will be mentioned at the end of this chapter. In this section we introduce the *multiple-channel or multiple-service model,* which is a logical extension of the single-channel model discussed in the preceding section.

In a multiple-channel queuing system we assume that two or more servers or service facilities are available to serve a *single* waiting line (see Figure 14–4). The formulas for the two-channel system are more complicated, although most of our basic assumptions are the same as those for the single-channel model. We now assume that there are C

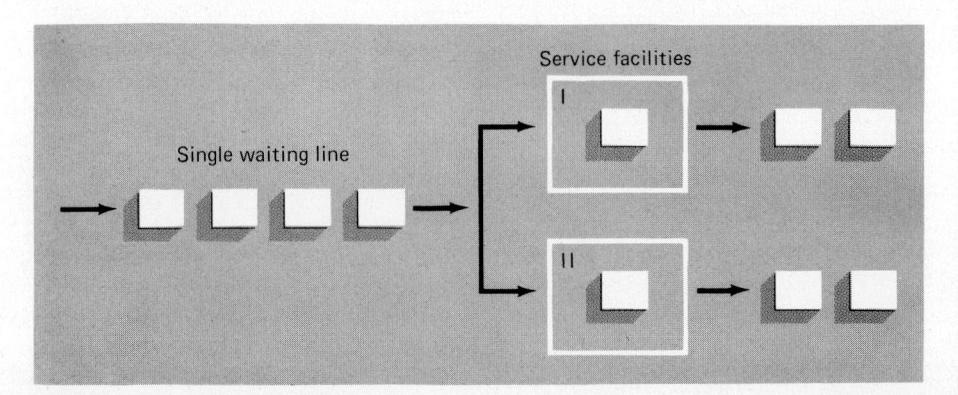

Figure 14–4. Two service facilities.

14.4 / Multiple-Channel Waiting Lines

service channels, and a single waiting line when all channels are busy; n is again the number of units in the system. For each service facility we assume identical service rates; that is, μ is the same for all C servers. The probability of having zero units in the system, that is, idleness of all C service facilities, is

$$P_0 = \left[\frac{(\lambda/\mu)^C}{C!\left(1 - \frac{\lambda/\mu}{C}\right)} + 1 + \frac{(\lambda/\mu)^1}{1!} + \frac{(\lambda/\mu)^2}{2!} + \cdots + \frac{(\lambda/\mu)^{C-1}}{(C-1)!} \right]^{-1} \quad (14\text{--}10)$$

and the probability of having n units in the system is

$$P_n = \begin{cases} P_0 \dfrac{(\lambda/\mu)^n}{n!} & \text{if } n \leq C \quad (14\text{--}11) \\[2ex] P_0 \dfrac{(\lambda/\mu)^n}{C! C^{n-C}} & \text{if } n > C \quad (14\text{--}12) \end{cases}$$

Again the service rate of all facilities, $C\mu$, must be larger than the arrival rate, that is, $\lambda/C\mu < 1$; otherwise the waiting line continues to increase without limit. When there is only one channel, that is, $C = 1$, we note that Eqs. (14–11) and (14–12) are identical with Equation (14–5) [in Eq. (14–1), $x!$ can then only be 0! or 1].

The average-number of units in the system is

$$E(n) = \frac{\lambda\mu(\lambda/\mu)^C}{(C-1)!(C\mu - \lambda)^2} P_0 + \frac{\lambda}{\mu} \quad (14\text{--}13)$$

The average time a unit spends in the system (waiting time plus service time) is

$$E(w) = \frac{\lambda(\lambda/\mu)^C}{(C-1)!(C\mu - \lambda)^2} P_0 + \frac{1}{\mu} = \frac{E(n)}{\lambda} \quad (14\text{--}14)$$

The average number of units waiting in line for service is

$$E(nq) = E(n) - \frac{\lambda}{\mu} \quad (14\text{--}15)$$

The average time a unit spends in the queue waiting for service is

$$E(wq) = \frac{E(nq)}{\lambda} \quad (14\text{--}16)$$

Let us return to the earlier example of the ABC company's parts distribution center. Suppose that as a third alternative they are considering the construction of a second loading dock. In this case the service rates for each dock would average 5 trucks per hour; that is, the combined capacity for both docks would average 10 trucks per hour, and $C = 2$. Using the preceding equations, we obtain the following operating characteristics:

$$\frac{\lambda}{\mu} = 0.8$$

The probability that both docks will be idle is

$$P_0 = \left[\frac{(0.8)^2}{2!(1 - 0.8/2)} + 1 + \frac{0.8}{1}\right]^{-1} = \left[\frac{0.64}{1.2} + 1.8\right]^{-1} = 0.429$$

The average number of trucks in the system is

$$E(n) = \frac{4 \times 5\left(\frac{4}{5}\right)^2}{(2 - 1)!(2 \times 5 - 4)^2} \times 0.429 + \frac{4}{5} = 0.9525$$

and the average time a truck spends in the system is

$$E(w) = \frac{0.9525}{4} = 0.238 \text{ hr} \quad \text{or} \quad 14.3 \text{ min}$$

The number of trucks waiting in line is

$$E(nq) = 0.9525 - \frac{4}{5} = 0.1525$$

and the average time spent in the queue is

$$E(wq) = \frac{0.1525}{4} = 0.038 \text{ hr or 2.3 min}$$

TABLE 14–5. Operating Characteristics

	Two Men, Two Forklifts, One Dock	Two Forklifts, Two Docks
1. Average unloading capacity, μ	8	10
2. Service utilization factor, λ/μ	0.5	0.8
3. Average number of trucks in system, $E(n)$	1	0.95
4. Average time trucks spend in system, $E(w)$	15 (min)	14.3 (min)
5. Average number of trucks waiting in line, $E(nq)$	0.5	0.15
6. Average waiting time for each truck, $E(wq)$	7.5 (min)	2.3 (min)

The earlier operating characteristics are summarized on Table 14–5 and compared with those of a system that uses two forklift trucks with only one dock. We note that the availability of a second loading dock would reduce waiting time from 7.5 min to 2.3 min, but would increase unloading time from 7.5 to 12 (14.3 − 2.3) min. Total time saved amounts to only 0.7 min, or (0.7/60) × $35 = $0.42 savings in truck operating costs. This, most likely, is not enough to justify the construction of a second dock.

14.5 Other Queuing Models

In our introduction to queuing theory we have presented two relatively simple models for single- and multiple-service facilities. There are numerous waiting-line situations that have been modeled by operations researchers. They differ from the ones we presented in terms of queuing discipline; ours was FCFS (first-come, first-served), but other assumptions include bulk arrivals, LIFO (last-in, first-out), and SOTO (shortest operating time, where the unit requiring the least amount of time for service is served first). They also differ in the probability distributions for arrival rates and service time and the number of waiting lines in the system.

Although there is a large number of queuing models available, it is still very difficult to find models that realistically describe many of the extremely complicated waiting-line situations encountered in real life. The models make many assumptions, for example, with regard to queuing discipline, service time distributions, and so on, that do not approximate actual situations. When no applicable queuing model can be found, it is usually possible to simulate specific waiting-line situations as discussed in Chapters 11 and 12. These simulation models also permit us to develop data on operating characteristics needed for an analysis of economic factors.

14.6 Summary

Queuing theory offers a large number of models that can be used for the analysis of many different queuing situations. We have presented a single- and a multiple-service-channel model. Crucial for all these waiting-line models are the underlying assumptions with regard to queue discipline, and arrival and service time probability distributions. Queuing models are descriptive; that is, they describe important operating characteristics, which in turn facilitate further analysis for decision making. When analytical models cannot be used because their assumptions make them unrealistic, a solution by simulation is usually possible.

Glossary

Arrival rate. The rate per unit of time at which calling units arrive at a service facility.
Operating characteristics. Key properties of a waiting-line system that describe its behavior.
Population to be served. Consists of all units that may demand to be served by a service facility.
Queue discipline. Defines the order in which arriving units will be served.
Queuing theory. The study and analysis with mathematical models of waiting lines or queuing systems.
Service rate. The rate per unit of time at which calling units are serviced.
Steady-state. The state when a system's operating characteristic are independent of the time elapsed.
Transient stage. A phase of a system's operations during which operating characteristics depend on and change with elapsed time.

Problems

For the following waiting-line problems, assume Poisson arrival times and exponential service times.
1. A book store on a college campus installed a coin-operated copying machine for use by students. During store hours there is an average demand of 10 copying jobs per hour.
   a. What is the probability that during an hour there will be no demand for the use of the machine?
   b. What is the probability that the demand will be for exactly two jobs? For exactly eight jobs?
   c. What is the probability that the demand will be for 10 or more jobs?
2. Refer to Problem 1. Assume that copying jobs require, on the average, 5 min.
   a. What percentage of copying jobs will be completed in less than 5 min?
   b. What percentage of jobs will require more than 15 min?
3. Refer to Problems 1 and 2 and answer the following questions.
   a. What is the utilization factor of the copying machine?
   b. What is the average waiting plus service time for a copying job?
   c. What is the average number of students waiting in line to get their copying done?
4. Ace National Bank has a drive-in teller window. The mean arrival rate of cars is 15 cars per hour, and the service rate is 18 cars per hour.

a. What is the teller's expected idle time?
  b. What is the expected number of cars waiting and being serviced?
  c. What is the average number of cars waiting in line?
  d. What is the probability that at least one is waiting in line?
  e. Suggest a cost/benefit approach to evaluate the current system.
5. A large power company operates a coal-fired power generating plant located on the Missouri River. More than half the coal used arrives on barges. The barges arrive at an average rate of 5 a day. There is a single unloading dock, and barges can be unloaded at the rate of 10 per day. (Assume Poisson arrival and exponential service times.)
  a. What is the average number of barges waiting to be unloaded?
  b. What is the average time a barge must wait to be unloaded?
  c. What is the average total time a barge spends waiting and being unloaded?
6. Refer to Problem 4. The company's management considers the construction of a second dock with an identical unloading capacity.
  a. What would be the average number of barges waiting?
  b. What would be the average waiting time for the barges?
  c. Assume that the cost of a waiting barge has been estimated at $1000 per day. What are the expected annual cost savings?
7. Refer to Problem 4. One of the company's engineers submitted a proposal to modify the existing unloading equipment at a cost of $150,000. This would result in an increased unloading rate of 15 barges a day.
  a. What would be the average waiting time for a barge?
  b. What would be the annual cost savings? (Assume the same cost of $1000 per day for waiting in line).
8. In a factory a clerk has the job of handing out special tools needed by mechanics. The mean arrival rate of mechanics is one a minute, whereas it takes the clerk an average of 50 sec to hand out the tools and to do the necessary record keeping. (Assume Poisson arrivals and exponential service times.)
  a. What is the average number of mechanics standing in line?
  b. What is the average time a mechanic spends waiting in line?
  c. What is the expected idle time of the tool crib clerk?
9. Refer to Problem 8 and assume that the crib clerk is paid $6 an hour and the mechanics earn an average of $12 an hour.
  a. How much do we have to pay for the mechanics waiting in line?
  b. How much do we pay the crib clerk while she has nothing to do?
  c. Calculate the costs under a and b assuming that we hire a second crib clerk for the same pay.
  d. Compare the total costs of using one or two crib clerks and make a recommendation.
10. OK Airlines has several daily flights to a midwestern city. The downtown reservations office is presently staffed with two clerks using telephones. When the two clerks are busy, a recording requests the caller to hold. When a line becomes available, the caller who has been waiting the longest is served first. Assume that incoming calls and reservations follow a Pois-

son process. Calls arrive at an average rate of 10 per hour, and the average time required for a call to be completed is 4 min.
   a. What is the average number of callers waiting?
   b. What is the average time a caller must wait before a reservations clerk answers the phone?
   c. What is the average total time required for a call to be completed?
11. Like many other airlines, OK will install a computerized reservations systems. In our midwestern city, one terminal with display screen will be installed. With the new equipment, it is estimated that *one* clerk can complete a call within 2 min.
   a. What is the average number of callers waiting under the new system?
   b. What is the new average waiting time before a caller gets to talk to the reservations clerk?
   c. What is the average total time required for a reservation to be completed?
   d. What cost estimates would be needed to justify the installation of the new system?
12. On the Illinois River there are a number of navigational locks for barge traffic. The one at La Grange is older, but in excellent repair. In a recent study of high load conditions it was determined that barges arrive at the rate of two per hour, each barge requiring an average of 20 min to pass through the locks (assume the Poisson distribution applies).
   a. What is the probability that no barge will arrive during an hour?
   b. What is the probability that exactly two barges will arrive during an hour?
   c. What is the probability that more than two barges will arrive during an hour?
13. Refer to Problem 12.

REQUIRED
   a. What percentage of the locks passages will take less than 15 min?
   b. What percentage of the locks passages will take less than 20 min?
14. Refer to Problems 12 and 13.

REQUIRED
   a. What is the utilization rate of the locks?
   b. What is the probability that there will be no barge in the system?
   c. What is the average time that a barge will require to pass through the system (waiting plus passage)?
   d. What is the average time that a barge will wait before entering the locks?
15. The Corps of Engineers have proposed a $3 million improvement project for La Grange. New high-speed gates and pumps would be installed to decrease the average passage time to 15 min per barge. Local barge companies and construction companies have given strong support to the proposed project. However, a representative from a western state has called it a "rip off" since it uses federal funds and only benefits the private interests of the local barge and construction companies. He would prefer that

Problems

the Corps of Engineers spend the money on a water conservation project in his home state.

REQUIRED
- a. With the improved locks, what would be the average time that a barge would require to pass through the system?
- b. What is the average time that a barge will wait before entering the locks?
- c. With a $200 per hour opportunity cost per hour per barge, what is the savings per barge passage with the improved locks?
- d. Assuming there are 13,000 such passages per year, what is the total savings that will accrue to the local barge companies annually?

16. Automatic Spinning Company runs its machines on a continuing basis. Machines break down at an average rate of one per hour. Mr. Jones, the maintenance engineer, and his swing and nightshift counterparts, require an average of 40 min to repair a broken machine.

REQUIRED
- a. What is the probability that no breakdown occurs during an hour?
- b. What is the probability that exactly one breakdown occurs during an hour?
- c. What is the probability that more than one breakdown occurs during an hour?

17. Refer to Problem 16.

REQUIRED
- a. What percentage of the maintenance repair jobs take less than 30 min?
- b. What percentage of the jobs take less than 20 min?

18. Refer to Problems 16 and 17.
- a. Mr. Bartlow, the owner, is concerned that Mr. Jones is idle (waiting for a breakdown) some of the time. What is the percentage of idle time?
- b. Yet Mr. Bartlow observes that not infrequently there is a broken machine awaiting repair. What is the expected number of machines awaiting repair?
- c. Mr. Bartlow has a difficult time reconciling there will be idle time and still there is an expected number of machines awaiting repair. Write a short explanation.

19. Refer to Problems 16, 17, and 18. Mr. Bartlow has been approached by Quickie Fix-up Trainees and Outfitters. QFT&O have guaranteed that Mr. Jones (and the other repairmen) will be able to repair machines in an average of 30 min after attending QFT&O's productivity in the maintenance course.

REQUIRED
- a. Mr. Bartlow wants to know whether the course will increase or decrease Mr. Jones' idle time.
- b. Mr. Bartlow, also, wants to know how many jobs will be waiting on average for repair.

20. Refer to Problems 16, 17, 18, and 19. Mr. Bartlow has decided to reject the QFT&O training course proposal if the idle time increases. Yet Mr. Harrington, the QFT&O, thinks this reason is shortsighted. Write a letter to Mr. Harrington outlining an analysis that he can present to Mr. Bartlow.
21. *(CMA)* Chadwest Manufacturing Company makes a single product that requires a significant amount of hand labor during final assembly. The standard production cost per unit is as follows:

Direct materials	$ 5.60
Direct labor (0.5 hr @ $8/DLH)	4.00
Overhead (120% of direct labor cost)	4.80
Total standard cost	$14.40

The firm employs 80 assembly workers, each of whom independently places finished units into a single conveyor slide for transportation to a single packing station. The actual assembly time required per individual unit varies. Arrivals of finished units at the packing station occur at random. If the packing station is busy at the moment an arrival reaches the station, the unit simply waits in a queue on the slide until it can be serviced. The slide is limited in length but it never fills to the extent that assembly work has to be interrupted to allow the packing station to catch up.

Due to strong demand for Chadwest's product, James Lew, the firm's general manager, is planning to add 20 more assembly workers to the present labor force. This will increase the average rate of assembly output by 25 percent. However, it will also increase the average arrival rate to the packing station by 25 percent. The packing station currently is operating near capacity.

Mr. Lew's thought on solving the packing station problem is to use overtime routinely after the regular day shift. He reasons that this approach amounts to increasing the capacity of the packing station and that this would solve the problem. However, he has hired an independent consultant to verify his judgment.

As a result of the preliminary examination of the problem, the consultant has concluded that Mr. Lew may be right, but the addition of a second packing station might be a better solution. The present plant layout could accommodate a second packing station identical to the first. Both stations could access the packing end of the conveyor slide. This alternative would essentially double the packing capacity. Even though this much extra capacity would not be needed at this time, the consultant still believes that it is worth investigating more carefully. The consultant has proposed that a more extensive analysis be conducted using quantitative modeling in the form of queuing (waiting line) theory.

Mr. Lew is unfamiliar with quantitative models and queuing theory. He is not sure modeling can assist in solving a "real-world" problem of this nature. Consequently, he is skeptical, but says he might consider the consultant's suggestion if he can be convinced of its merit.

Appendix

REQUIRED
- a. Explain in layman's terms how the queuing (waiting line) model works.
- b. Identify and explain what information will need to be collected in order to satisfactorily conduct the analysis regarding whether to use overtime after the regular shift or to add a second packing station.
- c. Explain what information Mr. Lew could realistically expect to learn by using the queuing model before he makes his decision to use overtime after the regular shift or to add a second packing station.

References

Deutsch, Howard, and Mabert, Vincent A. "Queuing Theory and Teller Staffing: A Successful Application." *Interfaces* 10, no. 5 (October 1980): 63–67.

Foote, B. L. "A Queuing Case Study of Drive-in Banking." *Interfaces* 6, no. 4 (August 1976): 31–37.

Grant, Floyd H., III. "Reducing Voter Waiting Time." *Interfaces* 10, no. 5 (October 1980): 19–25.

Hillier, F., and Lieberman, G. J. *Introduction to Operations Research*, 2d ed. San Francisco: Holden-Day, 1974.

Lee, Alex M. *Applied Queuing Theory*. London: Macmillan, 1966.

Page, E. *Queuing Theory in Operations Research*. New York: Crane, Russak, 1972.

Saaty, Thomas L. *Elements of Queuing Theory with Applications*. New York: McGraw-Hill, 1961.

Vogel, Myles A. "Queuing Theory Applied to Machine Manning." *Interfaces* 9, no. 4 (August 1979).

Wagner, H. M. *Principles of Operations Research*, 2d ed. Englewood Cliffs, N.J.: Prentice Hall, 1975.

White, J. A., Schmidt, J. W., and Bennet, G. K. *Analysis of Queuing Systems*. New York: Academic, 1975.

Appendix. The Poisson Process and Distribution; The Exponential Distribution

The Poisson Process and Distribution

The Poisson distribution results from a discrete process that generates a number of random events (successes) over a given distance, unit of time, or unit of products produced. The probability of occurrence of an event must be constant and independent of previous events. Examples of processes that may follow a Poisson distribution are arrivals of phone calls at a switchboard during a given period of time, the number of printing errors per page of a book, or the arrivals of workers asking for tools at a tool crib in the course of a workday. Given the average rate of occurrance per unit of time or space, for which the symbol λ (lambda) is used, we have

$$P(X = x) = \frac{\lambda^x e^{-\lambda}}{x!} \qquad x \geq 0$$

where x is the number of occurrences (events) per unit of time or space. The variance of the Poisson distribution is always equal to its mean λ. The Poisson probability distribution can also be used as an approximation to the binomial distribution.

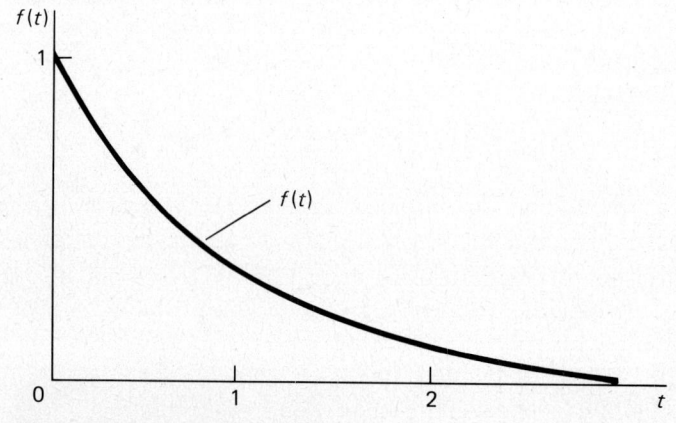

The Exponential Distribution

The exponential distribution is given by

$$f(t) = e^{-\mu t} \qquad (t \geq 0)$$

(See Figure 14–5). In the example of this chapter, μ is the expected number of events during a specified period of time and t, a time interval, is a random variable.

The mean of the exponential distribution is

$$E(t) = \frac{1}{\mu}$$

Experience has shown that the exponential can often be used as a realistic distribution of the time required for rendering certain processes. The right-hand tail of the distribution is

$$p(t > T) = e^{-\mu T}$$

Figure 14–5. Exponential distribution.

which represents the probability that the time between arrivals is larger than T. The time between arrivals can, of course, also be described as the time of no arrivals in a given period. We note that, using the Poisson distribution, this probability should not be surprising.

$$P(x = 0) = e^{-\lambda}$$

An average rate of 5 per hour means that the average time elapsed between arrivals is $\frac{1}{5}$ hr. Thus, we find that the Poisson distribution, which describes the arrival pattern per unit of time, and the exponential distribution for interarrival times are two alternative ways of describing the same process.

CHAPTER 15
Markov Processes

15.1 Introduction

15.2 Two Examples
A Brand-Switching Model
A Health-Planning Model

15.3 Markov Process Concepts and Terms
Calculating Steady-State Probabilities
An Intuitive Meaning for Steady-State Probabilities

15.4 Decision-making and Markov Processes
Brand Switching: An Advertising Decision
Health Planning: A Public-Sector Decision

15.5 Summary

Glossary

Problems

References

Key Concepts
"No memory" property
Probability transition matrix
Steady-state probabilities
Systems state
System steady-state property
Transition probability

Key Applications
Advertising decisions
Brand switching
Health-care planning
Production control
Public-sector decisions

15.1 Introduction

A Markov process models a well-defined system that may be in one of several possible states. Markov processes are concerned with the probabilities of the system being in a certain state at a given time and the probabilities of the system changing from one state to another. If we view the weather as a system, we find that it can be cloudy or sunny. The probability for tomorrow's weather being sunny or cloudy depends to some extent on today's weather. In general, a sunny day is often followed by another sunny day; and a cloudy day may often follow a cloudy day, but not always; it changes back and forth. This weather process can be described in conditional probability terms. In the context of Markov processes, such probabilities are called *transition probabilities*. The weather condition is the *system state*.

Markov processes can be applied to certain marketing, production, and finance problems as well as to health-care planning, and to situations and problems in the physical sciences. The brand-switching behavior of customers can be described by a Markov process. The health state of individuals, the condition of a production system, or changes in bond interest rates can also be modeled as a Markov process. In this chapter we develop the basic ideas of Markov processes using the context of brand switching and health-care planning as examples.

15.2 Two Examples

A BRAND-SWITCHING MODEL

A detergent manufacturer observes that customers switch detergent brands; some customers who use his brand, A, switch to his competitor's brand, B, and vice versa. Further, the manufacturer notes that there is a varying degree of brand loyalty as a number of people stay with their existing brand. Assume that this information has been summarized from customer household survey data in tabular or matrix shown in Table 15–1.

15.2 / Two Examples

TABLE 15–1. A Table of Transition Probabilities for a Customer Switching Detergent Brands*

Switch → To:
↓

From:	Brand A	Brand B
Brand A	0.7	0.3
Brand B	0.1	0.9

*This table may also be referred to as the probability transition matrix.

For a typical customer currently using brand A, we find that there is 0.7 probability that she will continue to use brand A, and a 0.3 probability that she will switch to brand B. For an individual currently using brand B, we find that there is 0.1 probability of switching to brand A, and a 0.9 probability of remaining with brand B. A casual observation is that customers of brand B have greater brand loyalty than customers using brand A. Table 15–1 entries can also be interpretated as conditional probabilities. Table 15–1 is a *probability transition matrix*. For example, if a customer currently uses brand A, there is a 0.3 probability she will switch to brand B, or

$$P(B|A) = 0.3$$

That is, there is a probability of 0.3 that a customer will use brand B given that she currently uses brand A. Similarly, the other three conditional probabilities are

$$P(A|A) = 0.7$$
$$P(A|B) = 0.1$$
$$P(B|B) = 0.9$$

Note that

$$P(A|B) + P(B|B) = 1$$

and

$$P(A|A) + P(B|A) = 1$$

In Table 15–1, the sum of the probabilities on any row must be 1. Intuitively, if a customer currently uses brand B, then she will "switch" to brand A or to brand B with certainty.

The detergent manufacturer is also interested in showing the long-run probability that a customer will use brand A. Call this probability π_A. Let π_B be the probability that a customer will use brand B. Now, the probability that a customer will use brand A is the probability that a customer who uses brand A remains with brand A times the probability that he uses brand A plus the probability that a customer who uses brand B switches to brand A times the probability that the customer uses brand B; that is,

$$\pi_A = P(A|A)\,\pi_A + P(A|B)\pi_B$$
$$= 0.7\pi_A + 0.1\pi_B$$

Now, the manufacturer observes that a customer uses either brand A or brand B; thus

$$\pi_A + \pi_B = 1$$

or

$$\pi_B = 1 - \pi_A.$$

Substituting this expression into the above equation yields

$$\pi_A = 0.7\pi_A + 0.1(1 - \pi_A)$$

This equation is easily solved to yield the probability that a customer will use brand A over the long run:

$$\pi_A = 0.25$$

The probability that a customer will be using brand B in the long run can be similarly calculated as

$$\pi_B = P(B|B)\pi_B + P(B|A)\pi_A$$
$$= 0.9\pi_B + 0.3\pi_A$$
$$= 0.9\pi_B + 0.3(1 - \pi_B)$$

where

$$\pi_A = 1 - \pi_B$$

Thus,

$$\pi_B = 0.75$$

That is, in the long run, there is a 0.75 probability that a customer will use brand B. Actually, this is not a new result, as we already knew that π_B must equal 0.75 from $\pi_A = 0.25$, as their sum must be 1. The probabilities for π_A and π_B are referred to as *steady-state probabilities*.

The detergent manufacturer can interpret this result that in the long run he will have a 25 percent market share, and the competition, brand B, will have 75 percent of the market. Let us assume that there are 1 million customers in total, or 250,000 who buy brand A. At an annual purchase for detergent of $20 per year, the manufacturer's estimated sales are $5 million. The given transition probabilities logically lead to steady-state probabilities that permit us to estimate market shares. In a later section we shall see how, through changing the transition probabilities, we may be able to increase the market share of a given brand.

A HEALTH-PLANNING MODEL

In Durham, North Carolina, an elderly individual who receives social security payments, meals-on-wheels, and attends a local social club can be in one of two conditions or states of health, referred to as state 1 or state 2. State 1 is generally considered to be a less desirable state, and further, it is difficult to recover from state 1 once an individual is there. State 2 is a "healthier" state, but there is a reasonable chance that an individual will move to state 1. These impressions have been made more precise in a recent community survey, which yielded conditional probabilities or a *probability transition matrix* as shown in Table 15–2. This table is completely analogous to Table 15–1 in the brand-switching model.

Table 15–2. Probability Transition Matrix for Elderly Individuals in Durham, North Carolina

	To: State 1 "Unhealthy"	State 2 "Healthy"
From: State 1 "Unhealthy"	0.95	0.05
State 2 "Healthy"	0.2	0.8

A health official wants to know the distribution of 10,000 elderly individuals between state 1 and state 2 in order to plan the allocation of resources for the elderly.

Let π_1 and π_2 be the long-run probability that an indiviual will be in state 1 or state 2, respectively. The probability that an individual will be in state 1 is the probability that an individual in state 1 remains, times the probability that he began in state 2, plus the probability that an individual in state 2 moves to state 1, times the probability that he began in state 2. Thus,

$$\pi_1 = 0.95\pi_1 + 0.2\pi_2$$

For the long-run state 2 probability, we have

$$\pi_2 = 0.8\pi_2 + 0.05\pi_1$$

Thus, we have two linear equations in two unknowns, but we cannot solve them because they are identical. Both of these equations reduce to

$$0.2\pi_2 = 0.05\pi_1$$

Our solution is that we know that $\pi_1 + \pi_2 = 1$, and thus we have two independent equations in two unknowns. Substituting $\pi_1 = 1 - \pi_2$ into the above equation, we have

$$0.2\pi_2 = 0.05(1 - \pi_2)$$

Then

$$\pi_2 = 0.2$$

and

$$\pi_1 = 0.8$$

That is, in the long run, we can expect 80 percent of the elderly individuals to be in state 1 and 20 percent to be in state 2. Thus in a population of 10,000, we can expect 8000 individuals to be in state 1 and 2000 to be in state 2.

15.3 Markov Process Concepts and Terms

Markov processes are models of systems that move from one condition or state to another following a probability distribution.[1] The descriptive terminology is identical to that used in Chapter 2 on probability concepts and in Chapter 11 on simulation. The probability that an individual moves to state 2 given that she is currently in state 1 is a conditional probability, that is, $P(\text{state 2}|\text{state 1})$. This table of conditional probability is called a probability transition matrix and can be written as

$$P = \begin{bmatrix} P_{11} & P_{12} \\ P_{21} & P_{22} \end{bmatrix}$$

where P_{12} is $P(\text{state 1}|\text{state 2})$, and so on; or P_{ij} is the probability of moving to state j given state i. State 1 and state 2, for example, denote the values of the state variable describing an individual's state of health. The state variable measures the condition of the system at a given time. In our examples we also calculated the probability that an individual would use brand A or brand B detergent and that an individual would be state 1 or state 2 for the health model. These long-run probabilities were called steady-state probabilities for the systems.

---

[1] In this chapter, we consider a special Markov process called a finite Markov chain.

CALCULATING STEADY-STATE PROBABILITIES

As pointed out, steady-state probability is the probability that the system will be in a given state in the long run. For the brand-switching model, the probability that a customer uses brand A, π_A, is a steady-state probability. The steady-state probabilities are useful descriptions of the system and have implications for decision making, as we shall demonstrate in a later section.

Previously, we calculated these steady-state probabilities for a two-state system. Now we want to consider a general approach that works for a system with any finite number of states. Let us return to the health model to illustrate the general approach. Now consider a three-state system: π_1, healthy; π_2, weak; and π_3, unhealthy. The steady-state probabilities can be obtained using this general approach. Let the transition matrix be

$$P = \begin{bmatrix} 0.7 & 0.2 & 0.1 \\ 0.3 & 0.6 & 0.1 \\ 0 & 0.3 & 0.7 \end{bmatrix}$$

and π_1, π_2, and π_3 are the steady-state probabilities. Writing out the three equations, we have

$$\pi_1 = 0.7\pi_1 + 0.3\pi_2 + 0\pi_3$$
$$\pi_2 = 0.2\pi_1 + 0.6\pi_2 + 0.3\pi_3$$
$$\pi_3 = 0.1\pi_1 + 0.1\pi_2 + 0.7\pi_3$$

There are three equations in three unknowns, but only two are independent. Thus, we must add the restriction $\pi_1 + \pi_2 + \pi_3 = 1$ to obtain absolute values for π_1, π_2, and π_3. Using the techniques given in the appendix on matrix algebra, we find that the steady-state probabilities are

$$\pi_1 = 0.375 \qquad \pi_2 = 0.375 \qquad \pi_3 = 0.25$$

We can now illustrate a more operational definition of a steady-state probability. Once a system state achieves the steady-state probability, it will remain at that probability level.

Let us again consider the health model. Let us assume that the steady state obtains as $\pi_1 = 0.8$ and $\pi_2 = 0.2$. Now, let us find the probabilities for state 1 and state 2 that result after an additional transition. The new probability for state 1 is given as the probability that an individual who is in state 1 remains, times the probability that an individual is in state 1, plus the probability that an individual who is in state 2 moves to state 1, times the probability that an individual is in state 2. This is

$$\pi_1(\text{new}) = 0.95\,\pi_1 + 0.2\pi_2$$

Letting $\pi_1 = 0.8$ and $\pi_2 = 0.2$ at steady state then

$$\pi_1(\text{new}) = 0.95 \times 0.8 + 0.2 \times 0.2 = 0.8$$

Thus, π_1 repeats itself. Similarly,

$$\begin{aligned}\pi_2(\text{new}) &= 0.05\pi_1 + 0.8\pi_2 \\ &= 0.05 \times 0.8 + 0.8 \times 0.2 \\ &= 0.2\end{aligned}$$

π_2 also repeats itself.

The system moves among its possible states according to the probability transition matrix. Roughly, in the long run, the system will be in state 1 for 80 percent of the time, and in state 2 for 20 percent of the time. Or, more precisely, there is a 0.8 probability for state 1 and 0.2 probability for state 2.

AN INTUITIVE MEANING FOR STEADY-STATE PROBABILITIES

A further characteristic of the steady-state probability is that it is independent of the beginning state of the system. This is not obvious, and a formal proof goes beyond this text. However, this property is easily demonstrated to strengthen our intuition.

Consider now the brand-switching model. Let us assume that we do not know which brand a customer uses, and A and B are equally likely; that is, $P(A) = P(B) = 0.5$. Now, what are the probabilities for the customer for the next period? The probability for brand A is the probability that a customer uses brand A times the probability that she continues to use brand A, plus the probability that she is using brand B times the probability that she switches. Thus,

$$P(A) = (0.5)(0.7) + (0.5)(0.1) = 0.4$$

Similarly, for brand B, we have

$$P(B) = (0.5)(0.3) + (0.5)(0.9) = 0.6$$

Let us continue to find new probabilities for A and B, given that currently $P(A) = 0.4$ and $P(B) = 0.6$. The new probabilities are

$$P(A) = (0.4)(0.7) + (0.6)(0.1) = 0.34$$

and

$$P(B) = (0.4)(0.3) + (0.6)(0.9) = 0.66$$

Continuing in similar fashion, for the third period we have

$$P(A) = (0.34)(0.7) + (0.66)(0.1) = 0.3$$
$$P(B) = (0.34)(0.3) + (0.66)(0.9) = 0.7$$

Let us summarize this information to note the progression of the state probabilities.

15.3 / Markov Process Concepts and Terms

State Probabilities

Beginning State	Period 1	Period 2	Period 3	...	Steady State Starting at Seventh Period
$P(A)$ 0.5	0.4	0.34	0.3		0.25
$P(B)$ 0.5	0.6	0.66	0.7		0.75

The probabilities are moving toward the steady-state probabilities. Now, we stated above that this will occur independent of the beginning state. So let us assume that the system is known to begin in state B, that is, the customer currently uses brand B. Then

$P(A) = 0$ and $P(B) = 1$

For the first period we have

$P(A) = (0)(0.7) + (1)(0.1) = 0.1$
$P(B) = (0)(0.3) + (1)(0.9) = 0.9$

For the second period we have

$P(A) = (0.1)(0.7) + (0.9)(0.1) = 0.16$
$P(B) = (0.1)(0.3) + (0.9)(0.9) = 0.84$

Again, we can note the progression of the state probabilities:

Beginning State	Period 1	Period 2	Period 3	...	Steady State Starting at Seventh Period
$P(A)$ 0	0.1	0.16	0.2		0.25
$P(B)$ 1	0.9	0.84	0.8		0.75

Again, we note the progression toward the steady-state probabilities.

In addition to the independence of beginning state, the steady-state property also generates a second Markov process property called the *"no memory" property.* That is, the transition probabilities do not depend on past events or how an individual arrived in state 1. One individual may have always been there; another individual may have changed states many times; the transition probabilities, however, are the same for the two individuals. Another meaning to this property is that history is not relevant. The only determinant for the next state of the system is the present state, not any previous state.

These two properties of Markov processes are important. The steady-state property permits us to consider decision-making situations involving Markov processes. The second property of "no memory" greatly simplifies the mathematics. However, one should make sure that the "no memory" property is met by the real-world system being modeled; otherwise, misleading results may result.

15.4 Decision-making and Markov Processes

In many situations it is possible to change the Markov process by using resources. For example, the detergent manufacturer can advertise brand A and change the transition probability matrix. For the health model, the transition probability may be changed by adding resources, say, for health care. In both situations, the question of whether the increased benefits justify the increased costs should be answered.

BRAND SWITCHING: AN ADVERTISING DECISION

Consider again the detergent manufacturer. An advertising agency has proposed a campaign that will change the probability transition matrix for 1 yr. (Then it returns to the condition given in Table 15–1.) The advertising campaign costs $250,000 and will generate a matrix as shown in Table 15–3.

TABLE 15–3. The New Detergent Brand-Switching Probability Transition Matrix with the Advertising Campaign.

From:	To: Brand A	Brand B
Brand A	0.7	0.3
Brand B	0.2	0.8

Intuitively, the campaign does not increase the brand loyalty for brand A but does decrease the brand loyalty for brand B, as those customers who use brand B are now more likely to switch to brand A. Clearly, the advertising campaign would benefit the manufacturer, but it is not possible to say whether the campaign is justified, as it is not possible to make comparisons with the information in this form. However, the information can be converted to market share information, which will facilitate comparison.

The detergent manufacturer calculates the steady-state probabilities for the system with advertising. The steady-state probabilities are given by

$$\pi_1 = 0.7\pi_1 + 0.2\pi_2$$
$$\pi_2 = 0.3\pi_1 + 0.8\pi_2$$
$$\pi_1 + \pi_2 = 1$$

where π_1 and π_2 are the steady-state probabilities for brand A and brand B, respectively. [Previously we used P(A) and P(B) for steady-state probabilities in the brand-switching model.] Of the first two equations, there is one independent relation:

$$3\pi_1 = 2\pi_2$$

Together with $\pi_1 + \pi_2 = 1$, this yields $\pi_1 = 0.4$ and $\pi_2 = 0.6$. Previously we interpretated these quantities as market shares. Brand A will have 40 percent and brand B will have 60 percent.[2] This is a 15 percent increase (40 percent with advertising minus 25 percent without advertising) in market share. For 1 million customers, this will be 150,000 additional customers spending $20 per year for an increase in sales of $3 million. From his accounting records the detergent manufacturer knows that profits are 15 percent of sales, so the increased profit is $450,000. This is greater than the advertising campaign cost of $250,000. So the detergent manufacturer should advertise and obtain a new profit of $200,000.

To review briefly, the detergent manufacturer can undertake an advertising campaign that will favorably change the probability transition matrix. By calculating the resulting steady-state probabilities, we were able to determine the increased market share, increased sales, and increased profits. These increased profits were greater than the advertising cost, and the manufacturer should therefore undertake the advertising campaign.

HEALTH PLANNING: A PUBLIC-SECTOR DECISION

In a city near Durham, North Carolina, the elderly have different services. In addition to social security, meals-on-wheels, and a social club, the elderly are monitored weekly for colds, flu, and changing blood pressure. This added service costs $100 per year per individual, and it would cost $1 million per year in Durham for its 10,000 elderly population. A group of public-sector local agencies wants to know the impact of this added service for the Durham elderly. The probability transition matrix for the other city is given in Table 15–4. With the monitoring, an individual in state 2 is less likely to move to state 1; and an individual in state 1 is more likely to move to the more desirable state 2. This information indicates that monitoring would be beneficial if monitoring in Durham would change the original probability transition matrix to the matrix in Table 15–4. Except for monitoring, the two elderly populations are similar, and past experience with changes suggests that the transition matrices adjust very quickly. Nonetheless, the planning

---

[2] In actuality, it is doubtful that the advertising campaign would change the market shares immediately, but we make the assumption to simplify the analysis.

agencies would like to know the impact of the change on the distribution of individuals in state 1 and state 2. The proposed program steady-state probabilities would be given by

$$\pi_1 = 0.8\pi_1 + 1.\pi_2$$
$$\pi_2 = 0.2\pi_1 + 0.9\pi_2$$
$$\pi_1 + \pi_2 = 1$$

Solving the three equations, of which the first two are redundant, we have

$$\pi_1 = 0.33\pi_2 = 0.67$$

Table 15–4. Probability Transition Matrix for Elderly Population for the Other City

	To: State 1	State 2
From:		
State 1	0.8	0.2
State 2	0.1	0.9

Thus, the 10,000 elderly in Durham would be expected to have 3333 individuals in state 1 and 6667 in state 2. Table 15–5 summarizes the changes.

TABLE 15–5. Present and Proposed System for Durham, North Carolina, Elderly Population

Alternatives	State 1	State 2	Increased Cost
Present care	8000	2000	
Proposed monitoring	3333	6667	$1,000,000

A review of Table 15–5 indicates that there are 4667 more individuals in the more desirable state 2 under the $1 million monitoring program. But does the increased benefit justify the additional cost? We cannot reduce the decision to a profit/cost criterion as we did for the detergent manufacturer. It is inappropriate to assign a priori a dollar value for an individual being in state 2 in lieu of state 1. The issue is much too complex to be reduced to such simple terms. The best we can do is to present the information in Table 15–5 to the appropriate agencies, and they will have to make a judgment.

15.5 Summary

In this chapter we discussed concepts and applications of Markov processes to management. The concepts of transition probabilities, system states, and steady-state probabilities were developed within the context of brand-switching and health-planning applications. Decision-making issues of advertising and health-care planning where systems follow Markovian behavior were considered. These analyses are useful to managers in the firm and also for choices in the public sector.

Glossary

"No memory" property. A property which states that the transition probabilities are independent of the path to move to the current system state.

Probability transition matrix. A table of transition probabilities for the system, for example, the transition probabilities of customer brand switching, or weather changes.

Steady-state probabilities. The long-run probabilities for the system states; for example, over the long run, the probability of a "sunny" day is 0.75.

Systems state. The present condition of the system; for example, one weather state is "sunny."

System steady-state property. One system steady-state property is that the long-run steady-state probabilities are independent of the beginning state.

Transition probability. The probability that a system will change (from a given system state) to another system state.

Problems

1. The Jones toothpaste marketing company hired a consulting firm to do a toothpaste market competition study. The consulting company included the following probability transition matrix in its report to Mr. Jones.

    REQUIRED

    a.

	To: Jones Toothpaste	Other Brands
From: Jones Toothpaste	0.6	0.4
Other Brands	0.5	0.5

    Mr. Jones is uncertain about the correct interpretation of the information in the table. Write a paragraph for Mr. Jones explaining the meaning of this information.

2. Calculate the steady-state probabilities for the probability transition matrix given in Problem 1.
3. For the brand-switching example, assume that the customer currently uses brand A; that is, $P(A) = 1$ and $P(B) = 0$. Calculate the probabilities $P(A)$ and $P(B)$ for the next three periods. Note that $P(A)$ and $P(B)$ progress toward the steady-state probabilities.
4. For the health-planning example:

REQUIRED

    a. Assume that an individual is in state 1; that is, $\pi_1 = 1$ and $\pi_2 = 0$. Calculate π_1 and π_2 for the next three periods and note the progression toward the steady-state probabilities.

    b. Assume that the individual is in state 2 and demonstrate the progression toward the steady-state probabilities.

5. A machine produces good items or defective items. When the machine is in adjustment, it produces good items. When it is out of adjustment, it produces defective items. The adjustment behavior of the machine follows a Markov process as shown:

	To: In Adjustment	Out of Adjustment
From: In Adjustment	0.9	0.1
Out of Adjustment	0.2	0.8

In steady state, find the probability that the machine produces good items.

6. Another machine of the same kind also produces good items and defectives. Its probability transition matrix is

	To: In Adjustment	Out of Adjustment
From: In Adjustment	0.85	0.15
Out of Adjustment	0.4	0.6

Find the probability that the machine is in adjustment in the steady state. Also, there has been considerable controversy over whether this machine or the machine in Problem 5 is better. Which machine is better? Why?

7. Calculate the steady-state probabilities for the following probability transition matrices:

Problems

a.

From:	To: State 1	State 2
State 1	0.7	0.3
State 2	0.3	0.7

b.

From:	To: State A	State B
State A	0.5	0.5
State B	0.5	0.5

c.

From:	To: State 1	State 2
State 1	0.9	0.1
State 2	0.4	0.6

d.

From:	To: State 1	State 2
State 1	0.75	0.25
State 2	0.4	0.6

8. A bond company has observed that the bond interest rate follows a Markov process. The monthly probability transition matrix is given as

From:	To: 4%	6%
4%	0.5	0.5
6%	0.4	0.6

REQUIRED
    a. Calculate the steady-state probabilities.
    b. What is the expected interest rate on bonds?

9. Calculate the steady-state probabilities for the following probability transition matrices:

a.

From: / *To:*

	State 1	State 2	State 3
State 1	0.8	0	0.2
State 2	0.2	0.6	0.2
State 3	0.1	0.2	0.7

b.

From: / *To:*

	State 1	State 2	State 3
State 1	0.6	0.2	0.2
State 2	0	0.7	0.3
State 3	0.1	0	0.9

10. A medical center has developed a Markov process matrix to explain an individual's chances of recovery. The annual probability transition matrix is given by

From: / *To:*

	Well	Cancer	Death
Well	0.95	0.03	0.02
Cancer	0.2	0.5	0.3
Death	0	0	1

REQUIRED
   a. The local cancer society is having difficulty understanding the matrix. Write a paragraph explaining the information in lay terms.
   b. In Markov process terminology, the state "Death" is referred to as an absorbing state. Using death as an example, write a definition for an absorbing state in a Markov process.
   c. For a population of 10,000, find the expected number of well individuals, cancer patients, and those who will die in 1 yr.

11. Mr. Jones, in Problem 1, has the opportunity to buy a new toothpast formula to replace his present formula. Test markets for the new formula indicate that the probability transition matrix is

Problems

	To:	
From:	New Formula	Other Brands
New Formula	0.8	0.2
Other Brands	0.4	0.6

REQUIRED

a. What are the steady-state probabilities for the new formula?

b. The toothpaste market has 30 million customers, and Mr. Jones estimates his profit to be $0.10 per customer per year. Dr. Dentblanche, the inventor of the new formula, want $2 million for exclusive rights to the formula for 1 yr. Should Mr. Jones purchase the formula?

12. The community health agency must decide whether it should invest in a telephone surveillance program. The program costs $120 per year for each individual. There would be 1000 individuals in the program. Basically, the program decreases the time required for a doctor to see an individual when the individual needs medical attention. Under the current setup, the community probability transition matrix is given as

	To:	
From:	State 1	State 2
State 1	0.7	.3
State 2	0.1	.9

State 2 is the more desirable state, as an individual is without pain and does not suffer from depression. In state 1 a patient is slightly depressed and has some pain. Under the surveillance program, the probability transition matrix would be

	To:	
From:	State 1	State 2
State 1	0.5	0.5
State 2	0.1	0.9

Basically, the surveillance program increases the probability that a depressed and pained individual will get better, but it has no preventive benefit because the same probability remains for a well individual to become depressed and pained. The community health agency is considering to implement the surveillance program.

REQUIRED

a. What are the steady-state probabilities and the expected number of individuals in each state at present?

b. What would be the steady-state probabilities and expected number of individuals in each state for the surveillance program?
c. Prepare comparative information on the two alternatives that would be helpful to the agency.
d. Write a short report for the agency explaining your analysis.

13. Currently, the distribution of population in the North and South is 60 percent and 40 percent, respectively. Each year some individuals in the North stay, whereas others move South. Similarly, some Southerners move and some stay. The population movement is summarized by the following probability transition matrix:

	To: North	South
From:		
North	0.9	0.1
South	0.03	0.97

a. Find the steady-state probabilities for the population.
b. Is the system in equilibrium? That is, is the current population distribution the same as the steady-state distribution?

14. The North Carolina beach is either sunny or cloudy in August. A local beach bum has observed that a sunny day is followed by a cloudy day with a probability of 0.1. A cloudy day is followed by a sunny day with a probability of 0.8.
a. Write out the probability transition matrix for an August beach in North Carolina.
b. Determine the steady-state probabilities for sunny and cloudy days.
c. The North Carolina tourist bureau advertises: "It is impossible to spend a week on a North Carolina beach in August and not see the sun." Comment.

References

Bessent, E. Wailand, and Bessent, Authella M. "Student Flow in a University Department: Results of a Markov Analysis." *Interfaces* 10, no. 2 (April 1980).

Bierman, Harold, Jr. "The Bond-Refunding Decision as a Markov Process." In *Financial Policy Decisions*. New York: Macmillan, 1970, pp. 221–31.

Burton, R. M., Dellinger, D., Damon, W., and Pfeiffer, E. "A Role for Operational Research in Health Care Planning and Management Teams." *Journal of Operational Research Society* 29, no. 7 (1978): 633–641.

Cyert, R. M., Davidson, H. J., and Thompson, G. L. "Estimation of the Allowance for Doubtful Accounts by Markov Chains." *Management Science* (April 1962): 287, 303.

References

Harary, F., and Lipstein, B. "The Dynamics of Brand Loyalty: A Markov Approach." *Operations Research* 10 (January–February 1962): 19–40.

Howard, R. A. *Dynamic Programming and Markov Processes.* Cambridge, Mass.: M.I.T. Press, 1960.

Kemeny, John G., Mirkil, Hazleton, Snell, J. Laurie, and Thompson, Gerald L. *Finite Mathematical Structures.* Englewood Cliffs, N.J.: Prentice-Hall, 1958, 1959.

CHAPTER 16
Organizational Implications for the Implementation of Quantitative Methods

16.1 Introduction

16.2 Extent of Practical Applications

16.3 Problems in Applying Quantitative Methods
Interaction Between Model Builder and Managers

16.4 Difficulty of Demonstrating a Satisfactory Cost/Benefit Relation

16.5 Difficulty in Obtaining Information Needed as Inputs for Quantitative Models

16.6 The Bottom Line

16.7 Summary

References

Key Concepts
Behavioral science
"Complete" systems scientist
Cost/benefit relation
Data analysis
Data needs
Implementation
Practical application
Requisites for successful application

16.1 Introduction

In this text we have studied various quantitative techniques that have application in management and accounting. Mastery of these techniques is necessary but not sufficient for successful implementation in real situations. In this chapter we review some recent studies on the extent of the use of quantitative methods in management. The use of quantitative methods is widespread and widely accepted. But that does not mean that implementation is easy. It is very difficult, and there have been more failures than successes. We review some reasons why quantitative methods are an interesting challenge for implementation. Basically, the challenge is to go beyond the techniques themselves to obtain a fuller understanding of the target organization itself. For the student, the next best step is twofold: a study of behavioral science and organization, and a better understanding of statistics and data analysis. Briefly, the materials in this text represent a good first step. There is considerably more to do if we are to realize the full potential of quantitative methods in organizations.

16.2 Extent of Practical Applications

In a 1972 survey (Turban, 1972) on the use of quantitative methods at the corporate level, the following problem areas where operations research techniques have been successfully applied were identified:

1. Distributions systems (e.g., transportation networks and plant warehouse locations)
2. Inventory ordering and stocking decisions.
3. Resource allocations for corporate activities
4. Capital investment analysis
5. Portfolio selection
6. Information systems design
7. Product mix and production decisions
8. New product analysis

A 1977 survey conducted by Ledbetter and Cox (1977) supported the results of other studies. It ranks the most frequently used quantitative methods in descending order as follows:

Regression analysis (statistical analysis)

Linear programming

Simulation

Network models (PERT/CPM)

Queuing

Dynamic programming

Game theory

Primary areas of application were inventory analysis, production scheduling, plant location, logistics, and project planning.

According to John Dearden and John Lastavice (1970), there are four basic operations research techniques:

1. Financial models
2. Statistical models
3. Mathematical programming
4. Simulation

Under financial models they include inventory models, capital budgeting, return on investment, financial statement analysis, and cash flow models. Simulation includes all techniques where a computer is used to evaluate multiple alternatives.

They make the following observations: "The only areas where linear programming has resulted in definite improvement in performance are mix models, such as gasoline blending by oil refineries and the selection of plants and warehouses in the distribution industry. These problems are prototypes of operational problems and should be distinguished from decision problems at the corporate level. . . . If we exclude the simulation techniques we are forced to conclude that OR is useful mainly in solving operational problems" (Dearden and Lastavice, 1970). They come to the following conclusions:

1. Present techniques can be used to solve only a limited kind of operating problem and are not adaptable at all to solving higher-level management problems.
2. No real progress has been made in the last 10 years or more in developing techniques that are more useful to business.

Recent new developments have occurred mainly through simulation and the use of microcomputers. One of the characteristics of this approach in the area of simulation is that the decision maker can perform the analysis. This has enforced better cooperation and communication between quantitative methods specialists and line managers. It has also brought about a decentralization of OR staffs.

A number of studies investigated the extent to which quantitative methods are applied to decision problems. Cook and Russel, in a survey of the *Fortune* 500 companies, found that, of responding companies, 95 percent indicated applications of linear programming, 88 percent used computer simulation, 91 percent used inventory control models, and 75 percent used the transportation method (Cook and Russel, 1977, p. 437).

A study published in 1974 by the Financial Executive Research Foundation (Traenkle et al., 1975), which investigated the use of financial models, found simulation, descriptive statistics, simple and multiple regression, and linear programming were among the most widely applied quantitative techniques. Kiani-Aslani (1977–1978) who surveyed the use of quantitative tools by the controllers of the *Fortune* 500 corporations, found that among the quantitative methods (as defined and covered in this text) used, forecasting techniques, simulation models, statistical techniques, inventory models, linear programming, and network analysis produced the most satisfactory results.

In more recent studies, Thomas and DaCosta (1979) report the growing acceptance, support, and application of quantitative techniques. They report from their answers that "93 percent of the firms use statistical analysis, 84 percent use simulation, 79 percent use linear programming and 70 percent use PERT/CPM" (p. 106). There were fewer, but significant applications of inventory, queuing, nonlinear programming, decision theory, and dynamic programming.

The areas of application include important business decision, forecasting, production scheduling, inventory, capital budgeting, transportation, plant location, advertising and sales research, equipment replacement, maintenance and repair, accounting procedures, and packaging. There has been significant growth in forecasting and accounting procedures.

Thomas and DaCosta also report on the organization and implementation of quantitative applications. Organizationally, it is becoming decentralized. They conclude "that Management Science is becoming a part of the everyday activities of the modern firm and therefore is no longer a specialized function to be undertaken by a separate specialized department" (p. 103). On implementation, they report that the user department acknowledges its needs and requests the study. It represents a higher level of acceptance (pp. 107–108). The results of this study suggest that quantitative studies are becoming an integral part of modern business management, integrated throughout the firm in many departments for many different applications.

McClure and Miller (1979) confirm the general thrust of these results for the banking community.

16.3 Problems in Applying Quantitative Methods

It is not surprising that over the years numerous problems have been encountered in the application of quantitative techniques to practical business decision problems. Some of the more important ones frequently discussed in the literature will be mentioned briefly.

INTERACTION BETWEEN MODEL BUILDER AND MANAGERS

Frequently operations research efforts fail because of lack of effective communication between the quantitative methods specialist and the managers who are supposed to benefit from the results of quantitative analyses. On the one hand, managers often fail to understand the underlying assumptions and limitations of the techniques employed. It is only natural that they hesitate to accept something they do not understand. Quantitative methods specialists, on the other hand, frequently fail to understand managers and the management process. This lack of understanding was often aggravated by an organizational and physical separation of the management science staffs from the line managers. In the article referred to earlier, Dearden and Lastavice (1970) state that: "In spite of the development of superior tools readily adaptable to a multitude of problems, operations research skill is not used as extensively as it should be. The answer, clearly, is to solve the people problem. Two things suggest themselves: one is to provide an organizational environment which facilitates communication, and the other is to structure studies so that communication flow is assured. These, in combination, will lead to more successful applications." To achieve this, they and many others suggest that operations researchers should work directly with and report to line managers.

16.4 Difficulty of Demonstrating a Satisfactory Cost/Benefit Relation

It is often difficult to measure the benefits of a modeling effort. For relatively simple operational problems, such as applications of linear programming to mix problems as encountered by oil refineries or developing shipping schedules from plants to warehouses, the benefits can usually be measured in terms of cost savings. For higher-level corporate decision problems, the benefits of a costly investment in developing complex optimization or simulation models are extremely difficult to quantify. This absence of readily discernible benefits is, in part, responsible for the reluctance of many top managers to employ models in complicated decision processes. Our experience suggests that the benefits argument is most frequently used when the manager was not involved in the process of developing the models.

16.5 Difficulty in Obtaining Information Needed as Inputs for Quantitative Models

By now the reader will have realized that the information inputs required by the various models covered in the text are usually not readily available. For example, the cost estimates needed for inventory models require a special study and analysis of the relevant costs involved; they are not readily furnished by the firm's accounting system. The same thing applies to the information needs for linear programming models. Many times special cost studies are needed to obtain the coefficients for the objective function and special engineering studies for the constraint equations. Nevertheless, estimates of varying degrees of accuracy must be made. The effort expended on this information gathering has a direct bearing on the reliability of the results of any quantitative analysis. Naturally, more accurate information will produce more reliable results, yet the cost of obtaining "accurate" information cannot be ignored.

Grinyer and Batt (1974) suggest the following six criteria against which models should be tested in order to assure their successful application:

1. Models should be understood by top management and provide output to it in as familiar a form as possible.
2. To gain and maintain a high level of management support, a fairly rapid payoff from the investment in model building should be secured.
3. Since many future alternatives cannot be foreseen at the time of model construction, models should be flexible.
4. The allowance should be made for the inaccurate and often subjective nature of projections and forecasts, of both costs and revenue, used or input to models. This in turn suggests that any model developed would be used in an explanatory, simulatory fashion . . . highly sophisticated and expensive approaches should not be used in such circumstances.
5. One should face the fact that objectives of top management are usually implicit, multiple, often incommensurate or conflicting, and always with the balance of political power in the boardroom and with the environmental influences that bear upon senior executives. It is

rarely possible to find an explicit objective function in strategic decision making that will be a true reflection of the goal of the board, let alone stable over time.
6. If it is to be extensively used and regularly updated, the model must be embedded in the existing planning system, and use a data base which already exists or may be built up and maintained without excessive cost or disruption. (pp. 150–151)

This list is significant both in what it contains and what it omits. There is no reference to proper application of the techniques and accurate calculations. This, of course, does not mean that techniques are not important. Proper applications of techniques and accuracy are a basic requirement.

16.6 The Bottom Line

The student has learned some important techniques and approaches for applying quantitative analysis in management and accounting. We have begun a long and difficult journey, but there is a long way to go, and many things remain to be considered:

1. A broader view of operations research and quantitative techniques for application and implementation; and
2. A more fundamental consideration of the mathematical techniques.

The two issues are important, and the interested student should pursue both. In our opinion, the development of the mathematical techniques far surpasses our ability to use the ones we have. Recall Dearden and Lastavice's (1970) earlier comment. That is, the cutting edge today is application and implementation of quantitative analysis.

There is no easy checklist on the implementation of operations research, although Grinyer and Batt's is appropriate. It is very difficult. It is an art, as well as a science. The successful practitioners learn through experience—experience of some successes, some failures, and numerous small errors that are correctable and corrected.

For the student, we suggest that the two most important areas of complementary study are behavioral science and data analysis. A study of behavioral science with an orientation to understanding how organizations operate and how they can be changed is most important. The cutting edge of quantitative analysis is implementation, and the successful practitioner has a good understanding of organizations. Quantitative analysis as discussed in this book is the natural complement to data analysis. By data analysis, we mean an understanding of statistics and its application. In real situations, data are abundant, but useful data are scarce and difficult to obtain. Every practitioner must be able to ferret out good data that can be used. This, too, is part art, as well as science. This triad of quantitative techniques, behavioral science, and data analysis position the student to become a successful practitioner, but a long apprenticeship and hard work lie ahead. This is the bottom line.

16.7 Summary

Quantitative approaches to management have been successfully applied and implemented, although there have been failures and errors—both in practice and education.

The general conclusions from a recent NATO Advanced Research Institute (ARI) in Systems Science (a management term to include operations research, management science, and quantitative analysis) education summarize both the problems and the opportunities.

We quote at some length, as we feel this summary captures our challenge very well (Bayraktar et al., 1979, pp. 15–16):

1.4.1   Successful practice of Systems Science requires knowledge and practical skills in many areas in addition to the mathematical and statistical tools usually associated with Systems Science (and sometimes, unfortunately, identified with it!).

1.4.2   The development of mathematical theories for Systems Science has, for the most part, advanced far beyond the requirements of real-world practice and educational programmes give too much emphasis to the mathematical aspects of Systems Science.

1.4.3   There is a general need to increase educational programme content and research effort in areas associated with the systems scientist's entry into and operation with the organization environments in which problems are embedded. This requires not only the knowledge and skills associated with "problem definition, structure and diagnosis" and "implementation and control of working systems" in a formal sense, but also an understanding of individual, group and organizational behaviour—including the value judgments implicit in the perceptions of problems and their possible solutions. In addition, the "complete" systems scientist needs to develop a range of personal skills and be familiar with basic management tools such as accounting and business economics.

1.4.4   Changing the emphasis of Systems Science education programmes requires more than reducing the number of mathematical courses and adding courses in the social sciences. There is a need for creative approaches to integrate formally acquired knowledge of the mathematical tools of Systems Science, the social sciences, management Skills, etc., with the practical experience (real or simulated) that is required to produce the well-rounded systems scientist. There is a need for research and experiment into a range of educational programmes for both specialists and non-specialists which achieve appropriate degrees of integration of theory, philosophy and practice. Examples of a few such programmes were given at the ARI. There is also a need for research experiment into the "softer" aspects of Systems Science, both to improve understanding of the processes at work in problem situations and to provide continually improving input to more practical Systems Science educational programmes.

1.4.5   Since the major responsibility for education in Systems Science rests at the university level, it was generally agreed that achievement of the changes in educational programme design indicated above will also require changes in the academic environment. In particular, the need to modify academic reward systems and to broaden the definition of scholarship.

References

Bayraktar, B. A., Muller-Merbach, H., Roberts, J. E., and Simpson, M. G. (Ed.). *Education in Systems Science: Report and Proceedings of the NATO Advanced Research Institute.* London: Taylor & Francis, 1979.

Cook, Thomas A., and Russel, Robert A. *Introduction to Management Science.* Englewood Cliffs, N.J.: Prentice-Hall, 1977.

Dearden, John, and Lastavice, John. "New Directions in Operations Research." *Financial Executive* (October 1970): 24–33. v. 38

Grinyer, Peter H., and Batt, Christopher D. "Some Tentative Findings on Corporate Models." *Operational Research Quarterly* 25, no. 1 (1974): 150–151.

Kiani-Aslani, R. "Do Corporate Controllers Use Quantitative Tools Currently Taught in Managerial Accounting." *The Accounting Journal* (Winter 1977–78): v.2

Ledbetter, W., and Cox, J. "Are OR Techniques Being Used?" *Industrial Engineering* 9, no. 2 (1977): 19–21.

McArthur, D. S. "Fantasies, Fundamentals, and a Framework in Corporate O.R.T." *Interfaces* 10, no. 4 (August 1980): 98–103.

McClure, Richard H., and Miller, Robert E. "The Application of Operations Research in Commercial Banking Companies." *Interfaces* 9, no. 2, part 1 (February 1979): 24–29.

PoKempner, Stanley J. *Management Science in Business.* 1977. The Conference Board, New York.

Thomas, George, and DaCosta, Jo Anne. "A Sample Survey of Corporate Operations Research." *Interfaces* 9, no. 4 (August 1979): 102–111.

Traenkle, Cox, et al. *The Use of Financial Models in Business.* Financial Executives Research Foundation, 1975.

Turban, E. "A Sample Survey of Operations-Research Activities at the Corporate Level." *Operations Research* 20 (1972): 708–721.

Ulrich, Werner. "The Metaphysics of Design: A Simon-Churchman 'Debate'." *Interfaces* 10, no. 2 (April 1980): 35–40.

APPENDIX A
A Review of Differential Calculus

This review is not intended to teach differential calculus. It will help those who have had a course in calculus recall the most important formulas of differentiation and some of their applications. We treat only algebraic functions, that is $y = f(x)$ where f is an algebraic function.

Differentiation of a Simple Function

1. The derivative of a constant is zero. More formally, we write the function:

$$y = a \quad \text{where } a \text{ is a constant}$$

The derivative is then

$$y' = 0$$

The derivative of y can be written as $\frac{dy}{dx}$, y', $\frac{df}{dx}$, $f'(x)$, or simply f'.

Consider two examples. Let

$$y = 5 \quad \text{then} \quad y' = 0$$
$$y = 2 + 3 \quad \text{then} \quad y' = 0$$

2. The derivative of a linear function is a constant. The linear function is

$$y = ax + b \quad \text{where } a \text{ and } b \text{ are constants}$$

The derivative is

$$y' = a$$

Consider three examples. If

$$y = 5x \quad \text{then} \quad y' = 5$$
$$y = 6x + 17 \quad \text{then} \quad y' = 6$$
$$y = x \quad \text{then} \quad y' = 1$$

3. The derivative of a power function is more complex. We have

$$y = ax^n \quad \text{where } n \text{ is a number and } a \text{ is a constant}$$

The derivative is then

$$y' = anx^{n-1}$$

Consider some examples. Let

$$y = x^{10} \quad \text{then} \quad y' = 10x^9$$
$$y = 5x^2 \quad \text{then} \quad y' = 5 \times 2x = 10x$$
$$y = 5x \quad \text{then} \quad y' = 5$$

(Note that the general derivative applies for the linear function as well.)

$$y = \sqrt{x} = x^{1/2} \quad \text{then} \quad y' = \frac{1}{2}x^{-1/2} = \frac{1}{2\sqrt{x}}$$

REVIEW PROBLEMS

Find the derivative for each of the following:
1. $y = 16$
2. $y = 13x$
3. $y = 2x^3$
4. $y = x^4$
5. $y = 18 \times 765$
6. $y = 17x^{18.5}$
7. $y = \sqrt{x+1}$

Rules for Differentiation

1. The addition rule:

   The derivative of a sum of two (or more) functions is the sum of the derivatives.

   For

   $$y = f(x) + g(x)$$

   the derivative is

   $$y' = f'(x) + g'(x)$$

   Consider some examples:

   $$y = x^{10} + x^9 \quad \text{then} \quad y' = 10x^9 + 9x^8$$
   $$y = 12x^2 + 13x \quad \text{then} \quad y' = 24x + 13$$
   $$y = 4x^3 + 16x^2 + 17x + 9 \quad \text{then} \quad y' = 12x^2 + 32x + 17$$
   $$y = x^3 - x^2 \quad \text{then} \quad y' = 3x^2 - 2x$$

2. The multiplication rule:

The derivative of the product of two functions is the derivative of the first function times the second function, plus the derivative of the second function times the first function.

For
$$y = f(x)\, g(x)$$
the derivative is
$$y' = f'(x)\, g(x) + g'(x)\, f(x)$$

Consider some examples:

$y = x^2(x + 3)$ then $y' = 2x(x + 3) + 1(x^2) = 3x^2 + 6x$
$y = (2x + 3)(x^5)$ then $y' = 2(x^5) + 5x^4(2x + 3) = 12x^5 + 15x^4$

3. The quotient rule:

The derivative of a quotient function is the denominator times the derivative of the numerator, minus the numerator times the derivative of the denominator, all divided by the denominator squared.

For
$$y = \frac{f(x)}{g(x)}$$
the derivative is
$$y' = \frac{g(x)\, f'(x) - f(x)\, g'(x)}{[g(x)]^2}$$

Consider an example:

$$y = \frac{1 + x}{x^2} \quad \text{then} \quad y' = \frac{x^2(1) - (1 + x)2x}{x^4}$$
$$= \frac{-x^2 - 2x}{x^4} = \frac{-(x + 2)}{x^3}$$

4. The chain rule:

The derivative of a function of a function is the product of the derivatives.

For
$$y(x) = [u(x)]^n$$
the derivative is
$$y'(x) = u[u(x)]^{n-1}\, u'(x)$$

Consider an example:
$$y = (4 - 2x^3)^4$$
Now, let $u = 4 - 2x^3$. Then write $y = u^4$. Then we have
$$y'(u) = 4u^3 \quad \text{and} \quad u'(x) = -6x^2$$
Combining according to the rule, we have
$$\begin{aligned} y'(x) &= 4u^3(-6x^2) \\ &= 4(4 - 2x^3)^3(-6x^2) \\ &= -24x^2(4 - 2x^3)^3 \end{aligned}$$

REVIEW PROBLEMS

Find the derivative for each of the following functions.
1. $y = 4x + 3$
2. $y = 18x^2 + 14x + 7$
3. $y^2 = x(x^2 + 4x^3)$
4. $y = (17x^2 + 10)(4x^5 + 12x)$
5. $y = \dfrac{17x^2 + 10}{4x^5 + 12}$
6. $y = \dfrac{1}{x^2 + 1}$
7. $y = x^2(x^3 + 10) + 14x^3 + 4$

Rules for Maximum and Minimum: Optimizing a Function

The derivative of a function is a measure of the rate of change of the function, that is, the slope in geometric terms. When the derivative of the function becomes zero, then the function itself is a local maximum, local minimum, or an inflection point. These are illustrated in Figure A–1. Note that the tangent line, or slope, at each point is zero.

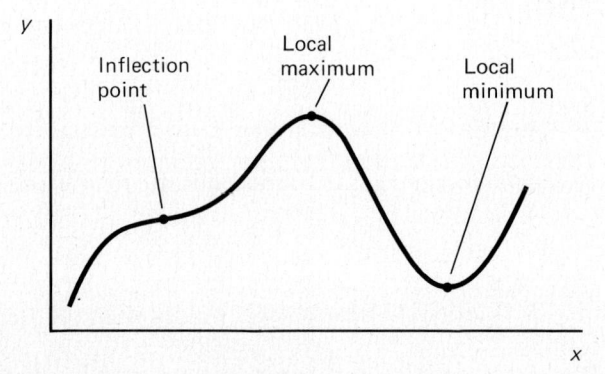

Figure A–1. The behavior of a function.

Appendix A / A Review of Differential Calculus   **507**

The conditions for a maximum and minimum point are summarized in Table A–1. The second derivative is the derivative of the first derivative.

TABLE A–I Conditions for Maximum and Minimum Points

Function	Maximum	Minimum
First derivative	$y' = 0$	$y' = 0$
Second derivative	$y'' < 0$	$y'' > 0$

MAXIMUM AND MINIMUM POINT CONDITION

Consider an example:
$$y = 2x^3 + 9x^2$$
Then
$$y' = 6x^2 + 18x \quad \text{and} \quad y'' = 12x + 18$$
$$y' = 0 = 6x^2 + 18x \quad \text{yields} \quad x = -3 \text{ and } x = 0$$
$$\text{at } x = 0, \; y'' = 18$$
$$\text{at } x = -3, \; y'' = -18$$

The function has a local maximum at $x = -3$ and a local minimum at $x = 0$.

Suppose that a firm's sales can be described by the following function, where x is the production quantity.
$$S = 12 - x$$
Its costs are
$$C = \frac{x^3}{3} - 3x^2 + 12x$$
Then the profit is
$$P = xS - C$$
or
$$P = 12x - x^2 - \left(\frac{x^3}{3} - 3x^2 + 12x\right)$$
$$= 2x^2 - \frac{x^3}{3}$$

The derivative of our profit function is
$$P' = \frac{dP}{dx} = 4x - x^2$$

Setting $P' = 0$, we have $4x - x^2 = 0$, which has two solutions, $x = 0$ and $x = 4$.

The second derivative is

$$P'' = 4 - 2x$$

Then

$$P'' = 4 - 2(0) = 4 \quad \text{at } x = 0$$
$$P'' = 4 - 2(4) = -4 \quad \text{at } x = 4$$

Thus, profit is maximized at a production quantity of 4. At $x = 0$, there is a minimum point.

REVIEW PROBLEMS

Find maximum and minimum points. Indicate whether the point is a maximum or minimum point.

1. $y = 3x^2 - \dfrac{x^3}{3}$

2. $y = (x - 8)^2$

3. $y = (x - 3)^2 + 8x$

4. $y = \dfrac{-x^4}{4} + 9x^3$

APPENDIX B
A Review of Matrix Algebra

A *matrix* is an ordered array of numbers. Examples are

$$A = \begin{pmatrix} 4 & 2 \\ 1 & 7 \end{pmatrix} \qquad B = \begin{pmatrix} 3 & 1 & 7 \\ -1 & 2 & 6 \end{pmatrix}$$

The *order* of a matrix is determined by the number of *rows* and *columns*. Thus, A is a 2×2 matrix and B is a 2×3 matrix. When the number of rows and columns is equal, we have a square matrix. For matrix elements we use small letters with two subscripts, the first referring to the row and the second to the column.

$$A = \begin{pmatrix} a_{11} & a_{12} & a_{13} \\ a_{21} & a_{22} & a_{23} \\ a_{31} & a_{32} & a_{33} \end{pmatrix}$$

The *transpose* of a matrix A, denoted by the symbol A^t, is a new matrix formed by interchanging the rows and columns.

$$A = \begin{pmatrix} 2 & 5 \\ 4 & 7 \end{pmatrix} \qquad A^t = \begin{pmatrix} 2 & 4 \\ 5 & 7 \end{pmatrix}$$

$$C = \begin{pmatrix} 3 & 6 & 7 \\ 2 & 4 & 3 \\ 1 & 8 & 5 \end{pmatrix} \qquad C^t = \begin{pmatrix} 3 & 2 & 1 \\ 6 & 4 & 8 \\ 7 & 3 & 5 \end{pmatrix}$$

Addition and Subtraction

Matrices can be added or subtracted *only* if they are of the same order. The resulting sum is obtained by adding or subtracting corresponding elements in each matrix.

$$\begin{pmatrix} 4 & 3 \\ 1 & 2 \\ 2 & 3 \end{pmatrix} + \begin{pmatrix} 5 & 0 \\ -1 & 2 \\ 3 & 1 \end{pmatrix} = \begin{pmatrix} 9 & 3 \\ 0 & 4 \\ 5 & 4 \end{pmatrix}$$

Multiplication

Multiplication by a scalar is given by taking each element and simply multiplying by the scalar:

$$A = \begin{pmatrix} 2 & -7 \\ 4 & 3 \\ 6 & 4 \end{pmatrix} \text{ then } 3A = 3\begin{pmatrix} 2 & -7 \\ 4 & 3 \\ 6 & 4 \end{pmatrix} = \begin{pmatrix} 6 & -21 \\ 12 & 9 \\ 18 & 12 \end{pmatrix}$$

Two matrices can be multiplied if and only if the *number of columns of the first is equal to the number of rows of the second*.

Procedure: Multiply the corresponding row element by the column element and then add these products.

1st row × 1st column, 1st row × 2nd column, . . ., 1st row × nth column

2nd row × 1st column, 2nd row × 2nd column, . . ., 2nd row × nth column

Examples:

1. $A = \begin{pmatrix} a & b & c \\ d & e & f \end{pmatrix} \quad B = \begin{pmatrix} g & i \\ h & k \\ i & m \end{pmatrix}$

$$C = AB = \begin{bmatrix} (ag + bh + ci) & (ai + bk + cm) \\ (dg + eh + fi) & (di + ek + fm) \end{bmatrix}$$

2. $A = \begin{pmatrix} 1 & 3 \\ 0 & 4 \end{pmatrix} \quad B = \begin{pmatrix} 0 & 2 \\ 3 & 3 \end{pmatrix}$

$$AB = \begin{pmatrix} 9 & 11 \\ 12 & 12 \end{pmatrix} \quad BA = \begin{pmatrix} 0 & 8 \\ 3 & 21 \end{pmatrix}$$

Note: $AB \neq BA$

Special Matrices

A matrix consisting of zeros is called a null or *zero matrix* (it is the matrix algebra equivalent of zero). An *identity matrix*, denoted by I, is a square matrix consisting of zero elements except for the diagonal from the left top to the right bottom, which is made up of ones.

$$I = \begin{pmatrix} 1 & 0 & 0 \\ 0 & 1 & 0 \\ 0 & 0 & 1 \end{pmatrix} \quad I = \begin{pmatrix} 1 & 0 \\ 0 & 1 \end{pmatrix}$$

The identity matrix is the matrix algebra equivalent of one.

Appendix B / A Review of Matrix Algebra

Matrix Inversion

The inverse of a matrix A is a new matrix A^{-1} such that $A^{-1}A = AA^{-1} = I$, where I is the identity matrix. The inverse of a matrix is the equivalent of a reciprocal in ordinary arithmetic. We can say that the reciprocal of a number a is that unique number which when multiplied by a yields 1, that is,

$$\frac{1}{a} a = 1$$

Using the Gaussian approach to finding the inverse, we transform a tableau A, I to a final tableau I, A^{-1}. Two operations are permitted in performing this transformation:

1. Any row can be multiplied or divided by a scalar.
2. A multiple of a row may be added to or subtracted from another row.

These two rules can be followed in any pattern to obtain the identity matrix on the left side of the tableau. An example will illustrate the procedure.

Example of matrix inversion:

$$A = \begin{pmatrix} 6 & 4 \\ 8 & 10 \end{pmatrix} \quad \text{Find } A^{-1}$$

1. Set up tableau A, I.

$$\begin{pmatrix} 6 & 4 \\ 8 & 10 \end{pmatrix} \begin{pmatrix} 1 & 0 \\ 0 & 1 \end{pmatrix}$$

2. Divide row 1 by a_{11}.

$$\begin{pmatrix} 1 & \frac{4}{6} \\ 8 & 10 \end{pmatrix} \begin{pmatrix} \frac{1}{6} & 0 \\ 0 & 1 \end{pmatrix}$$

3. Multiply row 1 by a_{21} and subtract from row 2.

$$\begin{pmatrix} 1 & \frac{4}{6} \\ 0 & \frac{28}{6} \end{pmatrix} \begin{pmatrix} \frac{1}{6} & 0 \\ -\frac{8}{6} & 1 \end{pmatrix}$$

4. Divide row 2 by a_{22}.

$$\begin{pmatrix} 1 & \frac{4}{6} \\ 0 & 1 \end{pmatrix} \begin{pmatrix} \frac{1}{6} & 0 \\ -\frac{2}{7} & \frac{3}{14} \end{pmatrix}$$

5. Multiply row 2 by a_{12} and subtract from row 1.

$$\begin{pmatrix} 1 & 0 \\ 0 & 1 \end{pmatrix} \begin{pmatrix} \frac{5}{14} & -\frac{1}{7} \\ -\frac{2}{7} & \frac{3}{14} \end{pmatrix}$$

We now have a tableau I, A^{-1}.

As an exercise, verify that $AA^{-1} = I$.

$$\begin{pmatrix} 6 & 4 \\ 8 & 10 \end{pmatrix} \begin{pmatrix} \frac{5}{14} & -\frac{1}{7} \\ -\frac{2}{7} & \frac{3}{14} \end{pmatrix} = \begin{pmatrix} 1 & 0 \\ 0 & 1 \end{pmatrix}$$

Matrix Solution of Linear Systems (Gaussian Method)

Assume a set of linear equations:

$$10x_1 - 4x_2 = 6$$
$$4x_1 + 10x_2 = 14$$

We now treat the coefficients of the left side of the equations as a matrix A and the constants to the right side of the equality signs as a vector of constants b.

$$A = \begin{pmatrix} 10 & -4 \\ 4 & 10 \end{pmatrix} \qquad b = \begin{pmatrix} 6 \\ 14 \end{pmatrix}$$

We now set up tableau A, b and solve it as in the Gaussian method for finding inverses to obtain a tableau in the form of I, x.

The first tableau is

$$\begin{pmatrix} 10 & -4 & 6 \\ 4 & 10 & 14 \end{pmatrix}$$

Divide row 1 by 10.

$$\begin{pmatrix} 1 & -\frac{4}{10} & \frac{6}{10} \\ 4 & 10 & 14 \end{pmatrix}$$

Subtract 4 times row 1 from row 2.

$$\begin{pmatrix} 1 & -\frac{4}{10} & \frac{6}{10} \\ 0 & \frac{116}{10} & \frac{116}{10} \end{pmatrix}$$

Divide row 2 by $\frac{116}{10}$.

$$\begin{pmatrix} 1 & -\frac{4}{10} & \frac{6}{10} \\ 0 & 1 & 1 \end{pmatrix}$$

Multiply row 2 by $\frac{4}{10}$ and add to row 1.

$$\begin{pmatrix} 1 & 0 & 1 \\ 0 & 1 & 1 \end{pmatrix}$$

Thus,

$$x_1 = 1$$
$$x_2 = 1$$

As an exercise, the reader should verify that this is a solution to the equations.

In general terms, the above can be stated as follows:

A = matrix of coefficients of unknowns $(x_1, \ldots, x_n)$
C = vector of constants on right-hand side of equation
$Ax = C$
$A^{-1}Ax = A^{-1}C$

We know that
$$A^{-1}A = I$$

Therefore
$$Ix = A^{-1}C$$
$$x = A^{-1}C$$

Another example will reinforce this point:

$$25x_1 + 50x_2 + 75x_3 = 1750$$
$$15x_1 + 25x_2 + 35x_3 = 850$$
$$0x_1 + x_2 + x_3 = 25$$

$$\overset{A}{\begin{pmatrix} 25 & 50 & 75 \\ 15 & 25 & 35 \\ 0 & 1 & 1 \end{pmatrix}} \overset{X}{\begin{pmatrix} x_1 \\ x_2 \\ x_3 \end{pmatrix}} = \overset{C}{\begin{pmatrix} 175 \\ 850 \\ 25 \end{pmatrix}}$$

Because $x = A^{-1}C$, we must find the inverse of A and multiply it by C to get the solutions for x_1, x_2, and x_3.

Finding the inverse is left to the student as an exercise. Having obtained the correct inverse, the solution is obtained by multiplying A^{-1} by C.

$$\overset{A^{-1}}{\begin{pmatrix} -\frac{2}{25} & \frac{1}{5} & -1 \\ -\frac{3}{25} & \frac{1}{5} & +2 \\ \frac{3}{25} & -\frac{1}{5} & -1 \end{pmatrix}} \overset{C}{\begin{pmatrix} 175 \\ 850 \\ 25 \end{pmatrix}} = \overset{A^{-1}C}{\begin{pmatrix} 5 \\ 10 \\ 15 \end{pmatrix}} = \begin{pmatrix} x_1 \\ x_2 \\ x_3 \end{pmatrix}$$

PROBLEMS

1. $\begin{pmatrix} 3 & 7 \\ 4 & 1 \end{pmatrix} + \begin{pmatrix} 8 & -1 \\ 0 & 3 \end{pmatrix}$

2. $\begin{pmatrix} 6 & 8 \\ 7 & 9 \end{pmatrix} - \begin{pmatrix} -8 & 1 \\ -2 & 2 \end{pmatrix}$

3. $4\begin{pmatrix} 3 & 6 \\ 2 & 1 \end{pmatrix}$

4. $\sqrt{4} \begin{pmatrix} 1 & 1 \\ 1 & 1 \end{pmatrix}$

5. $\begin{pmatrix} 5 & 6 \\ 7 & 8 \end{pmatrix} \begin{pmatrix} 1 & 0 \\ 0 & 1 \end{pmatrix}$

6. $\begin{pmatrix} 5 & 9 & -3 \\ -1 & 2 & 0 \end{pmatrix} \begin{pmatrix} 6 & 7 \\ 8 & 9 \\ 1 & 2 \end{pmatrix}$

7. $\begin{pmatrix} 3 & 4 \\ 7 & 2 \end{pmatrix}^2$

8. $\begin{pmatrix} 2 & 3 & 1 \\ 0 & 1 & 2 \\ 3 & 9 & 6 \end{pmatrix}^t$

9. $A = \begin{pmatrix} 2 & 3 \\ 1 & 5 \end{pmatrix} \quad B = \begin{pmatrix} 4 & 1 \\ 7 & -8 \end{pmatrix}$

Find:
a. AB
b. BA
c. B^2
d. BAB

10. Find the following inverses using the Gaussian method.

a. $\begin{pmatrix} 5 & 6 \\ 7 & 8 \end{pmatrix}^{-1}$

b. $\begin{pmatrix} 1 & 3 & 0 \\ 2 & 1 & 0 \\ 0 & 6 & 3 \end{pmatrix}^{-1}$

c. $\begin{pmatrix} 2 & 4 & 1 \\ 3 & 2 & 5 \\ 2 & 3 & 2 \end{pmatrix}^{-1}$

11. Using the Gaussian method, solve the following systems of equations.
 a. $\quad x - 10y + z = 0$
 $\quad\quad 0x \quad\quad 4x + 0z = 8$
 $\quad -3x - 4y + z = 0$
 b. $4x - 5y = 7$
 $\quad 2x + 7y = 13$
 c. $x_3 - x_2 = x_1 + 5$
 $\quad x_2 + 50 = x_3 + x_1 + 2x_2$
 $\quad\quad x_1 = 7x_2 + 15$

APPENDIX C
Tables

TABLE 1. Random Numbers

12651	61646	11769	75109	86996	97669	25757	32535	07122	76763
81769	74436	02630	72310	45049	18029	07469	42341	98173	79260
36737	98863	77240	76251	00654	64688	09343	70278	67331	98729
82861	54371	76610	94934	72748	44124	05610	53750	95938	01485
21325	15732	24127	37431	09723	63529	73977	95218	96074	42138
74146	47887	62463	23045	41490	07954	22597	60012	98866	90959
90759	64410	54179	66075	61051	75385	51378	08360	95946	95547
55683	98078	02238	91540	21219	17720	87817	41705	95785	12563
79686	17969	76061	83748	55920	83612	41540	86492	06447	60568
70333	00201	86201	69716	78185	62154	77930	67663	29529	75116
14042	53536	07779	04157	41172	36473	42123	43929	50533	33437
59911	08256	06596	48416	69770	68797	56080	14223	59199	30162
62368	62623	62742	14891	39247	52242	98832	69533	91174	57979
57529	97751	54976	48957	74599	08759	78494	52785	68526	64618
15469	90574	78033	66885	13936	42117	71831	22961	94225	31816
18625	23674	53850	32827	81647	80820	00420	63555	74489	80141
74626	68394	88562	70745	23701	45630	65891	58220	35442	60414
11119	16519	27384	90199	79210	76965	99546	30323	31664	22845
41101	17336	48951	53674	17880	45260	08575	49321	36191	17095
32123	91576	84221	78902	82010	30847	62329	63898	23268	74283
26091	68409	69704	82267	14751	13151	93115	01437	56945	89661
67680	79790	48462	59278	44185	29616	76531	19589	83139	28454
15184	19260	14073	07026	25264	08388	27182	22557	61501	67481
58010	45039	57181	10238	36874	28546	37444	80824	63981	39942
56425	53996	86245	32623	78858	08143	60377	42925	42815	11159
82630	84066	13592	60642	17904	99718	63432	88642	37858	25431
14927	40909	23900	48761	44860	92467	31742	87142	03607	32059
23740	22505	07489	85986	74420	21744	97711	36648	35620	97949
32990	97446	03711	63824	07953	85965	87089	11687	92414	67257
05310	24058	91946	78437	34365	82469	12430	84754	19354	72745
21839	39937	27534	88913	49055	19218	47712	67677	51889	70926
08833	42549	93981	94051	28382	83725	72643	64233	97252	17133
58336	11139	47479	00931	91560	95372	97642	33856	54825	55680
62032	91144	75478	47431	52726	30289	42411	91886	51818	78292
45171	30557	53116	04118	58301	24375	65609	85810	18620	49198
91611	62656	60128	35609	63698	78356	50682	22505	01692	36291
55472	63819	86314	49174	93582	73604	78614	78849	23096	72825
18573	09729	74091	53994	10970	86557	65661	41854	26037	53296
60866	02955	90288	82136	83644	94455	06560	78029	98768	71296
45043	55608	82767	60890	74646	79485	13619	98868	40857	19415
17831	09737	79473	75945	28394	79334	70577	38048	03607	06932
40137	03981	07585	18128	11178	32601	27994	05641	22600	86064
77776	31343	14576	97706	16039	47517	43300	59080	80392	63189
69605	44104	40103	95635	05635	81673	68657	09559	23510	95875
19916	52934	26499	09821	87331	80993	61299	36979	73599	35055
02606	58552	07678	56619	65325	30705	99582	53390	46357	13244
65183	73160	87131	35530	47946	09854	18080	02321	05809	04898
10740	98914	44916	11322	89717	88189	30143	52687	19420	60061
98642	89822	71691	51573	83666	61642	46683	33761	47542	23551
60139	25601	93663	25547	02654	94829	48672	28736	84994	13071

Source: The Rand Corporation, *A Million Random Digits with 100,000 Normal Deviates.* New York: The Free Press, 1955. Reproduced with permission of The Rand Corporation.

TABLE 2. The Standardized Normal Distribution Function, $F_N(Z)$

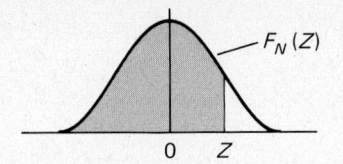

Z	0.00	0.01	0.02	0.03	0.04	0.05	0.06	0.07	0.08	0.09
0.0	0.5000	0.5040	0.5080	0.5120	0.5160	0.5199	0.5239	0.5279	0.5319	0.5359
0.1	0.5398	0.5438	0.5478	0.5517	0.5557	0.5596	0.5636	0.5675	0.5714	0.5753
0.2	0.5793	0.5832	0.5871	0.5910	0.5948	0.5987	0.6026	0.6064	0.6103	0.6141
0.3	0.6179	0.6217	0.6255	0.6293	0.6331	0.6368	0.6406	0.6443	0.6480	0.6517
0.4	0.6554	0.6591	0.6628	0.6664	0.6700	0.6736	0.6772	0.6808	0.6844	0.6879
0.5	0.6915	0.6950	0.6985	0.7019	0.7054	0.7088	0.7123	0.7157	0.7190	0.7224
0.6	0.7257	0.7291	0.7324	0.7357	0.7389	0.7422	0.7454	0.7486	0.7517	0.7549
0.7	0.7580	0.7611	0.7642	0.7673	0.7703	0.7734	0.7764	0.7794	0.7823	0.7852
0.8	0.7881	0.7910	0.7939	0.7967	0.7995	0.8023	0.8051	0.8078	0.8106	0.8133
0.9	0.8159	0.8186	0.8212	0.8238	0.8264	0.8289	0.8315	0.8340	0.8365	0.8389
1.0	0.8413	0.8438	0.8461	0.8485	0.8508	0.8531	0.8554	0.8577	0.8599	0.8621
1.1	0.8643	0.8665	0.8686	0.8708	0.8729	0.8749	0.8770	0.8790	0.8810	0.8830
1.2	0.8849	0.8869	0.8888	0.8907	0.8925	0.8944	0.8962	0.8980	0.8997	0.90147
1.3	0.90320	0.90490	0.90658	0.90824	0.90988	0.91149	0.91309	0.91466	0.91621	0.91774
1.4	0.91924	0.92073	0.92220	0.92364	0.92507	0.92647	0.92785	0.92922	0.93056	0.93189
1.5	0.93319	0.93448	0.93574	0.93699	0.93822	0.93943	0.94062	0.94179	0.94295	0.94408
1.6	0.94520	0.94630	0.94738	0.94845	0.94950	0.95053	0.95154	0.95254	0.95352	0.95449
1.7	0.95543	0.95637	0.95728	0.95818	0.95907	0.95994	0.96080	0.96164	0.96246	0.96327
1.8	0.96407	0.96485	0.96562	0.96638	0.96712	0.96784	0.96856	0.96926	0.96995	0.97062
1.9	0.97128	0.97193	0.97257	0.97320	0.97381	0.97441	0.97500	0.97558	0.97615	0.97670
2.0	0.97725	0.97778	0.97831	0.97882	0.97932	0.97982	0.98030	0.98077	0.98124	0.98169
2.1	0.98214	0.98257	0.98300	0.98341	0.98382	0.98422	0.98461	0.98500	0.98537	0.98574
2.2	0.98610	0.98645	0.98679	0.98713	0.98745	0.98778	0.98809	0.98840	0.98870	0.98899
2.3	0.98928	0.98956	0.98983	0.9^20097	0.9^20358	0.9^20613	0.9^20863	0.9^21106	0.9^21344	0.9^21576
2.4	0.9^21802	0.9^22024	0.9^22240	0.9^22451	0.9^22656	0.9^22857	0.9^23053	0.9^23244	0.9^23431	0.9^23613
2.5	0.9^23790	0.9^23963	0.9^24132	0.9^24297	0.9^24457	0.9^24614	0.9^24766	0.9^24915	0.9^25060	0.9^25201
3.0	0.9^28650	0.9^28694	0.9^28736	0.9^28777	0.9^28817	0.9^28856	0.9^28893	0.9^28930	0.9^28965	0.9^28999
3.5	0.9^37674	0.9^37759	0.9^37842	0.9^37922	0.9^37999	0.9^38074	0.9^38146	0.9^38215	0.9^38282	0.9^38347
4.0	0.9^46833	0.9^46964	0.9^47090	0.9^47211	0.9^47327	0.9^47439	0.9^47546	0.9^47649	0.9^47748	0.9^57843

For example: $F(2.41) = 0.9^22024 = 0.992024$.

Source: A. Hald, *Statistical Tables and Formulas* (New York: Wiley, 1952); reproduced by permission of Professor A. Hald and John Wiley & Sons, Inc.

TABLE 3. Student's t Distribution

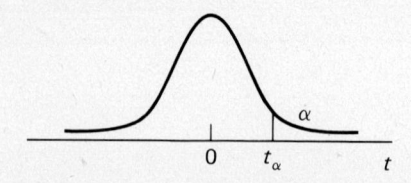

The following table provides the values of t_α that correspond to a given upper-tail area α and a specified number of degrees of freedom.

Degrees of Freedom	.4	.25	.1	.05	.025	.01	.005	.0025	.001	.0005
1	0.325	1.000	3.078	6.314	12.706	31.821	63.657	127.32	318.31	636.62
2	.289	0.816	1.886	2.920	4.303	6.965	9.925	14.089	22.327	31.598
3	.277	.765	1.638	2.353	3.182	4.541	5.841	7.453	10.214	12.924
4	.271	.741	1.533	2.132	2.776	3.747	4.604	5.598	7.173	8.610
5	0.267	0.727	1.476	2.015	2.571	3.365	4.032	4.773	5.893	6.869
6	.265	.718	1.440	1.943	2.447	3.143	3.707	4.317	5.208	5.959
7	.263	.711	1.415	1.895	2.365	2.998	3.499	4.029	4.785	5.408
8	.262	.706	1.397	1.860	2.306	2.896	3.355	3.833	4.501	5.041
9	.261	.703	1.383	1.833	2.262	2.821	3.250	3.690	4.297	4.781
10	0.260	0.700	1.372	1.812	2.228	2.764	3.169	3.581	4.144	4.587
11	.260	.697	1.363	1.796	2.201	2.718	3.106	3.497	4.025	4.437
12	.259	.695	1.356	1.782	2.179	2.681	3.055	3.428	3.930	4.318
13	.259	.694	1.350	1.771	2.160	2.650	3.012	3.372	3.852	4.221
14	.258	.692	1.345	1.761	2.145	2.624	2.977	3.326	3.787	4.140
15	0.258	0.691	1.341	1.753	2.131	2.602	2.947	3.286	3.733	4.073
16	.258	.690	1.337	1.746	2.120	2.583	2.921	3.252	3.686	4.015
17	.257	.689	1.333	1.740	2.110	2.567	2.898	3.222	3.646	3.965
18	.257	.688	1.330	1.734	2.101	2.552	2.878	3.197	3.610	3.922
19	.257	.688	1.328	1.729	2.093	2.539	2.861	3.174	3.579	3.883
20	0.257	0.687	1.325	1.725	2.086	2.528	2.845	3.153	3.552	3.850
21	.257	.686	1.323	1.721	2.080	2.518	2.831	3.135	3.527	3.819
22	.256	.686	1.321	1.717	2.074	2.508	2.819	3.119	3.505	3.792
23	.256	.685	1.319	1.714	2.069	2.500	2.807	3.104	3.485	3.767
24	.256	.685	1.318	1.711	2.064	2.492	2.797	3.091	3.467	3.745
25	0.256	0.684	1.316	1.708	2.060	2.485	2.787	3.078	3.450	3.725
26	.256	.684	1.315	1.706	2.056	2.479	2.779	3.067	3.435	3.707
27	.256	.684	1.314	1.703	2.052	2.473	2.771	3.057	3.421	3.690
28	.256	.683	1.313	1.701	2.048	2.467	2.763	3.047	3.408	3.674
29	.256	.683	1.311	1.699	2.045	2.462	2.756	3.038	3.396	3.659
30	0.256	0.683	1.310	1.697	2.042	2.457	2.750	3.030	3.385	3.646
40	.255	.681	1.303	1.684	2.021	2.423	2.704	2.971	3.307	3.551
60	.254	.679	1.296	1.671	2.000	2.390	2.660	2.915	3.232	3.460
120	.254	.677	1.289	1.658	1.980	2.358	2.617	2.860	3.160	3.373
∞	.253	.674	1.282	1.645	1.960	2.326	2.576	2.807	3.090	3.291

Source: E. S. Pearson and H. O. Hartley, *Biometrika Tables for Statisticians,* vol. 1 (London: Charles Griffin & Co., Ltd. 1976.)

Appendix C / Tables

TABLE 4. Cumulative Binomial Distribution $P(R \geq r \mid n, p)$

$n = 1$

p \ r	.01	.02	.03	.04	.05	.06	.07	.08	.09	.10
1	0100	0200	0300	0400	0500	0600	0700	0800	0900	1000

p \ r	.11	.12	.13	.14	.15	.16	.17	.18	.19	.20
1	1100	1200	1300	1400	1500	1600	1700	1800	1900	2000

p \ r	.21	.22	.23	.24	.25	.26	.27	.28	.29	.30
1	2100	2200	2300	2400	2500	2600	2700	2800	2900	3000

p \ r	.31	.32	.33	.34	.35	.36	.37	.38	.39	.40
1	3100	3200	3300	3400	3500	3600	3700	3800	3900	4000

p \ r	.41	.42	.43	.44	.45	.46	.47	.48	.49	.50
1	4100	4200	4300	4400	4500	4600	4700	4800	4900	5000

$n = 2$

p \ r	.01	.02	.03	.04	.05	.06	.07	.08	.09	.10
1	0199	0396	0591	0784	0975	1164	1351	1536	1719	1900
2	0001	0004	0009	0016	0025	0036	0049	0064	0081	0100

p \ r	.11	.12	.13	.14	.15	.16	.17	.18	.19	.20
1	2079	2256	2431	2604	2775	2944	3111	3276	3439	3600
2	0121	0144	0169	0196	0225	0256	0289	0324	0361	0400

p \ r	.21	.22	.23	.24	.25	.26	.27	.28	.29	.30
1	3759	3916	4071	4224	4375	4524	4671	4816	4959	5100
2	0441	0484	0529	0576	0625	0676	0729	0784	0841	0900

p \ r	.31	.32	.33	.34	.35	.36	.37	.38	.39	.40
1	5239	5376	5511	5644	5775	5904	6031	6156	6279	6400
2	0961	1024	1089	1156	1225	1296	1369	1444	1521	1600

p \ r	.41	.42	.43	.44	.45	.46	.47	.48	.49	.50
1	6519	6636	6751	6864	6975	7084	7191	7296	7399	7500
2	1681	1764	1849	1936	2025	2116	2209	2304	2401	2500

$n = 3$

p \ r	.01	.02	.03	.04	.05	.06	.07	.08	.09	.10
1	0297	0588	0873	1153	1426	1694	1956	2213	2464	2710
2	0003	0012	0026	0047	0073	0104	0140	0182	0228	0280
3				0001	0001	0002	0003	0005	0007	0010

p \ r	.11	.12	.13	.14	.15	.16	.17	.18	.19	.20
1	2950	3185	3415	3639	3859	4073	4282	4486	4686	4880
2	0336	0397	0463	0533	0608	0686	0769	0855	0946	1040
3	0013	0017	0022	0027	0034	0041	0049	0058	0069	0080

p \ r	.21	.22	.23	.24	.25	.26	.27	.28	.29	.30
1	5070	5254	5435	5610	5781	5948	6110	6268	6421	6570
2	1138	1239	1344	1452	1563	1676	1793	1913	2035	2160
3	0093	0106	0122	0138	0156	0176	0197	0220	0244	0270

For $p > 0.5$, the following identity holds:

$$P(R \geq r \mid n, p) = 1 - P(R \geq n - r + 1 \mid n, 1 - p)$$

For example, consider the probability of two or more heads in three tosses of a coin with P (head) $=$ 0.60; this is identical to one minus the probability of two or more tails in three tosses, with P(tail) $=$ 0.4, or $1 - 0.3520 = 0.6480$.

Source: By permission from R. Schlaifer, *Probability and Statistics for Business Decisions* (New York: McGraw-Hill, 1959).

TABLE 4. Cumulative Binomial Distribution $P(R \geq r \mid n, p)$ (Continued)

p\r	31	32	33	34	35	36	37	38	39	40
1	6715	6856	6992	7125	7254	7379	7500	7617	7730	7840
2	2287	2417	2548	2682	2818	2955	3094	3235	3377	3520
3	0298	0328	0359	0393	0429	0467	0507	0549	0593	0640

p\r	41	42	43	44	45	46	47	48	49	50
1	7946	8049	8148	8244	8336	8425	8511	8594	8673	8750
2	3665	3810	3957	4104	4253	4401	4551	4700	4850	5000
3	0689	0741	0795	0852	0911	0973	1038	1106	1176	1250

$n = 4$

p\r	01	02	03	04	05	06	07	08	09	10
1	0394	0776	1147	1507	1855	2193	2519	2836	3143	3439
2	0006	0023	0052	0091	0140	0199	0267	0344	0430	0523
3			0001	0002	0005	0008	0013	0019	0027	0037
4									0001	0001

p\r	11	12	13	14	15	16	17	18	19	20
1	3726	4003	4271	4530	4780	5021	5254	5479	5695	5904
2	0624	0732	0847	0968	1095	1228	1366	1509	1656	1808
3	0049	0063	0079	0098	0120	0144	0171	0202	0235	0272
4	0001	0002	0003	0004	0005	0007	0008	0010	0013	0016

p\r	21	22	23	24	25	26	27	28	29	30
1	6105	6298	6485	6664	6836	7001	7160	7313	7459	7599
2	1963	2122	2285	2450	2617	2787	2959	3132	3307	3483
3	0312	0356	0403	0453	0508	0566	0628	0694	0763	0837
4	0019	0023	0028	0033	0039	0046	0053	0061	0071	0081

p\r	31	32	33	34	35	36	37	38	39	40
1	7733	7862	7985	8103	8215	8322	8425	8522	8615	8704
2	3660	3837	4015	4193	4370	4547	4724	4900	5075	5248
3	0915	0996	1082	1171	1265	1362	1464	1569	1679	1792
4	0092	0105	0119	0134	0150	0168	0187	0209	0231	0256

p\r	41	42	43	44	45	46	47	48	49	50
1	8788	8868	8944	9017	9085	9150	9211	9269	9323	9375
2	5420	5590	5759	5926	6090	6252	6412	6569	6724	6875
3	1909	2030	2155	2283	2415	2550	2689	2831	2977	3125
4	0283	0311	0342	0375	0410	0448	0488	0531	0576	0625

$n = 5$

p\r	01	02	03	04	05	06	07	08	09	10
1	0490	0961	1413	1846	2262	2661	3043	3409	3760	4095
2	0010	0038	0085	0148	0226	0319	0425	0544	0674	0815
3		0001	0003	0006	0012	0020	0031	0045	0063	0086
4						0001	0001	0002	0003	0005

p\r	11	12	13	14	15	16	17	18	19	20
1	4416	4723	5016	5296	5563	5818	6061	6293	6513	6723
2	0965	1125	1292	1467	1648	1835	2027	2224	2424	2627
3	0112	0143	0179	0220	0266	0318	0375	0437	0505	0579
4	0007	0009	0013	0017	0022	0029	0036	0045	0055	0067
5				0001	0001	0001	0001	0002	0002	0003

p\r	21	22	23	24	25	26	27	28	29	30
1	6923	7113	7293	7464	7627	7781	7927	8065	8196	8319
2	2833	3041	3251	3461	3672	3883	4093	4303	4511	4718
3	0659	0744	0836	0933	1035	1143	1257	1376	1501	1631
4	0081	0097	0114	0134	0156	0181	0208	0238	0272	0308
5	0004	0005	0006	0008	0010	0012	0014	0017	0021	0024

TABLE 4. Cumulative Binomial Distribution $P(R \geq r \mid n, p)$ (Continued)

p\r	31	32	33	34	35	36	37	38	39	40
1	8436	8546	8650	8748	8840	8926	9008	9084	9155	9222
2	4923	5125	5325	5522	5716	5906	6093	6276	6455	6630
3	1766	1905	2050	2199	2352	2509	2670	2835	3003	3174
4	0347	0390	0436	0486	0540	0598	0660	0726	0796	0870
5	0029	0034	0039	0045	0053	0060	0069	0079	0090	0102

p\r	41	42	43	44	45	46	47	48	49	50
1	9285	9344	9398	9449	9497	9541	9582	9620	9655	9688
2	6801	6967	7129	7286	7438	7585	7728	7865	7998	8125
3	3349	3525	3705	3886	4069	4253	4439	4625	4813	5000
4	0949	1033	1121	1214	1312	1415	1522	1635	1753	1875
5	0116	0131	0147	0165	0185	0206	0229	0255	0282	0313

n = 6

p\r	01	02	03	04	05	06	07	08	09	10
1	0585	1142	1670	2172	2649	3101	3530	3936	4321	4686
2	0015	0057	0125	0216	0328	0459	0608	0773	0952	1143
3		0002	0005	0012	0022	0038	0058	0085	0118	0159
4					0001	0002	0003	0005	0008	0013
5										0001

p\r	11	12	13	14	15	16	17	18	19	20
1	5030	5356	5664	5954	6229	6487	6731	6960	7176	7379
2	1345	1556	1776	2003	2235	2472	2713	2956	3201	3446
3	0206	0261	0324	0395	0473	0560	0655	0759	0870	0989
4	0018	0025	0034	0045	0059	0075	0094	0116	0141	0170
5	0001	0001	0002	0003	0004	0005	0007	0010	0013	0016
6										0001

p\r	21	22	23	24	25	26	27	28	29	30
1	7569	7748	7916	8073	8220	8358	8487	8607	8719	8824
2	3692	3937	4180	4422	4661	4896	5128	5356	5580	5798
3	1115	1250	1391	1539	1694	1856	2023	2196	2374	2557
4	0202	0239	0280	0326	0376	0431	0492	0557	0628	0705
5	0020	0025	0031	0038	0046	0056	0067	0079	0093	0109
6	0001	0001	0001	0002	0002	0003	0004	0005	0006	0007

p\r	31	32	33	34	35	36	37	38	39	40
1	8921	9011	9095	9173	9246	9313	9375	9432	9485	9533
2	6012	6220	6422	6619	6809	6994	7172	7343	7508	7667
3	2744	2936	3130	3328	3529	3732	3937	4143	4350	4557
4	0787	0875	0969	1069	1174	1286	1404	1527	1657	1792
5	0127	0148	0170	0195	0223	0254	0288	0325	0365	0410
6	0009	0011	0013	0015	0018	0022	0026	0030	0035	0041

p\r	41	42	43	44	45	46	47	48	49	50
1	9578	9619	9657	9692	9723	9752	9778	9802	9824	9844
2	7819	7965	8105	8238	8364	8485	8599	8707	8810	8906
3	4764	4971	5177	5382	5585	5786	5985	6180	6373	6563
4	1933	2080	2232	2390	2553	2721	2893	3070	3252	3438
5	0458	0510	0566	0627	0692	0762	0837	0917	1003	1094
6	0048	0055	0063	0073	0083	0095	0108	0122	0138	0156

n = 7

p\r	01	02	03	04	05	06	07	08	09	10
1	0679	1319	1920	2486	3017	3515	3983	4422	4832	5217
2	0020	0079	0171	0294	0444	0618	0813	1026	1255	1497
3		0003	0009	0020	0038	0063	0097	0140	0193	0257
4				0001	0002	0004	0007	0012	0018	0027
5								0001	0001	0002

TABLE 4. Cumulative Binomial Distribution $P(R \geq r \mid n, p)$ (Continued)

p\r	11	12	13	14	15	16	17	18	19	20
1	5577	5913	6227	6521	6794	7049	7286	7507	7712	7903
2	1750	2012	2281	2556	2834	3115	3396	3677	3956	4233
3	0331	0416	0513	0620	0738	0866	1005	1154	1313	1480
4	0039	0054	0072	0094	0121	0153	0189	0231	0279	0333
5	0003	0004	0006	0009	0012	0017	0022	0029	0037	0047
6					0001	0001	0001	0002	0003	0004

p\r	21	22	23	24	25	26	27	28	29	30
1	8080	8243	8395	8535	8665	8785	8895	8997	9090	9176
2	4506	4775	5040	5298	5551	5796	6035	6266	6490	6706
3	1657	1841	2033	2231	2436	2646	2861	3081	3304	3529
4	0394	0461	0536	0617	0706	0802	0905	1016	1134	1260
5	0058	0072	0088	0107	0129	0153	0181	0213	0248	0288
6	0005	0006	0008	0011	0013	0017	0021	0026	0031	0038
7				0001	0001	0001	0001	0001	0002	0002

p\r	31	32	33	34	35	36	37	38	39	40
1	9255	9328	9394	9454	9510	9560	9606	9648	9686	9720
2	6914	7113	7304	7487	7662	7828	7987	8137	8279	8414
3	3757	3987	4217	4447	4677	4906	5134	5359	5581	5801
4	1394	1534	1682	1837	1998	2167	2341	2521	2707	2898
5	0332	0380	0434	0492	0556	0625	0701	0782	0869	0963
6	0046	0055	0065	0077	0090	0105	0123	0142	0164	0188
7	0003	0003	0004	0005	0006	0008	0009	0011	0014	0016

p\r	41	42	43	44	45	46	47	48	49	50
1	9751	9779	9805	9827	9848	9866	9883	9897	9910	9922
2	8541	8660	8772	8877	8976	9068	9153	9233	9307	9375
3	6017	6229	6436	6638	6836	7027	7213	7393	7567	7734
4	3094	3294	3498	3706	3917	4131	4346	4563	4781	5000
5	1063	1169	1282	1402	1529	1663	1803	1951	2105	2266
6	0216	0246	0279	0316	0357	0402	0451	0504	0562	0625
7	0019	0023	0027	0032	0037	0044	0051	0059	0068	0078

$n = 8$

p\r	01	02	03	04	05	06	07	08	09	10
1	0773	1492	2163	2786	3366	3904	4404	4868	5297	5695
2	0027	0103	0223	0381	0572	0792	1035	1298	1577	1869
3	0001	0004	0013	0031	0058	0096	0147	0211	0289	0381
4			0001	0002	0004	0007	0013	0022	0034	0050
5							0001	0001	0003	0004

p\r	11	12	13	14	15	16	17	18	19	20
1	6063	6404	6718	7008	7275	7521	7748	7956	8147	8322
2	2171	2480	2794	3111	3428	3744	4057	4366	4670	4967
3	0487	0608	0743	0891	1052	1226	1412	1608	1815	2031
4	0071	0097	0129	0168	0214	0267	0328	0397	0476	0563
5	0007	0010	0015	0021	0029	0038	0050	0065	0083	0104
6		0001	0001	0002	0002	0003	0005	0007	0009	0012
7									0001	0001

p\r	21	22	23	24	25	26	27	28	29	30
1	8483	8630	8764	8887	8999	9101	9194	9278	9354	9424
2	5257	5538	5811	6075	6329	6573	6807	7031	7244	7447
3	2255	2486	2724	2967	3215	3465	3718	3973	4228	4482
4	0659	0765	0880	1004	1138	1281	1433	1594	1763	1941
5	0129	0158	0191	0230	0273	0322	0377	0438	0505	0580
6	0016	0021	0027	0034	0042	0052	0064	0078	0094	0113
7	0001	0002	0002	0003	0004	0005	0006	0008	0010	0013
8									0001	0001

TABLE 4. Cumulative Binomial Distribution $P(R \geq r \mid n, p)$ (Continued)

p\r	31	32	33	34	35	36	37	38	39	40
1	9486	9543	9594	9640	9681	9719	9752	9782	9808	9832
2	7640	7822	7994	8156	8309	8452	8586	8711	8828	8936
3	4736	4987	5236	5481	5722	5958	6189	6415	6634	6846
4	2126	2319	2519	2724	2936	3153	3374	3599	3828	4059
5	0661	0750	0846	0949	1061	1180	1307	1443	1586	1737
6	0134	0159	0187	0218	0253	0293	0336	0385	0439	0498
7	0016	0020	0024	0030	0036	0043	0051	0061	0072	0085
8	0001	0001	0001	0002	0002	0003	0004	0004	0005	0007

p\r	41	42	43	44	45	46	47	48	49	50
1	9853	9872	9889	9903	9916	9928	9938	9947	9954	9961
2	9037	9130	9216	9295	9368	9435	9496	9552	9602	9648
3	7052	7250	7440	7624	7799	7966	8125	8276	8419	8555
4	4292	4527	4762	4996	5230	5463	5694	5922	6146	6367
5	1895	2062	2235	2416	2604	2798	2999	3205	3416	3633
6	0563	0634	0711	0794	0885	0982	1086	1198	1318	1445
7	0100	0117	0136	0157	0181	0208	0239	0272	0310	0352
8	0008	0010	0012	0014	0017	0020	0024	0028	0033	0039

$n = 9$

p\r	01	02	03	04	05	06	07	08	09	10
1	0865	1663	2398	3075	3698	4270	4796	5278	5721	6126
2	0034	0131	0282	0478	0712	0978	1271	1583	1912	2252
3	0001	0006	0020	0045	0084	0138	0209	0298	0405	0530
4			0001	0003	0006	0013	0023	0037	0057	0083
5					0001	0002	0003	0005	0009
6										0001

p\r	11	12	13	14	15	16	17	18	19	20
1	6496	6835	7145	7427	7684	7918	8131	8324	8499	8658
2	2599	2951	3304	3657	4005	4348	4685	5012	5330	5638
3	0672	0833	1009	1202	1409	1629	1861	2105	2357	2618
4	0117	0158	0209	0269	0339	0420	0512	0615	0730	0856
5	0014	0021	0030	0041	0056	0075	0098	0125	0158	0196
6	0001	0002	0003	0004	0006	0009	0013	0017	0023	0031
7						0001	0001	0002	0002	0003

p\r	21	22	23	24	25	26	27	28	29	30
1	8801	8931	9048	9154	9249	9335	9411	9480	9542	9596
2	5934	6218	6491	6750	6997	7230	7452	7660	7856	8040
3	2885	3158	3434	3713	3993	4273	4552	4829	5102	5372
4	0994	1144	1304	1475	1657	1849	2050	2260	2478	2703
5	0240	0291	0350	0416	0489	0571	0662	0762	0870	0988
6	0040	0051	0065	0081	0100	0122	0149	0179	0213	0253
7	0004	0006	0008	0010	0013	0017	0022	0028	0035	0043
8			0001	0001	0001	0001	0002	0003	0003	0004

p\r	31	32	33	34	35	36	37	38	39	40
1	9645	9689	9728	9762	9793	9820	9844	9865	9883	9899
2	8212	8372	8522	8661	8789	8908	9017	9118	9210	9295
3	5636	5894	6146	6390	6627	6856	7076	7287	7489	7682
4	2935	3173	3415	3662	3911	4163	4416	4669	4922	5174
5	1115	1252	1398	1553	1717	1890	2072	2262	2460	2666
6	0298	0348	0404	0467	0536	0612	0696	0787	0886	0994
7	0053	0064	0078	0094	0112	0133	0157	0184	0215	0250
8	0006	0007	0009	0011	0014	0017	0021	0026	0031	0036
9				0001	0001	0001	0001	0002	0002	0003

p\r	41	42	43	44	45	46	47	48	49	50
1	9913	9926	9936	9946	9954	9961	9967	9972	9977	9980
2	9372	9442	9505	9563	9615	9662	9704	9741	9775	9805
3	7866	8039	8204	8359	8505	8642	8769	8889	8999	9102
4	5424	5670	5913	6152	6386	6614	6836	7052	7260	7461
5	2878	3097	3322	3551	3786	4024	4265	4509	4754	5000
6	1109	1233	1366	1508	1658	1817	1985	2161	2346	2539
7	0290	0334	0383	0437	0498	0564	0637	0717	0804	0898
8	0046	0055	0065	0077	0091	0107	0125	0145	0169	0195
9	0003	0004	0005	0006	0008	0009	0011	0014	0016	0020

TABLE 4. Cumulative Binomial Distribution $P(R \geq r \mid n, p)$ (Continued)

$n = 10$

r \ p	01	02	03	04	05	06	07	08	09	10
1	0956	1829	2626	3352	4013	4614	5160	5656	6106	6513
2	0043	0162	0345	0582	0861	1176	1517	1879	2254	2639
3	0001	0009	0028	0062	0115	0188	0283	0401	0540	0702
4			0001	0004	0010	0020	0036	0058	0088	0128
5					0001	0002	0003	0006	0010	0016
6									0001	0001

r \ p	11	12	13	14	15	16	17	18	19	20
1	6882	7215	7516	7787	8031	8251	8448	8626	8784	8926
2	3028	3417	3804	4184	4557	4920	5270	5608	5932	6242
3	0884	1087	1308	1545	1798	2064	2341	2628	2922	3222
4	0178	0239	0313	0400	0500	0614	0741	0883	1039	1209
5	0025	0037	0053	0073	0099	0130	0168	0213	0266	0328
6	0003	0004	0006	0010	0014	0020	0027	0037	0049	0064
7			0001	0001	0001	0002	0003	0004	0006	0009
8									0001	0001

r \ p	21	22	23	24	25	26	27	28	29	30
1	9053	9166	9267	9357	9437	9508	9570	9626	9674	9718
2	6536	6815	7079	7327	7560	7778	7981	8170	8345	8507
3	3526	3831	4137	4442	4744	5042	5335	5622	5901	6172
4	1391	1587	1794	2012	2241	2479	2726	2979	3239	3504
5	0399	0479	0569	0670	0781	0904	1037	1181	1337	1503
6	0082	0104	0130	0161	0197	0239	0287	0342	0404	0473
7	0012	0016	0021	0027	0035	0045	0056	0070	0087	0106
8	0001	0002	0002	0003	0004	0006	0007	0010	0012	0016
9							0001	0001	0001	0001

r \ p	31	32	33	34	35	36	37	38	39	40
1	9755	9789	9818	9843	9865	9885	9902	9916	9929	9940
2	8656	8794	8920	9035	9140	9236	9323	9402	9473	9536
3	6434	6687	6930	7162	7384	7595	7794	7983	8160	8327
4	3772	4044	4316	4589	4862	5132	5400	5664	5923	6177
5	1679	1867	2064	2270	2485	2708	2939	3177	3420	3669
6	0551	0637	0732	0836	0949	1072	1205	1348	1500	1662
7	0129	0155	0185	0220	0260	0305	0356	0413	0477	0548
8	0020	0025	0032	0039	0048	0059	0071	0086	0103	0123
9	0002	0003	0003	0004	0005	0007	0009	0011	0014	0017
10								0001	0001	0001

r \ p	41	42	43	44	45	46	47	48	49	50
1	9949	9957	9964	9970	9975	9979	9983	9986	9988	9990
2	9594	9645	9691	9731	9767	9799	9827	9852	9874	9893
3	8483	8628	8764	8889	9004	9111	9209	9298	9379	9453
4	6425	6665	6898	7123	7340	7547	7745	7933	8112	8281
5	3922	4178	4436	4696	4956	5216	5474	5730	5982	6230
6	1834	2016	2207	2407	2616	2832	3057	3288	3526	3770
7	0626	0712	0806	0908	1020	1141	1271	1410	1560	1719
8	0146	0172	0202	0236	0274	0317	0366	0420	0480	0547
9	0021	0025	0031	0037	0045	0054	0065	0077	0091	0107
10	0001	0002	0002	0003	0003	0004	0005	0006	0008	0010

$n = 11$

r \ p	01	02	03	04	05	06	07	08	09	10
1	1047	1993	2847	3618	4312	4937	5499	6004	6456	6862
2	0052	0195	0413	0692	1019	1382	1772	2181	2601	3026
3	0002	0012	0037	0083	0152	0248	0370	0519	0695	0896
4			0002	0007	0016	0030	0053	0085	0129	0185
5					0001	0003	0005	0010	0017	0028
6								0001	0002	0003

Appendix C / Tables

TABLE 4. Cumulative Binomial Distribution $P(R \geq r \mid n, p)$ (Continued)

p\r	11	12	13	14	15	16	17	18	19	20
1	7225	7549	7839	8097	8327	8531	8712	8873	9015	9141
2	3452	3873	4286	4689	5078	5453	5811	6151	6474	6779
3	1120	1366	1632	1915	2212	2521	2839	3164	3494	3826
4	0256	0341	0442	0560	0694	0846	1013	1197	1397	1611
5	0042	0061	0087	0119	0159	0207	0266	0334	0413	0504
6	0005	0008	0012	0018	0027	0037	0051	0068	0090	0117
7		0001	0001	0002	0003	0005	0007	0010	0014	0020
8							0001	0001	0002	0002

p\r	21	22	23	24	25	26	27	28	29	30
1	9252	9350	9436	9511	9578	9636	9686	9730	9769	9802
2	7065	7333	7582	7814	8029	8227	8410	8577	8730	8870
3	4158	4488	4814	5134	5448	5753	6049	6335	6610	6873
4	1840	2081	2333	2596	2867	3146	3430	3719	4011	4304
5	0607	0723	0851	0992	1146	1313	1493	1685	1888	2103
6	0148	0186	0231	0283	0343	0412	0490	0577	0674	0782
7	0027	0035	0046	0059	0076	0095	0119	0146	0179	0216
8	0003	0005	0007	0009	0012	0016	0021	0027	0034	0043
9			0001	0001	0001	0002	0002	0003	0004	0006

p\r	31	32	33	34	35	36	37	38	39	40
1	9831	9856	9878	9896	9912	9926	9938	9948	9956	9964
2	8997	9112	9216	9310	9394	9470	9537	9597	9650	9698
3	7123	7361	7587	7799	7999	8186	8360	8522	8672	8811
4	4598	4890	5179	5464	5744	6019	6286	6545	6796	7037
5	2328	2563	2807	3059	3317	3581	3850	4122	4397	4672
6	0901	1031	1171	1324	1487	1661	1847	2043	2249	2465
7	0260	0309	0366	0430	0501	0581	0670	0768	0876	0994
8	0054	0067	0082	0101	0122	0148	0177	0210	0249	0293
9	0008	0010	0013	0016	0020	0026	0032	0039	0048	0059
10	0001	0001	0001	0002	0002	0003	0004	0005	0006	0007

p\r	41	42	43	44	45	46	47	48	49	50
1	9970	9975	9979	9983	9986	9989	9991	9992	9994	9995
2	9739	9776	9808	9836	9861	9882	9900	9916	9930	9941
3	8938	9055	9162	9260	9348	9428	9499	9564	9622	9673
4	7269	7490	7700	7900	8089	8266	8433	8588	8733	8867
5	4948	5223	5495	5764	6029	6288	6541	6787	7026	7256
6	2690	2924	3166	3414	3669	3929	4193	4460	4729	5000
7	1121	1260	1408	1568	1738	1919	2110	2312	2523	2744
8	0343	0399	0461	0532	0610	0696	0791	0895	1009	1133
9	0072	0087	0104	0125	0148	0175	0206	0241	0282	0327
10	0009	0012	0014	0018	0022	0027	0033	0040	0049	0059
11	0001	0001	0001	0001	0002	0002	0002	0003	0004	0005

$n = 12$

p\r	01	02	03	04	05	06	07	08	09	10
1	1136	2153	3062	3873	4596	5241	5814	6323	6775	7176
2	0062	0231	0486	0809	1184	1595	2033	2487	2948	3410
3	0002	0015	0048	0107	0196	0316	0468	0652	0866	1109
4		0001	0003	0010	0022	0043	0075	0120	0180	0256
5				0001	0002	0004	0009	0016	0027	0043
6						0001	0002	0003	0005
7										0001

p\r	11	12	13	14	15	16	17	18	19	20
1	7530	7843	8120	8363	8578	8766	8931	9076	9202	9313
2	3867	4314	4748	5166	5565	5945	6304	6641	6957	7251
3	1377	1667	1977	2303	2642	2990	3344	3702	4060	4417
4	0351	0464	0597	0750	0922	1114	1324	1552	1795	2054
5	0065	0095	0133	0181	0239	0310	0393	0489	0600	0726
6	0009	0014	0022	0033	0046	0065	0088	0116	0151	0194
7	0001	0002	0003	0004	0007	0010	0015	0021	0029	0039
8					0001	0001	0002	0003	0004	0006
9										0001

TABLE 4. Cumulative Binomial Distribution $P(R \geq r \mid n, p)$ **(Continued)**

p\r	21	22	23	24	25	26	27	28	29	30
1	9409	9493	9566	9629	9683	9730	9771	9806	9836	9862
2	7524	7776	8009	8222	8416	8594	8755	8900	9032	9150
3	4768	5114	5450	5778	6093	6397	6687	6963	7225	7472
4	2326	2610	2904	3205	3512	3824	4137	4452	4765	5075
5	0866	1021	1192	1377	1576	1790	2016	2254	2504	2763
6	0245	0304	0374	0453	0544	0646	0760	0887	1026	1178
7	0052	0068	0089	0113	0143	0178	0219	0267	0322	0386
8	0008	0011	0016	0021	0028	0036	0047	0060	0076	0095
9	0001	0001	0002	0003	0004	0005	0007	0010	0013	0017
10						0001	0001	0001	0002	0003

p\r	31	32	33	34	35	36	37	38	39	40
1	9884	9902	9918	9932	9943	9953	9961	9968	9973	9978
2	9256	9350	9435	9509	9576	9634	9685	9730	9770	9804
3	7704	7922	8124	8313	8487	8648	8795	8931	9054	9166
4	5381	5681	5973	6258	6533	6799	7053	7296	7528	7747
5	3032	3308	3590	3876	4167	4459	4751	5043	5332	5618
6	1343	1521	1711	1913	2127	2352	2588	2833	3087	3348
7	0458	0540	0632	0734	0846	0970	1106	1253	1411	1582
8	0118	0144	0176	0213	0255	0304	0359	0422	0493	0573
9	0022	0028	0036	0045	0056	0070	0086	0104	0127	0153
10	0003	0004	0005	0007	0008	0011	0014	0018	0022	0028
11				0001	0001	0001	0001	0002	0002	0003

p\r	41	42	43	44	45	46	47	48	49	50
1	9982	9986	9988	9990	9992	9994	9995	9996	9997	9998
2	9834	9860	9882	9901	9917	9931	9943	9953	9961	9968
3	9267	9358	9440	9513	9579	9637	9688	9733	9773	9807
4	7953	8147	8329	8498	8655	8801	8934	9057	9168	9270
5	5899	6175	6443	6704	6956	7198	7430	7652	7862	8062
6	3616	3889	4167	4448	4731	5014	5297	5577	5855	6128
7	1765	1959	2164	2380	2607	2843	3089	3343	3604	3872
8	0662	0760	0869	0988	1117	1258	1411	1575	1751	1938
9	0183	0218	0258	0304	0356	0415	0481	0555	0638	0730
10	0035	0043	0053	0065	0079	0095	0114	0137	0163	0193
11	0004	0005	0007	0009	0011	0014	0017	0021	0026	0032
12				0001	0001	0001	0001	0001	0002	0002

$n = 13$

p\r	01	02	03	04	05	06	07	08	09	10
1	1225	2310	3270	4118	4867	5526	6107	6617	7065	7458
2	0072	0270	0564	0932	1354	1814	2298	2794	3293	3787
3	0003	0020	0062	0135	0245	0392	0578	0799	1054	1339
4		0001	0005	0014	0031	0060	0103	0163	0242	0342
5				0001	0003	0007	0013	0024	0041	0065
6						0001	0001	0003	0005	0009
7									0001	0001

p\r	11	12	13	14	15	16	17	18	19	20
1	7802	8102	8364	8592	8791	8963	9113	9242	9354	9450
2	4270	4738	5186	5614	6017	6396	6751	7080	7384	7664
3	1651	1985	2337	2704	3080	3463	3848	4231	4611	4983
4	0464	0609	0776	0967	1180	1414	1667	1939	2226	2527
5	0097	0139	0193	0260	0342	0438	0551	0681	0827	0991
6	0015	0024	0036	0053	0075	0104	0139	0183	0237	0300
7	0002	0003	0005	0008	0013	0019	0027	0038	0052	0070
8			0001	0001	0002	0003	0004	0006	0009	0012
9								0001	0001	0002

TABLE 4. Cumulative Binomial Distribution $P(R \geq r \mid n, p)$ *(Continued)*

p\r	21	22	23	24	25	26	27	28	29	30
1	9533	9604	9666	9718	9762	9800	9833	9860	9883	9903
2	7920	8154	8367	8559	8733	8889	9029	9154	9265	9363
3	5347	5699	6039	6364	6674	6968	7245	7505	7749	7975
4	2839	3161	3489	3822	4157	4493	4826	5155	5478	5794
5	1173	1371	1585	1816	2060	2319	2589	2870	3160	3457
6	0375	0462	0562	0675	0802	0944	1099	1270	1455	1654
7	0093	0120	0154	0195	0243	0299	0365	0440	0527	0624
8	0017	0024	0032	0043	0056	0073	0093	0118	0147	0182
9	0002	0004	0005	0007	0010	0013	0018	0024	0031	0040
10			0001	0001	0001	0002	0003	0004	0005	0007
11									0001	0001

p\r	31	32	33	34	35	36	37	38	39	40
1	9920	9934	9945	9955	9963	9970	9975	9980	9984	9987
2	9450	9527	9594	9653	9704	9749	9787	9821	9849	9874
3	8185	8379	8557	8720	8868	9003	9125	9235	9333	9421
4	6101	6398	6683	6957	7217	7464	7698	7917	8123	8314
5	3760	4067	4376	4686	4995	5301	5603	5899	6188	6470
6	1867	2093	2331	2581	2841	3111	3388	3673	3962	4256
7	0733	0854	0988	1135	1295	1468	1654	1853	2065	2288
8	0223	0271	0326	0390	0462	0544	0635	0738	0851	0977
9	0052	0065	0082	0102	0126	0154	0187	0225	0270	0321
10	0009	0012	0015	0020	0025	0032	0040	0051	0063	0078
11	0001	0001	0002	0003	0003	0005	0006	0008	0010	0013
12							0001	0001	0001	0001

p\r	41	42	43	44	45	46	47	48	49	50
1	9990	9992	9993	9995	9996	9997	9997	9998	9998	9999
2	9895	9912	9928	9940	9951	9960	9967	9974	9979	9983
3	9499	9569	9630	9684	9731	9772	9808	9838	9865	9888
4	8492	8656	8807	8945	9071	9185	9288	9381	9464	9539
5	6742	7003	7254	7493	7721	7935	8137	8326	8502	8666
6	4552	4849	5146	5441	5732	6019	6299	6573	6838	7095
7	2524	2770	3025	3290	3563	3842	4127	4415	4707	5000
8	1114	1264	1426	1600	1788	1988	2200	2424	2659	2905
9	0379	0446	0520	0605	0698	0803	0918	1045	1183	1334
10	0096	0117	0141	0170	0203	0242	0287	0338	0396	0461
11	0017	0021	0027	0033	0041	0051	0063	0077	0093	0112
12	0002	0002	0003	0004	0005	0007	0009	0011	0014	0017
13							0001	0001	0001	0001

$n = 14$

p\r	01	02	03	04	05	06	07	08	09	10
1	1313	2464	3472	4353	5123	5795	6380	6888	7330	7712
2	0084	0310	0645	1059	1530	2037	2564	3100	3632	4154
3	0003	0025	0077	0167	0301	0478	0698	0958	1255	1584
4		0001	0006	0019	0042	0080	0136	0214	0315	0441
5				0002	0004	0010	0020	0035	0059	0092
6						0001	0002	0004	0008	0015
7									0001	0002

p\r	11	12	13	14	15	16	17	18	19	20
1	8044	8330	8577	8789	8972	9129	9264	9379	9477	9560
2	4658	5141	5599	6031	6433	6807	7152	7469	7758	8021
3	1939	2315	2708	3111	3521	3932	4341	4744	5138	5519
4	0594	0774	0979	1210	1465	1742	2038	2351	2679	3018
5	0137	0196	0269	0359	0467	0594	0741	0907	1093	1298
6	0024	0038	0057	0082	0115	0157	0209	0273	0349	0439
7	0003	0006	0009	0015	0022	0032	0046	0064	0087	0116
8		0001	0001	0002	0003	0005	0008	0012	0017	0024
9						0001	0001	0002	0003	0004

TABLE 4. Cumulative Binomial Distribution $P(R \geq r \mid n, p)$ (Continued)

p\r	21	22	23	24	25	26	27	28	29	30
1	9631	9691	9742	9786	9822	9852	9878	9899	9917	9932
2	8259	8473	8665	8837	8990	9126	9246	9352	9444	9525
3	5887	6239	6574	6891	7189	7467	7727	7967	8188	8392
4	3366	3719	4076	4432	4787	5136	5479	5813	6137	6448
5	1523	1765	2023	2297	2585	2884	3193	3509	3832	4158
6	0543	0662	0797	0949	1117	1301	1502	1718	1949	2195
7	0152	0196	0248	0310	0383	0467	0563	0673	0796	0933
8	0033	0045	0060	0079	0103	0132	0167	0208	0257	0315
9	0006	0008	0011	0016	0022	0029	0038	0050	0065	0083
10	0001	0001	0002	0002	0003	0005	0007	0009	0012	0017
11						0001	0001	0001	0002	0002

p\r	31	32	33	34	35	36	37	38	39	40
1	9945	9955	9963	9970	9976	9981	9984	9988	9990	9992
2	9596	9657	9710	9756	9795	9828	9857	9881	9902	9919
3	8577	8746	8899	9037	9161	9271	9370	9457	9534	9602
4	6747	7032	7301	7556	7795	8018	8226	8418	8595	8757
5	4486	4813	5138	5458	5773	6080	6378	6666	6943	7207
6	2454	2724	3006	3297	3595	3899	4208	4519	4831	5141
7	1084	1250	1431	1626	1836	2059	2296	2545	2805	3075
8	0381	0458	0545	0643	0753	0876	1012	1162	1325	1501
9	0105	0131	0163	0200	0243	0294	0353	0420	0497	0583
10	0022	0029	0037	0048	0060	0076	0095	0117	0144	0175
11	0003	0005	0006	0008	0011	0014	0019	0024	0031	0039
12		0001	0001	0001	0001	0002	0003	0003	0005	0006
13										0001

p\r	41	42	43	44	45	46	47	48	49	50
1	9994	9995	9996	9997	9998	9998	9999	9999	9999	9999
2	9934	9946	9956	9964	9971	9977	9981	9985	9988	9991
3	9661	9713	9758	9797	9830	9858	9883	9903	9921	9935
4	8905	9039	9161	9270	9368	9455	9532	9601	9661	9713
5	7459	7697	7922	8132	8328	8510	8678	8833	8974	9102
6	5450	5754	6052	6344	6627	6900	7163	7415	7654	7880
7	3355	3643	3937	4236	4539	4843	5148	5451	5751	6047
8	1692	1896	2113	2344	2586	2840	3105	3380	3663	3953
9	0680	0789	0910	1043	1189	1348	1520	1707	1906	2120
10	0212	0255	0304	0361	0426	0500	0583	0677	0782	0898
11	0049	0061	0076	0093	0114	0139	0168	0202	0241	0287
12	0008	0010	0013	0017	0022	0027	0034	0042	0053	0065
13	0001	0001	0001	0002	0003	0003	0004	0006	0007	0009
14										0001

n = 15

p\r	01	02	03	04	05	06	07	08	09	10
1	1399	2614	3667	4579	5367	6047	6633	7137	7570	7941
2	0096	0353	0730	1191	1710	2262	2832	3403	3965	4510
3	0004	0030	0094	0203	0362	0571	0829	1130	1469	1841
4		0002	0008	0024	0055	0104	0175	0273	0399	0556
5			0001	0002	0006	0014	0028	0050	0082	0127
6					0001	0001	0003	0007	0013	0022
7								0001	0002	0003

p\r	11	12	13	14	15	16	17	18	19	20
1	8259	8530	8762	8959	9126	9269	9389	9490	9576	9648
2	5031	5524	5987	6417	6814	7179	7511	7813	8085	8329
3	2238	2654	3084	3520	3958	4392	4819	5234	5635	6020
4	0742	0959	1204	1476	1773	2092	2429	2782	3146	3518
5	0187	0265	0361	0478	0617	0778	0961	1167	1394	1642
6	0037	0057	0084	0121	0168	0227	0300	0387	0490	0611
7	0006	0010	0015	0024	0036	0052	0074	0102	0137	0181
8	0001	0001	0002	0004	0006	0010	0014	0021	0030	0042
9					0001	0001	0002	0003	0005	0008
10									0001	0001

TABLE 4. Cumulative Binomial Distribution $P(R \geq r \mid n, p)$ (Continued)

p\r	21	22	23	24	25	26	27	28	29	30
1	9709	9759	9802	9837	9866	9891	9911	9928	9941	9953
2	8547	8741	8913	9065	9198	9315	9417	9505	9581	9647
3	6385	6731	7055	7358	7639	7899	8137	8355	8553	8732
4	3895	4274	4650	5022	5387	5742	6086	6416	6732	7031
5	1910	2195	2495	2810	3135	3469	3810	4154	4500	4845
6	0748	0905	1079	1272	1484	1713	1958	2220	2495	2784
7	0234	0298	0374	0463	0566	0684	0817	0965	1130	1311
8	0058	0078	0104	0135	0173	0219	0274	0338	0413	0500
9	0011	0016	0023	0031	0042	0056	0073	0094	0121	0152
10	0002	0003	0004	0006	0008	0011	0015	0021	0028	0037
11			0001	0001	0001	0002	0002	0003	0005	0007
12									0001	0001

p\r	31	32	33	34	35	36	37	38	39	40
1	9962	9969	9975	9980	9984	9988	9990	9992	9994	9995
2	9704	9752	9794	9829	9858	9883	9904	9922	9936	9948
3	8893	9038	9167	9281	9383	9472	9550	9618	9678	9729
4	7314	7580	7829	8060	8273	8469	8649	8813	8961	9095
5	5187	5523	5852	6171	6481	6778	7062	7332	7587	7827
6	3084	3393	3709	4032	4357	4684	5011	5335	5654	5968
7	1509	1722	1951	2194	2452	2722	3003	3295	3595	3902
8	0599	0711	0837	0977	1132	1302	1487	1687	1902	2131
9	0190	0236	0289	0351	0422	0504	0597	0702	0820	0950
10	0048	0062	0079	0099	0124	0154	0190	0232	0281	0338
11	0009	0012	0016	0022	0028	0037	0047	0059	0075	0093
12	0001	0002	0003	0004	0005	0006	0009	0011	0015	0019
13					0001	0001	0001	0002	0002	0003

p\r	41	42	43	44	45	46	47	48	49	50
1	9996	9997	9998	9998	9999	9999	9999	9999	10000	10000
2	9958	9966	9973	9979	9983	9987	9990	9992	9994	9995
3	9773	9811	9843	9870	9893	9913	9929	9943	9954	9963
4	9215	9322	9417	9502	9576	9641	9697	9746	9788	9824
5	8052	8261	8454	8633	8796	8945	9080	9201	9310	9408
6	6274	6570	6856	7131	7392	7641	7875	8095	8301	8491
7	4214	4530	4847	5164	5478	5789	6095	6394	6684	6964
8	2374	2630	2898	3176	3465	3762	4065	4374	4686	5000
9	1095	1254	1427	1615	1818	2034	2265	2510	2767	3036
10	0404	0479	0565	0661	0769	0890	1024	1171	1333	1509
11	0116	0143	0174	0211	0255	0305	0363	0430	0506	0592
12	0025	0032	0040	0051	0063	0079	0097	0119	0145	0176
13	0004	0005	0007	0009	0011	0014	0018	0023	0029	0037
14			0001	0001	0001	0002	0002	0003	0004	0005

$n = 16$

p\r	01	02	03	04	05	06	07	08	09	10
1	1485	2762	3857	4796	5599	6284	6869	7366	7789	8147
2	0109	0399	0818	1327	1892	2489	3098	3701	4289	4853
3	0005	0037	0113	0242	0429	0673	0969	1311	1694	2108
4		0002	0011	0032	0070	0132	0221	0342	0496	0684
5			0001	0003	0009	0019	0038	0068	0111	0170
6					0001	0002	0005	0010	0019	0033
7							0001	0001	0003	0005
8										0001

p\r	11	12	13	14	15	16	17	18	19	20
1	8450	8707	8923	9105	9257	9386	9493	9582	9657	9719
2	5386	5885	6347	6773	7161	7513	7830	8115	8368	8593
3	2545	2999	3461	3926	4386	4838	5277	5698	6101	6482
4	0907	1162	1448	1763	2101	2460	2836	3223	3619	4019
5	0248	0348	0471	0618	0791	0988	1211	1458	1727	2018
6	0053	0082	0120	0171	0235	0315	0412	0527	0662	0817
7	0009	0015	0024	0038	0056	0080	0112	0153	0204	0267
8	0001	0002	0004	0007	0011	0016	0024	0036	0051	0070
9			0001	0001	0002	0003	0004	0007	0010	0015
10							0001	0001	0002	0002

TABLE 4. Cumulative Binomial Distribution $P(R \geq r \mid n, p)$ (Continued)

p\r	21	22	23	24	25	26	27	28	29	30
1	9770	9812	9847	9876	9900	9919	9935	9948	9958	9967
2	8791	8965	9117	9250	9365	9465	9550	9623	9686	9739
3	6839	7173	7483	7768	8029	8267	8482	8677	8851	9006
4	4418	4814	5203	5583	5950	6303	6640	6959	7260	7541
5	2327	2652	2991	3341	3698	4060	4425	4788	5147	5501
6	0992	1188	1405	1641	1897	2169	2458	2761	3077	3402
7	0342	0432	0536	0657	0796	0951	1125	1317	1526	1753
8	0095	0127	0166	0214	0271	0340	0420	0514	0621	0744
9	0021	0030	0041	0056	0075	0098	0127	0163	0206	0257
10	0004	0006	0008	0012	0016	0023	0031	0041	0055	0071
11	0001	0001	0001	0002	0003	0004	0006	0008	0011	0016
12						0001	0001	0001	0002	0003

p\r	31	32	33	34	35	36	37	38	39	40
1	9974	9979	9984	9987	9990	9992	9994	9995	9996	9997
2	9784	9822	9854	9880	9902	9921	9936	9948	9959	9967
3	9144	9266	9374	9467	9549	9620	9681	9734	9778	9817
4	7804	8047	8270	8475	8661	8830	8982	9119	9241	9349
5	5846	6181	6504	6813	7108	7387	7649	7895	8123	8334
6	3736	4074	4416	4759	5100	5438	5770	6094	6408	6712
7	1997	2257	2531	2819	3119	3428	3746	4070	4398	4728
8	0881	1035	1205	1391	1594	1813	2048	2298	2562	2839
9	0317	0388	0470	0564	0671	0791	0926	1076	1242	1423
10	0092	0117	0148	0185	0229	0280	0341	0411	0491	0583
11	0021	0028	0037	0048	0062	0079	0100	0125	0155	0191
12	0004	0005	0007	0010	0013	0017	0023	0030	0038	0049
13		0001	0001	0001	0002	0003	0004	0005	0007	0009
14								0001	0001	0001

p\r	41	42	43	44	45	46	47	48	49	50
1	9998	9998	9999	9999	9999	9999	10000	10000	10000	10000
2	9974	9979	9984	9987	9990	9992	9994	9995	9997	9997
3	9849	9876	9899	9918	9934	9947	9958	9966	9973	9979
4	9444	9527	9600	9664	9719	9766	9806	9840	9869	9894
5	8529	8707	8869	9015	9147	9265	9370	9463	9544	9616
6	7003	7280	7543	7792	8024	8241	8441	8626	8795	8949
7	5058	5387	5711	6029	6340	6641	6932	7210	7476	7728
8	3128	3428	3736	4051	4371	4694	5019	5343	5665	5982
9	1619	1832	2060	2302	2559	2829	3111	3405	3707	4018
10	0687	0805	0936	1081	1241	1416	1607	1814	2036	2272
11	0234	0284	0342	0409	0486	0574	0674	0786	0911	1051
12	0062	0078	0098	0121	0149	0183	0222	0268	0322	0384
13	0012	0016	0021	0027	0035	0044	0055	0069	0086	0106
14	0002	0002	0003	0004	0006	0007	0010	0013	0016	0021
15					0001	0001	0001	0001	0002	0003

$n = 17$

p\r	01	02	03	04	05	06	07	08	09	10
1	1571	2907	4042	5004	5819	6507	7088	7577	7988	8332
2	0123	0446	0909	1465	2078	2717	3362	3995	4604	5182
3	0006	0044	0134	0286	0503	0782	1118	1503	1927	2382
4		0003	0014	0040	0088	0164	0273	0419	0603	0826
5			0001	0004	0012	0026	0051	0089	0145	0221
6					0001	0003	0007	0015	0027	0047
7							0001	0002	0004	0008
8										0001

p\r	11	12	13	14	15	16	17	18	19	20
1	8621	8862	9063	9230	9369	9484	9579	9657	9722	9775
2	5723	6223	6682	7099	7475	7813	8113	8379	8613	8818
3	2858	3345	3836	4324	4802	5266	5711	6133	6532	6904
4	1087	1383	1710	2065	2444	2841	3251	3669	4091	4511
5	0321	0446	0598	0778	0987	1224	1487	1775	2087	2418
6	0075	0114	0166	0234	0319	0423	0548	0695	0864	1057
7	0014	0023	0037	0056	0083	0118	0163	0220	0291	0377
8	0002	0004	0007	0011	0017	0027	0039	0057	0080	0109
9		0001	0001	0002	0003	0005	0008	0012	0018	0026
10						0001	0001	0002	0003	0005
11										0001

TABLE 4. Cumulative Binomial Distribution $P(R \geq r \mid n, p)$ (Continued)

p\r	21	22	23	24	25	26	27	28	29	30
1	9818	9854	9882	9906	9925	9940	9953	9962	9970	9977
2	8996	9152	9285	9400	9499	9583	9654	9714	9765	9807
3	7249	7567	7859	8123	8363	8578	8771	8942	9093	9226
4	4927	5333	5728	6107	6470	6814	7137	7440	7721	7981
5	2766	3128	3500	3879	4261	4643	5023	5396	5760	6113
6	1273	1510	1770	2049	2347	2661	2989	3329	3677	4032
7	0479	0598	0736	0894	1071	1268	1485	1721	1976	2248
8	0147	0194	0251	0320	0402	0499	0611	0739	0884	1046
9	0037	0051	0070	0094	0124	0161	0206	0261	0326	0403
10	0007	0011	0016	0022	0031	0042	0057	0075	0098	0127
11	0001	0002	0003	0004	0006	0009	0013	0018	0024	0032
12				0001	0001	0002	0002	0003	0005	0007
13									0001	0001

p\r	31	32	33	34	35	36	37	38	39	40
1	9982	9986	9989	9991	9993	9995	9996	9997	9998	9998
2	9843	9872	9896	9917	9933	9946	9957	9966	9973	9979
3	9343	9444	9532	9608	9673	9728	9775	9815	9849	9877
4	8219	8437	8634	8812	8972	9115	9241	9353	9450	9536
5	6453	6778	7087	7378	7652	7906	8142	8360	8559	8740
6	4390	4749	5105	5458	5803	6139	6465	6778	7077	7361
7	2536	2838	3153	3479	3812	4152	4495	4839	5182	5522
8	1227	1426	1642	1877	2128	2395	2676	2971	3278	3595
9	0498	0595	0712	0845	0994	1159	1341	1541	1757	1989
10	0168	0204	0254	0314	0383	0464	0557	0664	0784	0919
11	0043	0057	0074	0095	0120	0151	0189	0234	0286	0348
12	0009	0013	0017	0023	0030	0040	0051	0066	0084	0106
13	0002	0002	0003	0004	0006	0008	0011	0015	0019	0025
14				0001	0001	0001	0002	0002	0003	0005
15										0001

p\r	41	42	43	44	45	46	47	48	49	50
1	9999	9999	9999	9999	10000	10000	10000	10000	10000	10000
2	9984	9987	9990	9992	9994	9996	9997	9998	9998	9999
3	9900	9920	9935	9948	9959	9968	9975	9980	9985	9988
4	9610	9674	9729	9776	9816	9849	9877	9901	9920	9936
5	8904	9051	9183	9301	9404	9495	9575	9644	9704	9755
6	7628	7879	8113	8330	8529	8712	8878	9028	9162	9283
7	5856	6182	6499	6805	7098	7377	7641	7890	8122	8338
8	3920	4250	4585	4921	5257	5590	5918	6239	6552	6855
9	2238	2502	2780	3072	3374	3687	4008	4335	4667	5000
10	1070	1236	1419	1618	1834	2066	2314	2577	2855	3145
11	0420	0503	0597	0705	0826	0962	1112	1279	1462	1662
12	0133	0165	0203	0248	0301	0363	0434	0517	0611	0717
13	0033	0042	0054	0069	0086	0108	0134	0165	0202	0245
14	0006	0008	0011	0014	0019	0024	0031	0040	0050	0064
15	0001	0001	0002	0002	0003	0004	0005	0007	0009	0012
16							0001	0001	0001	0001

$n = 18$

p\r	01	02	03	04	05	06	07	08	09	10
1	1655	3049	4220	5204	6028	6717	7292	7771	8169	8499
2	0138	0495	1003	1607	2265	2945	3622	4281	4909	5497
3	0007	0052	0157	0333	0581	0898	1275	1702	2168	2662
4		0004	0018	0050	0109	0201	0333	0506	0723	0982
5				0006	0015	0034	0067	0116	0186	0282
6					0001	0002	0005	0010	0021	0038	0064
7							0001	0003	0006	0012
8									0001	0002

p\r	11	12	13	14	15	16	17	18	19	20
1	8773	8998	9185	9338	9464	9566	9651	9719	9775	9820
2	6042	6540	6992	7398	7759	8080	8362	8609	8824	9009
3	3173	3690	4206	4713	5203	5673	6119	6538	6927	7287
4	1282	1618	1986	2382	2798	3229	3669	4112	4554	4990
5	0405	0558	0743	0959	1206	1482	1787	2116	2467	2836

TABLE 4. Cumulative Binomial Distribution $P(R \geq r \mid n, p)$ **(Continued)**

p\r	11	12	13	14	15	16	17	18	19	20
6	0102	0154	0222	0310	0419	0551	0708	0889	1097	1329
7	0021	0034	0054	0081	0118	0167	0229	0306	0400	0513
8	0003	0006	0011	0017	0027	0041	0060	0086	0120	0163
9		0001	0002	0003	0005	0008	0013	0020	0029	0043
10					0001	0001	0002	0004	0006	0009
11								0001	0001	0002

p\r	21	22	23	24	25	26	27	28	29	30
1	9856	9886	9909	9928	9944	9956	9965	9973	9979	9984
2	9169	9306	9423	9522	9605	9676	9735	9784	9824	9858
3	7616	7916	8187	8430	8647	8839	9009	9158	9288	9400
4	5414	5825	6218	6591	6943	7272	7578	7860	8119	8354
5	3220	3613	4012	4414	4813	5208	5594	5968	6329	6673
6	1586	1866	2168	2488	2825	3176	3538	3907	4281	4656
7	0645	0799	0974	1171	1390	1630	1891	2171	2469	2783
8	0217	0283	0363	0458	0569	0699	0847	1014	1200	1407
9	0060	0083	0112	0148	0193	0249	0316	0395	0488	0596
10	0014	0020	0028	0039	0054	0073	0097	0127	0164	0210
11	0003	0004	0006	0009	0012	0018	0025	0034	0046	0061
12		0001	0001	0002	0002	0003	0005	0007	0010	0014
13					0001	0001	0001	0001	0002	0003

p\r	31	32	33	34	35	36	37	38	39	40
1	9987	9990	9993	9994	9996	9997	9998	9998	9999	9999
2	9886	9908	9927	9942	9954	9964	9972	9978	9983	9987
3	9498	9581	9652	9713	9764	9807	9843	9873	9897	9918
4	8568	8759	8931	9083	9217	9335	9439	9528	9606	9672
5	7001	7309	7598	7866	8114	8341	8549	8737	8907	9058
6	5029	5398	5759	6111	6450	6776	7086	7379	7655	7912
7	3111	3450	3797	4151	4509	4867	5224	5576	5921	6257
8	1633	1878	2141	2421	2717	3027	3349	3681	4021	4366
9	0720	0861	1019	1196	1391	1604	1835	2084	2350	2632
10	0264	0329	0405	0494	0597	0714	0847	0997	1163	1347
11	0080	0104	0133	0169	0212	0264	0325	0397	0480	0576
12	0020	0027	0036	0047	0062	0080	0102	0130	0163	0203
13	0004	0005	0008	0011	0014	0019	0026	0034	0044	0058
14	0001	0001	0001	0002	0003	0004	0005	0007	0010	0013
15					0001	0001	0001	0001	0002	0002

p\r	41	42	43	44	45	46	47	48	49	50
1	9999	9999	10000	10000	10000	10000	10000	10000	10000	10000
2	9990	9992	9994	9996	9997	9998	9998	9999	9999	9999
3	9934	9948	9959	9968	9975	9981	9985	9989	9991	9993
4	9729	9777	9818	9852	9880	9904	9923	9939	9952	9962
5	9193	9313	9418	9510	9589	9658	9717	9767	9810	9846
6	8151	8372	8573	8757	8923	9072	9205	9324	9428	9519
7	6582	6895	7193	7476	7742	7991	8222	8436	8632	8811
8	4713	5062	5408	5750	6085	6412	6728	7032	7322	7597
9	2928	3236	3556	3885	4222	4562	4906	5249	5591	5927
10	1549	1768	2004	2258	2527	2812	3110	3421	3742	4073
11	0686	0811	0951	1107	1280	1470	1677	1902	2144	2403
12	0250	0307	0372	0449	0537	0658	0753	0883	1028	1189
13	0074	0094	0118	0147	0183	0225	0275	0334	0402	0481
14	0017	0022	0029	0038	0049	0063	0079	0100	0125	0154
15	0003	0004	0006	0007	0010	0013	0017	0023	0029	0038
16		0001	0001	0001	0001	0002	0003	0004	0005	0007
17								0001	0001	0001

$n = 19$

p\r	01	02	03	04	05	06	07	08	09	10
1	1738	3188	4394	5396	6226	6914	7481	7949	8334	8649
2	0153	0546	1100	1751	2453	3171	3879	4560	5202	5797
3	0009	0061	0183	0384	0665	1021	1439	1908	2415	2946
4		0005	0022	0061	0132	0243	0398	0602	0853	1150
5			0002	0007	0020	0044	0085	0147	0235	0352
6				0001	0002	0006	0014	0029	0051	0086
7						0001	0002	0004	0009	0017
8								0001	0001	0003

TABLE 4. Cumulative Binomial Distribution $P(R \geq r \mid n, p)$ (Continued)

r \ p	11	12	13	14	15	16	17	18	19	20
1	8908	9119	9291	9431	9544	9636	9710	9770	9818	9856
2	6342	6835	7277	7669	8015	8318	8581	8809	9004	9171
3	3488	4032	4568	5089	5587	6059	6500	6910	7287	7631
4	1490	1867	2275	2708	3159	3620	4085	4549	5005	5449
5	0502	0685	0904	1158	1444	1762	2107	2476	2864	3267
6	0135	0202	0290	0401	0537	0700	0891	1110	1357	1631
7	0030	0048	0076	0113	0163	0228	0310	0411	0532	0676
8	0005	0009	0016	0026	0041	0061	0089	0126	0173	0233
9	0001	0002	0003	0005	0008	0014	0021	0032	0047	0067
10				0001	0001	0002	0004	0007	0010	0016
11							0001	0001	0002	0003

r \ p	21	22	23	24	25	26	27	28	29	30
1	9887	9911	9930	9946	9958	9967	9975	9981	9985	9989
2	9313	9434	9535	9619	9690	9749	9797	9837	9869	9896
3	7942	8222	8471	8692	8887	9057	9205	9333	9443	9538
4	5877	6285	6671	7032	7369	7680	7965	8224	8458	8668
5	3681	4100	4520	4936	5346	5744	6129	6498	6848	7178
6	1929	2251	2592	2950	3322	3705	4093	4484	4875	5261
7	0843	1034	1248	1487	1749	2032	2336	2657	2995	3345
8	0307	0396	0503	0629	0775	0941	1129	1338	1568	1820
9	0093	0127	0169	0222	0287	0366	0459	0568	0694	0839
10	0023	0034	0047	0066	0089	0119	0156	0202	0258	0326
11	0005	0007	0011	0016	0023	0032	0044	0060	0080	0105
12	0001	0001	0002	0003	0005	0007	0010	0015	0021	0028
13				0001	0001	0001	0002	0003	0004	0006
14									0001	0001

r \ p	31	32	33	34	35	36	37	38	39	40
1	9991	9993	9995	9996	9997	9998	9998	9999	9999	9999
2	9917	9935	9949	9960	9969	9976	9981	9986	9989	9992
3	9618	9686	9743	9791	9830	9863	9890	9913	9931	9945
4	8856	9028	9169	9297	9409	9505	9588	9659	9719	9770
5	7486	7773	8037	8280	8500	8699	8878	9038	9179	9304
6	5641	6010	6366	6707	7032	7339	7627	7895	8143	8371
7	3705	4073	4445	4818	5188	5554	5913	6261	6597	6919
8	2091	2381	2688	3010	3344	3690	4043	4401	4762	5122
9	1003	1186	1389	1612	1855	2116	2395	2691	3002	3325
10	0405	0499	0608	0733	0875	1035	1213	1410	1626	1861
11	0137	0176	0223	0280	0347	0426	0518	0625	0747	0885
12	0038	0051	0068	0089	0114	0146	0185	0231	0287	0352
13	0009	0012	0017	0023	0031	0041	0054	0070	0091	0116
14	0002	0002	0003	0005	0007	0009	0013	0017	0023	0031
15				0001	0001	0002	0002	0003	0005	0006
16									0001	0001

r \ p	41	42	43	44	45	46	47	48	49	50
1	10000	10000	10000	10000	10000	10000	10000	10000	10000	10000
2	9994	9995	9996	9997	9998	9999	9999	9999	9999	10000
3	9957	9967	9974	9980	9985	9988	9991	9993	9995	9996
4	9813	9849	9878	9903	9923	9939	9952	9963	9971	9978
5	9413	9508	9590	9660	9720	9771	9814	9850	9879	9904
6	8579	8767	8937	9088	9223	9342	9446	9537	9615	9682
7	7226	7515	7787	8039	8273	8488	8684	8862	9022	9165
8	5480	5832	6176	6509	6831	7138	7430	7706	7964	8204
9	3660	4003	4353	4706	5060	5413	5762	6105	6439	6762
10	2114	2385	2672	2974	3290	3617	3954	4299	4648	5000
11	1040	1213	1404	1613	1841	2087	2351	2631	2928	3238
12	0429	0518	0621	0738	0871	1021	1187	1372	1575	1796
13	0146	0183	0227	0280	0342	0415	0500	0597	0709	0835
14	0040	0052	0067	0086	0109	0137	0171	0212	0261	0318
15	0009	0012	0016	0021	0028	0036	0046	0060	0076	0096
16	0001	0002	0003	0004	0005	0007	0010	0013	0017	0022
17				0001	0001	0001	0001	0002	0003	0004

TABLE 4. Cumulative Binomial Distribution $P(R \geq r \mid n, p)$ *(Continued)*

$n = 20$

r \ p	01	02	03	04	05	06	07	08	09	10
1	1821	3324	4562	5580	6415	7099	7658	8113	8484	8784
2	0169	0599	1198	1897	2642	3395	4131	4831	5484	6083
3	0010	0071	0210	0439	0755	1150	1610	2121	2666	3231
4		0006	0027	0074	0159	0290	0471	0706	0993	1330
5			0003	0010	0026	0056	0107	0183	0290	0432
6				0001	0003	0009	0019	0038	0068	0113
7						0001	0003	0006	0013	0024
8								0001	0002	0004
9										0001

r \ p	11	12	13	14	15	16	17	18	19	20
1	9028	9224	9383	9510	9612	9694	9759	9811	9852	9885
2	6624	7109	7539	7916	8244	8529	8773	8982	9159	9308
3	3802	4369	4920	5450	5951	6420	6854	7252	7614	7939
4	1710	2127	2573	3041	3523	4010	4496	4974	5439	5886
5	0610	0827	1083	1375	1702	2059	2443	2849	3271	3704
6	0175	0260	0370	0507	0673	0870	1098	1356	1643	1958
7	0041	0067	0103	0153	0219	0304	0409	0537	0689	0867
8	0008	0014	0024	0038	0059	0088	0127	0177	0241	0321
9	0001	0002	0005	0008	0013	0021	0033	0049	0071	0100
10			0001	0001	0002	0004	0007	0011	0017	0026
11						0001	0001	0002	0004	0006
12									0001	0001

r \ p	21	22	23	24	25	26	27	28	29	30
1	9910	9931	9946	9959	9968	9976	9982	9986	9989	9992
2	9434	9539	9626	9698	9757	9805	9845	9877	9903	9924
3	8230	8488	8716	8915	9087	9237	9365	9474	9567	9645
4	6310	6711	7085	7431	7748	8038	8300	8534	8744	8929
5	4142	4580	5014	5439	5852	6248	6625	6981	7315	7625
6	2297	2657	3035	3427	3828	4235	4643	5048	5447	5836
7	1071	1301	1557	1838	2142	2467	2810	3169	3540	3920
8	0419	0536	0675	0835	1018	1225	1455	1707	1982	2277
9	0138	0186	0246	0320	0409	0515	0640	0784	0948	1133
10	0038	0054	0075	0103	0139	0183	0238	0305	0385	0480
11	0009	0013	0019	0028	0039	0055	0074	0100	0132	0171
12	0002	0003	0004	0006	0009	0014	0019	0027	0038	0051
13			0001	0001	0002	0003	0004	0006	0009	0013
14							0001	0001	0002	0003

r \ p	31	32	33	34	35	36	37	38	39	40
1	9994	9996	9997	9998	9998	9999	9999	9999	9999	10000
2	9940	9953	9964	9972	9979	9984	9988	9991	9993	9995
3	9711	9765	9811	9848	9879	9904	9924	9940	9953	9964
4	9092	9235	9358	9465	9556	9634	9700	9755	9802	9840
5	7911	8173	8411	8626	8818	8989	9141	9274	9390	9490
6	6213	6574	6917	7242	7546	7829	8090	8329	8547	8744
7	4305	4693	5079	5460	5834	6197	6547	6882	7200	7500
8	2591	2922	3268	3624	3990	4361	4735	5108	5478	5841
9	1340	1568	1818	2087	2376	2683	3005	3341	3688	4044
10	0591	0719	0866	1032	1218	1424	1650	1897	2163	2447
11	0220	0275	0350	0434	0532	0645	0775	0923	1090	1275
12	0069	0091	0119	0154	0196	0247	0308	0381	0466	0565
13	0018	0025	0034	0045	0060	0079	0102	0132	0167	0210
14	0004	0006	0008	0011	0015	0021	0028	0037	0049	0065
15	0001	0001	0001	0002	0003	0004	0006	0009	0012	0016
16						0001	0001	0002	0002	0003

r \ p	41	42	43	44	45	46	47	48	49	50
1	10000	10000	10000	10000	10000	10000	10000	10000	10000	10000
2	9996	9997	9998	9998	9999	9999	9999	10000	10000	10000
3	9972	9979	9984	9988	9991	9993	9995	9996	9997	9998
4	9872	9898	9920	9937	9951	9962	9971	9977	9983	9987
5	9577	9651	9714	9767	9811	9848	9879	9904	9924	9941

TABLE 4. Cumulative Binomial Distribution $P(R \geq r \mid n, p)$ *(Continued)*

r \ p	41	42	43	44	45	46	47	48	49	50
6	8921	9078	9217	9340	9447	9539	9619	9687	9745	9793
7	7780	8041	8281	8501	8701	8881	9042	9186	9312	9423
8	6196	6539	6868	7183	7480	7759	8020	8261	8482	8684
9	4406	4771	5136	5499	5857	6207	6546	6873	7186	7483
10	2748	3064	3394	3736	4086	4443	4804	5166	5525	5881
11	1480	1705	1949	2212	2493	2791	3104	3432	3771	4119
12	0679	0810	0958	1123	1308	1511	1734	1977	2238	2517
13	0262	0324	0397	0482	0580	0694	0823	0969	1133	1316
14	0084	0107	0136	0172	0214	0265	0326	0397	0480	0577
15	0022	0029	0038	0050	0064	0083	0105	0133	0166	0207
16	0004	0006	0008	0011	0015	0020	0027	0035	0046	0059
17	0001	0001	0001	0002	0003	0004	0005	0007	0010	0013
18						0001	0001	0001	0001	0002

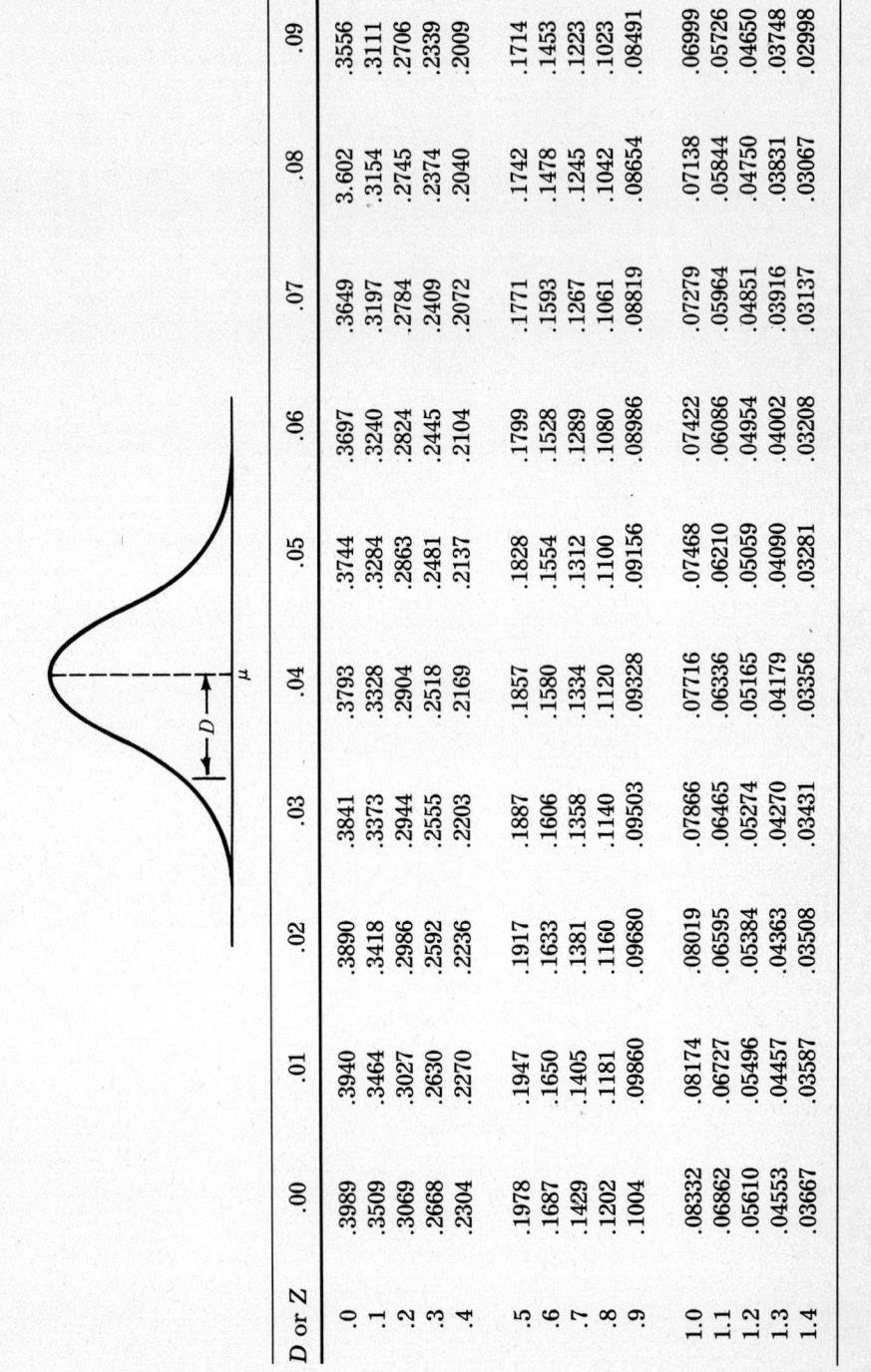

TABLE 5. Unit Normal Linear Loss Integral*

D or Z	.00	.01	.02	.03	.04	.05	.06	.07	.08	.09
.0	.3989	.3940	.3890	.3841	.3793	.3744	.3697	.3649	3.602	.3556
.1	.3509	.3464	.3418	.3373	.3328	.3284	.3240	.3197	.3154	.3111
.2	.3069	.3027	.2986	.2944	.2904	.2863	.2824	.2784	.2745	.2706
.3	.2668	.2630	.2592	.2555	.2518	.2481	.2445	.2409	.2374	.2339
.4	.2304	.2270	.2236	.2203	.2169	.2137	.2104	.2072	.2040	.2009
.5	.1978	.1947	.1917	.1887	.1857	.1828	.1799	.1771	.1742	.1714
.6	.1687	.1650	.1633	.1606	.1580	.1554	.1528	.1593	.1478	.1453
.7	.1429	.1405	.1381	.1358	.1334	.1312	.1289	.1267	.1245	.1223
.8	.1202	.1181	.1160	.1140	.1120	.1100	.1080	.1061	.1042	.1023
.9	.1004	.09860	.09680	.09503	.09328	.09156	.08986	.08819	.08654	.08491
1.0	.08332	.08174	.08019	.07866	.07716	.07468	.07422	.07279	.07138	.06999
1.1	.06862	.06727	.06595	.06465	.06336	.06210	.06086	.05964	.05844	.05726
1.2	.05610	.05496	.05384	.05274	.05165	.05059	.04954	.04851	.04750	.04650
1.3	.04553	.04457	.04363	.04270	.04179	.04090	.04002	.03916	.03831	.03748
1.4	.03667	.03587	.03508	.03431	.03356	.03281	.03208	.03137	.03067	.02998

TABLE 5. Unit Normal Linear Loss Integral* (Continued)

D or Z	.00	.01	.02	.03	.04	.05	.06	.07	.08	.09
1.5	.02931	0.2865	.02800	.02736	.02674	.02612	.02552	.02494	.02436	.02380
1.6	.02324	.02270	.02217	.02165	.02114	.02064	.02015	.01967	.01920	.01874
1.7	.01829	.01785	.01742	.01699	.01658	.01617	.01578	.01539	.01501	.01464
1.8	.01428	.01392	.01357	.01323	.01290	.01257	.01226	.01195	.01164	.01134
1.9	.01105	.01077	.01049	.01022	.0^{2}9957	.0^{2}9698	.0^{2}9445	.0^{2}9198	.0^{2}8957	.0^{2}8721
2.0	.0^{2}8491	.0^{2}8266	.0^{2}8046	.0^{2}7832	.0^{2}7623	.0^{2}7418	.0^{2}7219	.0^{2}7024	.0^{2}6835	.0^{2}6649
2.1	.0^{2}6468	.0^{2}6292	.0^{2}6120	.0^{2}5952	.0^{2}5788	.0^{2}5628	.0^{2}5472	.0^{2}5320	.0^{2}5172	.0^{2}5028
2.2	.0^{2}4887	.0^{2}4750	.0^{2}4616	.0^{2}4486	.0^{2}4358	.0^{2}4235	.0^{2}4114	.0^{2}3996	.0^{2}3882	.0^{2}3770
2.3	.0^{2}3662	.0^{2}3556	.0^{2}3453	.0^{2}3352	.0^{2}3255	.0^{2}3159	.0^{2}3067	.0^{2}2977	.0^{2}2889	.0^{2}2804
2.4	.0^{2}2720	.0^{2}2640	.0^{2}2561	.0^{2}2484	.0^{2}2410	.0^{2}2337	.0^{2}2267	.0^{2}2199	.0^{2}2132	.0^{2}2067
2.5	.0^{2}2005	.0^{2}1943	.0^{2}1883	.0^{2}1826	.0^{2}1769	.0^{2}1715	.0^{2}1662	.0^{2}1610	.0^{2}1560	.0^{2}1511
3.0	.0^{3}3822	.0^{3}3689	.0^{3}3560	.0^{3}3436	.0^{3}3316	.0^{3}3199	.0^{3}3087	.0^{3}2978	.0^{3}2873	.0^{3}2771
3.5	.0^{5}5848	.0^{5}5620	.0^{4}5400	.0^{4}5188	.0^{4}4984	.0^{4}4788	.0^{4}4599	.0^{4}4417	.0^{4}4242	.0^{4}4073
4.0	.0^{5}7145	.0^{5}6835	.0^{5}6538	.0^{5}6253	.0^{5}5980	.0^{5}5718	.0^{5}5468	.0^{5}5227	.0^{5}4997	.0^{5}4777

$N(D)$ is defined as follows:

$$N(D) = \int_{-\infty}^{-D}(-D-X)f^*(X)dX = \int_{D}^{\infty}(X-D)f^*(X)dX$$

where f^*X is the standardized normal density function and D is positive.

*From Robert O. Schlaifer, *Probability and Statistics for Business Decisions*. New York: McGraw-Hill Book Company, Inc., 1959. Copyright © 1959 by the President and Fellows of Harvard College. Reprinted by permission of the Harvard Business School.

Course Outlines

The text offers considerable flexibility in terms of topic selection and sequence, depending on course objectives. The following are examples of topical sequences for a one-quarter and a one-semester course (chapter numbers are in parentheses).

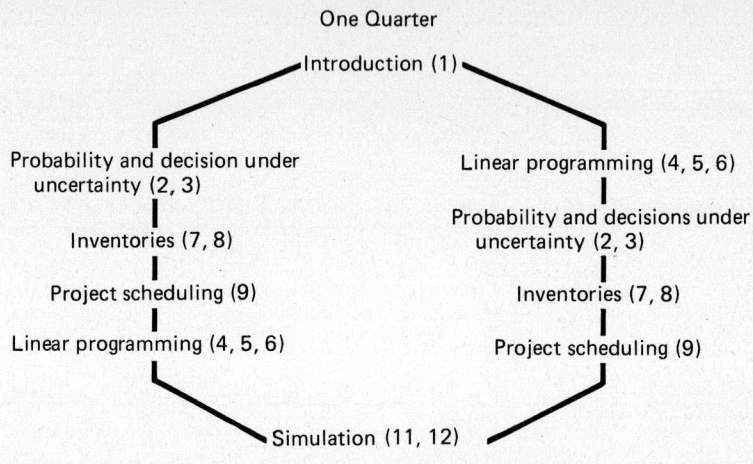

One Quarter

Introduction (1)

Left branch:
- Probability and decision under uncertainty (2, 3)
- Inventories (7, 8)
- Project scheduling (9)
- Linear programming (4, 5, 6)

Right branch:
- Linear programming (4, 5, 6)
- Probability and decisions under uncertainty (2, 3)
- Inventories (7, 8)
- Project scheduling (9)

Simulation (11, 12)

Previous course coverage of a given type may necessitate modification in a course plan.

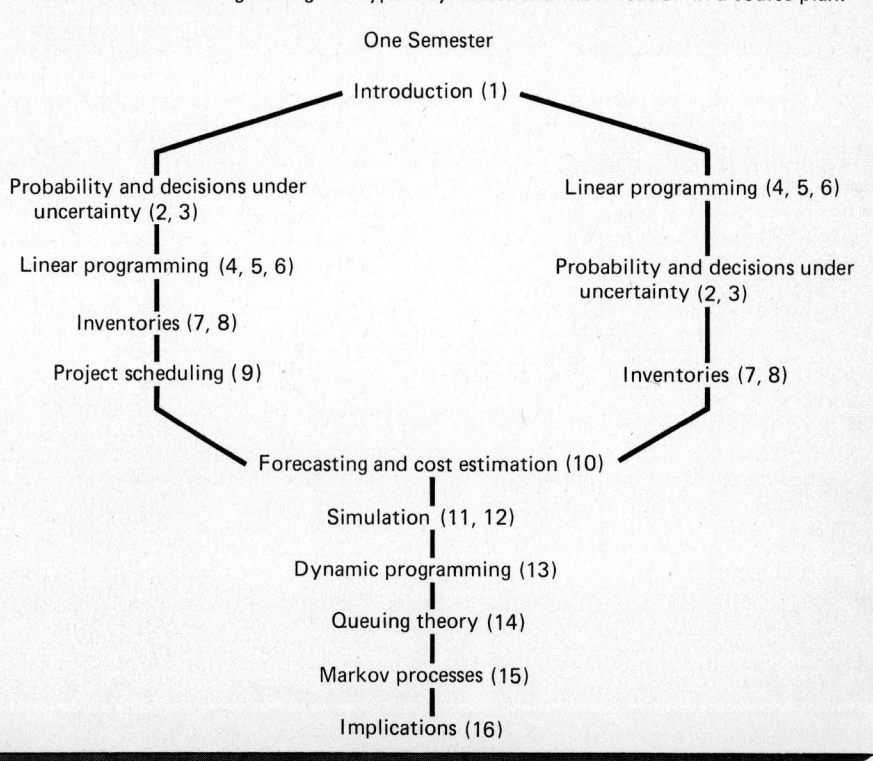

One Semester

Introduction (1)

Left branch:
- Probability and decisions under uncertainty (2, 3)
- Linear programming (4, 5, 6)
- Inventories (7, 8)
- Project scheduling (9)

Right branch:
- Linear programming (4, 5, 6)
- Probability and decisions under uncertainty (2, 3)
- Inventories (7, 8)

- Forecasting and cost estimation (10)
- Simulation (11, 12)
- Dynamic programming (13)
- Queuing theory (14)
- Markov processes (15)
- Implications (16)

Index

ABC inventory systems, 269–271
Analog model, 4, 9
Arrival pattern, 450
Arrival rate for a queue, 457, 464
Artificial variable, 169, 177

Basic solution
  in linear programming, 150, 177
  in transportation model, 211
Bayes' theorem, 23–25, 39
Binomial distribution, 63–67, 85
Buffer inventories, 220, 238

Carrying costs, in inventory models, 222, 238
Coefficient
  of correlation, 332, 344
  of determination, 331, 344
Computer spreadsheet, 404
Conditional loss, 27
Conditional probability, 18, 20, 39
Conditional profit, 26–27
Confidence interval
  for b in simple regression, 335
  for Monte Carlo simulation, 375, 384
  for y' in simple regression, 336
Constant order cycle, 267, 271
Constraint, 6, 9
  in linear programming, 100, 125
Continuous prob function, 61, 85
Corporate planning model, 409
Cost benefit of quantitative methods, 497
CPM (critical path method), 284, 287–290, 303
  critical path, 287, 303
  dummy task, 289, 303
  earliest completion time, 287, 303
  earliest start time, 287, 303
  latest completion time, 287, 303
  latest start time, 288, 303
  slack, 287, 303
CPM/limited resource model, 297–303
  crash time, 293
  resource conflict, 297

Crash time, 293
Critical path, 287, 303
Cumulative binomial table, 519–535
Cumulative distribution, 62, 85
Cycle inventories, 220–226, 238
  carrying cost, 222, 238
  order cost, 222, 238

Decision criteria, 73–76
  equally likely, 74, 86
  maximum expected value, 76, 86
  maximum likelihood, 75, 86
  maximax, 74, 86
  maximin, 74, 86
  minimax regret, 75, 86
Decision theory, 72–85
Decision variables, 7, 9
Definitional relation, 384, 398, 409
Degeneracy, in transportation model, 207–209, 211
Degenerate solution, in linear programming, 166, 177
Demand constraints, in transportation model, 192, 211
Dependent event, 18–20, 39
Deterministic model, 7, 9
Discrete probability function, 61, 85
Dual linear programming model, 117, 120, 126, 164
Dummy distributor, 206, 211
Dummy factory, 207, 211
Dummy task, 289, 303
Dynamic programming, 422, 439, 440, 495
  principle of optimality, 425, 440
  recursive relation, 429
  stage, 422, 440
  state variable, 422, 440

Earliest completion time, 287, 303
Earliest start time, 287, 303
Economic lot size, 229–232, 238
Economic order quantity, 220, 224, 238, 254–263
Empirical relation, 398, 409

Equal likelihood criteria, 74, 86
Event, 13
   dependent, 18–20, 39
   independent, 17
   mutually exclusive, 13, 15–17, 39
Expected monetary profit, 28–31, 39
Expected project time, 291, 303
Expected stockout per lead time $E(SPL)$, 258–263, 271
Expected value, 59, 60, 86
   with imperfect information, 33–39
   with perfect information, 31–32, 39
Exponential distribution, 456
Exponential smoothing, 320, 344
External variable, 398
Extreme point solution, in linear programming, 108, 126

Feasible region/area, 103, 126
Feasible solution
   in linear programming, 126
   in transportation model, 192, 211
Flowchart, 369, 384
Forecasting, 316–345

Heuristic model, 5, 9

Iconic model, 4, 9
Immediate predecessor, 285, 303
Imperfect information, 33, 39
Imperfect information, expected value, 33–39
Independent event, 17
Internal variable, 398
Inventory model, 217–239, 249–272
   ABC inventory, 269–271
   buffer inventories, 220, 238
   carry cost, 238
   constant order, 267, 271
   cycle inventory, 220–236, 238
   economic lot size, 229–232, 238
   EOQ (economic order quantity), 220, 224, 238, 254–263
   expected stockout per lead time, 258–263, 271
   lead time, 271
   order cost, 238
   periodic inventory review, 267, 271
   quantity discount, 232–234, 239
   reorder point, 220, 250–254, 258–263, 271
   safety stock, 253–263, 271
   seasonal inventory, 220, 239
   sensitivity analysis, 226–228
   service level, 266, 271
   stockout, 219, 234–239, 271
   stockout cost, 234, 239, 265, 271
Iso-profit line, 105

Joint probability, 17, 20–23, 39
Judgmental forecasting, 316, 344

Lagged variable, 398
Latest completion time, 287, 303
Latest start time, 288, 303
Lead time, 271
Learning curves, 339–344
Learning index, 341, 344
Learning ratio, 339, 344
Least squares, 324, 344
Linear programming, 97–120, 147–178, 495
   artificial variable, 169, 177
   basic solution, 150, 177
   constraint, 100
   degenerate, 166, 177
   dual formulation, 117, 120, 126, 164
   extreme point solution, 108, 126
   feasible region, 103, 126
   graphical solution, 100–110
   iso-profit line, 105
   marginal value, 114–117, 126
   minimization, 171, 177
   multiple optimal solution, 111, 168, 177
   nonnegativity constraint, 100, 126
   objective function, 99, 106, 126
   optimal solution, 110
   primal formulation, 117, 126, 163
   sensitivity analysis, 171–177
   shadow price, 115, 126
   slack variable, 149, 178
   simplex criterion, 153, 177
   simplex method, 148–163
   simplex tableau, 150
   surplus variable, 170, 178
   transportation model, 190–211
   unbounded, 165, 178
Loss
   conditional, 27
   opportunity, 27, 39

Marginal probability, 17, 20, 39
Marginal value, in linear programming, 114–117, 126
Markov process, 473–485
   no memory property, 481, 485
   probability transition matrix, 475, 485
   steady-state, 476, 479, 480, 485
Mathematical model, 4–9
Maximax criterion, 74, 86
Maximin criterion, 74, 86
Maximum expected value criterion, 76, 86
Maximum likelihood criterion, 75, 86
Minimix regret criterion, 75, 86
Minimization problem, 171, 177
Model, 4, 9
   analog, 4, 9

Index

deterministic, 7, 9
heuristic, 5, 9
iconic, 4, 9
inventory, 217–239, 249–272
linear programming, 97–126, 147–178
Markov process, 473–485
mathematical, 4, 9
project network, 284–303
queuing, 447–464
regression, 327–345
simulation, 5, 9, 362
stochastic, 7, 9
transportation, 189–211
validity, 5, 9
Monte Carlo simulation, 370–377, 384
confidence interval, 375
random number, 371
sample size, 376
sampling, 374
Moving average, 318, 344
Multiperiod simulation model, 369
Multiple optimal solution, 111, 168, 177
Multiple regression, 327, 337–339
Multiple-channel queuing model, 460–463
Mutually exclusive event, 13, 15–17, 39

No memory property, 481, 485
Nonnegativity constraint, 100, 126
Normal distribution, 67–73, 86
Normal distribution table, 517
Normal loss function, 264
Normal loss function table, 536
Northwest corner rule, 194, 211

Objective function, 6, 9
in linear programming, 99, 106, 126
Objective probability, 14, 39
Opportunity loss, 27, 39
Ordering costs, in inventory model, 222, 238

Parameters, 7, 9
Perfect information, 31–32, 39
Perfect information, expected value, 31, 39
Periodic inventory review, 267, 271
PERT (performance evaluation review technique), 284, 290–293, 303
expected project time, 291, 303
task variance, 291
PERT/cost, 293–297, 303
crash time, 293
Pivot element, in linear programming, 156, 177
Poisson distribution, 455
Population, 450
arrival pattern, 450
queue, 464
Prediction model, 316, 326, 344

Primal linear programming model, 117, 126, 163
Principle of optimality, 425, 440
Probability, 13–40
conditional, 18, 20, 39
joint, 17, 20–23, 39
marginal, 17, 20, 39
Probability distribution, 58–72, 86
binomial, 63–67, 85
continuous, 61, 85
cumulative, 62, 85
discrete, 61, 85
exponential, 456
normal, 67–72, 86
Poisson, 455
Probability transition matrix, 475, 485
Profit
conditional, 26–27
expected monetary, 28, 39
Project, 284, 303
Project network, 285–303

Quantitative forecasting, 316, 345
Quantity discounts, in inventory, 232–234, 239
Queuing, 448–464, 495
arrival rate, 457, 464
discipline, 451, 464
multiple-channel, 460–463
operating characteristics, 453, 464
population, 464
service rate, 464
simulation, 380
single-channel, 454
steady-state, 453, 464
transient stage, 453, 464

Random number, 371, 384
Random number table, 371, 516
Random variable, 58, 86
Recursive relation, 398, 409
in dynamic programming, 429, 440
Redundant constraint, in transportation model, 211
Regression analysis, 327, 345, 495
Reorder point, 220, 250–254, 258–263, 271
Resource conflict, in CPM, 297, 303
Risk averse, 83, 86
Risk neutral, 83, 86
Risk seeking, 83, 86

Safety stock, 253, 271
optimal level, 254–263
Sample size, in Monte Carlo simulation, 376, 384
Sample space, 14, 39

Sampling in, Monte Carlo simulation, 374, 384
Seasonal inventories, 220, 239
Sensitivity analysis
 in inventory models, 226–228
 in linear programming, 171–176, 177
 in simulation, 366
Sequencing constraint, 285, 303
Service facility, in queuing models, 451
Service level, 266, 271
Shadow price, 115, 126
Simple average, 318, 345
Simple regression analysis, 327–337
 coefficient of correlation, 332, 344
 coefficient of determination, 331, 344
 confidence interval of b, 335
 confidence interval on expected y', 336
 standard error of estimate, 333, 345
 standard error of regression coefficient, 335, 345
Simplex criterion, 153, 177
Simplex method, 148–163, 178
 iteration, 159, 177
 pivot element, 156, 177
 simplex criterion, 153, 177
 tableau, 150, 178
 technological rates of substitution, 153, 157–158, 178
Simplex tableau, 150, 178
Simulation, 362, 385, 495
 confidence interval, 375
 model, 5, 9, 365, 384
 Monte Carlo, 370–377, 384
 multiperiod, 369
 queuing model, 380
 random number, 371, 384
 sample size, 376, 384
 sampling, 374, 384
 sensitivity analysis, 366
 state variable, 365, 385
 system, 364
 transition variable, 365, 385
 validation, 365, 385, 407
 what-if questions, 396, 401, 409
 what-if response matrix, 402–404, 409
Single-channel queuing model, 454–460
Slack, 287, 303
Slack variable, 149, 178
Stage, in dynamic programming, 422, 440
Standard deviation, 60
Standard error of estimate, 333, 345
Standard error of regression coefficient, 335, 345
Standard normal deviate, 70, 86
State variable
 in dynamic programming, 422, 440
 in simulation, 365, 385
Steady state, in queuing models, 453, 464

Steady state probabilities, Markov models, 476, 479–480, 485
Stochastic model, 7, 9
Stockout, 219, 234–239, 271
Stockout cost, 234, 239, 265, 271
Student t distribution table, 518
Subjective probability, 14, 39
Supply constraints, in transportation models, 192, 211
Surplus variable, 170, 178
System, 364, 385
System state, in Markov models, 474, 485

Task, 284, 303
Task variance, 291
Technological rates of substitution, 153, 157–158, 178
Time series models, 316–326
Transient stage, 453, 464
Transition probabilities, in Markov models, 474, 485
Transition variables, 365, 385
Transportation model, 189–211
 basic solution, 211
 degeneracy, 207–209, 211
 demand constraint, 192, 211
 dummy distributor, 206, 211
 dummy factory, 207, 211
 linear programming formulation, 210
 northwest corner rule, 194, 211
 redundant constraint, 211
 simplex criterion, 199
 simplex method, 194–205
 supply constraint, 192
 Vogel's approximation, 195–199, 211
Trend models, 318–324
 exponential smoothing, 320–323, 344
 least squares, 324, 344
 moving average, 318, 344
 simple average, 318, 345
 weighted average, 319, 345

Unbounded solution, 165, 178
Utiles, 79–83
Utility, 79, 86
Utility function, 79–86
 risk averse, 83, 86
 risk neutral, 83, 86
 risk seeking, 83, 86

Validation, of simulation models, 365, 385, 407
Variance, 60, 86
Vogel's approximation method, 195–199, 211

Weighted average, 319, 345
"What-if?" questions, 396, 401, 409
"What-if?" response matrix, 402–404, 409